The Structure of
AMERICAN INDUSTRY

The Structure of
AMERICAN
INDUSTRY

FOURTH EDITION

edited by **Walter Adams**
MICHIGAN STATE UNIVERSITY

The Macmillan Company NEW YORK
Collier-Macmillan Limited LONDON

THE MACMILLAN COMPANY
866 Third Avenue, New York, New York 10022
COLLIER-MACMILLAN CANADA, LTD., Toronto, Ontario

Library of Congress catalog card number: 79-130019
FIRST PRINTING

PREFACE

When the first edition of this book was published in 1950, a lengthy preface seemed necessary to articulate the importance of studying the structure of industry. It was not the age of the political economist. Scientific model building was a more prestigious calling than the empirical study of economic power.

Today, this is no longer true. No apology is required for presenting a series of essays centering on industry structure, conduct, and performance, with an emphasis on policy alternatives and recommendations. The corporal's guard of 1950 has become almost respectable in the 1970's. And this is a tribute to our profession's receptivity to change—with a proper allowance for lag, of course.

Herewith, then, a collection of twelve industry studies—which I hope are representative of the structural spectrum of American industry.

East Lansing, Michigan   W. A.

CONTRIBUTORS

Walter Adams Distinguished University Professor, Professor of Economics, and President Emeritus, Michigan State University; Member, Attorney General's National Committee to Study the Antitrust Laws; erstwhile consultant to congressional committees.

Joel B. Dirlam Professor of Economics and Director of Institute for Study of International Aspects of Competition, University of Rhode Island; expert witness before congressional committees.

Kenneth Elzinga Assistant Professor of Economics, University of Virginia; special economic assistant to the Chief of the Antitrust Division, U.S. Department of Justice (1970–71).

Charles H. Hession Professor of Economics and Chairman of the Social Science Program, Brooklyn College.

Manley R. Irwin Professor of Economics, University of New Hampshire; consultant to Federal Communications Commission, Antitrust Division, and President's Task Force on Communications Policy.

Wyllis R. Knight Professor of Economics and Director of Bureau of Business and Economic Research, Georgia State University.

Robert F. Lanzillotti Professor of Economics and Dean of College of Business Administration, University of Florida; consultant to Federal Trade Commission and Attorney General of California.

Walter S. Measday   Lecturer in Economics, University of Maryland; economist, U.S. Senate Subcommittee on Antitrust and Monopoly.

Thomas G. Moore   Professor of Economics, Michigan State University; consultant to Council of Economic Advisers.

Elton Rayack   Professor of Economics, University of Rhode Island.

Frederic M. Scherer   Professor of Economics, University of Michigan; erstwhile consultant to National Aeronautics & Space Agency, Federal Council for Science & Technology, and Arms Control & Disarmament Agency.

Richard B. Tennant   Professor of Business Economics, Graduate School of Business, Columbia University.

Contents

1. Wyllis R. Knight

AGRICULTURE

I. INTRODUCTION

Agriculture is an industry whose economic characteristics approach those of pure competition. Within this highly competitive structure the industry has served the public interest especially well, but the rural families, only moderately well.

Historically, agriculture has been plagued with three main problems, the first being the long continued existence of many small-scale enterprises characterized by low output per worker. These farms accounted for the great bulk of the poverty which plagued rural society for many generations.[1]

Although the number of small-scale operators has shrunk rapidly over the last generation, many still remain. Largely because of them, the per capita income of farm people is now about 25 per cent lower than that of others in America.

The second problem concerns marked price instability for farm products. It is not unusual for the total value of individual crops produced in the nation to vary by 20 per cent from one year to the next because of price fluctuations, resulting in even greater variation in net income (because most of the farmer's costs are fixed). The resulting risk to the individual operator is large and, on occasion, may threaten to wipe out his equity.

The third problem is a persistent powerful tendency for agricultural production in the United States to expand faster than market demand would warrant—in other words, the chronic "surplus" conundrum.

HISTORICAL BACKGROUND   A look into this nation's agricultural history shows that small-scale farms have always been with us; in fact, much more so in the past than today. A network of small farms was established right from the outset of this country's development; the abundance of land (plus

---

[1] Lest the wrong impression be generated, looking at American agriculture as a whole, in terms of physical units produced, output per farmer has risen dramatically. Moreover, in terms of market-value productivity the trend upward has been very pronounced, especially over the last 20 years.

generous policies for its distribution) and the lack of cash markets for agricultural products favored this development.

Various schemes of farming on a large group basis were given a try, but economic and legal factors militated against them. The effects of both the Revolutionary and Civil Wars were such as to adversely affect big estates.

Almost anyone could secure on his own, at little or no cost, as much land as he could utilize, somewhere in America, from the time of the first settlements around 1620 until as late as 1875. With cash markets lacking, each family found it desirable not to push farm output to its maximum, but rather to be productive along many lines (spinning, weaving, dressmaking, herb gathering, food processing and preservation, soap making, hunting, and so on). Corn was the basic food and a relatively few acres of it sufficed each family.

Though these historical circumstances may explain their origins, they do not tell why a network of family-size farms still blankets America. The old circumstances which generated the system are gone; cash markets are now abundant, land is expensive, and machinery has largely eliminated the need for low-cost hired labor. Why has not agriculture taken a course of development similar to that of industry in general, that is, toward large-scale operations? Iron-making, too, was once a small-scale enterprise in America, but today it is performed only by big concerns. The best answer to the question seems to be that large farms have been unable thus far to demonstrate marked superiority, in terms of production efficiency, over well-managed, family-size farms. (In the case of a few "specialty crops" the large-scale farms probably are more effective.)

RISE OF COMMERCIAL FARMING   Since the middle of the nineteenth century, the major development in American agriculture has been a transition from self-sufficient to "commercial" agriculture.[2] Not all regions have shared in this evolutionary development to an equal degree; some of them, like the Appalachians and the Ozarks, still contain many subsistence farms.

Cash markets for farm products evolved as urban centers developed around manufacturing industry and commerce. To a lesser extent—yet vital in the cases of tobacco, wheat, and cotton—foreign markets comprised important cash markets.

With the appearance of cash markets, farmers became anxious to step up production, cut costs, and adopt the best techniques. Output per worker grew and living levels rose, as a rule. Fluid milk, fruit, vegetable, and poultry production developed around urban centers, almost without regard to the physi-

---

2   Commercial agriculture means production geared to cash markets. Since experience teaches that it pays to specialize, commercial agriculture also tends to mean the production of but one, or a few, products.

cal environment. Besides its great impact on the demand for agricultural products, urbanization affected agriculture in another respect that concerned the conditions of supply. It attracted labor away from the farms, thereby encouraging farmers to reorganize their methods and to use machinery. Moreover, the pull of good jobs in the city caused the gradual abandonment of the little farms on the hillsides, leaving only the better situated farms in operation. The combined effect of these revolutionary forces was strongly in the direction of larger productivity per worker in agriculture.

Commercial agriculture brought other changes, some of which were unfortunate. Whereas, under the subsistence pattern, the farmer had been able to erect a little economic island for his family—insulated from market disturbances—now he became linked to the ebb and flow of supply-and-demand fluctuations which were sensitive to dynamic developments throughout the nation (and the world). No longer his own master under his vine and fig tree, he became an anxious listener to the latest market reports, a heated participant in tariff controversies, and, finally, an advocate of a nationally sponsored system of guaranteed "fair" agricultural prices and production control.

There were offsets of other kinds, too. The heavy out-migration caused many rural hamlets to become virtual ghost towns and undermined the logic of further maintaining an extensive system of roads, schools, and a host of other service enterprises in rural areas. Worse yet, those left behind comprised a large ratio of older people and others who required public assistance. In truth, there has been a substantial breakdown of country life as farm population dropped and as those who remained became increasingly oriented—only partly by choice—to cities for their shopping, medical attention, education, church affiliation, and so on. It will require some time before the sociological impact of this change is clearly discerned.

On the other hand, commercial agriculture has brought great blessings to today's farmers, at least to those with managerial ability. It has made possible high production levels (and thereby high real incomes) undreamed of by their forefathers—levels of living impossible of attainment on the old, highly diversified, subsistence homesteads. While they have remained small in terms of ownership, management, and labor requirements, family-size farms in this new era of agriculture have been able to become large in terms of output, if judged by the standards of the past. It has been comforting to the American ideals of freedom and individualism that, despite the trend in so many industries toward production units involving the disciplined, specialized, cooperative efforts of thousands of men under one management, the great field of agriculture still offers a remunerative livelihood to a family-size enterprise (if conducted efficiently). The great strides in farm technology during the last century seem not to have placed the family-size farm at a disadvantage; in fact, it seems to have been strengthened, as a rule.

II. MARKET STRUCTURE

Aside from the government price support program, agriculture meets rather well the requirements of a perfectly competitive industry. Consider these characteristics: (1) There are a large number of sellers, no one of which can affect market price perceptibly by his production policy. (2) Farm products are standardized and sold by rather objective grades. Brand names are found only seldom, and advertising is but rarely attempted by an individual producer in the endeavour to boost the demand for his output. (3) Entry into the industry is easy. There are no patents to hinder the adoption of the best methods of production or in choosing the item to be produced. New methods have been introduced by competitive producers as fast as they are willing and financially able to do so. As a result, methods of preparing the soil, planting, cultivating, and harvesting many field crops have been revolutionized in the last couple of generations. Ease of entry is also facilitated because capital requirements, though large from the point of view of a young man wishing to farm, are small when compared with those of many other industries. (4) Within limits, prices of most farm products are determined by free markets in which many offers from sellers and bids from buyers are made. Prices change frequently within the course of a trading day, and they are often quoted in cents (and, sometimes, fractions of cents), indicating that tiny changes in supply and demand are reflected in price.

The competitive market structure is reflected in the process of price determination—the actual day-to-day mechanics that vary from product to product. Thus, the exact procedure of marketing and price determination varies in the cases of hogs and apples, but in each instance price is finally determined in a highly competitive way. However, if government price support and acreage limitation prevail in a given branch of agriculture, it cannot be termed "highly competitive" by the text definition; or, perhaps, it is highly competitive only within certain bounds.

VARYING SCALES OF PRODUCTION   Highly confusing is the wide variety in the levels of production existing among the units which it comprises (see Table 1). As a general rule, a well-managed, family-size farm in this decade should achieve a gross output of $20,000 or more, but only a minority are able to do so. (A gross output of $20,000 will yield a net income for family living of about $10,000, generally.)

Yet, a third of a million of the commercial farms had gross sales under $2,500 in 1964. Bad as this may seem, it represents a great improvement over past years. There were in 1964 less than half as many farms in Classes V and VI as there were in 1950.

Besides the commercial agriculture group, there are a large number—almost a third of the total—of part-time and part-retirement farmers. They

TABLE 1 FARMS—NUMBER BY
ECONOMIC CLASS, 1964

TYPES OF FARMS	VALUE OF SALES CLASS LIMITS ($)	THOUSANDS OF FARMS
Commercial		
Class I	40,000 and over	141,914
Class II	20,000 to 39,999	259,898
Class III	10,000 to 19,999	467,096
Class IV	5,000 to 9,999	504,614
Class V	2,500 to 4,999	443,918
Class VI	50 to 2,499[a]	348,272
Other		
Part-time		639,409
Part-retirement		350,558
Abnormal[b]		2,178
	Total	3,157,857

a Provided the operator was under sixty-five years
of age and did not work off the farm 100 or more days
during the year.
b Public and private institutional farms, and so on.
SOURCE *Census of Agriculture, 1964*, as reported
in the *Statistical Abstract, 1968* (Washington, D.C.:
U.S. Government Printing Office), p. 598.

may be excluded from a discussion of agriculture's problem situations because they supplement their incomes substantially with pensions, investments, and nonfarm jobs.

Nevertheless, after making these allowances, hundreds of thousands of
small-scale farms remain. They constitute one of the largest and most depressed groups in the nation; it may be added, a similar situation (and for
similar reasons) exists among the farm population in many other countries
(e.g., Canada).

For many decades the incidence of underemployment in agriculture (the
small-scale operators) has been greater in the South than elsewhere in the
nation. That is still the case for particular states, e.g., Kentucky, Tennessee,
Mississippi, Alabama, and North Carolina, but truly it is a nationwide phenomenon. Although poverty level agriculture was well nigh an endemic condition, the case is now much better. For example, income per farm in Georgia
is now on a par with that in Indiana and Ohio, in contrast to its 1944 ratio
of one-half.[3]

3 For income figures by states see
Economic Research Service, *Farm Income,*
State Estimates, 1949–1967, FIS 211
Supplement (Washington, D.C.: U.S.
Department of Agriculture, August 1968).

TABLE 2 INCOME PER FARM
OPERATOR FAMILY BY
MAJOR SOURCE, 1960–67

	REALIZED NET INCOME FROM FARMING ($)	OFF-FARM INCOME ($)
1960	2,962	2,140
1961	3,309	2,417
1962	3,424	2,702
1963	3,533	3,047
1964	3,802	3,349
1965	4,190	3,751
1966	5,000	4,176
1967	4,526	4,452

SOURCE U.S. Department of
Agriculture, Economic Research
Service, *Farm Income Situation*
(July, 1968), p. 72.

NONFARM INCOME The big change income-wise for farmers in the last
decade or two has been their rising earnings from pursuits outside of agriculture. Today the off-farm income received by farm operator families is
within an eyelash of being equal to that from agriculture (see Table 2).

PRICE MEASURING FUNDAMENTALS

LONG-RUN DEMAND The long-run demand for food[4] depends chiefly on
the level of population in the United States. In view of the experience of the
last couple of generations, it appears that rising incomes do not have a
primary influence on total demand; the income elasticity of demand for food
may be as low as one-tenth. (What this means is that if aggregate consumer
income were to increase, let us say, 10 per cent, the increased outlay for
food would be only 1 per cent.) The proportion of consumer spending going
for food, beverages, and tobacco shows a gradual decline: 30.9 per cent in
1940, 30.4 in 1950, 26.9 in 1960 and 24.8 in 1966. Not only is the trend downward, but more and more of the dollar spent goes for processing and marketing, not to the grower.

Per capita food consumption measured in calories is now estimated to be
at a point 10 per cent under that of the first decade of this century. Since it
is the *number* of people that makes the big difference, and since the national

---

4 Space does not permit an examination of the demand for tobacco and cotton crops, the combined value of which
normally amounts to about 9 per cent of
the total farm output of this nation.

level of population is currently expanding at a rate of about 1.5 per cent a year, there is considerable hope of a substantial boost in the demand for agricultural products in the long run.

Leaving aside the domestic scene for the moment, foreign purchases of American farm products are as apt to decline as to increase in the near future. The need exists but the means of payment are lacking.

HUNGER IN AMERICA? Is there a substantial unmet demand for farm commodities within our nation? In 1967 there was a flurry of excitement over "hungry" people, prompted particularly by a special TV program. The President appointed a Citizens Board of Inquiry into Hunger to examine the situation. The Board rendered its report in August 1968, finding no significant degree of starvation or acute hunger. It said that considerable malnutrition resulting from ignorance or parental neglect did exist.

Even if hunger on an appreciable scale is not a problem, what would a boost in income for poor people in the United States accomplish for agricultural demand? Available evidence indicates that demand would increase, but not markedly; therefore, as a long-run determinant, per capita income must be considered a factor of only secondary importance. Studies of consumer spending habits indicate that, if given more income, low-income groups would spend somewhat more for farm products, but they would not consume additional calories; rather they would eat slightly more of the animal products (like milk and beefsteak) and less bread, cornmeal, potatoes, and beans.[5]

There are some reasons to believe that a wider spread of nutritional knowledge might cause a decline in the demand for food because there are many Americans who eat too much, and nutritional science teaches people the how and why of substituting less expensive foods for the more costly ones (fats, proteins, minerals, and vitamins of vegetable origin in the place of nutrients from animal products). On the whole, nutritional science is apt to be a neutral factor in respect to the total demand for agricultural products.

Will manufacturing industries ever consume a large share of the farm output for nonfood uses? As matters now stand, farmers can be happy if new industrial uses are found fast enough to offset the replacement of farm products by synthetic fibers (which have cut deeply into the market for wool and cotton), by industrial processes that generate chemical detergents that replace soaps once made from animal fats, and so on.

---

5 This sort of substitution would mean a net increase in demand for farm products because it takes many more units of land, labor, and capital to produce a diet rich in animal foods than one of vegetable origin. Hence, a shift to the more expensive diet would mean an increased demand for the services farmers render, and more acreage would be needed.

LONG-RUN SUPPLY   If farmers were to adopt generally all the good management practices that are known now, production could be increased much faster than the expected increase in consumers' needs. The hard thing to predict is how fast improved methods will be adopted. Leaving aside the impact of government controls, it appears that the improved technology will spread, and the total production of farm products in this country will gradually continue to rise, as it has in the past, even if agricultural prices decline from current levels. This increase is probable even though many small-scale operators and hired workers leave agriculture for jobs in cities. In other words, the increased output is expected to come in the future, as it has for some years past, from greater yields per acre, per worker, and per livestock unit, not from new areas and new workers being applied to farming.

Over the past 30 years this nation's population has increased about 55 per cent, whereas its index of total farm output for human consumption has risen over 70 per cent. The large growth in production occurred despite a variety of Federal programs which have curtailed acreage devoted to cultivation. Of course, a tremendous amount of land was made available for humans as a result of replacing horses and mules by tractors. Moreover, the efficiency of production per acre and per animal unit has been importantly increased over the last three decades.

Farm groups have had a solid basis for fearing overproduction arising from improved technology, because of the inelastic demand for their products and the difficulty in transferring factors of production out of agriculture into other occupations. The greater supplies sent to market have tended to aid consumers more than they have benefited producers.

In summary, whereas total population and food output are both expanding significantly, the situation of recent decades—wherein agricultural production tends to grow slightly faster—is apt to continue in the foreseeable future.

SHORT-RUN DEMAND   One must distinguish between the behavior of prices of individual farm products and that of the conglomerate whole. Individual prices move frequently and widely over a short time period, but in recent decades (unlike the 1930's and 1940's) this has not been true of the index of the agricultural industry as a whole.

The behavior of prices for this industry is much affected by the price elasticity of demand. It varies from one product to another, being highly inelastic for potatoes, wheat, and milk, as examples, and elastic in the instance of fruits. For total food (and for total farm) products, the authorities contend that at the farm level, the demand is markedly inelastic. It is a pity that the demand for leading farm products is not elastic because, if it were, the problem of agricultural surpluses could be met by improving the efficiency of farm production; that is, by reducing the costs and selling prices, larger quantities of farm products could be marketed, still allowing normal profits for producers. Alas, this is not the case.

It will take only a simple exercise in economic graphics to demonstrate the underlying basics of the marked instability of prices that the agricultural industry confronts. Given these realistic assumptions for the short-run time period—an inelastic supply curve and an inelastic demand curve—the result will be wide price movement from a small change in either supply or demand.

What are the implications for the structure of the industry? Whenever a group of producers are confronted with a gyrating price for their output, they develop a longing for a regularized, fair pattern to replace the chaos—put an end to cut-throat competition. For farmers the risk from price uncertainty is so great that it is no wonder the producers came to demand orderly marketing. In manufacturing, where this problem existed years back, the usual response was to form monopolies or near monopolies, bringing into being follow-the-leader pricing. In agriculture this has not developed. Farmers have tried various things and finally turned to the Federal Government for a solution (Sections III and V).

CONSTANT SHORT-RUN SUPPLY   Agriculture is rather unique among American industries in regard to its short-run supply character. The supply of all farm products coming on the market varies little from year to year, even though the demand for them may drop drastically. Does this violate economic principles? On first glance, economic theory seems to indicate that when demand declines, bringing a drop in market price, a curtailment of production is to be expected. However, further inquiry indicates that a drop in production may not occur, in the short run, if most of the costs are fixed. This is the case with agriculture.

Most of the costs incurred by a farm operator do not vary with output. Real estate taxes, interest, and depreciation are all important costs, and they are fixed. The labor supply comes mostly from the operator's own family. The farmer cannot cut his costs by an appreciable amount, nor secure a higher price through curtailment of output. Only if a large number of farmers restrict production will price rise. This is not likely to happen, however, since it is usually to the individual farmer's interest to expand his own output if he thinks other farmers are reducing theirs.

Even in a depression, when prices fall to a very low level, a farmer can find little alternative use for his labor. Consequently, he continues to farm as long as he can cover his variable costs. He may shift from one crop to another, but he cannot profitably shift his resources into a nonfarm use to any feasible degree. Moreover, if one farmer goes bankrupt, another takes his place. These factors help to explain the powerful tendency for agricultural production to remain at a high level even when confronted by substantially lowered demand for farm products.

There are frequent and significant changes in the supply of a particular crop in the short run, mainly due to weather conditions. Domestic demand, largely a function of aggregate consumer income, and export demand (very significant for some commodities) fluctuate in the short run, and their combined change can be appreciable.

Hence, whether farmers' markets are "good" depends on the interaction of supply and demand at a particular moment—not on the President, or Congress, or support legislations, or men who are sympathetic with farmers' problems.

VARIABILITY ILLUSTRATED   To visualize how great the price variability can be, consider the price of hogs over the last 40 years. The average price received per hundredweight in 1924 was $7.34; in 1926, $11.79; in 1932, $3.34; in 1936, $9.37; in 1939, $6.23; in 1942, $13.04; in 1947, $24.10; in 1949, $18.10; in 1953, $21.60; in 1956, $14.50; in 1958, $19.60, in 1963, $14.90; in 1966, $22.80; and in 1967, $18.90. Note that within a period of 2 or 3 years price changes of 30 per cent or more would frequently occur. What other industry faces such price behavior?

INTERVENING IN THE MARKET

FORMULA PRICING AND FLUID MILK   A peculiar hybrid in pricing has become firmly established for the fluid milk industry (pasteurized and put in cartons for home use) in more than 70 major metropolitan areas—pricing under Federal orders. In essence all milk processors in a given market are required to pay farmers a certain price for the milk which goes into Class I use (cartons), and a lower price for the milk that is left over, which is processed into ice cream, cottage cheese, skim milk, cream for coffee, and so on.

The pricing pattern according to use usually involves a "formula," a basic factor of which is the price of "manufacturing milk" (for the making of cheese, evaporated milk, butter, and so on). That price is nationally competitive and low. Typically, add-ons are stipulated above the manufacturing base price to arrive at the various prices for milk according to the end use made of it by the particular processor in that market. The same milk sells at various prices; the farmer gets a "blend" price. For Class I milk the differential over manufacturing price is substantial, being $2.30 per hundredweight in the New York City region in 1967, for example.

The theoretical justification for the premium is that it is more costly and painstaking for farmers to produce a steady flow of Class I milk under the strict conditions set by state and city health officials. No doubt this is true. However, there is some reason to believe that these price structures allow more than a little premium, which only market power backed by law could make possible.

Nevertheless, over the past 50 years free market pricing for milk has been tried, and found wanting. That is why the Federal marketing orders and agreements came into being; they have achieved an orderly marketing and a workable pattern of pricing that is fair to all concerned. This approach has stood the test of time. How to categorize it in terms of industry structure is difficult. It is like public utility pricing, yet employs a system tied to a competitive base price. Frequently, the negotiation between big producer and processor interests influences the makeup of the formula. This is a unique pricing case, the product of long and bitter experience, not of economists' texts. It does not involve government subsidy from the Federal government.

FEDERAL PRICE SUPPORTS   Before attempting to analyze the government's role in the pricing of American farm products it is essential to get some understanding of the complexities involved. First, less than half of the volume of farm marketings gets price support (Table 3). Next, provisions are complex in that there are classes of commodities, degrees of certainty of support, and a multitude of means of support.

TABLE 3   FARM MARKETINGS BY
PRICE SUPPORT STATUS, 1968

CROPS	TOTAL MARKET SALES ($ MILLIONS)
Total	44,065
Under price support	17,892
Mandatory support	15,173
Basic commodities	7,418
Cotton	1,153
Wheat	1,823
Corn	2,447
Tobacco	1,169
Rice	519
Peanuts	307
Nonbasic commodities	7,755
Dairy products	5,981
Oats	185
Barley	266
Sorghum grain	577
Sugar beets	364
Others	382
Nonmandatory support	2,719
Soybeans	2,289
Cottonseed	211
Flaxseed	68
Dry beans	151
Not under price support	26,173

SOURCE   *Statistical Abstract of the United States,
1969* (Washington, D.C.: U.S. Department of
Commerce), p. 604.

There are a wide variety of government programs under which payments are made to farmers for their participation in actions demanded in agriculture's best interests. There are production curtailment devices: cropland diversion, conservation reserve, cropland adjustment (regular, public access, "greenspan"), cropland conversion, and acreage allotments. Then there are market propping measures: crop loan and storage; purchase and disposal through school lunch programs and wide-scale distribution of free (and/or almost free) foods to the poor; a variety of export subsidy programs.

Then there are payments to farmers under the Sugar Act.

Also important, but not involving subsidy, are a host of Federal orders and agreements, which have pricing implications and which affect in varying degrees the individual producer's freedom to market his product. The fluid milk case has already been mentioned. In addition, in 1967 there were 47 other orders involving fruits, vegetables, and nuts having a combined market value of over $1.5 billion.

CONCLUDING OBSERVATIONS American agriculture is so diverse in products and related government programs that it is hard to pin a market structure label on either the whole or its parts that will fit precisely. In some instances production is so restricted that freedom of entry is virtually gone, and marketing and pricing are so directly affected that we can hardly point to it as a "competitive" case. On the other hand, there are commodities (like apples) for which production, entry, pricing, and so on, are practically unrestricted.

One can assert that the great bulk of the government's support program concerns but a few crops, and therefore but a minority of agriculturalists. On the other hand, it can be argued that the effect of the support program spreads out and indirectly assists the price structure for most farmers. Further, it is claimed that the production restraint programs act chiefly to achieve the same end that much lower prices would accomplish, but which would occur more slowly and with great damage to the capital structures of farmers and of the thousands of small-town merchants, bankers, and service people who depend on agriculture.

Where does all this leave us? Here is an attempt to generalize about the whole: With several exceptions, the industry label "competitive case" fits American agriculture better than any other. Government assistance has softened for farmers what would have been the adverse reactions of the competitive market during the past generation but it has not altered fundamentally the structure of the industry.

Does a recitation of the agriculture industry's highly competitive characteristics have much to do with its economic ills? Indeed, there is a bearing! The competitive engine explains the persistent tendency to overproduce. Also, because of the large number engaged in the industry, it is virtually impossible (even through the medium of cooperative organization) for producers to achieve the regulation of output that would be necessary to achieve a stable price for their output. Because of *product standardization*, the individual producer has no chance to isolate himself from the market disturbances and achieve a stable adequate price for his output. The fact that prices are determined on free markets, in which a host of dynamic facts and fancies daily exert their influence without moderation, helps to explain why agricultural prices fluctuate so frequently and so widely. Because of ease of entry, it is possible for men to become farmers who—for reasons of either limited ability, poor health, laziness, old age, and so on—will never achieve output levels adequate for decent incomes. Truly, agriculture's basic economic ills are rooted in the structure of the industry.

III. MARKET CONDUCT
RESOURCE ALLOCATION
AND THE PRICE SYSTEM

There is a worldwide tendency for a chronic surplus of labor to adhere to the agriculture industry. Prices in a predominantly market economy are supposed to distribute land, labor, and capital among the various occupations and to place the proper quantities of these factors in such a way that they will make the greatest contribution to society's output (in terms of values). Moreover, a similar rate of pay should result for each grade of a factor.

Why does a surplus of labor persist so long and in such large numbers in the agriculture industry? Wages are very low where the surplus is greatest. Can't these people read the signals? Don't farmers respond to the movement of relative prices?

In the management of the farm enterprise, a farm operator does respond to the movement of relative prices, but the excess labor problem is more difficult. During periods of full employment, this equilibrating mechanism (the price system) functions fairly well, but during times of unemployment it hardly works at all. Today, after nearly 30 years of high level employment in cities, the excess of bona fide capable workers in agriculture is almost gone. True, there is still a considerable excess of people (from an economic point of view) in the countryside, and the resulting poverty is a national problem, but this is to be understood today more by the insights of sociology and psychology than by those of economics.

The virtual exodus of thousands of excess farm hands to the cities since 1940, forming inner-city communities too frequently characterized by cynicism, despair, ignorance, and unemployment, has raised many questions. Many wonder if it would have been preferable to have kept them down on the farm. From the standpoint of economics the answer is no, but from other considerations it could be yes. It is now clear that for thousands of these people the flight from Egypt was an exodus into a desert, indeed. Unfortunately, they have no Moses to lead them nor a real disposition to follow. Even under Moses it took 40 years, enough time to rear an entire new generation, to develop a disciplined, effective people who could enter the promised land. Then it took hard work to make the milk and honey flow.

In earlier generations the absorption of the immigrant and the farmhand into city life was left to itself with but meager aid from private and public welfare agencies. The record says it worked, though there was pain aplenty; today the transition seems harder to make for the groups involved. Despite public assistance on an unprecedented scale, headway has been made only slowly, and there is much evidence that large numbers are becoming adjusted to government support as a normal way of life.[6] More ominous are the signs of a breakdown of citizenship in some big cities.

RETURNS TO FARMERS

What a family earns from farming is a mixture of returns for its labor, an implicit return on its capital, and something for the management function. Relatively very few earn enough to equal the wages of craftsmen in cities. This is a primary reason why more and more of them have turned to non-farm jobs while still keeping the farm operating.

Counting earnings from all sources, per capita income of farm people in recent years has run about 70–75 per cent of that for the rest of the population. Viewed historically this is good! Remember, incomes of city folk have risen rapidly in the last 20–30 years; yet, farmers have gained on them—from 32.6 per cent in 1934 to 77.3 per cent in 1969 (Table 4).

Despite this remarkable progress, considerable poverty still exists within agriculture—especially if one includes all people who may be considered rural. As of the mid-1960's, government reports showed 46 per cent of America's families with incomes under $3,000 living in rural areas. In particular situations—i.e., camps where migrant farm workers used in harvesting vegetable and fruit crops lived, Appalachia, and Indian reservations—the low income problem among agricultural producers is chronic, indeed.

Even among typical commercial farms of various sorts, where good methods are employed, there is a wide diversity in earnings per hour of labor expended. In some cases earnings are very low (Table 5).

---

6 Actually, many people are making a normal upward climb on the socio-economic ladder. Currently, we are inclined to focus attention on our social failures. A basic fault may lie in our expectation. Another fault is inherent in the news industry; that is, troubles are dramatic and newsworthy, whereas upward mobility involves a long process of small humdrum middle-class bits of behavior.

TABLE 4 PER CAPITA
PERSONAL INCOME[a] OF
FARM POPULATION AS
A PERCENTAGE OF THAT
FOR THE NONFARM
POPULATION

	FARM AS A PERCENTAGE OF NONFARM
1934	32.6
1939	37.3
1944	54.7
1949	55.7
1954	52.8
1959	50.1
1964	62.5
1969	77.3

a Disposable income from all sources.

SOURCE U.S. Department of Agriculture, Economic Research Service, *Farm Income Situation* (July 1970), p. 50.

There is a considerable correlation between a farm's income and the amount invested in it, as economic analysis would suggest. So, why not supply more capital to low income farmers? Much attention has been devoted and a host of institutions have been created during the last 40 years to provide farmers with adequate access to capital funds, and it is hard to conceive what else can be done. Actually, the heart of the problem is not a capital shortage; rather, experience and analysis have shown that the big limiting factor is the low level of managerial ability usually possessed by those who need more capital and cannot get it. In other words, no credit institution can hand out thousands of dollars to a farmer just because he needs it unless there is abundant evidence that he will use it wisely. If additional capital is made available to many small-scale operators, it must be provided on a "supervised" basis; that is, some management direction from an outside source is needed—a ticklish and time-consuming matter for whatever agency undertakes the job.

The surplus population generated in rural areas is probably the most important reason why the small-scale farm problem is so persistent (around the world). Unless there is an out-migration, population pressure in the rural areas develops, resulting in the continued subdivision of good lands and the spread of farming to marginal soils. Carried to its ultimate, the result is such a low output per worker, and therefore such low real incomes, that death rates rise to equal birth rates.

TABLE 5   CAPITAL INVESTMENT, NET FARM INCOME, AND
EARNINGS PER HOUR OF FAMILY LABOR; TYPICAL COMMERCIAL
FAMILY-OPERATED FARMS, SELECTED TYPES: 1967

	CAPITAL INVESTMENT ($)	NET FARM INCOME ($)	RETURN PER HOUR TO OPERATOR AND FAMILY LABOR[a] ($)
Dairy farms, Grade A			
Central northeast	56,300	7,900	1.51
Eastern Wisconsin	89,520	10,114	1.62
Broiler farms			
Delmarva	67,940	8,347	2.14
Georgia	24,100	1,724	0.45
Corn Belt Farms			
Cash grain	229,500	13,902	2.05
Hog-beef raising	88,680	6,007	0.74
Cotton farms, nonirrig.			
High plains, Texas	95,920	15,885	5.59
Tobacco farms			
North Carolina coastal plains	48,330	6,421	2.10
Kentucky bluegrass			
Tobacco-dairy, inter. area	27,210	3,989	0.92

a   After deducting for family's invested capital at 4.1 per cent. If deducted at current interest rates, the amount left as a return for labor would decline a third or more,
with exceptions above and below that ratio.

SOURCE   U.S. Department of Agriculture, Economic Research Service, Bulletin 230,
Farm Costs and Returns (September 1960), pp. 2, 4.

Consequently, there is an urgent need for nonfarm employment to absorb the surplus farm population. When such employment exists, particularly if it is nearby, the healthy flow from farm to city takes place. That is
probably why statistics show that farm productivity and living levels are
highest in the vicinity of urban centers. However, distance alone does not
explain the rate of migration; apparently education, income per family,
health, and some other noneconomic factors bear upon it.

Birth rates tend to be highest in those states where farm productivity is
lowest, although this inverse relation is not perfect. In general, rural birth
rates in America are about 20 per cent higher in the low-productivity states
than in the high ones, and this tends to aggravate the man-land ratio in the
poorer areas. Historically, the birth rate among farm people has been twice
that of city residents. A constant migration of the excess rural population
to urban employment is essential if the small-scale farm problem is to be
avoided.

For the past 30 years the nation's demand for food and fiber, although
growing, has been met by a shrinking number of workers. Somewhere this
down trend must stop, but we are not at that point yet.

CONCLUDING OBSERVATIONS

Farming is a great laboratory where a competitive industry can be seen at work. The economic behavior, both of the individual producer and of the whole, is predictable in terms of the textbook analysis. Moreover, agriculture is becoming more rational—economic-wise—as the "way-of-life" farmers disappear or merely hang around the fringes of the main show.

In their search for profits, all the while being buffeted by shifting final demands, the individual producers have exhibited ever more sophisticated technique, expanded production, and released a constant supply of labor to other industries. Not only was society well served by their efforts, but they have made large strides in recent years toward the goal of parity in income vis-à-vis the nonfarm population.

IV. MARKET PERFORMANCE

Let us look at the record of the agriculture industry in terms of a number of key criteria.

1. Production adequacy The industry has kept America abundantly supplied with a great variety of farm commodities—no ordinary feat in today's world. The Federal program of aid for farmers, although trying to achieve limited production and fair prices, seems rather to have stimulated technological advance and heavy capital investment (perhaps because risk was reduced).

2. Adoption of new technique Between the late 1930's and the early 1960's the man-hours required per bushel of major grain crops was reduced by more than 80 per cent. For livestock and their products the cut in man-hours per unit of output was varied and usually less, but it was substantial in all cases: 90 per cent for broilers and turkeys, over 60 per cent for milk, and about 40 per cent for beef.

3. Prices of products In relation to the consumer's level of income, agricultural products have become cheap. Whereas the amount spent at retail, as a ratio of total consumer spending, has declined only a small amount over the past 30 years, a much larger portion of the expense is accounted for by processing, marketing, transportation, and taxes.

4. Freedom of entry Generally there is freedom of entry, but there are a few significant qualifications and exceptions. Often it is the right to market one's output which is curtailed. For tobacco especially, and for other less extreme cases, entry means paying a high premium for land, which carries with it the right to market the product. (These are instances where government power, fractionalized in individual hands, becomes wealth—an unintended and very unfortunate result.) For most farm products, however, entry is unrestricted.

5. Implications for payments balance   Agriculture has always been a major contributor to the nation's export earnings. Our farm exports potential is good today, and the nation will rely heavily on these exports in the years ahead.

6. Scale of operations   Although growing larger both in acreage and in the scale of investment, the family-size farm is in a strong competitive position, except for certain specialty crops. No monopoly problem is imminent.

7. Adequacy of income to members of the industry   Historically, earnings have been lower for farm people than for others in the economy. The situation has improved, both absolutely and relatively, and the current trend is hopeful. We cannot achieve equality between farm and nonfarm incomes. As long as farm communities produce an excess of labor there must be a differential to encourage an outward movement.

8. Price collusion   There is no price collusion except possibly where backed by government power in the name of economic justice. Whether certain producers have been able to use government power to achieve, in effect, higher prices by collusion depends on whether we think that an otherwise freely competitive price would have been right. The whole tenor of the legislation which authorizes government intervention reveals a conviction that free competition would not result in socially desirable prices and practices.

GOVERNMENT INTERVENTION
AND ASSISTANCE

The above highly favorable evaluation of this industry must not be seen as a hymn of praise for the competitive structure. Indeed, public interference of some sort in the markets that affect farmers has been extensive and persistent in American history. It is a long record worth reviewing.

In the last quarter of the nineteenth century, farmers desired government regulation of the railroads and other big businesses that they believed were exploiting them. In the seventies and nineties, when farm prices were low, farmers wanted to see railroad rates and industrial prices fall, so that farm products would continue to exchange for other goods in a ratio to which they had been accustomed.

Following World War I, farm prices fell drastically again, and demands for Federal aid were heard. A conservative group held that legislation could do little to restore farm prices to higher levels. Instead, they urged that the margin between prices paid by consumers and prices received by farmers be reduced through a variety of methods: preferred legislation for farmers' cooperatives; an improved system of intermediate credit; improved warehousing facilities and supervision; reduction of freight rates; the establishment of better grades and standards for farm products; and better farm roads. Also, to enable the farmer to adjust his production to market needs by supplying him with economic information concerning supply and demand conditions, an " outlook" service was sponsored by the United States Department of Agriculture (USDA). In the endeavor to find more foreign markets for farm products, the USDA set up a network of world reporters. Finally, in the 1920's, higher tariffs on farm products were erected.

Other farm groups, especially those from the hard-hit wheat districts, wanted much more direct aid through Federal legislation. They pressed hard for a program which would dump quantities of certain farm products on foreign markets but hold domestic prices above the world price by means of tariffs. Export subsidies—which were tried in the late 1920's, revived in the 1950's, and expanded in the 1960's despite serious drawbacks—generate ill will in other nations that have similar exports, encourage competitive subsidies by other governments, lower the world price structure for all exports of the affected items, and generate demands for more subsidy.

Still other farm spokesmen thought the solution to the farmer's price difficulties could be worked out through his own cooperative efforts, and they believed in what was called orderly marketing. Their idea was to set up large nationwide farmers' marketing cooperatives. If prices tended to sag, these marketing agencies would buy certain farm commodities in sufficient volume and place them in storage so as to elevate prices. Later, when prices were more favorable, these products would be sold. If production of some farm products appeared to be excessive year after year, the cooperatives were to advise farmers to alter their production plans. President Hoover favored this type of farm program and his administration set up the Farm Board, whose job it was to help finance the marketing cooperatives in their stabilizing efforts. Soon after the establishment of the Farm Board, however, the depression of the 1930's began. Prices of farm products fell badly, despite the efforts of the marketing cooperatives and the Farm Board to halt the decline. The Farm Board asked wheat farmers to reduce their production in line with the lower market demand, but farmers did not heed the request. The Board concluded that its price stabilization program would work only if it were accompanied by some sort of Federal production control.

In March 1933, the New Deal initiated new and bold measures to help agriculture out of the doldrums of low prices and low incomes. In meeting these problems, faith was no longer placed in the individual or cooperative efforts of farmers themselves. Instead, the coordinating power of the Federal government was used to accomplish needed programs. Legislation was passed that provided for farm income to be elevated to a position of equality with that of other large economic groups, a goal that was to be achieved by keeping agricultural prices up to parity levels. The method for attaining the desired goal was to be a system of direct production control.

Acreage allotments were determined for cotton, corn, wheat, rice, tobacco, potatoes, peanuts, and all other soil-depleting crops taken as a group. The national allotment was then broken down into allotments for the several states, and these, in turn, for counties and for individual farmers. In determining the size of these allotments, factors such as past production, type of farming, and kind of land was taken into consideration. Payments were made to those who participated in the acreage reduction program, payments which proved effective in eliciting the cooperation of farmers. Thus, paradoxically, a measure of national production planning was in a relatively short time established in the most individualistic and competitive sector of the American economy.

WEAKNESSES OF PRICE SUPPORTS AND ACREAGE LIMITATION   No matter how carefully parity price and acreage-limitation legislation may be drawn, serious weaknesses will remain.

1. Total income may not be increased   If prices are pegged above the free-market level, both theory and practice have demonstrated that the market will not absorb the whole crop. Production will have to be cut back, therefore offsetting higher prices.[7]

2. Production may not fall under acreage limitation   Of course, if acreage is cut back enough, production will certainly go down. Yet, acreage reductions of small magnitudes (such as 10 per cent) may not cause a reduction of crop output because average output per acre may rise enough to offset the smaller acreage. This has been the continuous experience.

3. Surpluses[8] may appear in different commodities   When corn is cut back, for example, the farmer will likely plant those acres with a soil-improving crop such as legume hay, which permits him to collect the soil conservation payment. When he gets a good crop of hay or pasture, he will expand his beef or dairy herd in order to make use of this roughage, or he may plant another grain. After a few years, beef, pork, and dairy product supplies may become so large (with price depressing effects) that producers of these products will call for production control.

Production of a few crops may be held back, but total agricultural output cannot be easily reduced.

4. Reduction of production is unpopular   Farmers claim that they do not like anyone to tell them what they can or cannot do with their land. (However, their satisfaction with the tobacco program which involves extensive controls, leads one to doubt their opposition.) City people do not like the idea of paying someone *not* to produce something.

---

7   This depends on the elasticity of the demand for the particular crop in question, and for corn (the number one crop) the question is complicated because most of it is fed to livestock on the farms where grown, not sold as grain.

8   By "surplus" is meant a quantity of product that will not go into consumption at a given price. It does not mean an amount beyond the nation's capacity to consume in some form, at some price; a surplus is a price phenomenon, basically, not a physical one.

Why was it that socially enlightened statesmen advocated lower production and higher prices during a depression period when many people were in dire want? The New Deal officials believed that the way to bring back prosperity was to raise prices. The farm program was but one aspect of a broader overall economic policy.

It was pointed out by the New Deal officials that the foreign demand for products, such as cotton, tobacco, wheat, and lard, had nearly vanished, making it unwise to continue producing the usual quantities.

Besides, should not farmers be allowed the same privileges as were already enjoyed by other important groups in the national economy? They had erected bulwarks to insulate themselves from price cutting and excessive competition—e.g., patents, tariffs, oligopoly pricing, labor union practices, and minimum wage laws. Did not social justice require that agriculture be guaranteed—with the help of the government—fair prices and thereby a fair share of the national income? If farmers were to receive higher incomes, the market for industrial goods would be strengthened, thus aiding the recovery in the cities.

Aside from the pros and cons, acreage limitation did not accomplish the desired objective. During the first term of the New Deal, production was indeed held back, but this was chiefly due to the effects of two great droughts in 1934 and 1936. As the weather returned to normal in 1937 and in subsequent years, the surpluses appeared (in spite of acreage reduction) with price-depressing effects. In the endeavor to support prices, the crop loan program under the Commodity Credit Corporation (CCC) assumed large proportions (e.g., so much cotton was put in storage that it equalled the entire U.S. consumption for 2 years). Millions of bushels of corn and wheat were also stored. But with the outbreak of World War II, demand began to rise and in a few years the grain stores were withdrawn. Agricultural prices rose sharply and, with rare exception, stayed above parity until the end of 1948; then the CCC found it necessary to engage in large-scale price support again. But in 1950 and 1951 the inflationary forces associated with the Korean War pushed prices generally above support levels, and some commodities moved out of storage, reducing the financial commitments of the CCC.

5. High prices stimulate substitutes High supported prices for butter and cotton have encouraged substitutes like oleomargarine and synthetic fibers to invade their markets.

6. Does not help farmers who need it most Like any other program in which benefits are tied to volume of output, this one does not significantly help the small-scale farmer.

7. Loss of foreign markets Foreign markets are important for tobacco, rice, cotton, and wheat. When prices are supported above the world price, foreign buyers tend to buy elsewhere.

8. Inflated land values The value of farm land follows the value of crops which can be raised on it. Acreage limitation schemes make land the one scarce factor of production, and supports tend to boost the value of output per acre. In consequence, support prices tend to become capitalized into higher land values, creating a windfall gain for the first owner, but making a higher overhead cost for the next one.

STEPS TOWARDS PARITY INCOME APPROACH   The price support program has remained a favorite public issue, almost constantly for 20 years. Numerous particular suggestions for change have been proposed and only a few can be mentioned here. One of the most durable has been to shift the emphasis from parity prices to parity incomes, an idea endorsed by a committee of the American Farm Economics Association in 1947. This distinction is important because support prices become capitalized into land values, a major problem today, and because higher prices help only those farmers who have a lot of output to sell. Most suggestions for providing parity incomes involve the issuance of a government check directly to individual farmers. How would the amount for each producer be determined? If it were somehow geared to his volume of productivity, the program would still fail to help the lowest income people. On the other hand, if the amount were calculated on some index of family need, with other income deducted, it would amount to a "minimum annual income" proposal—the merits and demerits of which are being currently debated in America as an alternative to existing welfare programs. It is a matter which lies beyond the scope of this chapter.

NEW DEVELOPMENTS   Significant alternatives in the price-propping approach were brought in national legislation between 1962 and 1965. Briefly, farmers were given more choice—grow as much as you want and get no direct help, or retire some acreage from certain crops and be paid income supplements directly from the U.S. Treasury.

Market prices for wheat, feed grains, and cotton were allowed to fall sharply, giving both domestic users and exporters the benefit of lower costs. For corn it meant a drop from $1.50 to $1.10 per bushel. Offsetting the lower price floors were the direct income supplements for the acreage-reduction cooperators.

For cotton, pegged at 21 cents, growers got a 9 cent per pound subsidy. The effect was to achieve a higher price for that portion of production which went into domestic consumption. In the case of wheat with a peg at $1.84, the grower got $2.57 per bushel (through supplements from the U.S. Treasury and a levy on millers) for that portion of the crop going into domestic use.

THE RURAL POVERTY PROBLEM

Thirty years ago millions of people lived on small-scale farms, which were run by operators who were essentially full-time workers, reasonably healthy, and under 65 years of age—that is, bona fide farm families. By current standards virtually all of them lived in poverty. Today, there are almost 800,000 farms with annual gross sales of less than $5,000, of which number 348,000 have a gross sales of under $2,500 (Table 1).

One cannot explain their continued adherence to agriculture at very low income levels in terms of economic behavior. In late 1968, with chronic labor shortages reliably reported across the nation, virtually anyone with a desire to work could have obtained a job—white or blue collar. Yet hundreds of thousands remained underemployed on the farms. Why?

Many remaining on the farms do have an economic logic which helps to explain their low level of participation in the economy; their current earnings (reported and unreported) plus the many free foods and other services that they get as recipients of public assistance, add up to a level of living that would be little, if any, surpassed by filling current job openings for which they would qualify. Their economic calculus has resulted in a reasonably satisfactory answer to them as individuals, but not for society. Moreover, a person dependent on the dole will likely deteriorate in body and spirit.

William H. Cooper, in a field survey of the poor in an agricultural section of Pennsylvania, found them to be people who either were bound by social mores and emotional ties of kinship and neighborhood to economically unproductive situations, or were suffering from personality disturbances which prevented them from participation in normal socio-economic life in America.[9] The latter group represented the really serious case, he felt. People in this group tended to withdraw into low- or no-rent fringes of society, and they generally lived in an economically irrational manner, the result being abject poverty.

Another survey of the many small farms in Appalachia found only a small percentage of farms with operators who seemed to have the potential of managing adequate size enterprises.

Moreover, recent reviews of the many research projects conducted in Appalachia stress the existence of a total culture that is inconsistent with that which economic rationality requires. Strong ties with relatives, a lack of respect for education and training (despite verbal affirmations of it), a strong preference for life in uncrowded hillsides rather than in cramped cities, certain religious attitudes, and so on, all add up to a society in which economic life tends to stagnate and from which migration is difficult.

What are the implications of all this? First, these unfortunate people are not needed in agriculture. As for the maladjusted individuals, if, from a psychiatrist's analysis, it is deemed best that many of them remain on small farms, aloof from close contact with others, busily engaged in a farm activity of some sort—in other words, a therapeutic prescription that could well fit thousands of individuals—that is an entirely different matter.

---

9 William H. Cooper, "Economics and Noneconomics of Poverty: A Clinical Economist in Rural Poverty," *American Economic Review*, **58**:521 (May 1968).

We have always known that farming offered a different way of life from that of the town dweller; for centuries this rural picture has exerted strong appeal. Wordsworth found health and a vision of truth in the countryside. Thoreau at his pond and in his garden found freedom from a seemingly absurd society—but he lived on a dire poverty level by current standards.

NEW CHALLENGES   Increasingly it has become apparent that the rural and urban poverty problems must be viewed together. When this is done the higher vantage point reveals quite different policy approaches from the methods that have been applied in the past. This is particularly true as the belief grows that the rash of problems now afflicting the big cities are not really solvable, that bigness itself creates unique dilemmas.

We are hardly ready to set a reverse tide of humans in motion, because the small towns are by no means prepared to receive them; indeed, they are continuing to generate a surplus of people. Therefore, an invigoration of the economies in the hundreds of small cities is clearly indicated. It will not happen as a natural response, urgent as the need may be. It will have to be planned and encouraged by appropriate means.

ABUNDANCE OF ASSETS   It would be a mistake to dwell wholly on the income shortcomings in American agriculture without even mentioning the surprising fact that farmers as a whole are well-to-do in terms of their net worth. Farm proprietors' net worth, estimated to be $231 billion in 1968, if divided by 3 million (the total number of farms) amounts to $77,000 each. In contrast, the average wealth per family for the total population was estimated to be about $21,000 in 1963.[10]

V. PUBLIC POLICY ALTERNATIVES
UNSTABLE PRICES AND THE SURPLUS PROBLEM

F ederal programs enacted over the last 50 years have aimed for agricultural price stability (usually called orderly marketing), the elimination of surpluses, and the lifting of a multitude of farm people out of poverty. It is clear now that the small-scale producers have been helped very little by the parity price approach, however.

Various programs have been devised to remove quantities of products from the normal trade channels to help dispose of surpluses. Federal funds were used to finance exports, school lunches, and free food for people on relief. These subsidy schemes were overshadowed by the foreign aid program during and right after World War II, which provided a marked stimulus to

---

10 For basic facts see the *Statistical Abstract, 1968* (Washington, D.C.: U.S.   Government Printing Office), pp. 333, 605.

American exports of numerous farm products. As this aid tapered off and exports tended to fall, the old schemes to help dispose of surpluses have all been revived and expanded full scale.

In the early 1950's, under a Republican President, there were moves to cut back on the expensive farm program, but the subsequent adverse political reaction in the "farm belt" was so pronounced that the administration quickly put together a new variation on the old theme—this time called the Soil Bank. The approach was simply to pay farmers to take land out of crops (and let trees take over, usually).

Since 1962, and especially since 1965, the program has been made much more complicated in order to allow for differing market conditions for the host of commodities involved and to please diverse producer interests and farm organizations. Meanwhile the dollar assistance in its multitudinous forms was gradually increased, possibly to aggregate $8 billion in fiscal 1969.

For a while in 1965 and 1966 it looked like a new day dawning for farmers as an invigorated foreign and domestic demand reduced CCC storage levels considerably. But in 1967 aggregate demand eased off and the price structure weakened, yet price inflation in the rest of the economy accelerated and continued through 1968.

A crack in the ranks of farmers became evident in the 1950's, and since then the split has widened and hardened; one major farm organization is demanding an end to the government's price props.[11]

No big upsurges of demand have come along now for 15 years to clear out the bulging warehouses of the stored surpluses. The taxpayer has had to shoulder a continuous series of large financial budgets, running generally in the range of $5–7 billion a year, an amount equal to about 40 per cent of the entire net income from farming in recent years. A condition of massive Federal aid has become "normal." New Deal programs launched 30 years ago under conditions of a deep depression were still in effect in the 1960's—after many years of unprecedented growth and prosperity. This says something about the durability of government assistance programs when once begun.

ALTERNATE APPROACHES

COMMITTEE FOR ECONOMIC DEVELOPMENT PROPOSAL   The Committee for Economic Development (CED) issued a report on agricultural policy in 1956 which recommended alternatives. It did not advocate a return to a completely free market price because that would expose farmers to "unnecessary risks and instability." The group did emphasize, however, that "a satisfactory farm price policy must retain as many of the desirable features

---

11 This organization, the Farm Bureau, is reported to be urging the government to engage on a much expanded program to retire acreage from production.

of a freely functioning price system as is possible," indicating that the free market price was a sort of norm from which the general level of agricultural product prices should not long depart.

To deal with the surplus problem the CED recommended continued price supports at gradually reduced levels combined with a program to pay farmers to take land out of crop production. To cope with the instability of prices it proposed a system of flexible price supports or income payments combined with a storage program; these devices were not expected to boost prices upward in the long run, but rather to bring about stability and orderly marketing. For the small-scale farmers there were suggestions whereby the operators would be aided in securing other kinds of employment and/or become more productive on their farms. A unique feature of the report was the recommendation to establish an Agricultural Stabilization Board whose members would be broadly representative of farm and nonfarm interests and who would serve for long terms on a staggered basis; the purpose in mind was to separate the formulation of policy (especially the setting of price support levels) from short-run political demands.

Although issued more than a decade ago, the CED proposal stands as, perhaps, the major alternative to that which exists.

NATIONAL COMMISSION ON FOOD AND FIBER   In 1966 President Johnson appointed a group of prominent leaders to review and make recommendations for the government's program for agriculture. In July 1967 the commission rendered its report. By a very slim majority the group backed the existing program (support prices at or slightly below world prices and direct income supplements to producers). The minority urged the phasing out of the entire control-support approach over a 5-year period, essentially recommending a return to the free market. It foresaw the inefficient producers being squeezed out of agriculture.

Looking beyond the horizons of today and tomorrow, the Rockefeller Brothers Fund, in a report released in December 1966, saw a need to bring idle farm acreage back into production. The dominant force behind this view, it held, was the massive population growth occurring around the world, a process which would lead to a great food crisis some years hence. (World population, it was estimated, would almost double between 1965 and 2000). In this milieu it saw a big role for America's "Food for Peace" (noncommercial) export program, the cost of which should be transferred from Agriculture to the State Department's budget.

Increasingly, as crop surpluses have accumulated in mammoth proportions, the question arises whether there should be a return to free-market pricing, pure and simple, in order to get crops into consumption, preserve this nation's position in foreign markets, and presumably to let the price system tell farmers not to produce so much. The repercussions would be felt in the case of wheat, the most troublesome surplus crop, in that its price would have to fall to the point where it would compete with corn and other feeds for livestock; the secondary reaction would be lower prices for feed grains, generally with a subsequent surge in livestock production and, consequently, lower prices for eggs, pork, milk, and beef. Cotton production would probably fall off sharply in the face of a drastically lower price on thousands of marginal farms in the Southeast; production in the Delta region of the Mississippi and in certain western states might expand.

Students of agriculture believe that: (1) total output would continue upwards, but at a slower pace than in recent years; (2) crop prices would fall more than those for livestock; (3) net farm income would fall approximately 25–30 per cent, the impact varying widely among different groups; (4) farm land values would experience a sharp drop from their present high level; (5) the gap between the incomes of efficient and inefficient producers would widen.

In view of the magnitude of disruptions, few agricultural economists would recommend the end of all supports and a return to a free-market pricing; but if they could turn the clock back and start 20 years ago, it is likely that many would. High supports have by now become so deeply imbedded in land values that any marked lowering of product prices will cause enormous capital losses to owners who have acquired land in good faith in the last 20 years. A drastic system of production control must be enacted if high support prices are to be continued and costly surpluses ended. This would mean a "public utility" approach involving the setting of national sales quotas for each principal agricultural commodity and then the giving to each farmer his pro rata share in the form of a marketing certificate.

CONCLUSION Standing in the way of finding a better approach than the current one is a serious conflict of objectives. What is it that is wanted? An end to rural poverty? Stability in prices? High prices? Is enterprise important in agriculture? Why be so concerned about the maintenance of the freedom in farming when in other areas of the economy (business and labor) the concept has been modified so much? (Some may answer that with entry freedom restricted in other industries there is more reason than ever to keep one great area, agriculture, open.) Regarding large subsidies for agriculture, even if it were granted that these subsidies were wrong in principle, should farmers abstain from seeking them when other groups within the ranks of business and organized labor have repeatedly sought to bolster their respective incomes through legislative devices?

Regarding the importance of the various objectives, farmers and their spokesmen are definitely divided. Evidence currently is conflicting as to what proportion would be inclined to surrender considerably more of their freedom of enterprise in exchange for assured high prices. Economists, on the other hand, appear to be much more anxious that economic freedom be maintained. It is apparent that the choice of a support program for agriculture hinges not only on economic but also on philosophical and political considerations.

ENDING RURAL POVERTY

Ending poverty in the countryside should now be viewed as but one phase of the nation's total program to uplift the poor. There are varieties of poverty, and in order to apply treatment it means placing people in various categories. Whatever cubby-holes are employed, we should have labels which clearly suggest the remedial steps appropriate for treating the ailment. This is a difficult criterion for analysis, but an essential one. Today it is likely that psychology and sociology, working through new educational curricula and methods, will provide more of the effective remedies than will economics.

Big cities can no longer be, in effect, the dumping ground for agriculture's excess people. In Carl Sandburg's *Chicago* the exfarmhands are standing around the street lights too much. The big challenge now is to find solutions for those surplus farm people who have a production potential, through vigorous economic development programs in the small cities. This will be difficult to bring about; not every village is a suitable site for an electronics factory or a veteran's hospital. Politically speaking, every town will demand growth, but this will fly in the face of sound economics. It would be easier to let resources be allocated by the free market, but the mounting problems of cities cast doubt on this alone.

The United States Department of Agriculture has taken a basic step in this direction by designating multicounty development districts. The Economic Development Administration has also encouraged the formation of development districts for planning and action. It has given significant amounts of aid to get the program underway, in many parts of the nation there are distinct evidences of growth. However, there is no real national policy to redirect a major portion of economic growth from the large to the small centers, and without such an approach the total picture will change little over the next decade or two.

An agriculture policy statement issued in August 1967 sets forth appropriate action steps, consistent with the analysis presented in the above paragraphs. This statement, prepared by a well-known agricultural economist, Professor Don Paarlberg, received extra attention in the press because it had the blessing of an official committee of a major political party. Its main points were the following:

1. Change the emphasis from parity price to a parity of opportunity as the proper goal.
2. Bring more manufacturing and other nonfarm employment into rural areas.
3. Provide more aid for rural schools (especially more and better vocational preparation).

4. Upgrade and expand the employment services for rural areas (to inform and assist people to get suitable jobs wherever they might be found).
5. Coordinate all public and private efforts to bring about needed changes in rural life.

NEW DIRECTIONS   With a rising tone of urgency, we are facing new challenges that will surely affect agricultural policy—though we cannot assess the impacts now; e.g., chemical fertilizer runoffs in river systems are causing great ecological damage. Are there any "safe" substitutes that farmers could employ?

A zero population growth policy will strongly affect farm people in general but it will strike most profoundly at the behavior of the poorest ones.

Since the pumping of large sums of money into schools for the culturally deprived accomplished little in the sixties, there is increasing talk of the need for "transition communities" where families would be subjected to a simultaneous package of medical-psychiatric-educational-vocational treatment.

We are on the verge of tackling socioeconomic disorders in the city and the country simultaneously as one problem. Official study committees are calling for a "national growth policy" by which to cope with an impending population explosion and its associated inevitable pollution of the natural environment. A larger role for rural communities will inevitably develop.

SUGGESTED READINGS

An Adaptive Program for Agriculture (New York: Committee for Economic Development, July 1962).

Banfield, Edward C. *The Unheavenly City* (Boston: Little, Brown and Company, 1970).

Cochrane, Willard W. *The City Man's Guide to the Farm Problem* (Minneapolis: University of Minnesota Press, 1965).

Heady, Earl O. *A Primer on Food, Agriculture, and Public Policy* (New York: Random House, 1967).

2. Joel B. Dirlam
FOOD DISTRIBUTION

I. INTRODUCTION
THE SIGNIFICANCE OF
FOOD DISTRIBUTION[1]

Food retailing is the most basic of the service industries. We spend about one fifth of our total consumption expenditure on food. Grocery store sales in 1967 were estimated at $74.2 billion, of which about $4 billion were non-foods.[2] In 1963, there were about 1 million employees and 234,000 active proprietors working in grocery stores.[3] Sharp jumps in the prices of key food items can evoke immediate reaction from housewives, who organize consumer boycotts. Retailers come under periodic fire from farmers because the farmer's share of the consumer's dollar is held to be insufficient.[4] Strategies invoked in the competitive warfare among the food retailers have affected all U.S. industry, through legislation such as the Robinson-Patman Act. The supermarket, a grocery store innovation, symbolizes the efficiency and wealth of the U.S. economic system.

With rising consumer incomes, food expenditures, though they have also risen in real terms, absorb a smaller and smaller proportion of disposable income, as shown in Table 1.

The food-chain era is usually dated from 1859, when George Gilmer and George Huntington Hartford launched the Great American Tea Company in a small store on Vesey Street in New York City. Originally, the firm had been a tea wholesaler; then the owners decided to sell directly to the public. A few years later they added a line of groceries. By 1869, the name was changed to The Great Atlantic and Pacific Tea Company. In 1912, the company introduced cash and carry, and the new "economy stores" were opened as quickly as possible. The stores were small, paid low rent, and were prim-

---

1 In writing this chapter, the author has leaned heavily on Professor William H. Wallace's expertise in food marketing, and on his preliminary draft of Parts I–III.

2 "35th Annual Report of the Grocery Industry," *Progressive Grocer*, 47:99 (April 1968).

3 *U.S. Census of Business 1963* (Washington, D.C.: U.S. Government

Printing Office, 1966), Vol. 1, Table 4–17.

4 In 1965 the spread between the farm and the consumer was about the same as in 1939, i.e., 61 per cent of the retail price. National Commission on Food Marketing, *Food from Farmer to Consumer* (Washington, D.C.: U.S. Government Printing Office, 1966), Table 9, p. 18.

TABLE 1 FOOD EXPENDITURES, 1937–1965

YEARS	PER CAPITA (1957–1959 = 100)	AS A PER CENT OF DISPOSABLE INCOME
1937–1939	78	23.1
1947–1949	95	24.7
1957–1959	100	20.6
1965	106	18.2

SOURCE   National Commission on Food Marketing, *Report* (1966), p. 9.

arily one-man operations with modest fixtures geared to low but steady profits. Only dry groceries were sold. For many years, chain stores that sold meat and produce did so on a concession basis.

Postdating A&P, the Grand Union Company, under the name of Jones Brothers Tea Company, was founded in 1872 in Brooklyn, New York; the Kroger Company followed in 1882, along with the Great Western Tea Company in Cincinnati. Safeway was founded as a proprietorship in American Falls, Idaho, in 1915, but was not incorporated until 1926.

The number of chain store units expanded from a few hundred in 1900 to a maximum of about 80,000 in 1934. Because the chains closed their small stores, the total fell to 18,000 in 1936. By 1968 the number of chain units (defined as owned by firms with 11 or more stores) had risen again to 27,860, and were responsible for 42 per cent of grocery store sales.[5] There were 258 food chains with 11 or more stores in 1963.[6] The largest, A&P, had 4,693 stores in 1967, and total revenue of $5.459 billion.

The term supermarket was first used in southern California during the early 1930's. It now designates large-volume retail food stores, predominantly self-service, having at least four departments—grocery, produce, meat, and dairy.

The self-service feature was introduced by Clarence Saunders in Memphis, Tennessee in 1912.[7] In his Piggly-Wiggly stores the customers would select their own merchandise and carry it to a check-out counter where they paid cash. Despite spectacular dollar volume in some units and an unprecedently low expense rate, the first chains of self-service stores were not financially successful. Their self-service feature was ignored by the national chains, which concentrated on acquiring and building small clerk-service stores.

The supermarket, as a retailing unit consciously setting a large volume

---

5 *Progressive Grocer*, op. cit., p. 236.
6 *U.S. Census of Business 1963* (Washington, D.C.: U.S. Government Printing Office, 1966), Vol. 1, Table 4–17.
7 R. J. Markin, *The Supermarket: An Analysis of Growth, Development,* *and Change*, (Pullman, Wash.: Washington State University Press, 1963), p. 4. See also, Super Market Institute, *The Supermarket Industry Speaks* (Chicago: Super Market Institute, 1960), p. 9.

target and using self-service to reach it, was conceived by Michael Cullen, who was a branch manager for Kroger in 1930. He proposed to build a 6,400 square foot store with ample parking space, which would sell about $12,500 worth of food per week. At that time the average store area was 500–600 square feet, with a volume of $500–$800 a week. Cullen planned to sell 300 items at cost, 200 at 5 per cent above cost, 300 items at 15 per cent above cost and 300 items at 20 per cent above cost. There were a few large-volume self-service stores operating in California and Texas by 1930, but they had made little impression on the retailing establishment.

When his idea was turned down by Kroger, Cullen opened his own store in Jamaica, Long Island, as "King Kullen the Price Wrecker." He lowered gross margins to 12–13 per cent of sales compared with the chains' 18–19 per cent. Net profits were higher than the chains'.[8] Supermarket prices were particularly attractive because of the depression; Big Bear, Giant Tiger, and Big Chief markets soon appeared in the larger cities. They were located in abandoned garages or warehouses with the merchandise set on rough pine tables or on the floor. Their techniques forced the large chains, but only after a long delay, to follow suit. As late as 1936, A&P had only twenty supermarkets. Replacement of the small store by the supermarket has continued to the present, except for an hiatus during World War II. Supermarkets now do about 72 per cent of grocery store dollar volume,[9] and they may be considered as the typical unit for producing food distribution service.

The King Kullen Grocery Company is still in existence with headquarters in Westbury, Long Island, and operates 50 stores.

In the early 1960's the food discount store made an appearance, imitating the selling appeal of the discounter in consumers' durables and apparel. It sells (or purports to sell) at lower average prices than typical supermarkets, has more restricted hours, offers about one-third fewer items, and gives no trading stamps. In 1967, Safeway converted 200 grocery stores to discount operation, and about 9 per cent of the new supermarkets that opened in 1967 were of the discount type, as against 6 per cent in 1966. The discounter became the King Kullen of the 1960's, bringing the "wheel of retailing" full circle once more.

In the early 1930's, the more progressive wholesalers began to join forces in larger buying groups in order to duplicate chain-store buying power, and management efficiency. Their retail customers are called "affiliated" independents. The affiliated independents' sponsor may be a voluntary, privately owned wholesaler group (like IGA or Super Valu), or their own cooperative wholesaler (like Certified Grocers of California, or Associated Grocers). Both types of wholesalers provide advertising, pricing and promotional services, and private label products. A bare 9 per cent of food store sales are

---

8 F. J. Charvat, *Supermarketing* (New York: Macmillan, 1961), pp. 18–25.

9 *Progressive Grocer*, op. cit., p. 84.

TABLE 2 NUMBER OF STORES, SALES, AND 5-YEAR RETURN ON EQUITY FOR 15 LARGEST FOOD CHAINS

	STORES, 1967		SALES, 1967			RETURN
	NUMBER	PER CENT OF CHAIN STORES	PER STORE ($ MILLIONS)	TOTAL PER CENT OF CHAIN SALES	SALES AS PER CENT OF GROCERY SALES	ON EQUITY 1963– 1968
A&P	4,724	17.1	1.2	17.6	7.4	8.7
Safeway	2,240	8.1	1.5	10.9	4.5	13.3
Kroger	1,458	5.3	1.9	9.1	3.8	9.6
Food Fare	566	2.0	2.3	4.2	1.7	6.8
Acme Markets	887	3.2	1.5	4.2	1.7	5.7
Jewel Tea	370[a]	1.3[a]	3.4[a]	4.0[a]	1.7[a]	9.6
National Tea	865	3.1	1.3	3.7	1.5	6.9
Winn Dixie	721	2.6	1.4	3.3	1.4	21.0
Grand Union	531[a]	1.9[a]	1.8[a]	3.0[a]	1.3[a]	9.8
First National	517	1.9	1.2	2.0	0.9	1.6
Lucky	202	0.7	3.0	2.0	0.8	19.3
Allied Supermarkets	324	1.2	1.8	1.9	0.8	8.7
Stop & Shop (Boston)	134[a]	0.5[a]	4.2[a]	1.8[a]	0.5[a]	7.7
Arden-Mayfair	240	0.9	2.3	1.8	0.8	5.2
Colonial	414	1.5	1.3	1.7	0.7	9.9

a Not wholly comparable because chain has substantial nonfood operations.

SOURCE *Moody's Industrials* (1968); *Progressive Grocer* (April 1968); *Forbes* (Jan. 1, 1969).

made today by nonaffiliated independents. Both affiliated independents and chains have grown at the expense of nonaffiliated stores.

Some voluntary wholesalers, like Super Valu in Minnesota, or Hannaford Brothers in Portland, Maine, have taken over some of their stores as wholly owned chains, while continuing to serve other independents as members of the voluntary group.

The volume of sales of the store is one basis for classification of retailers. Supermarkets (annual sales of $500,000 or more) are the largest, grading down to superettes and small stores. Among small stores, with annual volume of no more than $150,000, "convenience" stores have begun to show remarkable growth. A convenience grocery operates on high margins, carries a limited number of items (1,500–3,000), and remains open long hours, 7 days a week.[10] There are about 8,000 of these stores, concentrated mostly in the south.

10 *Progressive Grocer*, op. cit., p. 236.

II. MARKET STRUCTURE

In food distribution, as in other industries, the number of firms, their relative sizes, the proportion of business done by the largest firms in meaningful market areas, and the possibility of entry by new firms, are major structural characteristics. Together with the differentiation of products or services and the extent of vertical integration, these features provide the basic determinants that affect the reactions of firms to customers, to each other, and to potential entrants.

MARKET CONCENTRATION
CHARACTERISTICS

NUMBERS OF STORES AND FIRMS   In analyzing concentration, it is convenient to confine our attention to grocery stores, even though some specialized food stores compete with them. The specialized stores, such as meat markets, are comparatively few, and their numbers are decreasing. Grocery stores numbered about 226,000 in 1967. Their number has been falling for at least three decades, largely because of the decline in the number of independents. There were in 1940, about 405,000 independent grocery stores compared with 198,500 in 1967. Chains, too, with 27,600 units, are far below their 80,000 peak of 1934.[11] Actually, the number of small independent stores is not easily determined and national totals must be taken with a grain of salt. In many cases small stores are run by elderly operators, use antiquated equipment, and make small profits. If others in the family are uninterested in taking over, the store closes. A recent store-to-store survey in a New England county found only 347 food retailers in existence, although the names and addresses of 673 stores were supplied by town clerks and the state department of taxation.[12]

The number of firms has, of course, dropped correspondingly with the exit of the single-store independents. From 148 in 1948, the number of grocery chains rose to 258 in 1963. The chains operate a disproportionately large share of the larger stores. Approximately half the supermarkets are owned by chains, whereas 97 per cent of the small stores are independent.[13]

The more rapid growth of smaller chains has begun to affect the rank of older market leaders, although the first three national chains have not changed their relative position for at least 20 years. Food Fair, a newcomer, displaced Acme as number four in 1967, and both Grand Union and First National are being outdistanced by Winn-Dixie. The standing of the largest 15 chains in 1967 is shown in Table 3.

---

11   Ibid.
12   J. F. Farrell, and A. L. Owens, *The Rhode Island Food Industry, Output and*   *Costs, 1967* (Kingston R.I.: Rhode Island Agricultural Experiment Station, 1968).
13   *Progressive Grocer*, op. cit., p. 84.

TABLE 3 PROFITS OF LEADING GROCERY CHAINS, 1964-1967 BY SALES RANK IN 1967

NAME	RETURN ON NET WORTH				SALES (IN $ MILLIONS) 1967	PROFIT MARGIN 1967
	1964	1965	1966	1967		
A&P	9.0	8.8	9.2	8.9	5,458.8	1.0
Safeway	14.7	13.9	15.7	12.6	3,360.9	1.5
Kroger	11.9	12.8	11.3	9.6	2,806.0	0.9
Food Fair	10.4	9.3	11.6	10.7	1.296.6	0.9
Acme Market	8.4	6.6	5.8	5.1	1,293.8	0.6
Jewel Co.	12.1	12.8	12.2	12.3	1,244.4	1.4
National Tea	8.9	8.9	9.2	8.8	1,147.2	0.9
Winn-Dixie	21.3	22.1	23.5	20.2	1,020.3	2.3
Grand Union	10.7	11.2	10.4	10.0	935.9	1.2
First National	6.6	2.9	loss	loss	640.1	loss
Lucky Stores	19.5	14.0	11.6	26.4	627.3	1.8
Allied Supermarkets	12.1	7.5	6.2	9.5	591.0	0.8
Stop & Shop (Boston)	12.6	13.0	13.3	16.2	566.3	1.4
Arden-Mayfair				1.0	560.9	0.1
Colonial	13.2	12.1	11.6	11.8	531.7	1.3

SOURCE   *The Fortune Directory of the 500 Largest Industrial Corporations* (New York: Time, Inc., (1966, 1968)

MARKET SHARES   The most useful single index of market power is the share enjoyed by the most important firms. On the selling side, the food market is local, limited by the distance the shopper is accustomed to go for her major food shopping. Supermarkets tend to be patronized by middle- and upper-income customers, about 85 per cent arriving by auto.[14] Urban customers, many of them ghetto dwellers, are more likely to carry their groceries home on foot from non-affiliated independents.

In 218 Standard Metropolitan Statistical Areas (SMSA) surveyed by the census in 1963, stores of the top 4 firms accounted for 50.1 per cent of grocery store sales, the top 8 firms, 62 per cent; and the top 20 firms, 74.3 per cent.[15] These SMSA may be taken as proxies for local markets. The share of the national chains in many local markets, however, declined significantly during the 1958-1963 period, even though concentration ratios were rising.[16] Local or regional chains have taken the lead, as for instance in Providence, Rhode Island, where a local chain, Almacs, had 19 per cent of the grocery sales as against 10 per cent for the runner-up, A&P, in 1967.

---

14 E. R. Beem, and A. R. Oxenfeldt, "A Diversity Theory for Market Processes in Retailing," *Journal of Farm Economics*, **48**:69 (August 1966).

15 National Commission on Food Marketing, Technical Study No. 7,

Organization and Competition in Food Retailing (Washington, D.C.: U.S. Government Printing Office, 1966), pp. 44-51.

16 Ibid., p. 58.

These local concentration data are reinforced by studies of the Super Market Institute, showing that managers in new supermarkets on the average recognized direct competition from no more than three other supermarkets.[17] In measuring the buying power of food distributors, national sales concentration ratios are significant. Although the share of the four largest chains, including A&P, remained at about 20 per cent of food store sales from 1948 through 1963, the 20 largest chains increased their share from 26.9 to 34.0 per cent over the same period.[18] All chains had 41.0 per cent of the retail grocery store business in 1963 and 42.0 per cent in 1967.[19] The 70 largest retail organizations, including the 40 largest corporate chains, and members of the 15 largest cooperatives and of the 15 largest voluntary groups, had a 53.7 per cent participation in retail food sales in 1963.[20]

It seems unlikely that these national concentration rates will rise. The growth of sales of the 4- to 10-store chains exceeded that of all other size classifications from 1958 to 1964.[21]

The concentration ratios of wholesalers are not as significant as for retailers. It is highly inefficient for a retailer to deal with more than one general-line grocery wholesaler, because of the time consumed in ordering and receiving deliveries. It is interesting to note, however, that the privately owned voluntaries accounted for about 48 per cent of the volume of grocery wholesale business, with 24 per cent of the wholesaling firms, whereas cooperatives in 1967 did 30 per cent of the business with about 12 per cent of the firms.[22]

CONCENTRATION AMONG FOOD SUPPLIERS   The market power of the chains in their buying activities is affected by concentration among their suppliers. Such concentration differs widely from industry but is generally low. Meat packing is relatively unconcentrated; the four largest firms, ranked according to the red meat sales in 1963, accounted for only 29 per cent of shipments. It is not surprising, therefore, to find that large buyers have been able to obtain certain advantages, such as quantity discounts, advertising allowances, and price reductions. The National Commission on Food Marketing reported also the existence of cash payments, gifts to buyers, and bribery in wholesale meat marketing.[23]

In poultry production, the concentration of sellers is lower than in meat; approximately 18 per cent of chickens were slaughtered by the four largest

17   Super Market Institute, *Facts about New Supermarkets Opened in 1967* (Chicago: Super Market Institute, 1968), p. 10.
18   *Organization and Competition in Food Retailing*, op. cit., p. 41.
19   Computed from *Progressive Grocer*, op. cit., p. 236.

20   *Organization and Competition in Food Retailing*, op. cit., p. 71.
21   National Commission on Food Marketing, *Report*, op. cit., p. 143.
22   *Progressive Grocer*, op. cit., p. 100.
23   Information on concentration among food suppliers is taken from National Commission on Food Marketing, *Report*, op. cit., Ch. 4–9.

firms in 1963. Concentration is negligible in egg marketing, since there are about 8,000–10,000 egg handlers, and 13 firms handle about 10 per cent of the eggs.

The market share of the four largest processors in large milk markets in 1964 was about 53 per cent; in small markets 87 per cent. Ice cream concentration rates were lower. The advantage to a dairy of becoming a chain supplier is such that the milk handlers cannot exert the power commensurate with these high concentration rates prevailing in local markets.

In fruits and vegetables there is, of course, little concentration. Many of the same developments have occurred as in eggs and poultry. Terminal market auctions, which used to be characteristic of every large city and which provided a basis for pricing at the shipping point, have tended to disappear. Big buyers at shipping points reveal neither the volume they purchase nor their prices. "The trade has difficulty getting the feel of the market."[24] Large-scale growers have a larger share of production and have extended their operations into shipping, whereas shippers have moved backwards into growing.

The supply side is most highly concentrated in grocery manufacturing. "The four firms achieving the largest sales volume in each dry grocery product usually account for more than 50 per cent of total domestic sales."[25] Oligopolistic competition among grocery manufacturers has taken the form of heavy expenditures for new products, the concoction of coupons, free samples, cents-off deals, premiums, and allowances to retailers for newspaper advertising and point-of-purchase material. Salesmen spend much time servicing retail stores to make sure that the current "deals" or displays are meshing with the marketing program.

VERTICAL INTEGRATION IN
FOOD MARKETING

Partial vertical integration is quite common in the food retailing industry. In 1963, the 40 largest chains manufactured or processed food products, which had a wholesale value of 1.8 billion dollars. This was about 90 per cent of the food products manufactured by all chains. Eleven of the top 40 chains manufactured a sufficient volume to be included among the largest 200 food manufacturers, and two chains ranked among the 50 largest food manufacturers.[26]

The leading products manufactured or processed by chains are shown in Table 4. Baked goods, dairy products, and coffee are similar in that they can be blended or manufactured according to formula. There are a great variety of formulas available and a wide latitude in the quality and grade of the raw

---

24 Ibid., p. 50.
25 Ibid., p. 63.

26 *Organization and Competition in Food Retailing*, op. cit., p. 77.

TABLE 4   MANUFACTURING
ACTIVITIES OF FOOD CHAINS

INDUSTRY	NUMBER OF CHAINS REPORTING PRODUCTION	VALUE OF SHIPMENTS IN 1963 (IN $ MILLIONS)
Meat packing	4	216.8
Ice cream	18	90.1
Fluid milk	14	258.8
Bread	31	427.0
Coffee	21	157.7

SOURCE   *Organization and Competition in
Food Retailing*, op. cit., Table 4–6, pp. 82–83.

materials. Standardization can be achieved by controlling manufacturing processes. Bakery and dairy products also have high delivery costs, which many chains undercut with their own delivery system. Safeway's Lucerne milk processing plant is perhaps the largest of that chains' dairying operations. Safeway has been generally able to buy milk at whatever prices are Federally enforced, process and package it, and sell it at a highly competitive price.

Chains do less meat packing than they did immediately after World War II. At that time, some chains built packing facilities because they were worried about the availability and quality of the meat provided by the big packers. As time passed, the meat shortage disappeared, so the chains again became customers of the major packers and sold most of their plants to local-producer cooperatives. These plants were extremely efficient and, being located in the meat-producing areas, forced the large old-line packers into building new modern plants. The experiment of the chains has therefore shifted a good proportion of the slaughtering industry out of the large cities, like Chicago and St. Louis, to country areas in order to compete with the small cooperative plants. Nevertheless, meat packing remains the third most important manufacturing activity of chains.

Affiliated groups have failed to keep pace with their chain counterparts in the manufacture of food products. Only 7 of the top 15 voluntary and the top 15 cooperative groups manufactured any food products in 1963.[27] This inactivity reflects the fact that the voluntaries cannot require their customers to purchase products, nor do they have the organizational or financial stability of the chains.

---

27   *Organization and Competition in Food Retailing*, op. cit., p. 87.

CAUSES OF CONCENTRATION
IN FOOD RETAILING

ECONOMIES OF SCALE: THE STORE   According to Marshall, "an increase of capital and labor leads generally to an improved organization which increases the efficiency of the work of capital and labor."[28] As his theory of Increasing Returns has been refined, careful distinctions are made between the economies resulting from increased size of the plant and those economies associated with the expanded size of the firm. The savings resulting from the use of better and more expensive capital goods must not be confused with those deriving from the marketing, financial, and managerial advantages of a larger business organization.[29]

To determine the economies of scale in the store, the Federal Trade Commission (FTC) surveyed operating costs in nine cities. The Commission found the efficiency of the food stores was primarily affected by the size of store (in square feet) and by utilization (sales per square foot). After allowing for other influences, such as level of wages and unionization, the lowest ratio of expense to sales prevailed in stores with about 16,000 square feet of selling area; but the rates of utilization had a stronger influence on expense ratios than the size of a store. The Commission also found that utilization was not appreciably affected by size of store, in other words, larger stores did not tend to have higher sales per square foot. This conclusion seems to be belied by the surveys of the *Progressive Grocer*, according to which sales per square foot rise steadily with size of store, but these data are not stratified. They mix areas, ages, and types of ownership of store.[30]

Increasing the total volume, the Commission found, had only a small impact on unit cost. A 20 per cent rise in volume seems to result in a cost reduction of about 1 per cent. Since trading stamps raise costs by about 2 per cent, only if they produced a 40 per cent increase in volume could they pay for themselves. Such a volume increase, of course, is out of the question if all stores adopt stamps, and it is highly unlikely even if they do not use stamps.[31]

Yet there must be limits to the rise in net income that can be generated by raising utilization rates. Customers will not put up with what they regard as excessive delays at checkouts nor with overcrowded aisles. In a store

---

28   *Principles of Economics*, Book IV, xiii, 2 (London: Macmillan, 1910) (6th ed.), p. 318.
29   P. S. Florence, *The Economics and Sociology of Industry*, (Baltimore: Johns Hopkins, 1969) (rev. ed.), pp. 99–115.
30   Letter from Professor Daniel Padberg, January 17, 1969. Padberg suggests that in some cases, larger stores built in anticipation of population movement to the suburbs might have relatively low utilization during their first years of operation. He also points out that the small stores surveyed by the *Progressive Grocer* are mostly nonaffiliated independents; no stores of this size are being built by chains.
31   *Organization and Competition in Food Retailing*, op. cit., p. 148.

of a given size, there is an absolute limit to sales per square foot that is set by the speed with which customers can proceed through the aisles while examining the shelves. Confronted with long aisles and numerous products, many women become mesmerized, pass by approximately 800 items per minute, and fail to react either to prices or specific items, regaining full awareness only when they reach the cash register. This is a disadvantage of large-size stores.

Optimum size is affected by the tendency to shop on weekends, the number of items the typical customer wants to buy on a shopping trip, and the length of time she is willing to spend to make the weekly purchases. Although these variables are not easy to put into a precise quantitative relationship, we may accept the finding that the optimum-size selling area is close to 16,000 square feet, which means a total area of around 20,000–22,000 square feet. Yet the very factors that make a 20,000 square foot supermarket most efficient for customers doing a week's shopping may make it intolerable for small emergency purchases. Convenience stores, rapidly growing in number, fill the gap.

ECONOMIES OF SCALE: THE FIRM   When considering the variables affecting optimum size of the firm, we must take into account purchasing, marketing, and general administrative efficiency. If these activities permitted important economies of scale in food retailing, a negative relation could be discovered between the size of firm and these inputs per unit of output. No studies have shown any such reliable relationship. The National Commission on Food Marketing related inferred economies of scale in manufacturing to size of the chains. It concluded that to manufacture dairy products and baked goods efficiently, volume need not be high, but for jams, jellies, peanut butter, and mayonnaise, about $500 million annual volume of sales were required. Otherwise, their low turnover would not permit a sufficiently high rate of output to make an efficient manufacturing plant profitable. A similar volume was required for a successful private label program. These conclusions were based on opinions in the trade rather than upon a survey of unit costs behavior.[32]

In one respect larger chains have been thought to enjoy a significant advantage over smaller enterprises. They can set up a field-buying staff that will carry out direct-purchasing activities, enabling the chain to bypass brokers, or suppliers' salesmen. This was alleged to be an advantage that A&P, for instance, as the unquestioned giant of food retailing, enjoyed in comparison with its smaller rivals. With superior personnel, A&P could skim the cream off the produce that was marketed to retailers, leaving inferior quality to the rest of the trade.[33]

---

32   *Organization and Competition in Food Retailing*, op. cit., p. 152.
33   M. A. Adelman, "The A&P Case: A Study in Applied Economic Theory," *Quarterly Journal of Economics*, **63**:249 (May 1949).

Closer examination of these supposed advantages of giant chains, however, shows that, if one eliminates special concessions resulting from exertion of bargaining power, they permit little or no net saving of resources.[34] Although a single store can not supply itself efficiently by trying to deal directly with produce shippers, manufacturers, or canners, this handicap can be overcome by purchasing through a voluntary or cooperative wholesalers. Small chains can buy produce in carload lots of items, like potatoes or citrus, either from shippers or through brokers. The competition of other buyers is sufficient to ensure that premium quality produce or meat usually commands a premium price. Even a single-unit independent, making his meat purchases from a route salesman, can, by knowledgeable examination of the selection in the truck, consistently get better quality meat for lower prices. Dependent on purchasing in large volume according to grade classifications within which there are wide differences, the chains cannot get meats uniformly at the top end of the quality scale. A small buyer can be highly selective at the terminal market or when purchasing meat from a wholesaler, and at comparable costs, provide higher quality. The large packers have devised a system of permitting direct shipment of good quality meat to small buyers from their main plants, saving the cost of branch salesmen. Use of brokers requires payment of a fee, but, on the other hand, maintenance of a field-buying staff is not costless.

The more progressive smaller chains can often do a better job in expansion than the large chain because the latter cannot so easily allow for local differences by making changes in store plans or stock. The national chains—A&P, Safeway, Kroger, Food Fair, Acme, and Jewel—try to make up for their lack of flexibility by providing assurance to a mobile population that the store they go to in Los Angeles will be indistinguishable in layout from the one they patronize in Chicago or Newark.

Newspaper advertising is the predominant method used by food retailers to reach their customers. It accounts for 60 per cent of advertising expenditures for chains. Chains or cooperatives can run large attractive ads and share the price among all stores in a local market. The nonaffiliated independent finds most newspaper advertising expensive, unless the newspaper has limited distribution to his immediate market area. In many instances, the independent retailer has to resort to flyers or in-store signs for an advertising campaign.

Affiliated wholesale groups can and do, in many instances, compete with large chain warehouses quite favorably, and can deliver food products at a comparable rate. Some voluntary and cooperative wholesalers have managed to compress their costs to the point where they operate on a margin of 4 per cent. In 1967, the average for both groups was 5.5 per cent, which compares

---

34   J. B. Dirlam and A. E. Kahn, "Integration and Dissolution of the A&P Company," *Indiana Law Journal*, **29**:1 (Fall 1953).

favorably with chain warehouses, considering that affiliated wholesalers pay for private labels and prepare advertising posters and sales campaigns, including selection of specials for promotion by the retail stores.[35] Their salesmen have been converted to management consultants; their one-story warehouses are laid out to achieve maximum efficiency—their billing, delivery, and inventory control use electronic data processing, palletized selection and reserve storage areas, and installed conveyer systems. There is every reason to believe that affiliated independents, through IGA, Red & White, Clover Farms, and NAROG, have access to warehouses with operating costs matching those of the chains.

Although financial evidence of the success of small chains, and even large independents, is hard to come by because so many of these enterprises are closely held, there is enough to demonstrate that these smaller units are able to realize economies equalling those of the giant chains. Chains in the 4–10 unit classification had the highest sales growth rate of all chain sizes in 1964.[36] National Tea's profit rate in Memphis in 1959 was a little over 2 per cent; an independent supermarket operator, whom National had bought out earlier on condition that he not reenter for a 5-year period, had a volume of $12 million in a single store, with net profit on sales of 5 per cent.[37] In a midwestern city studied by Professor Bob Holdren, independents had profit targets, which they customarily reached, twice that of the national chains.[38] A Purdue study of independent supermarkets revealed extremely high earnings, in some years exceeding 100 per cent on equity.[39] After an intensive analysis of earnings by size of chain, the National Food Marketing Commission concluded that there was little difference between the medium and large-size chains.[40] Rates of return for some of the giants, particularly A&P, Acme, and First National have slumped sadly in recent years. A&P has begun to spin off unprofitable units, and is moving toward decentralization.[41]

MERGERS   Mergers have been an important cause of both national and local concentration in the retail food industry. In the 1920's the first major merger movement expanded the size and scope of operations of several leading food chains and increased their marketing operations to a broad regional or national scale. Through 1930, the seven largest food chains acquired over 5,800 stores, roughly a fifth of the stores they operated at that time.

---

35   *Progressive Grocer*, op. cit., p. 101.

36   National Commission on Food Marketing, *Report*, op. cit., p. 143, Table II.

37   Federal Trade Commission, Opinion, Docket No. 7453, *National Tea Co.* March 4, 1966, pp. 11–212.

38   B. Holdren, *The Structure of a Retail Market and the Market Behavior of Retail Units* (Englewood Cliffs, N.J.:

Prentice Hall, 1960), p. 100, fn. 32.

39   *Organization and Competition in Food Retailing*, op. cit., Table 15–16, p. 288.

40   Ibid., p. 304.

41   *Supermarket News*, **17**:1 (December 23, 1968).

Kroger led all other chains by acquiring over 2,200 stores. First National, starting with about 800 stores within a ten mile radius of Boston, by 1930 had over 1,600 stores in all six New England states, acquired largely through merger. In 1920 the four leading chains accounted for 5.7 per cent of grocery sales; by 1930 they accounted for 23.1 per cent. Except for A&P, only 300 of those 15,737 stores in 1930 had been acquired by merger, a good part of this rise in concentration may be attributed to chain store mergers.

Altogether, during the years 1949–1964, grocery chains made 621 acquisitions of enterprises with a total sales of over $4.5 billion. The 20 largest chains set the pace in the merger movement by acquiring 297 firms with a combined sales of $3.1 billion, which was 70 per cent of the business of all acquired stores during 1949–1964.[42]

Of the seven largest firms, those which have been active in mergers through the years have retained or improved their rank whereas those which have not merged as readily have declined in importance. A&P, which relies only on internal expansion, has retained first place in sales volume, although it has not gained in sales percentage. Most acquired firms had gone through a rapid growth period prior to their merger, which leads to the conjecture that the larger acquiring firms were looking for aggressive companies with which to merge.

DIVERSIFICATION Supermarkets have expanded the number of nonfood items they carry, coincidentally with their expansion of the total number of items, which amounted to 7,350 in 1967. The typical supermarket today carries 1,300 nonfood items that account for about 6–8 per cent of total sales.[43] Health and beauty aids, housewares, and soft goods, make up the bulk of the nonfood sales.

Many food chains have entered other retailing lines, combining their food stores and department stores in new shopping centers. By 1965 at least 11 large food chains had entered the discount department store business. These chains include Food Fair, Giant Food, Grand Union, Stop and Shop, and Red Owl (owned by Consolidated Foods). Diversification has been double-acting. The discount department chains have often set up a discount food store in their free-standing shopping center to pull patronage. Jewel Companies (once Jewel Tea) began with home-service routes and has expanded by acquiring a drug chain (Osco), Turn-Style self-service discount department stores, coffee and ice cream shops, franchised convenience stores, and wholesaling.[44]

Geographical diversification through acquisitions or by the opening of stores in a new market area adds to market power in established areas by providing an independent source of funds. And finally, prestige and image-

42 *Organization and Competition in Food Retailing*, op. cit., pp. 98–103.
43 *Progressive Grocer*, op. cit., pp. 82 and 99.
44 Dominick and Dominick, *Investment Notes* (December 1968).

building are undeniably important where the firm feels that bigness is something to be desired in order to keep its name before the consumer. The over-saturation of supermarkets that takes place when a chain opens a store close to competition is explicable in these terms. But is much quicker and easier for a firm to merge than to go to the trouble of building new stores and having to fight to enter a new market area. With a merger, there is a ready made and usually successful operation to take over.

PRODUCT DIFFERENTIATION OF RETAILING SERVICE   Service differentiation is not easy in an industry where, except with respect to location, most products are standardized and where it is not difficult to maintain cleanliness and cheerfulness. Reliance must be placed on devices such as a bizarre firm name or the provision of novel promotions not exclusively connected with food products—including games and trading stamps—but these moves can be easily countered. Alert managements attempt to differentiate the products by improving the quality of meat and taking care of the vegetables and fruits properly. Efforts to link discount supermarkets physically with discount department stores can be explained in part by a desire to differentiate the food retailing service, but this is a joint differentiation. John Schwegeman of New Orleans, the target of 70 injunction suits, who carried his fight against resale price maintenance to the Supreme Court, operates huge stores that do an annual business of over $15 million each and dwarfs his chain competitors.[45]

ENTRY BARRIERS   Entry barriers may be defined as the economic advantages that a firm already established in a market has over a potential entrant. These advantages can be measured by the costs new firms must incur to enter the market. Construction costs have risen substantially over the years as the size of the store has increased. The average chain investment in 1964 for a new supermarket was somewhat in excess of $500,000, including inventory. This indicates the amount that is necessary to enter the industry with a single store. Average construction cost was $13.96 per square foot and an overall investment of $28.27 per square foot. There are a number of ways that a firm can avoid or offset some of these costs, although these are less likely to be available to a single-store operator. In 1967, 63 per cent of the new stores were leased from independent landlords; 16 per cent were built by the food firms, sold, and leased back from the buyers; 21 per cent of the new stores were owned by the operator. Equipment and inventory purchased by independents may be partially financed by cooperative or affiliated wholesalers or equipment suppliers.

According to the National Food Marketing Commission, "initial financing requirements [in food retailing] are low compared with much of manu-

45   *Supermarket News,* **17**:1, 5 (October 28, 1968).

facturing."[46] By reinvesting profits and borrowing, it is possible for individual entrepreneurs to move fairly rapidly from small to large stores, providing they have ability. The *Progressive Grocer* recently reviewed the career of a Tennessee operator who expanded a 12′ × 12′ roadside stand, built in 1949, into a $500,000 volume store in 1957. He further expanded it and, after training with the Super Market Institute, built a new market in 1964 that reached annual sales of $2.5 million.[47]

Opportunities for independent entry have been kept open by the voluntaries and cooperatives. Wakefern Foods Corporation, a cooperative, was established in Elizabeth, New Jersey, in 1950. Wakefern has its own label, Shop Rite, and its members use Shop Rite advertisements and promotional materials. By 1955, it had 34 retail store members with a volume of $15 million. There were 200 Wakefern member stores with a volume of $400 million in 1968. This means that their stores had an average annual volume of well over $2 million per year, against the national sales average for supermarkets of $1.5 million.[48]

Barriers to entry are real, and, except by merger, almost impossible to surmount, if entry is regarded as the rapid creation of a national chain. At the local level, however, entry barriers are only moderate. Access to shopping centers is the major handicap for small firms. Once a chain manages to reach an annual volume of $20 million it faces no serious obstacles to further growth.

III. MARKET CONDUCT
INTRODUCTION

Market conduct consists of the practices by which firms attract customers, respond to each other's competitive practices, innovate, and grow. The most significant type of conduct, from the viewpoint of economics, is pricing behavior. Relative prices determine the distribution of purchases of consumers—depending upon the elasticity of demand—and the flow of sales, in turn, affects decisions of retailers and wholesalers and ultimately the allocation of resources to manufacturers.

Pricing practices also serve to decide which firms are successful in the competitive struggle and which will fall by the wayside. The options open to food retailers, both in pricing the thousands of items sold, and, for the larger chains, in setting margins among stores in different geographic areas, permit the adoption of widely varying competitive strategies. To the extent

46 *Organization and Competition in Food Retailing*, op. cit., p. 155.
47 *Progressive Grocer*, **44**:57 (April 1965).

48 *Organization and Competition in Food Retailing*, op. cit., pp. 161–163.

that the retailing oligopolist minimizes price competition, nonprice competition takes its place. The latter, too, must be evaluated according to its impact on consumer welfare.

The share of the consumer's food dollar that has been allocated to retail grocery service rose sharply from approximately 12–14 per cent in 1940 to 20–21 per cent in 1967. Food prices themselves have been rising, which means that the increase in the percentage going to retailing has been magnified in absolute expenditure. Explanation for the rising margins can be found in the costs of the retail stores. These include higher labor cost, higher rents in shopping centers, and higher capital costs, because of larger and more elaborate buildings, refrigeration, and display equipment. The rise in margins might measure a superior service. Whether it does will be considered in more detail in the succeeding section on economic performance.

THE NATURE OF RETAIL SERVICE

An analysis of food-retailing price behavior presents some difficulties because the retailing service is almost never priced separately from the products that are being marketed. We cannot be concerned solely with the final retail prices of meats, produce, cereals, and housewares because they reflect the invoice costs over which the retailer has little control and which do not measure or compensate for his performance of the retailing function. It is the margin between his payment to wholesaler or manufacturer and the price to the consumer that is the price of the retailer's service.

Following some future revolution in marketing technology this retail service might be sold separately. The consumer could pay an admission fee to the supermarket and an additional entrance fee for the privilege of selecting products in the different departments. In these departments each item might be priced at invoice cost plus the variable cost—consisting mostly of the labor required to the put the product on the shelves and the interest on the working capital tied up in it. The variable cost would tend to be inversely related to the turnover of the product in question. The admission fees would cover the capital costs of the building and each department's equipment, and the fixed costs of store labor and management. The separately priced retailing service would consist of storage, display, pricing, some limited quality information from newspaper and point-of-sale advertising, and amenities, varying with the intensity of nonprice competition. An additional charge might be made for assembling an order and carrying it to the automobile.[49]

This outline of a mythical price structure for food retailing helps to clarify the nature of the service as it now exists. The retailer today covers all of his

---

49   C. S. Bell, "Macroeconomics of Unbalanced Growth: Comment," *American Economic Review*, **58**:882 (September 1968).

costs from the margins included in price. A large part of these costs of providing the service cannot be traced to any single product or group of products.

The food retailer is a multiproduct firm, producing under conditions of common costs, a large share of which are fixed. Holdren found that as much as 90 per cent of the costs above invoice cost "do not vary with output."[50] This percentage may be excessive. If labor is regarded as largely variable, as are stamps, perhaps a third of the average gross margin is variable.

The demand of the shoppers, likewise, is seldom for one type of retailing service. Once a week shopping means that the housewife is purchasing a $15 or $20 composite. The margin (the difference between invoice cost and selling price) may vary widely from item to item without discouraging purchases. In the first place, the shopper is unlikely to substitute one commodity for another in order to reduce her expenditures on retailing service. There is little cross elasticity of demand between beer and ground beef. Second, once in the store, the customer is unlikely to consider immediately shifting part of her purchases to a different retailer unless she becomes aware of a wide difference in selling price of an important product. With respect to the customer on a weekly visit, the retailer is a monopolist.

HOW RETAILERS PRICE

Examination of price patterns reveals wide variations in margins among groups of items and products. measured in both cents and percentages. The retailer discriminates among products, selling some at margins very slightly above (or even on occasion under) invoice cost, and pricing others at substantial amounts above cost. Discrimination that is optimum from the point of view of profits maximization should equate marginal cost with the marginal revenue associated with each segment of demand. The demand for canned olives, for instance, may be less elastic than the demand for corned beef; the price of the retailing service associated with olives should therefore be higher. There is little to show, however, that retailers actually follow such discriminatory behavior. Because of interrelated demand among their products, they may accept a low price and margin on an advertised item in order to bring shoppers into the store, on the assumption that they can sell, as part of the composite "market basket," a substantial amount of other items. Total sales and profits may rise because of the pattern of purchases and the pricing structure on other items. There may be several combinations of margins that will, depending upon the number of shoppers attracted, result in the same profit.

Lack of knowledge, by both seller and customers, affects the retail pricing structure. Only a few studies have attempted to find the cost of providing

---

50 B. Holdren, *Structure*, op. cit., p. 40. He classified most labor costs as "discretionary fixed costs."

retail service for individual items, or even groups of items. Retailers are, of course, aware of the amount of shelf space occupied by a product and make judgments about the sales that could be realized by a substitute item. They also have some data on turnover, and realize that the service of displaying a slow-moving item absorbs more working capital than displaying a fast-moving item. But their detailed information with respect to these matters on the more than 7,000 items they sell is sketchy at best. Margins are not likely to be closely tailored to direct cost, because the time required to determine such cost would be prohibitive. The housewife is also afflicted by the lack of knowledge. There are about 1,750 grocery products that sell less than a half case a week in the typical supermarket. Customers are probably familiar with the prices of no more than 10 per cent, or 500, of the dry grocery items. Knowing this, the grocer feels relatively free to manipulate margins (or to leave them alone) to achieve management goals.

Retailers tend to imitate a leading competitor's prices. In many areas, A&P used to function as the price leader; in others, the leader was Safeway. Their leadership seems to have withered in recent years. A&P itself is responding to competition of smaller chains and even independents.

> Where stores need special attention because of unusually active competition . . . the stores in those towns should be put into a special zone and given the benefit of lower than average prices. In other towns a little better gross profit rate can be obtained.[51]

Conversely, A&P advanced prices in areas "where they felt competition was weak . . . ."[52] Safeway has followed price policies somewhat similar to those A&P had adopted in the 1930's. Price followership did not usually extend to the entire range of items. Other chains or independents, getting A&P's prices from headquarters, duplicated only those prices that they believed would be most instrumental in holding customers. At present, there may be emphasis only on matching the prices advertised in the Thursday paper by A&P (or another leader). Local and regional chains are often regarded as the most aggressive price cutters.

Studies of pricing have concluded that food retailers tend to price irrationally. According to Professor Holdren, the national chains neglect local conditions in setting margins, and allow managers little discretion in pricing. In his survey of pricing in a midwestern city in 1956, Holdren found that most retailers did not know "how they arrived at their prices."[53] They asserted that they attempted to realize a standard margin including a "satisfactory

---

51   *U.S.* v. *A&P*, 67 Federal Supplement 626, 665 (1946).
52   Ibid., p. 666.
53   B. Holdren, *Structure*, op. cit., p. 73, fn. 13. A composite expense statement shows the following breakdown of gross margin for representative chains, including voluntary groups, for 1966–1967:

profit" on each item, but examination of the prices showed this was not the case. Professor Preston could find no hypothesis that would account for margin variations among 20 products. "The individual store manager might be able to 'explain' in any particular instance how a series of historic circumstances has resulted in one 16-ounce can of pickled beets being priced at 19 cents and carrying a 30 per cent markup, another being priced at 25 cents carrying a 30 per cent markup, another priced at 21 cents carrying a 52 per cent markup . . . (A)n objective analyst is tempted to conclude that this array of prices . . . reflect(s) the pyramiding of essentially random responses." [54]

It should be pointed out that the average food store consumer spends 23.6 per cent of her money for meat, 11.58 per cent for dairy products, 8.10 per cent for produce, 4.99 per cent for cigarettes, and 4.63 per cent for frozen foods, and for health and beauty aids, 2.14 per cent. [55] A 1967 survey found that the average margins of independents were as follows: meat, 21.3 per cent; dairy products, 14.2 per cent; produce, 30.1 per cent; cigarettes, 6.0 per cent; frozen foods, 25.2 per cent; health and beauty aids, 29.2 per cent. [56] These averages conceal wide differences among stores, and among items within departments.

Many chains realize as net profit less than 1 per cent of sales after taxes. During 1967–1968, the gross margin for 51 food chains was 21.46 per cent with operating expenses of 20.97 per cent and a net operating profit of 0.49 per cent of sales. Other income from rebates and manufacturers' promotional and advertising allowances brought net earnings up to 0.99 per cent of sales. [57] Small differences in price can have substantial impact on

	PER CENT OF SALES		PER CENT OF SALES
Gross margin	22.29	*Depreciation*	0.97
Expenses		*Donations, ins., and so on*	4.08
Payroll	10.46	Operating expenses	20.65
Supplies	0.97	*Interest*	0.74
Utilities	0.76		
Services purchased	1.34	Net operating profit	0.90
Promotional giveaways	1.41	*Credits (allowances)*	1.33
Insurance		Net income before income taxes	2.23
Taxes (except income)	0.93	Income tax	1.04
Rentals (property)	1.78	Net earnings after income taxes	1.19

SOURCE *Progressive Grocer*, "*35th Annual Report of the Grocery Industry*," **47**:94 (April 1968).

54 L. F. Preston, *Profits, Competition and Rules of Thumb in Retail Food Pricing* (Berkeley, Calif.: Institute of Business and Economic Research, 1963), p. 40.
55 "35th Annual Report of the Grocery Industry," *Progressive Grocer*, **47**:109 (April 1968).
56 Ibid., p. 91.
57 E. Brown and R. Day, *1967–1968 Operating Results of Food Chains* (Ithaca, N.Y.: New York State College of Agriculture, 1968).

profits. Margin selection is therefore extremely important. Retailers are admonished at conventions and in trade publications to make use of multiple-unit pricing to raise prices (moving an item from 13 cents per unit to 3 for 40 cents, for instance) or to review their items so as to raise the non-featured ones by an average of 2 or 3 per cent.

The use of weekly ads with featured items or "specials" has become a characteristic of the retail food business. The practice seems to have begun in the late 1930's. It is a form of price competition, but subject to important limitations. The prices listed in the Thursday advertisements are part of the comprehensive margin and price structure. As late as 4 or 5 years after World War II, A&P still attempted to attract business by stressing its "every-day low-price" policy. Nevertheless, the tactic that had proved so successful for the independent supermarkets was eventually adopted by the industry including A&P. As the National Commission Food Marketing found,

> (The independent supermarket operator) met the chain store image
> yet sold enough of the higher priced items to cover his costs which
> might be higher than the chains'. This orchestration of prices, which is
> so important in supermarket merchandising, creates what is referred to
> as the "sales mix." . . . (I)t is possible to identify the store with the
> "lower price" only in the most simple, clear-cut cases.[58]

Surveys of the composite price of 105 items prominent in consumers' budgets, over half of which were featured in weekly ads, revealed roughly similar totals for chains in the same markets. This does not mean that the price of each product was the same in all stores. Even the advertised products are not uniformly priced. Some items are frequently purchased but not necessarily featured in ads: eggs, coffee, bacon, and butter. Most often featured—that is, given prominent position or type—are coffee, ground beef, sirloin steak, and mayonnaise. In many instances the "specials" actually are not priced at less than the customary level.[59] There is a tendency for items that are selected for almost continuous featuring, such as coffee, sugar, and soap powders, to be pushed to zero or negative margins.[60]

Discount food stores have reintroduced an indeterminate degree of across-the-board price competition into retailing. The discounter gives the impression of competing by price, frequently by ostentatiously dropping trading stamps, although he also endeavors not to sacrifice the comfort and cleanliness of modern supermarkets. Studies of discount store pricing have failed to disclose substantial differentials below composite purchases in conventional supermarkets, although there is, nevertheless, a slight saving.[61]

---

58 *Organization and Competition in Food Retailing*, op. cit., p. 169.

59 *Organization and Competition in Food Retailing*, op. cit., p. 174.

60 B. Holdren, *Structure*, op. cit., p. 95.

61 I. W. Dawson, "A study of the Discount Supermarket in Rhode Island," M.A. thesis in marketing, University of Rhode Island, 1965.

Convenience stores have higher margins than conventional supermarkets, averaging 25.4 per cent. Profit after taxes appears to be somewhat higher as a per cent of sales, with 2.8 per cent for independents and 1.6 per cent average for chains.[62] The convenience stores seem to be able to realize higher margins not only because they are patronized when their competitors are closed, but even at other times of the day they appeal to customers who are indifferent to price differences. In Washington, D.C., for instance the 7–11 convenience stores sell a half gallon of milk for 5 cents more than the consumer would pay in a High's immediately adjacent.

Despite an oligopolistic market structure, food retailers do not collude on prices. There are several reasons for their independent policies. First, entry is relatively easy, even for nonoptimal size firms. Second, the complimentarity of demand makes individual price cuts attractive. Because of the variety of competitive responses and ignorance of consumers, there is a long lag between the initiation of action and the time when competitors feel the results, so they are never sure what caused the change in sales. Finally, differences in product lines among stores and differences in location makes it very difficult for retailers to agree on price levels and structures that would satisfy each seller, even if there were no differences in personality and skill of entrepreneurs.[63] Nevertheless, consumers are sufficiently aware of the prices of key items, so that these cannot have wide differences among the stores they might patronize. Sizable differences in profits can be realized by making slight alterations in margins. Since most stores have excess capacity—at least during some hours of the day, or days of the week—a pricing structure that attracts more business can increase utilization, lower costs, and raise profits.

NONPRICE COMPETITION

Although the forms of nonprice competition can be discussed independently of price competition, they nevertheless form part of a continuum of management strategy, together with pricing policy and product line policy. Methods of nonprice competition may receive greater stress during times of affluence. Nevertheless, there was much recourse to premiums and gifts during the last decade of the nineteenth century; a Dayton, Ohio grocery gave vouchers redeemable in case of illness in the 1890's.[64]

Some types of nonprice competition attempt to upgrade the quality of service provided by food stores, or, perhaps more accurately, improve the environment in which shoppers make their choices about supermarket purchases. Air conditioning, parking lots, automatic door openers, music

---

62 *Progressive Grocer*, op. cit., p. 231.
63 B. Holdren, *Structure*, op. cit., p. 64.

64 S. Hollander, "Entrepreneurs Test the Environment: A Long Run View of Grocery Pricing" (mimeo., September 3, 1966), p. 6.

and soft lighting, rest rooms, "kiddie korners," check cashing, and package carry-out all make shopping a pleasanter experience. These services raise costs, although they may also result in increased volume. They are alike, however, in being easily imitated. They cannot be permanently associated with any particular store unless competitors decide not to make similar improvements. Nevertheless, in any local market there are perceptible differences among supermarkets. The newest or most recently reconditioned store is able to gain an advantage that may last for several years, particularly if his rivals are chain units whose managers have no power to make investments on store renovation.

By such variations, retailers try to differentiate the retailing service of stores whose interior layout has become pretty well standardized. All plans are designed to draw customers through the whole store. Shopping patterns ordinarily start at the right of the store with the meat department at the rear. Usually a few high-demand items are located at the beginning of the shopping pattern to get customers in the mood to buy. There is a tendency to put low-margin, high-demand items in less convenient spots, whereas high-profit candy or jam is placed where it can be easily reached.

Some nonprice competitive techniques are employed to keep the customers patronizing a particular store, and cannot be exactly duplicated. Encyclopedias, dictionaries, silverware, and dishes are offered piece by piece or part by part over a long period of time. Once the customer starts to buy the premiums she will continue shopping at the store until the set is complete. These lures may not always be economically priced, but the customer may think they are, or find it easy to purchase an expensive item on a weekly basis. A cookbook in thirteen parts, at the rate of 89 cents for the first and $1.49 for each of the others, adding up to a total of $18.77, is not cheap.

Trading stamps are like premiums in that they create customer loyalty. When stamps were a comparative novelty, in 1950, they drew customers with ease. At the peak of their popularity about 78 per cent of the supermarkets were obliged to adopt them, including even the giant chains like A&P and Safeway, which initially found them objectionable. Under most plans, retailers pay $2 to $3 per thousand stamps, which are given to customers at a rate of one stamp for each 10 cents in purchases. The stamp companies have tried to prevent exchanges, in order to preserve the attractiveness of the stamp plan to retailers, and limited the number of franchises in an area. Stamps add about 2 per cent to operating costs in a stamp-saturated market, where no increase in volume results.[65] The use of stamps is now declining; by 1968 less than half of the supermarkets were giving stamps.

---

65 *Food Retailing*, op. cit., p. 459. Prices rise to cover these costs. J. D. Bromley and W. H. Wallace, "The effect of Trading Stamps on Retail Prices," (Kingston, R.I.: Rhode Island Agricultural Experiment Station, 1964).

Some stores have made use of even more extravagant promotions, which seem to serve the purpose mainly of advertising the name of the store, or drawing a customer into the store in an irregular or sporadic fashion. Cash has been paid to supermarket customers holding winning numbers, and drawings have been held for new cars. After a 2-year study of games used by both groceries and service stations, the FTC found numerous situations that involved deception, principally in advertising. Chances of winning were overstated.[66] Games conceivably give some persons enjoyment but waste human resources of the specialists devising the games and the clerks administering them, and disappoint customers who do not win.

There is still another way in which food retailers can differentiate their stores. They can expand or contract the number of products they sell. By carrying gourmet foods, or an in-store bakery, or handling more nonfoods, the store may be differentiated from its rivals, and attract persons who will do their weekly food shopping at the store with the expanded product lines.

BRAND STRATEGY IN
FOOD MARKETING

Advertising firms have long sung the praises of the battle of the brands, referring to those well-known brands that battle for the consumers' dollar on a nationwide basis with one brand pitted against another. The battle of the brands is fought in the retail food stores as keenly as in hardware or drug stores but it is not necessarily between nationally known giants. Instead, the national brands compete against the private labels of the chain or wholesale group.

Private label products (also called distributor's label or house brand) are packaged to specifications either by a distributor or manufacturer for resale under a brand name owned by the distributor. In the case of the national label, the manufacturer has responsibility for the development and quality of the product, as well as for its movement through the distribution system, including the necessary advertising and promotion, and maintenance of a sales staff. For the private label product the chain or wholesaler takes over the functions of marketing and checks the quality of the product.

Private labels are used by retailers for two reasons: (1) To maintain a low-price image, since they can be sold less expensively than the national brands because of savings in distribution and promotion costs; (2) to build loyalty to the retailer (if the consumer is satisfied with the product).

When a chain or wholesale distributor adds private labels to its sales mix, in-store promotion and newspaper advertising are used to acquaint customers with the product. Private label products are given more facings on the shelves

---

than national or regional brands. The products are displayed on shelves that are eye level to the majority of shoppers so they can not miss seeing them as they travel the aisles.

Margins on private label products are slightly higher than on nationally advertised brands. A NFMC survey of a dozen items frequently sold under private label found the margin on the private label products was 24.8 per cent compared with 22.4 per cent for the national brands, but the retailer must pay for performance of functions incurred by the manufacturer of the national brand.[67] At the same time, the private label price averaged about 20 per cent lower. The private label products seem to sell as rapidly as their competition, although there are wide variations among products. The study showed, for example, that private label frozen orange juice sold twice as fast as the competitive national brand; private label peaches sold six tenths as fast.[68]

CONCLUSION: MARKET
CONDUCT

From the market structure of the food distribution industry, it could have been predicted that once the supermarket technological revolution had been assimilated, high concentration rates in local markets would lead either to collusion and identical pricing, or nonprice competition. Since collusion is difficult and illegal, the second alternative has been adopted. Moreover, with rising incomes many consumers do not think it worth their while to acquire the information or take the time necessary to minimize food expenditures. Only exceptionally rational and hard-pressed shoppers would increase their number of trips to supermarkets in order to pick up the special that each store advertised. Besides, the use of similar foods for specials would further reduce savings from shopping different stores for different products. Only if consumers were acquainted with the composite prices of "market baskets" of their weekly purchases at every store could price competition be effective. Even if information were improved to this extent and consumers shopped rationally, the fact that each consumer buys a different composite would probably prevent active price competition for all items. In present circumstances, firms compete when they adjust margins of some items to create an illusion of low prices, extend (or reduce, like discounters or convenience stores) the number of items carried, provide novel services and amenities, or maintain high quality in meats and produce.

---

67 *Organization and Competition in Food Retailing,* op. cit., p. 137.

68 *Organization and Competition in Food Retailing,* op. cit., p. 136, Table 6-2.

IV. MARKET PERFORMANCE

The performance of food distribution like that of other industries must be evaluated in several dimensions. It is not enough that the industry be efficient in the use of resources to satisfy a given pattern of consumer demand. It should be innovative, realizing potentials latent in technology and organization for reducing inputs required for marketing. It should also provide the variety and opportunity for choice that we have come to associate with maximum levels of consumption. Moreover, the industry must be judged on its competitive tactics. Financial success should be a consequence of efficient and imaginative management. Profits should not be generated by unethical, unfair, or predatory competition, including abuse of economic power to deceive or exploit the consumer.

EFFICIENCY

PROFITS AND EFFICIENCY The efficiency with which the industry uses resources can be determined by such measures as profit rates, unit costs, utilization of capacity, and the proportion of optimum size stores and firms to the total. Profit rates persistently above a competitive level are *prima facie*, though not conclusive, evidence that market power is being exploited. If excess capacity is found associated with normal profits, there is a strong indication that the consumer is paying for the maintenance of too many stores. Prevalence of stores smaller than the optimum size might suggest that the industry could give equivalent service with the use of fewer resources. These indexes will be successively examined.

The profit rates earned in the food retailing industry give no indication that consumers are being exploited by the large chains. Table 5 compares profits as a per cent of net worth for food chains and for other industries. In the past 4 years food chains have not earned substantially more than the

TABLE 5 PER CENT RETURN ON NET WORTH, BY INDUSTRY

INDUSTRY	1964	1965	1966	1967	1968
Food chains	12.5	12.5	12.3	11.0	11.5
Manufacturing	12.6	13.8	14.2	12.5	13.1
Electric power	11.0	11.4	11.5	11.5	11.2
Finance	5.6	5.4	5.4	6.0	5.6
Wholesale	11.4	13.4	15.2	15.1	16.5

SOURCE *National City Bank Letter* (April 1966; April 1968; April 1969).

manufacturing average, nor substantially less. They tended to earn more on net worth, however, from 1945–1965, than their suppliers and manufacturers, generally.[69]

During the years 1956–1962, demand by consumers shifted to the larger supermarkets. Until the number of supermarkets increased to respond to the demand, they may have earned a quasi-rent. This may have been reflected in the earnings of the larger chains, which had a noticeably higher return on net worth from 1956 to 1962 than in the following years.[70]

As more and more supermarkets were constructed, the returns of the larger chains dropped. As shown by Table 2, the very largest chains are not necessarily the most profitable. A study by the FTC showed that for 1964, there was no difference between the return of net worth among three size groups of chains, with $50–150 million annual sales, $150–500 million, and $500 and over. Each group averaged approximately 11.0 per cent, and all showed a declining trend, dropping approximately 30 per cent from 1948 to 1964.[71]

Internal indexes of efficiency are inconsistent. Annual sales per supermarket employee and sales per man hour have not increased by as much as the food price index from 1958 to 1967. At the same time, sales per square foot and inventory turnover have declined.[72] These changes are perhaps traceable to the increase in the number of items carried in supermarkets or to the additional services available. Curiously, the stock turnover of single-store operators appears to be higher than that of multistore operators whereas sales per man hour are about the same.[73]

CAPACITY UTILIZATION   Retailing inevitably suffers from unutilized capacity. Shoppers tend to patronize stores on the last 2 or 3 days of the week. Morning shopping is light. Consumers might be willing to change their buying habits if food prices were very low Monday through Thursday. Because of demand inelasticity with respect to the day of the week, however, the price reduction required to even out purchases would have to be so drastic that costs could not be covered. In these circumstances, a failure to use the physical facilities of the store all day, every day, cannot be regarded as anymore a waste of resources than is unutilized electric generating capacity at 3:00 A.M. There is no practicable pricing pattern that could completely eliminate the peak.

69 *Organization and Competition in Food Retailing*, op. cit., Figs. 15–8, p. 302.

70 *Organization and Competition in Food Retailing*, op. cit., Figs. 15–4, p. 292.

71 *Organization and Competition in Food Retailing*, op. cit., Table 15–7, pp. 290–291.

72 *Organization and Competition in Food Retailing*, op. cit., p. 232; *Progressive Grocer*, op. cit., p. 96.

73 Data are for supermarkets, taken from the Super Market Institute Figure Exchange. *Organization and Competition in Food Retailing*, op. cit., pp. 230–231. Chains with over $25 million annual sales had one-third higher per man-hour sales than single-store operators with less than $1 million sales, 1954–1964. Otherwise, differences among size classifications were negligible.

Scattered data suggest that most chain stores today are of optimum size, as are also most affiliated independents. Nevertheless, casual observation is sufficient to demonstrate that where there are clusters of supermarkets— three or four within a short distance of each other, as often happens—one store may be fully utilized at peak days, whereas the others remain partially patronized. In most cases, it is the older stores that have less than their full complement of customers. The steady decline in buying population per supermarket, which fell to 6,260 in 1965 compared with 11,770 in 1954,[74] increases the likelihood of this form of excess capacity. Low earnings of A&P and First National may reflect obsolescence of their older supermarkets; replacement may further intensify supermarket saturation of the market.

INNOVATION

Major innovations in food distribution have been (1) self-service retailing, (2) the supermarket or large-volume combination food store, and (3) automated and systemized wholesaling. All of these took root before World War II. Moves to larger and larger size stores in shopping centers and the addition of other types of products to the stock of food stores, which are the major differences between today's supermarkets and those of the late 1930's, can scarcely qualify as important innovations if the term is to be restricted to developments resulting in either a significant saving in resource inputs or an improvement in quality and service.

One-stop large-volume shopping made it possible to reduce sharply the average cost per transaction. Moreover, supermarket shopping took on elements of entertainment and excitement. Other developments, including suburban living and universal availability of home refrigeration and autos, created a favorable environment. Improvements in warehousing practices and layout (one-story warehouses, palletizing, and so on) cut wholesaling margins by 50 per cent or more. These changes were sparked by a new attitude toward their customers by the grocery wholesalers, who faced severe chain competition.

Some economists are reluctant to regard self-service and the supermarket as innovations that have reduced real costs. They argue that inputs which the store formerly provided, such as packaging and assembly of the items, are now performed by manufacturers and customers, respectively.[75] Yet the issue seems forced. Given a choice, the overwhelming majority of consumers simply would not patronize any retailer but a supermarket.

---

74 *Progressive Grocer*, **44**:61 (April 1965).

75 V. R. Fuchs, *The Service Economy* (New York: National Bureau of Economic Research, 1968), pp. 100–104. Fuchs is uncertain whether the unit by which productivity should be measured is the transaction itself or the amount of food (and associated services) purchased in the transaction. By the former standard, productivity has been diminished by once-a-week shopping; by the latter, it has increased.

In making these changes, the retail innovators seem to have been the independents rather than the large chains, although cooperative wholesalers and chains appear to have been equally active in cutting warehouse costs. The period of constructive innovation seems to have come to an end and has been replaced by increased emphasis on nonprice competition in the form of store frills and promotions.

Games, stamps, and premiums cannot increase the consumption of food. They merely serve to shift customers back and forth among existing stores. Since resources have to be hired to produce the promotional material and to distribute it, the inevitable consequence is to raise distribution costs and prices with little or no offsetting benefit. The customer therefore pays more in the end for the same product.

The use of trading stamps has been perhaps the most important manifestation of waste of resources in differentiation of service. The stamps serve to distinguish from each other giant supermarkets that otherwise would offer a combination of foods of much the same quality and advertised price. Once the housewives start collecting the stamps, they are loath to patronize a store that does not issue them. The procedure of marketing the merchandise sold by stamp companies is inefficient; their prices, translated into the dollar amounts paid by the food chains for the stamps, show that this is a very expensive way for the consumer to buy bathroom scales, blenders, or sets of china. When one takes account of the cost of handling stamps in the stores, and the consumers' time required to save and use them, there is little to be said in favor of stamps. They perhaps serve as a kind of forced saving that permits lower-income customers to purchase durable consumer goods.

An advantage claimed for games is that they cost less than stamps, but one is entitled to ask whether they are not as objectionable as any other form of gambling. The consumers who do not win bear the ultimate costs of the game.

PREDATORY TACTICS AND
UNFAIR COMPETITION

Chain-type operations dominate food retailing, even the convenience field, whereas unaffiliated independents have been relegated to interstices of the market. To what extend has this change been attributable to the use of unfair methods of competition?

In its chain store investigation, the FTC found that in the 1930's about one fifth of the difference in price between the chains and the independents (defining a chain as a group with two or more stores) resulted from lower buying prices available to the chains.[76] Although the National Commission

---

76 Federal Trade Commission, *Final Report on the Chain Store Investigation,* 74th Congress, 1st Session, Senate Document No. 4, 1934.

on Food Marketing made no quantitative survey of the significance of lower buying prices for chains, it concluded that "the discriminatory advantages of large buyers" contributed to the high levels of market concentration.[77]

BUYING TACTICS   It remains to be seen, however, whether the discriminatory lower prices received by the big chains from their suppliers have been economically justified.

Large chains, particularly A&P during the 1930's, demanded brokerage payments from their suppliers and actually qualified their field-buying personnel as brokers so they could receive rebates. If a supplier refused to pay "brokerage" he lost the sale. Under Section 2(c) of the Robinson-Patman Act, the FTC successfully attacked brokerage payments by suppliers not only to A&P, but to cooperative and voluntary groups. Nevertheless, A&P argued that because the suppliers directly contacted the A&P buyers, there was a saving of brokerage costs. Both FTC policy and the Robinson-Patman Act were alleged to be economically absurd. Forcing either A&P or IGA to pay the same price as other customers uneconomically discriminated against the big buyer, and in favor of the other customers.[78]

The "brokerage" received by A&P, however, was sometimes paid when the suppliers did not use brokers at all. Nor was there any evidence that the amounts paid as "brokerage" really measured actual cost savings. "Brokers as a group might be regarded as an overhead charge of the canning industry . . . whose function it is to keep canners independent of single buyers and to maintain a more perfect market."[79] Hence, although the economic underpinning for Section 2(c) may be weak (i.e., absolute prohibition of the payment of brokerage to buyers), A&P attempts to extract brokerage or equivalent price reductions as a systematic procedure could be justified only to the extent that all discriminatory concessions to buyers are economically defensible. It is necessary to turn, therefore, to the broader category.

In a Sherman Act proceeding, A&P was indicted and convicted in 1946, because (among other charges) it has "used its large buying power to coerce suppliers to sell to it at a lower price than to its competitors on the threat that it would place such suppliers on its private blacklist if they did not conform."[80] Other large chains, including Safeway and Kroger pleaded *nolo contendere* to similar indictments. The concessions condemned by the court were applauded by some economists because, it was said, A&P could thereby get suppliers to make reductions that would not otherwise be made available. The concessions would spread to all buyers when competing retailers

77 *Organization and Competition in Food Retailing*, op. cit., p. 436.
    78, Adelman, The A&P Case, op. cit., "The Great A&P Muddle," *Fortune*, **40**:122 (December 1949).

79 J. B. Dirlam and A. E. Kahn, "Antitrust Law and the Big Buyer: Another Look at the A&P Case," *Journal of Political Economy*, **60**:131 (April 1952).
    80 *U.S.* v. *A&P*, 173 F 2d 79, 82 (1949).

put pressure on their suppliers. A fuller utilization of manufacturing capacity would result, with lower cost, lower prices, and greater consumer welfare. Professor Galbraith erected his theory of "countervailing power" on the explicit assumption that A&P typified the big buyer who performed a public service by forcing concessions from oligopolistic suppliers.[81] Curiously enough, although it was strongly argued that the large size of A&P enabled it to get important discounts, at the same time, food retailing was said to exhibit no economies of scale, so that entry was easy and there was no danger of oligopoly or monopoly pricing at the retail level.

There was, in fact, little to show that A&P receipt of discriminatory concessions contributed to making competition more workable. Few discriminatory allowances were made by powerful sellers. "It was precisely the highly differentiated products which were the most rarely affected by discrimination."[82] Special discounts were obtained mainly from small canners and fruit and vegetable shippers. The nature of the canning business and of fruit and vegetable growing is such that when the pack or harvest is completed, marginal costs are negligible. Indeed, in a market dominated by large purchasers there may be no meaningful list or market price to undercut. In a discontinuous market dominated by monopsonists, sellers may be willing to accept prices far below long-run marginal costs rather than lose a sale entirely.

To the degree that the large chains benefit in the competitive struggle from concessions and allowances not justified by cost, resource allocation is distorted. Incentives and rewards do not reflect relative efficiencies.

SELLING TACTICS AND PRICE DISCRIMINATION   As chains have grown in size, spreading over more and more territory, they have been able to practice local price discrimination. Losses in one or more areas have been absorbed by profits elsewhere. There are two principal objections to local price discrimination. First, if a firm can charge a lower price after allowance for cost differences in one area, then the higher price elsewhere may be taken as evidence of exploitation of some degree of monopoly power. Second, competition with local (or territorial) price discrimination is economically undesirable because it makes it possible for the market to reward the inefficient. Transfer of patronage from a nondiscriminating small firm to a larger, discriminating firm would not assure the survival of the most efficient seller who uses fewer resources to perform food distribution. Rather, it would guarantee the success of a seller simply because he has greater financial power.

Local price discrimination has been defended on two grounds. First, it is said that when customers shift from independent to chain, the chain stores can realize economies of scale. In the short run, excess capacity would be

81   *American Capitalism* (Boston: Houghton Mifflin, 1952), Chs. IX, X, and *passim*.

82   J. B. Dirlam and A. E. Kahn, *Fair Competition: The Law and Economics of Antitrust Policy* (Ithaca, N.Y.: Cornell University Press, 1954), p. 238.

more fully used, thus spreading the overhead. This would enable the discriminating chain to earn profits with lower margins and prices than its competitors. The discrimination is viewed as simply another form of promotional pricing, designed to take advantage of demand elasticity. Second, regardless of its effect on competitors, it is argued that entry into food retailing is easy and permanent monopoly can never be achieved through local price discrimination.

It is important not to confuse desirable promotional pricing with objectionable price discrimination. To begin with, most small single-territory firms will be unable to use profits from one area to finance losses in another. A&P, however, carried out an avowed policy of "subsidizing" local price cuts, using funds from areas where competition was less keen. For instance, in September 1941, a sales manager in the Southern Division told his unit heads that . . . "Where stores need special attention because of unusually active competition or some other condition beyond our control, we feel that the store in those towns should be put into a special zone and given the benefit of lower than average prices. In other towns, where the conditions may not be quite as pressing, a little better gross profit rate can be obtained . . .." [83] In some units A&P lost money year after year. During the years 1932–1940, the Los Angeles unit lost $1,406,194.[84] The Boston and Springfield units failed to break even for 5 years in succession. These losses were real, that is, they were calculated after having allocated to the retail store or units discounts and allowances from headquarters and manufacturing profits.[85]

Local price discrimination by food chains did not end with the A&P conviction in 1947. Others have practiced it, notably Safeway and National Tea. In the 1950's Safeway was indicted for attempting to monopolize the food distribution business in Dallas and El Paso, Texas. The company had set as its objective the control of 50 per cent of grocery store sales, and used price wars as a means of achieving the objective.

Safeway had sold many items below invoice cost in several zones in Dallas, with the result that it suffered a loss of $2.3 million in 1954 in this division alone, and a $3 million loss in 1955. As the U.S. Antitrust Division attorney summarized the facts, "Safeway's rate of gross profit in its highest zone,

---

83 C. Fulda, *Food Distribution in the United States, The Struggle Between Independents and Chains* (Association of American Law Schools, 1951), p. 172, fn. 497. Footnote cited from A&P Transcript, Vol. 46, p. 9983.

84 J. B. Dirlam, and A. E. Kahn, "The Integration and Dissolution of the Company," *Indiana Law Journal*, 29:18 (1953).

85 It has been argued that in many cases the A&P units or stores that were

"in the red" actually broke even or made money after they were allocated their proportionate share of rebates paid to headquarters and profits on manufacturing subsidiaries. Retail stores should be credited only with that part of manufacturing profit attributable to combined operations of manufacturing and retailing. Normal manufacturing profits are part of the competitive costs that retailers should be expected to cover, whether they are integrated or not. Ibid., p. 18, fn. 62.

where there was no price war, was 15.62 per cent. . . . In the lowest price zone, it was 1.31 per cent. . . . (T)he defendant Warren [President of Safeway] has said . . . it takes 11 per cent just to meet the cost of running the store. . . ."[86]

Safeway's contention was that, far from attempting to monopolize the market, it was combating the competition of trading stamps. As the National Commission on Food Marketing has pointed our, however, a 2 per cent reduction in prices should be sufficient to match the trading stamp benefit; and this overall percentage cut could be achieved with a dramatic 10 per cent cut on 20 per cent of the volume. Safeway went much further than this, cutting by percentages sufficient to wipe out a store-wide normal 15 per cent margin.

Whether the large chains that have used local price discrimination have done so as a competitive response or initiated the practice to increase or maintain market shares is not crucial to an economic evaluation of the practice. To the extent that price discrimination takes patronage from efficient but less financially powerful firms, the price system is prevented from carrying out its normal functions. It is questionable whether society should disregard injuries inflicted upon nonconglomerates, even if over the long run rational discriminating firms erase their low prices and new firms enter to take the place of the casualties.

DISCRIMINATION AND LOW INCOME GROUPS   It has been alleged that, because they pay higher prices, ghetto residents suffer from exploitation at the hands of retail merchants, including food retailers.[87] There seems to be little evidence, however, to support this belief, as far as food stores are concerned. There are relatively few chain supermarkets in ghettos because it does not pay to invest where incomes, and therefore sales per store, are relatively low and where entry costs are high. Hence, Negro neighborhoods are more likely to be served by small independents, which tend to have higher costs and prices than chains. Surveys conducted by the Bureau of Labor Statistics and the FTC show that in poor neighborhoods, chain prices were 0.7 per cent higher, whereas small independents had slightly lower prices than elsewhere.[88] There was no conclusive finding with regard to quality of meat or produce. But there can be no question that ghetto residents are handicapped by their environment in selecting stores and in family food budgeting.

CONCLUSION: PERFORMANCE

That the introduction of the supermarket reduced inputs of clerical service per unit of food purchased is obvious. As manufacturers, processors, and

---

86   *Organization and Competition in Food Retailing*, op. cit., p. 407.

87   *Report of the National Commission on Civil Disorders* (New York: Bantam Books, 1968), p. 277.

88   *Food Retailing*, op. cit., pp. 336–338. See also Federal Trade Commission, *Economic Report on Food Chain Selling Prices in the District of Columbia and San Francisco* (Washington, D.C., 1969).

wholesalers have taken over more and more packaging functions, these types of inputs in retailing per dollar of sales have likewise tended to decline. Both these developments have changed the nature of the retailing service, by throwing on the consumer and the supplier responsibilities that used to be the retailer's. Yet, the display service and the greater array of items (up to the point where choice becomes fatiguing) provided by the supermarket undoubtedly represent improvements, except for confirmed addicts of Americana, over the environment of the homey old-fashioned grocery store, where prices varied from customer to customer and the cat slept in the cracker barrel.

If we consider the essential irrationality and indeterminancy of the pattern of food pricing and consumption, taking into account the inability of both the retailer accurately to allocate costs and estimate optimum pricing combinations and the shopper to perform quadratic linear programming as she moves her cart through the supermarket, it seems likely that we are far from reaching an economic optimum in food retailing. Although the Department of Agriculture has spent millions of dollars on extension work and research on food consumption, only one economist in the United States has made a systematic attempt to apply modern activity analysis to food purchases.[89] The housewife still sallies forth on her weekly shopping expedition abysmally ill-prepared for her job as the family purchasing agent.

V. PUBLIC POLICY
PUBLIC POLICY AND STRUCTURE

Public policy toward food distribution has focused mainly on acquisitions by large chains and on the competitive tactics in both buying and selling. Concern over market structure in retailing is soundly based. As we have seen, much of the recent increase in retail margins is attributable to attempts to differentiate retail service in oligopolized markets.

Economically justified opposition to large size must rest mainly on the assumption that giant chains will unfairly exercise their power, either by discriminatory pricing in local markets or in bargaining with suppliers. A reduction of concentration in local markets could perhaps reduce the pressures to spend on nonprice competition, and lead to a more efficient allocation of resources. Yet nothing in antitrust laws empowers either the Department of Justice or the FTC to initiate proceedings simply because concentration ratios are high. The leading firms are often local or regional chains that may have grown by internal expansion.

In the Von's case, decided in 1966,[90] the Supreme Court ordered the

---

89 V. E. Smith, *Electronic Computation of Human Diets* (East Lansing, Mich.: Michigan State University Press, 1964).

90 384 U.S. 270 (1966).

Los Angeles food chain to divest itself of Shopping Bag, another Los Angeles local chain. After the merger, the company accounted for 7.5 per cent of Los Angeles sales and ranked second in the market, and by 1965, it ranked 21st nationally in sales. The opinion held that, because of the disappearance of thousands of independent food stores, two leading local chains should not be permitted to expand by combination. The majority position was criticized by Justice Stewart on the ground that the Antitrust Division was trying to sweep back the tide of greater efficiencies associated with larger stores and retailing organizations.

The FTC has been particularly active in enforcing Section 7 of the Clayton Act against grocery mergers. It issued complaints against National Tea, Kroger, Grand Union, Consolidated Foods, and Winn-Dixie.

In the National Tea decision, although the FTC suggested that an expansion campaign of National Tea had been responsible for goading other chains into similar programs, and despite National Tea's acquisition of direct competitors in some markets, the company was allowed to keep its acquired stores on the condition that it expand no further by acquisition.[91] The prohibition was based on the finding that National Tea had used its market power to subsidize its operations in some localities and to extract discriminatory concessions.

The National Tea decision was generalized in a policy statement in 1967, after most of the merger cases had been closed by agreements to merge no more. On the basis of findings by the National Commission on Food Marketing, the FTC concluded that economies of scale in warehousing did not extend to chains with annual sales exceeding $100 million and that chains with more than $500 million annual sales could not realize further economies of scale in manufacturing operations, private label programs, and field buying of perishables. Accordingly, an acquisition raising the annual food store sales of a chain or a voluntary and cooperative group above $500 million is suspect, warranting "attention and consideration by the Commission . . .."[92]

Combinations with annual sales between $100 million and $500 million "warrant investigation," although the FTC did not, as in the case of the larger sales volume, indicate that there would be "questions regarding their legal status."

Even for smaller chains, a threat to competition would be posed when leaders in metropolitan areas merged with direct competitors which were also leaders. Mergers of not more than four stores, however, or representing grocery product sales of not more than $5 million or not more than 5 per cent of food store sales in any city or county, were given what amounted to a safe-conduct.

Mergers of food chains that have attracted the attention of the authorities

---

91   Federal Trade Commission Opinion, Docket No. 7453 (March 4, 1966).

92   Federal Trade Commission, "Enforcement Policy with Respect to Mergers in the Food Distribution Industries" (January 3, 1967), p. 8.

have rarely combined direct competitors (the Von's–Shopping Bag merger is an exception). The overwhelming number of acquisitions of the larger chains have been market extensions—joining together stores in different areas.

How shall we evaluate the market structure policy of the government? The Von's decision can be tested by the rough and ready measures of optimum size suggested by the FTC. Von's had 27 stores, Shopping Bag, 34. The combined sales of the two chains at the time of merger in 1960 were about $172 million, or less than the maximum amount at which they could realize economies of scale in manufacturing. With good management, however, a chain does not have to have mammoth size to be prosperous. While Justice Stewart is undoubtedly correct in arguing that the decline in the number of single unaffiliated independents may be traced to their inefficiencies, the Von's precedent will not, as he feared, "roll back the supermarket technological revolution." It simply checks mergers by direct competitors of substantial size and rank. This is not a policy that can hurt consumers. As the National Commission on Food Marketing pointed out, "... many of the small retailers taken over by the largest chains in the past 20 years were growing rapidly when acquired."[93]

PREDATORY TACTICS AND
UNFAIR COMPETITION

The small independent grocers did not passively accept replacement in the 1930's by the supermarkets and the chains. Joining forces with independent wholesale grocers and food brokers, they enlisted politicians to their aid. Supporting chain store taxation, Senator Huey Long proclaimed, "I would rather have thieves and gangsters in Louisiana than chain stores."[94] In 1935 the director of the National Association of Retail Grocers told the Judiciary Committee of the House of Representatives, "The present condition of affairs in the food industry has put thousands of salesmen out of work. It has driven many brokers out of business. It has closed the doors of many wholesale grocers and has shut up thousands of retail grocers .... Many of them are now on the relief rolls. And this was done, not to bring goods to the consumer cheaper but in order to fatten the income of a few chosen people who invested their money in chain stores."[95]

In 1936, Congress passed the Robinson-Patman Act, which was drafted by the counsel for the United States Wholesale Grocers Association. The Act amended Section 2 of the Clayton Act to outlaw price discrimination that made more than due allowance for differences in cost of manufacture,

---

93 *Organization and Competition in Food Retailing*, op. cit., p. 269.
94 Quoted in Beckman and Nolen, *The Chain Store Problem*, (New York: McGraw Hill, 1938), pp. 228–229.

95 Quoted in Fulda, *Food Distribution*, op. cit., p. 1.

sale, or delivery, where competition might be lessened or disadvantaged competitors injured. Meeting competition, however, excused otherwise illegal discrimination. Brokerage payments to buyers and promotional allowances not available to customers on a proportionate basis were outlawed unqualifiedly.

Though not sympathetic with the arcane intricacies of the Robinson-Patman Act, which seems to inhibit price competition if applied too rigidly, the Antitrust Division moved against giant chains under the Sherman Act. It succeeded in convicting the A&P Company. Other chains took warning so that discounts to big purchasers today are on a sporadic basis only. Most of the concessions are now given on the sales of fluid milk, ice cream, and bakery products,[96] the items most manufactured by chains. Between July 1954 and September 1965 the FTC made over 1,792 investigations of suspicious exertion of bargaining power. Complaints were issued in 101 cases alleging illegal preference by suppliers to food chains. There were 31 consent orders signed by chains among the top 20; 38 cases were contested.[97]

Prior to the passage of the Robinson-Patman Act, many voluntary or cooperative wholesalers were accustomed to collecting brokerage from suppliers. Relying on these allowances the cooperatives and voluntary wholesalers financed advertising and marketing assistance and helped their members to compete with the corporate chains.

The enforcement of Section 2(c), therefore, hurt not only A&P, but the affiliated groups. Commissioner Elman complained in his dissenting opinion in the *Central Retailer-Owned Grocers* case that the Robinson-Patman Act was being turned to a perverted use when it was applied against the voluntary or cooperative wholesaler. Although the chairman of the FTC had stated that "many independent food stores long ago would have withered before the competitive threat of large chains had they not formed retailer-owned cooperative wholesalers..." the "Commission's [CR-OG] opinion would most certainly have the effect of driving these groups out of existence. For what it holds is that any price concession to a cooperative buying organization—which of necessity performs functions which buyers' brokers would perform—will be deemed in lieu of brokerage in per se violation of Section 2(c)."[98]

SELLING TACTICS: PRICE DISCRIMINATION   The antitrust laws have been invoked against local price discrimination by large chains. In the A&P case an interrelated course of action was attacked by the Department of Justice. Discriminatory concessions from suppliers helped to finance low prices in certain territories where the company faced severe local competition or wanted

---

96   *Organization and Competition in Food Retailing*, op. cit., p. 422.

97   *Organization and Competition in Food Retailing*, op. cit., pp. 420–421.

98   *Dissenting Opinion*, Docket No. 7121 (May 14, 1962), pp. 10–11.

to attain a maximum market share. In the 1955 Safeway case, below-cost retail pricing resulted in conviction under the criminal provisions of the Sherman Act.

Below-cost sales are forbidden by many state statutes. Cost is usually defined to include a maximum markup. The statutes have been rarely applied. State attorneys do not act to enforce them. Proof of violation is difficult, and the remedy, usually an injunction, is of little value since it may be June before a Thanksgiving turkey special price is found illegal.

EVALUATION OF
PUBLIC POLICY TOWARD CONDUCT

One cannot muster much enthusiasm for the efforts of enforcement agencies to police buying concessions and the various forms of promotional and advertising allowances. True, many of the discounts were wrung from small sellers and cannot be defended as an exercise of countervailing power, and it is extremely unlikely that the proceedings have impeded the essential forces of grocery chain competition. ". . . (T)he benefit to the public from those aspects of company policy which the Department of Justice attacked has been greatly exaggerated. The great bulk of the good which grocery chains do—with their private labels, their large-scale coordinated operations, their low markups and intense competition with established manufacturers and channels of distribution—they may continue to do."[99]

Nevertheless, concessions and allowances today are one-shot affairs, against which a cease and desist order cannot be effective. More important, bureaucratic interference with price policy and formation at any level is fraught with dangers for a system depending on independence of enterprise decision-making. If public policy toward structure is efficiently and intelligently enforced, the supervision of pricing aspects can be minimized.

The consumer will still benefit, however, from government action to improve the quality of his information, protect him from deceitful and misleading selling tactics, and enable him to make more rational buying decisions.

PACKAGING AND LABELING It would be idle to pretend that retail food stores, despite their attractive decor and dreamy music, actually provide the buying information of the character necessary to enable the average housewife to maximize her returns for minimum expenditures. The calculations required are simply beyond the powers of most shoppers. As Marya Mannes put it, "Most of us are simply too busy or too tired or too harassed to take a computer, a slide rule, and an MIT graduate to market and figure out what we're buying." Consumers Union has conducted experiments

---

99 J. B. Dirlam and A. E. Kahn, "The Antitrust Law and the Big Buyer: Another Look at the A&P Case," *Journal of Political Economy*, **60**:132 (April 1952).

showing that even college-educated housewives cannot discover the lowest cost packaged items. In 1962, they made 34 wrong choices out of a possible 70; in 1968, 38 wrong choices."[100] This is because neither grocers nor manufacturers state prices per unit of the quantities usually purchased, such as ounces, pounds, or pints, although unit prices are available for meats, produce, and cheese in most stores. Senator Hart's Fair Packaging and Label Act requires net quantities to be printed in standard form in a well-defined place in reasonably legible type, so that unit prices could be provided, although the law does not require it.

Lack of standardization of sizes also makes price comparisons even more difficult. The Fair Packaging and Label Act directs the Secretary of Commerce to persuade manufacturers to voluntarily reduce the number of sizes. Soon there will be only (!) 12 different containers of peanut butter and 16 sizes of syrup.

The Act also gives the FTC discretionary authority to establish standards for "large," "small," "super," "giant," and so on. So far, no regulations have been issued.

Equally important is the authority given to the FTC to control claims of price savings on labels, such as "cents off." The "cents off" promotions are inherently deceptive. The manufacturer has no control over the retailer's price, and the consumer does not know and cannot remember the going price, if indeed there is such a thing. As the editor of *Sales Management* wrote, "To the best of my knowledge it all started several years ago with one of the makers of instant coffee who marked in big red letters on his jar '7 cents off.' Off what? I asked my wife and several shopkeepers. Nobody gave me an answer that made any sense. . . . I assume the practice has grown because manufacturers have found that it influences housewives. . . ."[101] The FTC is considering regulating "cents off" promotions, but has not yet acted.

Trading stamps are sold in a highly concentrated market with one firm, Sperry and Hutchinson, accounting for about 35–40 per cent of the stamps issued. Sperry and Hutchinson has forced its franchisees to limit their "double stamping" and generally has required that they observe a ratio of 1 stamp per 10 cents of purchase. It has stopped the exchange of its books for those of others and has prevented retailers from redeeming its stamps for merchandise. It has combined with other stamp companies to prevent unauthorized exchanges. In view of the concentration of the trading stamp market, the FTC was fully justified, though somewhat belated, in its 1968 finding that Sperry and Hutchinson had engaged in illegal activities under Section 5 of the Federal Trade Commission Act.[102]

---

100 News, *Consumer Reports* (December 20, 1968).

101 U.S. Senate Report of Antitrust Subcommittee, 88th Congress, 2nd Session, *Truth in Packaging* (1964), p. 17.

102 *Opinion*, Docket No. 8671, (July 25, 1968).

But the major economic issue associated with the use of stamps remains unresolved. By adding a second price dimension, stamps intensify the difficulties already faced by the housewife who attempts to make price and value comparisons. Sound public policy would seem to call for a complete ban on the issuance of stamps or at least for the enforced availability of an optional 2 per cent cash rebate for customers who do not want stamps.

CONCLUSION

The food distribution industry has performed quite well during the period covered in this analysis. Those inefficiencies and inequities that persist are traceable mainly to rising concentration. Merger guidelines may serve to keep concentration below the level where increasing concentration of purchases restricts the alternatives open to suppliers, stimulates compensating concentration on their part, and weakens the effectiveness of competition as a self-regulating device throughout the industry. Local oligopoly seems inevitable because of the relation between the most efficient size of store and the territory from which it can draw customers. Oligopoly will continue to be dynamic and noncollusive, however, as long as entry remains relatively easy, and personal ambition stirs entrepreneurs to expand their businesses. To the extent that consumers can be educated and assisted to purchase rationally, the food distribution industry's performance will be even better than it has been to date.

SUGGESTED READINGS

Holdren, Bob. *The Structure of a Retail Market and the Market Behavior of Retail Units*. Englewood Cliffs, N.J.: Prentice-Hall, Inc. 1960.

National Commission on Food Marketing. *Report, Food From Farmer to Consumer*. Washington, D.C.: U.S. Government Printing Office, 1966.

National Commission on Food Marketing. *Organization and Competition in Food Retailing*, Technical Study Number 7. Washington, D.C.: U.S. Government Printing Office, 1966.

Preston, L. F. *Profits, Competition and Rules of Thumb in Retail Food Pricing*. Berkeley, Calif.: Institute of Business and Economic Research, 1963.

3. Walter Adams

THE STEEL INDUSTRY

A I. INTRODUCTION

t the end of World War II in 1945, America's steel industry was the most powerful in the world. Its plant capacity was almost double that of all "iron curtain" countries combined, and there was no apparent chance that the devastated facilities in Germany and Japan would ever again rise to challenge American mastery. Today, only 25 years later, the situation is radically different. The U.S. produces only 22.8 per cent of the world's steel, closely followed by the U.S.S.R. with 19.2 per cent, the European Economic Community with 18.7 per cent, and Japan with 14.3 per cent. Indeed, if present trends continue in this decade, Japan may well dispute the U.S. among the world's steel powers.

HISTORY

Before 1898, the steel industry was the scene of active and, at times, destructive competition. In this early period, various gentlemen's agreements and pools were organized in an effort to control the production of steel rails, billets, wire, nails, and other products, but the outstanding characteristic of these agreements was the "frequency with which they collapsed."[1] Their weakness was that inherent in any pool or gentlemen's agreement, "60 per cent of the agreers are gentlemen, 30 per cent just act like gentlemen, and 10 per cent neither are nor act like gentlemen." If production and prices were to be controlled, these loose-knit agreements had to be superseded by more stable forms of organization. The latter came upon the industry with the suddenness and intensity seldom paralleled in American industrial history.

From 1898 to 1900, a vast concentration movement took place in the steel industry. Large companies such as Federal Steel, National Steel, National Tube, American Bridge, and American Sheet Steel were organized. Dominated by three financial interest groups—Carnegie, Morgan, and Moore—

---

1 H. R. Seager and C. A. Gulick, *Trust and Corporation Problems* (New York: Harper, 1929), p. 216. This book is an excellent source on the early history of U.S. Steel.

these consolidations did not succeed in bringing "stability" to the industry. In fact, a fight between the newly formed giants seemed unavoidable.

Since each of the major interest groups was peculiarly vulnerable in case a "battle between the giants" materialized, and since cooperation promised to be more profitable than competition, stubbornness yielded to reason. In 1901, with the initiative of Charles Schwab, J. P. Morgan, and a corporation lawyer named James B. Dill, the interested parties agreed to form the "combination of combinations"—the U.S. Steel Corporation which at the time of its formation controlled approximately 65 per cent of the nation's steel capacity.

Considerable disagreement has attended discussions of the motives behind the organization of the U.S. Steel Corporation. The announced motives were to form a completely integrated steel company; to secure the advantages of the most advanced technical organization; and to develop an extensive export trade. Judge Gary testified that the latter was the "dominating factor" favoring the creation of the corporation.[2] Most disinterested observers, however, agree that the "intent to monopolize" played a significant and perhaps dominant role. The policies of the corporation, subsequent to its organization in 1901, seem to bear out this opinion; for the corporation proceeded to acquire properties which would put it in a position to dominate the steel industry. Especially significant was the acquisition of essential raw material assets, particularly coking coal and iron ore mines.

By 1907, however, the corporation became concerned with more immediate problems than the long-run elimination of *potential* competition through a monopolization of some raw material supplies. It had to face a spasm of *active* price competition which had been brought on by the business panic of that year. To meet this challenge and to restore price stability under its own leadership, it innovated the famous Gary dinners. The purpose of these dinners—in the words of the host, the president of U.S. Steel—was "to maintain to a reasonable extent the equilibrium of business, to prevent utter demoralization of business and destructive competition."[3] Mr. Gary *achieved* this objective by urging "his guests, who represented fully 90 per cent of the industry, that they cooperate in holding prices where they were."[4] He exhorted them like a Methodist preacher at a camp meeting to follow the price leadership of U.S. Steel. There was no need for any formal agreements, no need to force a group of reluctant competitors into a cooperative arrangement. U.S. Steel merely assumed the lead incumbent on a firm its size; its rivals followed, fully realizing the security and profitability of cooperation. Under these circumstances, the Gary dinners were a singular success and

2 *Hearings before the House Committee on Investigation of the U.S. Steel Corporation*, 62nd Congress, 2nd Session (Washington, D.C.: 1911), Vol. 1, p. 104; hereafter referred to as *Stanley Hearings*.

3 *Stanley Hearings*, op. cit., Vol. I, p. 264.

4 Ida M. Tarbell, *The Life of Elbert H. Gary* (New York: Appleton, 1930), p. 205.

presented but another vivid illustration of Adam Smith's observation that "people of the same trade seldom meet together, even for merriment and diversion, but the conversation ends in a conspiracy against the public or in some contrivance to raise prices."

Available evidence indicates that the dinners were held at irregular intervals until 1911. However, when the government became increasingly suspicious of their price-fixing function and when it finally filed suit for the dissolution of U.S. Steel, the dinners were abruptly abandoned. But the damage had been done. The Corporation stood accused in the Federal courts as a monopoly, and the government demanded the extreme penalty—dissolution.

Due to the outbreak of World War I, the case was not decided until 1920 when the fervor of earlier trust-busting campaigns had died down. By a vote of 4 to 3, the Supreme Court decided against dissolution.[5] Without considering the effects of price quotation under the Pittsburgh-Plus system, the court declared that mere size was no offense. While conceding that U.S. Steel was guilty of an attempt to monopolize the steel industry, the court maintained that such a monopoly had never actually been achieved. However, if any one factor responsible for the court's rejection of the government plea were singled out, it would undoubtedly be the friendly attitude which U.S. Steel evidenced toward its competitors. This fact more than anything else probably explains why U.S. Steel was allowed to survive while the Standard Oil Company and the American Tobacco Company were unceremoniously dissolved. This was a vindication of a policy very close to Judge Gary's heart, a policy over which there was considerable dispute with the corporation's board of directors; for Gary's "Directors, worthy men but of a cruder age, were honestly puzzled. It was bewildering to hear their Chairman preach the community of interests of all steelmakers, to see him consistently refusing to use the Corporation's size as a club over the rest of the industry. Destructive competition, they pointed out, had made hundreds of millions for Rockefeller's oil trust. But the day came when Gary could point out that the oil trust was busted and that the steel trust had survived, and that its survival was largely due to his policy of 'friendly competition.'"[6]

After 1920, U.S. Steel continued to dominate the industry, although its percentage control over total industry sales declined steadily. The corporation remained sufficiently big, however, to keep its competitors "in line" without threats and without displays of force. The friendly competition, which had paid such handsome dividends in the past, endured as the basic characteristic of the industry.

Then, in 1929, came the big depression. For the steel industry, it was a traumatic experience causing widespread unemployment and a terrific drop

---

5   *United States* v. *United States Steel Corporation*, 251 U.S. 417 (1920).

6   "U.S. Steel: I," reprinted from *Fortune*, **13**:157 (March 1936), by special permission of the Editors. Copyright Time, Inc.

in production. In 1932, plants were operated at 19.5 per cent of capacity. Under the pressure of a rapidly falling demand, individual firms began to grant unofficial and secret price concessions in order to increase plant utilization and thereby spread fixed costs over a larger volume of output. Even the formerly effective basing point system seemed powerless to check the activity of panicky price cutters and "chiselers" with the result that the stable structure of uniform delivered prices broke down.

When anarchy seemed certain to gain control of the industry's price determination process, the National Industrial Recovery Act (NRA) of 1934 was passed. Under the NRA code of fair competition—drafted by steel leaders and approved by the President—the steel industry was almost totally immune against antitrust attack. It could, for the first time in its history, fix prices legally—or quasi-legally at any rate. So enthusiastic were steel executives over this government sanctioned price-maintenance scheme that Charles M. Schwab, former President of the Bethlehem Steel Corporation, claimed that never before in his 50 years' experience in the trade had he seen a year "when the business of the industry could be conducted on a common-sense basis." Little wonder can be expressed at this enthusiasm when it is considered that all price concessions under the NRA had to be approved by the Code Authority for the Steel Industry. This Code Authority consisted of none other than the Board of Directors of the American Iron and Steel Institute, the official trade association of the industry, in which the nine largest companies exercised majority (52 per cent) control.

Even government sanctioned price-fixing, however, could not provide more than a palliative for the depression ills of the steel industry. The fact remained that, given a low level of demand for producer goods, price rigidity alone could not solve the basic problems of the steel industry in the 1930's. The one sure way of getting steel out of the doldrums was by restoring full employment in the economy as a whole. This occurred only when production was stimulated by the outbreak of World War II and by the eventual entry of the United States into that conflict.

During the war, the industry made great forward strides in production and employment and by 1943, operated at 98.1 per cent of capacity. Prices, of course, were carefully regulated by the Office of Price Administration and intricate priority and allocation systems were worked out to govern the distribution of steel among essential users. After V-J Day it was generally expected that these regulations would be relaxed and the industry return to its "normal" methods of price determination. This expectation, however, never materialized simply because steel remained a scarce commodity during the postwar boom. A gray market, which by 1948 reached $500 million proportions,[7] developed due mainly to the insistence of industry leaders, the public, and the government that no substantial upward adjustment of steel prices take place. This

---

7 "That Daffy Gray Market," *Fortune*, 37:94 (May 1948).

decision necessitated the institution of a "private" OPA and allocation system to ration off the commodity's scarce supply. This, in turn, made it imperative that the government grant the industry temporary exemption from the antitrust laws to permit cooperation among the producers in the execution of the new allocation scheme. Eventually, with the outbreak of the Korean War in 1950, many of the detailed World War II controls were reimposed on the industry. But, with or without controls, the industry adhered to its basic pattern of rigid, administered prices. In the 1950's and 1960's, the industry continued to behave as if the world were not changing and its market control would never be challenged.

II. MARKET STRUCTURE

The iron and steel industry is divided into four principal branches—iron ore mining, pig-iron production, steel making, and steel rolling. Depending on the function performed, the individual companies composing the industry are classified as integrated, semiintegrated, and nonintegrated. Integrated companies are those which operate in all four of the industry's branches. Semiintegrated concerns do not make their own pig-iron, but purchase it to make steel and rolled products. Nonintegrated producers either make pig-iron exclusively (these are the so-called merchant blast furnaces) or buy ingots or semifinished steel for rolling and further processing.

The steel industry today is—structurally speaking—an oligopoly and is dominated by a relatively few, large, integrated producers. These, taken together, own or control about three-quarters of the nation's ore reserves,[8] blast furnace capacity, ingot and "steel for casting" capacity, and finished hot-rolled capacity. Both horizontally and vertically, therefore, steel is a highly concentrated industry.

Today, there are some 90 companies in the U.S. engaged in basic steel-making. As Table 1 shows, the 4 largest produce 54 per cent of the nation's steel tonnage, the 8 largest 75 per cent, and the 13 largest about 85 per cent. These percentages, however, understate the degree of concentration in particular product lines and particular market areas because not every steel company produces every steel product or sells in every section of the country. Thus, the four largest producers account for 54 per cent of the raw-steel

---

8 "Management and operation of iron-mining properties is concentrated in a few large companies which are either partly or wholly owned by the large iron and steel producers or otherwise closely affiliated with them." [U.S. Tariff Commission, "Iron and Steel," *War Changes in Industry Series*, Report No. 15 (Washington, D.C.: 1946), p. 88.] See also TNEC, *Hearings*, Pt. 18, p. 10426; Lake Superior Iron Ore Association, *Lake Superior Iron Ores*; also the *Mining Directory of Minnesota* (Minneapolis: Mine Experiment Station, University of Minnesota). Data on iron ore holdings in Michigan can be obtained from the Department of Conservation, Lansing, Michigan.

TABLE 1   RAW STEEL PRODUCTION IN THE U.S. BY COMPANY, 1968

COMPANY	RAW STEEL PRODUCTION	PER CENT OF TOTAL RAW STEEL PRODUCTION	NET INCOME AS PER CENT OF INVESTMENT
United States Steel Corporation	32,352,200	24.68	6.5
Bethlehem Steel Corporation	20,372,000	15.54	8.0
Republic Steel Corporation	9,748,688	7.44	7.2
National Steel Corporation	8,462,500	6.46	NA
Armco Steel Corporation	7,700,000	5.87	8.5
Jones & Laughlin Steel Corporation	7,688,000	5.86	3.6
Inland Steel Company	7,015,000	5.35	9.5
Youngstown Sheet & Tube Company	5,633,500	4.30	6.5
Wheeling Pittsburgh Steel Company	3,570,000	2.72	6.2
Kaiser Steel Corporation	2,925,000	2.23	10.2
CF & I Steel Corporation	1,639,000	1.25	6.7
Sharon Steel Corporation	1,490,212	1.14	4.2
McLouth Steel Corporation	1,452,000	1.11	7.3
Total for 13 Largest	110,048,100	83.95	7.0[a]
Grand Total	131,097,598	100.00	5.9

a   Unweighted average.
SOURCE   *Iron Age*, 1968 Steel Industry Financial Analysis.

output, but in some product lines—like skelp, tube rounds, steel piling, electrical sheets and strip, axles, joint bars, and so on—they contribute close to 90 per cent of the domestic production. Regional concentration in some cases is also higher than Table 1 might suggest.[9]

Historically, the share of the largest firms has decreased over the last 50 years, but there have been few dramatic changes in the concentration pattern during the post-World War II period. Since steel has typically been a capital intensive industry in which the capital cost of an efficient-sized plant is large, entry into the industry has been rare indeed. However, deconcentration trends have recently begun to appear that tend to attenuate the oligopoly control exercised by the integrated majors. Let us examine these trends, as well as the factors that have worked in the direction of solidifying the oligopoly control of the industry.

CONCENTRATION FACTORS

THE DISPOSAL OF WORLD WAR II STEEL PLANTS   At the end of World War II—as of October 8, 1945—the War Assets Administration held the following

9   Senate Subcommittee on Antitrust and Monopoly, *Administered Prices in Steel*, Senate Report No. 1387, 85th   Congress, 2nd Session (1958), pp. 67–72; hereafter cited as *Kefauver Committee Report*.

steel and related facilities: (1) 29 plants, valued at more than $5 million each, which were technically capable of disposal as independent operating units; (2) twenty plants, valued at more than $5 million each, which were classified as "scrambled with privately owned facilities"; and (3) plants, costing less than $5 million each, which were classified as partly "scrambled." The lion's share of the government's investment in steel facilities was in the first category. It amounted to $770 million and represented 59 per cent of the government's total investment in this area.[10]

Of the 29 larger plants capable of independent operation, four were integrated steel plants: the Geneva plant (erected at a cost of $202 million) whose wartime operator was U.S. Steel; a Chicago plant operated by Republic Steel during the war (costing $92 million); a plant at Houston, Texas, operated by Armco (valued at $37 million); and the Homestead, Pa., plant operated by U.S. Steel (valued at $124 million). These important plants, with the exception of Geneva, carried a purchase option by their wartime operators and two of the four might have been difficult to run by anybody else. Whatever the considerations which influenced the government's decision, however, the fact remains that these plants were sold to their wartime managers, i.e., to the large integrated producers of the industry. The effect of this action, whatever the justification for it, was to strengthen the hand of oligopoly in the steel industry and to encourage perpetuation of the status quo in the industry's economic structure. Especially significant is the fact that, in some areas—especially in the far West—the disposition of these plants allowed the major producers to increase considerably their percentage control of output in the local market. This is made clear when we consider that acquisition of the Geneva plant (built at a cost of $202 million to the government and sold to U.S. Steel for approximately $47 million) enabled U.S. Steel to increase its total capacity in the Pacific coast and mountain states from 17.3 to 39 per cent, and to bring its total of steel ingot capacity in the area up to 51 per cent.

The oligopoly structure of the steel industry was further strengthened by the Supreme Court decision in the Columbia Steel case.[11] This decision sanctioned the acquisition of a relatively small—small on a national scale—Pacific coast plant by United States Steel. The company in question (Consolidated Steel) accounted for 11 per cent of the total fabricated structural products made in the West. Together with United States Steel it would account for 25 to 30 per cent of total fabricated structural products produced in the 11-state Pacific coast and mountain states region. The merger of Consolidated with U.S. Steel constituted—in the minority opinion of the Supreme Court—a "purchase for control, a purchase for control of a market for which U.S. Steel has in the past had to compete but which it no longer wants left to the

---

10   U.S. Tariff Commission, p. 71.   11   See *U.S.* v. *Columbia Steel Company et al.*, 334 U.S. 495 (1948).

uncertainties that competition in the West may engender." The effect of the merger was not only to encourage concentration in the newly developing markets of the West, but to permit the growth of a major company which, according to Justice Douglas, was "big enough."

THE CONCENTRATION ON IRON ORE RESERVES   The concentrated ownership of iron ore reserves has also tended to fortify the oligopoly control of the integrated producers. Today, the nine largest integrated steel producers and the four major iron ore merchants account for over 95 per cent of the "measured" reserves in the nation's richest iron ore area—the Lake Superior District.[12] In the other iron ore districts—the northeastern, southeastern, and western—the integrated companies also exercise substantial control, at least with respect to high-grade ores. Of the nine major steel companies, only U.S. Steel has more than enough ore to support its steel making operations. Its competitors—including such companies as Bethlehem, Republic, Armco, and Inland,—lack adequate iron ore reserves and depend on the corporation for a portion of their supplies.

The four major ore merchants offer the small ore users and semiintegrated steel companies little hope of an assured iron ore supply. Nor are they likely to provide an open market in competition with the integrated majors. The fact is that, by 1948, the ore merchants had virtually become satellites of the major steel companies to whom they were tied by partnership arrangements, long-term supply contracts, and joint ownership. Approximately half of the ore handled by these houses went to the nine big steel companies under existing partnership arrangements. Almost all of the remaining ore was tied up under long-term contracts with the same nine companies. As a result, the spot market for iron ore, so far as sales by the ore merchants was concerned, has practically disappeared.[13]

In the control of foreign ore deposits the major integrated companies seem to enjoy a commanding lead. The extent of their deposits is indicated by the following estimates: (1) ten to fifteen million tons of Venezuelan ore controlled by U.S. Steel; (2) two to three million tons of Venezuelan ore controlled by Bethlehem; (3) two million tons of Liberian ore controlled by Republic; (4) ten million tons of Labrador ore controlled by the Iron Ore Company of Canada (a joint venture of Republic, Armco, Youngstown, National, Wheeling, and Hanna Ore Company). Only Kaiser's control over the recently developed Australian ores represents a breach in the oligopoly's dominance of foreign ore holdings.

---

12 Federal Trade Commission, *Report on the Control of Iron Ore*, 1952, p. 87, hereafter cited as *FTC Iron Ore Report.* For the entry implications of this concentration pattern, see Joe S. Bain, *Barriers to New Competition* (Cambridge, Mass.: Harvard University Press, 1956), pp. 153–154.

13 Ibid., p. 82.

In sum, the concentration of iron ore reserves helps explain the oligopoly structure of the steel industry, and the commanding role of its leader, the U.S. Steel Corporation. Whether technological innovations, or the substitutability of scrap for pig iron, or the availability of low grade (i.e., high cost) ores will change this picture, remains to be seen. It is noteworthy, however that a newcomer among the world's steel powers like Japan does not seem to have been hampered by its lack of control over iron ore reserves.

FORWARD INTEGRATION BY THE MAJORS   The forward integration by the major producers has also been a factor in the strengthening of the steel oligopoly. In the past, a good part of steel fabrication was left to the smaller independents—the semiintegrated and nonintegrated finishers. The dominance of the integrated companies in this branch of the industry was always much less than in the production of pig-iron, ingots, and semifinished steel. Since 1939, however, the situation has changed. Large steel producers have integrated forward; large steel consumers have integrated backwards; and independents have been subjected to a periodic vertical price squeeze. In periods of steel shortage, independent fabricators have also complained of a supply squeeze.

This forward integration—achieved largely through mergers and acquisitions—has, in some cases, resulted in the virtual disappearance of entire "small business" industries. Thus steel drum fabrication was almost completely absorbed by the basic steel producers, a process which *Iron Age* described as follows:

> Long, long ago, in 1939, before the words postwar and planning were wedded, the manufacture of heavy steel barrels and drums was a rather volatile business firmly in the hands of a large number of highly individualistic entrepreneurs. Most of these fabricators had started on a precarious shoe string and were justifiably vocal in their pride of success in the classical Horatio Alger Pluck and Luck Tradition.
>
> A few weeks ago, the purchase of Bennett Mfg. Co., Chicago, by the United States Steel Corporation pretty well completed the capture of the entire barrel and drum business by the major steel producers. Some 87 per cent of the business, representing about 435,000 tons of steel consumption yearly has been corralled by the mills and the remaining 64,500 tons of independent capacity will probably remain so for a variety of reasons.[14]

The significance of such forward integration is twofold: it tends, on the one hand, to extend the oligopoly of steel making into steel fabrication; and, on the other, to tie up an increasing portion of the semifinished steel that formerly was available on the open market. As a result, nonintegrated steel users,

---

14   *The Iron Age*, **154**: 103 (September 21, 1944); quoted in Federal Trade   Commission, *The Merger Movement: A Summary Report* (1948), p. 46.

dependent on the open market for their supplies, may be deprived of essential raw materials and find it increasingly difficult to stay in business.[15]

One other aspect of the vertical integration movement is noteworthy, viz., the price squeeze. When forward integration by the majors is combined with a vertical price squeeze against the independents, there are likely to be fatalities. For, the nonintegrated fabricator—caught by the denial of supplies, on the one hand, and manipulation of his profit margin, on the other—may find survival unduly expensive, if not altogether impossible.

An example of how the vertical squeeze works is afforded by the price changes instituted in the spring of 1948. In February of that year, U.S. Steel raised *semifinished* steel prices by an average of $5 per ton, and other companies promptly followed. Three months later, in May, U.S. Steel led the industry to a price reduction on *finished* steel, concentrating primarily on products made by semiintegrated and nonintegrated mills. This move, which *Iron Age* characterized as "one of the most unusual in steel history,"[16] elicited the following conclusion from the Federal Trade Commission:

It is apparent that by raising the prices of semifinished steel in February and by cutting the prices on the products made therefrom in May, United States Steel Corp. applied a double squeeze on the smaller semi-integrated and nonintegrated mills. The leadership of United States Steel was followed by the other large integrated companies in both instances, though apparently somewhat more reluctantly on the second occasion. These companies were themselves caught in the squeeze when the prices of finished steel products were cut. However, their loss of revenue at the finished-steel level was partially offset by larger receipts for semifinished steel, whereas the nonintegrated companies, as a result of the double action, were squeezed at both the semifinished and finished levels.[17]

---

15 This is especially true in times of steel shortage, when the independents complain about the alleged increase in steel shipments to the steel companies' own fabricating subsidiaries; the alleged increase in steel shipments to the steel companies' own warehouses; and the alleged increase in the proportion of steel sold in the more expensive cold-rolled and other highly finished types at the expense of the less costly hot-rolled types. See Federal Trade Commission, *The Distribution of Steel Consumption, 1949–50* (1952). On this point, see also Simon N. Whitney, *Antitrust Policies* (New York: Twentieth Century Fund, 1958), Vol. 1, pp. 319–321.

16 *The Iron Age*, **161**:125B (May 6, 1948). That this was a price squeeze

seems clearly to have been recognized by the late Senator Robert A. Taft who was then chairman of the Joint Committee on the Economic Report. See the interesting colloquy between Senator Taft and Benjamin Fairless, then president of U.S. Steel, in *Hearings before the Joint Committee on the Economic Report*, 80th Congress, 2nd Session (1948), pp. 14–15. Some time after this hearing, Senator Taft is reported to have said that the power of the steel companies over prices seems to be such as perhaps to require some supervision in the public interest.

17 Federal Trade Commission, *Monopolistic Practices and Small Business*, 1952, pp. 53–54.

More recently, the independent nonintegrated fabricators accused their integrated supplier-competitors of raising the price of raw materials (wire rods) at a faster rate than the prices of finished products (wire fence, nails, barbed wire, and so on.) One of the independents testified to the nature of the squeeze in a 1963 proceeding before the U.S. Tariff Commission:

Mr. Reagan: . . . I have here in front of me a quotation on wire rod from Bethlehem Steel Company to Florida Wire Products Corporation, and one from United States Steel Corporation to Florida Wire Products Corporation, which roughly amount to a price of $156 per ton for the raw material f.o.b. Miami, Florida.

The sales price for our finished product f.o.b. Miami and the sales price of U.S. Steel for their finished product f.o.b. Miami is $150 a ton.

Mr. Graubard: Just to get this straight, you are saying that U.S. Steel Corporation is selling the finished product at less than it offers to sell you wire rod?

Mr. Reagan: Yes, sir.

Mr. Graubard: These are delivered prices?

Mr. Reagan: Yes, sir.[18]

Such vertical price maneuvers are but one manifestation of the vertical integration movement and the entry of the major producers into steel fabrication. The effect is to impose a serious handicap on the independent whose predicament arises from the fact that he is dependent on the integrated producers for his supply of raw materials, while simultaneously competing with them in the sale of finished products.

DECONCENTRATION FACTORS

THE DECLINE OF U.S. STEEL   The relative position of U.S. Steel in the industry has been declining ever since its formation in 1901. Several factors are responsible for this development. First, U.S. Steel did not want to become too big for fear of prosecution under the antitrust laws. Judge Gary was impressed with the William Jennings Bryan rule that no business should be allowed to control more than 50 per cent of an industry. Gary felt that if U.S. Steel confined itself "voluntarily to a size approved by the most popular and trusted of radicals, [it] surely cannot be attacked for monopoly."[19]

Second, starting the 1920's, the "independents" in the industry took part in an aggressive consolidation movement. In 1922, Bethlehem acquired all the properties of the large Lackawanna Steel Company near Buffalo, N.Y.;

---

18 W. Adams, "Vertical Power, Dual Distribution, and the Squeeze: A Case Study in Steel," *Antitrust Bulletin*, 9:503 (1964). See also W. Adams and J. B.

Dirlam, "Steel Imports and Vertical Oligopoly Power," *American Economic Review* (September 1964).
19 Tarbell, pp. 257–8.

it erected extensive modern facilities at Sparrows Point, Md.; it acquired the large Cambria Steel Company (1923); and, in 1930, bought the assets of the Pacific Coast Steel Company and the Southern California Iron and Steel Company. (Its attempt to merge with Youngstown Sheet and Tube, the nation's sixth largest steel producer, was blocked by judicial decree in 1958.) In 1930 another powerful independent arose when a merger between the Republic Iron and Steel Company, the Central Alloy Steel Corporation, the Donner Steel Company, and the Bourne Fuller Company was consummated. A third important merger during this period resulted in the formation of the National Steel Corporation (1929), which united steel plants in the West Virginia and Detroit areas and the blast furnace properties of the M. A. Hanna Company of Cleveland.[20]

A third factor contributing to the relative decline of the U.S. Steel Corporation was the gradual transformation in the demand for steel from heavy products (such as rails, plates, and structural shapes) to lighter products (such as sheets and strips). This shift in demand had important repercussions on the position of U.S. Steel which was deeply committed, as far as plant capacity was concerned, to the production of heavy products. What made this shift in demand even more painful for the corporation was the geographic source of the new demand—especially that of the growing auto industry— which was often located at a considerable distance from the corporation's main plants. To the extent that the smaller companies were more flexible, they could, of course, accommodate themselves more readily to these changing patterns of steel consumption and thus improve their position relative to U.S. Steel.

A fourth factor affecting the position of the industry's giant was the impact of changing technology. Here U.S. Steel lagged significantly behind its integrated rivals. In 1926, the American Rolling Mill Company bought the patents on the continuous rolling mill process which was the major American advance in steel technology during the interwar period. Republic Steel became the leader in the growing alloy steel field. Finally, technological innovations which permitted an increasingly large use of scrap in the production of steel ingots tended to reduce the value of U.S. Steel's heavy investment in iron ore mines and blast furnace capacity. The growing use of scrap also tended to shift the most advantageous location pattern for the industry away from coal-producing regions and toward consumption areas, which were rich sources of scrap.[21]

---

20 For a history of the merger movement in the steel industry, see "Steel —Acquisitions, Mergers, and Expansion of 12 Major Companies, 1900 to 1950," *Hearings before the House Small Business Committee*, 81st Congress, 2nd Session, (1950).

21 See W. Isard, "Some Locational Factors in the Iron and Steel Industry since the Early Nineteenth Century," *Journal of Political Economy* (June 1948); also W. Isard and W. M. Capron, "The Future Locational Pattern of Iron and Steel Production in the United States," *Journal of Political Economy* (April 1949).

A final factor contributing to the relative decline of U.S. Steel was the depression of the 1930's which made the maintenance of price conformity under the basing point system more difficult. The corporation was not completely successful in protecting its recognized position as the industry's price leader against the inroads of "chiselers" and secret price cutters.

NEW TECHNOLOGY AND THE MINI-MILL   Recent technological changes have substantially reduced the barriers to entry and deprived the integrated producers of their dominant position vis-à-vis the potential newcomer. As long as the open hearth was the work horse of raw steel production, companies which owned extensive ore reserves, coke ovens, efficient blast furnaces (to make pig iron), and large open hearths (to make steel) had a decisive advantage deriving from size and vertical integration. The capital investment required by new facilities made entry by small producers virtually impossible.

In the last 20 years, however, the introduction of the basic oxygen furnace and the adaptation of the electric furnace to the production of carbon steel substantially reduced the cost of entry.[22] The electric furnace, especially, has made it possible to construct mini-mills—without the necessity of integrating backward into iron ore, coke ovens, and blast furnaces.

The electric furnace, originally used primarily for producing specialty steels, now enjoys considerable popularity as a low cost, high-tonnage steel producer. First, it is an efficient and versatile producer of both specialty (alloy and stainless) and carbon steels. Second, it operates efficiently on a 100 per cent scrap charge, thus obviating the need for facilities making pig iron and molten metal. Third, it can be built in small sizes and can produce steel in small batches, without the same cost penalty for smallness as other steelmaking methods. This is especially true for the new electric furnaces operating on 80,000 kilovolt-amperes—compared to the 35,000-kilovolt-ampere units common 5 years ago. Fourth, an associated technical development, the continuous and other direct methods of casting steel as it comes from the furnace, makes it possible to transform molten steel directly into semi-

---

22   The dramatic shift in the relative popularity of different raw steel production techniques in the last 20 years is indicated by the following percentages:

YEAR	OPEN HEARTH	BASIC OXYGEN	ELECTRIC
1950	89.1	—	6.2
1955	90.0	.3	6.9
1960	87.0	3.4	8.4
1965	71.6	17.4	10.5
1968	50.4	37.1	12.5
1970[a]	38.5	46.3	15.2

a   First seven months.

finished shapes. By displacing intermediate steps formerly necessary, it reduces capital costs, operating costs, and space requirements.[23]

Professor William Haller, Jr., an expert on the electric furnace, summarizes its impact on competition as follows: "Yet for actual or potential steel producers without their own supplies of hot metal, and for those with limited or obsolescent facilities for producing it, the cost advantage of the scrap charged electric furnace seems almost conclusive. The cost penalty for small-scale production is moderate: The Battelle study finds that a 200,000-ton electric furnace plant can produce a ton of steel at a cost of only $3.08 greater than a 1,500,000-ton plant. Therefore, a moderate widening of the gap between scrap and hot metal prices, or a limited or geographically isolated market may offer opportunities for moderate- or small-size plants.

The cost penalty of small-scale production becomes even less if continuous casting is used. The Battelle study estimates that a 500,000-ton plant with continuous casting can produce 8 × 8-inch blooms for $14 a ton less than can a 1,500,000-ton plant using conventional casting methods, and for only 10 cents a ton more than a 1,500,000-ton plant also using continuous casting. The advantage for small billets is apparently at least as great. The president of Roblin Steel Corporation claims that his electric furnace and continuous casting plant will produce about 120,000 tons of billets a year for a 'safe $20 a ton less than the $115 per ton that is the market price for billets.'[24]

Given low-cost scrap, a reasonable power rate, and proximity to local markets—combined with ultrahigh power on the electric furnace and continuous casting—the mini-mill seems to be cost competitive with respect to the giant producers. Thus, Georgetown Steel Corporation in South Carolina, a $20 million venture with a 300,000 ton capacity of bar and wire products, is a mini-mill that faces the future unafraid. By using electric furnaces and continuous casting, it claims to be producing at a cost of 5–10 per cent lower than the big steel companies. It counts on its lower overhead and greater flexibility in meeting changing market conditions as distinct advantages in battling its stodgy domestic competitors and the aggressive challenge of imports.[25]

---

23   U.S. Senate Antitrust and Monopoly Subcommittee, Hearings, *Economic Concentration*, 90th Congress, 1st Session, Part 6 (Washington, D.C.: 1967) pp. 2692–2694; 3163–3197 [hereinafter cited as *Economic Concentration Hearings*]. See also "On Come the Electrics," *Steelways* (Nov./Dec. 1969).

24   *Economic Concentration Hearings*, part 6, op. cit., p. 3169.

25   Willy Korf, the German entrepreneur who controls Georgetown Steel, has little doubt about the competitive viability of the company. He recalls that when he first entered the German steel industry, his large competitors reacted by slashing the price of reinforced bar by 25 per cent. The reaction of Mr. Korf, who accounts for 20 per cent of Germany's output, was typical. "This price will still give us a profit. But the big mills will lose money on it. Next year we will supply 30 per cent of the market," he said. *New York Times*, p. F1 (January 26, 1969).

Other technological advances—such as the SL/RN method for direct reduction of iron ore—also point toward lowering the high capital costs, which in the past have been a formidable entry barrier.[26] However, it would be premature to predict that the new technology will be more than a peripheral check on oligopolistic giantism in steel. Its procompetitive impact is clear, but so far, at least, the impact is only at the margin.

STEEL IMPORTS   During the 1960's, steel imports began to play a major role in modifying the oligopoly structure of the domestic industry. Prior to 1958, annual steel imports into the United States remained below the 2 million ton level (except in 1951, a Korean war year, when 2.18 million tons were brought in). The 1959 steel strike, it seems, opened the floodgates and witnessed the importation of 4.4 million tons. From then on, imports steadily increased, reaching a total of 6.4 million tons in 1964, 10.8 million tons in 1966, and a high of slightly less than 18 million tons in 1968. Only with the imposition of "voluntary" quotas in 1969 did the total recede to 14 million tons (see Table 4).

Two aspects of the burgeoning import trend are structurally noteworthy: (1) The steel imported in the early 1960's consisted mainly of products like rods and bars, which could be produced with comparatively old equipment and simple technology. Since 1965, however, flat-rolled products, requiring large and complex processing equipment and advanced technology, accounted for an increasing share of steel imports. (2) During the 1960's, steel imports captured a steadily rising share of the U.S. domestic market: 4.7% in 1960, 7.3% in 1964, and 16.7% in 1968. The share of imports in the U.S. market for particular steel products is shown in Table 2.

The structural impact of imports on the steel oligopoly had rather pronounced implications for the industry's competitive strategy, as we shall see in the following sections. However, the industry's success in obtaining a "voluntary" quota system in 1969 will undoubtedly mean at least a partial return to the *status quo ante*—an oligopolistic structure substantially insulated from the Schumpeterian gales of creative destruction.

OTHER FACTORS

Three other factors which have some bearing on the structure of the steel industry deserve some mention *en passant*. First, some large steel consumers

---

26   Usually iron ore and iron ore pellets go directly into a blast furnace where they are converted into pig iron. Then the pig iron goes into an open-hearth or basic-oxygen furnace where it is converted to steel.

The new process substitutes a rotary kiln, basically a 250-ft. long oven, for the blast furnace. The kiln bakes iron ore concentrate at 1,100°F, producing pellets which can be converted directly into steel in an electric arc furnace.

With the kiln, it is claimed, a producer could build a 200,000-ton-a-year steel mill that is economically competitive with the industry giants. It would cost at least 40 per cent less than a conventional steel mill. ["Will Kilns Give Steel a New Cast?" *Business Week* (December 7, 1968) p. 149.]

TABLE 2 IMPORTS OF SELECTED
STEEL PRODUCTS AS A PER CENT
OF APPARENT CONSUMPTION IN
THE UNITED STATES

PRODUCTS	1959	1961	1968
Wire rods	NA	32.7	54.7
Structural shapes and piling	3.5	6.1	20.0
Plates	0.4	0.6	17.7
Reinforcing bars	19.0	19.4	18.7
All other bars and tool steel	2.6	4.1	13.8
Pipe and tubing	3.2	7.1	14.2
Wire—drawn	6.1	6.6	17.8
Wire—nails and staples	32.3	42.8	44.8
Wire—barbed	51.9	53.0	34.7
Wire—woven wire fence	20.4	32.9	34.9
Sheets and strip	0.1	0.7	17.1
Average of all steel products	2.9	4.7	16.7

SOURCE AISI, *Foreign Trade Trends*
(New York: American Iron & Steel Institute),
1959, 1962, and 1969 eds.

like the Ford Motor Company and International Harvester Company have integrated backward and become raw steel producers. Other firms in that category—primarily the automobile and agricultural equipment makers—represent potential entrants into the steel industry. Second, substitute materials like aluminum, plastics, cement, and glass pose some threat to the steel oligopoly—at least at the margin. Although it is difficult to predict technological change, it would appear that substitute materials can contend effectively for about 5 per cent of the market now held by steel. Third, the steel industry, like American industry generally, has been immersed in the conglomerate merger movement of the 1960's. Major companies have either merged with, or been acquired by, firms outside the steel industry, viz., Jones & Laughlin (LTV), Youngstown Sheet & Tube (Lykes), Colorado Fuel & Iron (Crane), Sharon (NVF), Crucible (Colt), and so on. Also, many steel companies have announced their intention to diversify into other industries in order to obtain better returns on investment than they think is available in steel. (National has already made a commitment in aluminum and expects to be a joint owner of the 5th largest primary aluminum producer by 1971. Armco has acquired an equipment leasing subsidiary.) The effect of these conglomerate trends in the structure of the steel industry cannot yet be assessed with scientific assurance.

Summarizing our discussion of market structure, we may conclude that, due to a variety of competitive forces, a single firm no longer dominates the steel industry; that this dominance is now shared by a dozen large, integrated producers who operate in an oligopoly framework; and that this oligopoly is subject to peripheral checks primarily from some entry by small producers and from import competition.[27] The implications of this oligopolistic structure for market conduct becomes apparent in an analysis of the industry's price policy.

III. MARKET CONDUCT

Price policy, especially in a basic industry like steel, is of crucial importance. It influences the amount of steel consumed in a given year and the extent to which capacity is utilized. It stimulates or retards steel-using industries. It sets a pattern for other basic industries, and thus plays a central role in the economy. Without too much exaggeration, one can say that "as steel goes, so goes the nation." Hence it is important to understand the industry's price policy and the underpinnings on which it rests, viz., basing points, price leadership, and price stability.

THE MECHANICS OF
BASING POINT PRICING

Although it was officially abandoned in 1948, the basing point system is deeply imbedded in the philosophy of the steel industry and may again be used, at least in modified form, in times of recession. The mechanics are simple. Under the single-basing point (Pittsburgh-Plus) system, steel prices at any given delivery point were uniform—regardless of where the steel was shipped from. To achieve this uniformity, sellers did not have to meet in a smoke-filled room or preview each others' bids. They simply had to adhere to the basing point formula of (1) uniform base prices, (2) uniform delivery charges, and (3) uniform prices for "extras" and "deductions."

1. The base price was the charge for a ton of steel applicable at designated basing points and measuring up to standard specifications (gauge, thickness, length, chemical composition, and tolerance). Until 1924, Pittsburgh was the only basing point and all steel prices were quoted in terms of the Pittsburgh base plus the cost of transportation to the point of delivery. As a rule, base prices were set by U.S. Steel and widely publicized in the trade press, so that other companies would have no difficulty in following the leader.

---

27 This conclusion is corroborated by Professor Haller's observation that "(c)learly the big eight hold a powerful and secure position in the industry's competitive structure. There is little indication that any of them will be forced to a lower rank, or that the medium or small firms individually will match them in size. But the slight decline in their group share, the more marked decline in the individual share of the largest firm and the indications of growth and new entry among the medium and small firms are symptoms of potential competition emerging at some points into actuality." (*Economic Concentration Hearings*, Part 6, op. cit., p. 2690).

2. Transportation charges, the second element in the formula, had to be uniform in order to make delivered prices identical at any one destination. Obviously, the delivered price in Detroit would not be identical if one company charged an all-rail rate whereas its competitors charged a part-rail, part-water rate. Moreover, if one company charged the actual transportation costs and another collected "fictitious" freight charges, it would be impossible to maintain uniform delivered prices. For many years, therefore, the American Iron & Steel Institute published a book of freight rates showing the rail cost for transporting a ton of steel from Pittsburgh to every delivery point in the United States.

3. Extras and deductions, the third element in the formula, were merely additions to, or deductions from, the base price—in order to make allowance for special variations from standard specifications. Here again, the objective was to assure uniform delivered prices and U.S. Steel, often after consultation with other companies, set up and publicized its schedule of extras which its rivals chose to follow with amazing regularity.

Here is a concrete example of how the Pittsburgh-Plus system operated: In 1920, the Pittsburgh price for steel was $40 per ton, and the freight charge from Pittsburgh to Chicago (then not a basing point) was $7.60. The delivered price in Chicago, therefore, was $47.60—regardless of where the steel was shipped from and regardless of which company happened to make the sale. In an extreme case, where steel was wheeled through a party wall opening from a Chicago producer to a Chicago consumer, the latter still had to pay $7.60 for transportation even though no transportation cost had been incurred. Such "phantom freight" came into being whenever steel was shipped from a mill nearer than the basing point to the place of delivery. The amount of phantom freight was measured by the excess of the "official" over the actual transportation cost.[28]

To carry our example a step further: If the Chicago producer shipped to a customer in Pittsburgh, he would get a delivered price of $40 (base price plus cost of transportation from the *basing* point to the point of delivery). He would be unable to collect any freight charges, even though it cost him $7.60 to transport the steel to Pittsburgh. He would have to "absorb freight" —the exact amount being the excess of the actual over the "official" freight charges. On this transaction, therefore, he would receive a mill net price of $32.40—in contrast to the mill net of $47.60 on his sale to the Chicago customer.[29] He would discriminate against the nearby (well-located) consumer and in favor of the distant (poorly-located) consumer.

---

28 Phantom freight also arose when a producer charged his customer an all-rail rate while actually using cheaper transport means, such as water or truck.

29 Mill net is defined as the price received at the mill after the payment or allowance for the actual transportation from mill to destination has been deducted from the invoiced delivered price.

In 1924, this Pittsburgh-Plus system was superseded by a multiple basing point system. The principle of quoting uniform delivered prices, however, remained intact. The only modification was to create new basing points like Chicago, Birmingham, and Sparrows Point, and to quote prices in terms of the *nearest* basing point (called the governing basing point) plus the transportation cost to the point of delivery. In Des Moines, therefore, the delivered price would be computed on a Chicago instead of a Pittsburgh base, but all mills shipping into Des Moines would still quote identical prices at the point of delivery.

THE CASE FOR BASING POINT PRICING

Steel industry executives have defended the basing point system with uncompromising consistency.[30] They have supported the efforts to legalize the system even after the Supreme Court declared it to be a violation of the antitrust laws. Their arguments are as follows:

1. The basing point system is the quintessence of perfect competition, since it results in one price in one place at one time: "Competition is at its perfection of expression when all of the sellers are on the same level."[31]
2. The system cannot be harmful because it does not work. Thus the president of U.S. Steel told a Congressional Committee that " [i]f base prices as announced were followed in every transaction, and . . . the nearest basing point to the consumer governed, and . . . rail freight was added from that point, and the delivered price actually arrived at in that manner, there wouldn't be any competition in the steel industry. It would be a one-price industry, pure and simple."[32] Industry spokesmen point out, however, that basing point prices are "fictitious"; they are prices "we want to get"—"prices that we feel fair." "We don't succeed in getting those prices because competition won't permit it,"[33] the spokesmen contend.

30 In this, they have had the support of some distinguished economists. See, among others, J. M. Clark, "Imperfect Competition Theory and Basing Point Problems," *American Economic Review*, 33:283 (June 1943), and "Law and Economics of Basing Points," ibid., 39:430 (March 1949); A. Smithies, "Aspects of the Basing-Point System," ibid., 32:705 (December 1942); H. G. Lewis and T. O. Yntema in *TNEC Papers* (United States Steel Corporation, 1940).

31 TNEC, *Hearings*, Part 5, p. 1882. To this argument, TNEC members replied that, under perfect competition, a single price in a given market at a given time is the result of an interplay of many buyers and sellers, whereas under the basing point system—by contrast—there prevails a single *bid* price at a point of delivery, a price quoted *outside* the market and then imposed *on* the market. It is further contended that this basing point price in fact results in variable mill net prices; that it is therefore, in effect, a discriminatory price based on a predetermined formula collusively derived. Compare: Ibid., pp. 1862–63, 1873, 1882, 1911–1913.

32 TNEC, *Hearings*, Part 27, p. 14172.

33 Ibid., Part 19, pp. 10511–10512.

In times of slack demand, there is some truth in this argument. The deeper the recession, the greater is the pressure on steel firms to shade the list prices computed under the basing point formula.

3. The basing point system some say, is necessary—not to promote competition but to prevent its excesses. In the steel industry, overhead costs are a significant portion of total costs, and profits depend largely on the extent to which capacity is utilized. As steel output goes up, average costs decline and profits increase. The converse is also true. It is imperative, therefore, that steel companies operate as close to full capacity as possible in order to maximize profits, and here is the rub. Given high overhead costs and in the face of a slack demand, steel companies will be tempted to secure additional sales by offering price concessions. They will tend to accept additional orders at any price in excess of variable cost (out-of-pocket expenses). If one company does this, there are no adverse effects; but if all resort to the same solution of their overhead cost problem, the inevitable result is a devastating price war—waged without regard to average costs.[34] Such a war may cause prices on *all* sales to be cut below average total costs and may eventually result in a victory for the financially most powerful producers (those who can sustain short-run losses because of their financial staying power) rather than in the survival of the industry's most efficient firms. Such a war would only lead to cut-throat competition, the extinction of some producers, and a further tendency toward concentration in the industry.

At this point the clincher is applied to the overhead cost argument. Steel producers, it is said, are under constant pressure to spread their overhead costs over as large an output as possible. Since they dare not cut prices and thus invite certain retaliation and perhaps a disastrous price war, they have only one alternative—to discriminate.[35] By following the basing point system—by absorbing freight in their invasion of distant markets—steel producers can solicit additional sales without incurring the dangers of price competition. In order to stimulate volume, they can accept a lower mill net price on sales outside their "natural" market areas in the hope of solving their overhead cost problem. The only difficulty with this solution is that freight absorption has to be paid out of the producer's

34 This argument is based on the assumption of an inelastic and cyclically derived demand.

35 J. M. Clark describes the paradox of price confronting a firm burdened by high overhead costs as follows: "If any business that would pay its own particular costs is refused because it will not pay its share of overhead, there is a loss. Yet prices must be charged, which will cover overhead, so long as industry depends on private enterprise. There is only one answer to this dilemma—discrimination. The overhead costs must be levied on such parts of the business as will stand the burden, while other parts of the business, which cannot otherwise be had at all, are charged whatever they can pay, regardless of overhead costs. However," Clark significantly concludes, "this is only a partial answer to the question, and creates more problems than it solves." *The Economics of Overhead Costs* (Chicago: University of Chicago Press, 1923), p. 23.

pocketbook. Moreover, it may prove self-defeating if other producers resort to the same solution as they inevitably will and must.

4. The basing point system, steel leaders point out, is a necessary instrument of price stability, because the demand for steel is highly inelastic; i.e., price cuts will not bring about a proportionate increase in steel consumption. To be sure, the individual producer faces an elastic demand schedule; if he cuts prices, he can increase sales. But, if all producers do the same thing, they cannot increase their sales sufficiently to overcome the inelastic demand for the industry as a whole. Therefore, it is argued, it is desirable to prevent price competition through some stabilizing mechanism like the basing point system.

Steel spokesmen cite the following evidence for the inelasticity of steel demand. First, they point to the fact that steel is a raw material the demand for which is derived from the demand for other products. Hence, if the aggregate demand for such items as automobiles and washing machines is depressed (because of a recession), cutting the price of steel is futile as a demand stimulant.

Second, they argue that "substitution of steel for other materials, or a reverse substitution, is not an important factor in the cyclical fluctuations in the demand for steel."[36] Since the substitution factor is not very important in the demand for steel, "price reduction would result in very little additional steel being sold as substitutes for other products, and a price advance, unless abnormal, probably would not result in additional competition from substitute products."[37]

Third, so runs the argument, the demand for steel is inelastic because steel generally constitutes a very small portion of the total cost of the products in which it is contained as a raw material. It is pointed out, for example, that, under 1948 conditions, "a $5 per ton change in the price of all steel products going into a $1,500 automobile would affect the cost of producing the automobile about $8; a $20 electric toaster would be affected by less than 1 cent; a $285 electric refrigerator by 61 cents; a $184 gas range by 49 cents; and a $130 washing machine by 25 cents while the cost of building a 35 story steel frame office building would be affected by six tenths of 1 per cent."[38]

---

36 Study by the United States Steel Corporation, Exhibit No. 1410, TNEC, *Hearings*, Part 26; reprinted in the TNEC Monograph No. 42, *The Basing Point Problem*, p. 15.

37 TNEC Monograph No. 42, op. cit., p. 16. This argument is, of course, at loggerheads with the industry's contention, that steel is subject to intense interindustry competition.

38 Statement by Arthur B. Homer, President of the Bethlehem Steel Corporation, *Hearings before the Joint Committee on the Economic Report*, March 2, 1948. Cf. also T. Yntema, "A Statistical Analysis of the Demand for Steel, 1919–1938" in the United States Steel Corporation, *TNEC Papers* (New York: United States Steel Corporation, 1939); General Motors Corporation, *The Dynamics of Automobile Demand* (New York: General Motors Corporation, 1939).

It is for these reasons that industry leaders hold the demand for steel to be inelastic, and consider the price stabilizing functions of the basing point system to be vital to the preservation of a healthy price structure for steel products.

5. Another favorite argument in defense of the basing point system alludes to the dangers of local monopoly in case the system were abandoned and replaced by f.o.b. mill pricing. F.o.b. mill prices, it is charged, "would put [the consumer] generally at the mercy of the nearest mill," because the latter could make the shipment of steel into its "natural" delivery area unprofitable to rivals. The nearest mill could eliminate competition in its immediate vicinity by setting a price so low that no competitor could meet it.[39]

THE CASE AGAINST BASING POINT PRICING

In its legal skirmishes against the basing point system which lasted some 30 years, the Federal Trade Commission (FTC) relied on the following major arguments:

1. The system, according to the Commission, promotes collusion and results in the elimination of price competition. The system worked so well that companies located at widely separated points, and in ostensible competition with one another, would submit sealed bids to the Federal government which were identical to the fourth decimal place.[40] At any given destination, there would be no price competition—regardless of which company made the sale or where the steel was actually shipped from.

The basing point formula, according to the FTC, is a more effective instrument of collusion than old-fashioned price agreements. It is the eye which discovers the chiseler and the hand which wields the punishing

---

39 If it were the inevitable result of f.o.b. mill pricing, however, the consumer can certainly be no worse off than under the basing point system; for, if the local mill ever attempted to exploit its regional monopoly by charging exorbitant prices at a given point "A," producers located in nearby areas would again find it profitable to make deliveries at "A," thus destroying the potentially evil effects of local monopoly. A local monopoly in steel, therefore, would be no more serious than the monopoly enjoyed by the neighborhood grocer due to his strategic location in respect to the market. Under these conditions, "The mercy of the nearest mill might be preferable to the mercy of a whole industry united on one price." Compare: "U.S. Steel II: Prices," reprinted from *Fortune*, 13:136 (April 1936), by special permission of the Editors. Copyright Time Inc.

40 See TNEC, *Hearings*, Part 5, p. 1897. While the commission does not consider the basing point formula illegal per se (i.e., when used by *one* or a *few* producers independently), the formula is held to become unlawful when it serves to implement collusion and price-fixing among *all* the producers in an industry. [*Notice to Staff* (October 12, 1948).] As such it is deemed illegal under Section 5 of the Federal Trade Commission Act, since the commission believes it to be "an obvious fact that the economic effect of identical prices achieved through conscious parallel action is the same as that of similar prices achieved through overt collusion." (Ibid., p. 3.)

whip. Under its rules price cutting does not pay and, in its enforcement, price cutting is not "necessary." Price cutting does not pay because the chiseler's reduced price immediately becomes the base price in his area and is "matched" by all his competitors. This means that "all delivered prices are identical again and the fellow hasn't gained anything by cutting his price except a headache."[41] Moreover, price cutting is not neccessary because the steel industry's "live and let live" tradition makes for a protective umbrella that is high and wide enough for everyone—including the inefficient producers.

2. The system, according to the FTC, is artificial and discriminatory. The customer located nearest to the production site from which the steel is actually shipped does not always get the lowest price and often "would be as cheaply supplied if the nearby mill did not exist."[42] Moreover, he suffers discrimination even if he is located right at the basing point. This is so, because base prices must be high enough to permit mills to absorb freight on sales to less fortunately located customers. Such discrimination would persist, even if all production points were to become basing points. While phantom freight would disappear, the system of uniform delivered prices would still result in freight absorption and hence differential (discriminatory) mill nets.

3. The system, the FTC charges, results in wasteful cross-hauling—i.e., the reciprocal invasion of the "natural" market areas of steel mills producing identical products.[43] As Charles Schwab, former president of Bethlehem Steel Corporation, candidly observed, it "is manifestly uneconomic for a steel manufacturer in Chicago to ship 100,000 tons of steel to Pittsburgh at a time when a Pittsburgh manufacturer is shipping a like quantity of like material from Pittsburgh to Chicago."[44] Not only is such cross-hauling self-defeating, it also dissipates part of the producer's revenue on unnecessary transportation and imposes an additional burden on the consumer who ultimately has to pay for this wasteful extravagance. Competition is diverted from base price reductions which would benefit *all* consumers to increased freight absorption which entails no price advantage to *any* consumer.

4. The basing point system is also said to result in uneconomic location of both steel producers and consumers. The latter may locate at an unfavor-

---

41 TNEC, *Hearings*, Part 5, p. 1868.
42 TNEC Monograph No. 42, op. cit., p. 2.
43 In this connection it is interesting to note the attempt of Professor Smithies of Harvard to show that a rational monopolist would certainly have eliminated the wasteful practice of cross-hauling. Smithies regards the preservation of cross-hauling under the basing point system as one item of evidence that the basing point system is not necessarily an instrument of collusion. A. Smithies, "Aspects of the Basing-Point System," *American Economic Review*, 32:423 (December 1942).
44 Quoted in C. D. Edwards, "Basing Point Decisions and Business Practices," *American Economic Review*, 38:840 (December 1948).

able site just to be close to a basing point, whereas under a different pricing system they might have chosen a better location near a steel mill which was *not* a basing point. Similarly, steel producers can afford to maintain their investment in anachronistic locations because "under the umbrella of a controlled price system the test of profitable plant location ceases to be essentially a matter of cost of production and distribution. . . . Plants thereby may be established at uneconomic points in terms of production costs."[45]

Why, some critics ask, should Detroit have only 5 per cent of the nation's steel capacity when Detroit industries consume nearly three times as much? Why should Pittsburgh produce almost twice as much steel as is needed in its market area? Can the present location of steel plants be explained purely in terms of proximity to raw materials and markets? Obviously not. The basing point system bears part of the blame for whatever distortion exists, because it allows "every steel mill to compete on a substantially equal footing for any piece of business anywhere in the country," thus tending to neutralize the advantages of location.

PRICE LEADERSHIP

Although most of these arguments against the basing point system are valid, it would be a mistake to carry them too far. In an industry like steel, geographic price discrimination and restraints on price competition can be explained not so much in terms of the basing point system but by the fewness of sellers, the homogeneity of steel products, the importance of overhead costs, the difficulty of entry, the substantial concentration on the buyer's side of the market, and the danger of cut-throat competition (especially when firms are hungry)—in short, by the structure of the industry. It is a fundamental fact that steel is an oligopoly and that its prices will therefore be "administered." This can be done "in many different ways. There may be no other technique of price administration that is so elegantly simple to operate as the basing point system, but there may be many others that will yield socially equivalent results."[46]

With or without a basing point system, price leadership is a pervasive characteristic of the steel industry. Typically, U.S. Steel sets the pace and the other companies follow in lockstep—both in their sales to private customers and in their secret bids on government contracts. Often, steel producers shipping from different locations will quote delivered prices identical to the thousandth of a cent per pound. Mr. Blough, president of U.S. Steel, explained this phenomenon by citing a Naval Gun Factory contract as an example:

45 Reprinted from David Lynch, *The Concentration of Economic Power*, p. 191. Copyright 1946 by Columbia University Press, New York.

46 J. K. Galbraith, "Light on a Hot Subject," reprinted from *Fortune*, **39**:211 (April 1949) by special permission of the Editors. Copyright Time, Inc.

"United States Steel offered a delivered price to meet the lowest delivered price it anticipated would be bid on this item. From its prior knowledge of dealings with the Naval Gun Factory and of the market, U.S. Steel could and did expect that Bethlehem would offer a bid on this invitation. Upon evaluation of these competitive circumstances, U.S. Steel found that if Bethlehem bid its announced price for the item at its producing mill at Sparrows Point, Md., from which it could be expected to offer to ship, plus freight from that mill to the Naval Gun Factory, its delivery price would be $0.07205 per pound. U.S. Steel accordingly reduced its own delivered price for shipment from its Fairless Works to the Naval Gun Factory by an amount which would enable it to meet the equally low price of its competitor."[47]

"Meeting competition" is the industry's euphemism to explain this price uniformity. On the downside this is understandable. Given the high degree of standardization of steel products and the negligible differences in quality, price cuts by one producer must quickly be matched by his competitors. "There isn't certainly any steel company in the first ten or in the first twenty," says the president of U.S. Steel, "that couldn't require us to change our prices overnight simply by taking action which is different than the action that we take."[48]

But what about "meeting competition" on the upside? Why do powerful companies like Bethlehem or National seldom challenge U.S. Steel's decisions to increase prices? Such price followership seems anomalous especially in those lines and those areas where these companies surpass U.S. Steel in production volume. In 1957, for example, Bethlehem held 72.2 per cent of the capacity for rolled steel piling (compared to U.S. Steel's 26.6 per cent), yet it dutifully followed U.S. Steel's price leadership. In the northeastern states, National ranked first (18.9 per cent) and U.S. Steel sixth (7.2 per cent) in cold-rolled sheets capacity, yet National was not inclined to challenge the price leader.[49] This price followership is also anomalous because different steel companies have different costs, and earn different profits.

Meeting the price *increases* of a competitor is what the steel executives call competition. They liken it to the Gimbels-Macy's rivalry. But Senator O'Mahoney calls it "upside-down competition," and Senator Kefauver rejects the Gimbels-Macy's analogy: "Would New Yorkers," he asks, "have the benefit of greater competition, of greater freedom of choice, if the prices of Macy's and Gimbels were invariably identical? Would . . . competition . . . be greater if every price increase by Macy's was immediately matched by Gimbels? If Macy's and Gimbels turned to what we have heard here about the steel industry, then a new Macy's slogan might wave over Herald Square, 'Our prices are always exactly as high as Gimbels.'"[50] Price uniformity in a competitive industry is one thing. In an oligopoly, it is quite another.

---

47 *Kefauver Committee Report*, op. cit., p. 122.
48 Ibid., p. 78.

49 Ibid., pp. 90–94.
50 Ibid., p. 100.

PRICE RIGIDITY

This tendency toward price uniformity is reinforced by a tendency toward price rigidity. In comparison to other industries, where prices are more responsive to automatic, competitive market forces, steel prices appear remarkably stable and inflexible. Contrast steel with textile and agricultural products, for example. In these industries, a cyclical change in demand tends to result in relatively drastic price changes without a similar effect on output and employment. In steel, the process is reversed. Production and demand are equated by an administered price which results in relatively wide output and employment fluctuations and proportionately smaller price fluctuations. In other words, price stability is obtained at the expense of instability in output (see Figure 1).

Such stability, of course, is not natural or inevitable, but the result of conscious administrative direction. In the past, U.S. Steel has tended to resist substantial price increases in times of high demand and opposed any marked reductions in times of slack demand. It has tried to hold prices constant—often for months and years. In the case of Bessemer steel rails—to take an extreme example—annual average prices fluctuated from $67.52 to $17.62 per ton between 1880 and 1901, i.e., during the competitive era preceding the organization of U.S. Steel. From May 1901, however, less that 60 days after the founding of the Corporation, a price of $28 per ton was in effect until April 1916 (a period of 180 months). After some fluctuations, a price of $43 per ton was announced in October 1922, which remained in effect until October 1932 (a period of 121 months).[51] Other steel products have experienced similar, though less pronounced, price stabilization. "Unless impelled by sharp increases in direct costs or dangerous sniping by rivals," say Kaplan, Dirlam, and Lanzillotti, U.S. Steel has generally preferred to resist "either price increases or decreases," and to sacrifice stability "only when the decision [was] unavoidable."[52]

In recent years, however, this policy seems to have undergone some change. According to the Kefauver Committee, steel prices have tended to become more flexible—but flexible in an upward direction only. Since 1947, the Committee reports, there has emerged a fairly consistent pattern of "stair-step" price increases at regular intervals—with base prices usually going up in midsummer and extra prices rising in midwinter. Moreover, this upward flexibility has at times been achieved in the face of declining demand. Thus, between December 1955 and August 1957, the price index on cold rolled sheets rose 20 points while the production index declined 80 points; on cold rolled strip, the price index advanced 23.8 points, while the production index slumped

---

51 See A. R. Burns, *The Decline of Competition* (New York: McGraw-Hill, 1936), pp. 205 ff.

52 A. D. H. Kaplan, J. B. Dirlam, and R. F. Lanzillotti, *Pricing in Big Business* (Washington, D.C.: The Brookings Institution, 1958), p. 175.

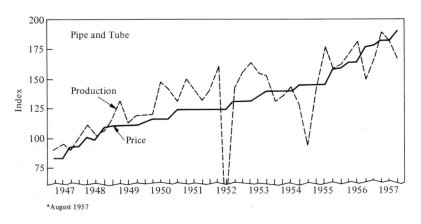

*August 1957

Figure 1

**TRENDS IN THE PRICE AND PRODUCTION OF PIPE
AND TUBE, 1947–1957 (1947–1957 = 100)**

SOURCE   Subcommittee on Antitrust and Monopoly, "Administered
Prices: Steel," *Senate Report No. 1387*, 85th Congress, 2nd Session, 1958,
p. 21.

45.6 points; on hot rolled sheets, the price index rose 30.4 points, while the production index fell 58.6 points. Similar trends were observed in hot-rolled bars, pipe and tube, rails, plates, and other steel products.[53]

Since World War II, it seems, steel prices have not only shown a remarkable insensitivity to market conditions but have risen with virtually unbroken regularity. They have increased even when demand and production declined (as in 1949, 1954, and 1957). They continued their climb even when unit labor costs declined (as in 1950 and 1955). According to the Kefauver Committee, "no matter what the change in cost or in demand, steel prices since 1947 have moved steadily and regularly in only one direction, upward." The fact that prices were raised again in 1957, and that this increase was "made to stick" in the face of a general recession, was further "tribute to the perfection with which price leadership in the steel industry maintains price rigidity."[54] With few exceptions, events during the 1960's only served to buttress this generalization.

IV. MARKET PERFORMANCE

PRICE ESCALATION AND LOSS OF COMPETITIVENESS

The persistent price escalation of steel prices during the 1950's has been the primary cause of the industry's lackluster performance during the 1960's —resulting in the erosion of domestic markets by substitute materials and imports, the loss of export markets not tied to Agency for International Development (AID) control, and the decline in return on investment.

The facts on steel pricing are beyond question. According to the Council of Economic Advisers, "Steel prices played an important role in the general price increases of the 1950's. Between 1947 and 1951, the average increase in the price of basic steel products was 9 per cent per year, twice the average increase of all wholesale prices. The unique behavior of steel prices was most pronounced in the mid-1950's. While the wholesale price index was falling an average of 0.9 per cent annually from 1951 to 1955, the price index for steel was rising an average of 4.8 per cent per year. From 1955 to 1958, steel prices

---

53 *Kefauver Committee Report*, op. cit., pp. 17–26. Prices of different steel products are, of course, adjusted to varying market elasticities. In general, prices and profit margins are highest on items facing less intense competition, like steel rails and cable. "Stainless steel, galvanized sheets, and tin plate, on the other hand, which are in direct or potential competition with substitutes from aluminum to lumber, had narrower profit margins." The same holds true for products like cold rolled sheets which are sold to buyers (e.g., automobile and farm equipment manufacturers) "who are able to exert strong pressures because of size and ability to threaten, at least, to make their own." See Kaplan, Dirlam, and Lanzillotti, op. cit., p. 172 ff.

54 *Kefauver Committee Report*, op. cit., p. 129. Again, it should be noted that those prices subject to more intense competition or buyer pressures have increased less than others, but the composite index for *all* steel products has clearly risen.

were increasing 7.1 per cent annually, or almost three times as fast as whole-sale prices generally. No other major sector shows a similar record."[55] After a quiescent stage during the early 1960's, characterized by the "jawboning" moral suasion of the Kennedy Administration, steel prices resumed their upward movement in 1964—on a gradual selective product-by-product basis at first, and on a general across-the-board basis after 1968. The imposition of "voluntary" import quotas in 1969 renewed prosperity in the world steel market, and the Nixon Administration's refusal to engage in government-industry confrontations simply accelerated the trend.

The industry followed its traditional course, increasing prices as a response to rising costs and lagging profits. It justified this policy by arguing that its competitive position could be improved only by increasing profits which would enable it to attract the necessary capital for investment in more efficient plants and equipment.[56] During the period from 1953 to 1958, the policy of increasing prices (at an average rate of more than 6 per cent per year) did produce the desired profit results. It did so, because cost-plus pricing is workable in the absence of effective competition. But it left the industry vulnerable to both substitute competition and imports, and as such competition increased, steel's rate of output growth and capacity utilization declined. So did its profits.

TABLE 3   PRICE CHANGES IN STEEL AND
COMPETITIVE MATERIALS, 1947 TO 1967

MATERIAL	PERCENTAGE CHANGE IN WHOLESALE PRICE, INDEX, 1947 TO 1967	PRICE IN 1967 RELATIVE TO STEEL (PER CENT)[a]
Steel mill products	119.9	100.0
Cement	70.0	77.3
Glass, flat	52.4	69.2
Plastic materials	−5.5	43.0
Aluminum ingots	75.6	79.8

a   Based on 1967 prices on a 1947 base.
SOURCE   Department of Labor and Council of Economic Advisers.

55   Council of Economic Advisors, *Report to the President on Steel Prices* (Washington, D.C.: April 1965), pp. 8–9. [Hereafter cited as *CEA Steel Report.*]

56   Roger Blough, in defending the industry's 1962 abortive price increase, clearly articulated this philosophy: "While the price rise might have appeared to intensify our competitive difficulties with cheaper foreign steel, that steel is usually priced in relation to ours anyway, and in the long run, the increase would have improved our competitive strength. By using the added profits produced by the price increase to help obtain the most modern and efficient tools of production, we could hope eventually to narrow the gap between American and foreign steel prices." [*Look* (January 29, 1963), p. 23] Thus, Mr. Blough proposed to meet the competition of cheaper foreign steel by *raising* prices.

SUBSTITUTE COMPETITION   Part of steel's woes can be traced to the deterioration of its price competitiveness vis-à-vis substitutes (see Table 3). "On a comparative basis," reports the Council of Economic Advisers, "the price of basic steel products rose substantially relative to the prices of competing materials. Relative to plastics, the price of basic steel products was over twice as high in 1963 as it was in 1947. The prices of cement, glass, plastic materials, and aluminum all rose substantially less than steel. With this sharp deterioration in the relative price position of steel products vis-à-vis other materials, failure of iron and steel production to keep pace with the growth of the economy is not surprising."[57]

It is not surprising, therefore, that between 1947 and 1967, the aluminum industry increased sixfold, the plastics industry twentyfold, and the glass, cement, and brick industries about doubled in size—whereas iron and steel output rose only 35 per cent. In the 3 years from 1964 to 1967, whereas the level of steel production remained unchanged, total industrial production increased 19 per cent, the production of glass 10 per cent, cement 4 per cent, aluminum 28 per cent, and plastics 33 per cent. While other than price factors undoubtedly played a role, steel's deteriorating relative position is partly attributable to its upward-rigid price policy.

LOSS OF EXPORT MARKETS   In the mid-1950's, the United States exported about four times as much steel as it imported. By 1960, the United States had become a net importer of steel and, by 1968, imports exceeded exports by a margin of 8 to 1. (See Table 4.) Even so, the lion's share of our exports represented "tied" sales under the AID program. Here, again, the noncompetitive price policy of the steel industry was the primary factor explaining this performance record.

Typically, American steel exports were priced at U.S. list prices (f.o.b. producing mill or service centers) plus freight costs to the point of delivery.

TABLE 4   STEEL EXPORTS AND IMPORTS, 1958–1969 (NET TONS)

YEAR	EXPORTS ($)	IMPORTS ($)	TRADE BALANCE ($)	IMPORTS AS PER CENT OF U.S. MARKET
1958	2,822,910	1,707,130	1,115,780	2.9
1960	2,977,278	3,358,752	− 381,474	4.7
1962	2,012,590	4,100,039	− 2,087,449	5.6
1964	3,442,014	6,439,635	− 2,997,621	7.3
1966	1,723,958	10,753,022	− 9,029,064	10.9
1968	2,169,792	17,959,886	−15,790,094	16.7
1969	5,229,337	14,034,287	− 8,804,950	13.7

SOURCE   AISI, *Foreign Trade Trends*, various years.

57   *CEA Steel Report*, op. cit., p. 28.

As the Senate Finance Committee concedes, "generally no attempt is made to align export pricing on the substantially lower prices quoted in third markets by the European or Japanese steel producers."[58] This means, of course, that American steel exports carry the albatross of high prices and rigid prices into the arena of international competition.

All available studies corroborate this conclusion. "With the sole exception of cold-rolled sheets," Professor Egon Sohmen found, "steel export prices in the United States were up to 30 per cent higher than in the ECSC during the early 1960's. As noted with much chagrin by the High Authority in its 15th annual report (1967, item N. 195), steel prices in the Common Market were about the same as in 1953 while they had risen by an average of 40 per cent in the United States and also in England whose steel industry is notoriously uncompetitive."[59] Similarly, the National Bureau of Economic Research found that U.S. export prices on steel rose approximately 3 per cent between 1957 and 1964, whereas the export prices of Common Market steel producers declined about 6 per cent.[60] In yet another study, it was found that between 1962 and 1968, U.S. export prices for selected carbon steel products went up by an average of 18 per cent, whereas world market prices for similar products declined by about 2.5 per cent.[61]

Not only the level, but also the rigidity of American steel export prices stands in remarkable contrast to that of Common Market prices. Between 1955 and 1967, according to Professor Sohmen, "steel prices were almost completely rigid in the United States (for all practical purposes, they were adjusted only in an upward direction) while they were remarkably flexible in Europe . . . . Largely as a consequence of this rigidity in price, the level of production suffered major setbacks in the United States whenever business activity receded so that steel works operated at less than two thirds of capacity for many years. Steelmakers in Europe, on the other hand, were able to operate near capacity more or less continuously until recently [late 1960's]."[62] Table 5 and Figure 2 underscore this point, showing that the U.S. turned from

58   U.S. Senate Finance Committee, Staff Study, *Steel Imports*, 90th Congress, 1st Session (Washington, D.C.: 1967), p. 126.

59   *Economic Concentration Hearings*, Part 7, 1968, op. cit., p. 3444.

60   *American Economic Review*, **57**:486 (May 1967). After surveying four main product groups (iron and steel, nonferrous metals, and nonelectric machinery), the National Bureau of Economic Research economists found that the largest changes in international competitiveness "have taken place in iron and steel." Between 1953 and 1963, there was an almost 20 per cent decline in the price competitiveness of American steel relative to European pro-

ducers. Although a reversal of the trend began to appear in 1964, the price posture of U.S. steel in world markets "remained considerably worse than in 1953 and 1957."

61   Unpublished M.A. thesis by Jean Louis Kruseman, University of Rhode Island, 1969.

62   *Economic Concentration Hearings*, Part 7, op. cit., p. 3444. The Organization for Economic Cooperation and Development (OECD) Iron and Steel Committee observed in its 1960 report, "[there seems to be] a fundamental difference in the export price policy pursued by producers in the various exporting areas . . . the producers in the E[uropean] C[oal and]

a net exporter to a net importer of steel precisely during a period—the late 1950's and early 1960's—when its own steel producing capacity was seriously underutilized. No wonder that U.S. Steel exports became progressively restricted to AID financed sales and the export of specialty steel products.

EROSION OF DOMESTIC MARKETS BY IMPORTS The dramatic rise in steel imports during the 1960's, and the increasing share of the domestic market captured by imports, is further evidence of the industry's counterproductive (and even, suicidal) price policy (see Table 2).[63] Given the price differential between domestic and imported steel—ranging from $10 to $40 per ton, depending on the product and the state of the market—and given the industry's refusal to meet such price competition in the market place (except under the rarest circumstances), the erosive impact of steel imports was an almost foregone conclusion. It explains the industry's persistent and unrelenting pressure on the government for protection—whether through "antidumping" measures, "temporary" tariffs, mandatory or "voluntary" quotas, "buy American" policies, and so on.

This demand for government protection centers on the claim that the domestic steel industry cannot be expected to compete against foreign producers enjoying substantially lower labor costs. The claim, though plausible, is not substantiated; like most protectionist arguments, it borders on the disingenuous. Thus, Professor Richard Thorn, although conceding the wage-cost differential between U.S. and foreign producers, found that this differential is more than offset by the lower material costs, capital costs, transportation costs, and prevailing tariff rates—both vis-à-vis the European and Japanese producers. The explanation for the lower price of steel imports must be sought in directions other than in the lower costs of foreign producers, Thorn concludes. "For most steel products, American steel products are already 'cost competitive' in U.S. markets. For most of those foreign steel products that have a present cost advantage, the American industry has it in its power to eliminate this advantage in most products through a higher rate of new investment and greater research and development expenditure. 'Cost competitiveness,' however, cannot be equated with price competitiveness. What

S[teel] C[ommunity] and Japan, seem to adopt a much more flexible policy . . . to try to expand their share of the export market by making sacrifices . . . . This policy is in marked contrast to that followed in the United States and, it would seem, in the United Kingdom where the steel industries seem less disposed to offer heavy cuts in prices to overseas consumers." (*The Iron and Steel Industry in Europe*, (Paris: 1960), p. 97) Nor, one can add, are they inclined to readily reduce prices to domestic consumers to meet foreign competition.

63 *Fortune*, for example, finds it curious that, "while complaining about the low costs and the low prices of foreign steel, leading steel companies have chosen this particular time, of all times, to *raise* their own domestic prices when their mills are still working at well under full capacity. Put all this together and one is reminded of that old British march to which Cornwallis surrendered at Yorktown called *The World Turned Upside Down*." *Fortune*, **76**:116 (October 1967).

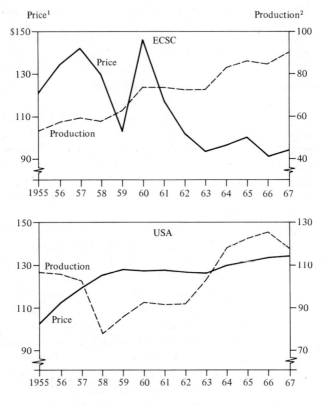

1. Average export prices, open-hearth grade, beginning of year, per metric ton.
2. Millions of metric tons.

Figure 2

STEEL EXPORT PRICES AND PRODUCTION, EUROPEAN COAL AND STEEL COMMUNITY AND U.S.A., 1955–1967

SOURCE   Economic Concentration Hearings, Part 7, p. 3445

102

TABLE 5 STEEL PRICES, OUTPUT, AND USE OF CAPACITY IN THE UNITED STATES AND THE EUROPEAN COAL AND STEEL COMMUNITY, 1955 TO 1967

[Average prices in U.S. dollars per metric ton of 5 rolling-mill products; outputs in millions of metric tons]

	1955	1956	1957	1958	1959	1960	1961	1962	1963	1964	1965	1966	1967
Average export prices:													
ECSC	122	135	144	129	102	147	117	101	93	96	100	91	94
United States	103	112	119	125	128	127	127	126	126	130	131	133	134
ECSC:													
A. *Output*	53	57	59	58	63	74	74	73	73	83	86	85	90
B. *Capacity*	56	59	64	69	70	78	80	83	88	92	102	109	112
C. *Per cent use of capacity*	96	96	94	86	90	96	92	88	83	90	84	78	80
United States:													
A. *Output*	106	105	102	77	85	92	91	91	102	118	122	125	118
B. *Capacity*	115	119	124	131	134	138	139	140	143	145	150	152	155
C. *Per cent use of capacity*	93	90	85	61	63	67	65	64	71	81	81	82	76

SOURCES ECSC, Annual Reports, 1955–67, and unpublished EEC statistics; Steel Prices, Unit Costs, Profits, and Foreign Competition, Hearings before the Joint Economic Committee, 88th Congress, 1st session, Washington, 1963, pp. 186 and 339. All prices refer to open-hearth quality steel (beginning of year values). Domestic prices in the ECSC countries were at all times close to export prices, the official price lists of steel producers in Europe (required by the ECSC treaty) being a mere formality. (Table appears in *Economic Concentration Hearings*, part 7, op. cit., p. 3811.)

is lacking is an aggressive price competitiveness to match the high cost competitiveness of the American industry."[64] In short, like most observers, Thorn views the rise in steel imports as a dramatic and highly visible index of the American steel industry's aversion to price competition.

SUMMARY: PRICE POLICY AND PERFORMANCE   It is difficult to resist the conclusion that the American steel industry during the last 20 years has tended to price itself out of the market and that, as a consequence, it has suffered from incursions into its domestic market from imports and substitutes and from a significant loss of exports. The magnitude of the damage inflicted by the industry's noncompetitive behavior on the U.S. balance of trade has been estimated by Professor Sohmen: "Had the industry worked at capacity during the early sixties, and had it exported the additional steel at world market prices, the additional export revenue (taking into account the fact that steel prices on the world market would have been somewhat lower as a consequence) would have eliminated the U.S. balance-of-payments deficit during these years. One need hardly go into details of what the United States would have been spared in this event . . . . This comparison is, if anything, likely to understate the contribution of high steel prices to the U.S. balance-of-payments troubles. If steel prices in the United States had uniformly been at the lower world market levels, many important American industries using steel (the automobile or the machinery industries, to name only a few) could have reduced their prices. This would have entailed a rise of exports of these industries and a fall of competing imports, further improving the U.S. trade balance."[65]

In a nutshell, here is an example of how an oligopolistic industry structure militates toward a noncompetitive price policy which, in turn, results in a deplorable industry performance.

TECHNOLOGICAL PROGRESSIVENESS

Historically, according to the American Iron & Steel Institute, American steel has been able to compete in world markets because of its technological

---

64   "Steel Imports, Labor Productivity, and Cost Competitiveness," *Western Economic Journal*, **6**:383 (December, 1968). Thorn found that the total cost advantage of American steel producers ranges from $1.64 to $6.25 per metric ton over Japan, and from − $0.28 to $15.24 over the Common Market. These figures take into account a unit-wage cost differential of − $17.63 and − $18.62 to − $10.72, respectively (Ibid., p. 380).

65   *Economic Concentration Hearings*, Part 7, op. cit., p. 3446. According to

Sohmen's calculations, "The officially recorded aggregate deficit of the U.S. balance of payments during the years 1960–1963 (decrease of official resources plus increase in liquid liabilities to foreigners) amounted to $10.6 billion. The American steel industry could without difficulty have produced an additional 30 million tons of steel per year during these years which it could have sold at world market prices of at least $90 per ton." (Ibid.)

superiority. Steel spokesmen assure us that they have done "everything in the book to make this industry as efficient and as competitive as it is possible for any industry to be." U.S. Steel calls itself the company "where the big idea is *innovation*," and its general counsel claims that the "distinguishing characteristic of the American steel industry is its tremendous productiveness, a quality which other countries have been unable to emulate so far"—that U.S. Steel, in particular, "is fully aware of, and has continuously studied and tried out, new processes developed both in this country and abroad."[66]

Unfortunately, the facts do not support this boastful *hubris*:

1. A 1966 report of the National Science Foundation shows that the steel industry ranks shockingly low in its research and development expenditures. In 1964, it spent only 60 cents of every $100 in sales revenue on research and development compared to a $1.90 average for all manufacturing industry. Moreover, all the industries producing steel substitutes—aluminum, cement, plastics, and glass—invested more in research and development than did the steel industry, sometimes five or six times as much.

2. The major steel inventions in recent years—including the basic oxygen furnace, continuous casting, and vacuum degassing—came from abroad. They were not made by the American steel giants.

3. In innovation, as in invention, the American steel giants seem to lag, not lead. The oxygen furnace, for example, the only major technological breakthrough in basic steel making since the turn of the century, was invented and innovated by the miniscule Austrian steel industry in 1950. It was first installed in the United States in 1954 by a small company (McLouth), and not adopted by the steel giants until more than a decade later: U.S. Steel in December 1963, Bethlehem in 1964, and Republic in 1965. (See Table 6 which shows that, as of September 1963, the largest steel companies, operating more than 50 per cent of basic steel capacity, had not installed a single LD furnace, whereas smaller companies, operating only 7 per cent of the nation's steel capacity, accounted for almost half of the LD installations in the United States.)

   Indeed, despite the fact that the new oxygen process entailed operating cost savings of roughly $5.00 per ton, as well as capital cost savings of $20–25 per ton of installed capacity, the U.S. steel industry during the 1950's "bought 40 million tons of the wrong kind of capacity—the open hearth furnace."[67] As *Fortune* observed, much of this capacity "was obsolete when it was built" and the industry, by installing it, "prepared itself for dying."[68] Or, as *Forbes* put it more mildly, "In the Fifties, the

66   W. Adams and J. B. Dirlam, "Big Steel, Invention, and Innovation," *Quarterly Journal of Economics*, **80**: 175 (May 1966).

67   *Business Week* (November 16, 1963), p. 144.

68   *Fortune*, **74**: 130 (October 1966); **74**: 135 (October 1966).

TABLE 6 DISTRIBUTION OF L-D OXYGEN CAPACITY AMONG
UNITED STATES STEEL PRODUCERS, SEPTEMBER 1963

U.S. STEEL COMPANY'S RANK IN THE INDUSTRY[a]	OXYGEN STEEL CAPACITY (TONS)	PERCENTAGE OF U.S. OXYGEN STEEL CAPACITY	PERCENTAGE OF TOTAL U.S. STEEL CAPACITY[a]
1st, 2nd, 3d	0	0	52.27
4th, 5th, 6th	6,550,000	50.62	14.76
9th, 10th, 12th, 15th, 19th	6,390,000	49.38	7.06
All companies	12,940,000	100	100

a Based on company ingot capacity as of January 1, 1960.
SOURCE American Iron and Steel Institute, *Iron and Steel Works Directory of the United States and Canada* (1960); Kaiser Engineers, *L-D Process Newsletter* (September 27, 1963).

steel industry poured hundreds of millions of dollars into equipment that was already obsolete technologically—open hearth furnaces."[69] The technological blunder may have cost close to $1 billion in "white elephant" facilities.

4. The belated adoption of continuous casting by the steel giants is a further illustration of their technological lethargy. Again it was a small company (Roanoke Electric), with an annual capacity of 100,000 tons, that pioneered in introducing this European invention in the United States in 1962. Other small steel companies followed, so that by 1968, firms with roughly 3 per cent of the nation's steel capacity accounted for 90 per cent of U.S. continuous casting production.[70] The record was embarrassing to the giant firms. Said William P. Hill, engineering executive of National Steel: "There were eight companies operating continuous casting machines before 1965 handling small tonnage. The outstanding thing was all of these companies were small independent companies. They are competing by continuous casting their entire tonnage. These companies are demanding the low cost, low operating and first cost in order to produce small tonnage. It is a little embarrassing to some of us when we see this." As for the continuous casting of slabs, Mr. Hill warned his colleagues in Big Steel: "This means that we have to be a little more progressive. The larger companies will have to help develop these large slab casting machines and not depend on the small independent companies to carry the load."[71]

5. Even defenders of the American steel giants concede that it was the cold winds of competition rather than the sheltered atmosphere of protectionism which ultimately forced the domestic majors (belatedly) to follow the

---

69 *Forbes*, **99**: 23 (March 1, 1967).
70 "Continuous Casting," *Iron and Steel Engineer*, **33**:52 (May 1968).

71 Quoted in R. Easton and J. W. Donaldson, "Continuous Casting," *Iron and Steel Engineer*, **43**:80 (October 1966).

path of technological progress. Thus, Professor Alan McAdams admits that by "1962 it appears that the costs to United States producers for *not* innovating were significantly raised by actual and threatened competition from both domestic and foreign oxygen steelmakers."[72] Competition, not protection, broke down the industry's habitual lethargy and resistance to change.

Summing up the industry's performance with respect to technological progressiveness, it is fair to conclude that the giant companies lagged, not led, both in invention and innovation—both vis-à-vis their smaller domestic rivals and their foreign competitors.

PROFITS

Reported profit rates, as the Council of Economic Advisers warns, provide a very limited basis for comparison of the real profitability of an industry over the years or for comparison with other industries. Changing accounting practices and different rates of capacity utilization over the years tend to distort meaningful comparisons. Cash flow—i.e., the sum of profits after tax plus depreciation and depletion allowances—is a better, though far from perfect, measure of profitability.

Whether we examine steel's reported profits or cash flow, however, the industry's record is far from impressive. On both counts, steel ranks below the average for all manufacturing—primarily because of its technological lethargy and the inadequate capacity utilization, attributable to a noncompetitive price policy. As Figure 3 shows, there is a very strong positive relationship between capacity utilization and cash flow. According to the Council of Economic Advisers, a "four-point improvement in operating rate leads to over a one-point improvement in cash flow as a percentage of equity. Thus, if the steel industry were back to the operating rates of the mid-1950's, both the ratio of cash flow to equity and the relative position of the industry compared with others would be much more favorable than at the present time [1965]."[73]

It seems safe to predict that once the industry begins to benefit from its belated efforts at technological modernization and if it adopts a more realistic (i.e., more competitive) price policy to achieve a higher rate of capacity utilization, it will successfully overcome the profit doldrums of the 1960's.

SUMMARY

Summarizing, then, steel is a concentrated industry. Its behavior conforms closely to the oligopoly pattern. Price uniformity is assured through price leadership (with or without resort to the basing point system). Price stability

72 *Quarterly Journal of Economics,* **81**:473 (August 1967).

73 Council of Economic Advisors, *Steel Report,* op. cit., p. 56.

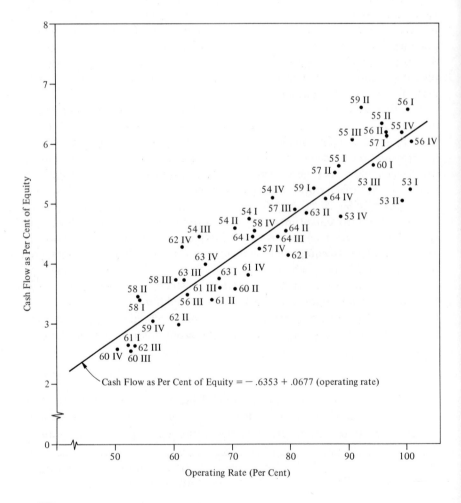

Cash Flow as Per Cent of Equity = − .6353 + .0677 (operating rate)

is attained, often at the expense of extreme fluctuations in production and employment. Price levels are geared to a break-even point of 50 per cent or less of capacity, and only remotely influenced by natural market forces. The industry leader sets prices like a public utility, aiming for a predetermined profit target (after taxes), and the other firms usually follow in lockstep. In short, the industry's performance hardly measures up to the standards of workable competition. As George Stocking correctly concludes, the industry's "structure contribute[s] to conduct incompatible with an effective interplay of market forces, and its structure and conduct [result] in unacceptable performance."[74]

V. PUBLIC POLICY

What should be the public policy toward the steel industry? Is the performance of the industry sufficiently good to justify a policy of noninterference? Could performance be improved by a change in structure, or is it enough to press for a rehabilitation of behavior? Above all, is effective competition in the steel industry possible, and/or desirable? If so, how can it be promoted?

Ever since the Supreme Court's refusal to break up U.S. Steel in 1920, the government has confined itself mainly to combating collusive, discriminatory, and exorbitant prices. For more than 50 years, the Justice Department and the FTC have battled in the courts—first to eliminate the single- and then the multiple-basing-point system. These battles were eventually won. The Pittsburgh Plus system was proscribed in 1924, and the multiple-basing-point system and systematic freight absorption were banned in 1948. These rulings have not caused havoc in the industry. Nor have they assured the competitive pricing of steel products. Now, as before, price leadership and collusion in the economic sense are hallmarks of this industry.

As of today, the steel industry has operated for two dozen years under a modified sort of f.o.b. pricing. Despite the dire predictions of 1948, this has caused little, if any, hardship. The issue is far from settled, however. With a slackening in the demand for steel or a major recession, the industry is almost certain to insist that stabilization of competition is imperative, and that such stabilization requires basing point pricing. In the face of such agitation it may

---

74 "The Rule of Reason, Workable Competition, and Monopoly," *Yale Law*   *Journal*, **64**:1136 (July 1955).

Figure 3

RELATIONSHIP BETWEEN CASH FLOW AS PER CENT OF EQUITY AND OPERATING RATE, STEEL INDUSTRY
SOURCE American Iron and Steel Institute and Council of Economic Advisers.

be well to remember, however, that recessions cannot be cured by basing points and competition cannot be achieved through collusion. In the light of our recent experience, it would be difficult to justify the return to a collusive, discriminatory, and wasteful pricing method. It would be difficult to justify a reversal from our present opposition to basing points and systematic freight absorption.[75]

On the other hand, it is unrealistic to suppose that mere abstention from the basing point system will achieve either price competition or price flexibility—a fact illustrated by the recurrent official inquiries into steel prices and profits. Congress has investigated, exposed, and condemned. The President has pleaded, admonished, and warned. Steel labor and steel management have been exhorted to exercise restraint and to forego desired wage and price increases in order to combat inflation and thus preserve the American way of life. "The response," as Ben Lewis observes, "has been not only less than spectacular; it has been imperceptible." Voluntary restraint, creeping admonitionism, and economizing by conscience have simply not worked. They have become, as Lewis says, "a symptom of, and not a cure for, organic disabilities which are beginning to be plainly discernible in our economic body."[76]

From society's point of view, the objective is not to keep steel prices low in prosperity and high in depression. The function of steel prices, as of all prices, should be to promote a proper allocation of society's resources—to channel resources into those uses where the consuming public most wants to have them. Thus, given a high demand for steel, an uncompetitively low administered price brings in its wake grey markets and allocation problems. Such a price is, in effect, a subsidization by the steel industry of steel-consuming industries. It distorts the allocation of resources in accordance with the dictates of the market. It strikes at the central nervous system of a free enterprise economy. The same is true in times of slack demand. At such times, the effort by the steel industry to stabilize prices and to maintain prices at higher levels than the market justifies again results in distortions of the allocation process. It represents an unwarranted tax on steel-using industries imposed by steel producers. It is an attempt to cure recessions by cartel-like restraints on the free market. Not only are such attempts futile, as history amply demonstrates, but they represent a crucial deviation from the fundamentals of free enterprise.

No! Creeping admonitionism, voluntary restraint, and the corporate soul are not likely to solve the basic problem. Nor will a conscientious adherence to f.o.b. pricing make the steel industry a paragon of competition. The prob-

75 This recommendation is supported by the findings of the most definitive and thoroughgoing study of the basing point problem. See F. Machlup, *The Basing Point System* (New York: McGraw-Hill, 1949).

76 "Economics by Admonition," *American Economic Review Proceedings*, **49**:384 (May 1959).

lem goes deeper. It is inherent in the structure of the industry. It is the problem of "size," and any attack on oligopoly pricing without an attack on oligopoly structure will be no more effective than the treatment of a symptom instead of the disease itself. In other words, public policy toward this industry must concern itself with the basic problem of structure and how it can be changed. This, in turn, raises questions about the relation between the size of firms and technological efficiency—in short, the feasibility of increasing the number of competitors. If it is possible to increase the number of firms and thus create a more competitive industry structure, this would enhance the prospects for more competitive behavior and the likelihood of nonconformity in pricing and other aspects of business policy. Whether this can be done is the problem to which we now turn.

THE PROBLEM OF SIZE

On the basis of information which is available it seems reasonable that iron and steel making requires firms of considerable size—firms which are not only significant horizontally (i.e., within any one branch of the industry) but which are also integrated vertically. Vertical integration seems economically justifiable due to the "geographic concentration of the industry, the magnitude of individual operations necessary for efficiency in mining and manufacture, and the economies obtained by continuous operation, which makes possible the immediate use of the end product of one stage of production as the material in the next stage."[77] Thus there are very definite economies to be obtained from a combination of the operations of blast furnaces and steel works. These economies are obtained (1) by transforming pig iron into steel by a continuous process without permitting the iron to cool, thus using it in a molten state; (2) by recovering the valuable by-product gasses from blast furnaces and coke ovens; and (3) by avoiding the cost of transporting pig iron, a cost which is high in comparison to its value.

On the other hand, there is little evidence to indicate that firms must be of Brobdignagian size to be efficient. Professor Bain, for example, estimates that an integrated steel mill of "optimal size" need have a capacity of not more than 1–2.5 million ingot tons.[78] Other studies indicate that (1) operational efficiency, (2) technological progressiveness, and (3) profitability might best be promoted not by preserving, but by reducing the size of some steel giants.

First, with respect to operational efficiency, it is interesting that the capacity of the giant steel companies is not concentrated in a handful of large plants. Thus, when a total of 51 steel making plants belonging to the 8 largest companies were classified according to size, it was found that only 5 had

---

77 U.S. Tariff Commission, p. 42.
78 Bain, p. 236. On this point, see

also *Celler Report*, p. 69, which corroborates Bain's estimate.

annual capacities of more than 3 million ingot tons; 24 had ingot capacities from 1 to 3 million tons; and the remaining 20 plants had capacities of less than 1 million tons.[79] These, remember, were plants owned by the eight largest steel companies.

Moreover, it is doubtful if the combination of spatially and functionally separate plant units yields any significant economies. To be sure, there are advantages in integrated steel production at Pittsburgh or Gary or Birmingham; but is there any technological justification for combining these three functionally independent plant units under the administration of one firm?

Consider for a moment that U.S. Steel's Gary plant alone is bigger than the total operations of Jones & Laughlin, Youngstown, Armco, and Inland. One plant of the nation's largest steel producer is bigger than all the plants of the fifth largest producer. This inevitably raises the question, whether Jones & Laughlin and other companies of similarly substantial size are big enough to be efficient. If they are, then certainly U.S. Steel's Gary plant—standing on its own feet and divorced from the industrial family of U.S. Steel—should also be capable of efficient operation. The same goes for the corporation's integrated units at Pittsburgh and Birmingham. Divorcement of these plants from the home office should hardly result in a loss of efficiency.[80]

In fact, such divorcement may result in more, not less, operational efficiency—at least, if the evidence in the hitherto unpublished Ford, Bacon & Davis report is reliable. This report was prepared by Ford, Bacon & Davis (a private management consulting firm) at the request of U.S. Steel itself, and was of course undertaken at the corporation's expense. Its findings, as summarized by Professor George Stocking before the Celler Committee, pictured the corporation as

> a big sprawling inert giant, whose production operations were improperly coordinated; suffering from a lack of a long-run planning agency; relying on an antiquated system of cost accounting; with an inadequate knowledge of the costs or of the relative profitability of the many thousands of items it sold; with production and cost standards generally below those considered everyday practice in other industries; with inadequate knowledge of its domestic markets and no clear appreciation of its opportunities in foreign markets; with less efficient

---

79 Bain, pp. 236–237. The data are for 1952.

80 See the very interesting testimony of Benjamin Fairless on this question in *Hearings before the Subcommittee on Study of Monopoly Power*, 81st Congress, 2nd Session, 1950, Serial No. 14, Part 4A, pp. 498–505. Also interesting in this connection is the testimony by Professor George Stigler that "all the largest steel firms, and most of the oligopolies in other industries, are the product of mergers. Not one steel company has been able to add to its relative size as much as 4 per cent of the ingot capacity of the industry in fifty years by attracting customers. Every firm that has gained four or more per cent of the industry's capacity in this half century has done so by merger." (Ibid., p. 996.)

production facilities than its rivals had; slow in introducing new processes and new products.

Specifically, according to the engineers, it was slow in introducing the continuous rolling mill; slow in getting into production of cold-rolled steel products; slow in recognizing the potentials of the wire business; slow to adopt the heat-treating process for the production of sheets; slow in getting into stainless steel products; slow in producing cold-rolled sheets; slow in tin-plate developments; slow in utilizing waste gases; slow in utilizing low-cost water transportation because of its consideration for the railroads; in short, slow to grasp the remarkable business opportunities that a dynamic America offered it. The corporation was apparently a follower, not a leader, in industrial efficiency.[81]

On the basis of the powerful indictment in this engineering report (as well as other evidence), Stocking concluded that "the Steel Corporation has lagged, not led"; that "it was neither big because it was efficient, nor efficient because it was big."[82] This conclusion was supported by the testimony of other leading economists who maintained that the dissolution of U.S. Steel into at least three separate integrated units was technologically quite feasible. They assured the committee that "one can be opposed to economic bigness and in favor of technological bigness in most basic industries without inconsistency."[83]

Second, with respect to technological progressiveness, it is noteworthy that the small- and medium-sized steel companies compare quite favorably with U.S. Steel. Thus it was Bethlehem which patented the sensational Gray beam; it was Republic which became the leader in alloy steels; it was Armco which patented the continuous rolling mill process (invented by Naugle and Townsend); it was the Cold Metal Process Company which patented the Steckel reversing mill; and it was Europe which taught us how to make stainless steels and how to save millions with by-product coke ovens. European inventors, not the American steel giants, developed the revolutionary basic oxygen process and continuous casting.

Third, with respect to profitability, it is significant that some of the medium-sized companies have fared considerably better than the giant U.S. Steel Corporation.[84] To the extent that profit figures are valid as measures of

---

81 Ibid., p. 967.
82 Ibid., p. 969. See also W. S. Bowman, "Toward Less Monopoly," *University of Pennsylvania Law Review*, **101**:590 (March 1953). In fairness, it should be said that the Corporation has done much to correct the situation described in the Ford, Bacon & Davis report. Today it is a far more efficient organization than it was 30 years ago.

83 Ibid., p. 996. This was the statement of Professor Stigler who argued that Bethlehem, and possibly Republic, might also be subjected to dissolution proceedings.
84 Care must be exercised in making profit comparisons the measure of relative efficiency in corporations of different size. Profit rates often do not measure relative efficiency, since "the rate of profit is affected by bargaining advantages and various other factors as well as efficiency.

efficiency, the record would show a balance in favor of the medium-sized firm. Moreover, multiplant companies seem to have performed no better than single-plant organizations. Thus, Professor Bain found that between 1936–40 and 1947–51 there was "apparently no significant relation of profit rate on equity to size of firm among the 15 largest steel firms in the United States, although these firms ranged in size from U.S. Steel, with about 19 mills, down to single-plant firms. Although these profit-rate data are not conclusive," says Bain, "they are consistent with the hypothesis that economies did not result from expansion beyond a single integrated plant with from one to 2.5 million ingot tons capacity." [85]

On the basis of the little authoritative information available, we can say that whereas large firms may be necessary for efficient steel production, and whereas a considerable degree of vertical integration may be imperative for maximum efficiency, the optimum size of firm is substantially smaller than that of the largest companies today. Although there can never be enough firms in the steel industry—from the point of view of the technological and economic optimum—to assure even an approximation to perfect competition, there can nevertheless be enough firms to assure more intense competition than prevails today. There can be enough decentralization of power to assure a basic minimum of freedom for individual action "so that new ideas, new men, and new organizations will have the bona fide chance to introduce themselves." [86]

One more point is relevant here. Even if we hesitate to achieve greater decentralization through antitrust surgery, some structural reform is nevertheless easily attained. Foreign competition, as our experience with steel imports has demonstrated during the 1960's, can provide some moderating influence on oligopolistic excesses and a valuable yardstick for improving industry performance. Such competition should be encouraged, not stifled. Thus there is no justification for steel tariffs, quotas, or similar government

---

of operation. Since bargaining advantage tends to grow with size, a corresponding increase of profits might be attributable to corporate power, whereas a failure of profits to increase, too, might be a persuasive indication that the level of efficient operation had been passed." From *Maintaining Competition* by C. D. Edwards, p. 119. Copyright 1949. Reprinted by courtesy of the McGraw-Hill Book Company, New York. For a general discussion on the relation between size and efficiency in multiple-plant enterprises, see Edwards, op. cit., pp. 113–120.

85 Bain, op. cit., p. 255. Medium-sized firms have an advantage especially in times of depression when an organization like U.S. Steel finds itself too big to limit its operations only to the successful branches of the industry. "When the current is adverse, small companies can make headway in the eddies, but the Steel Corporation must breast the main stream. Furthermore the bigger a company the harder to keep it operating at a satisfactory percentage of capacity, if for no other reason than that buyers of steel tend to divide their orders equally among steel companies rather than on a basis prorated to capacity." Reprinted from *Fortune*, 13:170 (March 1936), by special permission of the Editors. Copyright Time, Inc.

86 D. McC. Wright, "What's Best for the Competitive Enterprise System" in U.S. Chamber of Commerce, p. 205.

restraints on competition. Let public policy not be misused as a protector and promoter of monopoly!

What makes the achievement of more effective competition in the steel industry so compelling is a consideration of the alternatives. Once we grant the unworkability of competition, the only alternatives seem to be: (1) a supervision of steel prices by a government commission (along the Interstate Commerce Commission pattern);[87] (2) a government counterspeculation agency;[88] (3) direct government participation in the steel industry; (4) industry self-government along NIRA lines, and (5) outright socialization. A perusal of the choice available should convince us that experimenting with the workability of competition is worthwhile, Only after fair trial and definitive failure, should we consider abandoning a competitive plan for the steel industry.

CONCLUSION

In conclusion, let us note that the steel industry today stands at an important cross-road. It is on the horns of the proverbial dilemma. If it concedes that effective price competition is feasible, it must go out and play the capitalistic game according to its naked, shameless, yet vitalizing and invigorating rules. If, on the other hand, it follows Judge Gary's lead and insists that competition in steel is impossible, that competition must somehow give way to cooperation, the industry must then accept some form of government regulation to protect the public interest. In any event, the industry can hardly continue with a structural organization under which every price change becomes the subject of a congressional investigation, every labor dispute the cause of a national emergency. The brutal choice before the steel industry seems to lie between the painful rigors of competition and the anguished frustrations of bureaucratic regulation.

SUGGESTED READINGS
BOOKS AND PAMPHLETS

Burns, A. R. *The Decline of Competition.* New York: McGraw-Hill Book Company, Inc., 1936.

Clark, J. M. *The Economics of Overhead Costs.* Chicago: University of Chicago Press, 1923.

Daugherty, C. R., M. G. de Chazeau, and S. S. Stratton. *Economics of the Iron and Steel Industry.* 2 vols. New York: McGraw-Hill Book Company Inc., 1937.

---

87 This proposal was advocated by Judge Gary, former president of United States Steel, before the Stanley Committee.

88 See A. P. Lerner, *The Economics of Control* (New York: Macmillan, 1944).

Fetter, F. A. *The Masquerade of Monopoly*. New York: Harcourt, Brace & World, Inc., 1931.
Machlup, F. *The Basing Point System*. New York: McGraw-Hill Book Company, Inc., 1949.
Seager, H. R., and C. A. Gulick. *Trust and Corporation Problems*. New York: Harper and Row, Publishers, Inc., 1929.
United States Steel Corporation, *TNEC Papers*. 3 vols. New York: 1940.

GOVERNMENT PUBLICATIONS

Council of Economic Advisers, *Report to the President on Steel Prices*, Washington, D.C.: April 1965.
Federal Trade Commission. *Report on the Control of Iron Ore*. Washington, D.C.: U.S. Government Printing Office 1952.
Hearings before the Subcommittee on Antitrust and Monopoly, Senate Judiciary Committee. *Administered Prices: Steel*. Parts 2, 3, 4. Washington, D.C.: 1957.
———, *Economic Concentration*, Parts 6 and 7, Washington, D.C.: 1967.
Hearings before the Subcommittee on the Study of Monopoly Power, House Judiciary Committee. *Steel*. Serial 14, Parts 4-A and 4-B. Washington, D.C.: 1950.
Hearings before the Temporary National Economic Committee. *Iron and Steel Industry*. Parts 19, 20, 26, 27. Washington, D.C.: 1940.
Senate Finance Committee, Staff Study, *Steel Imports*, Washington, D.C., 1967.
Subcommittee on Antitrust and Monopoly, Senate Judiciary Committee. *Administered Prices: Steel*. Washington, D.C.: 1958.
Subcommittee on the Study of Monopoly Power, House Judiciary Committee. *The Iron and Steel Industry*. Washington, D.C.: 1950.
Temporary National Economic Committee. *Price Discrimination in Steel*. Monograph No. 41. Washington, D.C.: 1941.
———. *The Basing Point Problem*, Monograph No. 42 Washington, D.C.: 1941.
U.S. Tariff Commission. "Iron and Steel." *War Changes in Industry Series*. Report No. 15. Washington, D.C.: 1946.
U.S. v. *Bethlehem Steel Corp., et. al.*, 168 F. Supp. 576 (1958).

JOURNAL AND MAGAZINE ARTICLES

Adams, W., and J. B. Dirlam. "Steel Imports and Vertical Oligopoly Power," *American Economic Review*, 54:626 (September 1964).
Adams, W., and J. B. Dirlam. "Big Steel, Invention, and Innovation," *Quarterly Journal of Economics*, 80:167 (May 1966).
Iron Age, New York, various numbers.
Smithies, A., "Aspects of the Basing-Point System." *American Economic Review*, 32: 705 (December 1942).

4. Thomas G. Moore

THE PETROLEUM INDUSTRY

T
I. INTRODUCTION

he petroleum industry, one of the most important and vital industries in the United States, supplied 43 per cent of the nation's energy requirements in 1965.[1] The assets involved in petroleum refining alone exceeded $70 billion at the end of 1968, almost three times the assets in iron and steel and about twice the assets involved in the manufacture of automobiles and equipment. Over $2 billion of personal income in the United States in 1967 was earned in crude petroleum and natural gas production, more than half of which was distributed in Oklahoma and Texas alone. In the same year, almost $9 billion of national income originated in oil and gas production and refining alone.

Actually, the petroleum industry is not one industry but many, with no firm spanning all activities and many specializing in only one branch. Although the industry could be considered to include natural gas as well as liquid petroleum, because of space limitations this chapter will focus on the latter. But bear in mind that in many cases natural gas and crude oil are produced jointly from the same wells, that natural gas can be liquefied and transported like oil, that natural gas is an excellent substitute for many of the uses of oil such as heating, cooking, and generation of electricity.

The oil industry consists of four industries: crude oil production (or imports), transportation by pipeline or tanker, refining, sales to distributors or to filling stations and then to consumers. The structure of the industry differs at each vertical stage and for each final product. Some firms operate at all stages, some at just one. Production of crude oil provided 63 per cent of the profits of integrated companies in 1967, 6 per cent came from transportation, 21 per cent from refining and marketing, and 10 per cent from petrochemicals.[2] About 49 per cent of refined output is gasoline, 21 per cent is distillate fuel oil, 7 per cent is residual fuel oil, and the rest is kerosene

---

1 American Petroleum Institute, *Petroleum Facts & Figures* (1967), p. 25. Most of the data on the petroleum industry were secured from this source.

2 *Oil and Gas Journal* **66**:36 (September 30, 1968).

(6 per cent), jet fuel (2 per cent), asphalt (4 per cent), and petrochemicals (3 per cent).

HISTORY

The petroleum industry originated in the United States on August 29, 1859 when exrailroad conductor "Colonel" E. L. Drake struck oil at 69 feet near Titusville, Pennsylvania. His discovery made possible the production of a cheap illuminating oil to replace whale oil and tallow candles. Industry sales from the Titusville area jumped from a production of 2,000 barrels in the first year to 4 million 10 years later.[3] Federal help to the burgeoning industry arrived almost immediately in the form of a 40 cents per gallon protective duty on kerosene, the principal product. The industry was characterized by individual enterprise or partnerships specializing in drilling, producing crude, barrelmaking, or refining one of the final products, kerosene, naphtha, or lubricants. Capital requirements were small and competition was vigorous.

A disastrous early development was the application of common law to the production of crude oil—those who brought the crude oil to the surface owned it. This led to a multiplication of wells and rapid and wasteful production.

The chaotic conditions of the early oil industry led to widely fluctuating prices, bankruptcies, and fortunes made overnight. As a result, oil men attempted to protect themselves by forming combinations and agreements on prices, production, and investment. The most successful of these combinations was the Standard Oil Company of Ohio, organized in 1870 as a million dollar corporation. Starting with a handful of refineries, Rockefeller and his associates bought up or combined with leading refiners in Cleveland and in the East. Having achieved control over a large volume of oil, they obtained significant reductions in rates from railroads; they built pipelines to the fields; and they induced the cooperation of leading stockholders in rival

TABLE 1 PER CENT OF CONTROL
OVER REFINERY CAPACITY BY
STANDARD OIL

1880	1899	1906	1911
90–95	82	70	64

SOURCE Harold F. Williamson and Ralph L. Andreano, "Competitive Structure of the Petroleum Industry, 1880–1911: A Reappraisal," *Oil's First Century* (Boston: Harvard Graduate School of Business Administration, 1960), pp. 70–84.

3 H. F. Williamson, R. L. Andreano, A. R. Daum, and G. C. Klose, *The American Petroleum Industry: The Age of Energy 1899–1959* (Evanston, Ill.: Northwestern University Press, 1963).

refineries. Standard Oil increased its dominance of refining by buying plants, leasing others, and making quota agreements with still others. By 1880 Standard had almost a complete monopoly of refinery capacity.

Folklore would have it that Standard Oil achieved and maintained a monopoly from 1880 to 1911. Folklore would also have it that the monopoly was achieved and maintained by unscrupulous business practices, especially secret railroad rebates, predatory and discriminatory pricing policies, dummy companies which sold its product and were ostensibly in competition with the firms publicly identified with Standard, secret price cuts, and the use of threats to induce customers to shun Standard's competitors. Like most folklore these beliefs have an element of truth but are exaggerated. Standard slowly lost its market share after 1880, and especially after 1900. Although Standard did use its large size to induce railroads to provide it with a favorable rate, most of the discriminatory price cutting appears to have been the result of Standard's offering lower prices to meet the lower prices of a competitor. The fact is that Standard achieved and maintained its monopoly by buying out its competitors at far from ruinous prices. New firms continued to enter the industry, and in one case, a former Standard employee went into the business of building refineries, threatening to compete with Standard, and then selling out to Standard.[4]

Nevertheless, in the eyes of contemporaries Standard became the prototype of greedy monopoly and big business. Inevitably the Sherman Act was invoked and in November 1906, the Federal Government filed suit in the U.S. Circuit Court for the Eastern District of Missouri against the holding company, Standard Oil Company of New Jersey, and its leading directors, including John D. Rockefeller. Charged with violating Sections 1 and 2 of the Sherman Act, they were found guilty on November 20, 1909, after some 12,000 printed pages of testimony and exhibits. Upheld in a landmark decision by the Supreme Court in 1911, the holding company was ordered dissolved and its stock passed through to its stockholders so that each stockholder in the holding company would receive a proportional amount of stock in each of the 33 successor companies.[5]

The result of this decree was to produce 33 companies all owned by the same stockholders with considerably different market power and integration. Only Jersey Standard and California Standard were fully integrated. Twelve of the successors were primarily pipeline companies, a few of which had crude-oil producing capacity. They did, of course, have to continue to deal with their former associated refining firms. Ten of the successors had refining capacity but each operated primarily in a different territory. In the short run, therefore, little competition was introduced by this decree. Jersey

---

4 See John S. Magee, "Predatory Price Cutting: The Standard Oil Case" *Journal of Law and Economics*, 1:137 (October 1958) for a discussion of Standard Oil's behavior.

5 *Standard Oil Company of New Jersey* v. *United States*, 221 U.S. 1 (1911).

Standard by itself kept about 43 per cent of the assets of the parent company. However, after a time each successor grew and competition developed between them. In part, this was due to the unequal distribution of facilities, which led successor companies to build new facilities, often in competition with other ex-Standard companies. In addition, new firms, such as Gulf Oil, Texaco, Shell, Phillips, Cities Service, and Sun Oil, were entering the industry, mainly based on Texas crude, the crude in the Gulf area, and California crude. Probably even more important in making the industry more competitive was the rapid growth of the automobile, with a skyrocketing demand for gasoline that could not be met by any one company, even the old Standard Oil Corporation.

II. MARKET STRUCTURE

As was pointed out above, the oil industry really consists of four separate industries: crude oil production, transportation, refining, and marketing. Twenty firms which are completely integrated through all of these steps are called majors.[6] Some of the independents are almost as large as the majors and are also integrated. The division between majors and independents is somewhat arbitrary but this chapter will continue it. Many other firms, however, specialize in one or the other of these subindustries. The major companies are huge vertically integrated operations with worldwide sales and production. Four of the largest industrial firms in the United States are oil companies. Standard Oil (N.J.) is the largest industrial firm in terms of assets in the world and Royal Dutch/Shell is the third largest with assets just slightly less than that of General Motors.

PRODUCTION

Crude oil is found throughout the world, but particularly in the Middle East, North Africa, the U.S.S.R., Venezuela, United States, Canada, and Indonesia. Tanker costs of moving crude and refined products are low and falling with the introduction of super tankers of over 250,000 tons. Consequently, the market for petroleum products would be worldwide in the absence of trade barriers. The United States limits imports of both crude and refined petroleum. As a consequence the U.S. market is isolated from the rest of the world. Thus this chapter will focus primarily on U.S. production.

Concentration nationwide in crude oil production is very low. Over

---

6   Standard Oil Co. N.J., Socony Mobil Oil, Texaco, Gulf, Standard Oil (Indiana), Standard Oil (Calif.), Shell, Phillips, Sinclair, Cities Service, Continental, Sun, Tidewater, Atlantic Richfield, Union, Standard Oil (Ohio), Sunray, Marathon, Skelly, and British Petroleum.

TABLE 2 CRUDE PRODUCTION BY STATES (1966)

	VALUE OF CRUDE ($ BILLIONS)	PRODUCTION OF CRUDE (MILLIONS OF BARRELS)	NUMBER OF PRODUCING WELLS
Texas	3,141	1,058	196,308
West Texas	1,421		66,910
Gulf Coast	632		19,255
East Coast	138		16,843
Rest of state	951		93,300
Louisiana	2,097	674	31,063
California	813	345	41,348
Oklahoma	654	225	80,583
Wyoming	344	134	8,434
New Mexico	352	124	16,504
Kansas	306	306	46,016
U.S. Total	8,028	3,028	583,302

SOURCE   American Petroleum Institute, *Petroleum Facts and Figures* (1967), pp. 41, 46, and 31.

16,000 firms are involved in oil and gas extraction.[7] The largest eight crude oil firms shipped about 47 per cent of crude output, but these same firms accounted for only 26 per cent of the wells drilled.

As Table 2 shows, concentration is actually considerably higher geographically than it is by ownership. Texas has almost 35.5% of the producing oil wells in the United States, with west Texas having approximately one third of that amount. Other major oil producing states are Louisiana, California, Oklahoma, and Wyoming.

The newly discovered north slope field in Alaska may in the future dominate production, provided the oil can be brought to market cheaply. Being located in a remote area with extreme weather conditions may reduce its commercial feasibility. Geologists have estimated that the Alaskan find contains at least 10 billion barrels, considerably exceeding the 5 billion barrel east Texas found in 1930. The latter was the largest oil field in the United States. Moreover, few large fields are found in isolation. The Cabinet Task Force on Oil Import Controls, established by President Nixon in March 1969, to review the oil import program (hereafter referred to as the Cabinet Task Force), estimated that the Alaskan north slope area contains conservatively 40 billion barrels.

The economic potential of these new finds lies in being able to move the oil cheaply to market. The major companies involved are already committed

7   Bureau of the Census, *1963 Census of Mineral Industries* (Washington, D.C.: U.S. Government Printing Office, 1967), Vol. I, Summary and Industry Statistics, p. 13 A-4.

to building a pipeline, estimated to cost about $900 million, from the north slope to the Gulf of Alaska. Studies are under way on the feasibility of constructing a 2,600-mile pipeline from Puget Sound to Chicago and to the East Coast. Humble Oil took the lead in a $40 million experiment to modify the 115,000 ton tanker, the S.S. Manhattan, to test the feasibility of developing a northwest passage to the deposits. The results of these tests and studies are not yet in but whatever their results, this major find should have a substantial impact on the U.S. oil industry.

Wildcatting or exploration is the search for new oil fields. This search is carried out by the major companies, the independents, and individual wildcatters. All it takes to search for oil is a few thousand dollars, the rights from property owners to drill, and much luck. In 1965, for example, there were 676 wildcat wells of less than 1,250 feet drilled in the United States, but only 25 produced oil and 11 produced gas. The average cost, however, of such wells was less than $7,500.

It is not possible to get accurate information on the proportion of exploratory drilling that is completely independent of the major companies. In 1962, about 20 per cent of all exploratory drilling was done by the 20 largest companies. Although the rest was performed by independents, many of whom are quite large companies, some exploratory drilling is financed by the majors.

The largest companies do most of the exploratory drilling in offshore areas and in remote areas like Alaska. Small independents confine their wildcatting to shallow wells, mostly in the contiguous 48 states. Consequently, the largest companies account for a much larger percentage of the expenditures on exploratory drilling than they do of the number of wells.

Except for Alaska, the major new oil fields have been found in recent years offshore of Louisiana and California. Although oil was first produced in the offshore area of southern Louisiana in 1938, it was not until 1954, when the Federal Government's claim to all resources outside of the three-mile limit was established, that offshore production became an important factor.

As techniques for deep water drilling have developed, the government has offered for sale the right to drill for oil on selected acreage. To the highest bidder goes the privilege of searching for oil. Between 1954 and 1965 over $1 billion was paid in bonuses for the right to drill offshore of Louisiana. Alaska received $900 million in the fall of 1969 on the tracts offered on the north slope area.

Currently, offshore techniques permit drilling in water depths up to 400 feet. The dollar expense of such operations is staggering. Such drilling involves constructing platforms costing $2 or $3 million dollars a piece. To the $1 million in bonus payments for offshore rights must be added about $600 million for the cost of exploratory drilling offshore of Louisiana between 1951 and 1965.

OFFSHORE PRODUCTION   Crude production from offshore wells has been growing rapidly. In the 5 years between 1958 and 1963, crude output from offshore wells tripled but still remained less than 6 per cent of total industry output. Offshore output, though, will become more important in the future. In the last few years, about half of the increase in U.S. reserves has stemmed from offshore output.[8] It is considerably more costly to drill offshore than onshore. The average cost per offshore well was $380,000 in 1963, compared to an average of about $56,000 for all wells. Many onshore wells, however, are shallow with limited output. The average footage drilled for offshore wells was just over 10,000 feet in 1963. For that depth the average cost for all wells was $224,750. Costs rise rapidly with increased depth. From onshore to 100 feet of water capital costs double. They rise another 70 per cent in 400 feet of water.[9] Because of the cost and because leases are auctioned only in large lots, the total number of establishments operating offshore amounted to only 49 in 1963, with 2,708 wells.

ONSHORE PRODUCTION   Well drilling is divided into exploratory drilling or wildcatting and development drilling. In 1966, 1,030 exploratory wells were sunk out of a total of 37,881. Only about 16 per cent of all exploratory wells are successful, and for new field wildcats only about 10 per cent are successful.

Once in operation, wells are generally classified as stripper wells if maximum production is less than 10 barrels per day. In 1965, there were almost 400,000 such wells, which produced an average of about 4 barrels per day. These strippers produce about 20 per cent of the nation's output.

Almost 90 per cent of all oil wells use some type of artificial means of pumping oil to the surface. Sometimes water or gas is pumped down to force oil to the surface. In other cases natural gas is recycled back into the reservoir to maintain pressure.

TRANSPORTATION

Crude oil producers generally sell their oil either to one of the major refiners or to one of the independents. About three quarters of crude oil flows from the field by pipeline to the refinery; the rest moves by tanker, 17 per cent; or trucks, 8 per cent. Pipelines also carry about 27 per cent of all refined petroleum transported in the U.S.; water carriers, 30 per cent; and trucks, 42 per cent. Pipeline concentration is considerably higher in any given market than that of crude oil production, refining, or marketing. Generally the major fields are served by more than one pipline; in the majority of

---

8 *Oil and Gas Journal* **65**:48   **9**   Ibid., p. 49.
(September 18, 1967).

very large fields, three or more pipelines compete. In the east Texas field there are 17 major lines and several smaller ones.[10]

The major pipeline owners are also the major refiners and crude producers. Although nationwide the pipeline of the largest four companies—Standard Oil of New Jersey, Texas Company, Gulf, and Standard of Indiana—carry only 26 per cent of the crude transported by pipelines, these same companies also are deeply involved in joint pipeline ownership with other firms.[11]

Pipelines have been treated in law as common carriers obligated to carry the oil of any independent refinery. As a consequence, pipelines have been regulated since 1906 by the Interstate Commerce Commission. However, the Interstate Commerce Commission up until the 1930's never bothered to investigate pipeline rates. In fact, to this day crude oil pipelines are regulated nominally at best.

The concentration in pipelines is understandable in light of the large economies of scale inherent in pipeline transportation. When the diameter of a pipeline is doubled, the volume of fluid that can be carried increases fourfold, yet the cost per mile of pipeline installation goes up much less. For example, the average cost per mile in recent years for a 6-inch pipe has been $20,000; for a 12-inch pipe, $40,100; and for a 24-inch pipe, $104,700.[12] Per inch of diameter the average cost increases only for pipes bigger than 16 inches. Moreover, there is less friction per unit volume of oil flowing through the pipeline, hence operating costs decline with size. Given these large economies of scale, therefore, the most efficient organization for the industry is a few large pipelines serving each major oil field.

Almost all pipelines constructed in recent years have been owned by integrated oil companies either outright or as joint ventures. But because of the increased number of pipelines serving each area, pipeline transportation has become readily available to even small independent refiners.

PETROLEUM REFINING

Concentration in petroleum refining is somewhat higher than that in crude oil production. In 1966, the four largest petroleum refining companies controlled 32 per cent of the output of refining and the largest eight controlled 57 per cent.[13] On January 1, 1968, 145 petroleum refining companies controlled 269 refineries. The 20 largest had 119 of the refineries with 83 per

---

10   Wallace T. Lovejoy and Paul T. Homan, *Economic Aspects of Oil Conservation Regulation* (Baltimore: Johns Hopkins Press, 1967), p. 245.

11   Interstate Commerce Commission, *Transportation Statistics in the United* *States*, Part 6, Oil Pipe Lines (Washington, D.C.: 1965).

12   *Oil and Gas Journal*, **66**:104 (July 29, 1968).

13   U.S. Bureau of the Census Annual Survey of Manufacturers by Industry, *Value-of-Shipment Concentration Ratios* (Washington, D.C.: 1968).

cent of capacity.[14] Most of the small independents sell their gasoline or refined products to independent service stations.

In contrast to crude production, entry into refining takes little luck but much capital. Although exact estimates are not possible, it has been estimated that the cost of entering the refining industry was $225 million in 1951.[15] Refineries can be built for $100 million or less today, but entry is still expensive. Moreover supplies of crude must be guaranteed either through pipeline construction or access to tankers.

Even though an efficient size plant is large absolutely, it is not large compared to the industry size. Bain estimated that the minimum efficient size in petroleum refining was only $1\frac{3}{4}$ per cent of the industry output and that there are no efficiencies involved in multiplant operations.

CRUDE OIL MARKETS

Modern refineries need a continuing supply of crude oil. It is also important that the quality of the oil be homogeneous. Oil comes in different qualities. Some crudes are called sweet and others sour, depending upon the admixture of sulfur; their specific gravity can vary considerably; impurities such as minerals in the oil affect the quality and the potential end use of the oil.

On the other hand, many producers are small and have a small storage capacity. As a consequence, they need a continuous outlet for their crude.

The major refining-marketing companies have field buying organizations that purchase crude on division orders from the individual producers. The oil is purchased at the wellhead rather than at the refinery. The shipper, that is the field buying organization, combines the small production of numerous producers into a big batch of oil of similar quality. Approximately 90 per cent of the crude oil transported by pipeline comes through pipelines owned by major marketing and refining companies. The independent refiners secure their crude through the field buying organizations of the major companies who charge the independent refiners for the service. The oil is then transported through pipelines, by tank cars, or by water carriers to the refinery.

The division order is an agreement between the producers and the buyer, establishing how prices are to be set and how the settlement is to be made between royalty owners. The prices to be paid are normally the posted prices of the buying company itself. Sometimes they may be the posted prices of some other specific company or the highest posted prices in the area. These posted prices are in effect offers to buy by the major companies. Once the oil is purchased, sales are made at different points in the pipeline to independent refiners or other majors.

---

14 *Oil and Gas Journal,* **66**:126 (April 1, 1968).

15 J. S. Bain, *Barriers to New Competition* (Cambridge, Mass.: Harvard University Press, 1956), p. 159.

REFINED PRODUCTS MARKETING

The refinery market is being increasingly dominated by the major companies. The Justice Department has estimated that less than 10 per cent of crude oil refining is done currently by nonintegrated refineries.[16] Refined products are normally shipped by pipeline or tanker to a refiner's product terminal. At this point the products of different major companies, even though they may differ somewhat chemically, are substantially fungible for heating or for automobiles. When gasoline leaves the product terminal, additives are usually added which supposedly distinguish one brand from another. Fuel oil, on the other hand, remains essentially homogeneous.

A large share of the refiner's product is sold to independent marketing firms called jobbers. The rest is marketed directly by the refining companies at "tank wagon prices" to its own retail outlets. The jobbing firms pick up fuel or gasoline by truck, barge, or tank car and transports it to area bulk stations. They then sell gasoline at "tank wagon" prices to filling stations.

Although a substantial portion of a jobber's business is at wholesale, most jobbers operate at the retail level as well. There are two types of jobbers. One handles brand-name gasoline products of the refiner and supplies brand-name filling stations. The other buys gasoline on specification and markets the product as off-brand or no-brand gasoline. Although there are many fewer private-brand jobbers than brand-name jobbers, they are of vital importance in the industry. Most price wars, and, in fact, most price competition stem from the competitive efforts of private-brand jobbers.

Name-brand jobbers are constrained to operate within narrow established margins. The refiner usually suggests the expected retail price as well as the price to the jobber. On the other hand, private-brand jobbers have more leeway to reduce prices and initiate competition.

MARKETING SHARES

In gasoline marketing the largest company in the United States, Texaco, had $8\frac{1}{2}$ per cent of the market in 1966.[17] The largest four companies had 32 per cent of the market. However, gasoline is marketed regionally and, as Table 3 shows, on a regional level concentration increases considerably. The most concentrated market in the United States is the Middle Atlantic area consisting of New York, Pennsylvania, Maryland, Delaware, New Jersey, and West Virginia in which Jersey Standard was the largest company

---

16   Report of the Attorney General pursuant to Section 2 of the Joint Resolution of September 6, 1963, Consenting to an Interstate Compact to Conserve Oil and Gas, July 1967 in *Hearings before the Subcommittee on* *Communications and Power*, House of Representatives, 90th Congress, 1st Session, April 18, 1967.
   17   *Oil and Gas Journal*, **65**:56 (February 6, 1967).

TABLE 3 PERCENTAGE OF SALES, SECOND QUARTER, 1966, TOP TEN PRODUCERS IN NINE REGIONS

	PER CENT OF U.S.	NEW ENGLAND	MIDDLE ATLANTIC	SOUTH ATLANTIC	MIDWEST	NORTH CENTRAL	SOUTH CENTRAL	ROCKY MOUNTAIN	SOUTH-WEST	WEST COAST
Texaco	8.5	11.2	7.9	9.6	5.6	5.1	8.0	13.2	15.9	8.5
Shell	8.0	10.9	6.0	7.8	9.7	2.3	5.3	4.9	4.6	15.8
Jersey Standard	7.8	10.6	17.7	13.0			5.4	11.7	14.0	
Indiana Standard	7.6	4.0	6.5	7.4	13.8	14.9	6.3		10.1	3.5
Gulf	7.2	9.4	10.0	12.5	5.6		7.3	3.9	7.0	8.1
Mobil	6.4	13.0	9.8		5.5	7.6	4.0	9.5	5.2	22.5
Socal	4.9			5.4						
Sinclair	3.8		5.0	5.4	4.5	2.9	3.9	4.5	4.4	
Phillips	3.4			5.0		8.1	6.1	8.9	5.3	9.3
Atlantic Richfield	3.3	5.8								
Union (Pure)	3.2		8.0	5.5	3.6					9.6
Sun	3.0	6.6	8.6		4.4					
Cities	2.3	6.2	3.2	2.6		2.4				
Continental	2.1					4.7	4.4	11.9	5.1	
Tidewater	1.9	8.4			7.7					7.1
Sohio					4.05					
Marathon										
Skelly						4.5				
DX Sunray						3.5	3.6			
Frontier								4.32		
Tenneco								2.5		
Petrofina									2.8	
Signal										3.2
Continental (Douglas)										2.1
Total for top ten	73.5	86.2	82.4	74.1	64.2	55.8	54.2	75.4	74.1	86.7

SOURCE *Oil and Gas Journal*, **65**:56 (February 6, 1967).

127

with almost 18 per cent of the market and the largest four firms had 46 per cent of the market. Four-firm concentration within the states varies from a little under 50 per cent to about 35 per cent.[18]

Since World War II, independent gasoline companies, receiving their refined petroleum from either independent refiners or as surplus from major companies, have increased their share of the market. Competition in retailing has grown considerably. However, in the last few years the share of the market held by the major companies seems to have stabilized.

VERTICAL INTEGRATION

In summary then the major companies are integrated from crude production to marketing the final product. Generally, they supply most but not all of the crude they need. Either individually or in joint ventures they control the pipelines through which almost all the crude oil flows. They substantially dominate the refinery business; the largest 20 companies have 83 per cent of the capacity. They market most but not all of the refined products they produce.

Nevertheless, the independents are important factors in the industry. With the largest four firms controlling less than a third of the refinery capacity, the petroleum industry is far from one of the more concentrated industries in the United States. Yet with their huge size and by being vertically integrated from exploration and development to refining and marketing, the majors are in a position to dominate the industry and perhaps to control it.

III. CONDUCT

Almost from the beginning the oil industry was faced with the law of capture: he who pumped oil from the ground kept it. From the point of view of economic efficiency, conservation, or technological efficiency the law of capture is disastrous. A producer who may desire to pump oil slowly from the ground either because he expects its value to increase with time or because the more slowly the oil is removed, the greater the total that can be recovered, will lose oil to others by pumping slow. Oil not taken today may be lost to a neighbor. Consequently, oil producers are compelled to pump oil from the ground as rapidly as possible.

This is not only economically wasteful, but it is technically wasteful. The faster oil is removed from the ground, the less oil can be recovered from a given pool. This is due in part to the wasteful use of gas under pressure, which forces the oil up. In addition, the efficient exploitation of a given oil pool will

---

18   Ibid., p. 58.

usually mean a relatively small number of wells producing oil and possibly a well to pump air down to increase pressure. If a number of individuals own the land above the oil pool, it is often difficult to secure agreement on such practices.

Even if the rule of capture did not lead to a reduction in the potential output from a given oil field as a result of its rapid exploitation, it would lead to an uneconomic use of resources in the oil industry. Oil, like most other natural resources, is a scarce commodity. It is valuable to society. But the result of uncontrolled oil well production is that the value of oil in the ground is driven to zero. This startling result becomes clear when one considers that each potential oil well owner will continue to sink wells as long as the expected revenue from the next well is greater than the cost. With a fixed stock of oil in the pool, the more wells drilled, the less the average amount of oil for each well, and hence the less the average per well. Thus as each producer sinks wells, output per well falls and with it, average revenue. Thus average revenue of the oil will tend to equal average cost of drilling and operating the wells, including a return to capital, with the result that the value of crude in the ground at that point is zero—obviously an extremely wasteful economic practice.

If oil pools were managed as a unit, these inefficiencies would not arise. There would be no temptation, then, to pump oil too fast nor would it be profitable in an unregulated market to sink excessive wells. Unitization would therefore not only increase the potential output of any given field, but would maximize the value of a scarce resource—crude oil.

Notwithstanding the benefits from unitization, it is often difficult to achieve. For example, from the beginning exploration and development of the giant Fairway Field in east Texas was carried out in such a way as to facilitate unitization. The chief reservoir engineer estimated that unitization might increase ultimate recovery from 70 million barrels to about 200 million. Yet it took 5 years and a cut in allowable production by the Texas Railroad Commission from 12,000 barrels daily to 2,000 before the more than 150 owners would agree to a plan for unitization.[19]

Although the industry has long been aware that such unitization would improve efficiency, the individual nature of most production and the wildcat aspects of the industry prevented unitization or other concerted methods of dealing with the problem. However, the economic situation of the oil industry became disastrous in the early 1930's when, in the face of declining demand from the depression, the great east Texas oil pool was discovered. Oil flooded the market. Crude oil prices plummeted to 10 cents per barrel; producers abandoned their property in the face of bankruptcies. In desperation the states, producing organizations, and the Federal Government attempted to

---

19 W. F. Lovejoy and P. T. Homan, *Economic Aspects of Oil Conservation* *and Regulation* (Washington, D.C.: Resources for the Future, 1967), p. 81.

stabilize production. The outcome was the prorationing system bolstered by the Connally "Hot Oil" Act which prohibited the interstate shipment of oil produced in violation of state statutes.

Basically prorationing is state control over crude output in accordance with estimated demand. The process starts with the Bureau of Mines' monthly estimate of next month's demand for petroleum. These estimates are based on final consumption of oil, on existing stocks, and on desired stocks. Of course, such estimates are made on the assumption that prices remain constant. No estimates have been made on what consumption would be at different price levels.

Texas, Louisiana, Oklahoma, New Mexico, and Kansas, major producing states, are "market-demand states." In each of these states regulatory commissions establish the amount of oil that can be produced and sold at current prices. In making their decisions, each of the regulatory commissions receives the Bureau of Mines' forecast. In addition, the major oil companies furnish the regulatory commissions with estimates of their need for crude petroleum. Although these estimates are not binding on the oil companies, there is considerable pressure to ensure that they are lived up to. Each of the market-demand states also considers existing and desired stocks of oil.

Having determined total output, the regulatory commissions allocate the total among wells. Within each market-demand state there are prorated pools and wells and exempt wells. The exempt wells include discovery wells, statutory marginal wells, and other stripper wells. The discovery wells are new and are exempted temporarily, partly as an incentive to finding new wells and partly in order to determine the size and capacity of the field for later prorationing purposes.

Statutory marginal wells are defined as wells with limited output. For example, a well with a depth of under 2,000 feet and a daily maximum production of 10 barrels would be defined as a marginal well in Texas. If the well was between 6,000 and 8,000 feet, its maximum would be 30 barrels per day.[20] Other stripper wells include relatively old pools and wells tapping small and shallow pools. Some of these stripper wells are in the secondary recovery stage in which water flooding is taking place.

Production of exempt wells has declined from $43\frac{1}{2}$ per cent of Texas output in 1963, to about 32 per cent in 1967, caused primarily by increased total demand, by a less liberal attitude towards drilling marginal wells, and by more unitization. Almost 90 per cent of the exempt output in recent years in Texas has come from marginal wells, which are normally the most expensive type.

---

20   Lovejoy and Homan, op. cit., p. 154.

The state regulatory commission, having determined the appropriate state output in light of current price, subtracts expected exempt output from the total. The rest is prorated among remaining wells. For the prorated wells the state regulatory commission has determined a yardstick or allowable from a schedule, which depends both on the depth of the well and the spacing of wells over any pool. The deeper the well, the greater the allowable. Offshore yardsticks average 1.7 times land allowables.[21] The more closely spaced the wells the less the allowable per well. All market-demand states have established minimum spacing requirements. For example, in Texas the wells in a pool less than 1,000 feet deep with 10 acres per well would receive a yardstick of 21 barrels per day.[22] If the spacing of the wells were on the basis of 20 acres, yardsticks would increase to 39 barrels per day for the 1,000-foot well and 96 barrels per day for the 10,000 foot well.[23]

Having determined the yardstick for each well, the state regulatory commission can then simply set the percentage of the yardstick that the well is permitted to produce during the month. For example, the Texas market-demand factor in December, 1968, was 41.3 per cent, which meant that the prorated wells during that month were allowed to produce 41.3 per cent of their monthly total allowable. This market-demand factor fell slowly during the 1960's prior to the Vietnamese War as exempted wells increased their proportion of total output. With the war and especially with the closing of Suez Canal in June 1967, demand increased. In May 1967, the market-demand factor in Texas was 33.8 per cent; by August it had reached 54 per cent. Although it has fluctuated since, the market-demand factor reached a record of 87 per cent in October 1970.

IMPORTS

Partly as a result of a prorationing, which maintains prices, and partly as a result of discoveries of vast amounts of oil in the Middle East and Venezuela, United States changed from the exportation of crude oil to a net importing country after World War II. Oil imports rose steadily throughout the postwar period with the exception of brief periods in the Korean War and during the first Suez Crisis. By the end of 1956, imports were threatening the stability and the very existence of the prorationing system. As imports took a larger and larger proportion of the domestic market, the regulatory commissions had to restrict output further and further, in order to maintain prices. Therefore on February 26, 1957, President Eisenhower announced "voluntary" quotas on oil imports. These voluntary quotas worked only moderately well to hold down imports, and in March 1959, the President established mandatory quotas ostensibly to preserve the domestic industry

---

21 *Oil and Gas Journal*, **65**:48 (September 18, 1967).

22 Lovejoy and Homan, op. cit., p. 145.

23 Ibid., p. 145.

for national defense reasons. Since that time there have been strict quotas with a few exceptions on imports of crude oil into the United States.

For the purpose of imports the United States is divided into two areas, Districts I–IV and District V. District V consists of Alaska, Arizona, California, Hawaii, Nevada, Oregon, and Washington. Separate allocations are made for both areas. For Districts I–IV the allocation is 12.2 per cent of the estimated U.S. production of crude oil and natural gas liquids during the ensuing year; for District V, it consists of the difference between supply and demand, or 322,000 barrels per day in 1968.[24]

Refined petroleum products are treated separately from crude. Finished products such as gasoline, home heating oil, jet fuel, lubricating oils, and asphalt are permitted to be imported by historical importers in proportion to the level of 1957 imports. They represent only about 3 per cent of total imports and their total is subtracted from the permitted crude imports.

Residual fuel oil, which is used mainly by power plants and in large industrial and commercial boilers, is in the main free from import control.

From the total allowed imports are subtracted the estimated Canadian and Mexican imports to derive the licensed crude imports. Canadian imports have informally been limited in recent years and mandatory quotas were imposed in the spring of 1970. In addition, an allocation is set aside for petrochemical imports. For example, in the second half of 1968, total U.S. production was expected to be about 9,028,000 barrels per day. Imports for Districts I–IV were 12.2 per cent of this or 1,101,000 barrels per day. With Canadian and Mexican imports into Districts I–IV estimated at 310,000 barrels and with 79,000 barrels per day for petrochemical allocation—plus other minor set asides—there were 565,000 barrels divided up among refineries.[25]

Under the voluntary import restrictions, the allocation of the quotas among companies was on an historical basis. The Department of Interior has been phasing out that system and basing quotas on refinery capacity. The formula for 1969 is shown in Table 4.

These import allocations have been very valuable. During most of the 1960's, crude oil could be landed on the East Coast at about $1.25 per barrel less than the cost of U.S. oil. On the West Coast, because of higher transportation rates, the value of an import license was about 80 cents per barrel.

The actual difference between imported oil and domestic oil depends on tanker rates and the price of crude in Venezuela and in the Persian Gulf. With skyrocketing tanker rates that difference diminished considerably right after the June 1967, Middle East war, which closed the Suez Canal. Since then the rates have fallen as the market adjusted but trouble in the Middle East in 1970 raised tanker rates again.

---

24 Department of Interior Oil
Import Administration, News Release,
July 9, 1968.

25 Ibid.

TABLE 4 IMPORT FORMULA 1969

AVERAGE BARRELS PER DAY INPUT OF REFINER	PER CENT OF INPUT IMPORTED	
	DISTRICTS I–IV	DISTRICT V
0–10,000	19.5	40.0
10–30,000	11.0	9.3
30–100,000	7.0	4.1
100,000 plus	3.0	1.9

SOURCE   Cabinet Task Force on Oil Import Control, *The Oil Import Question* (Washington, D.C.: U.S. Government Printing Office, February 1970), p. 12.

Although quota holders are not permitted to sell their quotas, trades between imported and domestic oil are possible and are widely used by inland refineries. Oil landed on the East Coast is traded for oil located near an inland refinery with a premium paid for the imports.

The import program clearly favors the small refiner. Many small refiners survive only on the profits from their quotas. But this bias in favor of small refiners encourages the uneconomic survival and entry of small firms.

Notwithstanding the bias in favor of small refiners, the large companies also benefit. Standard Oil of New Jersey received a crude import allocation that resulted in a windfall gain of about $14 million in 1968, which although small relative to Standard's operations is still pure profit. Recent quota allocations for the largest companies are given in Table 5. Based on a value of $1.25 for Districts I–IV and 80 cents for District V and annualizing the results, Table 5 also shows the windfall gain to the recipients.

TAX TREATMENT

To encourage oil exploration and because oil production leads to a diminishing asset, the oil industry receives special tax treatment. Basically the difference between the taxation of oil and gas well operators and businesses in other fields lies in the provision that certain capital costs may be deducted immediately rather than being deducted over the life of the assets, and second, that the annual deduction for depletion is related to income and not to the cost of the assets.

Intangible drilling costs, except for the cost of depreciable property used in drilling, are deductible whether the oil well is dry or producing. Lease rentals are deductible at the time they occur. Generally, exploration studies are also deductible at the time they are incurred. Other capital costs must be depreciated as in other businesses. Lease acquisition costs and exploration expenses on nonproductive properties are capitalized and charged off only

TABLE 5 IMPORT QUOTAS FOR SECOND HALF OF
1968 (BARRELS PER DAY)

	DISTRICTS		TOTAL QUOTAS	ANNUAL WINDFALL[a] ($ MILLIONS)
	I–IV	V		
Gulf Oil Corporation	42,795	7,323	50,118	21.7
Standard Oil California	25,605	16,137	41,742	16.4
Mobil Oil Corporation	27,225	9,488	36,713	15.2
Standard Oil N.J.	30,639	—	30,639	14.0
Atlantic Richfield	22,590	11,340	33.930	13.6
Shell	20,789	11,208	31,997	12.8
Standard Oil Indiana	26,407	—	26,407	12.0
Sinclair	23,850	—	23,850	10.9
Phillips	14,099	10,118	24,217	9.4
Union Oil Company	11,035	11,774	22,809	8.5
Total all U.S.	560,193	153,066	713,259	300.3

a Computed on the basis of $1.25 per barrel for Districts
I–IV and 80 cents per barrel for District V. The calculation
assumes that the companies receive the same quotas for the entire
year.

SOURCE Department of Interior, Oil Import Administration,
News Release, July 9, 1968.

when the property is abandoned. The cost of drilling equipment is capitalized
and taken as annual depreciation. Exploration costs and lease acquisition
costs on productive property are capitalized and taken as a cost depletion.

Oil well owners are permitted to deduct each year the greater of cost
depletion minus the amount taken as depletion in previous years or percentage depletion. Cost depletion is computed by adding the capitalized cost of
the property to the lease acquisition cost, including any exploration costs,
and taking a portion each year equivalent to the ratio of oil extracted to the
estimated recoverable reserves of the property. Percentage depletion is
computed as the lesser of 22 per cent of the gross value of the oil at the
wellhead or 50 per cent of the net income from the property.[26] Normally
percentage depletion is considerably greater than cost depletion except on a
property that was purchased after it began to produce.

An example may clarify the tax benefits (see table, facing page). With
lifetime earnings of $4 million, percentage depletion would be $880,000.
The producers' costs (not discounting), therefore, would be $750,000
($550,000 for sinking 11 wells and $200,000 for lifting costs). His net
income would then be $3,250,000, which would be subject to tax in other

---

26 Prior to 1970, the percentage
depletion was the lesser of 27½ of the

gross value or 50 per cent of the net
income.

industries. However, his taxable income in this case would be only $2,395,000 ($4,000,000 minus $880,000 depletion and minus $725,000 for deductible costs). Almost a million dollars would be tax-free income.

ITEM	TOTAL COST ($)	TAX TREATMENT ($)
10 dry wells @ $50,000 each with $35,000 intangible cost	500,000	350,000 deduct currently 150,000 to be depreciated
1 successful well	50,000	25,000 intangibles deduct currently 25,000 caplitalized and taken as cost depletion
Lifting costs over well lifetime	200,000	200,000 deduct

This calculation does not present all the advantages of the tax laws. Note that $375,000 of capital costs can be deducted immediately. The ability to write off in 1 year a substantial part of capital costs is a major advantage, compared to investment in other industries.

CRUDE OIL PRICES

The crude-oil-buying firm is normally also a major producer. As such, it is in its interest, because of the tax laws, to divert part of its bookkeeping profits from refinery operations to crude oil production. But not all the oil the majors purchase comes from their own wells. So higher crude prices increase their costs. As a consequence, the companies are limited in the extent to which they can post high prices by the competition of other companies at the retail level. If a major's posted prices are excessive, it will find that independent refiners will secure their oil elsewhere. In the long run the buyer must ensure that his prices are adequate or he will be unable to secure new suppliers in any area. But such prices cannot be too high or he will find himself with excess supplies of oil that he cannot efficiently market.

In addition, there are small buyers in each of the markets ready to buy at above or below posted prices, depending upon supply conditions. If supply is greater than that which buyers want at posted prices, the small buyer can buy at significant discounts. Discounts of up to 50 cents per barrel from posted prices have been reported. On the other hand, when the market is tight the small buyer must often pay a premium of 10 to 25 cents to secure crude oil.[27] But since the small buyer must usually rely on the major companies for transportation, his competitive position is not strong.

---

27 *A Study of Conservation of Oil and Gas in the United States* (Oklahoma City, Okla.: Interstate Oil Compact Commission, 1964).

The major companies secure only about two thirds of their necessary supplies from their own production. In addition, buying extensive amounts of oil for independents is profitable since the pipeline investments and operating costs may be spread over a larger base. Moreover, state prorationing requires that a company take a proportionate amount of oil from nonowned wells in the same reservoir.

The efficiency of the market is also considerably enhanced by the integration of crude oil pipelines. Since World War II, major pipelines have been increasingly tied together in an intricate network. Oil flows are regulated by computer operations to minimize costs and to ensure the continuous flow of the appropriate quality of crude to the right refinery. The efficiency of this system is also enhanced by swap agreements. When crude oil in one area is needed more than in some other areas, swap agreements can be arranged. If a refinery has too great a supply of one quality of crude and not enough of another quality, trades can be and are made. Trades are also made over time. In other words, oil may be provided to one refinery at one time with an agreement that a quantity of oil will be provided to the supplier at some future time in exchange.

In fact, even for the most integrated companies, much of the oil refined is acquired from other companies. Although an integrated company may produce or buy the volume it refines, it rarely supplies its actual entire needs. As the oil moves in pipelines, it is traded among integrated companies, each seeking to maximize the particular types of crude which its refiners can most efficiently process.

REFINED PRODUCTS PRICING

In setting the prices of refined petroleum the large integrated companies would prefer not to engage in price competition. Consumers tend to believe there is little difference between different types of branded gasoline, so the elasticity of demand for any one gasoline is quite high. On the other hand, the overall demand for gasoline is generally believed to be inelastic. Thus price reductions by one producer will lead to immediate imitation by other producers and lower revenues for all with only modest increases in sales.

The result is typical of a cartel-like market. Prices are established by the major at profitable levels. The most efficient company sets the price that will maximize its profits, and other firms conform. Additional sales at the established price mean additional profits with the result that the major companies compete through advertising, credit cards, and trading stamps and games. Since the major's price is above average costs, new firms seek to enter the industry. Independents arise and attempt to secure part of the market through cut-rate stations.

The effect of these activities is to increase average costs. Advertising expenditures alone cost the industry about $250 million a year, and the largest firms account for almost all of this sum. In effect, then, this cartel arrangement deprives the consumer of lower prices without providing the major companies with the expected profits, since much of the profits are eaten up by nonprice competition. Indeed, profit rates for the industry are close to those earned in all manufacturing. For example, in the first quarter of 1968, the annual profit rate on stockholders equity before taxes was 15 per cent for petroleum refining and 19.4 per cent for all manufacturing. On an after tax basis, because of the tax benefits, the industry rate was 12.9 per cent, a little higher than the 11.5 per cent earned in all manufacturing.

Private-brand jobbers not only purchase at published prices from the refiners, but are often in a position to buy gasoline at "distress" prices. Marginal costs for operating the refinery up to capacity are below average costs. Operating costs are very small and fixed cost can be spread over a larger volume when operating near capacity. Moreover, the refining industry has often operated with considerable excess capacity. Capacity in excess of production has varied in recent years from 20 per cent in 1961 to 10 per cent in 1967. In addition, the more domestic crude oil processed by a refinery, the larger the import quota for the refining company. In total the incentives to operate a refinery near capacity and dispose of the product in the best way possible are large. Refiners often try to market such distress gasoline in areas where they are not strongly represented at the retail level.

With cheaper gasoline, independent jobbers are in a position to reduce prices to their retail outlets. Although nonbranded gasoline normally sells for around 2 cents per gallon less than branded, the differential can widen when the independent jobber has sufficient quantities of distress gasoline. A wider differential, however, will often force the major companies into lowering prices. Notwithstanding the fact that most gasolines at retail are essentially fungible products, consumers will buy the more expensive-branded gasoline at a differential of 1 to 2 cents. However, at larger differentials sufficient consumers switch to make it important to the major company to respond.

One recent response to the growth of independent gasolines has been the introduction of subregular by several major companies. These subregular gasolines are designed to sell for about 1 cent less a gallon than regular and about 1 cent more than independent prices.

In some cases though, the majors must reduce their retail prices across the board in response to competition. The burden of lower prices is normally shared by the supplier and the retailer until a minimum profit margin is reached for the retailer. Up to this "down stop" point the major bears 70–80 per cent of the reduction in prices and the station owner the rest. Independent refiners normally bear about 60 to 70 per cent down to the "down stop."[28] When a major or large independent reduces its price to meet

---

28 Federal Trade Commission, *Report on Anticompetitive Practices in* *the Marketing of Gasoline* (Federal Trade Commission, n.d.), p. 20.

the competition of nonbranded gasoline, other majors usually follow suit and a price war develops. Price wars normally last only as long as refiners are willing to continue to offer pricing assistance.

Such price wars often lead to complaints of unfair practices and unfair competition by independent refiners or filling station operators. A good example of this occurred in 1955 in Jacksonville, Florida. An independent cut-rate station, Super Test Oil, opened across the street from a Sunoco station, operated by Gilbert McLean. At this time the McLean station bought its oil from Sun at 24.1 cents per gallon and resold it at 28.9 cents. The Super Test station sold "regular" at 26.9 cents. At the margin of 2 cents the Sunoco station could survive. When the independent operator reduced his prices further, McLean secured a price concession of 1.7 cents per gallon from Sun Oil and lowered its price to 25.9 cents, 1 cent more than Super Test. McLean thus absorbed 1.3 cents to give him a gross margin of 3.5 cents—the minimum Sun believed should be earned by its dealers. Super Test followed by reducing its price to 23.9 cents. Two months later Super Test reduced its price to 22.9 cents. About this time the price war became general throughout the Jacksonville areas as other refiners made price concessions to their dealers. Before the price concession became general other Sunoco stations within a radius of $3\frac{1}{2}$ miles complained of a loss of customers to the McLean station. The Federal Trade Commission accused Sun Oil of illegal price discrimination and injuring competition. Sun Oil argued that it was meeting in good faith the lower prices of a competitor. However, in ruling on the case the Supreme Court held that the competitor to Sun would be the supplier to Super Test. Since there was no evidence that this supplier had lowered its prices, the Supreme Court upheld the Federal Trade Commission.[29]

IV. PERFORMANCE

The effects of prorationing, import quotas, and tax advantages are mutually reinforcing and work to maintain prices. Although not explicitly designed to do so, each policy helps to maintain a cartel-like arrangement.

RESULTS OF PRORATIONING   The objective of the state regulatory commissions is to ensure an "orderly market." That is, supply is to be kept in check so that prices do not fall. Each regulatory commission carefully considers the oil its state can produce without causing a price reduction. In effect then the regulatory commissions assure prices higher than would exist in a free market. Without regulatory restraint each producer would increase production as long as the price for crude exceeded the additional cost of produc-

---

[29] *FTC* v. *Sun Oil Company*, 371 U.S. 505.

ing it. Thus considerably more output would be forthcoming, at least from the efficient wells that are prorationed. With the higher output prices would decline. This would result in marginal wells being shut down and abandoned as crude prices fell below their operating costs. A new balance would eventually be reached with lower prices, higher output from the efficient currently prorationed wells, reduced output from marginal facilities, and somewhat increased consumption caused by lower prices. Thus fewer wells would be producing more output. Neither the major companies nor the small producers are enthusiastic about a free market since prices would be lower and many small producers would be forced out of the business.

Each well owner including the majors would like to increase their own production to earn greater profits. To ensure that the buyers of crude do not satisfy their needs mainly from their own wells, the commissions require that buyers take a proportional output from all wells in a field. Thus the benefits of the maintained prices are spread to all producers and cannot be cornered by the "majors."

The method of allocating oil production output among wells tends to foster gross inefficiencies. Since each well receives a quota subtracted from the output of other wells, prorationing encourages the drilling of excess wells. A few years ago the Texas Railroad Commission which regulates oil output in that state was urged to close down seven-eighths of the wells in the east Texas field and produce the same output with the remaining wells.[30] Although profits would obviously be increased, the Texas Railroad Commission ruled against the proposal on the grounds that it would have an unfavorable impact on employment and earnings in many communities.

The exempt wells are mostly, but not all, high-cost wells, yet they are allowed to produce unlimited amounts. The most efficient wells are restricted in order to permit the high-cost wells to produce and to ensure price stability.

Since allowable output of a well depends in part on the depth of the well, there is an incentive for producers to drill deeper wells rather than shallower wells. Again, deeper wells are more expensive. The cost of a well rises at an increasing rate; although in 1964 it cost less than $9 per foot for wells less than 5,000 feet deep, it cost $18.34 per foot for wells between 7,000 and 10,000 and over $43 per foot for wells deeper than 15,000.[31] Moreover, since allowables are greater for offshore wells, prorationing encourages the drilling of these more expensive units.

In other words, the prorationing system encourages the expansion of the number of wells since each well gets an allocation which is subtracted from other wells. It encourages the production from the most costly wells—the strippers, the deep wells, and those offshore. State commissions that regulate

---

30 Lovejoy and Homan, op. cit., p. 121.

31 *Petroleum Facts and Figures,* op. cit., p. 29.

prorationing are increasingly recognizing this problem and restricting the drilling of unnecessary wells.

As Table 2 illustrates, Texas is the primary producing state in the nation. As such it is pivotal in maintaining prices and, in fact, acts as the supplementary oil producer. Given the output of crude from other states, Texas then sets its production such that prices remain stable. Naturally this has led, over a period of time, to a gradual expansion of the output of other states and a reduction in Texas' share.

Like any cartel which distributes production on the basis of capacity, prorationing encourages the sinking of excessive numbers of wells and the production from inefficient producers. Basically the chief beneficiaries have been the small inefficient producers who own a substantial part of the stripper production. But there is something in the system for all producers.

The large integrated companies, which own a major share of all crude production, have little or no incentive to attempt to secure lower prices. The higher the price of crude oil relative to the price of the final product, the greater the tax advantage that will accrue to the oil companies. Since the crude oil producer can take 22 per cent of his gross revenue as a depletion deduction, it is in the interest of the oil companies to maintain high crude prices. Independent refiners, which are generally small, do not have the leverage to secure lower crude prices. Since the majors benefit from higher prices, the usual competitive pressures from buyers for lower prices are reduced.

RESULTS OF IMPORT QUOTAS

Without oil import quotas, foreign oil would destroy the prorationing system and produce lower prices. Although major oil companies control substantial amounts of foreign oil, it is still in their interest to maintain oil import restrictions. Without such restrictions foreign oil would enter the United States at approximately the cost of production plus shipping, or about $1.25 a barrel less than the current domestic price. The U.S. prices would decline to the world level and importers would earn only a competitive profit on crude. With oil import restrictions those companies that secure quotas reap the windfall profit described above. Since oil imports are based on refinery capacity, the major companies receive most of the import quotas. As a consequence, they have no desire to free imports.

RESULTS OF TAX TREATMENT

The tax advantages are extremely costly to other taxpayers. The treasury estimated that had the depletion allowance been removed on all minerals completely in 1968, taxes collected would have risen by $1½ billion (most of the increase would come from oil and gas). Had percentage depletion never been instituted, tax payments would have been about $1.3 billion higher.

If capitalization of exploration and development expenses had been required, the increase in taxation in 1968 would have been about $750,000; but in the future the increase in tax receipts would have been only $300,000 as depreciation would be substituted.

The effect of percentage depletion is to increase the profitability from oil production. But does it encourage exploration? The major benefit from the tax advantage arises when oil is being produced. The depletion allowance therefore works toward encouraging more exploratory drilling as well as wildcatting. But the depletion allowance and other tax advantages do not appear to have increased reserves. The ratio of proved reserves to annual production, the Life Index, has been steady for decades. The Life Index was 12.7 years in the 1920's, 13.8 years in the 1930's, and 12.5 in 1946–1962.[32] By 1966 the ratio had declined to 11.0. Although it is possible that the ratio might have declined further in the absence of tax benefits, it is clear that it has not increased reserves relative to production. However, the ratio of capacity to reserves has grown fairly steadily, as can be seen in Table 6.

It is obvious that the tax advantage must have affected reserves. Any such tax advantage could be converted to an equivalent price increase which would give producers the same net revenue. With the present price of crude oil at about $3.00 per barrel the depletion allowance is the equivalent to the producer of about a 75 cent rise in the receipts per barrel. The effect of allowing an immediate write off for intangible capital expenses depends on interest rates and the period over which such intangibles would have to be spread. But since the present value of a sum spread over 20 years at 8 per cent interest is less than half the value of the original sum taken in the first year, the effect of this provision must be substantial. Moreover, over two thirds of the expense of oil well drilling consists of intangibles.[33] For an average well that cost about $50,000 to sink, about $35,000 would be intangible expense and deductible. Thus the gain on average from this provision must be about $17,500 per well or, for an average producer of about 14.2 barrels per day (1966), the equivalent of about a 50 cents per barrel rise in the price of oil.

In other words, for oil producers to receive the same net income without

TABLE 6   PER CENT CAPACITY OF RESERVES
AS OF JANUARY 1 FOR
SELECTED YEARS

1951	1953	1957	1960	1963	1967
9.7	9.7	11.8	12.2	11.8	12.8

SOURCE   A. E. Kahn, *American Economic Review.* **54**:302 (June 1964); *Petroleum Facts and Figures* (1967).

32 A. E. Kahn, "Depletion Allowance in the Context of Cartelization," *American Economic Review*, **54**:304 (June 1964).

33 *Petroleum Facts and Figures*, op. cit., p. 29.

these tax advantages, the price per barrel of oil would have to go up about $1.25, which means about 3 cents per gallon if spread equally over all refined products.

There have been several studies of the responsiveness of oil supplies to price changes. Franklin Fisher found that a 1 per cent increase in the price of crude at the wellhead resulted in a 0.3 per cent increase in barrels of new discoveries.[34] Edward Erickson followed up Fisher's work with additional data and a somewhat improved approach found that a 1 per cent increase in price leads to a 0.89 per cent increase in discoveries.[35] A study done by the Consad Research Corporation for the U.S. Treasury concluded that a 1 per cent increase in price brings about a 0.27 per cent increase in desired reserves.[36]

Using the Consad figures which deal directly with reserve levels we can estimate the effect of the tax provisions on reserves. A $1.25 tax benefit per barrel is equivalent to about a 42 per cent price increase. Thus desired reserves are increased by about 7 per cent.

The Cabinet Task Force on Oil Import Control recently estimated that the abandonment of oil import controls would reduce the U.S. wellhead price to about $2.00 a barrel and that this in turn would reduce U.S. production from 10.6 million barrels a day in 1968, and 12.4 and 13.5 million barrels per day in 1975 and 1980, respectively, to 11.2 million in 1975 and 9.5 million in 1980. In particular, they predicted that at $2.00 per barrel prorationing would be abandoned as useless, resulting in increased output from the currently existing excess capacity of 1.7 million barrels per day, and an addition of 2.0 million barrels per day from Alaska—offset in part by an abandonment of 500,000 barrels per day of high-cost stripper well production. Outside of Alaska new additions to reserves would be expected to fall to less than half their current rate within 6 years.

RESULTS OF VERTICAL INTEGRATION Vertically integrated companies, partly for tax reasons, find it profitable to increase the price of crude relative to the prices for final products. This of course squeezes independent refiners who must pay the higher crude price and sell in competition with the major integrated companies.

This relationship was demonstrated by Alfred Kahn before a Senate subcommittee. Kahn examined the pattern of crude oil and gasoline price

34 *Supply and Costs in the U.S. Petroleum Industry* (Resources for the Future, 1964).

35 Economic Incentives, *Industrial Structure and the Supply of Crude Oil Discoveries in the U.S., 1946–58/59,*

Ph.D. thesis, Vanderbilt University, 1968 (unpublished).

36 *Effects of Special Federal Tax Provisions on Selected Aspects of Oil and Gas Industry,* a special report of the Consad Research Corporation to the U.S. Treasury (June 1967).

rises in February 1969. He found that the first five companies to raise their crude prices supplied between 63 and 93 per cent of their own crude needs. But the three companies who initiated raised product prices—but not crude prices—supplied only 40 to 58 per cent of their needs from their own wells.

The combination of vertical integration and import controls has worked to reduce competition in a number of areas. New England, for example, is particularly dependent on oil for heating and energy. About 76 per cent of the residential commercial energy demand is met by oil, compared to 33 per cent for the nation as a whole. No oil pipeline serves New England, however, and most products reach the area by barge or tanker from the East or Gulf Coasts.

In the 1950's and early 1960's there were a number of independent deep-water terminal operators who brought in products to compete with the integrated majors. Since most of them lacked a historical basis for claiming a quota, they have become increasingly dependent on the majors for supplies. Quite a number of such operators have disappeared through acquisition by the majors in recent years. Moreover, demand has caught up with refinery capacity and less distress gasoline has become available. As a result, independent marketers have had difficulty in securing supplies to compete with the majors. Two major independent marketers, Citgo and Bay State, have been acquired by major companies with a concomitant reduction in competition.

The problem of the independent marketers is partly a result also of the problems of the independent refiners. These refiners have been squeezed by the majors and the number of such refiners have decreased. Moreover, east coast refining capacity has decreased since the 1950's with the abandonment by Esso of a 50,000 barrel refinery.

At least partly as a result of the decline in competition and partly as a result of the oil import program, prices for final products are significantly higher in New England than in most other areas. Price margins for fuel oil dealers in New England are about 0.9 cent higher than the U.S. average. Retail gasoline in Montreal which receives unlimited imports of oil at world prices is about 3 cents per gallon less than in major east coast cities.

Even more serious monopoly problems have existed in the Hawaiian market. Standard Oil of California has the only refinery in Hawaii and supplies a minimum of 60 per cent of all the gasoline retailed by other firms. The output of the refinery is equal to the consumption in Hawaii, but some gasoline is hauled to the West Coast and some imported from the West Coast.

Standard is, therefore, in a position to limit competition. Posted prices, exclusive of taxes, are set on the basis of Los Angeles' posted prices plus the freight. Freight amounts to about 1 cent a gallon. But in Los Angeles, transaction prices often differ substantially from posted prices, whereas in

Honolulu the transaction price and the posted price have been identical. In 1967, for example, transaction prices in Los Angeles ran about $3\frac{1}{2}$ cents less than posted prices but Honolulu prices remained based on posted prices. Tank-wagon prices for regular gasoline were 11.5–12.5 cents per gallon in Los Angeles in 1967–1968, whereas retail dealers were charged 18.4 cents in Honolulu. Other product prices also reflect the lack of competition. Asphalt costs $35 a ton in Honolulu at the refinery and from $18 to $20 on the West Coast. Bunker fuel used by ships costs $2.77 per barrel in Honolulu and $2.20 in Los Angeles.

As a consequence, the State of Hawaii has brought an antitrust suit against Standard Oil of California, Shell, and Union. They are charged in a civil suit with violation of Sections 1 and 2 of the Sherman Act.

COSTS OF THE SYSTEM

Although this cartel arrangement has benefits for all in the petroleum industry, it is terribly costly to the economy and to the consumer. Professor Adelman has published some very enlightening estimates of the cost of the system.[37] On the basis of 9.4 million barrels of crude and natural gas liquid consumption per day, and on the basis of a net premium on imported oil of $1.16 per barrel ($1.25 minus pipeline costs of $0.09 per barrel to cover half the U.S. market), he computed the cost to the consumer per year at about $4 billion annually.

The Cabinet Task Force on Oil Import Control estimated the total costs to consumers in 1969 as $4.85 billion and the per capita cost at $24. The Office of Emergency Preparedness in the Executive Office of the President estimated the consumer cost at $5.26 billion, whereas Standard Oil of New Jersey in defending the system estimated the cost at $3.45 billion. Whatever the exact amount, it is clear that it costs consumers a lot.

A second resulting waste stems from the restriction of U.S. coastal trade to U.S. ships. Such ships cost about twice as much to build in America and twice as much to operate as foreign tankers. As a result the cost of shipping oil from the Gulf Coast to the East Coast by water is about 35 cents per barrel, considerably above a competitive charge. As a consequence, oil companies have constructed two large diameter pipelines from the Gulf, a considerable waste of resources.

Kahn reports that "industry representatives estimate that on the order of $500,000 annually are spent drilling unnecessary development wells.[38] In addition, the system encourages the drilling of costly deep wells, the production from inefficient wells, and the production from too many wells. Adelman has estimated that in 1961 simply transferring output to non-

---

37 M. A. Adelman, "Efficiency of Resource Use in Petroleum," *Southern*   *Economic Journal*, **31**:101 (October 1965).
38 Kahn, op. cit., p. 310.

stripper wells in Texas would have produced a gain for them of $2.41 billion and a loss to strippers of $1.12 billion with a net gain for all of Texas of $1.29 billion. This would have been in addition to anything saved on preventing the drilling of unnecessary wells. Adelman concludes that over drilling costs each year around $1.31 billion in development costs and $800 million in producing costs. In total unitization and efficient production would bring savings of about $2.15 billion annually or about 85 cents to $1.00 per barrel.

The tax provisions are also costly. The increase in reserves due to these provisions was estimated to be only 7 per cent. To maintain a 1:12 ratio between consumption and reserves with a 3 per cent growth rate in demand, it is necessary that discoveries be equal to 136 per cent of consumption annually. A 7 per cent decline in reserves implies that the ratio between consumption and reserves would fall to about 1:11. With this ratio and a 3 per cent growth rate, discoveries should equal 133 per cent of consumption, a fall of about 2.2 per cent in annual discoveries. Since the value of reserves in the ground is about $1.00 per barrel and since about 4.5 billion barrels of new reserves are developed annually, the annual value of reserves is $4.5 billion. A reduction in new reserves of 2.2 per cent would reduce the market value of new reserves about $0.1 billion. Thus about $1.6 billion is being lost annually in taxes to gain a resource worth about $0.1 billion, a poor benefit-cost ratio. Most of the benefits of the tax treatment go to increasing the rents of oil land owners.

Thus eliminating the favorable tax treatment would produce a net gain of about $1.6 billion to taxpayers. Rationalizing the domestic industry might bring savings of about $2.15 billion to the economy. Elimination of the import quota with unitization of the domestic industry might bring an additional $1.85 billion gain to consumers on top of the $2.15 billion from a more efficient local industry for a net gain of $4.0 billion.

V. PUBLIC POLICY

The objective of the above system is twofold. Since unlimited individual drilling and pumping under the rule of capture can lead to great waste, prorationing has been instituted. But prorationing in turn has led to great waste with efficient producers being restricted while inefficient producers have been permitted to produce. Unitization of oil pools could eliminate or reduce these wastes and obviate the need for prorationing.

Since there are thousands of oil pools, unitization of each would not limit competition. Each pool could operate as a unit in competition with each other pool. Economic and technological waste could be avoided. With a multitude of oil pools and with a fairly large number of buyers, in the absence of prorationing, competitive forces would establish prices probably significantly below existing levels.

The extensive use of barter in crude—it is also extensively used for refined products—is surprising. Barter is costly. Bookkeeping is complicated. Barter may be used to avoid establishing market prices for crude that might differ from posted prices. If such market prices were lower than posted prices, tax deductions under the percentage depletion allowance would be smaller.

Of course, if posted prices were set competitively then trading could be done at such prices. However, in most oil fields only a very small number of buyers operate. Although such a situation might result in monopsony pricing, there are several factors working against this result. First, entry is possible and small nonintegrated buyers do exist. Second, prorationing assures that supplies will be restricted enough to maintain prices. Third, it is in the interest of integrated companies to pay high prices for crude and increase their net profits at that level due to the depletion allowance.

The Cabinet Task Force evaluated war contingencies and the need for a large domestic oil supply. They concluded that a nuclear war was unlikely and that the continuity of oil supply in its event would not likely be a matter of major significance. In the event of limited wars such as Korea and Vietnam they concluded that dependence on foreign oil supplies does not lead to protracted supply interruptions. A general non-nuclear war was evaluated to be unlikely. In its event the risk to tanker shipments from Venezuela was viewed as no greater than from the Gulf Coast to the East Coast, and less than the risk through the northeast passage from Alaska. Shipments across the Atlantic in either direction or from the Middle East to Europe would be highly vulnerable to submarines. The Task Force concluded that with spare capacity, normal inventories, and potential expansion of output, the U.S. would be able to cover its normal consumption, even if all import controls were abandoned and if all Arabian and Iranian oil was cut off. The principal shortages would appear in Western Europe. In the case where all Eastern Hemisphere oil was lost and North America received a smaller share of Venezuela oil, as some Latin American oil was diverted to substitute for the precrisis Eastern Hemisphere shipments, the U.S. and Canada would face a 5 per cent deficit in the no controls situation. Only where all Eastern Hemisphere and Latin American oil is lost would the U.S. find itself in a situation not easily handled by tolerable rationing of domestic consumption.

The elimination of import quotas would not lead to the abandonment of all domestic oil production. Many marginal producers would cease production but this would permit an increase in production by the more efficient wells. The Task Force estimated that by 1980, in the absence of import controls, U.S. production would be 9.5 million barrels per day, whereas a continuation of the status quo would result in a U.S. production of 13.5 million barrels per day.

It is also argued that the tax advantages are necessary to increase domestic capacity. It is clear that such advantages do increase the profitability of oil production. Since supply is undoubtedly not completely inelastic, reserves are bound to be increased by these tax favors.

A major effect of the tax provisions is to increase the rents going to owners of petroleum deposits. Such rents now constitute approximately 25 to 30 per cent of the total value of crude oil production.[39] With freer imports, rents would fall even further. The question then arises whether the marginal increase in reserves and in production that results from these policies is worth the added cost. It is clear that the consumer is paying considerably extra for gasoline and other oil products due to these policies. Only a small share of this extra payment is going to domestic producers since much of it is swallowed up in the inefficiencies inherent in the system.

A more efficient method of protecting U.S. production capacity would be to shift from a quota system to a tariff, as recommended by the Cabinet Task Force. A shift to a tariff would eliminate the need and ability of market demand prorationing to establish domestic prices. Paradoxical as it might seem, a shift to a tariff would probably lead to a reduction in imports and, depending on the tariff level, a reduction in domestic prices. Since domestic prices would be set by world prices plus tariff, prorationing would no longer be able to maintain fixed prices. For example, if the tariff were increased by $1.35 per barrel as the Task Force majority recommended, the effect would be a price for domestic crude of around $3.00 per barrel. The regulatory commissions could increase domestic production in this case without affecting prices. Increased U.S. output would simply displace foreign production.

A tariff would also eliminate the existing problem of allocating valuable import quotas. With a tariff the entire gain from the import restriction would go to the taxpayer. Consequently, the majority of the Task Force supported abolishing the quota system and substituting a tariff. The Chairman of the Task Force recommended shifting to a tariff of about $1 per barrel which would lead to some reduction in prices.

There are three public props to this system: prorationing, import quotas, and tax advantages. Prorationing could be removed without eliminating import quotas or changing the tax laws. Similarly the tax advantages could be changed without affecting either of the other policies. Freer imports, however, would mean at least major changes in prorationing if not its abandonment. From a public policy point of view we can consider changes in only one of these policies, in two of them, or in all of them.

For example, the tax laws might be amended to eliminate the depletion allowance and the favorable treatment of certain capital expenses for a net long-run saving of about $1.6 billion per year for the taxpayer. To predict the result it is necessary to estimate the political reaction of regulatory commissions. It might be that regulatory commissions would encourage higher

---

39 Kahn, op. cit., p. 290.

prices to offset the resultant higher taxes. On the other hand, some rationing of production might take place with higher-cost wells being shut down to maintain the profits of the system. Some wells would clearly close unless higher prices were substituted. However, without the tax advantage, major oil producers would be less interested in maintaining crude oil prices.

VERTICAL INTEGRATION   The major companies dominate the market and are likely to continue to do so. A relaxation of import controls and of prorationing might help independents, but there is no certainty.

Each stage of the industry, crude production, transportation, refining, and marketing involves tremendous investments. There does not seem, however, to be any great efficiency in vertical integration. Independent refiners can and do exist despite the tax advantages of the majors. Most pipelines are not wholly owned subsidiaries but joint ventures. Numerous independent marketers exist.

Since there do not appear to be great economies in vertical integration, it seems likely that the industry would be more competitive and perform better without the existing vertical integration. As a practical matter, however, antitrust policy is not likely to be effective in reducing or eliminating the vertical relationships. Courts and the antitrust division of the Justice Department have naturally been conservative in restructuring successful enterprises and there is no reason to believe they will become more radical.

Not only is the vertical integration troublesome, but the increasing number of joint ventures involved in exploration, development, and in transportation creates a community spirit not conducive to vigorous competition. Joint bids are numerous on offshore tracts and most of the winning bids in the Alaskan north slope lease sale were joint ventures involving the major companies. Almost all the product pipelines built since the early 1950's have been joint ventures.

Large-scale joint venture pipelines have reduced the amount of distressed products offered for sale. With a large number of partners a major company with excess gasoline, for example, can probably find another company on the line to take the product in a trade. Thus independent marketers have found that their supplies of distress products have been drying up. Of course, such arrangements may result in savings to the companies and to society yet they have had a significant impact on the independents.

There seems to be little public policy can do about such situations under current law. Nor are such exchanges necessarily bad. However, an elimination of the independents would undoubtedly reduce competition and, consequently, the advantages of joint ventures should be carefully weighed against any anticompetitive effects.

An elimination of the prorationing system, on the other hand, without a change in other public policies could significantly improve efficiency. Lower prices might even result in higher profits for some producers if unitization were substituted for prorationing. Not all producers would benefit, however; those with marginal wells might suffer. It would, of course, take considerable time to rationalize the industry since much excess capacity has been installed. Many wells would simply be abandoned whereas a few efficient ones would produce.

As has been pointed out above, the elimination of the import quota system would force major changes in prorationing. At a minimum, many marginal wells would shut down. Efficient producers would be able to increase their production. On net the domestic industry could be expected to shrink. Initially, domestic output would probably increase, but over a period of time with less exploration, output would become smaller relative to what would be produced with import controls.

NATURAL GAS   Although this chapter deals only with liquid petroleum, some attention must be paid to natural gas policy. Natural gas is often found jointly with crude oil. In many cases wildcatters are searching for either natural gas or oil. In addition, within limits well owners can alter the ratio of gas and oil produced from a given well. As a consequence the profitability of natural gas will affect exploratory activity as well as the profitability of crude oil.

Since World War II the demand for natural gas has expanded tremendously. Prior to World War II much natural gas was burned at the well or vented into the atmosphere since no economical way to market existed. After the war the pipeline network expanded tremendously bringing natural gas into most areas of the country. Under the spur of a Supreme Court decision [40] which directed the Federal Power Commission (FPC) to regulate natural gas, the FPC has moved actively into regulating rates at the production level, at the transmission level, and at the wholesale level. After some experimentation with different methods of regulation, the FPC has settled on area-wide pricing for natural gas production, that is, it determines an average cost for an area and bases prices upon that cost. Since the early 1960's, possibly as a consequence of Federal regulation, prices for natural gas have leveled off.

As in oil production, there are thousands of natural gas producers. Also, as in oil production, there are only a limited number of gatherers and pipelines. Offhand, the industry would appear to more monopsonistic than monopolistic.[41] If anything, it must be highly competitive on the production side. Thus the regulations of the FPC if they are having any effect, must be holding natural gas prices below competitive levels, or below those that

40   *Phillips Petroleum Co.* v. *Wisconsin*, 347 U.S. 672 (1954).
41   See Paul W. MacAvoy, *Price Formation in Natural Gas Fields* (New Haven: Yale University Press, 1962) for a discussion. He concludes that "Monopsony prevailed . . . at some time, but pricing was generally becoming more competitive during the later 1950's." p. 243.

would be achieved under monopsonistic practices. The FPC has set up a two-price system: a low price for gas already discovered and a somewhat higher price for new discoveries.

In wells producing both natural gas and crude oil the owners have some flexibility in the relative proportions of each they produce. Natural gas left in the ground helps push crude to the surface. Alternatively, less crude can be produced if more natural gas is taken. Holding down the price of already discovered natural gas will tend to increase the desired production of crude oil. In prorated states, of course, crude oil production is already limited by regulatory control, and the producers are barred from exercising this option. In states without prorationing, however, crude oil production is encouraged at the expense of natural gas production, adding to the problem of over-production.

If the price for new gas production is being held below long-run competitive prices, it will discourage the search for new gas. Since gas and oil are found jointly, future reserves of oil will be less than if gas prices had been higher. Thus the regulation of natural gas partially thwarts the objective of increasing reserves.

Natural gas is also a competitive fuel with oil. Both natural gas and oil can be used for heating and for the production of electricity. A decrease in the price of natural gas due to regulation means an increase in the quantity of natural gas demanded and a decrease in the demand for petroleum. Such a result presents problems for both industries. If prices are being held below market equilibrium for gas, shortages in the long run can be expected for natural gas. Of course, this is at least partly offset by the regulation of crude oil, which increases the incentive to find crude and, as an accident, natural gas. In addition, the same tax treatment that benefits the oil industry also applies to natural gas and helps to encourage the discovery of natural gas. Nevertheless, regulation could present problems in the long run for the supply of natural gas.

Lower natural gas prices mean a reduced demand of oil for heating and power. Thus prorationing must restrict output more than it would in the absence of such regulation.

To sort out the end effect of these government regulations on the production of oil and the production of natural gas is almost impossible. Nevertheless, it is clear that the system, as it is currently organized, is extremely wasteful, contradictory, and in the long run may be self-defeating.

THE FUTURE

As this chapter was completed the Cabinet Task Force on Oil Import Control submitted its report to the President. If the President accepts the recommendations of the majority, major changes, as indicated above, are likely in the oil industry. On the other hand, if the minority view that the quota system has worked effectively and only needs better policy guidance and better administration is accepted, the market situation can be expected to remain much as described above.

The future of the petroleum industry, as we currently know it, may be affected, however, by the development of other sources of oil besides crude production and of other sources of power. To the extent that the system inflates oil prices, these substitutes are encouraged.

The most economical sources of additional oil are secondary recovery from existing fields and the development of tar sands. Oil is being produced from both sources currently. It is estimated that oil from tar sands is feasible at present prices using conventional mining techniques. In the future, however, oil may come from other sources.

OIL SHALE[42] A major potential source of petroleum that might become plentiful in the next decade is oil shale. The Department of Interior has estimated that there are 1.8 trillion barrels of oil in the oil shale deposits in Colorado, Wyoming, and Utah. This is sixty times the size of the proved U.S. reserves. There is enough oil locked in the shale to meet the U.S. needs for hundreds of years. It is clear that if this oil can be economically extracted from the shale, the U.S. need never fear running out of oil.

Oil has been produced from shale for years; in fact, oil was produced from shale before it was extracted by wells from the ground. When oil shale is heated to 900°F, oil flows out. Today shale oil industries operate in both Red China and the USSR.

The U.S. oil shale resources consist of 11 million acres located in Colorado, Wyoming, and Utah. Of these acres 72 per cent are Federally owned with about 80 per cent of the known oil shale resources. The richest deposits are in Colorado with 1,359,000 acres, of which 26 per cent are in private hands.

Oil shale quality varies considerably. Some shale has as much as 60 gallons per ton, whereas some has as little as 10 gallons per ton; it averages 25 gallons per ton. The thickness of the oil shale deposits in Colorado ranges up to 2,000 feet at depths of over 1500 feet from the surface. This shale also contains a wide number of other valuable minerals, some of which may be efficiently extracted with oil from the shale.

Extracting the oil is not easy. Much of the shale is deep in the ground. Thick deposits of shales are not suitable for normal mining activity where rooms are carved and supported by pillars. How can a 2,000-foot thick seam be removed from deep in the ground? Once mined and brought to the surface and the oil extracted, what can be done with the spent shale? The pollution problems and the destruction of natural scenery that would result from bringing vast quantities of shale to the surface and from piling up large mounds of spent shale are obvious.

---

42 The data in the section were taken from U.S. Department of Interior, *Pros- pects for Oil Shale Development: Colorado Utah, and Wyoming* (May 1968).

It may be possible to extract oil from the shale while it is still in the ground. Several methods have been considered and discussed, including atomic blasts to crush and heat the shale sufficiently to make the oil flow out. However, such extraction methods would leave in the ground the other valuable minerals found in oil shale.

The Department of Interior study on oil shale development indicates that at the moment with current oil prices and current technology, the economic extraction of this oil is marginal at best. It estimated that the cost of simply mining and extracting the oil, assuming no payments to land owners, would, with current technology, produce oil at a cost of $2.68 to $3.28 per barrel by 1972. With expected technological improvements and with some experience in the production of oil from shale, it predicts that by 1976 the cost of oil from shale would drop to $1.91 to $2.33 per barrel.

Private industry has not moved actively in the development of oil shale, which indicates that the Interior Department may be correct when it asserts that extraction of oil from oil shale is marginal. It is clear that private industry could develop an active industry if it were profitable. As the Interior study says:

> Since most of the deposits for which the tested mining technology is well suited (at reasonable recovery of the resource and at lowest mining costs) are in private ownership, development of this resource could be undertaken by the private sector without use of Federal land if other significant factors (Continental Shelf leasing, import restrictions, tax provisions, etc.), remain generally as they are. The study indicates that no serious barriers exist for private development other than investing in a high technologic risk venture.[43]

Notwithstanding the availability of privately owned oil shale deposits, there have been claims that Federal deposits would have to be made available to make the industry viable. In response to this demand, the Interior Department in the fall of 1968 put three leases up for private bids. The Department had expected bids in the order of millions of dollars such as it receives on offshore acreage. The largest bid was $650,000 for one 1,250 acre tract in Colorado. One of the three tracts received no bids at all.[44] The fact that the bids were so small supports the proposition that at the moment the production of oil from shale is marginal.

There is one company, however, the Shale Oil Corporation, using private lands in producing oil from shale. Currently, it produces 800 barrels per day. It has claimed that the cost of oil from shale may fall to approximately

---

43 Ibid., p. 36.

44 *Wall Street Journal* (December 27, 1968), p. 4.

$1 per barrel in the near future.[45] Were this possible, it would have serious repercussions on the rest of the oil industry.

It has been alleged that the major oil companies have been attempting to stifle the growth of the oil shale industry because it threatens their own large holdings of crude.[46] Even if the allegations were true, it is difficult to see how the majors have prevented other private companies from bidding on Interior leases for developing shale oil, and, in fact, they have been unsuccessful since the Oil Shale Corporation is actually operating. In addition, the Union Oil Company of California is building a 140,000 barrel per day refinery near Chicago to handle shale oil. The Union Oil Company plant is designed to accommodate tar-sand oil from Canada if shale oil does not become available.

In the very near future the government must decide whether refineries processing oil from shale will receive import quotas. Since import quotas are based on the quantity of crude refined, considerable crude would be displaced by including shale oil in this system. If shale oil on the other hand does not become eligible for quotas, then oil from shale, to be competitive, will have to sell at somewhat less per barrel than crude.

OTHER SOURCES OF OIL   Research efforts are currently being undertaken to improve the process of producing oil from coal. Coal has certain advantages over oil shale in that the product yield from coal is about 100–150 gallons per ton compared to 25–40 gallons per ton for oil shale.[47] In addition, the waste disposal problem is smaller for coal than for shale oil. Finally, coal deposits are located considerably nearer to fuel markets than are shale oil deposits.

The Department of Interior has estimated that the operating costs of extracting oil from coal are currently about $3.22 per barrel before byproduct credits and $1.47 a barrel with byproduct credits.[48] The cost of extracting oil from natural gas is considerably higher at over $4.00 per barrel.[49]

The future of the current oil regulation system is also clouded by the development of large-scale production of Alaskan oil, which to be accommodated in the prorationing system might mean that Texas and Louisiana allowables would have to be cut back sharply. Canadian oil also may cause problems. In recent years, an informal agreement between the U.S. and Canada has attempted to limit Canadian imports. The Canadian "quota," however, has been consistently exceeded and by March 1970, it became so large that quotas had to be imposed on Canada to protect the system. In addition, other sources of energy such as atomic energy may also substitute for oil.

---

45   Chris Wells, "Oil Shale: Hidden Scandal or Inflated Myth?" *Harper's* p. 62 (August 1968).
46   Ibid., p. 62.

47   Interior, *Prospects for Oil Shale Development*, op. cit., p. 75.
48   Ibid., p. 76.
49   Ibid., p. 76.

The present system of maintaining a relatively high price for crude oil is, of course, encouraging the development of these substitute supplies. As with any cartel, maintaining prices encourages new entry and the development of substitutes. In the long run then the current high price for oil may lead to major changes in the crude oil industry as it is now known. From the point of view of the crude oil producing states, it may be best for them to move actively to rationalize the industry by unitization, and they will, of course, be forced to move in this direction if the President accepts the recommendation of the majority of the Cabinet Task Force on Oil Import Control.

SUGGESTED READINGS
BOOKS AND PAMPHLETS

Day, W. H. (ed.) *Petroleum Market Practices and Problems* (Tulsa, Okla.: Commercial Publishers, 1966).

DeChazeau, M. G., and A. E. Kahn. *Integration and Competition in the Petroleum Industry* (New Haven: Yale University Press, 1959).

Fisher, F. M. *Supply and Costs in the U.S. Petroleum Industry* (Washington, D.C.: Resources for the Future, 1964).

Geddens, P. H. *Standard Oil Company (Indiana): Oil Pioneer of the Middle West* (New York: Appleton-Century-Crofts, 1955).

Lovejoy, W. F., and P. T. Homan. *Economic Aspects of Oil Conservation Regulations* (Baltimore: The Johns Hopkins Press, 1967).

MacAvoy, P. W. *Price Formation in Natural Gas Fields* (New Haven: Yale University Press, 1962).

McLean, J. C., and R. W. Haigh. *The Growth of Integrated Oil Companies* (Boston: School of Business Administration, Harvard University, 1954).

Rostow, E. V. *A National Policy for the Oil Industry* (New Haven: Yale University Press, 1948).

Sell, A. *The Petroleum Industry* (New York: Oxford University Press, 1963).

Williamson, H. F., R. L. Andreano, A. R. Daum, and G. C. Klore. *The American Petroleum Industry: The Age of Energy 1899–1959* (Evanston, Ill.: Northwestern University Press, 1963).

GOVERNMENT PUBLICATIONS

Cabinet Task Force on Oil Import Control. *The Oil Import Question*, A Report on the Relationship of Oil Imports to the National Security (Washington, D.C.: U.S. Government Printing Office, February 1970).

Consat Research Corporation. *Effects of Special Federal Tax Provisions on Selected Aspects of Oil and Gas Industry*, a special report to the U.S. Treasury (June 1967).

Federal Trade Commission. *Report on Anticompetitive Practices in Marketing of Gasoline* (Federal Trade Commission, n.d.).

Federal Trade Commission. Staff Report, *The International Petroleum Control* (Washington, D.C.: 1952).

Interstate Oil Compact Commission. *A Study of Oil and Gas in the United States* (Oklahoma City, Okla.: Interstate Oil Compact Commission, 1964).

Report of the Attorney General pursuant to Section 2 of the Joint Resolution of September 6, 1963, converting to an Interstate Compact to Conserve Oil and Gas, July 1967. In *Hearings before the Subcommittee on Communications and Power*, House of Representatives, 90th Congress, 1st Session, April 18, 1967.

U.S. Department of Interior. *Prospects for Oil Shale Development:* Colorado, Utah, and Wyoming (May, 1968).

ARTICLES

Adelman, M. A. "Efficiency of Resource Use in Petroleum," *Southern Economic Journal* **31**:101 (October 1965).

Kahn, A. E. "Depletion Allowance in the Context of Centralization," *American Economic Review* **54**:286 (June 1964).

McGee, J. S. "Predatory Price Cutting: The Standard Oil Case," *Journal of Law and Economics*, Vol. 1:137 (October 1958).

Wells, C. "Oil Shale: Hidden Scandal or Inflated Myth?" *Harper's* p. 62 (August 1968).

5. Walter S. Measday

THE PHARMACEUTICAL INDUSTRY

I. DEVELOPMENT OF THE INDUSTRY

One of the more widely quoted remarks attributed to the late Sir William Osler is that the desire to take medicine is perhaps the greatest feature which distinguishes man from the animals. Any practicing physician will confirm that there is at least a strong ring of truth to Osler's exaggeration. Some of the more cynical writers of advertising copy for over-the-counter remedies for acid indigestion, headaches, constipation, or tired blood would question whether Osler exaggerated at all.

Given man's awareness of the problems of illness and his propensity to seek cures, it is not surprising that the story of pharmaceutical remedies is as old as recorded history. Macbeth's witches, to say nothing of a modern physician, might shrink in horror from some of the concoctions served up to patients in the past. Most of these remedies were useless; their efficacy rested upon the psychological satisfaction which a large segment of humanity derives from taking medicine. Lest we think too harshly of our ancestors, it can be noted that more than a few drugs on the market today have been shown to have no greater therapeutic effects than placebos—pills manufactured from inert ingredients known to generate no physiological response. A number of the ancient remedies are still in use, albeit in purified form. Quinine, digitalis, strychnine, colchicine, reserpine, and the opiates, among others, have genealogies which can be measured in centuries or even millenia.

To speak of the ancient history of drugs, however, is a far cry from describing the pharmaceutical industry, which is a comparatively recent development. Well into the nineteenth century, botanical drugs as well as the few early chemical remedies were collected and compounded by the physicians and apothecaries who dispensed them. It is no accident that the first United States Pharmacopoeia, published in 1820 (with texts in both English and Latin) described more than 200 drugs in terms useful to the doctor or druggist who, so to speak, "rolled his own."

As medicine itself became more scientific, its practitioners found a need for standardized drugs. It was to meet such needs that the ethical drug industry was founded during the nineteenth century. One of the earliest "industrialists" was a German apothecary, H. E. Merck, who began the production for wholesale distribution of morphine, quinine, strychnine, and a growing list of other drugs in 1827; the U.S. branch of the firm was established some 65 years later. In the U.S., Edward R. Squibb developed a process for distilling ether of uniform purity and strength in 1854, and gave up the practice of medicine shortly thereafter to concentrate on supplying the drug requirements of his colleagues. By the end of the nineteenth century, factory production had supplanted the art of the individual apothecary in the preparation of ethical drugs.

This is not to say that the modern pharmaceutical industry was created full-blown in the nineteenth century; a more appropriate date for this purpose would be World War II. Through the 1930's, botanical products remained an important part of the manufacturer's business. The work of Louis Pasteur and others had provided an impetus to the production of biologicals (serums antitoxins, and vaccines). Paul Ehrlich can lay the greatest claim to the foundation of modern chemical pharmacology. His discovery of arsphenamine or Ehrlich 606, the first successful treatment for syphilis, is most widely known to the laymen. Of greater importance was his development of the earliest systematic theory of selective drug action, which provided a logical basis for the search for new chemical drugs. The search proceeded slowly, however, for many years.

There were differences other than the pace of development between the pre-World War II industry and that of the postwar period. Today more than 97 per cent of all prescription drug items reach the retailer in finished form. Before World War II, however, the production of finished medications was largely confined to the proprietary field. The typical ethical drug manufacturer then purchased his basic chemicals from a "fine chemical" firm, such as Merck, Pfizer, or Mallinckrodt. From these he prepared the active drug ingredients, which he sold in bulk form almost exclusively through wholesalers, to the retail trade.

The pre-World War II pharmacist was not so far removed from the apothecary of an earlier century, in that he still had to compound most of the prescriptions he sold. Using the bulk powders and crystals obtained from the drug manufacturers, the pharmacist added excipients and binders, rolled his own pills, filled capsules, or prepared liquid suspensions and tinctures. For most products, since the skill of the local pharmacist contributed as much to the finished item as did that of the manufacturer, brand names (as distinct from a general reputation for reliability) played a much smaller role than they do today.

The industry underwent a veritable revolution in the 1940's, generated in part by an upsurge in new drug discoveries and in part by the production requirements of World War II. Sulfanilamide, the first of the modern "wonder drugs," appeared on the market in 1936. Possessing remarkable antibacterial properties in comparison to other drugs then available, it came into wide use and was the principal antiinfective drug used by the military through 1943. Sulfanilamide's usefulness, despite its toxicity, encouraged research for other safer and even more effective drugs. Success came with the production of penicillin, the first of the antibiotics which have contributed so much to modern drug therapy. The story of penicillin provides an excellent illustration of the factors which revolutionized the drug industry during and after World War II.

Penicillin was first observed by Alexander Fleming in 1928, when bread mold spores accidentally contaminated a staphylococcus culture, destroying staph germs in the vicinity of the spores. Investigation continued on a small scale, but not until 1940 did Chain and Florey, at Oxford University, succeed in preparing enough pure penicillin to try it on human patients and establish its invaluable pharmaceutical efficacy. With Britain fully mobilized, Florey came to the United States in the hope of persuading American drug companies and the government to develop commercial production. His hope was realized through industry-government cooperation on a large scale, which provided sufficient penicillin capacity to meet military requirements by early 1944. The War Production Board's target was 3,600 billion units of penicillin, a level which it was feared would create a serious postwar problem of idle capacity. (Today, despite the competition of a number of other antibiotics, annual penicillin production is nearly 400 times the wartime target.)

Considerable research effort, both publicly and privately supported, was directed to the discovery of other antibiotics. The effort, which involved the mass screening of thousands upon thousands of different molds, paid off handsomely. Selman Waksman and Albert Schatz, at Rutgers University, found streptomycin, which was being commercially produced by the end of the war. Merck, which had financed Waksman, later developed dihydrostreptomycin. Bacitracin was isolated at Columbia University and chloramphenicol by a research team at Yale.

The most important of the post-penicillin discoveries, however, have been the tetracyclines. These are "broad-spectrum" antibiotics, i.e., they are active against a much wider range of organisms than is penicillin. The first, chlortetracycline (Aureomycin), was marketed by American Cyanamid's Lederle Laboratories in 1948. It was followed by a variant, oxytetracycline (Terramycin), introduced by Pfizer in 1950. By 1954 tetracycline itself had been prepared by several firms, including American Cyanamid, Heyden (whose antibiotic facility was acquired by Cyanamid), Pfizer, and Bristol Laboratories. A number of other antibiotics, some of considerable use and others of only minor importance, were discovered in the 1950's; by 1960 the impetus given to antibiotic research by World War II and the later commercial success of antibiotics appeared to have run its course, and few new products have appeared since.

World War II not only stimulated research and production of antibiotics and other drugs, but it changed the industry in other ways as well. The exigencies of military medical practice left no room for local compounding of prescriptions from bulk drugs. To meet military needs, the drug manufacturers had to invest in the mixing, tableting, and encapsulating equipment necessary to provide finished drugs, ready for administration to the patient. By the end of the war, the compounding function of the retail pharmacist was irrevocably passing into history. More important, once the original manufacturer had come to provide drugs in the form in which they reached the ultimate consumer, the value of brand names was immeasurably enhanced; ethical drug advertising and promotion to the medical and allied professions surged upward toward the levels which now prevail.

World War II and a quarter of a century of postwar prosperity for the industry also attracted a number of newcomers. Entry in many cases has been accomplished through the acquisition of existing drug firms, to secure both a sales force familiar with the unique problems of pharmaceutical merchandising and the entree of a name with which the medical profession is acquainted. Several distinct groups of entrants can be identified.

First, some of the fine chemical companies secured wartime contracts under which they had supplied drug products in finished form. Thus, at the end of the war, they themselves had become drug manufacturers rather than simply suppliers of chemicals to the industry. Merck & Company and Chas. Pfizer & Company provide excellent examples. Each had been a manufacturer of drug-grade chemicals for the pharmaceutical industry before World War II, and each came out of the war as a leading producer of drugs, particularly in the antibiotic field. Each solved the problem of entry into the civilian market by acquisition of an established firm. Pfizer, which had only a dozen chemical salesmen, purchased J. B. Roerig, a well-known drug firm with a large pharmaceutical sales force. Merck sold its products to other firms for distribution until it acquired Sharp & Dohme, one of the largest drug manufacturers and distributors, with a reputation dating from the Civil War. Today the two companies rank first and second, respectively, in industry sales of ethical pharmaceuticals.

Next, a number of companies, known primarily as proprietary firms, entered or greatly expanded their activities in the ethical field. In 1939, manufacturers' shipments of proprietary drugs exceeded shipments of ethical products; by 1967 shipments of ethical drugs were nearly triple the volume of proprietaries. The proprietary companies had the advantages of familiarity with production techniques and retail drug distribution; their major problem has been to overcome the longstanding distrust of the medical profession towards patent medicine hucksters.

To solve this problem, they have utilized what had been minor pre-World War II ethical subsidiaries, the establishment of new divisions, and to a lesser degree, acquisitions. Thus American Home Products has employed Wyeth Laboratories (acquired in 1931) and Ayerst (purchased shortly after World War II), to promote ethical products in a manner which minimizes physician identification of these products with the corporate producer of such items as Anacin, Bi-So-Dol mints, and Kolynos toothpaste. Bristol-Myers (Sal Hepatica, Bufferin, Ipana, Mum, Ban, and so on) established Bristol Laboratories, which has prospered on the basis of tetracycline and semisynthetic penicillins. In a similar manner, Norwich Pharmacal Company has created Eaton Laboratories to overcome any reluctance of physicians to prescribe drugs supplied by the manufacturer of Pepto-Bismol. The Vick Chemical Company, which had coated the chests of untold millions of Americans with Va-Po-Rub, has even changed its corporate name to Richardson-Merrell in order to develop a new image as an ethical, rather than a proprietary, manufacturer.

Finally, mention should be made of the entry of companies with little or no primary relationship to either the ethical or proprietary fields. In such cases a customary route of entry has been the acquisition of existing ethical drug firms. Mathieson Alkali, for example, acquired the venerable E. R. Squibb firm in 1952, shortly before the Olin-Mathieson merger (the drug operations were spun off into Squibb-Beechnut in 1967). Johnson & Johnson, the largest manufacturer of surgical dressings and similar textile products, acquired McNeil Laboratories in 1959, and has since become a major factor in the oral contraceptive market. Phillips Electronics Company, controlled by Phillips Incandescent Lamp Company of the Netherlands, became Phillips Electronics and Pharmaceutical Industries (now PEPI, Inc.) through the purchase of the Columbus Pharmacal Company. Since the mid-1960's, such cosmetic manufacturers as Revlon Inc. have been moving into pharmaceuticals, presumably because this is the only other industry offering a comparable rate of return on investment. Given the profitability of drug manufacturing, it is not surprising that plants within this industry are operated by companies which themselves are classified primarily in such other diverse industries as animal feeds, women's and children's underwear, soaps and detergents, plastics products, household appliances, or photographic equipment.[1]

It should be noted that the invasion of the ethical drug field by outsiders has been paralleled in recent years by a growing diversification movement among the traditional ethical drug houses. Not surprisingly, a major area of diversification has been into the proprietary market. An obvious factor here is, of course, the profitability of proprietary drugs. Related to this is the fact that an ethical drug company which develops a product safe enough for over-the-counter (nonprescription) sale is faced with a choice: it can keep its ethical image by promoting the drug to physicians and pharmacists, relying upon them to recommend it, or it can advertise directly to the consuming public. In most cases, the latter alternative is chosen.

Some companies, such as Upjohn and Squibb, market proprietary items

---

1   Cf. U.S. Bureau of the Census, *1963*   (Washington, D.C.: U.S. Government
Enterprise Statistics, Part 1, Table 6   Printing Office, 1968).

under their own names, on the theory that the consumer can be more easily persuaded of a drug's quality if it is advertised by the same firm whose products are prescribed by his own doctor. Other companies fear that any broad promotion of over-the-counter remedies will contaminate their carefully nurtured ethical images in the eyes of the medical profession. Using the same strategy as proprietary manufacturers entering the ethical sector, but moving in the opposite direction, these ethical companies have either formed or acquired subsidiaries to market proprietaries in a manner which will minimize any physician identification of their proprietary activities.

The combination of pharmacological advance, marketing changes, and new entrants has markedly changed the character of the pharmaceutical industry. Before World War II, ethical drug manufacturing was dominated by a handful of "old-line" companies, usually family-controlled, such as Lilly, Abbott, Squibb, Upjohn, and Parke, Davis. Very little effort was expended on research, and advertising, even in reputable professional journals, was considered dangerously akin to the promotional activities of the proprietary segment of the industry. In the words of one author: "Conservative and steeped in tradition, they put great emphasis on public responsibility, product quality, and close association with physicians. These segments of the industry, in fact, gave the industry many of the aspects of an exclusive gentlemen's club."[2] Developments since World War II have drastically altered the "gentlemen's club" image of the industry. It has become highly competitive, although this competition among the major companies is seldom on the basis of prices. Research and product development, as a marketing strategy rather than for its own sake, has become one accepted form of competition. The other is advertising and promotion directed to the medical profession on a scale which rivals that of any other industry in the economy.

II. MARKET STRUCTURE

It is difficult to define the "drug industry" with any degree of precision. While this chapter is principally concerned with the ethical sector of the industry, the available statistics include both ethical and proprietary output; indeed, this is unavoidable since today the same companies often operate in both areas. The Bureau of the Census includes both in the "Pharmaceutical Preparations" industry.

The growth of the market for human use alone since before World War II is shown in Table 1.

Over a period of 30 years, the industry expanded its shipments from $301 million to $4.5 billion. It may be a commentary on our society that shipments of tranquilizers alone in 1968 exceeded the entire output of the industry in

---

2   David M. Kiefer, "Prognosis for the Drug Houses," Part 1, *Chemical &*   *Engineering News*, **42**(68):73 (August 10, 1964).

TABLE 1 PHARMACEUTICAL PREPARATIONS FOR HUMAN USE,ᵃ VALUE OF SHIPMENTS, SELECTED YEARS 1939-1968

	DOMESTIC SHIPMENTS ($ MILLION)		EXPORT SHIPMENTS[b] ($ MILLION)	TOTAL ($ MILLION)
	ETHICAL	PROPRIETARY		
1939	148.5	152.4	c	301.0
1947	520.7	317.6	c	838.3
1954	1,088.9	368.3	c	1,457.2
1958	c	c	c	2,256.9
1963	2,001.6	787.1	99.3	2,888.1
1964	2,145.8	797.4	103.6	3,046.8
1965	2,468.9	880.5	112.7	3,462.1
1966	2,684.9	1,000.3	121.6	3,806.9
1967	2,885.8	999.5	112.7	3,998.0
1968	3,223.0	1,123.4	103.5	4,450.0

a   Except biological products.
b   Includes shipments to foreign subsidiaries.
c   Not separately reported.
SOURCE   Bureau of the Census, *Census of Manufactures* (Washington, D.C.: U.S. Government Printing Office, various years); *Current Industrial Reports*, Series MA-28G.

1939 by a wide margin. What is especially notable, as suggested earlier, is the rapid growth of the ethical drug sector, at a rate three times that of the proprietary sector. Not included in Table 1 are veterinary products (ethical and proprietary), which have accounted for a relatively constant 3–4 per cent of the total market. Although they will not be discussed further, it is worth noting that the current level of sales ($151 million in 1968) has become large enough to attract the participation of most of the leading manufacturers of drugs for human use.

Within the ethical sector of the market, several groupings of companies can be distinguished. Leading the list are perhaps 25–30 large companies which promote their products to physicians on a national scale; their emphasis is almost always upon brand names rather than price, and they tend to dominate the private prescription market. Next there is a great number of smaller manufacturers who cannot afford the cost of heavy promotion. Although they occasionally have some local or regional brand reputation, their products are normally sold by generic name either to the retail trade through wholesalers[3]

3   The extent to which wholesalers rely upon small generic drug manufacturers has been increasing in recent years. Most major companies now try to bypass the wholesaler and sell directly to the retailer. Of the largest companies, only Eli Lilly still sells exclusively through wholesalers. Others sell direct (with a modest minimum order) at the same prices they charge the wholesaler—e.g., the direct-buying retailer saves 15–20 per cent of the wholesaler's resale price.

or to governmental and nongovernmental institutions on the basis of competitive bidding. Finally there is a fringe of about 150 "repackaging houses" usually controlled by physicians. The repackaging house buys generic drugs from the lowest-cost source and resells them under its own brand names at much higher prices (frequently above the prices charged by the leading firms in the industry). By prescribing these brands, the stockholding physicians assure a market for the firm and dividends on their own investments at the same time.

Entry into the industry is not inherently difficult. The technical expertise and ability to maintain the high quality necessary for drug manufacturing are well within the reach of small enterprises. Nor are capital requirements for production any barrier. Of the drug companies filing income tax returns in 1964, 38 per cent had no more than $50,000 in assets and 95 per cent were below the $5 million mark.[4] The problem lies not in becoming a drug manufacturer but in becoming a drug marketer. It is only in this context that questions of industry structure and patterns of competitive conduct can be understood.

DEMAND FOR DRUGS

It is desirable to preface the analysis of market structure in the pharmaceutical industry with some mention of the nature of market demand. Little need be said about proprietary drugs, since these are not markedly different from such other consumer nondurables as soft drinks, breakfast foods, cosmetics, toiletries, and so forth. The demand for proprietaries depends largely upon the extent to which consumers suffer, or can be persuaded that they suffer, from headaches, indigestion, insomnia, nervous tension, acne, vitamin deficiency, nasal congestion, or a host of other real or imagined ailments. The consumer diagnoses his own need and then shops around for a product that hopefully will meet this need.

The nature of demand for individual ethical drugs, however, is very nearly unique, at least where private buyers are concerned. With most consumer products, the consumer himself makes the buying decision. For ethical drugs, in the words of the late Senator Kefauver, "He who orders does not buy; he who buys does not order." The decision is made for the consumer by his physician when the latter writes out a prescription, generally by brand name. The pharmacist is obligated to fill the prescription exactly as it is written.[5] If, for example, the physician has specified Achromycin, the druggist must

---

4 Pharmaceutical Manufacturers Association, *Prescription Drug Industry Fact Book, 1968* (Washington, D.C.: Pharmaceutical Manufacturers Association, 1968), p. 15.

5 Although it has always been unethical for a pharmacist to substitute a different drug for the one prescribed, the protection of individual brands of the same drug is of recent origin. As late as 1953, only four states had laws prohibiting brand substitution. Since that time the National Pharmaceutical Council, representing major companies, has managed to secure such laws or pharmacy regulations in all 50 states and the District of Columbia.

supply American Cyanamid's brand of tetracycline and not the identical product offered by Pfizer, Bristol, Squibb, or Upjohn. The average patient may not even know what he has purchased, apart from the fact that it is a bottle of small pink pills, or large white ones, or yellow capsules; in the majority of cases neither the physician nor the pharmacist tells him clearly what has been prescribed.

The customer's ignorance of the product is matched by his ignorance of prices. The most prevalent retail markup on ethical drugs is 40 per cent of the retail price (i.e., $66\frac{2}{3}$ per cent above the cost to the druggist). In any major metropolitan area, however, a given prescription may be filled over a wide range of prices. Some druggists may accept much lower margins, offering substantial savings to customers. Others, especially in the case of less expensive prescriptions, may employ a minimum "professional fee," which results in a higher markup. A quantity of pills that cost the druggist $1.50 would usually be retailed at $2.50, but might be available in some outlets for $2.00 or in others for as much as $3.50, depending upon the pricing policy of the retailer. Comparatively few customers will shop around to have a prescription filled at the lowest price. Even those who are willing to do so find it a difficult task, since in 48 of the 50 states (as of 1969) pharmacists are forbidden by law to advertise prescription drug prices.[6]

Next, consider the physician, who is frequently described as the "purchasing agent" for his patient's drug requirements. In contrast to other purchasing agents, most physicians have little knowledge of price or price alternatives. This stems from what is probably a distortion of an ancient and excellent principle: the physician's prescription of a drug should be based solely upon his judgment as to the best therapy for his patient. Thus, in the flood of advertising and promotional literature with which the major drug companies inundate the medical practitioner, there is never any mention of price, nominally on the ground that such commercialism might be interpreted as an attempt to taint professional judgment. The physician who is concerned about drug prices must find them out in the same way as anyone else; and, with the best will in the world, he simply has no time to engage in economic research.

Finally, remember that the patient has visited his doctor in the first place because he is experiencing certain symptoms which worry him even if they do not incapacitate him; the doctor's prescription offers him the hope that these symptoms can be cured. The patient will have the prescription filled, unless he has absolutely no resources (either of his own or through public aid) to pay the cost. When this underlying reason for seeking medical advice is viewed in juxtaposition to the inability of either the physician or the patient

---

6 The Florida statute, declared invalid in February 1969 by the State Supreme Court, was typical in that it gave the Florida Board of Pharmacy the power to revoke the license of any retail outlet that "promotes or advertises the use or sale of prescription drugs." Only Ohio has never passed a law prohibiting the advertising of prescription drug prices.

to include price as a factor in the buying decision, we can see that the demand for prescription drugs, either in the aggregate or as individual products, approaches closer to complete inelasticity with respect to price than the demand for any other commodity which readily comes to mind.

In the institutional sector of the market (hospitals and governmental agencies), the demand for ethical drugs in the aggregate is probably as inelastic as it is in the private prescription sector. Total demand will depend upon such factors as hospital patient loads or the number of people eligible to receive drugs through governmental channels rather than upon drug prices. Within the aggregate framework, however, the demands for many individual drugs and particularly for different brands of the same drug may exhibit considerable elasticity.

A majority of the nation's hospitals have adopted formularies from which staff physicians are expected to prescribe as a means of holding down hospital costs. The purpose of a formulary can be understood from the foreword to one issued by the Baltimore City Health Department: "The principal criteria for admission of substances to this formulary are therapeutic efficacy, simplicity and economy." Therapeutic efficacy is clear enough. Simplicity is achieved by limiting the number of drugs in the formulary. If, say, 40 or 50 drugs on the market are available to treat the same illness, the formulary committee will choose four or five for inclusion. In this connection it may be noted that there are upwards of 7,000 ethical drug products (single drugs and combinations of two or more active ingredients) offered to the medical profession by the industry. The director of one of the leading hospitals in the country has stated that a formulary containing only 400 of these products covers more than 99 per cent of patients' drug requirements.[7] Economy is achieved both through simplicity and through a common provision that the hospital pharmacy may fill any prescription on a generic basis—i.e., if a staff physician prescribes Meticorten, the pharmacy may dispense equally reliable, but much less expensive, generic prednisone.

In the institutional market as distinct from the private prescription market, therefore, price becomes an important influence in the choices made by purchasing authorities. The degree of this influence may vary considerably according to the ability and objectivity of the decision-makers, and drug manufacturers woo these decision-makers even more assiduously than they do individual practicing physicians. Some hospitals and agencies have done an excellent job; at the other extreme, the state of New Mexico uses the *Physicians' Desk Reference* as its official "formulary."[8] This is a commercial advertising compendium, distributed free to physicians and utilized almost

---

7 U.S. Senate, Select Committee on Small Business, *Hearings on Competitive Problems in the Drug Industry*, Part 2 (Washington, D.C.: U.S. Government Printing Office, 1967), p. 676.

8 Task Force on Prescription Drugs, "The Drug Prescribers," *Background Papers* (Washington, D.C.: U.S. Government Printing Office, 1968), p. 46.

exclusively by the major drug companies. Despite such variations in standards, it is clear that price elasticity of demand can be a significant factor in the institutional market. It is likely to become even more significant as both hospital costs and public expenditures for out-of-hospital prescription drugs for the needy and elderly continue to rise.

To summarize, two submarkets for ethical drugs can be distinguished. The private prescription market accounts for between two thirds and three fourths of total demand, and the institutional market for a quarter to one third. In the former, demand—whether considered in the aggregate for different drugs within the same therapeutic class, or for individual brands of the same drug— is extraordinarily inelastic. In the latter, since price is a factor in decisions involving choices among different drugs for the same therapeutic purpose and in choices among alternative brands of a given drug, an important element of price elasticity may be introduced into the demand functions for individual products and brands.

MARKET CONCENTRATION

Company concentration ratios, developed by the Bureau of the Census and the Senate Subcommittee on Antitrust and Monopoly are shown for the pharmaceutical industry in Table 2. It should be noted that the shipments portrayed are those of plants classified within the industry; i.e., they include both ethical and proprietary products for human or veterinary use, as well as any other products (biologicals, chemicals, flavorings, cosmetics, and so on) manufactured in pharmaceutical plants.

There are approximately 800 firms in the industry. The majority are small enterprises; other data suggests that at least 80 per cent have fewer than

TABLE 2 PHARMACEUTICAL PREPARATIONS INDUSTRY CONCENTRATION RATIOS, 1947–1966

YEAR	NUMBER OF COMPANIES	VALUE OF SHIPMENTS ($ MILLIONS)	PERCENTAGE ACCOUNTED FOR BY THE LARGEST:			
			4	8	20	50
1967	791	4,696.4	24	40	73	90
1966	n.a.	4,432.4	24	41	n.a.	n.a.
1963	944	3,314.3	22	38	72	89
1958	1,064	2,533.4	27	45	73	87
1954	1,128	1,643.1	25	44	68	n.a.
1947	1,123	941.3	28	44	64	n.a.

n.a. = not available.
SOURCE   U.S. Bureau of the Census, *1967 Census of Manufactures*, Special Report Series, *Concentration Ratios in Manufacturing*, MC67(S)–2.1 (Washington, D.C.: U.S. Government Printing Office, 1970).

20 employees.[9] No more than 50 companies today would account for 90 per cent of the industry's output. Nevertheless, on the surface, the industry's structure is not inconsistent with a reasonable expectation of competition. The four largest firms have less than a quarter of the market, and the eight largest about 40 per cent. Further, it is obvious that in the years for which 20 firm ratios are available, the medium-sized firms grew far more rapidly than the industry leaders. Companies in the 9–20 size group increased their market share of total shipments from 20 per cent in 1947 to 34 per cent in 1963, whereas the share of the four largest declined and the next four remained reasonably constant.

Although some drug companies are much larger than others, there do not appear to be any industry-wide dominant firms such as those one finds in automobiles, steel, or a number of other industries. Instead, the bulk of the market is shared among 20–30 leading firms, with a substantial fringe of competitors.

This is the view of the industry emphasized by the Pharmaceutical Manufacturers Association and not a few outside observers. To accept such a view uncritically, however, is to ignore the fact that the overall drug market is fragmented into a number of separate, noncompeting therapeutic markets: antibiotics are not substitutes for antidiabetic drugs, and tranquilizers are not substitutes for vitamins. Manufacturers do not compete on an industry-wide basis, and hence concentration must be evaluated within the various therapeutic groups of drugs in which competition does occur.

When this is done, even on the basis of the fragmentary data available, it is clear that high levels of concentration within important therapeutic classes are a more meaningful element of structure than the relatively moderate level for the industry as a whole. Examples can be found from the overly broad therapeutic classes used by the Bureau of the Census.[10] The four largest producers of central nervous system drugs (including a wide variety of products from aspirin and other analgesics through tranquilizers to anesthetics) accounted for 44 per cent of the market in 1963, whereas the eight largest had 65 per cent. In the anti-infective drug class (including antiparasitic products, antibiotics, antimalarials and even simple antiseptics), the four largest firms held 47 per cent and the eight largest 72 per cent of the market. For preparations affecting neoplasms, endocrine system, and metabolic diseases (lumping together drugs for the treatment of cancer, arthritis, diabetes, with the oral contraceptives, anti-obesity drugs, and others) the four and eight company concentration ratios were, respectively, 53 and 74 per cent. These are high, not low, concentration ratios, and they would be much higher still were Census to compute them on the basis of realistic therapeutic divisions rather than agglomerating widely diverse products into broad categories.

---

9 U.S. Bureau of the Census, *1963 Enterprise Statistics*, Part 1 (Washington, D.C.: U.S. Government Printing Office, 1968), Table 9.

10 U.S. Senate Subcommittee on Antitrust and Monopoly, *Concentration Ratios in Manufacturing Industry, 1963*, Part I (Washington, D.C.: U.S. Government Printing Office, 1966), Table 4.

Another aspect of the pharmaceutical industry, concentration of bulk drug production, is an important consideration even when there may be an impressive number of suppliers of any given finished drug on the market. The nature of this type of concentration may be readily illustrated.[11] Ascorbic acid (Vitamin C) is offered in dosage form by upwards of 150 companies; the entire output of the vitamin itself, however, is produced by Merck, Pfizer, and Hoffman-LaRoche. Finished reserpine products are offered by at least 85 suppliers; S. B. Penick is the sole U.S. manufacturer of the active drug. Meprobamate (Miltown) tablets are now available from over 50 sellers; the actual drug is manufactured by Abbott, Penick, and Millmaster Onyx. It is obvious in such cases that the bulk producers may have considerable power to influence the effectiveness of competition by their selling policies.

In the first two instances, ascorbic acid and reserpine, the bulk manufacturers are selling under conditions that appear to permit remarkably effective price competition at the dosage form level. In the case of meprobamate, there is a very real limit to price competition through control over supply by the patent holder, Carter-Wallace, Inc. With the unfortunate blessing of the Justice Department, the licenses of the three bulk meprobamate manufacturers require that they sell all of their output to Carter; they did so in 1966 at an average price of $2.54 a pound. All compounders of meprobamate products, in turn, must purchase the meprobamate from Carter at a price of $20 or more a pound, or eight times the price which Carter pays the actual manufacturers. In other words, the meprobamate for, say, a thousand 400-mgm tablets costs Carter about $2.35 (including a wastage allowance) and Carter's competitors $18.75, not an inconsiderable advantage to the firm that controls the bulk supply.

In short, concentration ratios for the pharmaceutical industry as a whole convey a somewhat misleading impression of the industry, although they are useful in the broad sense of supplying information on the number and approximate size distribution of drug firms. From a standpoint of the influence of industry structure on competitive behavior, however, it is necessary to go beyond the industry-wide ratios and examine concentration in therapeutically significant categories and in bulk drug production. On this basis it appears that high concentration in these separate categories, rather than the moderate concentration of the entire industry, is the dominant structural characteristic.

GOVERNMENTAL BARRIERS TO COMPETITION

Underlying the types of nonprice competition developed by the major drug companies are a variety of governmental policies which facilitate monopolis-

---

11   Seller information from *Drug Topics Red Book* (New York: Topics Publishing Co., 1966), bulk producer identities from U.S. Tariff Commission, *Synthetic Organic Chemicals, 1966* (Washington, D.C.: U.S. Government Printing Office, 1968).

tic practices in the industry. Especially important are policies with respect to patents, trademarks, and new drug approval. The first two have nothing at all to do with the protection of consumers' health, whereas the third is sometimes administered in such a manner as to go beyond its primary essential purpose.

Patents were not an important factor in the drug industry prior to World War II. Only in part can this be explained by the slow pace of innovation and the relative scarcity of novel drugs at that time. More important, a long tradition in the medical profession and the industry considered that patenting an essential drug was a questionable practice. The United States Pharmacopoeial Convention, for example, held to this position for the first 120 years of its existence; not until 1940 was a patented drug admitted to the United States Pharmacopeia. The reversal of this tradition and the subsequent proliferation of drug patents have created a significant new element in the structural characteristics of the industry over the past quarter century.

A patent monopoly may be exploited in several different ways. The patent-holder can, and often does, if he is an established manufacturer, preserve his monopoly to himself. Frequently, however, the patent is licensed to one or a few other manufacturers. Although such arrangements may provide alternative sellers in the market, they rarely lead to price competition. Finally, licenses are occasionally granted to a number of competitive sellers for reasons not necessarily related to a spirit of benevolence. Thus, Ciba granted an unrestricted license to S. B. Penick to make reserpine, which Penick sells in bulk to a large number of other firms; it is possible that this was motivated to some degree by the desire to avoid legal challenge to a patent on the active ingredient of a botanical product in use for at least 2,000 years. Again, in recent years Carter-Wallace has freely licensed competitors to market meprobamate products (compounded from bulk meprobamate purchased through the company), but only in settlement of an antitrust case brought by the Department of Justice.

Even a dubious patent held by a major company can be a source of great profit, since the mills of justice grind slowly. There is no clearer example of this than the patent on tetracycline, the leading broad-spectrum antibiotic. The basic tetracycline patent was awarded to Pfizer in 1955, following the settlement of complex claims and counterclaims by American Cyanamid and Bristol. Pfizer licensed Cyanamid and Bristol to manufacture and sell tetracycline products; Bristol received the additional right to sublicense Squibb and Upjohn to market finished products made from Bristol's bulk tetracycline. Under this happy arrangement the five companies marketed the drug at identical high prices for a number of years.

In 1958, three years after the patent was issued, the Federal Trade Commission (FTC) challenged the methods used to obtain the patent and the subsequent licensing arrangement. Ten years later, in September 1968, the Sixth Circuit Court of Appeals affirmed a final order of the Commission directing that any qualified manufacturer desirous of producing tetracycline be licensed to do so at a royalty rate not exceeding 5 per cent. The compulsory licensing order became effective when the Supreme Court declined to review the case on April 2, 1969; the patent on tetracycline expires on January 10, 1972. Despite a unanimous FTC decision that the patent was obtained, in the words of Commissioner Jones, "by fraud . . . and by deliberate misrepresentation and withholding of essential and relevant data relating to the patentability of tetracycline . . . ," it has served its purpose as well as any more valid patent for nearly all of the 17 years it could possibly run. There is one solid bit of evidence for a bare minimum indication of the profits involved. In an attempt to settle a collateral price conspiracy case brought by the Department of Justice, early in 1969 the five companies voluntarily offered to establish a $120 million fund to reimburse tetracycline buyers for overcharges.

Although there are thousands of unpatented drugs on the market, the patented products occupy a strategic position. A good indication of this is provided by the so-called Master Drug List assembled by the Task Force on Prescription Drugs. The list contains 366 drugs most frequently prescribed in 1966 for persons aged sixty-five years and over, and accounts for nearly 90 per cent of both the number and cost of prescriptions filled by retail pharmacies for the elderly.[12] Of this number, 293 products (80 per cent of the total) were "still under patent, available only under brand name from a single supplier."[13] In addition, despite an erroneous conclusion of the Task Force to the contrary, many of the drugs available from more than one supplier were also covered by patents, under licensing arrangements not conducive to price competition. Although such a list for the entire population would be somewhat different from that for the elderly, there is no reason to believe that the relative significance of patented products would be any less. The patent system either bars or severely controls entry into the largest part of the prescription drug market and confines meaningful competition to what is quantitatively a small segment of that market.

The use of trademarked brand names, as distinct from the generic, or "official" names of drugs, introduces another governmentally sanctioned interference with the competitive process. While virtually all patented drugs are sold under brand names, the trademark can be particularly valuable to a manufacturer in marketing a drug which either cannot be patented or, if patented, has been so freely licensed as to minimize the competitive barrier of the patent itself. The Master Drug List for the elderly offers numerous examples of each situation.[14] Thus, chloral hydrate is unpatentable since it

---

12 Task Force on Prescription Drugs, "The Drug Users," *Background Papers* (Washington, D.C.: U.S. Government Printing Office, 1968), p. 31 ff. As published the Master Drug List contains 409 items, but with extensive duplication of brand names for identical products (e.g., Miltown, Equanil, and meprobamate are separately entered).

13 Ibid., p. 36.

14 Ibid., appendices B and N.

has been used medicinally as a hypnotic, or sedative, for a full century. It is available from a number of suppliers; nevertheless, Squibb's Noctec brand of chloral hydrate had more than half of the market in the Task Force survey— and at wholesale prices from three to four times the cost of the generic product offered by reliable small firms. Meprobamate has been mentioned as a patented drug freely licensed. Despite this, American Home Products (Equanil) and Carter-Wallace (Miltown and Meprospan) appear to retain 80 per cent of the market, at prices to the druggist which are more than double the prices charged by generic suppliers. Ciba's brand of reserpine (Serpasil) outsells generic reserpine by a wide margin at wholesale prices which are up to forty times those charged by some of its competitors.

It can be argued that brand names are a pervasive characteristic of the American economy, and hence one should not be surprised to see them used in the pharmaceutical industry. This ignores the very basic distinctions between the marketing of prescription drugs and, say, detergents or gasoline. In the first place, official standards for drugs establish the identity of products from different suppliers to a degree not found in most other consumer goods. Confirmed cases in which branded and generic versions of the same drug have not been chemically and biologically equivalent are exceedingly rare.

More important, we return to the basic fact that the physician makes the buying decision for the patient. Jersey Standard undoubtedly would be happy to get twice as much per gallon for Esso gasoline as independent dealers get for their products, but the company knows that this is impossible. No matter how heavily it is promoted, the value of the Esso trademark in the minds of consumers is at most three or four cents a gallon over the price of "generic" gasoline; if the differential widens in any market, the company is forced to cut prices to hold its market position. Since physicians are to a large degree insulated from price considerations, however, the major pharmaceutical companies can achieve and hold dominant positions in ethical drug markets, solely through promotion of their brand names; further, a firm that has established itself as a leading seller of a drug can enjoy average revenues per unit of output that are two, three, ten, or more times those that can be realized by its generic competitors. There is no other industry in the economy in which a trademark can be so successfully exploited to the benefit of the seller.

A third influence of government on market structure and conduct is the New Drug Application (NDA) procedure of the Food and Drug Administration (FDA). Unlike patents and trademarks, this procedure is essential to the protection of the public, and thus, to a large extent, its impact on the industry is unavoidable. Old drugs (or in good bureaucratese, "not-new" drugs) may be marketed by any registered manufacturer so long as they meet established standards of purity, strength, and quality. It is unlawful, however, for any manufacturer to offer for sale a new drug unless he holds an effective NDA for the product, i.e., one approved by the FDA.

Proof of safety and efficacy required for FDA approval of an application necessarily requires an elaborate program of animal and clinical (human) testing at a cost that is beyond the reach of most smaller companies. Thus the introduction of new drugs and the marketing advantages accruing from them tend to be confined to the major companies. In an industry so marked by the rapid introduction of new products as drug manufacturing has been, this gives an inevitable competitive edge to size.

The FDA practice, however, may serve to magnify restrictive effects of New Drug procedure beyond what is essential for the protection of consumers. A drug may remain on New Drug status indefinitely, in some cases even beyond the term of a patent. Throughout this period not only the innovator, but also any subsequent marketer must hold an effective NDA, supported by adequate clinical tests. The cost of repeating such tests on a drug whose safety and efficacy have been presumably established by the original applicant can be a powerful deterrent to potential small competitors. Among the major companies, on the other hand, there appears to be an active trade in so-called letters of authorization—a device by which an original applicant, company A, permits a second applicant, company B, to avoid the expense of further testing by offering A's tests as proof of the safety and efficacy of B's own product.[15] Such letters are usually an integral part of licensing agreements and product exchange arrangements, or may on occasion be purchased in an outright cash transaction.

The nature of demand for drugs would tend to produce high levels of concentration in meaningful therapeutic markets. This tendency is reinforced to a significant degree by a variety of governmental policies. What remains to be explored are the patterns of market conduct which both flow from and maintain these levels of concentration.

III. MARKET CONDUCT AND PERFORMANCE

The major ethical drug manufacturers, like their compatriots in other industries, are convinced that they operate in an intensely competitive environment. From a businessman's viewpoint, they are certainly correct. The number of persons suffering from a given illness represents the ultimate market for drugs used to treat that illness. A new product can gain a place in the market only by winning a share away from other products with similar therapeutic uses. Any product, no matter how well established, may find its market position eroded almost to the vanishing point by the successful introduction of a new product. This rivalry among the major firms seldom expresses itself in the price competition of classical economics, at least so far as the

---

15   The fact that FDA accepts such arrangements undermines any logical basis for requiring repetitive clinical tests from subsequent NDA applicants.

private prescription market is concerned; the fields of combat are product development and product promotion.

RESEARCH AND DEVELOPMENT

The stimulus to research and new drug development provided during World War II carried over into the postwar era, although by 1950 there had occurred a very real change in its focus. There were no product patents on the original penicillin G, and the basic process patents were held by the government which freely licensed all interested manufacturers. Two of the largest producers, Merck and Pfizer, were still fine chemical manufacturers, who sold bulk penicillin and finished dosage forms to other drug companies rather than marketing under their own brand names. As a result the penicillin market was highly competitive. When the drug was released by the War Production Board for sale through normal channels in 1945, Merck's bulk price was $6,000 per billion units (BU). By December 1948 the bulk price had dropped below $1,000 per BU, and in another 4 years the $100 level was reached. In 1965 the average sale value of the principal medicinal salts (procaine and potassium) of penicillin G was below $15 per BU.[16] Competition and the absence of patent restrictions ensured that the benefits of technological progress in the manufacture of penicillin G reached the market, through price reductions of nearly 99.8 per cent.

Any check provided to research incentives by the price erosion of competition in the case of penicillin was soon offset by American Cyanamid's success with chlortetracycline (Achromycin), followed by Parke, Davis's chloramphenicol (Chloromycetin) and Pfizer's oxytetracycline (Terramycin) in 1949 and 1950. Here the combination of private patent monopoly and heavy promotional campaigns demonstrated the amazing capacity of new drugs to make profits for their innovators. It was at this point that the major pharmaceutical firms discovered the importance of research and development, not so much for its own sake, but as a basic element in competitive strategy.

The dimensions of the research revolution can be seen in the annual research activity surveys conducted by the Pharmaceutical Manufacturers Association (PMA) since 1951.[17] In that year firms which conducted nearly all of the industry's research reported expenditures (excluding government contracts) of $50 million. By the end of the decade, company financed research outlays for human-use drugs were close to $200 million, whereas by 1968 they had risen to $472 million.

---

16 U.S. Tariff Commission, *Synthetic Organic Chemicals 1965* (Washington, D.C.: U.S. Government Printing Office, 1967).

17 Pharmaceutical Manufacturers Association, *Prescription Drug Industry*

Fact Book 1968, op. cit. p. 39 and "Research and Development Activity, 1967–1968," (Washington, D.C.: Pharmaceutical Manufacturers Association, 1969).

Company-financed research and development expenses, like sales, tend to be highly concentrated within the larger firms. Within the PMA group in 1967, more than three fourths of the total outlay was accounted for by 17 companies with budgets of $10 million and over. Forty-two companies with research and development budgets of at least $1 million a year reported 97 per cent of the total. The use of research as a competitive strategy is primarily the prerogative of the major companies. This should not be surprising in view of the nature and the cost of drug research and development.

Even at the basic research stage, costs are high. The principal starting point is one of "mass screening," i.e., the investigation of hundreds or thousands of substances on the random chance that a few might have some desirable therapeutic effect. In large part this reflects the fact that pharmacology is still in its infancy, better equipped to describe effects than to explain causes. We know a great deal about what a large number of drugs will do in the treatment of illness and very little about how these drugs accomplish their results. With a weak theoretical foundation on which to build, there can be little alternative to mass screenings as a means of developing new products.

An appreciation of this research approach may be gained from the PMA detailed survey for 1967. In that year the companies who replied to the PMA questionnaire indicated that they had investigated nearly 176,000 chemical substances for possible therapeutic use. A total of 1,370 showed sufficient promise to be advanced to a stage of clinical trials. Of this number it may be predicted that 20–25 will reach the market, where, with a little bit of luck and a lot of promotion, perhaps 10 or 12 will achieve some commercial success. This is an extraordinarily expensive way to develop "new models" for the marketing department to sell.

The new-model analogy is hardly farfetched. Few of the new chemical entities marketed in any year are truly original. The majority are congeners (new salts or other minor molecular variations) of existing drugs. These may, but more often do not, represent any real improvement over the drugs on which they are modeled. What the molecular variants do offer is the basis for additional patents, through which rivals can enter a field from which they would otherwise be foreclosed and the opportunity for promotion as "significant therapeutic advances." The benzothiazide diuretics can provide an illustration. Chlorothiazide (Diuril), introduced by Merck in 1957, secured a major share of the diuretic market almost overnight. Within 3 years eight other closely related compounds were on the market, with two more added in 1961 and 1963. Merck itself marketed two of the variants, for in the pharmaceutical industry the developer of a successful original drug cannot rest on his laurels; knowing what his competitors' reactions will be, he must exert every effort to produce his own new models.

There are two sides to any evaluation of the research performance of the industry. On the one hand, the industry can rightly claim that its research effort is impressive (with a higher ratio of privately financed research to sales than can be found anywhere else) and that the result has been a flow of products which have revolutionized the practice of medicine. Even the oft-maligned molecular manipulation can be defended in numerous instances where the goal of experimentation has been to produce a drug that has a broader range of therapy or less toxicity than one already in use. On the other hand, the proliferation of "me-too" drugs arising from molecular manipulation, aimed solely at product marketing, involves an unfortunate waste of extremely scarce resources and talents. This view is not confined to extramural critics of the industry. Nowhere has it been better expressed than by the research director of one of the finest firms in the industry:

We cannot ignore the criticism that we have created an abundance of new drugs, related structurely and therapeutically, which in the minds of many serious-minded clinicians contribute little but confusion. . .

In viewing the congener-drug developments of recent years, I have often wondered why medicinal chemists in so many laboratories had chosen to direct their efforts into molecular modification of new drugs discovered by others. Although this massive surge has created new knowledge for the medicinal chemists at an almost explosive rate, its productiveness in the field of medicine can be questioned.[18]

ADVERTISING AND PROMOTION OF DRUGS

The layman often assumes that because ethical drugs are not advertised to the general public, they are not advertised at all. Nothing could be further from the truth. No other products on the market are promoted as intensively as ethical drugs. Like so many other aspects of the industry, this has been a post-World War II development. Prior to the war the promotional efforts of the old-line drug companies were limited to a small amount of restrained advertising in professional journals with occasional visits to physicians by company sales representatives, stressing the quality of the companies' product lines.

The change came in 1948, when American Cyanamid's Lederle Laboratories first used the blitz technique to introduce Aureomycin to the medical profession. The 142,000 physicians then in active practice were inundated with journal advertisements, direct mail, and ten freight car loads of samples which alone were said to have cost $2 million.[19] The blitz approach was adopted by Merck and Pfizer, both of whom were then making the difficult transition from fine chemical manufacturing to ethical drug marketing. During the following decade, aggressive sales promotion became the principal

---

18 Task Force on Prescription Drugs, "The Drug Makers and the Drug Distributors," *Background Papers* (Washington, D.C.: U.S. Government Printing Office, 1968), p. 22.

19 Charles E. Silberman, "Drugs: The Pace is Getting Furious," *Fortune*, **61**:140 (May 1960).

characteristic of market conduct. The newer entrants found it an effective way of penetrating the market, and the old-line companies followed defensively.

"Educational effort" (as the industry prefers to call drug promotion) is directed almost entirely to the select group of about 200,000 practicing physicians who are in a position to decide what drugs and what brands will be purchased by the ultimate consumers. The effort begins when the physician is still a medical student and continues throughout his active career. For the leading companies, drug promotion has been successful in developing brand and company loyalties within the profession, which can be far more effective in maintaining sales than the therapeutic value of the particular drugs promoted. Further, it is a mode of competition requiring enormous resources beyond the reach of all but the major firms in the industry.

The funds devoted to drug promotion can only be guessed. In the course of the Kefauver investigation, 22 companies reported that advertising and promotional expenses for their drug operations alone amounted to $580 million in 1958; the subcommittee staff estimated that the industry total was $750 million.[20] Allowing for increases in salesmen's salaries and expenses, advertising rates and mailing costs, as well as a growth of over 80 per cent in manufacturer's shipments in the following decade, a conservative estimate for 1969 would be well over $1 billion. The magnitude of this sum can be appreciated best in terms of the small audience courted by the drug companies—the expenditure averages at least $5,000 per physician.[21]

Perhaps half of the total expenditure is used for advertising as such. This includes advertising in the Journal of the American Medical Association (AMA) and other AMA publications. Such advertising, together with the rental of membership lists to drug companies for direct mail campaigns, provides half of the AMA income. Over a hundred other professional journals are published by medical specialty groups and by regional, state, and even county medical societies, as well as pharmacy and dental associations. In addition, there are a number of "controlled circulation" publications, distributed free to physicians and supported entirely by advertising. These periodicals contain articles ranging from laudatory reviews of particular drugs to helpful hints for the tired physician as to the best European golf courses for his vacation.

Heavy as it is, journal advertising is dwarfed in dollar volume by direct mail promotion, particularly in the introduction of new products. For example, in promoting Achromycin, its brand of tetracycline, Lederle Laboratories spent nearly $900,000 (at 1954 prices) in direct mail advertising during the first year that the product was on the market; this included an average of two

---

20   U.S. Senate, Subcommittee on Antitrust and Monopoly, *Report on Administered Prices—Drugs* (Washington, D.C.: U.S. Government Printing Office, 1961), p. 157.

21   A slightly more modest estimate, $4,500 per physician, was provided to the Task Force on Prescription Drugs by Dr. James Goddard, former FDA Commissioner. See Task Force on Prescription Drugs, "The Drug Makers and the Drug Distributors," op. cit., p. 28.

mailings a week to every physician in the country.[22] An advertising executive estimated that by 1962, the average doctor was receiving 4,000 promotional pieces a year.[23]

The very magnitude of journal and direct mail advertising causes it to lose much of its impact. The average physician is too busy to do more than glance at the mass of material that comes into his office, and much of it is thrown away unopened. For this reason, the key element in any major company's promotional effort is the sales representative, or "detailman." Most people have seen a detailman without realizing it—he is a conservatively dressed gentleman with an attache case, sitting quietly in the doctor's waiting room until the physician can spare him 5 or 10 minutes between patients. His function in that brief period is to persuade the doctor to prescribe his company's drugs, especially any new products that are being marketed.

This persuasion function may be considered either "education" or "brainwashing," depending on how one views the industry. There is some evidence for the latter point of view. The detailman has neither enough of the doctor's time nor the qualifications to present a balanced scientific report on the product he is pushing. At best he will give a one-sided but reasonable presentation of the benefits of the drug. At worst his approach raises serious ethical questions.

In 1968 the Nelson Subcommittee reprinted a series of bulletins from a regional sales manager to his detailmen, regarding promotion of an antirheumatic drug, indomethacin.[24] The scientific level of these documents is illustrated by his description of elderly patients as "the real crocks and cruds of everyday practice." At one point he informed his superior: "Our guys are using a real expanded claim"—translated, this means that his salesmen were making therapeutic claims to physicians which went far beyond any clinical evidence submitted by the company to FDA. Coupled with this was a slanderous attack on the leading competitive product, including the implication that any physician using the rival drug "is a gambling sole" (sic) willing to risk a malpractice suit. The "educational" theme of the campaign is best expressed in the conclusion of one bulletin: "Tell 'Em Again and Again and Again—Tell 'Em Until They're Sold and Stay Sold."

Nevertheless, the detailman does provide an educational service in the present state of pharmacological communication. Few physicians have the time to keep up with professional literature in the drug field, and not many more are influenced solely by company advertising. A number of surveys of

22 U.S. Senate, Subcommittee on Antitrust and Monopoly, *Hearings on the Drug Industry Antitrust Act*, Part 2 (Washington, D.C.: U.S. Government Printing Office, 1961), p. 783.

23 Pierre S. Gerai, "Advertising and Promotion of Drugs," *Drugs in Our Society* (Baltimore: Johns Hopkins Press, 1964), p. 192.

24 U.S. Senate, Subcommittee on Monopoly, *Hearings on Competitive Problems in the Drug Industry*, Part 8 (Washington, D.C.: U.S. Government Printing Office, 1968).

drug information sources are in agreement that the majority of doctors get their first knowledge of new drugs from detailmen. It is for this reason that the industry devotes so much of its promotional outlays to the support of detailing. The cost of this promotion is high. The Kefauver subcommittee learned that in 1958 there were some 15,000 detailmen in the industry. The cost of keeping a single detailman in the field, salary, expenses, training, and so on, was about $16,000. By 1968 the number of detailmen had grown to 20,000 and the cost may be estimated to be $25,000–30,000 per detailman. The total annual detailing outlay by the industry was between $500 million and $600 million a year at this time.

From the standpoint of market performance, the issue of drug advertising and promotion has a significance which transcends its economic cost. Almost any drug good enough to be useful has some potential for toxicity. A number of distinguished pharmacologists are in agreement that drug company promotional efforts have led to overprescribing on a large scale, which has created an increasingly serious problem of illness and hospitalization caused by the drugs themselves. It is in the area of product promotion that the basic conflict between the goal of the drug company as a profit-seeking organization and its function of meeting a vital human need is most evident.

PRICING POLICIES

Drug companies, like other firms, are in business to make profits; this means, simply enough, that any firm's overall price structure must be sufficient to provide revenue that more than covers costs. The nature of these costs can be illustrated by two surveys of leading firms made some 8 years apart and covering different but overlapping groups.[25]

The two surveys are in substantial agreement. Both sets of figures show that production costs absorb a minor portion, roughly one third, of total revenue for the leading firms. The costs of nonprice competition (research and brand promotion) are of the same order of magnitude as manufacturing costs. Within this area, advertising and selling expenses account for a far larger share of the corporate budget than research into new or improved drugs. This has led observers to suggest that, for the major pharmaceutical companies, prices determine costs rather than the other way around—i.e., a company tries to establish a price structure high enough to finance the degree of nonprice competition required to maintain its market position.

Table 4 provides some illustrations, from the HEW Task Force study, of differences between the costs to druggists of brand-name prescription quantities and the identical drugs from generic suppliers. Since the generic drugs on

---

25 The Subcommittee's 1958 survey was based on detailed financial reports, covering drug operations only, from 22 companies. The Task Force's survey, including 13 of the companies in the subcommittee's sample, was derived from published information for 17 companies.

TABLE 3 BREAKDOWN OF SALES DOLLAR, LEADING DRUG COMPANIES

	1958 (22 COMPANIES)	1966 (17 COMPANIES)
Net profit	13.0%	13.5%
Income taxes	12.8	10.0
General and administrative expense	10.9	35.0
Advertising and selling expense	24.8	
Research and development	6.3	6.5
Cost of goods sold	32.1	35.0

SOURCES U.S. Senate, Subcommittee on Antitrust and Monopoly, *Report on Administered Prices: Drugs* (Washington, D.C.: U.S. Government Printing Office, 1961), p. 31; Task Force on Prescription Drugs, "The Drug Manufacturers and the Drug Distributors," *Background Papers* (Washington, D.C.: U.S. Government Printing Office, 1969), p. 14.

the list are regularly offered at the prices shown, we can assume that these prices are sufficient to cover costs and to provide a reasonable profit margin to the supplier. The table thus provides an illustration of the influence of brand-names promotion on manufacturer's pricing policies, despite the existence of competitive suppliers. It may be noted that for half the drugs shown,

TABLE 4 BRAND NAMES VERSUS LOWEST PRICE GENERIC DRUGS: COST TO DRUGGIST OF TYPICAL PRESCRIPTION, 1966

BRAND NAME; GENERIC NAME	COST TO DRUGGIST	
	BRAND ($)	GENERIC ($)
Achromycin; tetracycline hydrochloride	2.04	.66
Chlor-Trimeton; chlorpheniramine maleate	.71	.15
Decadron; dexamethasone	3.10	1.36
Dexedrine; dextroamphetamine sulfate	2.71	.19
Miltown; meprobamate	2.75	1.01
Nembutal; sodium pentobarbital	.46	.12
Noctec; chloral hydrate	1.08	.29
Pentids; penicillin G potassium	1.99	.23
Peritrate; pentaerythritol tetranitrate	2.42	.10
Prolixin; fluphenazine	1.91	.09
Seconal Sodium; secobarbital sodium	.49	.12
Serpasil; reserpine	2.04	.05

SOURCE Task Force on Prescription Drugs, "The Drug Users," *Background Papers* (Washington, D.C.: U.S. Government Printing Office, 1969), Appendix N.

the generic version was not prescribed often enough to gain a place on the Task Force's list of those most frequently prescribed, and in most other instances brand-name products held the lion's share of the market.

In sales to institutional buyers, much depends on the nature of competition and the desire of a company to move its products into these channels. The influence of competition was explored by the Kefauver subcommittee in respect to sales to the Military Medical Supply Agency, then the drug procurement agency for the Armed Forces.[26] A significant inverse relationship was found between the number of bidders and prices offered. Thus, Squibb's bids on hydrocortisone (five bidders) and cortisone acetate tablets (ten bidders) were, respectively, 25 per cent and 28 per cent of the company's prices to direct buying retailers; in the case of the oral antidiabetic drug tolbutamide (Orinase), for which Squibb was the only supplier, the company's price to the government was 90 per cent of the price to the druggist. More recently, the City of New York was purchasing 50-mg Benadryl capsules from Parke, Davis at a price of $15.63 per 1,000; as soon as the city adopted the generic specification (diphenhydramine capsules), it was able to buy the same item for $3.00—from Parke, Davis.[27]

Meeting competitive prices in the institutional market has a significance beyond the immediate sale. Prescribing habits acquired by military physicians, medical students and interns in teaching hospitals, and staff physicians in community hospitals are carried over into private practice. George Squibb, a former marketing director himself, has stated:

> We know that if a certain product is used in a teaching hospital, where a large proportion of the physicians of a community practice, that the use of this product outside the hospital on private practice prescriptions will be larger. . . this is a real factor in the success of a product.[28]

Many companies view entry into important segments of the institutional market as a logical extension of their overall promotional program. Discriminatory pricing in this area (Robinson-Patman restrictions exempt sales to governmental or nonprofit agencies) may be one of the less expensive methods to develop a market for a product.

Given the nature of demand and the limitations of price competition in the pharmaceutical industry, pricing policy appears to be the weakest area of performance. Monopolistic competition has created a situation in which a large part of the private consumer's outlay goes for prices which are higher

26 U.S. Senate, Subcommittee on Antitrust and Monopoly, "Report on Administered Prices: Drugs," op. cit., pp. 88–97, 262.

27 U.S. Senate, Subcommittee on Monopoly, *Hearings on Competitive Problems in the Drug Industry*, Part 1 (Washington, D.C.: U.S. Government Printing Office, 1967), p. 389.

28 U.S. Senate, Subcommittee on Monopoly, *Hearings on Competitive Problems in the Drug Industry*, Part 5 (Washington, D.C.: U.S. Government Printing Office, 1968), p. 1566.

than they need be by any standards, such as the costs of production or product improvement, prices to institutional buyers, or the prices at which competitive products are available.

DRUG COMPANY PROFITS

The profitability of an industry provides an important clue to its economic performance. Note that this clue is susceptible to two interpretations, particularly when the industry maintains a high level of profits over a long period of time. A financial analyst would take such performance as evidence of good management, sound marketing, and an excellent investment prospect. An economist, on the other hand, might well view the same performance as evidence of a market structure and pattern of conduct which deviates significantly from any competitive norm. Suffice it to say that the profit record of the pharmaceutical industry is impressive to financial analysts.

Table 5 shows the average rates of return on stockholders' investment from 1958 to 1968 for 12 large companies, the drug industry as a whole, and all manufacturing. Over the entire period, the annual rates of return for all manufacturing averaged 10.8 per cent, compared to 18.0 per cent for the entire drug industry and 19.1 per cent for the 12 large companies shown.[29]

TABLE 5 RATES OF RETURN ON AVERAGE STOCKHOLDERS' INVESTMENT,[a] PHARMACEUTICAL INDUSTRY AND ALL MANUFACTURING, 1958–1968

YEAR	12 LARGE COMPANIES AVERAGE (%)	RANGE (%)	DRUG INDUSTRY (%)	ALL MANUFACTURING (%)
1968	18.8	9.0–26.1	18.3	12.1
1967	19.0	10.4–28.1	18.7	11.7
1966	21.1	14.4–29.8	20.3	13.4
1965	21.0	14.3–32.7	20.3	13.0
1964	18.9	13.6–33.0	18.2	11.6
1963	17.8	11.2–32.7	16.8	10.3
1962	17.1	6.3–33.0	16.8	9.8
1961	17.6	10.3–32.7	16.7	8.8
1960	18.4	10.3–31.6	16.8	9.2
1959	20.3	11.5–37.5	17.8	10.4
1958	20.3	13.3–35.4	17.7	8.6

a Net profit as a per cent of the average of net worth at the beginning and the end of each year.

SOURCES Federal Trade Commission, *Rates of Return for Identical Companies in Selected Manufacturing Industries* (Washington, D.C.: U.S. Government Printing Office, annual); FTC-SEC "Quarterly Financial Reports."

29 The 12 companies are Abbott Laboratories, American Home Products, Eli Lilly, Merck & Co., Parke, Davis & Co., Chas. Pfizer, Rexall Drug & Chemical, Richardson-Merrell, Smith, Kline & French Laboratories, Sterling Drug, Upjohn Co., and Warner Lambert Pharmaceutical Co.

Further, as Table 5 suggests, there has been relatively less variation in drug industry profits than in all manufacturing. Drug industry profits after taxes rose in every year from 1958 ($343 million) to 1968 ($973 million), including those years in which net manufacturing income as a whole declined. Few, if any, industries in the economy can match this record.

A coterie of distinguished economists, retained by the PMA, explained to the Nelson Subcommittee in 1968 that the rate of return in this industry reflects a substantial risk factor. If this were so, over a reasonable period of time losses would presumably offset extreme profits, so that something approaching the average rate of return in the economy would result. Among the 12 companies for which individual rates of return have been published by FTC, the least profitable, Rexall, averaged 12.6 per cent from 1958 to 1968, whereas Smith, Kline, & French averaged 32.0 per cent; in general, nine of the 12 firms managed to do at least half again as well as the 10.8 per cent average for all manufacturing over the 11-year period.

Thus, although considerable variation among company profits does exist, the risk appears to lie between earning a normal rate of return and some significant multiple of a normal rate. This would seem to support what has been said earlier concerning the barriers to effective price competition in the industry.

A CONCLUDING NOTE ON PERFORMANCE

Many aspects of the pharmaceutical industry's economic performance can be criticized. Market-oriented research has been wasteful of scarce technical and professional talents, promotional methods leave much to be desired, price and profit levels are difficult to defend on any rational basis. Yet no evaluation of performance can be complete without recognition of what may truly be called "the facts of life." A baby born in 1920 had a life expectancy of 54 years; one born in 1965 could reasonably hope for a life span of more than 70 years. Medical advances, better nutrition, higher educational levels, and a host of other factors have been of great importance, but the drug industry is entitled to no small share of the credit for this improvement.

A number of the dreaded diseases of the past are much less serious problems today. In the early 1930's, for example, pneumonia was treated in a manner which was more sophisticated (leeches and emetics had been discarded) but hardly less rudimentary than had been the practice for centuries. Basically, the infection ran its course, with physician and relatives gathering around the bedside for "the crisis" to learn whether the patient would live or die. Since then penicillin and the broad-spectrum antibiotics have reduced the mortality rate of pneumonia by more than 60 per cent. In just 15 years from 1950 to 1965, the death rate from tuberculosis was cut by 80 per cent, from syphilis and its complications by nearly 75 per cent, from complications of pregnancy and childbirth by 70 per cent, and from nephritis by 67 per cent.

The development of preventive serums and vaccines has been of incalculable value, especially in the protection of children. Diphtheria antitoxin has reduced the incidence of this often fatal disease from 85,000 cases in 1929 to 164 in 1965. The Salk and Sabin vaccines have virtually eliminated the horror of poliomyelitis; more than 33,000 cases were reported during the polio epidemic of 1950, and only 72 cases in 1965. The sharp reduction in measles cases since 1960 offers the hope that this disease, too, may join the ranks of those that the medical student must learn from a textbook because they are so rarely seen in clinical practice.

Tranquilizers and other psychotherapeutic drugs have shown excellent results in the treatment of mental illness. Persons who formerly would have been hospitalized for extensive periods are now treated in out-patient clinics while retaining their status as self-supporting members of society; the period of confinement has been dramatically reduced for many of those who still require hospital treatment. Despite an increase in the number of persons treated for mental illness, the patient population of mental institutions has fallen steadily from its 1955 peak to the point where many of these facilities are being converted to general hospitals.

In still other areas life has been made somewhat more comfortable through drugs. The oral antidiabetic products have freed many victims of diabetes from the discomfort and inconvenience of daily insulin injections. Oral contraceptives have introduced a new degree of certainty in family planning. The antihistamines have relieved the sufferings of millions of allergy patients.

The examples suggested, and many others, can best be judged in terms of the prevention of disease, the mitigation of physical mental suffering, and the extension of life itself. In these terms the ethical pharmaceutical industry has made a magnificent contribution to human welfare. The function of the economist is to analyze what exists, in the hope that improvement in the allocation and management of resources may lead to even greater progress in the future, but not to deny the very real accomplishments of the industry to the present.

IV. PUBLIC POLICY

Public policy has been concerned primarily with the safety and efficacy of drug products. Safety is a less simple matter than it might appear to be. Any drug, from aspirin through the spectrum of pharmaceutical remedies, has some potential for toxicity, so that safety is a relative term, and the determination of safety standards is an extraordinarily complex problem. Efficacy refers to the probability that a drug will have the therapeutic results for which it is prescribed. More is involved here than the waste of money in buying safe but useless drugs; treatment with such drugs can lead to serious or fatal delays in the institution of effective therapy.

The Pure Food and Drugs Act of 1906 was the first significant Federal drug legislation. Passage of the Act required years of work by its supporters (who included most ethical drug companies), the crusading efforts of Dr. Harvey W. Wiley, and, ultimately, a catalyst for public opinion in the form of Upton Sinclair's novel *The Jungle*. This book described conditions in the meatpacking industry so graphically that public consumption of meat dropped sharply, the press entered the fray, President Theodore Roosevelt called for reform, and Congress was moved to speedy action, passing first a meat inspection bill in 1905 and then the omnibus food and drug bill a year later.

The 1906 act established the United States Pharmacopeia, the National Formulary, and the Homeopathic Pharmacopeia (seldom used today) as official compendia, establishing enforceable standards for the purity, strength, and quality of drugs. All drug products had to be clearly labeled as to identity and composition, and no drug could be described as "U.S.P.," "N.F.," or "H.P." unless it could be demonstrated by tests and assay that it was identical to the official drug included in the appropriate compendium. For the first time, physicians could have some confidence that the patient would receive the drug prescribed by his doctor.

From a modern point of view, the 1906 act was woefully inadequate, lacking either safety or efficacy provisions. Any drug, no matter how dangerous or worthless it might be, could be freely marketed. The government could not move against a toxic product, and then only by a lengthy process, until the product had actually caused injuries or deaths in use. In this respect it is interesting to note that the Biological Serums and Antitoxins Act of 1913 required manufacturers of these products for veterinary use to demonstrate both the safety and the efficacy of items they proposed to market. It took Congress another half century to extend the same protection to human consumers.

In 1933 President Franklin D. Roosevelt proposed new legislation which would require food processors and cosmetic manufacturers (not covered by the existing law) to prove the safety of any chemical additives or cosmetic mixtures used; for drug products the proposed requirements included both safety and efficacy. Although leading ethical drug producers supported the safety provisions, they balked at the efficacy proposal, and this was quietly dropped. There was strong opposition to any change in the law from the proprietary drug, the food, and the cosmetics industries. The bill languished for several years, until once again an event occurred to arouse public opinion and galvanize the Congress into action. This time the catalyst was the "Elixir Sulfanilamide" disaster.

Sulfanilamide, first of the "wonder drugs," appeared in 1935. With any such drug there is great demand for a liquid suspension for children and adults who find it difficult to swallow tablets or capsules. Unfortunately, sulfanilamide proved to be insoluble in water, alcohol, or any other known drug solvent. A chemist employed by S. E. Massengill Company found that the drug would dissolve in diethylene glycol, a sweet syrupy liquid used primarily as a dye solvent. The elixir, which was rushed to the market without safety tests, claimed 107 known victims, nearly all of whom were children.

In the wake of this tragedy, Congress passed the Food, Drug, and Cosmetics Act of 1938 which, as amended, is still the basic law of the land. The act greatly expanded the powers of the Food and Drug Administration to protect the public against unsafe products. In broad terms, this was accomplished by defining foods, drugs, or cosmetics as adulterated if they contained any substances found by FDA not to be demonstrably safe for human use. So far as drugs are concerned, since 1938 any manufacturer who wishes to market a new drug must first secure an Effective New Drug Application; note that "effective" does not mean "efficacious" in this context.

Under the 1938 act the NDA had to include (1) reports of animal tests and clinical investigations made to determine the safety of the drug; (2) a list of substances used as components of the drug; (3) a full statement of the composition of the finished product; (4) a description of manufacturing methods, facilities, and quality controls used in producing the drug; (5) samples required by FDA for testing; and (6) specimens of all proposed labeling for the drug. If the application was not disapproved by FDA, it automatically became effective at the end of 60 days unless the agency exercised an option to extend its review for up to another 120 days. In any event, the power of the FDA was essentially a negative one of rejection, rather than a positive approach of approval. Should the application be rejected, of course, the applicant was entitled to judicial review.

The act had a number of shortcomings in addition to its failure to require any proof of efficacy. Since the FDA jurisdiction began with the marketing stage, dangerous drugs could be widely distributed to unqualified investigators for clinical testing; such drugs might even reach the market from some companies which included only favorable clinical reports in their applications. Medical advertising was unregulated and tended to be both inaccurate and misleading.[30] Although the act provided the first statutory basis for factory inspection, enforcement required a lengthy criminal prosecution, which was seldom employed. These shortcomings were intensified by an FDA leadership that, in the case of the ethical drug industry, failed to enforce vigorously the powers that it did possess.

Once again any reform needed both a crusader and a catalyst. The crusade was provided by Senator Estes Kefauver, whose hearings on the ethical drug industry, beginning in December 1959, attracted wide public attention. The senator's legislative proposals, however, appeared to be a lost cause until another near disaster occurred.

---

30 The FDA held that responsibility for medical advertising, as distinct from labeling, rested with the FTC; the FTC, in turn, could not or would not regulate advertising directed solely to an audience professionally qualified to evaluate its merits.

Thalidomide was a sedative-type drug developed by Chemie Grunenthal of West Germany and widely marketed throughout Europe. Richardson-Merrell secured a U.S. license, distributed clinical testing quantities to nearly 1,300 physicians, and filed a NDA for marketing in this country. Fortunately, the FDA scientist responsible for this application delayed action as long as she could, in light of foreign reports that pregnant women treated with thalidomide delivered horribly deformed infants with disturbing frequency. The entire case, including the pressure on Dr. Kelsey from her superiors to approve the application, made newspaper headlines before the drug was released. As a result, a compromise bill, the Kefauver-Harris Amendments to the Act of 1938, was passed by Congress and signed by the President in October 1962.

Under the amendments, positive approval of a NDA is required before a drug can be offered for sale. Approval cannot be granted unless the applicant offers "substantial evidence" of therapeutic efficacy in addition to proof of safety. Further, the Secretary of Health, Education and Welfare may withdraw approval of any drug marketed between 1938 and 1962 if the manufacturer is unable to furnish satisfactory evidence of its efficacy. The impact of this provision became evident in 1968 and 1969 when FDA took steps to remove from the market a number of products, including 90 popular and profitable combinations of antibiotics, following authoritative review of therapeutic evidence.

The FDA received the power to regulate clinical testing to ensure maximum safety and quality. Before beginning such tests a manufacturer must now have carried out thorough animal toxicity tests and hold an approved Investigational New Drug (IND) application. The IND describes the nature of the tests, as well as the names and qualifications of investigators. Careful records must be kept, with unfavorable as well as favorable results made available to FDA.

Governmental control over drug quality has been vastly improved. The FDA is empowered to issue and enforce "good manufacturing practices" regulations covering both production methods and quality control procedures. Every manufacturer or packager is required to register his plants annually, and these establishments must be inspected at least every two years. Federal courts are now authorized to issue injunctions against refusals to permit inspection. In the special case of antibiotics, the FDA must sample and certify every batch produced before it can be used in finished products; this is an extension of earlier amendments covering penicillin and four other antibiotics.

Finally, the Kefauver-Harris Amendments as implemented by FDA regulations have raised the standards of prescription drug advertising. Advertisements of brand names must also feature prominently the generic names of drugs. They must contain summaries of side effects and contraindications (i.e., conditions such as pregnancy, heart trouble, or diabetes, in which a given drug should not be administered). Advertising claims must not go beyond the therapeutic evidence submitted to the FDA for a drug's efficacy. Any drug that is improperly advertised is considered to be misbranded, subject to seizure and removal from the market.

Present legislation, if properly enforced, can ensure the quality and the utility of drugs reaching the consumer. Little attention has been paid, however, to the economic conditions under which drugs are distributed. Public concern in this area will grow as governmental funds are increasingly committed to the purchase of drugs. Federal and State funds paid for more than 16 per cent of the ethical drug industry's output in fiscal year 1968; if comprehensive drug coverage is added to Medicare, governmental payments could account for half the industry's output by 1975.[31] Under similar circumstances a number of foreign nations have adopted cost-reducing measures ranging from an emphasis on generic prescribing, restrictive formularies, compulsory licensing of high-priced patented drugs, and the regulation of profit margins, to direct price control. This will be the area of debate over public policy in the U.S. during the 1970's. In the author's opinion, it is to be hoped that the debate will be resolved in terms which do not impair the individual physician's right to prescribe as he sees fit but which will enable him to exercise this judgment in a more competitive environment than has heretofore existed.

SUGGESTED READINGS

BOOKS AND PAMPHLETS

Drugs in Our Society. Ed. by Paul Talalay. Baltimore: The Johns Hopkins Press, 1964

Garb, Solomon, and Betty Jean Crim. *Pharmacology and Patient Care*. New York: Springer Publishing Company, Inc., 1962.

Harris, Richard. *The Real Voice*. New York: The Macmillan Company, 1964.

Harris, Seymour E. *The Economics of American Medicine*. New York: The Macmillan Company, 1964.

Mintz, Morton. *By Prescription Only*. New York: Houghton Mifflin Com-Company, 1967.

GOVERNMENT PUBLICATIONS

Task Force on Prescription Drugs, *Background Papers* (Washington, D.C.: U.S. Government Printing Office, 1968, 1969):
   "Approaches to Drug Insurance Design."
   "Current American and Foreign Programs."
   "The Drug Manufacturers and the Drug Distributors."

---

31 Task Force on Prescription Drugs, "Approaches to Drug Insurance Design," *Background Papers* (Washington, D.C.: U.S. Government Printing Office, 1969), pp. 20, 21.

"The Drug Prescribers."

"The Drug Users."

Task Force on Prescription Drugs. *Final Report.* Washington, D.C.: U.S. Government Printing Office, f 1969.

U.S. Senate, Subcommittee on Antitrust and Monopoly. *Hearings on Administered Prices.* Parts 13–24. Washington, D.C.: U.S. Government Printing Office, 1960–1962.

U.S. Senate, Subcommittee on Antitrust and Monopoly. *Hearings on the Drug Industry Antitrust Act.* Parts 1–7. Washington, D.C.: U.S. Government Printing Office, 1962.

U.S. Senate, Subcommittee on Antitrust and Monopoly. *Report on Administered Prices: Drugs.* Washington, D.C.: U.S. Government Printing Office, 1962.

U.S. Senate, Subcommittee on Monopoly. *Hearings on Competitive Problems in the Drug Industry.* Parts 1–14. Washington, D.C.: U.S. Government Printing Office, 1967–1970.

ARTICLES

Kiefer, David M. "Prognosis for the Drug Houses." *Chemical & Engineering News.* **42**:68 (August 10, 1964).

Kiefer, David M. "The Challenge of Change in the U.S. Drug Industry." *Chemical & Engineering News.* **42**:114 (August 17, 1964).

May, Charles D. "Selling Drugs by 'Educating' Physicians." *Journal of Medical Education.* **36**:1 (January 1961).

Reese, K.M. "Drug Prices." *Chemical & Engineering News.* **46**:66 (January 29, 1968).

Silberman, Charles E. "Drugs: The Pace Is Getting Furious." *Fortune.* **61**:138 (May 1960).

Steele, Henry. "Patent Restrictions and Price Competition in the Ethical Drug Industry." *Journal of Industrial Economics.* **12**:198 (July 1964).

6. Kenneth Elzinga
THE BEER INDUSTRY

I. INTRODUCTION

The beer industry and college education have an interesting historical relationship. For example, Robert Sedgwick, one of the first commercial brewers in the colonies, helped endow Harvard.[1] Matthew Vassar's fortune made in brewing enabled him to start Vassar. Obviously, some educational institutions owe a part of their success to the beer industry.

One might also argue that the beer industry owes part of its success to college education—due to the obvious reciprocity displayed by college students toward the brewing industry and their seeming devotion to its economic well-being. Whether this devotion stems from the generosity of Sedgwick and Vassar or from some characteristic of the industry's product, is a question economics is not suited to answer. What economic analysis can yield, however, is some conception of the structure and level of competition in this industry.

THE DEFINITION OF THE INDUSTRY

Beer is a potable product with four main ingredients.

1. Malt, which is simply barley (or some grain) that has been germinated in water and dried.
2. Flavoring adjuncts, usually hops and corn or rice, to give beer its lightness and provide starch which the enzymes in malt convert to sugar.
3. Cultured yeast, which ferments the beverage and feeds on the sugar content of the malt to produce alcohol and carbonic acid.
4. Water, which acts as a solvent for the other ingredients.

Since the process of *brewing* (or boiling) is so intrinsic to the making of beer, the industry is often called the brewing industry.

---

1 From the 1670's until the end of the 1700's, there was a series of three brew houses on the Harvard grounds to furnish what was, even then, a familiar beverage for college students.

Generically the term beer means any beverage brewed from a starchy (or farinaceous) grain.[2] Because the grain is made into a malt which becomes the main substance of the beverage, another broad term for beer is malt liquor or malt beverage. In this study the terms beer, malt liquor, and malt beverage will be used broadly and interchangeably to include all such products as beer, ale, porter, stout, and malt liquor. Because the terms beer and malt liquor also have meaning in a narrow sense, i.e., as specific products that are distinct from each other and from other malt beverages, to avoid confusion these terms in the narrow sense will be preceded by the word "product," e.g., the product beer, the product malt liquor.[3]

For this study, then, beer includes a variety of products. It includes those products that are branded as beer; it also includes products branded as ale and malt liquor. The factor common to the beverages of this industry, and that which differentiates them from all other alcoholic and nonalcoholic beverages, is that all are brewed by a process of fermentation applied to a basic grain ingredient.

Note, however, that a unique production process is not the key to defining an industry. The concept of an industry implies a group of firms (or conceivably one firm) supplying a set of products that consumers, voting in the marketplace, find to be close substitutes for each other. To be sure, some avid drinkers of the product beer may not prefer to substitute, say, ale, but these people would prefer to substitute milk even less! The cross-elasticity of demand is high between malt beverages. And it is upon this fungible characteristic of all malt beverages that its distinction as a separate industry can be made.

The distinction is supported, moreover, by the high cross-elasticity of supply between the separate products of this industry. If a firm is producing some brand of beer and notices that ale production is very profitable, its management can shift to ale production with only moderate difficulty. A brewer would be much more hard pressed to shift into some other nonmalt beverage such as milk. For that matter, to shift even to another alcoholic beverage such as wine or distilled spirits would be expensive. The cross-elasticity of supply between malt beverages and other alcoholic beverages is low.

EARLY HISTORY

The history of beer in America originated with the founding of America. Beer was a very common beverage in England and the early settlers had not only

---

2   The grain is generally barley, sometimes wheat, rye, or millet. In what were presumably distressing times, pumpkins and potatoes were used—or perhaps *tried* is the better word.

3   The product beer is the most commonly consumed malt beverage in the United States. In fact, the product beer commands such an overwhelming share of all malt beverage consumption that, for many purposes, the study of the beer industry is the study of the product beer.

a taste for beer but also a supply of it on the ships that brought them. In 1630, in New Amsterdam, the first recorded public brewery was established. Other commercial brewing followed, though considerable brewing was done also in the homes of seventeenth century America. All that was needed in the way of equipment at the time were a few vats, one for mashing, one for cooling, and one for fermenting. The resulting product would be scarcely recognizable (or consumed) as beer today. The process was very crude. The end result uncertain. Small wonder brewing was referred to as "an art and mystery."

Brewing was often publicly encouraged in early America. For example, the General Court of Massachusetts passed an act in 1789 to support the brewing of beer ". . . as an important means of preserving the health of the citizens . . . and of preventing the pernicious effects of spirituous liquors." James Ogle-thorpe, trustee of the colony of Georgia, was even blunter: "cheap beer is the only means to keep rum out."

LAGER BEER: THE JUMPING OFF POINT   The 1840's and 1850's were important decades in the brewing industry. The product beer, in the basic form consumed today, was introduced in the 1840's with the brewing of lager beer.[4] Prior to lager beer's introduction, malt beverage consumption in America resembled English tastes—heavily oriented toward ale, porter, and stout. Lager beer represented the influence of German tastes and brewing skills. The influx of German immigrants provided not only skillful brewers but also eager customers for this type of beer.

In 1850, there were 431 brewers in the U.S. who produced 750,000 barrels of beer.[5] By the end of the decade, 1,269 brewers produced over a million barrels of beer, dramatic evidence of the high expectations held by many of this industry's future.

In 1851, Valentin Blatz bought the City Brewery. Four years later another German, Frederick Miller, purchased the Menomonee Valley Brewery. A year later the Krug Brewery came under the control of Joseph Schlitz. All this took place in Milwaukee, Wisconsin. In St. Louis, in 1857, a soap manufacturer named Eberhard Anheuser joined with his son-in-law Adolphus Busch, to begin what became a not unsuccessful brewery. These are names now familiar to all beer drinkers.

The latter half of the nineteenth century saw not only the successful innovation of lager beer in America. The industry prospered through the adoption of several important technological advances affecting the production and marketing of malt beverages. Mechanical refrigeration greatly aided the production process as well as the transporting of beer. Pasteurization, originally

---

4 Lager beer is bottom fermented, i.e., the yeast settles to the bottom during fermentation. Also lager beer is aged (or "lagered") to mellow. The result is a lighter, more effervescent brew.

5 A barrel of beer contains 31 gallons or 446 8-oz. glasses (allowing for spillage) or almost 14 cases of 24 12-oz. bottles.

a process proposed to preserve wine and beer, was adopted during this period. This meant beer did not have to be kept cold, could be shipped into hot areas, and stored for a longer period of time without refermenting. Once the stability of beer was secured through pasteurization, the way was opened for wide-scale bottling and off-premise consumption of beer. In addition, developments in transportation technology enabled brewers to expand production beyond their local markets. The twentieth century saw the rise of the national brewer.

PROHIBITION   The twentieth century also saw the legal banning of beer sales. The temperance movement, which began as the promotion of voluntary moderation and abstention from hard liquors, slowly moved towards a goal of universal compulsory abstention from all alcoholic beverages. The beer industry seemed blissfully ignorant of the movement. Many brewers thought (or hoped) the movement would lead to a ban only on liquor.

In 1919, 36 states ratified the 18th Amendment to enact national prohibition of alcoholic beverages. This led many brewers to simply close up shop; some produced other products. Schlitz sold candy; Blatz produced industrial alcohol. Pabst made cheese, soft drinks, even machinery. Anheuser-Busch and others built a profitable business selling malt syrup which was used to make "home brew." Since a firm could not state the ultimate purpose of malt syrup, the product was marketed as an ingredient for making baked goods, such as cookies.

Prohibition lasted until April of 1933. The rapidity with which brewers reopened after repeal was amazing. By June 1933, 31 brewers were in operation; in another year, the number was 756

THE DEMAND FOR BEER IN THE
POST-WORLD WAR II PERIOD

The total market demand for beer exhibits seasonal fluctuations due to the greater thirsts during hot weather. On an annual basis, the overall demand began a slow decline in 1948 from a 1947 record sales of 87.2 million barrels. The 1947 figure was never surpassed until 1959 with sales of 87.6 million barrels. During this period, per capita consumption fell from 18.5 to 15.0 gallons in 1958. In the 1960's, total demand began to grow again at an average rate of better than 3 per cent per year. The year 1965 marked the first year with over 100 million barrels sold, and the figure for 1968 was 111.4 million barrels. Per capita consumption has crept up from 1958's level of 15 gallons to 1968's level of 16.7 gallons. Still, the industry has never fully recovered from prohibition. Per capita consumption during the decade prior to prohibition (1908–1917) averaged 19.9 gallons.

Demand is not only seasonal but also varies from region to region. The East North Central and Middle Atlantic States show the highest per capita consumption; the East South Central and South Atlantic the lowest. By states, the demand for beer varies strongly. Alabama and North Carolina had per capita consumption of 8.0 and 9.5 gallons in 1968, respectively. Needless to say, with a national per capita consumption in 1968 of 16.7 gallons, some states register a heavy demand to compensate for the more moderate southern states. In fact, nine states have per capita figures of over 20 gallons; of these, Wisconsin far outdistances the others with a per capita consumption of 27.2 gallons.

Though economists are never able to measure price elasticity exactly, a statistical estimation indicates the total demand for beer to be inelastic. However, brand attachment is not so strong as to make the demand for any particular malt beverage inelastic. Demand for individual brands of malt beverages is elastic.[6]

One indication of how responsive consumers have been to price changes is seen from the records of a price discrimination case to be discussed later. Table 1 shows the percentage of the St. Louis market recorded on various dates by Anheuser-Busch, three important rival brewers, and the combined total of the other brewers. At the close of 1953, Anheuser-Busch's Budweiser beer was selling for 58 cents per case more than the three rivals and had 12.5 per cent of the market. Early in 1954 the price of Budweiser was cut 25 cents; but, since this was a wholesale price, it had only a small impact upon the retail price. Still, the Anheuser-Busch market share increased.

In June 1954, Anheuser-Busch cut its price to $2.35 per case, the same as its rivals. By early in 1955, Budweiser was the largest beer seller in St. Louis. At that time, prices were increased by all the sellers in such a manner that Budweiser again sold at a differential of 30 cents per case. Note that the Anheuser-Busch market share then dropped, evidence that consumers will shift brands in response to price incentives.

TABLE 1

	DECEMBER 1953 (%)	JUNE 1954 (%)	MARCH 1955 (%)	JULY 1955 (%)
Anheuser-Busch	12.5	16.6	39.3	21.0
Griesedieck Bros.	14.4	12.6	4.8	7.4
Falstaff	29.4	32.0	29.1	36.6
Griesedieck Western	38.9	33.0	23.1	27.8
Others	4.8	5.8	3.9	7.2

SOURCE Taken from *Federal Trade Commission* v. *Anheuser-Busch*, 363 U.S. 536 at 541. Subsequent evidence indicated that factors in addition to price accounted for the Griesedieck Bros. drop in market share.

6 Ira Horowitz and Ann R. Horowitz, "Firms in a Declining Market: the Brewing Case," *Journal of Industrial Economics*, 13(129):138 (March 1965).

II. MARKET STRUCTURE

One general conclusion of economic analysis is that the consumer is more apt to be able to buy the exact product he wants at the lowest price when he faces a large number of independent rivals, all willing and able to sell to him. When he faces a monopolist (or tight-knit oligopoly) his choice is reduced; he must pay its price or go without. Because of this, the question of the *structure* of the beer industry, the total number and size distribution of firms arrayed before beer consumers, is of interest and importance. Is the beer industry unconcentrated, with its customers courted by many firms, or concentrated, forcing beer drinkers to do business with but a handful of brewers?

Though the structure of the beer industry has altered substantially in the post-World War II period, no easy answer can be given to the above question. There have been two opposing forces at work in the industry, one leading to increased concentration, the other in the opposite direction. On the one hand, there has been a marked decline in the number of brewers in the U.S. The forces behind this decline cause beer drinkers to face fewer sellers. On the other hand, there has been an increase in the size of market area served by existing brewers, so that brewers now offering their products in larger geographic areas create competition with rivals who previously did not face them. The result of this trend is to offer beer consumers a wider choice. The exact extent to which these two forces offset each other is not certain.

THE DECLINE IN NUMBERS

The decline in the number of individual plants and the number of independent companies in the brewing industry has been substantial. In 1935, shortly after repeal, there were 750 brewing plants operating in the U.S. Since that time the number has declined, dropping in every single year with the exception of three, to a total of 163 in 1968. Table 2 shows the decline in the number of companies in the industry. Note that in a 20-year period the number of independent brewers more than quartered though beer sales increased by almost 20 million barrels. Few other American industries have undergone a similar structural shakeup.

TABLE 2

YEAR	NUMBER OF COMPANIES
1947	404
1954	263
1958	211
1963	150
1967	93

SOURCE   Adapted from United States Senate, Committee on the Judiciary, *Report, Concentration Ratios in Manufacturing Industry, 1963*, Part I (Washington, D.C.: U.S. Government Printing Office, 1966); *Modern Brewery Age: Blue Book Issue* (Stamford, Conn.: Modern Brewery Age Publishing Co., 1968).

TABLE 3

YEAR	PERCENTAGE OF VALUE ADDED ACCOUNTED FOR BY TOP BREWERS		
	4 LARGEST	8 LARGEST	20 LARGEST
1963	34	52	78
1958	28	44	68
1954	27	41	60
1947	21	30	44

YEAR	PERCENTAGE OF SALES ACCOUNTED FOR BY TOP BREWERS		
	5 LARGEST	10 LARGEST	25 LARGEST
1969	47.8	69.1	95.5
1966	42.6	63.2	90.4
1963	38.4	58.2	84.3
1958	28.5	45.2	66.7
1954	24.9	38.3	59.1
1947	19.0	28.2	43.3

SOURCES   United States Senate, Committee on the Judiciary, *Report, Concentration Ratios in Manufacturing Industry, 1963*, Part I (Washington, D.C.: U.S. Government Printing Office, 1966); I. Horowitz and A. R. Horowitz, "The Beer Industry," *Business Horizons*, **10**:14 (1967); *Marketing/Communications*, **298**:27 (January 1970).

Concomitant with the decline in the number of companies has been the increasing share of national business held by a handful of the largest brewers. As Table 3 shows, in 1947 the top 4 companies accounted for 21 per cent of the industry's value added; in 1963 their share was 34 per cent. The top 20 brewers increased their market share in this 16-year period from less than one half to over three fourths of the national market. On the basis of sales, the top five brewers have increased their share steadily. Table 3 also shows the increasing dominance of the top five and ten brewers.

THE WIDENING OF MARKETS

To understand the offsetting structural factor to this decline in brewing companies one must realize that in the days of hundreds of brewing companies, most beer drinkers faced an actual choice of only a few brewers. This was because the majority of brewers were small and the geographic market area they served was severely limited. Beer is an expensive product to ship, relative to its value, and few brewers could afford to compete in the "home markets" of distant brewers.

Thus at one time it was very meaningful to speak of local, regional, and national brewers. Of these, the local brewer was the most common. He brewed for a small market, perhaps smaller than a single state, often only a single metropolitan area. The regional brewer was multistate, but usually encompassed no more than two or three. The national brewers, those selling in all or almost all the states, were very few in number. In addition, it was very uncommon for a firm to operate more than one plant.

Today, to talk of local, regional, and national brewers is still meaningful and common parlance in the industry, but much less so than in the past. The average geographic market served by one brewer from one plant has, so to speak, "exploded," because of the economies of large-scale production and, to some extent, marketing. With the average-size brewing plant much larger today, the brewing company "reaches out" geographically to sell sufficient beer to maintain capacity operations.

For example, the Olympia Brewing Company operates out of one plant in Olympia, Washington. In 1957, it sold beer in 8 states; in 1968 it sold in 11 states and considers it possible to ship to all states west of the Mississippi on a profitable basis, an example of the exploding scope of market served by regional brewers.

Supporting the ability to enter new geographic regions is the rather recent propensity on the part of large brewers to operate more than one plant. In 1955 the top ten brewers operated ten plants. In 1961 the top ten operated 40 plants; by 1968, 48 plants. Of the top 20 brewers in 1967, 15 were multiplant operations. The Carling Brewing Company, for example, had four plants in 1957; a decade later it had seven plants and sold in 47 of the 50 states.

The problem of determining the degree of concentration in brewing is inextricably tied up with delineating just how wide the markets for beer are. If there is one market, a national one, then the concentration statistics for the entire nation are relevant. But if brewing, like cement or milk, has regional markets, then delineating their boundaries is necessary before the industry's structure can be ascertained.

The federal courts have to solve this problem when deciding antimerger cases in the brewing industry.[7] A couple of examples taken from their attempts will indicate that to understand the supply and demand forces in this industry, one must look to a wide geographic market, but not so wide as to include the entire country.

In evaluating the merger of Schlitz with a California brewer and its stock control over another western brewer, a California district court, noting that freight rates were important in beer marketing, singled out an eight western

---

7 In order to determine the possible effect of a merger on competition, a relevant geographic market has to be determined.

state area as a separate geographic market.[8] The judge was impressed by the fact that, in 1963, 80 per cent of the beer sold in this area was also produced there and 94 per cent of the beer produced in the area that year was sold there. The Continental Divide was seen as a transportation barrier of sorts from outside the area, as evidenced by those brewers who, having plants both in the eight state area and outside, generally supplied the eight state area from their western plants only.

Given these figures, most economists would agree that if one wants to see what determines the supply and demand for beer in this eight state area, one need be concerned only slightly, if at all, by supply and demand conditions in the regions east of the Continental Divide. Even here, however, the geographic area is not perfectly clear cut. Adolph Coors Company, located in Colorado outside the eight state area, was the leading seller of beer in the eight state area in 1963, with 13.6 per cent of the total sales; it can certainly be argued that any market area that overlooks this important seller overlooks an important force on the supply side. The market, in its economic sense, should include all the buyers and sellers that are important in explaining the supply and demand conditions in any one place.

In another court case involving the merger of two brewers located in Wisconsin, the government was able to convince the Supreme Court that the state of Wisconsin alone is ". . . a distinguishable and economically significant market for the sale of beer."[9]

Although Wisconsin may be a separate market for legal purposes, to single it out as a meaningful market in the economic sense is to draw the market boundaries too narrowly. In 1966, brewers in the state of Wisconsin sold 14.7 million barrels of beer; that year consumers in Wisconsin bought 3.6 million barrels of beer.

Since beer is also "imported" into Wisconsin from brewers in Minnesota and Missouri, obviously more than three fourths of Wisconsin beer is "exported" to other states. To say then that Wisconsin is a separate geographic market is to overlook the impact of over three fourths of the production in that state, not to mention the impact upon supply of beer coming into Wisconsin and competing with the "home" brewers. In 1961, roughly 25 per cent of the beer consumed in Wisconsin was not produced there.[10]

One simply cannot explain the price of beer in Wisconsin without looking at the supply and demand conditions in other states that buy the bulk of Wisconsin's beer production. In this case, the court erred by singling out the state of Wisconsin as an economically meaningful market.

---

8 See *U.S.* v. *Jos. Schlitz*, 253 F. Supp. 129 (1966); aff'd. 385 U.S. 37 (1966). The states were: California, Oregon, Washington, Nevada, Idaho, Montana, Utah, and Arizona.

9 *U.S.* v. *Pabst*, 384 U.S. 546 (1966) at 559.

10 *U.S.* v. *Pabst*; trial transcripts. M. A. Adelman testimony, p. 2007.

Despite the difficulties of ascertaining with numerical exactness the magnitude of the increased geographic scope of the marketing efforts of brewers, brewing *is* a concentrated industry. Consider the case of a beer consumer in Wisconsin. In 1955 there were 43 breweries operating in Wisconsin, and beer was sold in Wisconsin by 77 breweries, i.e., 34 breweries shipped beer into Wisconsin to compete with the breweries located there. There has been a steady decline in the number of breweries operating in Wisconsin, down to 17 breweries in 1968, a drop of 60 per cent. However, the decline in the number of breweries "exporting" to Wisconsin was not as great. In 1968, 32 breweries "exported" to Wisconsin, a drop of only 6 per cent. Nevertheless, in spite of the increased ability of brewers to ship into Wisconsin, the Wisconsin beer drinker is now courted by fewer suitors. It is probable, though the evidence is sketchy, that the forces which work to increase concentration are more than offset by the force of widening markets.

THE REASONS FOR THE DECLINE
IN THE NUMBER OF BREWERS

What are the reasons for the precipitous drop in the number of rival brewers? In a sense, each brewer's demise is somewhat unique. But many have common characteristics. In this section, two factors leading to the decline in brewers will be considered: economies of scale and mergers. In a later section, the impact of advertising on the industry's structure will be assessed.

ECONOMIES OF SCALE   Economies of scale pertain to the size of production plant necessary to produce at relatively low unit costs. Economies of scale exist if "big plants" produce at lower unit costs than small ones. In a broad sense, economies of scale relate not only to some finite productive capacity but also to management's ability to use the capacity efficiently.

In markets where competitive pressures are present, firms that do not operate with internal efficiency or exploit potential economies of scale are squeezed out. To a considerable extent, this was the fate of many brewers since repeal; they have been eased out because of poor management, inefficient plants, or both.

Shortly after repeal in 1933, there was a flood of entrants into the brewing industry, all expecting to be faced with thirsty customers. However, the demand for beer was unexpectedly low in the immediate post-repeal period, far below the expectations and hopes of the brewers. From the high of 750 breweries operating in 1935, almost 100 were quickly eliminated in but 5 years.

Quite a few of the post-repeal breweries had operated before prohibition, but many were under new management. Some were family-owned firms and heredity had been cruel to the second or third generations, not endowing them with the brewing and/or managerial capabilities of their fathers or grandfathers. Competitive pressures, no respecter of nepotism, eliminated such breweries.[11]

Most of these new entrants were small producers, selling in local or, at most, single-state areas. As economies of scale became more pronounced, those who expanded their production survived. The brewer who could continue to operate profitably on a small scale became rarer and rarer.

The extent to which inefficient plants were forced out is evidenced by a study of brewing plants that ceased operations from 1950 to 1961.[12] During this period there were 182 such plants. Of the 182 plants, 119 simply closed their doors and ceased producing beer—*prima facie* evidence that they were not operating on an economically efficient scale, for if they were, some enterprising management presumably would have reopened them. In 41 of these closings, the company that owned the brewery continued to operate from another location—again *prima facie* evidence that the closed plant was not of an optimum size. Thus it appears that roughly 88 per cent of these closings represented plants that were either too small or had insufficient managerial talent.

The inability of small plants to produce efficiently is also borne out by the substantial increase, since repeal of prohibition, in the average-size plant in the brewing industry. In 1947 the average plant had 188 employees; in 1963, in spite of considerable automation, the average plant had 312 employees. In 1947, brewing plants had an average value of shipments of $4.09 million; by 1963 the average value of shipments, in constant dollars, had increased more than twofold to $11.48 million.

The increasing importance of the larger plant in brewing is also indicated in the simple "survivor test" shown in Table 4. This Table shows the number

TABLE 4

PLANTS WITH AVERAGE EMPLOYMENT OF:

YEARS	TOTAL PLANTS	1–19	20–99	100–499	500–999	1000–2499	2500+
1947	440	47	196	166	23	5	3
1954	301	35	107	120	26	9	4
1958	258	34	88	97	27	9	3
1963	201	21	61	85	23	8	3

SOURCE   Adapted from *Census of Manufactures* (Vol. 2; Part 1, 1947, 1954, 1958, 1963).

11   Alfred Marshall saw this phenomenon as one of the important factors limiting the growth and size of firms, and an important determinant in the preservation of competition. See Alfred Marshall, *Principles of Economics*, ed. by C. W. Guillebaud (New York: Macmillan, 1961), pp. 315–17.

12   *U.S.* v. *Pabst*, trial transcripts, R. I. Tenney testimony, pp. 2593–2601.

of plants existing in four different years by employment size. Note first the already mentioned decline in the total number of plants in the U.S. Now note where the decline has been the severest. The plants with 1–19 employees have more than halved in number. The plants with 20–99 employees have diminished by more than two thirds. Those with 100–499 have almost halved in number. Only those plants with 500+ employees have shown stability in their numbers—indicating that these plants have, over the period 1947–1963, been better suited for survival than their smaller counterparts.

Using some crude estimations, the capacity of the 500-employee brewery is over 700,000 barrels per year. Two other observers place the minimum efficient scale of a brewing plant at 100,000 barrels and estimate that the lowest average cost range is around 1 million barrels per year.[13] Another observer estimates the minimum efficient scale of plant to be 1 million barrels per year.[14] Still another economist has estimated that a brewery of roughly 500,000 barrels per year could produce at low average unit costs.[15] A cost study done for the Brewer's Association of America offered this general comment on economies of scale:[16]

> The only relationship between the large and small brewery was that there was a tendency towards the larger brewery realizing a lower beer cost than the smaller brewery.

The Report added that this was a general conclusion not a constant condition. In some cases, small brewers operated at less cost than their larger counterparts.

Of course, no definitive answer can be given to this question of optimality since the optimum plant will vary depending upon the density and growth of the market served, the intensity of competition, the management's ability to produce a quality brew and still cut costs, and the condition of the brewing facilities. Conceivably, a small brewer in a metropolitan area, by serving only that area and keeping transportation costs at a minimum, could survive by finding a special niche for itself.

Nevertheless, these various studies and estimates on economies of scale support three general but important conclusions.

> The present state of technology for brewing and packaging beer is such that large breweries, of at least 500,000–1,000,000 barrels of capacity, are probably necessary to exploit this technology. Brewers with less than

13 Horowitz and Horowitz, "Firms in a Declining Market: the Brewing Case," op. cit., p. 145.

14 Leonard W. Weiss, "An Evaluation of Mergers in Six Industries," *Review of Economics and Statistics*, **47**(172):177 (May 1965).

15 *U.S.* v. *Pabst*, trial transcripts, M.A. Adelman testimony, pp. 2944 and 2045.

16 Roger L. Goettsche, A Report to the Brewers' Association of America *1958 Brewery Cost Report* (Chicago: Brewers' Association of America, 1959), p. 5.

this capacity may survive but not under less than excellent management that can compensate for what will tend to be higher production costs. The days of the brewer of less than 100,000 barrels, barring unusual circumstances, are numbered.

Of the 200 firms that left the industry between 1947–1964, 151 firms had sales of less than 100,000 barrels per year; only 19 firms had sales exceeding 200,000 barrels per year. Since plants of this relatively small capacity are vanishing from the industry, presumably many are of inefficient size or lacking in adequate management. Consequently, what may seem to be a sharp drop in the number of rivals in brewing is actually a disappearance of many of the least efficient brewers, whose impact as a competitive force is *de minimus*.[17]

THE CONDITION OF ENTRY   The ease with which outsiders can enter an industry is a structural characteristic of great importance in ensuring competitive performance. If entry is easy, if potential rivals are lurking in the wings so to speak, existing firms will be reluctant to use what market power they may have to raise prices—lest they encourage an outbreak of fresh competition. On the other hand, if entry is barred, perhaps by a patent or government license, existing firms will find the potential for garnering monopoly gains greatly enhanced.

Entry into the beer industry is not hindered by the traditional barriers of patents and exclusive government grants. Nor is the monopolization of key resources or economies of scale so important that an efficient entrant would have to supply a significant share of industry output. Yet entry is not likely. In part, this is explained by the relatively low profits, the slow increase in demand, and the fatality rate of small firms in the industry. Given these factors, rational investors will probably find better opportunities elsewhere for their funds.

The sheer expense of entering the beer industry is, no doubt, a barrier, though it would be less of one were profits higher, thereby making credit easier to acquire. Still, with the expiration of the small brewery has come the demise of the inexpensive brewery. The price of a modern million barrel brewery is $35 million to $40 million.

Once the brewery is built, the cost of introducing the new brew will also be high, since entrants will have to overcome the entrenched product differentiation of the established brewers. One example of the high promotional costs involved in marketing a new beer is Rheingold's introduction of its Gablinger's brand. In 1966, Rheingold spent more than $5 a barrel promoting Gablinger's.

A look at the record indicates the low probability of any potential threat facing existing producers of beer from outside aspirants. Since World War II,

17   See Ann Horowitz and Ira Horowitz, "Entropy, Markov Processes and Competition in the Brewing Industry," *Journal of Industrial Economics,* **16**(196): 210 (July 1968).

four firms have tried to enter the American beer market. Three of these were American firms; all failed. The only successful entrant was Carlings of Canada. Entry certainly is not impossible, and there are many industries with much higher barriers to entry. The beer industry can be classed as one with moderate, though increasing, barriers to entry.[18] The most promising source of new competition is that of the established brewer moving into a new geographic market.

MERGERS IN THE BREWING INDUSTRY Mergers have one of three effects on competition:

1. Strengthening it, by forming a viable rival where one previously did not exist;
2. No recognizable effect;
3. Lessening it, by removing from the scene an important established or potential rival.

Mergers in brewing have been of all three types.

In some cases, brewers have been strengthened through their acquisition program. Falstaff for example acquired a series of five geographically dispersed small to moderate size breweries in 1948–1956. To these five, with their original capacity of 1,620,000 barrels, Falstaff added 2,105,000 barrels of new capacity, making Falstaff one of the more vigorous brewers of less than national scope.

Many of the mergers in brewing represent no more than the demise of an inefficient firm, salvaging some remainder of its worth, perhaps only a brand name, by selling out to another brewer. This type of merger has no measureable impact upon competition, and should be allowed—even encouraged. Allowing mergers of this type eases freedom of "exit" from an industry; if exit were made more costly, potential aspirants will be less apt to enter. Some inefficient brewers have had the penalty of inefficiency lightened by the merger exit route. For example, two of the breweries acquired by Drewrys, Limited in 1961–1962, if not acquired, would have gone into receivership.

Not all of the mergers in brewing can be dismissed as having salutary or *de minimus* effects on competition. In fact the Department of Justice has attacked several mergers in this industry as violating the antimerger provision of the Clayton Act.

In 1950 the antimerger law was strengthened. The first government action in the beer industry subsequent to this was taken in 1958 against the industry leader Anheuser-Busch. Anheuser-Busch had purchased the Miami, Florida brewery of American Brewing Company. Florida, because of its unique geography, faces potential competition from out-state brewers from only one

---

18 See H. Michael Mann, "Seller Concentration, Barriers to Entry, and Rates of Return in Thirty Industries, 1950–1960," *Review of Economics and Statistics*, **48**:299 (August 1966).

direction. The government argued that this merger would eliminate American Brewing as an independent brewer and remove its rivalry with Anheuser-Busch in Florida. The final judgment called for Anheuser-Busch to sell this brewery and refrain from buying any others without court approval for a period of five years.[19] Due to this action, Anheuser-Busch has foregone any policy of acquiring rival brewers and has since undertaken an extensive program of building new plants in Florida and other locations.

Two other national brewers have been involved in important merger cases. The Schlitz Brewing Company, the second largest brewer in the country, made two acquisitions in violation of the antimerger law. In 1961, Schlitz acquired Burgermeister Brewing Corporation, a large brewer of popular price beer in San Francisco with brewing capacity of about 1 million barrels per year. In 1964, it purchased controlling interest in John Labatt, a Canadian brewery that in turn controlled, through stock interest, General Brewing Corporation, a U.S. firm. Schlitz therefore gained control of General Brewing.

Both Burgermeister and General Brewing (brewer of Lucky Lager beer) were large regional brewers in the West. Lucky Lager, a popular price beer, was the 12th largest seller in the U.S. with better than 2 per cent of national sales. Its strength in the west is obvious from its share of California sales: 18.4 per cent in 1961. In addition, Labatt was attempting to introduce its own premium price Canadian beer into the U.S. through the General Brewing sales organization. Schlitz had, at one time, planned to introduce its own popular price beer in the western market. But the merger route had more appeal since through it Schlitz could quickly become the dominant seller of popular price beer in the west, eliminate two large rival sellers of popular price beer in the process, and be able to stop the further introduction of Labatt premium price beer in competition with its own premium brand.

The impact of the merger was to increase concentration in the beer industry, both nationwide and in the west, and to eliminate the rivalry between the four companies involved. A district court found both acquisitions would likely lessen competition in the beer industry. The Supreme Court, on an appeal by Schlitz, affirmed the lower court and Schlitz was ordered to sell the Burgermeister assets and divest itself of the Labatt stock. In 1969 Burgermeister was sold to Meister Brau.

Pabst Brewing Company, a national brewer, acquired Blatz Brewing Company in 1958. In 1957 Pabst was the 10th largest brewer in the country; Blatz was the 18th. The acquisition catapulted Pabst to number five in the industry and eliminated the Pabst-Blatz rivalry in the 40 states in which Blatz sold as well as the potential rivalry of Blatz in the remaining states. By 1961, the combined Pabst-Blatz amalgamation was the 3rd largest seller of beer in the nation with 5.8 per cent of the market. In 1959 the Department of Justice challenged this merger, charging that it violated the Federal antimerger law.

---

19   *U.S.* v. *Anheuser-Busch*, 1960 CCH Trade Cases, para. 69, 599.

The wheels of justice revolved sluggishly in this case. After more than a decade, during which three Court decisions were made, Pabst was finally required to sell Blatz. Essentially, the Blatz brewery had already been closed down, so only the brand could be sold and this was done in 1969 to Heileman Brewing Company, another Wisconsin brewer.

Mergers have contributed to the structural shakeup in the beer industry, causing in part the declining number of independent companies and in part the increasing concentration at the national level. Between 1946 and 1964, there were 68 acquisitions in the beer industry, with approximately one half of these being made by the 10 largest firms.

But a word of caution in interpreting merger figures in this industry is in order: these figures, alone, tend to exaggerate the impact of mergers in this industry. One study found that increases in concentration from 1947 to 1964 were better explained by internal growth than by merger, and that the majority of capacity acquired during this time consisted of less than optimum-size plants or firms with declining sales.[20] For example, at least 37 of the 68 mergers mentioned above involved the acquisition of failing breweries, breweries of under 400,000 barrels per year capacity, or both.

III. MARKET CONDUCT AND PERFORMANCE
PRICING

Judging from the early records of the preprohibition beer industry, life in the industry was very competitive. Entry was easy and producers were many. Economic theory would predict a competitive industry given these two characteristics and the evidence bears this out. Some brewers made a fortune and perhaps held some market power; they were also the ones that pioneered new techniques for producing and marketing quality malt beverages.

In fact the early beer industry offers a classic example of the predictions of price theory. Given the inelastic demand, brewers saw the obvious advantages to monopolizing the industry, raising prices, and gleaning monopoly profits. Various types of loose- and tight-knit cartels were seen as advantageous, but the difficulty of coordinating so many brewers and the lack of any barriers to entry prevented any of these efforts from being successful, at least for long. The degree of competition is evidenced by reading this plea from Adolphus Busch to Captain Pabst:

> . . . I hope also to be able to demonstrate to you that by the present way competition is running we are only hurting each other in a real foolish way. The traveling agents . . . always endeavor to reduce prices and send

20 Horowitz and Horowitz, "Entropy, Markov Processes and Competition in the Brewery Industries," op. cit. pp. 206–11; see also Weiss, op. cit., pp. 177 and 178.

such reports to their respective home offices as are generally not correct and only tend to bring forth competition that helps to ruin the profits ... all large manufacturing interests are now working in harmony ... and only the brewers are behind as usual; instead of combining their efforts and securing their own interest, they are fighting each other and running the profits down, so that the pleasures of managing a brewery has been diminished a good deal.[21]

This is the sort of letter a competitive market structure should elicit. A year earlier, the Western Shipping Brewers' Association was formed to divide markets and maintain prices in the midwest. There is no evidence that it was successful—except in abolishing the trade practice of giving away expensive novelties such as knives and ash trays to retail dealers.

The beer industry also escaped the horizontal mergers that transformed the structure of so many industries such as steel, whiskey, petroleum, tobacco, farm equipment, and so on, during the first great merger movement. There were attempts, mostly by British businessmen, to combine the large brewers during this time. One attempt called for the amalgamation of Pabst, Schlitz, Miller, Anheuser-Busch, and Lemp into one company, a feat which, had it been successful, would have greatly altered the structure and degree of competition in the industry. But the attempt failed and brewing entered prohibition with a competitive structure responding with competitive prices.

THE PRICING PATTERN   Uniform delivered pricing systems, which have been common in industries like steel and cement, have never been representative of pricing in the beer industry. Instead beer is generally sold f.o.b. the brewery; and prices vary according to differences in transportation costs, taxes, and competitive conditions.

There is a pattern or structure to prices in this industry, though it is not so distinct that a clear-cut description can be offered. Regional beer markets exist, and prices may vary between these markets for the reasons cited. But in addition, there is a pattern to beer prices within these individual markets. Beer is neither sold at a uniform price across the country nor in the separate beer markets.

The existing pattern of prices dates back to the turn of the century when certain Milwaukee brewers, notably Pabst, Schlitz, and Blatz, brewed beer for markets other than their immediate brewery localities. Since beer had relatively high transportation costs relative to its value, to sell in distant markets required either a higher price or a smaller margin for brewers. Opting for the former alternative, these brewers were able to obtain higher prices than the local beers, having established in the customers' minds a measure of superiority for Milwaukee beer, in general, and their own brands in particular. To

---

21   Thomas C. Cochran, *The Pabst Brewing Company* (New York: New York   University Press, 1948), p. 151. (Letter of January 3, 1889).

some extent, this differential has withstood the years for those beers considered "premium" beers.

Note that the pattern for beer prices is different than the price differentials that exists between various grades of lumber, steel, or aluminum. In these latter cases the differential is attributable to some identifiable physical characteristic of the product. In the case of malt beverages, price differences are in part due to customers' tastes and are subjective for there are no important differences in the cost of labor or materials for the various grades of beer.[22] A preference for beer X, either because of its advertising, package, or taste, apparently induces some to pay an extra amount for this brand vis-à-vis another.

Today a handful of national producers generally charge a higher price than the beers with local or regional distribution. For example, in California, Schlitz and Labatt's are premium price beers, Lucky Lager is a regional or popular price beer. Fisher is a "price" or "local" or "shelf" beer.

This is not to say that the differential is an exact and easily predictable phenomenon. Some beers do not seem to fit into this tripartite pattern. Coors and Olympia beer have sold in California at a price between the premium and popular price beers. Miller High Life has sold at prices above the Schlitz premium price. Occasionally a beer will move from one category to another or to an in-between level.

In April 1965, the national brewers lowered their prices in New England, New Jersey, and New York. Prior to this, six-packs of the national brewers' products were selling for $1.25 retail. Popular price beer of the regional brewers such as Rheingold, Schaefer, and Piels was selling for $1.09 and some "price" or local beers at 99 cents. The price drop by the premium brewers was sufficient to cause their retail six-pack prices to drop to 99 cents. Some of the regional brewers responded with price cuts but Rheingold and Schaefer elected to remain at $1.09—thus becoming a premium beer at that time![23] Some regionals lowered prices until their six-packs sold for 85–89 cents. In short, beer X may be higher priced than beer Y in market A, sell at the same price in market B, and conceivably lower in market C.

In spite of these situations, it is still meaningful to talk of the three-part price pattern. Anheuser-Busch once conducted a survey involving 113,305 price comparisons in 78 areas. In over 100,000 comparisons, a differential of 5 cents per can or per 12-oz. bottle existed between Budweiser and the popular priced beers. In over 90 per cent of the comparisons, a 10 cent differential existed over local beers.

The differential has narrowed over the years. Pabst, one of the initiators of

---

22 For an illuminating study of how extraordinarily subjective these tastes might be, see J. Douglas McConnell, "An Experimental Examination of the Price-Quality Relationship," *Journal of Business*, 41:439 (Oct. 1968).

23 *U.S.* v. *Rheingold Corp.*, Pleading files, Affidavit of Berhard Relin, December 20, 1965, pp. 2 and 3.

the premium price beer, is now sold at popular prices in many areas, as is Blatz. Premium beer now accounts for about 20 per cent of total beer sales.

PRICE DISCRIMINATION In 1955 the Federal Trade Commission (FTC) issued a complaint against Anheuser-Busch charging it with unlawful price discrimination. Anheuser-Busch had dropped the price of its premium brand to all buyers in the St. Louis area; but it did not make this reduction in any other areas. The FTC maintained this was price discrimination and the result would be to impair the intensity of competition by diverting beer sales from the Anheuser-Busch regional rivals in St. Louis to Anheuser-Busch.

The charge against Anheuser-Busch was brought under Section 2(a) of the Robinson-Patman Act. Proof of such a violation involves answering three questions:

1. Is there price discrimination?
2. If so, does the respondent have a defense?
3. If not, might the discrimination lessen competition?

Reasonable men disagreed strongly on each of these questions in this case.

There was no doubt that after the price cut Anheuser-Busch's Budweiser brand beer was selling for less money per case in St. Louis than anywhere in the country, and that this differential could not be explained fully by the lower transportation costs from the Anheuser-Busch brewery in St. Louis. Query: is this automatically price discrimination?

The circuit court of appeals said no. It argued that price discrimination, as construed in antitrust, could not exist unless different prices were charged to *competing* purchasers. The circuit court put it this way:

> Anheuser-Busch did not thereby *discriminate* among its local competitors in the St. Louis area. By its cuts Anheuser-Busch employed the same means of competition against all of them. Moreover, it did not discriminate among those who *bought* its beer in the St. Louis area; all could buy at the same price.[24]

This court argued that a mere price differential is not price discrimination unless some competitive relationship exists between the customers paying different prices, so that the ones paying the lower price have a competitive advantage.

The FTC and ultimately the Supreme Court disagreed with this interpretation. The Court said price discrimination is "selling the same kind of goods cheaper to one purchaser than to another" and thereby overruled the circuit court.[25]

---

24 *Anheuser-Busch, Inc.* v. *Federal Trade Commission*, 265 F. 2d 677 (7th Cir., 1959) at 681.

25 *Federal Trade Commission* v. *Anheuser-Busch, Inc.*, 363 U.S. 536 (1960) at 549.

Ever since the "Detroit case,"[26] a defense to a charge of price discrimination was to show that one's lower price was offered to meet the equally low price of a rival. Prior to the FTC complaint, Budweiser was selling at $2.93 per case in St. Louis; its rivals were three regional brewers selling at $2.35 per case. In two successive cuts, Anheuser-Busch dropped to $2.35. Query: could not Anheuser-Busch argue that it was only meeting the equally low price of its rivals?

Anheuser-Busch tried, but interestingly, the FTC rejected this defense. Note what this implies: Anheuser-Busch is going on record that its premium beer, Budweiser, is the same as regional beer, i.e., "beer is beer." The FTC, however, argued that at $2.35 a case Anheuser-Busch "was selling *more value* than its competitors were . . . the consumer has proved . . . that [he] will pay more for Budweiser than . . . for many other beers."[27] Note that this statement comes very close to saying that Budweiser, because of its "superior public acceptance," should and must be priced at a differential over regional and local beers.

After the Supreme Court ruled that Anheuser-Busch had priced in a discriminatory fashion, the circuit court had to decide whether competition might be lessened by Anheuser-Busch's St. Louis pricing practice. The FTC, arguing from the figures given earlier on the changing market shares in St. Louis, said yes, that this practice would give Anheuser-Busch market power in St. Louis by increasing its market share.

The circuit court disagreed, ruling that the simple diversion of business was not an indication that competition in St. Louis was being lessened. The court's decision pointed out that Anheuser-Busch was not subsidizing St. Louis with revenues from other markets, and that none of the Anheuser-Busch rivals in St. Louis had felt so "pushed" as to lower their prices in response to the Anheuser-Busch cut. The only result was that consumers of beer in St. Louis could buy Budweiser for less money which, the court felt, is what market competition is all about.

Consider one final important issue here: what if the FTC had won its case and Anheuser-Busch had been barred from making this price cut in St. Louis? One might argue that competition would be increased, for companies would be prevented from making selective price cuts to eliminate smaller rivals or to enforce price leadership. But there is another possible implication of this per se approach to selective price cutting in the beer industry. Barring selective price cuts *may* come dangerously close to barring price competition. How is Anheuser-Busch to respond to the loss of sales in its own back yard? True, it could cut prices across the board all over the country. But as one observer put it, "If a seller by law must lower all his prices or none, he will hesitate long to lower any."[28]

---

26 *Federal Trade Commission* v. *Standard Oil*, 355 U.S. 396 (1958).

27 In the matter of Anheuser-Busch, *FTC DKT.* 6331, p. 19; italics mine.

28 F. M. Rowe, "Price Discrimination, Competition, and Confusion: Another Look at Robinson-Patman," *Yale Law Journal* **60**:929 (1951), p. 959.

ADVERTISING

One indicator of the relative amount of advertising done by industries is the ratio of advertising expenditures to sales. One economist has called any percentage over 5 per cent as a "significantly . . . substantial level."[29] For some companies in the soap, cosmetic, and drug industries, this ratio is over 10 per cent. For the beer and malt industry in 1962, this ratio was 6.8 per cent as compared to a 1948–1958 average of 5.2 per cent. This is higher than the same ratio for all beverages combined and for all food and kindred products. Of the top 100 advertisers in television, magazines, and newspaper supplements in 1967, four were brewers who spent an average of $9.57 million in these three media alone.

The exact implications of extensive advertising are uncertain. But there is evidence of a relationship between rising concentration and rising advertising expenditures.[30] The extent of a causal relationship between these two phenomena is also uncertain. Professor Yang found that the brewing industry has had, over time, an increasing advertising to sales ratio and an increasing share of advertising done by the largest firms.[31] His study indicates that there is a relationship between increasing advertising intensity by the largest firms and increasing concentration, with the chain of causality running from the former to the latter. If this is so, the trend to heavier advertising by the major producers of beer will strengthen the trend towards increasing concentration.

The amount spent on advertising beer is large, and this is not surprising. There are millions of actual and potential beer drinkers that a brewer wants to inform of the quality and availability of his product. New customers come of age and producers seek to inform them; old customers may forget and producers seek to remind them.

Nevertheless, at some stage massive advertising offers only inframarginal information, and will have the effect of entrenching the industry leaders. Unfortunately, economic analysis does not provide a tool for determining at what stage advertising becomes redundant and wasteful. The drawback to advertising in this industry is its apparent tendency to enhance the forces leading to increased concentration. Whether the amount of advertising is non optimal, in an informational sense, is unknown.

MARKETING

While all industries are subject to various Federal and state laws that affect the marketing of the industry's product, the brewing industry faces an

---

29 Joe S. Bain, *Industrial Organization* (New York: Wiley, 1959), pp. 390 and 391.
30 H. M. Mann et al., "Advertising and Concentration: An Empirical Investigation," *Journal of Industrial Economics*, **16**:34 (November 1967).

31 Charles Yang, *Economic Concentration*, Hearings before the U.S. Senate Subcommittee on Antitrust and Monopoly, Part 5, (Washington, D.C.: U.S. Government Printing Office, 1966), pp. 2153–2163.

especially variegated pattern of laws and regulations concerning labeling, advertising, credit, container sizes, alcoholic content, tax rates, and even in some states, container deposit requirements.

For example, Michigan does not permit a beer label to show alcoholic content; Minnesota requires an accurate statement of alcoholic content; in Indiana, advertising is strictly regulated; Louisiana has no advertising restrictions. Some states require sales from the brewer to wholesaler to retailer to be only on a cash basis; others allow credit. The size of containers, both maximum and minimum, are stipulated in some states. Alabama permits no package beer containers larger than 16 ounces; Colorado permits a giant 128 ounce container. States have varying requirements on the permissible alcoholic content, ranging from no limit to 3.2 per cent by weight. To complicate this, in some states alcoholic content may be different for different types of outlets.

All of this complicates the marketing of beer. This is perhaps the only area in which the local brewer is at an advantage. He has a small set of state rules with which to comply. The regional and national brewers face a web of various, and varying, restrictions, which require them to keep close watch on sales to various states in order to comply with the rules.

The governmental scrutiny applied to the beer industry also includes taxation. The Federal tax alone on a barrel of beer is $9.00 and in 1968 U.S. Treasury Department coffers gathered over $960 million in beer taxes. The state taxes on beer vary substantially but average about $3.90 per barrel. In addition, brewers, wholesalers, and retail outlets pay Federal, state, and sometimes local occupational taxes. Taxes represent the largest single-cost item in a glass of beer, about 35 per cent of its price.

There is little vertical integration in the beer industry. The brewing industry is the customer of the agricultural sector, companies producing brewing and packaging equipment, and containers. A few brewers partly own their own container manufacturers and one brewer hopes to cut transportation costs by manufacturing cans right at its breweries. But generally a brewer buys too little of the manufactured brewing and packaging equipment to warrant integration in this area. A few brewers have integrated backwards into grain and hop production and some brewers do own their malting operations. One brewer even grows his entire own supply of malting barley. But backwards integration has not proven popular and is the exception, not the rule.

Similarly, there is little forward integration in brewing. In principle, possibilities here include owning distributors and owning retail outlets. But a brewer is barred by law from owning retail outlets, which leaves the wholesale distribution of his product as the only possible forward vertical integration route.

Most brewers rely on independent distributors to channel their brew to the retail outlets. In 1968 there were over 6,600 wholesalers of beer, the vast majority of these being independent merchant wholesalers. Some brewers own a portion of their wholesale distribution channel. For example, Anheuser-Busch distributes about 75 per cent of its beer through independent wholesaler-distributors; the remainder is marketed through branch offices in large metropolitan areas.

The retailing of beer is done through two general types of outlets: those allowing on-premise consumption and those allowing only off-premise consumption. In 1968 there were over 132,000 retail beer outlets.

The beer wholesaler at one time distributed mainly kegs of beer for on-premise draught consumption. In 1935 only 30 per cent of beer sales were packaged, i.e., in bottles or cans suitable for on- or off-premise consumption. Since that time there has been a steady increase in the percentage of beer sold packaged, relative to draught; by 1968 over 84 per cent of beer sales were packaged. The popularity of the can and one-way bottle, the changing consumption habits of the male, the apparent loss of the "saloon habit" during prohibition, and the preferences of the female mean that the beer distributor, today, will make more delivery trips to the grocery store than the tavern.

This trend in beer marketing works to the disadvantage of the small brewer. When beer sales were primarily by the keg for on-premise consumption, the small brewer could survive by selling to taverns in his immediate area. But packaged beer sales are primarily for off-premise consumption and distribution of packaged beer increases the importance of product differentiation and brand emphasis.

Moreover, the consumption trend away from draught beer lessens the survival prospects of the small brewer. Competitive forces in the industry, of course, dictate the adoption of low-cost packaging techniques. In the packaging of liquids, both bottling and canning, technological advances have been such that modern equipment could bottle or can the entire output of the 100,000 barrel producer in a month or less! For example, low unit costs in canning require units that churn out up to 1,200 cans per minute; in bottling, about 800 per minute. Consequently, the small brewer, if he acquired such packaging equipment, would have to increase his brewing capacity to keep these packaging machines from lying idle.

Finally, the increasing emphasis in the industry on product differentiation via package "innovations" is to the disadvantage of the small brewer. The rapidity with which new openers, new shapes, and new materials are introduced into beer bottling and canning, and the advertising flourish with which they are promoted, cannot be matched by the resources of the small brewer.

Whether these changes in cans and bottles are meaningful in the sense of making the beer customer better off is an open question. But there is no doubt that these marketing changes have been to the detriment of the small brewer, who, even though he may efficiently brew relatively small batches of beer, can no longer survive in the race to market it.

PROFITS

If an industry is effectively monopolized, we might expect to see this reflected in its profits. This is not, of course, necessarily so since: (1) demand might not

TABLE 5   PER CENT OF NET
PROFIT TO GROSS SALES (AFTER
FEDERAL INCOME TAXES) FOR THE
BEER AND MALT INDUSTRIES AND
ALL CORPORATIONS

YEAR	BEER-MALT	ALL CORPORATIONS
1954	2.8	3.8
1956	2.4	4.0
1958	2.6	2.9
1960	2.4	2.8
1962	2.2	3.0
1964	3.4	3.9
1966	3.4	3.9

SOURCE   United States Brewers
Association, *Brewers Almanac* (New York:
U.S. Brewers Association, 1969), p. 40.

be sufficiently high to yield profits in spite of monopoly; (2) the monopolists
may be inefficient; (3) or the accounting records might not show the monopoly
gains, the gains having been eaten up by large expense accounts or other types
of in-kind benefits.

The profit figures for the beer industry itself are unavailable since not all
of the firms in the industry make their profit figures public. However, the
Treasury Department does publish data which give some idea of the industry's
relative profitability. Unfortunately, the profit figures given in Table 5 include
not only beer industry but also the malt industry. But since the malt
industry is small relative to brewing, the figures do give a rough indication
that profits in brewing are less than those for all corporations, *prima facie*
evidence of the competitive nature of the industry.

IV. PUBLIC POLICY

The statistics on the structure of the beer industry, the conduct of its
members, and the profits it has earned indicate that the American beer consumer does not face a monopolized industry. On the other hand, the distinct
trend toward industry dominance by the top ten firms should serve as a
caution light to antitrust authorities, calling forth particularly stringent
enforcement of the antimerger law.

In an industry where supply conditions have led to a decreased number of
rivals, the trend must not be artificially enhanced by allowing large brewers
to expand via the systematic purchase and elimination of rivals. Even if the
merger participants are not in direct rivalry, such as two large regional brew-

ers selling in different regions, allowing their amalgamation may have anti-competitive effects by removing each as a *potential* rival in the other's territory.

The top 20 brewers have gained an increasing share of the brewing business in the post-World War II period. Mergers either among or by brewers of this group will lead to even greater concentration of the beer industry. It is the purpose of the antimerger law

> . . . to arrest the trend toward concentration, the tendency to monopoly, before the consumers alternatives [disappear] through merger . . ..[32]

The increasing concentration at the national level and the unlikely entrance of new rivals poses a threat to the future level of competition in this industry. Thus far there is no evidence of collusion in the beer industry. But as the industry becomes populated by fewer and fewer companies, the possibility and likelihood will be enhanced of their engaging in tacit or direct collusion—given the inelastic nature of demand—to establish a joint profit maximizing price and output. Similarly, the chances will become slimmer that individual firms in the industry will follow a truly independent price and production strategy, vigorously striving to take sales away from rival brewers. With only a few sellers will come the increasing awareness that parallel business behavior might be feasible.

With many sellers, an aggressive price-cutting firm in the beer (or any other) industry can expect to substantially increase his sales due to the high cross-elasticity of demand between various brands. Moreover, with many firms, a price cutting firm will go relatively undetected since the sales losses he inflicts on rivals will be diffused over many firms. But in the case of few sellers, the price cutter is more easily recognized, since his gains are at the expense of but a handful of firms. The increased chances of recognition concomitant with fewer sellers is likely to dissuade most price cutters due to a fear of retaliation.

With the weapon of price cutting sheathed, the seller will have to select some nonprice method of gaining sales, such as advertising. The beer industry's increasing reliance on advertising as its form of rivalry also has public policy implications. Emphasis on advertising rivalry, if seen as a substitute for product and price rivalry by brewers, will provide beer customers with a narrower range of genuine choices. As was mentioned earlier, many economists believe that in highly concentrated markets where rivalry takes the form of advertising and slogan emulation, the costs of such endeavors are excessive and provide no meaningful benefit to the consumer of the product who ultimately pays for them.

Moreover, the emphasis on advertising rivalry and efforts to differentiate products on some basis other than price or physical product differences will

---

32 *U.S.* v. *Phil. National Bank.*, 374 U.S. 321 (1963) at 367.

increase the barriers to entry into this industry. As brand names become more entrenched in customers' minds, newcomers will find it more difficult to pierce this entrenchment. Professor Bain found that the advantages of established firms over possible entrants due to product differentiation constitutes the prime elevator of barriers to entry.[33]

Rivalry from foreign producers has never been a strong force in the beer industry. The amount of beer imported into the U.S. in 1968 was only approximately 775,000 barrels. But this represents a better than 175 per cent increase over imports a decade ago and provides a serious source of potential rivalry. Presently, imported beer faces a tariff of approximately $3.85 per barrel. To preserve the present degree of concentration, it is important that foreign rivalry remain a threat. Consequently, the tariff on beer should not be increased—and preferably removed.

All this is not to overlook the present degree of competition in the industry. The Wholesale Price Index in brewing has increased only 7.7 points from 1955 to 1967, indicating that even the large firms have been unable to raise prices in the presence of excess capacity and the high cross-elasticity of demand between brands. The level of profits in the industry is not that of an industry with great market power.

SUGGESTED READINGS
BOOKS AND PAMPHLETS

Arnold, John P., and Frank Penman. *History of the Brewing Industry and Brewing Science in America*. Chicago: privately printed, 1933.

Baron, Stanley Wade. *Brewed in America*. Boston: Little, Brown and Company, 1962.

Mathias, Peter. *The Brewing Industry in England, 1700–1830*. New York: Cambridge University Press, 1959.

Thomann, Gallus. *American Beer*. New York: United States Brewers Foundation, 1909.

Weeks, Morris Jr. *Beer and Brewing In America*. New York: United States Brewers Foundation, 1949.

GOVERNMENT PUBLICATIONS

Anheuser Busch v. *Federal Trade Commission*, 265 F.2d 677 (1959); 363 U.S. 536 (1960); 289 F.2d 835 (1961).

U.S. v. *Anheuser Busch*, 1960 CCH Trade Cases, Par. 69,599.

U.S. v. *Jos. Schlitz*, 253 F. Supp. 129 (1966); 385 U.S. 37 (1966).

U.S. v. *Pabst*, 233 F. Supp. 475 (1964); 384 U.S. 546 (1966).

---

33   Joe S. Bain, *Industrial Organization* (New York: Wiley, 1968), 2nd ed., p. 284

ARTICLES

Brewers Almanac. New York: United States Brewers Association, an annual.
Horowitz, Ira, and Ann Horowitz. "Firms in a Declining Market: the Brewing Case," *Journal of Industrial Economics*, **13**:129–153 (March 1965).
———. "The Beer Industry," *Business Horizons*, **10**:5 (Spring 1967).
McConnell, J. Douglas. "An Experimental Examination of the Price-Quality Relationship," *Journal of Business*, **41**:439–444 (October 1968).
Modern Brewery Age: Blue Book Issue. Stamford, Conn.: Modern Brewery Age Publishing Co., an annual.
Modern Brewery Age. Stamford, Conn.: Modern Brewery Age Publishing Co., tabloid edition, 40 times a year.

7. Richard B. Tennant

THE CIGARETTE INDUSTRY

T

I. INTRODUCTION

he cigarette industry[1] is worth studying for several reasons. First, its economic magnitude is significant to consumers, distributors, farmers, and government revenues. Second, the industry has long been caught up in controversial issues of public policy, earlier in the development and application of the antitrust laws, and more recently with issues of public health. Third, the long history of this industry offers useful insight into economic principles and the forces affecting industrial structure, conduct, and performance. The cigarette industry has existed under different economic and social conditions and different legal rules, and in the course of time has shown substantial differences in its structure and behavior. But also in this long history, stable patterns are to be observed. An examination of this industry casts useful light on the question of how firmly industry characteristics are dictated by fundamental economic constraints and how much they are free to vary according to social policies and the free action of business managers.

ECONOMIC IMPORTANCE

The significance of the cigarette industry to various sectors of the economy may be seen from Table 1, which provides an approximate breakdown of total industry proceeds in 1967.

In 1967 the American people consumed 527.8 billion cigarettes for which they spent $8,432 million through normal channels of trade.[2] Cigarettes accounted for 1.1 per cent of the gross national product and for 3.9 per cent of consumer expenditures for nondurable goods. Federal tax yields were

---

1 This chapter is based in large part upon the author's book, *The American Cigarette Industry* (New Haven: Yale University Press, 1950). Recent brand statistics are based on estimates by John C. Maxwell, Jr. published annually in *Marketing Communications*.

2 Another 49.0 billion worth $261 million at wholesale were withdrawn tax free for export, or use on ships at sea. Other tobacco products accounted for another $1016 million of consumer expenditure.

TABLE 1 TOTAL INDUSTRY PROCEEDS
IN 1967

TAXES	($ BILLIONS)
Federal excise tax	2.1
State excise tax	1.6
Corporate income tax	0.4
Total taxes	4.1

EXPENDITURES	
Wholesale and retail margins	1.9
Farm value of tobacco used	0.8
Other manufacturing and selling costs	1.4
Manufacturer's net profit	0.5
Total expenditure	8.7

SOURCE Based on various government and
industry publications. For method, see Tennant, op.
cit., pp. 389 ff.

larger than the proceeds of all internal revenue taxes for any year prior to
1918; tobacco was the sixth most important cash crop in American agriculture; the distribution network involves about 7,000 jobbers and more than
1.5 million retail outlets.

This economic importance is a relatively recent development. Two
generations ago cigarettes were a minor branch of the tobacco industry,
ranking in value below plug smoking tobacco and cigars, but above snuff,
fine cut chewing tobacco, and little cigars. In 1900 cigarettes accounted for
3.4 per cent of the leaf tobacco consumed, 6.7 per cent of tobacco tax receipts and 4.1 per cent of the value of tobacco products. In 1967 the analo-
gous figures were 77.2 per cent, 98.5 per cent, and 89.2 per cent. Total
expenditure on cigarettes in 1900 was only $12.8 million or about 0.15 per
cent of sales in 1967.

Yet although cigarettes were relatively unimportant in 1900, their history
goes back much further. Cigarettes were first introduced to this country
about the time of the Civil War, and since 1870, they have grown steadily
in favor. In almost every year the consumption of cigarettes has been higher
than in the year preceding, and the industry experienced rapid percentage
growth in the early years when absolute consumption was small. Cigarettes
came into general acceptance among men during World War I, and the later
growth was based upon the spread of smoking among women, the progressive
displacement of other forms of tobacco, and the general growth in population.

INVOLVEMENT WITH PUBLIC POLICY

From early days the cigarette industry has been closely involved in the development of the antitrust laws. James B. Duke founded the Tobacco Trust in

1890, the same year the Sherman Act was passed and he built the kind of monopolist dominance that was the target of much antitrust agitation in that period. In 1911 the American Tobacco and Standard Oil cases involved landmark Supreme Court decisions, which established the "Rule of Reason" in antitrust law, but also set a precedent for active industrial reform by splitting those companies into a substantial number of smaller enterprises. A later prosecution in 1941, upheld by the Supreme Court in 1946, again found this industry to be guilty of monopolization and conspiracy in restraint of trade. Antitrust action has since been minor but there remains some possibility of further antitrust problems because of basic characteristics of this industry's structure and behavior.

The most important current issues of public policy of course center about questions of public health rather than of competition. The increasing accumulation of evidence since 1953 that cigarettes contribute significantly to the incidence of cancer and certain other diseases raises a direct threat to industry markets and has already led to some limitations on the industry's freedom to advertise its products as it sees fit.

This unfavorable public image and the danger of adverse legislation also have a very long history. In the early days, cigarettes were regarded as unmanly as well as unhealthy and, even after World War I, they were widely regarded as immoral at least when used by women.

STABILITY AND CHANGE

The influence of managerial ambition, social climate, legal developments, economic conditions, and medical discoveries have created successive periods of time in which industry structure, competitive objectives, competitive methods, and profit performance have been significantly different. At the same time, common elements of industry structure and behavior have persisted. The following section presents a summary of industry history as a guide to the sources of industry structure and conduct.

HISTORY OF THE INDUSTRY

The basic design of the cigarette industry was already well established before James B. Duke established the Tobacco Trust. From the earliest times output has been concentrated in a few firms.

EARLY YEARS   In the early 1880's four firms dominated the industry. Allen & Ginter of Richmond, Virginia; William S. Kimball & Company of Rochester, New York; and Kinney Tobacco Company and Goodwin & Company, both of New York City, together produced about four fifths of the national total. Between 1880 and 1885, the firm of W. Duke Sons &

Company, which had previously produced only smoking tobacco, secured a foothold in the industry through the extraordinary persistence and sales-manship of James B. Duke. The predominance of all these firms was based upon their ability to expand markets. The product was new and strange, and it was necessary both to educate consumers and to open distribution channels through tobacco jobbers and retailers, so that goods would actually be available to satisfy the new demand. The position of the five leading firms was based upon their advertising ability and on their power to keep the channels of distribution open.

In these years, however, when the industry was young, even the leading firms were quite small, and it was probable that the existing concentration of output could not be long continued. At this time all cigarettes were made by hand, and a skilled workman could roll no more than 3,000 in a 10-hour day. Labor costs for hand rolling were about 75 cents per thousand in 1885, and the process of manufacture required the supervision of numbers of skilled workmen, which would have caused difficulties in the operation of really large plants. As the industry continued its growth, the leading firms could maintain their position only by an equivalent increase in their own size. If technological methods had remained unchanged, it seems unlikely that cigarette companies as large as those we know today could have grown up. The old firms would have found their expansion blocked by rising costs. New firms would have come in and much less concentration of output would have resulted.

In the early 1880's, however, a great technological change occurred with the invention of suitable cigarette-rolling machinery. The most successful of several inventions was patented in 1881 by James Bonsack, and it came into general use after 1884. The Bonsack machine could produce 200 to 220 cigarettes per minute and was usually rented, complete with operator, for 30 or 33 cents per thousand depending on whether a printing device was used. Even with royalties the cost of fabricating was cut in half, and the labor cost alone was cut to 2 cents per thousand. With such significant cost savings it was inevitable that machine methods should supplant hand methods on all but the highest-priced brands.

With the introduction of machinery the problem of supervising hand labor was removed, and the principal obstacle to continued industrial con-centration disappeared. It was possible to increase the output of a firm simply by adding more machines, and the firm was free to expand to the extent that its sales would allow. In this purely negative sense the adoption of machinery removed potential barriers to the scale of enterprise.

Machinery also gave positive encouragement to increased concentration by the advantages it conferred on particular manufacturers. James B. Duke was the first to adopt machines for his factory, in spite of a general belief that consumers opposed machine-made goods. This gave him a considerable cost advantage over those firms that lagged in introducing new methods.

Moreover, in return for assuming the risk of consumer disfavor, he secured a secret contract with the Bonsack Machine Company that provided for a rebate to reduce the net royalty to 20 cents per thousand whether printed or not, and a later clause guaranteed that the royalty charged Duke should always be 25 per cent less than that paid by anyone else.

This advantage itself was not so important as was the use that Duke made of it. The savings in costs were reinvested in the industry, as was the major part of all operating profits. Duke spent large sums on advertising and on deals and inducements to jobbers, and he was himself extremely active in visiting the retail trade to promote his business. The resources that Duke commanded because of his secret contract and the extraordinary persistence and energy with which he applied them brought him rapidly to the front of the industry. By 1889, W. Duke Sons & Company was the largest cigarette manufacturer in the country.

THE TOBACCO TRUST   The other companies found their businesses invaded and fought back as best they could, but Duke invested $800,000 in advertising in 1889 alone, and the struggle grew increasingly unattractive for the other companies. Unable to defeat Duke, they agreed to join him. In 1890, the American Tobacco Company was incorporated in New Jersey and exchanged its securities for the properties of the five leading companies.

The new company, which quickly became known as the Tobacco Trust, controlled at the outset more than 90 per cent of the national output of cigarettes, and it maintained essential monopoly control for the next 20 years. The same aggressiveness that Duke had shown in forming the combination was used to preserve it and to expand its activities. The Trust at first secured exclusive rights to the Bonsack machine in return for royalty payments of $250,000 a year, bought up and sequestered patents on other machines, and sought to prevent the use of still other machines by suits for patent infringement. Adverse legal decisions removed this protection by 1895, but in any event it does not seem to have been a principal source of the Trust's power.

Such competition as arose was subjected to ruthless attack. The Trust cut prices drastically to discipline local competition. Thus, in 1900, the American Beauty brand was sold in North Carolina for $1.50 per thousand at a time when the internal revenue tax was $1.50. The Trust also secured favor treatment from jobbers, sought to deny wholesale facilities to competitors, fomented strikes in competing factories, bid up prices on local leaf tobacco markets where competitors secured their supplies, and in other ingenious ways made life difficult for independent manufacturers. The knowledge that measures of this kind would be used was a powerful deterrent to such potential competitors as might be attracted by the high level of Trust profits.

Perhaps the most important advantage of the Trust was the consumer loyalty to its many popular brands.[3] A large number of these were inherited from constituent companies and given further heavy advertising promotion. By 1898, one of the old Kinney brands, Sweet Caporal, accounted for more than 50 per cent of the total national consumption. Consumer loyalty and the market pressure developed through advertising were probably even more effective than the various methods of unfair competition in maintaining the position of the Trust. By 1899, the Trust's output had risen to 95 per cent of the national total.

Most of the Trust's brands of cigarettes were made of straight domestic Virginia tobacco, and after 1900, a shift of public taste in favor of Turkish tobacco subjected the Trust to a temporary loss of business. Turkish cigarettes were relatively expensive because they were made from imported leaf and rolled by hand in small shops operated by Greeks, Egyptians, or other Levantine manufacturers.[4] The Trust had no established position in such brands and by 1906 its share of the national output had fallen to 80 per cent. However, the Trust redoubled its competitive efforts, bought up several of the leading independents and supported their brands with heavy advertising and with attractive prices to jobbers.[5] A number of completely new brands of Virginia tobacco or of blended Virginia and Turkish tobacco were also introduced.[6] By 1910, the independent Turkish manufacturers were no longer a threat and the Trust had regained complete dominance of the cigarette industry.

Although the Tobacco Trust was initially a combination of cigarette manufacturers, the Trust took early measures to invade the other large branches of the tobacco industry. Using its large cigarette profits for heavy advertising and cut-throat price warfare and employing many other forms of market and financial pressure, the Trust secured dominant control of the rest of the industry. Around the turn of the century it established the Continental Tobacco Company, the American Snuff Company, and the American Cigar Company to monopolize the plug, snuff, and cigar branches. By 1910, the Trust had achieved almost complete control of various tobacco products (see Table 2).

The failure to achieve monopoly control of cigars stands in interesting contrast to the Trust's accomplishments with other tobacco products. In 1890, plug, smoking tobacco, and snuff were already concentrated in a

---

3 The most important were Richmond Straight Cut, Pets, Virginia Brights, Duke's Best, Cameo, Sweet Caporal, Vanity Fair, High Grade, and Old Judge. The Trust produced about 100 brands of cigarettes in all.

4 The leading independent brands were Natural, Melachrino, Milo, Condax, Rameses, and Philip Morris. These were manufactured in the order named by

Schinasi Brothers, M. Melachrino & Company, Surburg Company, Eli Condax & Company, Stephano Brothers, and Philip Morris & Company, Ltd.

5 Trust Turkish brands included Pall Mall, Egyptian Deities, Murad, Mogul, Egyptian Straights, Helmar, and Turkish Trophies.

6 The most important were Piedmont, Hassan, Mecca, and Fatima.

TABLE 2   PERCENTAGE OF
TRUST CONTROL OVER
TOBACCO MARKETS
%

Cigarettes	86.1
Plug	84.9
Smoking	76.2
Fine cut	79.7
Snuff	96.5
Little cigars	91.5
Cigars	14.4

SOURCE   U.S. Bureau of
Corporations, *Report of the
Commissioner of Corporations on
the Tobacco Industry*, Part III
(Washington, D.C.: U.S.
Government Printing Office,
1915), p. 2.

moderately small number of firms, and it was possible for the Trust, by aggressive competition, to force them to combine further into single monopolies. The cigar industry, however, was not concentrated for reasons of technology. Adequate cigar-making machinery did not exist, and hand production methods involved serious administrative difficulties if large numbers of skilled workers were to be supervised. Cigar factories were characteristically small and remained so for many years. Even the aggressive tactics of the Trust were not sufficient to establish monopoly in cigars, and the Trust never enjoyed either the control or the profits that it had secured elsewhere. The persistence of industrial decentralization in cigars indicates the importance of the Bonsack machine in making possible the heavy concentration of the cigarette industry.

In the course of its expansion, the Trust absorbed some 250 companies operating throughout the world. Some were continued as subsidiaries, some were consolidated, and some closed down. In 1909, 86 companies were doing business as members of the Tobacco Trust in the continental United States, Puerto Rico, and Cuba, and at least 33 companies were operating in other parts of the world. In addition to tobacco manufacture, the Trust had important interests in cigarette and cigar machinery, in licorice paste, in box manufacture, and in a large chain of retail stores.

The Trust was regarded with hostility by tobacco farmers, by distributors, by the competitors whom it suppressed, and by the public at large. There were several investigations of its affairs and a number of states instituted fruitless legal proceedings. At length the Federal Government intervened, and in 1911 the Supreme Court held the American Tobacco Company and all its subsidiaries and its affiliates to be in violation of the Sherman Act.

A subsequent circuit court decree divided the assets and business among sixteen "successor companies." The principal direct tobacco business of the Trust fell to only four companies: R. J. Reynolds Tobacco Company, Liggett & Myers Tobacco Company, P. Lorillard Company, and a much reduced American Tobacco Company. Reynolds had been a plug and smoking tobacco subsidiary of the Trust and was now removed from Trust control. Liggett and Lorillard, bearing names of companies acquired by the Trust, were newly organized for the express purpose of receiving a portion of the assets of the American Tobacco Company. Only these last three companies were engaged in the cigarette business.

THE CAMEL REVOLUTION   Scarcely had the new competitive regime been established when a second revolution occurred. In 1913 the R. J. Reynolds Tobacco Company, which had not previously produced cigarettes, introduced a new brand, Camel, that immediately swept the country. Reynolds expanded production as fast as it was able. New machines were added as rapidly as they could be obtained, and by 1917, Camel accounted for 35 per cent of the national output of cigarettes. By 1923 the proportion had risen further, to 45 per cent.

A principal reason for this sudden popularity was the new blend of Virginia, Burley, Turkish, and Maryland tobaccos from which Camels were made. Burley had previously been used in smoking tobacco and in plug, where its capacity to absorb quantities of sweetening sauces gave it a special usefulness. This characteristic was now turned to account in the manufacture of cigarettes and it appealed to the public taste.

There were also several contributory reasons for Camel popularity. Wartime shortages forced consumers to abandon their favorite Turkish brands and to try something new. By the end of the war, habit had reinforced natural liking. Camel was put up in a package of twenty like that in use today, rather than in the cardboard slide and shell box commonly employed at the time. This new package had previously been used only for expensive blended cigarettes, yet Camel was priced at 10 cents compared with 15 cents for Fatima. Finally, Camel abandoned the use of redeemable coupons and prizes, which had been a principal method of advertising in earlier years and which had increasingly come to be regarded as an unsatisfactory form of market pressure. Camel advertising was restricted to newspapers, magazines, and billboards, and on its pack was printed the slogan which it still bears: "Don't look for premiums or coupons as the cost of the tobaccos blended in Camel cigarettes prohibits the use of them." Reynolds was thus able both to abandon an unsatisfactory medium of advertising and to obtain an unfavorable implication regarding the quality of products which continued to use the older methods.

Whatever the reasons, Camel's success was overwhelming and it revolutionized the industry. The American Tobacco Company and Liggett & Myers

Tobacco Company brought out Lucky Strike and Chesterfield, respectively, made of similar tobacco blends and similarly packed and advertised them. Although these retaliatory brands were quite successful from the start, Camel held undisputed sway for several years. By 1925, however, the new brands as a group completely dominated the industry. Their combined sales were 82.3 per cent of the national total, whereas the many brands inherited from the Trust steadily declined.

In 1925, George Washington Hill, one of the great advertisers of all time, became president of the American Tobacco Company and his subsequent advertising campaigns directed especially to women with the slogan "Reach for a Lucky instead of a sweet" caused a rapid increase in sales. In 1930, Lucky Strike first surpassed Camel in volume, and for the next 25 years the leadership alternated between these two brands. For most of that same period, Chesterfield was sometimes in second and sometimes in third place.

Equally as dramatic as the rise of Camel was the decline of the Lorillard brands. This company had inherited most of the Trust's leading Turkish business, and in 1913 sold 22 per cent of the industry total. However, Lorillard developed no suitable answer to Camel, and when the Turkish brands decayed, Lorillard's sales declined too, and by 1925 they were only 1.9 per cent of the national consumption. The introduction of Old Gold in 1926 accompanied by unusually heavy advertising outlays was marked by a rise to 7 per cent of the national output in 1930, but this proportion was never again reached. For many years Old Gold enjoyed substantial success but remained in fifth place, far behind the leaders.

By the end of World War I, the cigarette industry had achieved a new and apparently stable structure. The three leading companies had emerged in a position of complete dominance, and three new leading brands had emerged, which were not seriously challenged during the interwar period. Advertising through national media became the principal method of competition. The change from advertising by the package to general publicity on a national scale helped to reinforce the supremacy of the new brands. The selling pressure developed in concentrated promotion of a single brand was greater than that developed by the same total expenditure scattered over a number of brands; the latter method dissipated much of its power in self-competition. The efficiency of large-scale advertising as an instrument of market pressure was sufficient for many years to maintain the supremacy of the major brands.

With secure market control there was little need for aggressive price tactics to restrain independents. Price discipline among the Big Three was strong and net profits as a percentage of equity ran at double the average rate for manufacturing corporations. Rapidly growing demand carried absolute profits to record heights. In terms of profits, prices, and extent of market control, it is difficult to see much difference between the Old Trust and the new industrial regime which matured in the 1920's.

A PRICING ERROR AND NEW COMPETITION This comfortable state of affairs was disrupted by the Great Depression and by a major strategic error in pricing the effects of which are still felt. In 1931, declining incomes were severely affecting consumer spending, and cigarette consumption showed one of its rare declines, dropping below the level of the preceding year. Leaf tobacco prices were the lowest since 1905, and cigarette manufacturing costs were correspondingly reduced. Reynolds chose this time to raise the price of Camel to $6.04 per thousand net, the highest level in 10 years, involving a rise of 1 cent per pack at retail. The other companies followed.

This interesting experiment in extreme monopoly pricing probably had little effect on the total consumption of cigarettes but it did make possible the rise of new competition. Given the existing leaf prices, an acceptable cigarette could be made for 10 cents per pack at retail and the difference between this and 14 or 15 cents for the standard brands made it possible to sell the new cigarettes. A number of brands were introduced of which Wings of the Brown & Williamson Tobacco Company and Twenty Grand of the Axton-Fisher Tobacco Company were the most important. By the end of 1932, sales of the 10-cent brands had risen to 23 per cent of the national total. In spite of this invasion and in spite of the decline in total consumption, net profits for the Big Three companies were $100 million in 1932, or the second highest on record.

In January 1933, American cut the price of Lucky Strike to $5.20 net and the others followed. In February there was a second cut to $4.85. Efforts were made to see that the major brands were sold for 10 cents a pack at retail, even though this allowed distributors a markup of only 15 cents a thousand. The 10-cent brands wilted under the attack and their sales fell to less than 10 per cent of the total. During the price war, both Lucky Strike and Camel were sold at a loss, and when the enemy was under control, Reynolds, in January 1934, led a rise back to $5.38.

Although the 10-cent brands were repulsed, they were not eliminated, but recovered some ground when the extreme price pressure was removed. For most of the decade these brands sold around 11 per cent of the industry total. New 10-cent brands were introduced, and by 1939 the market share had increased to 13 per cent, and the absolute quantity sold was more than twice as large as in 1932.

New competition began stirring in the 1930's, attracted partly by the price umbrella of the Big Three and partly by the growing national market, which now had room for more than three brands, each receiving heavy advertising. In 1933, Philip Morris & Company, Limited, Incorporated, an independent manufacturer of Turkish cigarettes in the days of the Trust, introduced a new blended cigarette, which by 1939 was the country's fourth largest brand with 6.1 per cent of industry sales. The Brown & Williamson Tobacco Company, an independent plug manufacturer in the days of the

Trust,[7] introduced a number of cigarette brands: Raleigh, filter tipped Viceroy, and metholated Kool in addition to its 10-cent brands. From 1932 to 1942, Brown & Williamson was the fourth largest producer in the country with 10.6 per cent of industry sales in 1939, altogether none of the brands individually was of the first rank. Axton-Fisher was moderately successful with mentholated Spud. In 1938, the Riggio Tobacco Company, a newly organized firm, introduced Regents, the first successful king-size brand, though its share of market was very small.

As a result of this new competition, the relative position of the Big Three weakened. Their market share declined steadily throughout the decade from 91 per cent in 1930 to 69 per cent in 1939. The control of the Big Three in 1930 had not in fact been as secure as it had seemed, and the error of pricing beyond what their power would support imposed serious penalties.

Still further trouble arose from increased vulnerability to antitrust action. Largely as a result of this price behavior, the major companies in 1941 were convicted of conspiracy in restraint of trade and of monopolization under Sections 1 and 2 of the Sherman Act. This conviction was upheld by the Supreme Court in 1946.

Neither the direct business setback nor the antitrust conviction were seriously damaging in the short run. Despite the loss in market share, the major companies' absolute sales continued to grow as did total profits. Return on equity, once the price war was out of the way, was well above the average manufacturing level. Moreover, part of the decline in market share was due to special depression conditions, which made 10-cent cigarettes possible and helped to sell them. With higher incomes and higher leaf tobacco prices after the war, the cheaper cigarettes declined, and by 1947 the market share commanded by the Big Three companies had recovered to 84.7 per cent. The pricing error reduced their sales and profits below what they might have been, but the companies' basic power and profitability was not seriously hurt. The price war may even have served as a warning to smaller companies not to compete too aggressively and especially not through price.

The antitrust convictions also had limited direct effect. Fines of $250,000 were imposed, a matter of no particular moment in so rich an industry. At one time, it appeared that the government might seek to reform the industry through further proceedings in equity but 22 years have passed without specific action and it seems unlikely that any will now come.

Yet for the long run both the business changes and the antitrust litigation have had important consequences. The unsettling of brand loyalties and competitive relationships in the 1930's laid the basis for major industrial

---

7 Since 1927 Brown & Williamson has been a subsidiary of the British American Tobacco Company, Ltd., one of the successor companies to the old Trust.

changes after World War II, and the antitrust conviction has placed important limits on competitive behavior and profits. As was true of the first Tobacco Case of 1911, the second Tobacco Case of 1946 marked the end of an era in the cigarette industry.

THE MULTIBRAND REVOLUTION   Since 1946 the cigarette industry has seen a revolution in product and comparative standings comparable in importance to the earlier Camel revolution. The dominance of the three leading brands has been broken and the bulk of the market has been taken over by a proliferation of new brands, king-size, filtered, and mentholated. The share of the market accounted for by Camel, Lucky Strike, and Chesterfield regular has fallen from the post-World War II high of 82.5 per cent in 1947 to 11.6 per cent in 1968. Reynolds and American remain the two largest cigarette companies but Liggett & Myers has fallen to sixth position with Brown & Williamson, Philip Morris, and Lorillard ranking ahead of her in that order. The industry is now composed of a Big Two, each selling more than 115 billion cigarettes, a second four with sales in the range of 40–80 billion, and a few smaller companies with less than 1 billion in total. The current rankings, which have been in effect for about 4 years, followed a period in which substantial reversals of competitive standings were common.

This violent dislocation of the competitive pattern that existed so long before World War II was the result of important changes in the economic conditions affecting the industry.

One source of change was the unsettling of old-brand preferences by the competitive maneuvers of the 1930's. The growth of Philip Morris and of Brown & Williamson showed that it was possible for smaller companies with different brands to grow despite the concentrated promotion of the three leading brands. The growth of menthol cigarettes like Kool, filter cigarettes like Viceroy, and king-size brands like Regents indicated that there was a market for new types of product and that if the leading firms did not supply them, other companies would.

A second important influence was the greatly increased absolute size of the cigarette market which in 1946 was 78 per cent, or 140 billion cigarettes larger than in 1940. Each of the companies had grown along with the market and some of the secondary companies were now as large in absolute terms as the market leaders had been a few years before. Thus, there was now increased financial muscle for any competitive moves that might be required, and the greater absolute size of markets and of companies meant that advertising expenditures could now be productively expended on more than one significant brand per company. A contributing influence in the same direction was probably exerted by the new availability of television advertising and the opportunity it offered for the rapid creation of consumer acceptance for a new brand.

A third major influence was a decline in the industry rate of growth to only 3.4 per cent annually for the years 1947–1952. This contrasted with a growth in total production of 11.8 per cent annually for the war years 1941–1945, and of 5.3 per cent for 1946. This slowing down imposed increased competitive pressures and meant that if any company was to maintain its previous rate of growth, a much larger proportion would have to come at the expense of competitors rather than simply out of the absolute expansion of a constant market share.

Of course, wartime conditions are unusual and in the previous peacetime years of 1930–1940, the average annual growth had been only 3.9 per cent. However, the 1930's were depression years and the modest growth then contrasted favorably with the experience of other industries. In previous years of prosperity growth had been much higher, amounting to 14.3 per cent annually for 1912–1915, and to 12.2 per cent for 1923–1929. The years since World War II have generally been years of high prosperity and for cigarettes to show this modest rate of growth undoubtedly signified that maturity had set in and that the industry could no longer expect the ebullient markets of its earlier decades.

Finally, the recent antitrust experience directly encouraged heavier competition. The nonaggressive posture behind established leading brands was under some kind of legal cloud with possible dangers if it continued. It was clear that the major companies were unable to engage in any power play to preserve their existing market share, and the second-ranking companies were free to use their new financial strength aggressively without fear of over-muscular retaliation.

For all these reasons the industry pattern began to change. The leading companies moved quickly to develop the market for king-size cigarettes. As early as 1939, American Tobacco converted Pall Mall[8] to a king-size brand and later followed with Herbert Tareyton. Liggett & Myers converted its old brand, Fatima. Lorillard brought out Embassy, and Philip Morris introduced Dunhill Majors. In 1949 Reynolds finally abandoned its policy of exclusive concentration on one brand by bringing out Cavalier.

Of all these brands only Pall Mall and Herbert Tareyton were successful, accounting for 15.9 per cent of the total cigarette market by 1953. In 1952 the king-sized Chesterfield was introduced and in 1953 Raleigh, Philip Morris, and Old Gold appeared in the large size, thus attempting to capitalize on existing brand acceptance in a new market. Meanwhile, mentholated and filter sales had been growing. By 1953 the market share of Camel,

---

8 Pall Mall had been the leading Turkish brand of the old Trust and marked George Washington Hill's first great advertising and promotion success as a young man. Revived as a domestic blend in 1936 and entrusted to a subsidiary of the American Tobacco Company where it would not interfere with the promotion of Lucky Strike, Pall Mall showed moderate but satisfactory growth with very little advertising support.

Lucky Strike, and Chesterfield regular had fallen to 54.3 per cent, and the share of the three leading companies to 75.6 per cent.

CANCER AND BUSINESS STRATEGY These developments were only partly complete when the industry was suddenly subjected to serious new pressures by the so-called "cancer scare" of late 1953 and 1954. The charge by reputable medical authorities that cigarette smoking is an important factor in lung cancer and heart disease confronted the industry with major problems of public relations, market tactics, and long-range competitive strategy.

The immediate market impact was sharp but temporary. By 1954 annual consumption fell 24 billion cigarettes, or 6.4 per cent, but the market then recovered and total consumption in 1963 was 115 billion above that of 1952. This recovery did, however, amount to an annual rate of only 3.6 per cent from the low point in 1954.

The Surgeon General's report in 1964 and continuing publicity on the dangers of smoking seem to have had a more serious long-term effect. The average annual growth in the years 1964–1968 has been only 0.6 per cent with the most recent year showing a small absolute decline. The longer term outlook is doubtful. Existing smokers may not reduce consumption substantially but there is considerable likelihood that fewer nonsmokers will be converted to cigarettes in the future. Governmental action to restrict the advertising and promotion of cigarettes is not beyond the bounds of possibility.

These developments have imposed serious pressures on the companies. They may face a declining market, and even if the health menace is eventually removed, the concern over cancer has reinforced a tendency toward maturity and stagnation in the total cigarette market, which was already in existence.

The immediate response of the industry was to dispute the validity of the medical charges and simultaneously to promote filter brands, which yield less of the supposedly harmful tars and other combustion products. Filter brands rose from less than 1 per cent of the market in 1952, to 73 per cent in 1968; seven of the ten leading brands in 1968 were filter cigarettes.

One of the first effects of the cancer scare in 1953 was to double the sales of Viceroy, the old Brown & Williamson filter, and to sharply accelerate the growth of Lorillard's Kent, which had been introduced in 1952. Liggett & Myers introduced L & M in 1953. American's filter version of Herbert Tareyton, Reynolds' Winston, and Lorillard's Old Gold filters all appeared in 1954. Philip Morris' Marlboro filter was introduced in 1955. In 1956, Reynolds, and Brown & Williamson introduced menthol flavored filters in Salem and Kool.

The growth of filter cigarettes stopped the rapid growth of plain king-size brands, and since 1953, they have declined as a class. Pall Mall, however, rose against the trend for some years, and even though it has declined substantially since 1965, it is still the second largest cigarette brand of any type and accounts for 80 per cent of the plain king-size class. Chesterfield king accounts for half the remainder.

American's success in the king-size market has not been matched in the more important class of plain filter cigarettes. Here Reynolds has enjoyed the outstanding success with Winston and in 1968 sold around 85 billion plain filter cigarettes. With Brown & Williamson selling Viceroy and Raleigh; Philip Morris selling Marlboro; Benson & Hedges and Lorillard selling Kent, True, Newport, and Old Gold, each of these companies sold about half as many filter cigarettes as Reynolds. American producing Tareyton and Pall Mall filters was far behind, with Liggett & Myers still further back.

In the menthol filter class Reynolds was again far ahead with their brand, Salem and Winston menthol; Brown & Williamson's Kool was the only serious rival.

These differences in successful adaptation to new market pressures have been directly reflected in company fortunes. In the years prior to 1954 American was supported by its king-size brands and was industry leader by a substantial margin. Although subject to the stronger competition of the secondary producers after World War II, the American Tobacco Company retained its market share; it only declined from 34.2 per cent in 1947 to 32.6 per cent in 1953. Thereafter American's failure to win a leading position in filter cigarettes resulted in an erosion of market share to 21.8 per cent in 1968.

In contrast Reynolds suffered a significant loss in its market position in the immediate post-World War II years as a result of its failure to develop a successful king-size. By 1953 its market share had fallen from 29.4 per cent to 26.4 per cent. Subsequent success with filter and menthol cigarettes raised its percentage to 32.1 per cent, and since 1957 Reynolds has been the industry leader in sales, significantly ahead of American in second position. Liggett with no outstanding success in any area has seen its share decline from 21.7 per cent to 7.2 per cent. Again in contrast, the former Little Three have all more than doubled their market share, Philip Morris increasing from 6.9 per cent to 13.6 per cent, Lorillard from 4.3 per cent to 10.1 per cent, and Brown & Williamson from 3.9 per cent to 15.1 per cent.

These major shifts in competitive standing are evidence of the strong destabilizing forces that have been at work in this industry. This is even more apparent when we look at the path by which the new set of competitive standings was reached. During the past 10 years Reynolds and American have always been in the first two positions but Liggett, Lorillard, and Brown & Williamson have each occupied every ranking from three to six in at least 1 year. Philip Morris has never been third but it has been sixth three times, fifth three times and fourth four times in 10 years.

Equally significant of changed conditions is an apparent change in the whole focus of competitive effort. The old aim was to build an impregnable brand and to profit by its growth and promotion. This remained the objective as the early king-size, menthol, and filter brands were introduced. Reynolds, with its outstanding success in Winston and Salem and its continuing strength in Camel seems to have used the same approach until very recently. The company's introduction of Brandon in 1962 and Tempo in 1964 did little to disturb the continuing cultivation of existing brands.

Other companies, however, with less secure brand positions have been introducing new brands at an increasing rate. Between 1959 and 1963 Brown & Williamson introduced Bellair, Life, Kentucky Kool, Kool King. Philip Morris brought out Alpine and Paxton. Lorillard introduced Spring, Old Gold King, and York. Liggett & Myers' new brands were Duke and Lark. Since 1963 the number of new products has increased dramatically not only with new brands like Carleton, Galaxy, True, or Masterpiece, but with the development of variations of old brands like Pall Mall Menthol, Lucky Strike Menthols, Lucky Strike 100's, and Lucky Strike Menthol 100's. New sizes, new filters, new flavors, new packages, new shapes have all been used as marketing appeals. American Tobacco has been especially active the last 2 years, and appears to have a longer line of product variants than any other company. Even Reynolds, with a small number of brand names, has provided variation in boxes and lengths, a filter version of Camel and menthol flavor in Winston as well as Salem.

The significance of this product proliferation lies not merely in sheer number and complexity, but in the different competitive objectives sought. These products appear to be designed to appeal to a temporary public whim, to respond to relatively minor and special demands, and to appeal to customers by novelty of product without any particular expectation that the product will become a long-lasting well-established brand. This approach to skimming a profit by repeated new product innovation is quite different from the market strategy originally employed on Camel, Lucky Strike, and Chesterfield; it is more like the multiproduct competition of the Trust and its predecessor companies.

If this is indeed the shift that marketing efforts have taken, it is consistent with the kinds of pressures operating upon the cigarette market; it is quite similar to the developments in other mature consumers' goods like detergents, breakfast foods, and cookies, where continuous new-product introduction with relatively short expected life cycles is an essential marketing tool.

The cigarette industry has also come closer to other mature industries in its strategic decisions. In this day of conglomerates it should not be surprising to find the cigarette industry expanding outside the range of its own historical interests. It has especially strong motives to do so because of the slowing down of cigarette growth, the very serious possibilities of market decline in the future, and the strengthening of competitive pressures in the present. The cigarette industry is still highly profitable but it would not appear to be an attractive location for the reinvestment of those earnings. Management is well advised to look abroad and this they have done, some to foreign tobacco markets where domestic pressures are not yet felt, and others to different industries where the outlook is more favorable and where, hopefully, the skills and techniques learned in the cigarette industry can be put to profitable use. The proportion of nontobacco business now ranges from 5 per cent to more than 25 per cent of sales and some company spokesmen have identified 50 per cent as a common target.

Most companies have some interest in packaging and packaging materials for sale to others as well as for their own use. Philip Morris has major foreign tobacco interests and domestic interests in shaving supplies, chewing gum, and industrial chemicals. American and Reynolds are interested in packaged foods. American has a stake in the manufacture and Liggett in the distribution of distilled liquors. Pet food is a concern of Liggett and Lorillard, Lorillard has acquired two candy companies and has itself been acquired by Loews Theatres.

II. MARKET STRUCTURE

The present market structure of the cigarette industry is partly the result of historical development and accident. The personality of James B. Duke created the Tobacco Trust, the Supreme Court destroyed it, and the character of the men who succeeded to control determined the pattern of power among the successor companies. Industry maturity and growth, specific pricing decisions, changes in public taste, and the concern over health have contributed to major changes in the product itself and in the methods of competition.

Yet, in addition to accident and the heavy hand of the past there have been constant influences upon the industry throughout its history. In all phases of its existence the industry has shown a high concentration of output and marked similarities of competitive techniques and policies. The principal factors responsible have been the technology of cigarette manufacture and the nature of cigarette demand.

It has long been common knowledge that the demand for all tobacco products taken together is highly inelastic. Ever since the first discovery of the weed, tobacco has been a favorite object of taxation and of state or private monopoly because of the heavy charges that it can bear without appreciably diminishing consumption. The urgency of the wants that tobacco satisfies, the small cost even of relatively expensive tobaccos, and the complete lack of substitutes make the volume of tobacco consumption independent of prices over a wide range.

For a single tobacco product like cigarettes other tobacco products are possible substitutes; pipes, cigars, plug, and even snuff can be used in place of cigarettes, and over the years wide shifts have occurred in the relative use of these various products. Between 1900 and 1958 the consumption of tobacco in the form of cigarettes rose from 3.4 per cent to 88 per cent of total tobacco consumption. Yet, it appears that in any short period of time very little substitution takes place in response to economic incentives. Changes in tobacco usage appear to be carried along on broad social currents of fashion and taste, and do not seem to be greatly influenced either by relative prices of tobacco products or by advertising activity. In the longer study on which this chapter is based the author has demonstrated that the consumption of cigarettes is almost wholly insensitive to changes in price or in advertising pressures within the range of changes that can be observed.

In contrast, the demand for individual brands of cigarettes is highly elastic in its response to price. In the 1930's the major companies found that a difference of more than 3 cents per pack between the standard brands and the 10-cent brands was injurious to the business of the former, and they tried to prevent the recurrence of so large a differential. This sensitivity existed despite real differences in product quality, for the leaf tobacco used in standard brands was sometimes more than twice as expensive as that in the cheaper cigarettes. Between brands of the same quality class, price sensitivity is even higher. In 1918, for example, Lucky Strike was sold for a short time at a higher retail price than Camel or Chesterfield, and rapidly lost half its business. There were other occasions that indicated high sensitivity of demand for the standard brands to slight retail price differences.

Though individual brand demand is highly elastic there are some limits to this elasticity. Between different product types, i.e., regular, king-size, filter, and menthol, there are significant physical differences that allow different prices. The leading brands in any one type are almost identical, yet they have slight differences in leaf blend and flavoring treatment. Customers show preferences for individual brands based in part of these differences and in part on intangible and even nonexistent qualities. The existence of irrational brand preference renders demand highly susceptible to advertising. The shifting fortunes of the leading brands within the same product type reflect both autonomous fluctuations in taste and the varying pressures of advertising.

These basic characteristics of cigarette demand give important market advantages to the large firm. It is possible to compete either through price cutting, advertising, or through the development of new products, and all methods have been used at one time or another. Whichever is used, the large firm holds a competitive advantage over the small firm, and it is to be expected that the industry will be dominated by large firms.

If prices are cut to gain business, as was the frequent practice under the Trust, it forces other firms to follow suit if they are not to lose a large portion of their business. This means that no firm can expect to gain customers by price cutting without inviting retaliation. But if prices are cut until all companies are losing money, it is the largest and strongest that can hold out and endure losses until the small firms go under.

On the other hand, when competition is conducted through advertising, its effectiveness depends largely on the total amount spent in promoting a given brand. Skillful salesmanship may allow one company to achieve the same results as another with only half the expenditures, for the persuasiveness of the advertising depends as much on the sales message as on the loudness with which it is shouted. Where advertising abilities are evenly distributed, however, the larger expenditures win, and it is the big company that can afford these outlays.

Still another advantage to large companies arises from the requirements of distribution. With thousands of wholesalers and a million and a half retail outlets, and with the heavy dependence of cigarette purchase upon convenient access, the maintenance of complete distribution requires expensive field sales activities. The major companies each employ many hundreds of salesmen to visit wholesalers and retailers for order taking, stock supervision, point of sales displays, and other promotion. The expenses of such activities are more easily borne by large companies. A small producer can avoid some of these costs by accepting narrower distribution but he then reduces his market opportunities.

Again, if competition is conducted through product changes, it is the large firm that can mobilize the necessary advertising and assure the necessary distribution.

For all these reasons we would expect the output of the cigarette industry to be concentrated unless the large firm suffered a serious disadvantage in production costs. This does not appear, however, to be the case. The development of cigarette making machinery removed the technological impediments to the growth of the individual firm. Much of the process of manufacture is concerned with handling masses of tobacco in simple operations with close control of humidity and temperature. The machinery and equipment are readily adapted to quite small or very large factories. Cigarette making machines are highly complicated but the output of the individual machine is small with respect to that of the enterprise as a whole. A modern machine can produce 750–1,600 cigarettes per minute and the American Tobacco Company was operating about 600 machines in 1942. The output of the firm can be quite small or very large simply by varying the number of machines; and although large firms may have significant cost advantages compared to very small ones, there is no evidence of a significant cost advantage between a moderately small or a very large firm. Since large firms are better able to apply market pressure, the consequently expand until they have secured a large proportion of the national output.

III. MARKET CONDUCT

The concentrated structure of the cigarette industry and the peculiarities of cigarette demand have a profound influence upon industry behavior. When firms are large, they need not and in fact cannot, as in the theoretical model of perfect competition, accept the going market price and demand conditions as something given and outside their own control. Each firm must set its policy with the knowledge that its own action will affect the industry as a whole. With this understanding, two entirely different types of behavior are possible. Policy may be directed either to eliminate weaker competitors by outright warfare or to ensure maximum profits on the assumption that all firms will survive. Price and advertising policies provide adequate tools for either task, and at various times in history both ends have been pursued and both tools have been used.

When Duke was a power in the industry, competitive measures were directed at injuring competitors so that they would either abandon business or agree to join forces. Usually extreme pressure by price cutting and advertising was combined with relatively generous offers to buy, and most competitors went out of existence by sale to the Trust rather than through the bankruptcy courts. Once control was achieved selling pressures were relaxed, and the Trust was able to enjoy a comfortable level of monopoly profits. So long, however, as control was incomplete, Duke used price and advertising primarily as weapons of commercial warfare rather than as instruments of short-run profit maximization.

After the dissolution, on the other hand, competitive strategy was directed to increase profits rather than to injure competitors. The effect of the 1911 decree narrowed the range of practicable business policy. There were now three or four major competitors, any one of whom possessed the resources to withstand prolonged price warfare. At the same time the decree forbade any recombination of the severed parts of the Trust. It was now possible neither to eliminate competitors nor to join them, and the major successor companies were forced to adapt their policies to a situation in which each others' continued existence and independence must be taken for granted.

In these circumstances price cutting has serious disadvantages as a competitive weapon. These disadvantages stem from its very efficiency which would force competitors to retaliate, and from the small unit of sale which makes any retail price reduction a large percentage decline, imposing a serious drain on profits. At present prices a reduction of 1 cent in the single package price would amount to 9 per cent of the manufacturers' net receipts excluding excise tax, and to more than the manufacturers' net profit after income taxes. A reduction in the price per carton can be more delicate but it is difficult to see how a price reduction attractive to consumers could also be attractive to manufacturers, especially since competitors must cut in turn, so that no competitive advantage could result. A headlong drive to absorb losses may be useful for purposes of commercial warfare, but it is an unsatisfactory way of competing for business during normal times.

Advertising, on the other hand, can be a much less expensive method of competition. Even large changes in advertising outlays may amount to only a fraction of a cent per package. Advertising is as unlikely a tool as pricing for changing the total consumption of cigarettes, but competitive advertising campaigns designed to change the division of the market need not result in a purposeless draw. The effectiveness of a given expenditure depends on skill and good fortune in discovering an effective sales message, and each firm has a chance to win. The frequent changes in relative position among the leading brands, even during the period of Big Three supremacy, testified to the erratic influence of advertising. Moreover, heavy advertising outlays by the leading firms make it more difficult for new competitors to grow, and thus serve a function that is in the joint interest as well as in the competitive interest of the leading companies. For all these reasons it is evident why cigarette firms prefer to match prices and compete through advertising.

The disadvantages of using retail price as a competitive tool do not apply so strongly in the case of wholesale prices. Cigarettes are normally sold to jobbers at a price set by the manufacturer, whereas the prices at which jobbers resell to retailers and the latter resell to the public are set by competition among distributors modified by occasional collusive agreements. Although a large change in the manufacturer's price will normally be reflected in a similar change at retail, a manufacturer's change of only a few cents per thousand may not be reflected in the retail price per pack, but may be added to or subtracted from the distributors' margins. Thus, although the major firms almost always strive to maintain identical retail prices, it is possible that one of them may seek the goodwill of jobbers and retailers by shaving his net price. On the other hand, a slightly higher manufacturer's price, obtained by squeezing distributor's margins, may make additional advertising funds available while leaving retail prices unchanged. Since both dealers' goodwill and advertising campaigns affect brand sales, there has sometimes been a problem of deciding in which direction funds could be employed most profitably.

The greatest opportunities for the use of price as a competitive tool occur in connection with new product introductions. Consumer goodwill attaches to a brand rather than to the company that makes it, and hence a new and untried brand, even from a well-known firm, is not equivalent to an established brand in the eye of the consumer. His willingness to try a new brand may not be greatly increased by a low price or hindered by a high price. In fact, since price is sometimes regarded as an indicator of quality, price incentives at some times or for some people may work in reverse. A new brand may be effectively promoted with prices that are below or above established brands. Once a brand is well known and accepted in a given class, interbrand elasticity becomes higher and uniformity of prices within the class is almost certain to be established.

Camel was introduced at 10 cents compared with Fatima, the nearest comparable brand at 15 cents. The directly competitive Lucky Strike and Chesterfield were introduced at the same 10-cent retail price, but in the years before 1928 the price to jobbers of Lucky Strike was consistently several cents higher than the price of the other brands. At this time Lucky Strike sales were much smaller than Camel sales. As mentioned before, market position depends upon massive advertising expenditures, and if outlays for Lucky Strike were to be comparable in size to those for Camel, this required a higher level of expense per thousand. George Washington Hill's great skill in advertising and his even greater confidence in its value caused the company to set aside funds for that purpose, even though this involved a higher price and some distributor ill will. As sales increased, the necessity for additional funds declined and the dealer's goodwill could be taken into consideration. After 1928, Lucky Strike was maintained at the same price as Camel. In 1922 experiments with Chesterfield prices above and below Camel indicated that a differential in either direction from the industry leader was not worthwhile and identical prices were thenceforth set.

The initial promotion of Philip Morris extended further the price and advertising pressures that Lucky Strike had earlier employed. Philip Morris was introduced at a higher manufacturer's price and a higher retail price than the standard brands. An additional 1 cent per pack price to wholesalers made additional advertising funds available. A 2-cent higher price to consumers increased the dealer's interest, which was important for a new brand. The higher retail price did not at first injure consumer demand because the new cigarette was named for an old expensive Turkish brand; by "trading down" on an established reputation, it was able to secure a special quality market. As the brand grew in size and was accepted as a counterpart to the standard brands the special quality appeal (which was due in part to the high price) no longer had validity, and Philip Morris was brought to sell at the same wholesale and retail price as the other brands.

In normal competitive situations in the 1920's and 1930's when the major brands had achieved maturity and when all were selling comparable volumes, the major manufacturers were content to set identical wholesale prices, to strive through the auction markets to pay approximately the same prices for leaf tobacco, and to devote the difference between these two principal elements of receipts and costs to advertising outlays and to net earnings, as competitive pressures and stockholder requirements allowed. In this way price was not intended to serve the competitive function of shifting customers. The rise and fall in prices of particular brands depended primarily on the use that the various companies could make of approximately equivalent advertising resources. The early behavior of Lucky Strike and Philip Morris represented departures from this pattern in order to compensate for lower sales; the Old Gold effort to buy a market outright represents a similar departure by its sudden heavy expenditures financed through bond and stock issues.

The multiplication of brands since World War II has given many opportunities for price experiment, and the antitrust conviction has provided incentives to demonstrate price independence. With major new product classes assuming importance, it was necessary to establish workable differentials between them, and this involved testing and experimentation. The pattern of experimentation and some of the forces at work are seen quite clearly in the price record.

When price controls were abolished in 1946, all major brands bore the same price. In the first free-price revisions, the manufacturer's net price of Camel was kept 3 cents per thousand below the prices of the other brands. The difference was small and made little sense in view of Camels' leading position, but was probably occasioned by the antitrust case. The companies protested bewilderment at what that case implied concerning their proper conduct, and this may have been an attempt to demonstrate noncollusive independence in pricing. In any event, the differential was eliminated in 1949.

In the early post-World War II period, Pall Mall was sold at the same net price as the standard brands, but in 1950 it was advanced to a differential of 4 cents per thousand above them. Cavalier, which had been introduced in 1949 at the standard brand price, stayed at that level, whereas Pall Mall raised its differential to 9 cents in 1953, and 44 cents in 1955. This attempt to win a market for Cavalier by a low price was unsuccessful, and in 1956 Cavalier joined Pall Mall at 44 cents. Raleigh kings were introduced in 1953 at a 9-cent differential and held at that level when Pall Mall advanced in 1955. At the cheaper price Raleigh sales did not improve and in 1957 the price was raised to equal Pall Mall.

Meanwhile, Chesterfield King was introduced in 1957 at a 47 cent differential when Pall Mall was at 4 cents. In 1953 the Chesterfield King differential was reduced to 30 cents when Pall Mall was at 9 cents. Philip Morris King and Old Gold King were also set at 30 cents when introduced in 1953. When Pall Mall's differential was raised to 44 cents in 1955, these other brands followed. The king-size differential remained at 44 cents until 1963 when it was reduced to 17 cents. In 1966 the differential went back up to 20 cents, and in 1968 was eliminated entirely with king-size brands at the same price as standard.

King-size brands thus showed both low- and high-price approaches to new market development. The low-price approach of Cavalier and Raleigh was ineffective and was dropped. The higher-price approach of Chesterfield and the others did not prove harmful and was taken over by the leaders. Experiment had established a workable price structure and identical prices once more ruled. Once these brands became thoroughly mature, both the need and the opportunity for special prices weakened and the differentials disappeared.

Filter cigarettes show an opposite type of behavior. Viceroy as an old small-volume brand was priced in the early post-World War II years at various differentials between 45 and 62 cents over the standard brands. When Kent was introduced in 1952, it was priced $3.02 higher than the standard brands. This differential was reduced to $2.64 by a regular brand price-rise in 1953. Viceroy stuck at 88 cents during this period. Liggett & Myers attempted to go along with the $2.64 differential when L & M filters were introduced in late 1953, but when Winston was introduced in early 1954 with massive promotion at an 88 cent differential, L & M capitulated at once and also established an 88 cent differential. Kent held on to the extra margin but lost more than half its sales in 1955 and joined the others in 1956. All other new filters were thereafter set at 88 cents until 1958 when the uniform differential was reduced to 53 cents. Even Parliament, an old premium brand acquired by Philip Morris, was reduced to the 53-cent level. The filter differential was set equal to the plain king-size differential in 1966, with final elimination in 1968.

Thus, the filter brands traced out the same ultimate pattern as plain king-size brands but with somewhat different pricing maneuvers along the way. For a time differentials rose moderately above the early Viceroy level but the attempt of Lorillard and Liggett to get much higher margins was defeated. Again experiment established workable differentials and price uniformity ruled, with the differentials ultimately eliminated by brand maturity.

At the present time only the new 100 millimeter cigarettes have special prices. Introduced in 1967 at an adverse differential of 70 cents, they have been reduced to 50 cents in 1968 by an increase in the price of all other brands.

Apart from such occasions in introducing a new product and apart from the price war of 1933, price has seldom been used as a competitive tool. Prices among brands in the same class are normally identical and price is not intended to affect the division of the market among competitors.

An interesting exception to this pattern occurred in 1928 when Reynolds led a price cut from $5.64 to $5.29 per thousand net. At this time Camel advertising was not proving effective whereas Lucky Strike advertising was having extraordinary success. The cut had the effect of reducing the advertising funds available to both firms, and was probably designed to cripple a successful American campaign. Lucky Strike advertising did fall off but sales continued to expand and in 1929 Reynolds raised the price to $5.64 once again. This is one of the few cases in which price seems to have been used as a competitive tool among the major firms, though even here it is not the kind of tactic usually thought of in connection with the term price competition.

PRICE LEADERSHIP

For many years the actual prices were determined by Reynolds. As the largest cigarette producer, this company was in a position to enforce its will on other companies. In 1918 an attempt was made by American to lead a large price rise. Reynolds refused to follow and American was forced to retract. In 1921 American cut its price but Reynolds seized the initiative by cutting still further. Thereafter Reynolds made the important changes with Liggett setting an identical price and American setting a related but slightly higher price. Reynolds led all later price changes until 1933 and all price rises until 1946. Since World War II American has led most of the price increases with Reynolds occasionally taking the lead, especially with respect to filter cigarettes. Attempts by other companies to initiate price changes have not been successful.

In 1956 Liggett & Myers attempted to lead a price rise of 50 cents per thousand on all brands. Liggett had never done this before and her executives had testified in the antitrust trial that they felt compelled by market forces to follow the lead of the other companies whether up or down. This contention was received skeptically by the courts and Liggett may have intended its lead as a declaration and demonstration of independence. Whatever its purpose the attempt was a failure. The other companies refused to follow and in two weeks Liggett retracted the rise.

In 1965 Lorillard attempted to increase the price of filter cigarettes by 35 cents and was immediately followed by Philip Morris and Liggett. Reynolds and American, however, refused to follow and a month later Liggett & Myers led the others back to the old price. It is not clear whether this pattern reflected an attempt by the two majors to discipline Lorillard and reassert leadership or whether it was simply a difference of opinion. At any event, the role of price initiator has remained restricted to the two front runners.

Another interesting example of the price setting minuet occurred in 1966 when American attempted a 40-cent increase and all the rest followed. When the President of the United States requested a rollback, Reynolds gave in and cut price all the way to the original level. American, however, gave up only 20 cents of the rise and the smaller companies followed this pattern. Several weeks later Reynolds moved up to the 20-cent level.

COMPETITION AND COOPERATION

The 1933 price war against the economy brands, waged in a manner reminiscent of the old Trust, was a highly unusual occurrence. Price policy in this industry since the Trust has normally been noncompetitive in character. For the most part, price has been set with a view to good profits rather than to divide the market.

The absence of price competition does not necessarily imply collusion by the manufacturers to fix prices. It is clear that all have an interest in high prices and that there is no joint interest in low prices. The possible interest that each might have in cutting prices lower than the others is eliminated except in some cases of new-product introduction when it is known that the other manufacturers will follow any cut and that the net effect will be to the detriment of all without profit to any. In regard to pricing, the interests of the leading firms are cooperative rather than competitive, and their small number makes effective price discipline possible without the need for outright collusion. As we have remarked before, the elimination or combination of the leading firms has not been a practicable object of market policy since the Dissolution Decree of 1911. Each firm must count on the continued existence of its competitors. Each firm needs merely to take into consideration the effect that its actions must inevitably have on the others, and in a mature market judicious self-restraint can eliminate price competition as efficiently as explicit agreement among them.

This common interest does not extend to all aspects of the firm's behavior. The major companies are in vigorous competition for the favor of consumers and for an increased share of the market. They have a joint interest in erecting barriers against new competition, but the difficulties of entry for a small firm are so great that little direct attention to this joint interest is needed. In any event the companies' diverse interest in market shares induces them to make much larger expenditures for advertising and product changes than they would if they were concerned solely with maximizing the profits of the industry as a whole. The industry is unlike a monopoly in the resources it devotes to market competition through advertising and product innovation, but price behavior—once brands are well established—would probably not be very different if the major firms were governed by a single head.

IV. MARKET PERFORMANCE

Considered simply as business enterprises, there is no doubt that the leading tobacco companies have been highly successful. Under shifting conditions of product demand and of competitive pressure, industry leaders have shown a high degree of marketing skill and an ability to adapt to demands of the market place. With benefit of hindsight it is easy to see that major strategic errors were made in the price manipulations of the 1930's and the response of the industry to the cancer problem has been defensive and unimaginative. Whatever the strategic deficiencies, however, the leaders have been highly successful in the short term. This is measured in high profitability over long periods of time.

PROFITS

The effect of noncompetitive pricing of the 1933 price war and of changing competitive patterns are clearly visible in the profit results. Figure 1 presents a comparison between the percentage return on equity for the three principal cigarette companies and that for manufacturing corporations in general.

The three leading companies earned yearly net profits after interest and taxes equal to 18 per cent of their average tangible net worth from 1912 to 1941, despite the pressure of severe economic depression in the last decade of the period. In the 20 years before World War II, cigarette profits appear to have been at more than double the rate for the manufacturing industry in general.

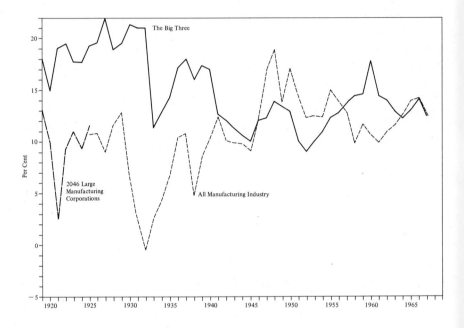

Figure 1

NET PROFITS AS A PERCENTAGE OF NET WORTH,
1919–1967

SOURCE   R. C. Epstein, *Industrial Profits In The United States*, New
York, National Bureau of Economic Research, 1934, p. 56; Moody's
Industrials; First National City Bank, *Monthly Letter*.

The superiority of cigarette earnings in the 1930's partly reflected the stability of cigarette demand in the face of lower incomes. Even an industry characterized by flexible price competition would show superior profits if its demand were of this character. But in the 1920's when most industries were prosperous, the cigarette industry also earned at double the average rate.

From 1941 through 1955 cigarette profits were substantially lower and ran generally at a rate about equal to that of the manufacturing industry in general. This reduction can be explained by wartime price controls, by a cautious market policy, probably induced by the monopoly conviction of 1941, by market maturity, and by the costs of the active multibrand competition of the first post-war years.

From 1956 to 1960, as the first adjustment to the filter revolution was completed, profit rates of the old Big Three again soared, whereas all manufacturing declined. But in later years with slowing growth and accelerated new product competition, profit ratios again returned to the all-manufacturing level.

The rate of return on equity, of course, differs among the companies as shown in Figure 2.

Reynolds has shown ordinarily high profitability as well as a dominant market share. American, under pressure from Reynolds has fared only slightly better than all-manufacturing industries. Surprisingly, Liggett with its rapidly eroding market position has nonetheless been able to maintain reasonably favorable profit ratios. Philip Morris and Lorillard have matched rapid growth with above-average profitability.

Comparisons of profit figures over long periods of time are somewhat confused by changes in excise and corporate income taxes. To avoid these complications and to provide a basis for comparison between the modern industry and the old Trust, Table 3 presents a series of profit ratios for significant time periods.

It appears that though in the 1920's the leading successor companies secured a higher return on sales than did the Trust, they had a somewhat lower return on assets. Taking both of these measures of profitability together, it appears that the rate of earnings of the successor companies was somewhat reduced by their competition and by the heavy advertising expenditures involved. Yet profits in the industry remained remarkably high and testified to an almost unimpaired degree of market control.

Throughout the history of the industry profits have been limited by the possibility or actuality of outside competition. Thus when the Trust was first organized and was enjoying its secure monopoly of cigarettes, operating profits were running at the ample rate of 30 per cent of net sales less tax. Between 1894 and 1900 when successive price wars were extending the Trust's control over other branches of the tobacco industry profits fell sharply to 20 per cent and below. Once the position of the Trust was consolidated, the profits on sales rose near its former level. Again in 1933 the operating profits of the American Tobacco Company were 34 per cent of net sales

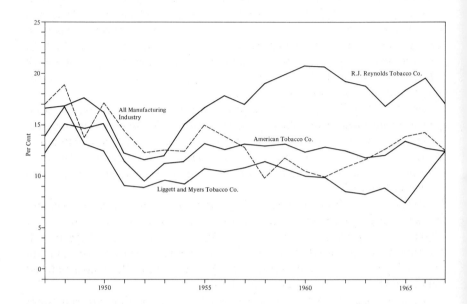

Figure 2

NET PROFITS AS A PERCENTAGE OF NET WORTH,
1947–1967

SOURCE   Moody's *Industrials*; First National City Bank *Monthly Letter*.

TABLE 3 SELECTED PROFIT RATIOS FOR THE TRUST
AND THREE SUCCESSOR COMPANIES (%)

	TRUST	AMERICAN	LIGGETT	REYNOLDS
Net earnings (before interest, after taxes) as percentage of net tangible assets:				
1890–1908	19.7			
1912–1941		15.1	14.7	20.0
1942–1947		8.9	8.9	12.0
1948–1958		7.4	9.3	8.5
1959–1967		9.5	6.9	12.8
Operating profit as percentage of net tangible assets in direct business:				
1890–1908	32.7			
1931–1941		20.8	17.3[a]	23.8[b]
1942–1947		17.0	15.8	20.1
1948–1958		14.3	13.6	18.7
1959–1967		18.1	14.4	25.8
Operating profit as percentage of net sales less tax:				
1890–1908	25.8			
1931–1941		27.0	21.2[a]	25.0[b]
1942–1947		18.5	17.9	18.4
1948–1958		19.7	20.6	24.0
1959–1967		20.5	17.5	28.1

a 1933–1941.
b 1932–1941.
SOURCE Compiled from company reports and from U.S. Bureau of
Corporations, *Report of the Commissioner of Corporations on the
Tobacco Industry*, Parts II, III (1915).

less tax, and this excessive margin allowed the 10 per cent brands to prosper.
Subsequent price cuts repelled the invasion but reduced profit margins to
around 25 per cent for most of the period, though they were back to 33 per
cent in 1941. In the post-World War II period, slower market growth, heavy
competition on new brands, and shifting market shares put American and
Liggett profit margins under heavy pressures, but Reynolds results were as
favorable as ever.

From the usual analysis of nonaggressive oligopoly, which was the
characteristic posture of the industry between the wars, we would expect
cigarette firms to maintain their prices as high as the elasticity of demand

allows. The relevant elasticity which would make price rises inadvisable in this case would not be the elasticity of demand for cigarettes as a whole but the long-run elasticities for the brands of established companies. These were influenced by the possibility of new entrants into the industry when the margin between cigarette prices and leaf costs became too wide. This seems to have been the basis of pricing during the long interval between the two World Wars. In the affluent economy since World War II, the threat of small entrants with cheaper cigarettes does not seem to have exerted a realistic restraint upon profit margins. It seems more likely that the absolute margins between manufacturing costs and price have been limited on the top side by prudent regard for what would be defensible if antitrust activity again stirred, and on the low side by what would be required to return moderate net profits after paying the extraordinary promotional expenditures of the new multibrand competition. The price that would allow moderate profit rates to beleaguered American and Liggett, allowed outstanding returns to the surpassing success of Reynolds.

IMPLICATIONS FOR PUBLIC POLICY

Although high profits are a badge of business success and although business managers are supposed to try to make them as high as possible, there may also be a question of whether profits in any given industry are too high for effective economic performance or whether they reflect interference with desirable competitive mechanisms. Twice in its history the cigarette industry has been involved in major antitrust cases and this suggests a way of approaching the economic evaluation of this industry. Both cases were important in the development of antitrust law and both have had significant effect upon industry structure and behavior. It is the purpose of this section to comment briefly on the nature of the antitrust cases and to consider the industrial reforms that followed or that might follow in the future.

THE 1911 CASE   The 1911 Supreme Court opinion in *United States* versus *American Tobacco Co.* was a classic statement of antitrust principles and the subsequent circuit court decree was a classic example of industrial reform through dissolution. The courts were faced with a pattern of monopoly power deliberately created and predatorially used, and although this was one of the cases, along with the Standard Oil Case, in which the "rule of reason" was first developed, the pattern of industrial buccaneering was clearly outside the bounds of that rule. Legal remedy through dissolution—the breaking up of the monopoly into many segments—found one of its applications here. The consequences for the industry were of fundamental importance.

THE 1946 CASE   The Supreme Court opinion in *American Tobacco Company* versus *United States* in 1946 had less clear effects either on antitrust law or on the industry than was the case with the 1911 decision. The problems involved may be indicated by a brief discussion of the case itself.

The leading companies and 13 of their officers were convicted under Section 1 of the Sherman Act of a conspiracy or combination in restraint of trade, and under Section 2 of conspiring to monopolize, attempting to monopolize, and monopolizing the trade in cigarettes. The conviction in all its parts was based upon a finding by the jury that conspiracy or combination existed among the various defendants both to fix prices and to exclude competitors from the business.

Problems both for antitrust law and for effective remedy arose from the fact that no specific evidence was introduced during the trial to show that the defendants had met together or had made any explicit agreement on any important aspect of their businesses. Instead, the conspiracy was to be inferred from a pattern of common behavior. As we have shown, the common price policy of the leading companies follows naturally from their individual interests and need not imply collusion.

Three possible interpretations of the jury verdict and the later Supreme Court opinion may be advanced.

1. The jury based its verdict on insufficient evidence. In the words of one of the defense attorneys the companies were "judicially lynched."
2. The kind of common action on price practiced by the industry and understood by all its members represented a kind of combination or conspiracy in restraint of trade without the need to prove an explicit agreement or without even the need for such an agreement to exist. Under this interpretation the cigarette industry is obviously monopolistic in economic terms and with new developments in legal thought, the fact of economic market power becomes nearly the same as legally defined monopoly.[9]
3. The jury convicted and the Supreme Court sustained the conviction because of a pattern of common oligopoly action, lying quite outside the bounds of acceptable competitive behavior.

If the first interpretation is correct, it implies a miscarriage of justice. For reasons to be developed below, this interpretation is not persuasive.

If the second interpretation is correct, it raises peculiar problems of public policy for if rational oligopoly behavior is the same thing as illegal conspiracy or combination, it makes futile a direct attack on the conspiracy itself. The conspiracy is merely symptomatic of a market structure that confers illegal power and the violation of the act arises from the structure of the industry itself not merely from deliberate illegality in the details of market behavior. This suggests that civil action to secure changes in the

9 See E. V. Rostow, "The New Sherman Act: A Positive Instrument of Progress," *University of Chicago Law Review*, **14**:584 (June 1947).

industrial structure would have been more appropriate than the criminal penalties on behavior actually enforced.

It seems doubtful, however, that the second interpretation is valid either for the meaning of the law or as an explanation of the cigarette case itself. The appeals courts did not say that the pattern of common action on pricing was illegal but merely that a pattern of common action was grounds upon which a jury could properly infer conspiracy. It is doubtful that the jury was sufficiently impressed by common price behavior to bring a conviction on these grounds alone, although the jury may well have entertained dark suspicions. In the cigarette trial, however, more than mere suspicion was present. There were clearly established indications of collusion on minor matters such as the sending of leaf buyers to market towns; the price behavior from 1931 to 1934 indicated the presence of monopoly power and the use of that power for its own increase.

The 1931 price rise in the midst of depression clearly could have occurred only if the manufacturers had strong administrative discretion over their prices and were prepared to act cooperatively. It was this kind of use of monopoly power that popular thought has always opposed and feared. So too, the 1933 price war against the economy brands, altogether it indicated the actual weakness of this monopoly power, was a classic case of monopoly price raiding. The occasions of minor collusion and the aggressive use of monopoly power gave the jury something to strike at and probably served to increase the jury's willingness to infer collusion from a pattern of common price behavior.

It seems likely that the third interpretation is nearest the truth and that the 1946 antitrust case penalized the abuse of power rather than its mere existence. Later antitrust cases have not made cooperative oligopoly pricing illegal per se, and the cigarette conviction does not appear to have depended on such a principle.

Regardless of the explanation of the antitrust conviction itself, that conviction opened up a wide range of possibilities of industrial reform. Through further proceedings in equity, the government could have sought to modify industry behavior. Structural reform through the breaking up of existing companies into a number of smaller ones would have had a classic precedent in the cigarette industry itself. The fact that no further legal action has been taken raises some interesting questions. In what ways is the existing organization and behavior of the industry unsatisfactory? What opportunities for useful reform have been missed? What have been the effects of antitrust policy as it has actually worked?

INDUSTRY BEHAVIOR

An evaluation of the behavior of the cigarette industry might start from a consideration of the kinds of unsatisfactory behavior that traditional economic analysis leads us to expect from a monopoly. According to that analysis the economic results of monopoly are inferior in several respects. to those that a perfectly competitive industry would yield. The monopolist sets prices higher than the competitive level and these high prices discourage consumption and result in the exclusion from the industry of resources that otherwise would be employed there. The monopolist operates on the downward sloping section of a U-shaped average cost curve so that excess capacity exists, causing unit costs to be higher than they need be. The ability of the monopolist to do these things depends on the exclusion of outside competition, and measures may be taken to reinforce the barriers to entry. The consequence is excessive profits. Thus the monopolist secures pay for the antisocial functions of restricting opportunity, increasing costs, and disturbing the optimum allocation of resources.

At least one of the characteristics indicated by traditional analysis is true of the cigarette industry. For most of its history it has earned at about double the average profit rate. Market control has been reflected in high profits. In recent years, however, other pressures have forced cigarette profits to average levels, and this may be accounted, in part, as one of the accomplishments of antitrust prosecution.

With this exception the failings attributed to monopoly do not seem to be characteristic of the cigarette industry. The extremely inelastic demand means that high prices and high profits do not reduce consumption (and with the cancer threat we might be glad if they did). The firm does not exhibit a U-shaped cost curve, for the small producer is as efficient as the large and the long-run average cost curve is flat. Thus no burden of higher cost is imposed on the industry by its pricing practices, and the excess capacity does not exist from any other cause than fluctuations in brand demand.

A question arises, however, whether large advertising outlays may not represent a special kind of waste in this industry. Considerable sums are involved and have been growing larger. In the early post-World War II years the industry spent around $50 million annually on advertising, and between 1954 and 1958 total expenditure doubled from $74 million to $142 million.

A small part of this expense serves to inform consumers of what is available and thus to make possible a more intelligent choice. But most of the expenditure is for other competitive purposes. Some of it results in indirect entertainment benefits, but this raises other issues concerning the organization and functioning of television and other communications industries that are beyond the scope of this chapter. Massive advertising also serves to strengthen large producers vis-à-vis small ones and is an important factor in maintaining the highly concentrated structure of the industry.

A complaint might be made about the resources devoted to the introduction and promotion of new brands and products. We can scarcely complain about the development of new filter types if these make cigarettes less damaging, or new menthol types if these taste better to the consumer. But much of the innovation in terms of brand names and cleverly contrived images seems to have no wider purpose or utility than expanding the manufacturers' sales. As a mere sales device, new product introduction can be just as wasteful as advertising.

If, however, advertising expenditures or innovation costs are to be considered a waste, it is important to note that they are wastes of competition. The expenditures are designed to capture the public attention, to sell goods, and perhaps to foster brand loyalties. Advertising and product innovation serve as weapons in the competitive struggle and help to shift customers among nearly identical commodities. This shifting may be on an irrational basis but so long as competition exists, some method for providing this shifting is necessary. If these methods were not used in interbrand competition, substitutes would have to be found. Other forms of sales promotion are also expensive. So long as the present structure of the industry exists, substantial marketing expenses are necessary. Although questions might be raised about the volume, it is not easy to arrive at a judgment as to how much is superfluous and wasteful.

INDUSTRY STRUCTURE

Most cigarette industry behavior patterns are implicit in the industry's present structure, and any substantial change in the functioning of the industry would probably require a change in the number of firms and their relationships to each other. What kinds of structural reform might have been undertaken?

It should be noted at the outset that no possible reorganization of the cigarette industry could bring it close to the theoretical model of perfect competition. Perfect competition requires, among other conditions, that a commodity be homogeneous in quality and that marginal costs rise sharply at a small scale of output. Rising marginal costs keep the firm small, and small size and homogeneous product yield a perfectly elastic demand curve for the firm. The perfectly competitive firm has no effect on price, no concern with price policy, and no problem of sales. It can sell any amount it wishes at the going price and need only decide how large an output it is profitable to produce.

The cigarette industry obviously does not and cannot operate under such conditions. Long-run marginal costs do not rise and there is no limit to the size of the firm except that set by the market. The products of rival manufacturers although similar, are not identical in the public eye and cannot be made so. The firm cannot merely sell at a going price all that it wishes, but must fight for markets; this is the function of brand names, advertising, and other methods of distribution competition.

Since perfect competition cannot exist in the cigarette industry, all possible alternative forms of market structure that might be set up in place of the present oligopoly must contain some other kind or degree of monopolistic element. If the present firms were merged into one, reversing the 1911 dissolution, monopoly would result. If they were broken into very small segments the nonhomogeneous product would ensure a state of Chamberlinian monopolistic competition, at least in the short run.

We may note that the industry has already moved some distance from the tight oligopoly of three overwhelmingly dominant firms to a looser arrangement of six very strong competitors. If this is not satisfactory, we might consider further changes with a still larger number of sizable competitors and perhaps with different competitive relationships among them.

If the cigarette industry were a complete monopoly under either private or government auspices the wastes of competition would disappear and there would be little need for advertising. This single possible advantage would be balanced by all the other disadvantages normally attributed to secure monopolies. Prices would be high and profits excessive unless restricted by regulation, which has its own wastes and disadvantages. Government-run monopolies in other lands do not occasion confidence in the idea that full monopoly would be economically superior to the existing organization.

If the industry were composed of a large number of small firms, profits would be expected to be at a competitive level, which would not be far below the level where Liggett and American are now. There is a serious probability that costs would be higher. There is no guarantee that an industry made up of small firms would have lower total advertising expenditures. In the past, very small companies have usually spent less per thousand cigarettes, because, in the years when they were successful, they produced mostly lower quality cigarettes, which were sold to a different market where price was the primary appeal. A large number of small companies competing for the business of the present large companies would be just as likely to have equally high unit advertising expenditures.

Regardless of the effect on advertising, an industry with many small firms would probably have significantly higher total distribution costs. Nonadvertising selling expenses would probably increase; the costs of field sales overhead are likely to be lower per unit for companies with large sales volumes. Moreover, other costs of distribution would probably be sharply higher. In 1910 when the Trust was promoting a large number of different brands, the margins between the manufacturer's price and the retail price ranged from 22 per cent to 35 per cent of the latter; some years earlier when competition was more active, the margins were as high as 42 per cent. In 1934 the NRA code established margins ranging from 10 per cent to 17 per cent of the retail price depending on whether the sale was by the carton or pack. In the early post-World War II years, the single-pack margin excluding state taxes was about 20 per cent. This reduction in margin was possible because of the general growth of the business and because of the establishment of a few leading brands with a large steady volume of trade. Wholesalers' inventories normally turned over weekly and retailers retained only a few days' supply. Rapid turnover allowed a small markup per package.

The multiplication of brands in the last few years has already led to major increases in distribution costs. Wholesale and retail margins on cigarettes were $534 million in 1946 and are estimated at $1,900 million for 1967. A part of this is due to the inflationary rise in all types of service costs but most of it must be attributed to the costs of higher inventories, larger storage space, more complicated bookkeeping, and large proportions of deliveries in broken cases and cartons. The rise in average distribution margins from 18 per cent of retail sales in 1946 to 23 per cent in 1967 constitutes a return to the levels of distribution costs attained by the Trust. The present level of costs or something higher would have to be expected if the cigarette industry were composed of many small firms.

If advertising expenditures were reduced in an industry with many small firms, the effects on distribution costs might be even worse. Other forms of sales promotion would probably expand and the selling activities of jobbers and retailers would become more important. Distributors' costs and margins would thus be increased not only by the greater mechanical complexity of distributing a large number of small brands, but also by the necessity of resuming once more the same functions of sales promotion that distributors used to fulfill in the days before national advertising was fully developed.

It is illuminating to examine the possible gains and losses from establishing a regime of monopolistic competition in comparison with the tight oligopoly of 1939. In that year the three major companies earned net profits, after taxes, of $73 million. If we take this as twice the competitive level, the possible savings from eliminating monopoly profits would have been $36 million. In the same year those companies spent $41 million for advertising. Distributors' markups on their sales were about $180 million. Thus a rise of even 25 per cent in wholesale and retail margins would more than have erased the savings in monopoly profits. Any savings in advertising outlays would have been highly problematical and could easily have been offset if the rise in distributors' margins had been larger than 25 per cent.

A regime of monopolistic competition does not look any more desirable under present circumstances. Cigarette profits on the average are only moderately above competitive levels, so that competitive savings would be relatively small. We have already experienced a massive increase in distribution costs, and it is probable that a substantial increased fragmentation could lead to serious additional increases.

A third possibility of a still looser oligopoly seems to have relatively little attraction. It is difficult to see how it could do more than reduce profits somewhat and lead to a still further increase in the wastes of competition which are the principal disadvantages of the present structure.

The present organization and behavior of the cigarette industry thus appears in relatively favorable light when compared with possible alternative market structures or alternative types of behavior. Perfect competition is not an attainable alternative. Monopolistic competition or still looser oligopoly would probably result in substantially increased costs. On economic grounds there does not appear to be a case for increasing the competitive pressures in this industry. Savings could probably be obtained by a full monopoly or even by a return to the tighter and less aggressive oligopoly that existed before World War II. These alternatives are not likely to be seriously proposed.

The major wastes in this industry are wastes of competition and they could not be removed without eliminating competition or seriously restricting it. At one time, the present author urged that a direct limit on the volume of advertising would be an effective way of loosening competitive relations and directly reducing waste. He does not now hold to this opinion. Quite apart from the political obstacles to imposing such a limit, we are without criteria for determining what it should be. If we accept competition as desirable in itself, we must accept associated costs. There are also no obvious guides to define when competition becomes too intense or cost too excessive. In any event, this does not seem the kind of reform that would be appropriately sought as a remedy in antitrust proceedings.

There is one minor change in industry circumstances that might yield an improvement in its economic results. The present Federal excise tax of $4.00 per thousand, or 8 cents per pack, plus smaller state excises reinforce the least desirable features of the industry. The specific tax rate, which is the same regardless of the price of the cigarette, reduces the incentive to produce brands of different qualities with different prices. Some premium price brands are always sold, but it is unusual for cigarettes that are cheaper than the standard brands to have extensive sale. No savings that can be made either by shrinking profit margins or by lowering leaf quality and advertising costs can be enough to reduce price sufficiently to attract consumers when so large a fraction of unit costs is absolutely fixed. The replacement of a flat excise by an *ad valorem* tax would remove an artificial limit on product variety and give price variation a larger role in the industry's product and marketing activities.

V. PUBLIC POLICY

Twice in its history, the cigarette industry has been a party to spectacular Sherman Act proceedings. In view of the preceding analysis what can be said about the desirability and effectiveness of these applications of public policy?

It has long been an article of faith in American political thought that competition is desirable and monopoly and restraint of trade undesirable, quite apart from narrow economic effects. The economist's view that monopoly is objectionable because it distorts the proper allocation of resources has been an increasingly important element in antitrust thought. However, the protection of the public and other competitors against the tyranny and extortions of a monopolist have played a larger role in legal thought and in the political support for antitrust policy.

In terms of these objectives, the applications of the Sherman Act to the cigarette industry have been outstandingly successful. The old Tobacco Trust was not immune to the winds of competition, but its power was too great and its exercise of power too tyrannical to survive a confrontation with the law. The second antitrust case 30 years later involved similar though smaller abuses of power, and it taught a useful lesson on the limits of power in market behavior. The major companies are not likely to act in concert either explicitly or tacitly to exclude competitors in this generation.

Though the 1911 dissolution destroyed the overwhelming power of the Trust, the successor companies retained strong market power and price discipline, as the price and profit history of the 1920's testifies. But the competitive struggles and loss in market share by the Big Three in the 1930's indicated serious limits to their market power. These limits were further strengthened by the second Tobacco case, and the price and profit pattern since World War II indicates that the lesson has been learned.

One measure of the degree of competition in an industry is the ability of smaller firms to overcome larger firms and for industrial leadership to change. Immediately after the 1911 dissolution, the rise to importance of Camel and the R. J. Reynolds Company testified to a flexible competitive system. In the 1920's it seemed that a new and stable competitive dominance had been established for the Big Three, and the rise of Lucky Strike to equality with Camel could be interpreted merely as the expected revival of a company already well established in the industry and a member of the club. In the 1920's, it appeared that the leadership of the three top companies was permanent and unchangeable.

In the 1930's the rise of Philip Morris and Brown & Williamson from very small beginnings showed that competitive opportunities still existed. The serious inroads by Philip Morris, Brown & Williamson, and Lorillard in recent years and the decline of Liggett & Myers indicate that the position of the leading companies is not automatically guaranteed by a position of superior power, but depends on the outcome of a competitive struggle that will go on into the future and for which the final result may never be known.

In terms of changing relationships among firms and in terms of the influences of competitive maneuvers upon profits, the cigarette industry seems to be as competitive as many industries. This is largely the effect of two important antitrust cases that changed the structure of the industry and set some de facto rules for competitive behavior.

Of course, throughout its history the number of leading firms has been quite small since it is not an easy industry for a small firm to enter and secure a substantial foothold. There are substantial economies of scale in marketing. It would require great antitrust pressure to force the industry into any other mold, and in terms either of traditional antitrust objectives or narrower concerns with economic efficiency, it is difficult to see why this should be done.

SUGGESTED READINGS

BOOKS AND PAMPHLETS

Cox, R. *Competition in the American Tobacco Industry.* New York: Columbia University Press, 1933.

Nicholls, W. H. *Pricing Policies in the Cigarette Industry.* Nashville, Tenn.: Vanderbilt University Press, 1951.

Robert, J. C. *The Story of Tobacco in America.* New York: Alfred A. Knopf, Inc., 1949.

Tennant, R. B. *The American Cigarette Industry.* New Haven: Yale University Press, 1950.

Tilley, N. M. *The Bright Tobacco Industry, 1860–1929.* Chapel Hill, N.C.: Yale University Press, 1950.

Whitney, S. N. *Antitrust Policies: American Experience in Twenty Industries,* New York: Twentieth Century Fund, 1958.

GOVERNMENT PUBLICATIONS

U.S. Bureau of Corporations, *Report on the Tobacco Industry,* 3 vols. Washington, D.C.: U.S. Government Printing Office, 1909–1915.

U.S. v. *American Tobacco Co.,* 164 F.700 (1908); 221 U.S. 106, 328 U.S. 781 (1946).

8. Robert F. Lanzillotti
THE AUTOMOBILE INDUSTRY

O

I. INTRODUCTION

ver the past half-century the automobile industry has introduced more than a new form of transportation into American life—it has accounted for new work and living habits, new standards of comfort, style, and affluence, and vastly altered social attitudes and problems.[1] The automobile has influenced the lives of people and the organization of society to perhaps a greater extent than any other mechanical invention of the past century.

The pivotal position of the industry in the U.S. economy is underscored by such considerations as the following: One out of every seven workers in this country is said to be dependent directly or indirectly on the automobile industry;[2] the industry consumes about one fifth of the nation's steel production, one out of every fourteen tons of copper, more than two out of every five tons of lead, more than one out of every four tons of zinc, one pound in seven of nickel, one-half the reclaimed rubber, almost three fourths of the upholstery leather, and substantial proportions of total national output of glass, machine tools, general industrial equipment, and forgings.

The automobile is the prototype of the modern "durable" product. Regular model changes make it obsolete; it passes down the ladder of affluence in a "used" market; "gadgets" and decorative chrome relieve its standard design; it is purchased on installments, and its newness, novelty, and gadgetry distinguish the social status of its owner.

HISTORY

The production of automobiles represents one of the nation's most highly concentrated manufacturing industries. Consider the statistics: (a) In the early 1900's, 181 companies manufactured and sold automobiles. (b) By

---

1 Parts of this chapter are taken from Donald A. Moore's chapter on "The Automobile Industry" which appeared in a previous edition of this book. Both the author and editor are grateful

to Professor Moore for this contribution.
2 *Automobile Facts and Figures*, Automobile Manufacturers Association, 1958, 38th ed., p. 65, and 48th ed., p. 1.

1927, 137 of these had retired from the industry. (c) Since 1939 only two new companies have ventured into the industry (both of which have since disappeared). (d) Today only four companies remain in business, of which the three largest account for over 90 per cent of total output.

Broadly speaking, the history of the industry can be divided into several distinct stages with respect to growth patterns, market structure, and competitive behavior: the first, the period up to about 1910, was one of pioneering, experimentation, and early growth, during which numerous firms entered and withdrew, with no single firm able to sustain a position of prominence; the second, 1911 through the end of World War I, was the period of the development of a mass market, with Ford reaching prominence, but with the market structure remaining fluid as both new entrants and failures remained high; the third, the 1920's and 1930's, during which the number of producers declined sharply, and the industry's concentrated structure took its basic form; and the fourth, the post-World War II period, in which industry concentration reached new heights, and General Motors attained an increasingly dominant position.

EARLY GROWTH, MARKET EXPANSION, AND ENTRY   It cannot be said that any one man invented the automobile. The idea is an old one, but more than a century of experimentation with power vehicles preceded commercial success. Early efforts began in Europe with steam vehicles, which provided regular "bus" service in Great Britain as far back as 1831. These did not prove to be popular, however, which was no doubt due in part to new restrictive legislation requiring that there be three operators and a man proceeding on foot with a red flag.[3] By 1885, gasoline automobiles were being produced commercially in Europe, and, by 1893, were being exported to the United States. In the United States, Charles and Frank Duryea in 1893 successfully operated a buggy-like gasoline vehicle which is generally regarded as the first built in this country.

The early manufacturers not only designed and produced vehicles, but found it necessary to demonstrate their sturdiness and utility. Some interest in autos was generated by the moneyed aristocracy of the period, who imported and raced the European models at Newport, Rhode Island, but these were expensive, dashing, and generally regarded as useless playthings.

Between 1900 and 1910, demand expanded rapidly and total sales increased from 4,000 to 187,000. The competition to produce vehicles for this new market was vigorous as the number of new companies mushroomed. Between 1902 and 1909 the number of firms increased from 12 to 69 (Table 1),[4] despite a relatively high rate of failures. In 1910, the rate of failure

---

3 C. F. Kettering and Allen Orth, *The New Necessity* (Baltimore: Williams & Wilkins, 1932), p. 4.

4 Estimates of the number of early automobile manufacturing firms run to more than 1,000, but many of these were only "paper" firms, or companies that produced only one or two automobiles,

**TABLE 1 EARLY STRUCTURE OF THE
AUTOMOBILE INDUSTRY**

YEAR	NO. OF ENTRANTS	NO. OF EXITS	NO. OF FIRMS REMAINING	FAILURES AS % OF TOTAL
1902	—	—	12	—
1903	13	1	24	4
1904	12	1	35	3
1905	5	2	38	5
1906	6	1	43	2
1907	1	0	44	0
1908	10	2	52	4
1909	18	1	69	1
1910	1	18	52	26
1911	3	2	53	4
1912	12	8	57	12
1913	20	7	70	10
1914	8	7	71	9
1915	10	6	75	7
1916	6	7	74	9
1917	8	6	76	7
1918	1	6	71	7
1919	10	4	77	5
1920	12	5	84	6
1921	5	1	88	1
1922	4	9	38	10

SOURCE Ralph Epstein, *The Automobile Industry* (Chicago: Shaw, 1928), pp. 176 and 177.

reached 26 per cent, which was considerably higher than the rate that prevailed following the 1920 crisis and recession. There are several good reasons to explain this fluid structure. The steady increase in the number of firms reflected the relatively easy entry conditions in the early days—the nature of automobile manufacturing required only limited capital requirements to begin operations.[5] Manufacturing amounted to designing and assembling, with orders for engines, bodies, and other members and parts farmed out to many machine shops and carriage works then in existence.

or were essentially stock promotion schemes. The most reliable estimates are those of Epstein, who lists a total of 181 firms producing cars at some time between 1903 and 1926. See R. M. Cleveland and S. T. Williamson, *The Road is Yours* (New York: Greystone, 1951), pp. 270–291, and Ralph C. Epstein, *The Automobile Industry* (Chicago: Shaw, 1928), p. 164.

5 The Ford Motor Company experience is typical: It was incorporated in 1903 with 12 people subscribing to $100,000 in stock, of which $51,000 was paid for with patents, machinery, and supplies. It is said that only $28,000 was actually paid in cash.

Competition, from the beginning, ran partly in terms of product variation and vigorous selling effort. Price was an important selling point as soon as automobiles began to be advertised as "pleasure cars" for the moderately well-to-do, but the models were individually priced for different purses and tastes. It was at this stage of development that a large number of well-financed dealers across the country was recognized by producers as essential for survival.

The increased failures around 1910 reflected another development—the changing conditions of auto manufacture. The trend to higher-powered engines, from the single- and two-cylinder to the four-cylinder, required redesigning the axles, transmission, and other parts, as well as the motor. The change to higher power also involved heavy expenses in order to buy new dies, jigs, and machinery. The resistance by many firms to undertaking the extensive changes involved in higher-powered motors resulted in loss of reputation and sales. The picture was further complicated by the uncertainty in the industry as to the kind of vehicle to produce and the best price class in which to place cars.

EARLY ATTEMPT AT MONOPOLY   An attempt at monopoly control of the industry was made in 1903, reflecting the general tone and industrial trend of the period. The effort centered around the formation of the Association of Licensed Automobile Manufacturers (ALAM) with 30 members. Ford was refused admission to ALAM on the grounds that he was a "fly-by-night" operator, and sued by the Association as an unlicensed operator. Ford joined a smaller association of eighteen producers to fight the ALAM, but when a court ruled against Ford in the patent suit, his association deserted him. In January 1911, however, a U.S. circuit court of appeals reversed the lower court's decision,[6] and the ALAM disintegrated.

The ALAM episode left its mark upon the structure of the industry in several ways. First, the notion that patent rights should be allowed to cover a generic commodity such as the automobile became repugnant and, following the demise of ALAM, a new association was formed, Automobile Manufacturers Association, Inc., whose patent pooling practices enjoy the stamp of approval of the Federal Trade Commission.[7] Second, the early engineering activities of the defunct ALAM resulted in the formation of the Society of Automotive Engineers (SAE), whose achievements in standardizing metals, metal fabrication units, screw and bolt threads, fuels, lubricants, and related items, has materially reduced costs for everyone connected with the

---

6   The court held that Selden had used the Brayton two-cycle engine, whereas all current autos were using variations of the Otto four-cycle engine. Cf. 184 Fed. 893–916.

7   See Federal Trade Commission, *Report on the Motor Vehicle Industry* (Washington, D.C.: U.S. Government Printing Office, 1939), p. 62, where an officer of the AMA is quoted, tracing the practice of patent pooling to the lessons of the Selden case.

industry. A third effect was to set Ford upon a maverick course of non-cooperative behavior. Ford's personality perhaps would have made him quite uncooperative in any case, but, as one historian put it, he "had a mad on," and was beginning to enjoy his public role as the champion of the little man. Ford's attitude left its imprint on the industry in several important ways: he did not guard production secrets and thus contributed much to the technology of the whole industry. More important was Ford's now famous announcement in 1909 that:

> . . . in the future we were going to build only one model, that the model was going to be "Model T", and that the chassis would be exactly the same for all cars, and I remarked:
> "Any customer can have a car painted any color that he wants so long as it is black."
> I cannot say that anyone agreed with me.[8]

FORMATION OF GENERAL MOTORS   One other significant development of this period should be mentioned: the formation of General Motors by William Crapo Durant, a financial genius who had previously reorganized and revived the Buick Motor Company. Durant organized General Motors hoping eventually to control all the principal auto manufacturers, in the manner of the great "trusts" of the period.

By the end of 1909, General Motors controlled more than twenty automobile and accessory companies (including Buick, Cadillac, Oldsmobile, and Oakland) and was bidding for Ford and others. Ford was willing to sell in 1909 for $8 million in cash. The General Motors Board of Directors approved the purchase, but Durant's Wall Street backers thought the Ford enterprise was not worth so big a cash risk. Once again, Ford's intransigence had a decisive effect on the industry's structure.[9]

1911–1922: THE GROWTH OF
FORD AND GENERAL MOTORS

PRODUCING FOR A MASS MARKET   This period witnessed the transformation of America to an "automobile society." Ford felt that the Model "T" was a utility vehicle, and by freezing its design, he could concentrate all his energies on mass production at low cost. Motor and chassis parts were completely

---

8 Henry Ford, *My Life and Work* (New York: Doubleday, 1923), p. 72.

9 It has been observed that Ford and James Couzens (who together owned 68.5 per cent of Ford stock) still did not fully grasp the significance of their "Model T." [K. Sward, *The Legend of Henry Ford* (New York: Holt, 1948),

p. 28.] This would appear to be correct, since the net earnings after taxes in 1911 were $7,579,334, and were to reach a peak of more than $120 million in 1922. (Federal Trade Commission, op. cit., pp. 634 and 645.) It might also be observed that Durant's backers did not fully appreciate the "Model T" either.

TABLE 2 PRICES AND SALES OF THE MODEL "T" FORD, 1909–1925

YEAR	PRICE OF MODEL "T" TOURING CAR	TOTAL FORD SALES	TOTAL INDUSTRY SALES	FORD SALES AS % OF TOTAL
1909	$950	12,292	130,986	9.38
1911	690	40,402	210,000	19.24
1913	550	182,809	485,000	37.69
1915	440	355,276	970,000	36.62
1917	450	802,771	1,874,000	42.85
1919	525	782,783	1,934,000	40.48
1921	355	933,720	1,683,916	55.45
1922	298	1,351,333	2,655,624	50.88
1923	295	1,917,353	4,034,012	47.53
1925	290	1,771,338	4,265,830	41.52

SOURCE Federal Trade Commission, op. cit., pp. 27, 632. The 1909 and 1922 totals are from Lawrence H. Seltzer, *A Financial History of the Automobile Industry* (Boston: Houghton Mifflin, 1928), pp. 75, 84.

interchangeable and remained so for all models from 1909 through 1926. By 1914 Ford had a moving-belt production line fed by other moving belts with parts that were, in turn, mass produced. Other manufacturers employed the same principles, and the price of many automobiles declined rapidly. Ford's policy of reaching for larger total net profit through smaller margins on increased sales volume is shown in Table 2—the price of the Model "T" was reduced from $950 in 1909 to under $300 in the early 1920's with the result that sales jumped from around 12,000 to almost 2 million or roughly 50 per cent of the market.

Noting Ford's success, in 1915 Durant formed the Chevrolet Motor Company of Delaware. Then Jonah swallowed the whale. Durant traded Chevrolet stock for General Motors stock until he had control of a majority of the outstanding common stock of General Motors. When General Motors refused to take in the Chevrolet enterprise, Durant exercised his control and again became president of General Motors. It was in this venture that the du Pont family of Delaware gave backing to Durant, and Pierre S. du Pont later became chairman of the board. At this point, the General Motors Corporation of Delaware, a holding company, was formed, in what is essentially the present organization of General Motors.

In 1917 and 1918, the du Pont Company invested $50,000 in General Motors, which provided some lucrative captive markets for du Pont products, and, years later, ample grounds for an antitrust suit. An important condition of the investment was that the du Pont Company would assume responsibility for the financial policies of General Motors and that Durant would assume responsibility for operations.[10]

The number of active producers continued to increase during this period, but the rate of failures remained high (Table 1). The level of concentration increased moderately despite this new entry, mainly as a result of Ford's successful price policy and the growth of General Motors.

THE TWENTIES: RISE

OF THE BIG THREE

Ford's relative position in the industry began to decline after 1921 (Table 2), although during most of the period from World War I to the end of the 1920's it was the leading producer; more cars were manufactured by Ford than all other companies combined. Ford's product and price policies had paid off handsomely.[11] However, the failure of Ford fully to appreciate the changing nature of consumer demand in the 1920's, lead to a weakening in its market position. Ford's market share fell from 55 per cent in 1921 to 41 per cent in 1925, and to slightly more than one third in 1926. Ford resumed its leadership briefly with the changeover to Model "A" at the end of the 1920's. In 1929, Ford and General Motors each held about one third of the market, and in 1930 Ford's share increased to over 40 per cent; but this proved to be the last year in which Ford was the leading auto producer. General Motors took the lead in 1931 with 43 per cent—a leadership position it has retained ever since.

Chrysler, the third member of the Big Three, was formed in 1925. The first Chrysler car created a sensation with a "high-compression" engine and four-wheel brakes. In 1928 Chrysler acquired the estate of the Dodge Brothers. Chrysler soon developed into a strong competitor, with the introduction of the Plymouth and De Soto cars, and the contest between what had become the Big Three worked hardship on the other producers in the industry. As in the case of the change to the Model "A" in 1928, Ford, again belatedly, abandoned the "A" for his "V-8" in 1932. By 1937, Chrysler had taken second place in the industry from Ford.

THE DISAPPEARANCE OF THE INDEPENDENTS

AND THE CLOSURE OF ENTRY

Meanwhile, the number of firms in the industry declined sharply—partly because of combinations, but mainly because of failures.

---

10   See *Report of the Federal Trade Commission on du Pont Investments* (Washington, D.C.: U.S. Government Printing Office, 1929), pp. 15–23.

11   See Allan Nevins and Frank E. Hill, *Ford, Expansion and Challenge, 1915–33* (New York: Scribner, 1957), p. 264.

The depression decade gave rise to a new kind of rivalry among the few surviving producers. There were some price reductions,[12] but competition was confined mainly to other channels. The race for market share through model changes was intensified, and annual changes became the policy. In addition, great pressure was placed on cost reductions, and the speed of the production line was considerably stepped up. Wages were cut, workers downgraded, and older men replaced. With long shutdowns for model changes, automobile workers learned the meaning of seasonal unemployment. These kinds of pressures on the labor force—while well known in the depression economy—were, according to the Henderson Report,[13] especially widespread in the automobile industry.

II. MARKET STRUCTURE
SURVIVAL OF THE FEW

The growth of the automobile industry has been characterized by the concentration of production in progressively fewer hands, so that today there are only four domestic producers, the largest three of which account for about 90 per cent of total industry output (see Table 3). Moreover, since 1931, General Motors usually has accounted for over 40 per cent of automobile registrations, and since 1950 its share has been from 45 to 50 per cent of total registrations, *including* all foreign makes. There has not been a successful new entry into the U.S. industry since the formation of the Chrysler Corporation after World War I.

For a considerable time prior to World War II the independents shared about 10 per cent of the market, and in the immediate post-World War II period their total share reached about 22 per cent of the market. That the independents' temporary resurgence was the result of the temporary shortage of new and used cars is all too clear today. The 1950's saw the gradual disappearance of several of the independents and mergers among the others. Kaiser attempted to bolster its rapidly deteriorating position by the acquisition of Willys, but soon only the Jeep remained available; and in 1949, production of Kaiser passenger cars was discontinued. In 1954, Studebaker and Packard merged, and Hudson joined with Nash to form American Motors—both mergers being approved by the Department of Justice and Federal Trade Commission on the premise that the new firms possibly

---

12 Ford's intransigence on prices persisted into the 1930's. As an official of General Motors and the AMA pointed out in 1932, "... Mr. Ford, who won't play, is pretty much the price setter in this industry. I'll bet if Mr. Ford's cars were $50 higher, ours would be $50 higher. We care about Ford. We have been struggling with him for years." Federal Trade Commission, op. cit., p. 33.

13 *Preliminary Report on Study of Regularization of Employment and Improvement of Labor Conditions in the Automobile Industry*, NRA (Washington, D.C.: U.S. Government Printing Office, January 1935).

TABLE 3   PASSENGER CAR MARKET SHARES, BY COMPANY,
SELECTED YEARS, 1950–1967

COMPANY	1950	1954	1958	1962	1966	1967	AVERAGE 1958–1967
General Motors	45.4	50.7	46.4	51.9	50.1	49.5	47.8
Ford	24.0	30.8	26.4	26.3	26.1	22.2	26.1
Chrysler	17.6	12.9	13.9	9.6	15.4	16.1	13.2
American Motors	4.9	2.1	4.3	6.1	2.9	2.8	4.9
Studebaker-Packard	5.4	2.4	1.1	1.1	—	—	1.0[a]
Kaiser-Willys	2.3	0.5	—	—	—	—	—
Foreign Makes	0.4	0.5	7.9	5.0	7.4	9.9	7.2

a   Based on years 1958–1962 only.

SOURCES   Almanac Issue, *Automotive News*, **22**:55 (Detroit 1958); **23**:46 (Detroit 1959); and Hearings before the Subcommittee on Antitrust and Monopoly of the Senate Judiciary Committee, 85th Congress, 2nd Session, "Automobiles," *Administered Prices*, Pt. 6 (Washington, D.C.: U.S. Government Printing Office, 1958), p. 2405.

would have a better chance of survival. It is also noteworthy that although American and Studebaker-Packard's market position appeared stronger as of the late 1950's, the *gap* in size of firm and market share between the independents and the Big Three has remained persistently enormous (Table 3).

The gap in the market share between American Motors and Studebaker-Packard widened even further in the 1960's. American Motors' share reached a high of 6.4 per cent in 1960, but by 1967 it dropped to less than 3 per cent. Studebaker-Packard's share dropped steadily from 2.2 per cent in 1959 to 0.1 per cent in 1965. In December 1963, Studebaker closed its plant in South Bend, Indiana, but continued to build cars in Canada. However, in March 1966 the company discontinued manufacturing of cars altogether.

On a percentage basis, imports now account for approximately 10 per cent of the market, matching their peak percentage penetration of 1959. Volkswagen alone sells over one half of the imports.

How can the rigidity of the automobile industry's structure, the increasing prominence of General Motors, and the lack of domestic entry into this industry be explained? Do the changes in the structural and operational aspects of the industry during the last three to four decades explain the inability of new firms to effect entry and of the remaining independents to make serious inroads on the "90 per cent" market of the Big Three? What reasons can be given for the failure of the relatively high profitability of the auto manufacturers to perform its traditional function of attracting new outside resources to this industry? In essence, what are the conditions for entry and survival in this industry, and to what are "natural"—i.e., economies of scale—as against "artificial" barriers responsible for the high degree of concentration that persists?[14] The principal barriers to entry and conditions for survival are (1) size of operations necessary to realize the economies inherent in the mass production of cars; (2) large capital required for an optimum-sized operation; (3) the high degree of differentiation among the products of established sellers (which generally favors General Motors products over all others and Big Three products over the remainder); (4) need for a diverse product line covering a considerable range of prices; (5) the nature of resale value determination on used cars; and (6) the impact of government contracts and preferential treatment afforded established firms by suppliers of some basic materials.

SCALE ECONOMIES AND
OPTIMUM PLANT SIZE

Economies of scale constitute a very important barrier to entry in automobile manufacture. Our interest here concerns "economic efficiency"; that is, ability of a firm to make the most economical use of resources and produce at the lowest possible unit cost. Essentially, we wish to know how large an automobile manufacturing plant must be in order to realize optimum efficiency. For this purpose the appropriate unit for study is the plant, or integrated plant complex, i.e., "a related complex of facilities for manufacturing components [principally engines and bodies] normally integrated by the assembler and then assembling them."[15]

Some degree of integration in automobile production has proved strategically advantageous and has served also to broaden the profit base. In the interest of providing some immunity from total interruption in the supply of any one component or part, producers have developed what may be best described as "tapered integration," as contrasted with *complete* integration. Tapering means that producers will attempt to keep their parts factories operating at predetermined output rates, filling in additional supplies through "contract" suppliers. The automobile companies usually maintain at least two sources of supply for essential parts, and also reserve "shop rights" to manufacture given parts themselves in case a strike ties up the supplier.[16] This means that the parts suppliers are continuously placed in a very precarious position since orders from the auto producers fluctuate with anticipated

---

14 See Harold G. Vatter, "The Closure of Entry in the American Automobile Industry," *Oxford Economic Economic Papers*, **4**:213 (October 1952), and Report of the Subcommittee on Antitrust and Monopoly of the Committee on the Judiciary, 85th Congress, 2nd Session, *Administered Prices: Automobiles* (Washington, D.C.: U.S. Government Printing Office, 1958)

(hereafter *Administered Prices: Automobiles*).

15 Joe S. Bain, *Barriers to Competition* (Cambridge, Mass.: Harvard University Press, 1956), pp. 244–245.

16 Simon N. Whitney, *Antitrust Policies: American Experience in Twenty Industries* (New York: Twentieth Century Fund, 1958), p. 497.

auto sales. Moreover, there has been a rather clear trend toward further integration in the automobile industry. Whitney estimates that the percentage share of dollar sales of producers originating in outside purchases has been declining secularly.[17]

How important are economies of scale in automobile production under present technology? According to a study by Bain, the minimum size of auto plant—i.e., an integrated plant complex—necessary to realize lowest per unit costs would be 300,000 passenger cars per year (as of the mid-1950's) with some probable additional increase in efficiency up to 600,000 units. A plant complex of this size represented from 5 to 10 per cent of national output in the 1950's. The economies of scale arise from greater efficiency in the production of major components, especially engines and bodies.[18] Scale economies are relatively unimportant in assembly operations; 60,000 to 180,000 units per year are considered to be an optimal size for assembly alone.

Similar estimates of optimum plant size were disclosed by Mr. George Romney when he was President of American Motors:

> Our studies based on our own experience and that of our competitors, is that optimum manufacturing conditions are achieved with a production rate of 62.5 cars per hour per assembly line. To absorb the desired machine-line and press-line rate, two final assembly lines would be required. . . .
>
> A company that can build between 180,000 and 220,000 cars a year on a one-shift basis can make a very good profit and not take a back seat to anyone in the industry in production efficiency. On a two-shift basis, annual production of 360,000 to 440,000 cars will achieve additional small economies, but beyond that volume only theoretical and insignificant reductions in manufacturing costs are possible. It is possible to be one of the best without being the biggest.
>
> . . . [My] point is that when you get up to 180,000 to 200,000 cars a year, the cost reduction flattens out, from a manufacturing cost standpoint, and from 360,000 to 400,000 on up it is a negligible thing.[19]

The Bain-Romney estimates relate to the minimum size necessary to attain optimum production efficiency, but do not indicate whether, once minimal

---

17 The strength of the trend is underestimated, as Whitney points out, because the figures used included purchases of basic materials like iron and steel, transportation, and other services—none of which involves the parts industry. Ibid., pp. 498–499.

18 Bain, op. cit., pp. 245–246; *Admin-*

istered Prices: Automobiles, op. cit., p. 85.

19 Hearings before the Subcommittee on Antitrust and Monopoly of the Senate Judiciary Committee, 85th Congress, 2nd Session, "Automobiles," *Administered Prices*, Pt. 6 (Washington, D.C.: U.S. Government Printing Office, 1958), p. 2851.

optimum scale is reached, unit costs rise or remain constant. The most we can say about scale economies and diseconomies is that unit costs are fairly constant in the output ranges cited.

On the basis of these estimates, General Motor's divisions with total annual production in recent years of 4–4.5 million cars are all well within the optimal range or above, with the exception of Cadillac, as shown in Table 4. (This assumes the minimal optimum scale has not changed significantly since the studies were made.) Ford and Chrysler are several times the minimum on an overall production basis, and their respective makes generally fall within the optimal range, with the exception of their luxury lines, Lincoln and Imperial. Production rates for almost all of the individual makes of cars fall within the minimum efficient size for assembly operations—60,000 to 180,000 units. Since there are very important plant economies in both engine and body production, the apparent inefficiency in the production of some makes, e.g., Lincoln and Chrysler, is offset as an operational matter by the utilization of common components for more than one make.

There is some evidence that extensive integration of parts manufacture—going well beyond the integration of bodies and engines—may provide additional absolute cost advantages to the established firms. Ford and

TABLE 4 COMPARISON OF ANNUAL PRODUCTION OF AUTOMOBILE MANUFACTURERS AND ESTIMATED OPTIMUM PLANT SCALE, BY MAKES, FOR YEARS 1965–1967

COMPANY AND MODEL NAME	1965–1967 OUTPUT RANGE	RELATION OF OUTPUT TO OPTIMUM SCALE (300,000–600,000)
General Motors	4,027,000–4,599,000	
Buick	563,000– 600,000	Within range
Cadillac	181,000– 200,000	Below minimum
Chevrolet	1,900,000–2,382,000	Above maximum
Oldsmobile	546,000– 593,000	Within range
Pontiac	802,000– 831,000	Above range
Ford	2,143,000–2,472,000	
Ford	1,742,000–2,093,000	Above range
Lincoln	40,000– 50,000	Below minimum
Mercury	323,000– 355,000	Within range
Chrysler	1,254,000–1,448,000	
Chrysler	189,000– 240,000	Below minimum
Dodge	427,000– 551,000	Within range
Imperial	14,000– 18,000	Below minimum
Plymouth	590,000– 683,000	Within range
American Motors	236,000– 391,000	Within range

SOURCES Production Data, *Automotive News*, **43**:60 (Detroit, 1967); **44**:62 (Detroit, 1968).

General Motors are highly integrated on parts and they (General Motors in particular) also supply various parts to other car manufacturers. Thus, unless a firm can secure parts from independent suppliers it will likely experience increased parts costs. The alternative is integration of parts manufacture, which would mean that the minimum optimal scale would be higher, i.e., closer to the upper limit (10 per cent of the national market).

It appears from the foregoing that the company size of the Big Three automobile manufacturers, and General Motors in particular, are not explained by plant-complex efficiency alone. This does not mean that the companies are inefficient, or that they have necessarily run into diseconomies of scale. It does suggest rather that if scale economies justify the size of these producers, there must be other economies arising out of the operation of several plant complexes, such as plant specialization, mass buying, marketing, and advertising. No quantitative information is available on the importance of these types of savings in automobile manufacture, nor is there any evidence regarding the extent to which these economies of company size represent real cost-savings in the economic sense, or merely private savings or pecuniary gains (money "transfers" to the Big Three from various suppliers).

CAPITAL REQUIREMENTS

Entry into the automobile industry is further influenced by large capital requirements. In the early days, very slender resources were necessary, and working capital requirements were supplied by firms other than the car manufacturers—i.e., parts suppliers who furnished credit, and dealers who made cash deposits and paid the balance on delivery. As the industry matured, these relationships were upset. Automobile companies, which had been merely assemblers of purchased parts, began making their own components and parts, and later moved into the credit field to finance the inventories held by dealers and installment buying by consumers. The installment finance capital, although essential to the industry, could well be supplied entirely by independently owned finance companies. There are, however, other factors which require an automobile producer to command sizable resources.

Bain estimated that a firm with a plant complex of efficient scale as previously described would require an initial investment of 250–500 million (as of 1952) and might in addition need to invest another $150 million or more in "break-in" losses—all in the face of a substantial risk of ultimate failure.[20] Mr. Romney, former president of American Motors, has stated that a new company breaking into this industry for the first time, with an output of 250,000 cars per year, would require $576 million as of 1958, based upon reproduction costs for building, machinery, equipment, and standard tools and dies, plus organization expenses and estimated first-year losses.[21] An

---

20 Joe S. Bain, *Industrial Organization* (New York: Wiley, 1959), p. 254; *Barriers to Competition*, op. cit., p. 129.
21 Ibid., p. 17.

estimated additional $326.2 million would be involved in establishing a system of dealers and distributors.[22] However, in the past these requirements have been supplied by the dealers themselves, so they should not appropriately be included in the total.

Just how much does a capital requirement of this magnitude deter entry into this industry? The history of the Kaiser Motor Company is illustrative— bearing in mind that it started operating at a most propitious time (when there was a high backlog of demand that could not be satisfied by existing capacity of the established firms). It seems generally agreed that without the financial resources derived from many other Kaiser enterprises, augmented by a timely loan from the Reconstruction Finance Corporation, Kaiser could hardly have attempted entry into this industry. Kaiser's first two stock issues were successful in raising 53.5 million dollars capital, but this was inadequate to finance the period of losses while market acceptance was developing.[23] In 1950, when survival depended upon the launching of a new model, the old model was still not selling in sufficient volume to finance the retooling costs. Bankers and investment houses have been reluctant to participate in the financing of new automobile concerns which means that the required capital must come from other financial intermediaries or from substantial retained earnings by an established concern in some other field.

PRODUCT DIFFERENTIATION

Automobiles have been characterized by an extremely high degree of product differentiation, which constitutes a third important barrier to entry and survival in the industry. The primary sources of product differentiation in autos are (1) physical design and related advertising outlays, (2) manufacturer's reputation among buyers, and (3) sales and service operations through a system of controlled dealers.[24]

1. Physical product differences in body design, general appearance, engines, transmissions, suspension, and braking systems, and the like have reached a position of primary importance in this market, and seem to gather increasing momentum over time. Although perceptible physical differences exist among various makes, the product policies of American manufacturers seem generally to be based on "protective imitation" in style, engine design, power, and other features. Similarities usually are more striking than the differences.

---

22 The amount is distributed as follows: $262,500,000 for 3,500 domestic dealers, $18,750,000 for 350 Canadian dealers, and $45,000,000 for 3,000 export distributors. Cf. Romney testimony, *Administered Prices: Automobiles*, op. cit., p. 16.

23 *Fortune*, 44:74 (July 1951).
24 Cf. Bain, *Barriers to Competition*, op. cit., Ch. IV; Bedros P. Pashigian, *The Distribution of Automobiles, An Economic Analysis of the Franchise System* (Englewood Cliffs, N.J.: Prentice-Hall, 1961).

Changes in automobile design have become almost inextricably bound with advertising. Large sums are spent on various advertising media in an effort to impress the buyer with the unique appearance and features of what are fundamentally very similar products. A former president of the Bureau of Advertising, American Newspaper Publishers Association, has criticized these claims as follows:

Last year the ads bristled with coined-name exclusive features. Today the glitter of chrome is equalled only by the glitter of generalities. The claims seem to come off the same copywriter's typewriter.

. . . Do automobile advertisements talk in terms of the prospects of daily needs and problems? With very few notable exceptions, the answer is negative. Apparently, automobile advertising isn't aimed at the consumer. Judging by what one sees and hears, the major objective of automobile advertising is to impress—and, preferably, frighten—one's fellow members at the Detroit Automobile Club.[25]

2. The car buyer must evaluate the respective properties and claims concerning such a complex and expensive product, which forms the basis for a second source of product differentiation—*the tendency for buyers to rely upon the established reputations of manufacturers.* Consequently, automobile producers, and the Big Three in particular, tend to have a loyal group of buyers.
3. A third important source of product differentiation and an essential prerequisite for survival in this industry is a *national system of dependable, adequately financed, and strategically located dealers with service facilities.* In promoting sales and providing specialized maintenance and repair services the dealers provide further differentiation of the delivered product. The nature of the differentiation varies from community to community, and the degree of success in differentiation nationally will be a function of the scope and density of dealer representation. As of 1968, General Motors had 46 per cent, Ford 25 per cent, Chrysler 22 per cent, and American Motors 9 per cent of the auto dealers.[26]

The market strength of the Big Three rests on many of the various factors cited earlier, but, as Bain observes.

. . . perhaps more largely on reputation, conspicuous-consumption moves and superior strength and size of dealer systems than on demonstrable superiority in design or quality of products. Independents have generally encountered difficulties in keeping up with

25 Harold S. Barnes, "Why Doesn't Detroit Bring Out a 1958 Model Marketing Philosophy?" *Advertising Age,* **29**:75 (June 23, 1958).

26 Almanac Issue, *Automotive News,* **32**:73, 92 (Detroit, 1968).

the Big Three in the matter of product design only after their market shares and profits had sunk so low that they had difficulty in financing periodic improvements and design changes in an adequate fashion.[27]

A DIVERSIFIED PRODUCT-LINE

Another condition for survival appears to be a well-diversified product line. This was recognized by Durant when he formed General Motors and by Chrysler in his firm's rise into the class of the Big Three. To Ford, diversification was less important because of his early success in pioneering mass production. Since 1935, however, the Ford Company has introduced various models to complete its line. Mercury, and Lincoln to a somewhat lesser extent, have been successful, but the Edsel introduced in 1957 and discontinued in 1959, was a failure. The independents have repeatedly attempted to cover wider segments of the market, with varying degress of success. Such familiar but now defunct makes as the Terraplane (Hudson), and Lafayette (Nash), and the Rockne (Studebaker) attest to the futile efforts during the 1930's to enter the low-price range. The sales volume of these makes was too low to meet the minimum conditions for economies of large-scale production and hence—despite increasing sales—they were discontinued or absorbed into the medium-priced lines. In recent years, American Motors made a bid for the low-price market, with stress on economy in operating costs.

Increasing emphasis upon product differentiation and product diversification has led to an overlapping of price classes, except at the high-end luxury cars. At the other end, European producers have had the under $2,000 market largely to themselves ever since the end of World War II. The increasing penetration of the imports finally has induced Ford, General Motors, and American Motors to enter the field.

RESALE VALUE OF USED CARS

It has often been observed that the market for new cars is supported by the used-car market. Since 60–70 per cent of all new car purchases involve trade-ins, the depreciation value of a used car in relation to the price of the new car is a major determinant of demand and a survival condition in the industry. If more rapid depreciation occurs in some makes than in others, brand loyalty—regardless of the impact of product differentiation and personal preferences—will be subjected to a most severe test. Among used cars of roughly comparable quality and age, whose new-car factory suggested list prices were approximately the same, General Motors cars for many years

---

27 *Industrial Organization*, op. cit., pp. 226–227. See also Pashigian, *The*   *Distribution of Automobiles*, pp. 1–51.

TABLE 5 RESALE AND ORIGINAL RETAIL PRICES OF CHEVROLET, FORD, AND PLYMOUTH

MODEL	Chevrolet Biscayne			Ford Custom 6			Plymouth[c]		
YEAR	FADP[a] ($)	ARP[b] ($)	ARP/ FADP (%)	FADP ($)	ARP ($)	ARP/ FADP (%)	FADP ($)	ARP ($)	ARP/ FADP (%)
1968	2,623	2,025	77.2	2,642	2,030	76.1	2,483	1,930	77.7
1967	2,484	1,485	59.8	2,496	1,495	59.9	2,356	1,505	63.9
1966	2,431	1,140	46.9	2,533	1,170	46.2	2,315	1,130	48.8
1965	2,367	880	37.2	2,366	835	35.3	2,236	895	40.0
1964	2,417	605	25.0	2,415	615	25.5	2,280	640	28.1
1963	2,376	490	20.6	2,378[d]	480	20.2	2,262	490	21.7

a Factory adjusted dealer price.

b Average retail price, central region (Illinois, Indiana, Kansas, Kentucky, Michigan, Missouri, Ohio, Wisconsin).

c Savoy model in 1963–1964 and Belvedere model in 1965–1968.

d Ford 300–6.

SOURCE National Automobile Dealers Association, *Official Used Car Guide, Central Edition*, 35:39 (December 1968).

generally experienced the lowest depreciation, with Ford and Chrysler somewhat larger. Since the early 1960's, however, General Motors cars no longer evidence a consistent advantage in resale value.[28] Resale prices of comparable Big Three models (central U.S.) and original retail prices of full-size six-cylinder four door cars are shown in Table 5.

Other influences buttressing the position of established auto producers have been government defense contracts and the preferential treatment afforded the Big Three by steel suppliers in times of shortages. Defense contracts for both research and production provide a number of advantages to contractors, which among others things, (a) make it possible for a firm to keep its plant operating at most efficient (lowest cost) output rates; (b) if expansion of productive facilities is required, incentives are offered that are not normally available in private contracts; (c) marketing costs are reduced because of bulk sales; (d) financial risks are minimized; and (e) inestimable byproducts are realized from research knowledge and patent rights associated with the defense work.[29]

---

28 Bain found that during the 1946–1950 period, General Motors brands occupied preferred positions on trade-in values over Ford and Chrysler brands. Pashigian studied data for 1955 and 1956, which basically substantiated Bain's findings that General Motors autos invariably have lower depreciation rates. Bain,

op. cit., p. 304; Pashigian, op. cit., pp. 8–9.

29 From June 1950 through June 1957, General Motors realized 4.5 per cent, Ford 1.5 per cent, and Chrysler 1.4 per cent of the net value of military prime contracts—ranking first, twelfth, and thirteenth, respectively, among the

As a result of loans and investments in steel companies General Motors and Chrysler have enjoyed preferential positions with respect to the supply of steel in times of shortage. In 1951, for example, General Motors loaned 28 million dollars to Jones & Loughlin and $40 million to Republic Steel, and Chrysler made some investment in Pittsburgh steel. The arrangement was for the automobile companies to be guaranteed a certain percentage of the increased capacity, under which the steel companies would pay back on a per-ton basis against those loans. The importance of this matter has decreased in recent years with increased foreign competition in steel.

CONCLUSION ON ENTRY CONDITIONS

In summary, the importance of the economies of scale and the magnitude of capital requirements constitute substantial barriers to entry. At present levels of demand, i.e., 9 million cars annually, at least ten firms of efficient size would appear to be economically feasible. The other main barrier to the attainment of an industry of this size would appear to be product differentiation. The only entry threat in many years, which has a good chance of survival (assuming the revival of national protectionism does not spread), is that of the foreign producers in the "dinky" or "mini" car field. As of 1968, foreign makes have captured about 10 per cent of the market (compared to less than 1 per cent in 1955), and appear to be firmly entrenched. It is of special interest to note that sales of the leading import make, the German Volkswagen, constitute more than one half of all imports (see Table 6). The success of the imports in capturing this corner of the U.S. market reflects a number of factors, including the disenchantment of buyers with U.S. styling, size, planned obsolescence, quality of product, price, and cost of operation and maintenance. The fact that the import brands made large absolute as well as relative gains in the U.S. market during the recession years of 1958–1959 and since the mid-1960's is indicative of more than just transitory changes in demand. The introduction of the Big Three "compact" models in 1960, and their announcement of plants to introduce mini-cars in 1969 and 1970, would tend to support this observation.[30] The compacts actually are in a larger-size and higher-price class, and have encroached as much on the Chevrolet, Ford, and Plymouth as on the foreign brands. Nonetheless, with the introduction of the mini-cars it does not seem likely that the foreign

---

largest recipient companies. Moreover, the Big Three, and especially General Motors, have been among the largest beneficiaries of experimental, developmental, and research work—General Motors ranking twenty-fourth, twenty-ninth, and seventeenth in 1955, 1956, and 1957, respectively. Cf., ibid. pp. 37–45, and see *Administered Prices* (Hearings), op. cit., pp. 2598–2599; 2855–2857.

30 The market strategy behind General Motors and Ford's belated entry may appear puzzling, but it should be noted that both had made provisions earlier against import penetration of the U.S. market by establishing subsidiaries in England and Germany—the English Ford and General Motors Opel are among the top ten imports (Table 6).

TABLE 6   FOREIGN CAR SALES IN THE UNITED STATES, 1967

MAKE	LOWEST-PRICED MODEL[a] ($)	SALES	% OF TOTAL
Volkswagen	1,699	446,060	58.2
Opel	1,766	50,186	6.5
Datsun	1,996	33,908	4.4
Volvo	2,775	33,189	4.3
Toyota	1,870	32,996	4.3
MG	2,215	22,036	2.9
Mercedes-Benz	4,360	19,356	2.5
Renault	1,745	19,156	2.5
English Ford	1,993	15,992	2.1
Triumph	2,385	15,562	2.0
All others	—	78,551	10.3
Total	—	766,992	100.0

a   U.S. port of entry.

SOURCE   Almanac Issue. *Automotive News,* **32**:78 (Detroit, 1968).

producers will increase their share much further, and holding on to what they now have may become more and more difficult in the future.

III. MARKET CONDUCT

The oligopolistic structure of the automobile industry means that since none of the producers can afford to ignore the actions and reactions of rival firms to given price of product policies, the pattern of interfirm behavior—under General Motors' leadership—has become largely a function of industry custom, convention, and tacit understandings. The activities of the Automobile Manufacturers' Association (AMA) the principal trade association of the industry, also serve to discourage independent behavior. Trade associations generally provide avenues for cooperation; the AMA is no exception. Some activities, such as the cross-licensing agreements, may have increased the degree of effectiveness of competition in the industry. On the other hand, the Sales Manager's Committee of AMA over the years has discussed such things as methods of quoting prices, used car problems, the "pack" to be allowed dealers,[31] and related matters. It is difficult to determine the net

---

31   The "pack" is the amount of additional charges a dealer may add to the delivered price of a car. It has included a "handling" charge, a "markup" on the freight cost, a share of any freight saving realized through the use of cheaper transport medium, and a share of the finance company's charges.

effect of the activities of these and other departments. Much cooperative effort can be channeled through these committees without adversely affecting the consumer, but a solid front emanating from one of them could exceed the bounds of safety in the exercise of economic power by one manufacturing group.

Within this rather close-knit industry matrix is found a rather unique pattern of rivalry of both price and nonprice varieties. Interestingly, although there would appear to be a rather wide berth for price differences at the manufacturing level—reflecting advertised differences in quality and mechanical complexity—the existing form of rivalry has limited price differences among firms on comparable models. Instead, there has been an ever-increasing emphasis on various forms of nonprice competition, particularly stylistic variations.

DEMAND

The demand for new automobiles is a complex phenomenon, reflecting the influence of many factors, including the prices of new and used cars, income of consumers, prices of other goods (both complementary and substitute goods), the stock of automobiles people own, availability, and terms of credit, and the design of new models. Those that appear to be of greatest interest and importance in determining the level and responsiveness of demand are:

1. *A new auto is a replacement for an old auto.* The demand for automobiles, like the demand for all durable goods, is essentially a replacement demand, i.e., a demand for "ownership," and thus does not follow any simple laws of demand.

2. *Size of outlay* The magnitude of expenditure involved for a new automobile is another distinguishing feature of demand. No other commodity, save the purchase of a home, entails such a large outlay in relation to the typical consumer's income and savings. This means that the average consumer may not be in a position to buy a new car unless credit is available.

3. *A new auto is purchased out of "supernumerary" income.*[32] Although the automobile as such competes with all goods to one degree or another, the purchase of a new car is a major item for most buyers. As a result, purchase is considered only after provision has been made for other costs of maintaining minimum desired living standards. Thus, a new auto is apt to be competing with a vacation trip, the remodeling of a home, or even a fur coat. The important thing here is that an automobile purchase involves some explicit

---

32 Supernumerary income has been defined as disposable income less subsistence living costs (rent, fuel, food, clothing, and so on). See C. F. Roos and Victor Von Szeliski, "Factors Governing Changes in Domestic Automobile Demand," *Dynamics of Automobile Demand* (New York: General Motors, 1939), p. 41.

TABLE 7 ELASTICITY OF NEW
CAR PURCHASES WITH RESPECT
TO PRICE AND INCOME

	PRICE	INCOME
Roos & Von Szeliski	−1.5	+2.5
Atkinson	−1.4	+2.5
Chow	−1.2	+3.0
Suits	−0.6	+4.2
Nerlove	−0.9	+2.8
Veno & Tsurmi	−1.6	+2.9

or implicit weighting of expectations by the household, so that anticipated changes in income and economic activity generally may be as important as actual changes.

4. *A new automobile is a means of acquiring distinction and of expressing one's personality.* In a very real sense, an automobile has become part of a family's general appearance; to some, it may be more important than a fine house or attractive furniture. However, conspicuous consumption motives and tastes also tend, at any one time, to place a ceiling on possible new car sales. If model changes are too rapid or extreme, some buyers will shift to "economy" type models. Finally, as tastes have moved away from extreme ostentation, the most expensive cars have declined in relative importance. But even in these cases, it is noteworthy that buyers elect many expensive options like automatic transmission and air conditioning.

Statistical studies of the elasticity or responsiveness of demand to price and income changes, both for the pre- and post-World War II periods,[33] are in substantial agreement in their findings with respect to price elasticity and income elasticity of demand.

Except for Suits' and Nerlove's analysis, the results indicate a range of price elasticity between − 1.2 and − 1.5, and income elasticity in the range of +2.5 to +3.9.[34] Thus, as between the two most important variables affect-

---

33 The pre-World War II studies were Roos and Von Szeliski, ibid.; L. Jay Atkinson, "Consumer Markets for Durable Goods," *Survey of Current Business*, 32:19 (April 1952). The postwar studies are Gregory C. Chow, *Demand for Automobiles in the United States* (Amsterdam: North-Holland, 1957); Daniel B. Suits, "The Demand for New Automobiles in the United States, 1929–1956," *Review of Economics and Statistics*, 40:273 (August 1958); M. Nerlove, "A note on Long-Run Automobile Demand," *Journal of Marketing*

22:57 (July 1957); H. Veno and H. Tsurmi, "A Dynamic Supply and Demand Model of the U.S. Automobile Industry, 1921–1945," Economic Research Service Unit Discussion Paper No. 58, University of Pennsylvania (July 1957).

34 A reworking of Suits' study using the BLS index of retail prices of new cars (deflated by the Consumer Price Index) instead of the price series constructed by Suits, yielded a price elasticity coefficient of − 1.2 and income elasticity coefficient of +4.2. See *Administered Prices: Automobiles*, op. cit., pp. 142–144.

TABLE 8 ESTIMATED PERCENTAGE CHANGES IN
ANNUAL PURCHASE OF AUTOMOBILE
AS RELATED TO PERCENTAGE CHANGES IN INCOME
AND THE RELATIVE PRICE OF AUTOMOBILES
(PER CAPITA IN CONSTANT DOLLARS)

		PERCENTAGE CHANGE IN INCOME:					
		− 8	− 6	− 4	− 2	0	+ 2	+ 4
PERCENTAGE CHANGE IN PRICE:	+10	−36	−30	−24	−18	−12	− 6	0
	+ 5	−30	−24	−18	−12	− 6	0	6
	0	−24	−18	−12	− 6	0	6	12
	− 5	−18	−12	− 6	0	6	12	18
	−10	−12	− 6	0	6	12	18	24
	−15	− 6	0	6	12	18	24	30
	−20	0	6	12	18	24	30	36

SOURCE   Testimony of Gregory Chow in Hearings
before the Subcommittee on Antitrust and Monopoly of
the Senate Judiciary Committee, 85th Congress,
2nd Session, "Automobiles," *Administered Prices*, Pt. 6
(Washington, D.C.: U.S. Government Printing Office,
1958), p. 3193.

ing automobile demand, sales evidently are more responsive to changes in
income than to changes in price.

A rough approximation of the responsiveness of demand to various possible price changes by the automobile industry, given various possible
changes in income, is shown in Table 8 (based upon Chow's elasticities of
− 1.2 for price and +3.0 for income). The data suggest that if income remains the same, a 5 per cent increase in price would mean a 6 per cent decrease in sales, whereas a decline in income of 2 per cent, coupled with a 5 per
cent increase in price would produce a drop of 12 per cent in sales, and so on.

COSTS AND SUPPLY

The most significant features of the supply of automobiles are the magnitude
and structure of manufacturing costs. An estimated breakdown of the major
cost components of the "average" General Motors car in 1957 is shown in
Table 9.[35]

Recent figures presented to U.S. senate committees, purportedly as official
Ford Motor Company cost data for the 1966 model year, indicate that direct

---

35   Ibid., p. 129.

TABLE 9 COST COMPONENTS OF A GENERAL MOTORS CAR

	($)
Overhead cost	550
Materials and other direct costs	950–1,050
Hourly-rated labor cost	300– 400
Average total unit cost	1,750–2,000

SOURCE *Administered Prices: Automobiles*, op. cit., p. 129.

labor and manufacturing overhead are a much smaller component of unit production costs than the 1957 estimates for General Motors. Unit standard costs for a 1966 Ford Model 54A Galaxie 500, 4-door sedan are reported in Table 10.

Considerable interest centers on the unit costs of model changes. Data compiled for the late 1950's indicated that estimated styling costs averaged about $250–300 per unit.[36] More recent data supplied by General Motors to a Senate subcommittee indicated style change costs to be no greater than $134 per vehicle in 1967.[37]

TABLE 10 COSTS FOR 1966 FORD GALAXIE 500, 4-DOOR SEDAN

	AMOUNT ($)	PER CENT
Materials and parts	1,397.03	86.1
Direct labor	57.85	3.6
Manufacturing overhead	147.12	9.1
Inbound transportation and usage and delivery charges	20.50	1.2
Total	1,622.50	100.0

SOURCE *Congressional Record—Senate*, September 25, 1968, p. S11358.

36 Ibid., pp. 115–124.
37 "Responses of General Motors Corporation to the Eleven Points Stated by Senators Morse and Nelson," Chairmen, respectively, of the Subcommittee on Retailing, Distribution and Marketing Practices, and of the Subcommittee on Monopoly of the Senate Select Committee on Small Business, October 18, 1968.

PRICE MAKING

Certain basic questions on automobile pricing of particular interest can be stated as follows: How does each firm arrive at a price for each of its models? Do all firms follow a common procedure or objective in determining prices? What relationships exist between the pricing process among the various producers, the major producers in particular?

General Motors reportedly sets its prices on the basis of *cost-plus-profit*. But average total unit costs themselves are determined by the price decision. This interrelationship between costs and prices results from the method of price determination and the effects of price-induced changes in output on the company's overhead costs.[38] The pricing method employed by General Motors, similar in many ways to rate setting by public utilities,[39] is as follows: Unit costs (i.e., direct labor and material costs plus unit overhead costs) are projected on the basis of "normal" or "standard" volume (generally set at around 80 per cent of capacity), and a profit margin per car is added to this unit cost to yield a predetermined total target rate of return to the company. The important thing to notice here is that current *actual* costs are not used in pricing. The rate of return on which General Motors prices are based is 20 per cent on net worth. This is a long-run pricing objective of the company; no attempt is made to "maximize" the return in any given year. The target objective applied to the standard volume is basic in the pricing decision because long-run corporation planning of physical capacity and expansion are premised on a target flow of funds to support the investment plans.

General Motors' approach implicitly makes certain necessary assumptions about (1) the percentage of capacity at which other producers operate—i.e., over time, General Motor's capacity must be built with a view to rivals' expected sales. Thus, pricing will be partly a function of investment. (2) It assumes further that given rival producers' sales, General Motors will, on the average, be able to sell—at direct cost plus overhead (assuming 80 per cent of capacity), plus a margin to realize 20 per cent return on net worth —enough cars to realize the target return. (3) Hence General Motor's pricing assumes a share of the market. Is this share based upon assumptions regarding the level of rivals' costs (i.e., their marginal costs)? Evidently not; as we shall see, rivals' "costs" apparently do not determine their prices or sales, since they are price followers. General Motors must also assume

---

38 See A. D. H. Kaplan, J. B. Dirlam, and R. F. Lanzillotti, *Pricing in Big Business* (Washington, D.C.: Brookings Institution, 1958), pp. 48–55 and 131–142, and *Administered Prices: Automobiles*, op. cit., pp. 104–130. See also "Responses of General Motors to the Eleven Points Stated by Senators Morse and Newson," Ibid., p. 7.

39 There is, of course, one important difference: A public utility is a regulated monopoly, whose costing and pricing practices are subject to governmental supervision and control. General Motors on the other hand, has considerable economic power like a public utility, but is essentially free to set its own prices.

TABLE 11   FACTORY SUGGESTED LIST PRICES OF 1968 MODELS OF
THE BIG THREE (4-DOOR SEDAN, 8-CYLINDER MODELS)[a]

GENERAL MOTORS MODELS	($)	FORD MODELS	($)	CHRYSLER MODELS	($)
A. Compact					
Chevrolet Chevy II	2,593	Ford Falcon	2,623	Plymouth Valiant	2,609
		Ford Futura	2,752	Plymouth Signet	2,755
				Dodge Dart	2,669
B. Intermediate					
Chevrolet Chevelle Deluxe	2,840	Ford Fairlane	2,848	Plymouth Belvedere	2,874
Chevrolet Chevelle Malibu	2,919	Ford Fairlane 500	2,927	Plymouth Satellite	2,963
Oldsmobile F-85	2,695			Dodge Coronet Deluxe	2,916
Oldsmobile Cutlass	3,079	Ford Torino	3,072	Dodge Coronet 400	3,010
Pontiac Tempest	2,905	Mercury Montego	2,900		
Pontiac Tempest Custom	2,988	Mercury MX	3,053		
Pontiac Tempest Lemans	3,312				
Buick Special Deluxe	2,969				
Buick Skylark	3,071				
C. Specialty					
Chevrolet Corvair 500	2,396				
Chevrolet Corvair Monza	2,620				
Chevrolet Camaro	2,973	Ford Mustang	2,993	Plymouth Barracuda	2,993
Pontiac Firebird	3,177	Mercury Cougar		Dodge Charger	3,341
		XR-7	3,534		
		GT	3,639		

that, given the price at which it intends to sell various models (determined
as indicated above), it will realize 40 per cent to 50 per cent of the market.
It has been able to realize its target market share through stylistic changes
and advertising which are reflected in cost. Therefore, the pricing problem
for General Motors is one of simultaneous determination of target profits,
based upon its estimation of industry demand, factors previously mentioned,
industry capacity, and respective market shares of its competitors.

PRICE LEADERSHIP AND
PRICE UNIFORMITY

Chrysler and Ford executives have indicated that their companies do not
have profits goals like General Motor's, which provide an objective for price
determination, although Ford utilizes a "standard cost" procedure which is

GENERAL MOTORS MODELS	($)	FORD MODELS	($)	CHRYSLER MODELS	($)
Buick Riviera	5,036	Ford Thunderbird	5,143		
Oldsmobile					
Toronado	5,171				
Cadillac Eldorado	7,121	Lincoln Continental			
		Mark III	6,910		
D. Full-sized "low-priced"					
Chevrolet Biscayne	3,018	Ford Custom	3,045	Plymouth Fury I	3,066
Bel Air	3,118	Custom 500	3,144	Fury II	3,163
Impala	3,241	Galaxie 500	3,267	Fury III	3,296
Caprice	3,561	LTD	3,431	VIP	3,627
Pontiac Catalina	3,346			Dodge Polara	3,324
Ventura	3,451			Monaco	3,613
E. Full-sized "medium priced"					
Oldsmobile Delmont	3,662	Mercury Monterey	3,631	Chrysler Newport	3,820
Delta	3,909	Montclair	3,883	Newport Custom	4,007
Delta Custom	4,105	Park Lane	4,017	300	4,240
Ninety-Eight	4,422	Brougham	4,343	New Yorker	4,500
Buick LeSabre	3,696				
Custom 400	3,790				
Wildcat	3,960				
Electra	4,330				
Electra Custom	4,509				
Pontiac Executive	3,834				
Bonneville	4,055				
F. Full-sized luxury					
Cadillac Calais	6,007				
DeVille	6,301	Lincoln Continental	6,474	Imperial Crown	6,608
				LeBaron	7,433

a Including Federal excise tax, dealer preparation, and standard equipment.
SOURCE General Motors Press Release, September 23, 1968; *Consumer Reports*, **33**:199 (April 1968).

similar to General Motor's—perhaps because Ford's former chief operating executive was an alumnus of General Motors.[40] All three firms plan production of a new model with clearly defined cost targets based upon current prices of competitive makes. The primary concern in the early stages of production planning evidently is to make sure that a particular model can be mass-produced at costs that are considered suitable in relation to current prices. Final cost estimates are made on the basis of average volume of past years, after which production is started on the new model. The actual decision on prices, however, is not made until the last minute before models are placed on sale, so that ample time is available to study the actual or probable pricing action of rivals.

40 For a summary of Ford's standard cost procedures, see A. R. Oxenfeldt, *Industrial Pricing and Market* *Practices* (Englewood Cliffs, N.J.: Prentice-Hall, 1951), pp. 135 and 136.

List price differentials are rather small among models of the three firms in most model classes, as shown in Table 11. This is especially true in the compact class, in the intermediate class (for Chevelle, Fairlane, and Plymouth models), in the specialty class (Camaro, Mustang, and Barracuda) and class "D" (Chevrolet, Ford, and Plymouth models). In all of these cases the list price differentials vary from 1 per cent to less than 3 per cent. This pattern of list price differentials apparently is the result of market strategies of the major firms reflecting the effectiveness of product differentiation, advertising, and other forms of nonprice competition. The close similarity of list prices in the particular instances mentioned also reflects price leadership-followership and pure oligopolistic interdependence.

There is no evidence of a consistent pattern of one firm announcing new prices first, with the others following; the role of first announcing price changes appears to have been about equally divided among the three companies. However, other evidence suggests that even where Ford or Chrysler announce new prices first, their basic aim is to anticipate and, as necessary, follow, the price actions of General Motors.[41] Three instances illustrate Ford and Chrysler's desire to keep prices in line with those of General Motors. On September 29, 1956, Ford announced its suggested price list for 1957 models, averaging a 2.9 per cent increase, ranging from $1 to $104 over 1956 models. Two weeks later, General Motors announced its new prices for Chevrolets, averaging 6.1 per cent over 1956 and ranging from $50 to $166 higher. One week later Ford revised its prices upward, with the result that on ten models the new price differences with Chevrolet were only $1 to $2, and on two models, $10 to $11. A week later Chrysler announced Plymouth prices, which conformed to the traditional Chrysler pattern of around $20 higher than Chevrolet.

TABLE 12   PRICING PATTERNS, 1968

DATE		RANGE OF DOLLAR CHANGE ($)	AVERAGE DOLLAR CHANGE ($)	AVERAGE % CHANGE
9/16/68	*Chrysler*	−66 to +164	+84	2.9
9/23/68	*General Motors*	− 1 to +144	+49	1.6
9/25/68	*Ford*	−89 to +149	+47	1.6
9/26/68	*Chrysler* (revised)	−69 to +188	+53	1.8
9/27/68	*American Motors*	−74 to +437	+37	1.5

SOURCE   A statement by General Motors Corporation, prepared for the Subcommittee on Retailing, Distribution and Marketing Practices and the Subcommittee on Monopoly of the Select Committee on Small Business, U.S. Senate, "The Automobile Industry: A Case Study of Competition," October 1968, p. 34.

---

41   *Administered Prices* (Hearings), op. cit., pp. 2777, 2683, 2785.

In pricing 1966 models, Chrysler made the first move by increasing the prices of most models, justifying its increases by citing "improvements" in the cars and the inclusion of a "safety package" as standard equipment. Several days later General Motors said it was reducing its prices for 1966 models compared to comparably equipped 1965 models, since it was not passing on the full cost of the safety package. The actual difference between General Motors and Chrysler prices was small in dollar terms. Ford, the last to announce, fell in line with General motor's price cuts.

TABLE 13 MARKETING AND SALES INCENTIVE PROGRAMS CONDUCTED BY CHEVROLET, FORD, AND PLYMOUTH, 1968 MODEL YEAR[a]

MAKE	DATE OF CAMPAIGN	TYPE OF CAMPAIGN	MODELS AFFECTED	RANGE OF ALLOWANCES ($)
Plymouth	Jan. 1–End of Model Run	Special product promotion	Valiant	33
Plymouth	Jan. 1–End of Model Run	Special product promotion	Barracuda	81–128
Plymouth	Jan. 1–End of Model Run	Special product promotion	Fury III	61–116
Plymouth	Jan. 1–End of Model Run	Special product promotion	Belvedere (Satellite)	65–97
Ford	Jan. 21–End of Model Run	Special product promotion	Mustang	13–31
Chevrolet	Feb. 1–Mar. 31	Special product promotion	Impala	15–30
Plymouth	Feb. 1–Apr. 30	Cash incentive	Valiant, Barracuda, Belvedere, and Fury	10–40
Ford	March 1–May 31	Cash incentive	Mustang and Falcon	40–70
Ford	March 1–May 31	Special product promotion	Fairlane and Ford XL	50
Chevrolet	Apr. 1–June 30	Special product promotion	Chevrolet Regular and Chevelle	20–55
Ford	Apr. 1–May 31	Cash incentive	Ford Regular	45–125
Plymouth	May 1–End of Model Run	Cash incentive	Valiant, Barracuda, Belvedere, and Fury	10–40
Ford	June 1–End of Model Run	Cash incentive	All models	50–250
Chevrolet	July 1–End of Model Run	Cash incentive	Chevrolet Regular	50–150

a Merchandise and trip incentive programs were initiated by Plymouth in December 1967 with Chevrolet and Ford beginning on January 1, 1968. These programs extended through most of the remainder of the model year.

SOURCE Statement by General Motors Corporation, "The Automobile Industry A Case Study of Competition," October 1968, p. 49.

In 1968, Chrysler rolled back its prices after earlier announcing price increases that General Motors did not follow. The pattern is shown in Table 12.

Despite the year-to-year price increases that have occurred, the U.S. Bureau of Labor Statistics (BLS) wholesale and retail prices indexes for new cars (by making allowances for improvement in car quality) show a slight decline from 1959 to 1969, during which period wholesale and retail prices on the average rose by 8 per cent and 20 per cent, respectively. This, of course, does not mean that the 1969 dollar price of a new car is actually less, but rather by BLS reckoning the consumer was getting slightly more car for his dollar in 1969 than in 1959, even though he had to make a larger total outlay to realize this gain in utility.

List prices of new cars rarely are changed during the model year, but from time to time manufacturers utilize various merchandising programs with dealers such as (a) special sales campaigns involving cash bonuses to dealers for cars sold above established quotas, (b) special product promotions involving reduced prices for specified optional equipment, and (c) merchandise and trip prizes to sales managers and car salesmen. General Motors has cited in Table 13 "sales campaigns and special product promotions" of the Big Three during the 1968 model year as illustrative of the rough and tumble of the marketplace in the pricing of new automobiles.

Additionally, a large number of "special product and sales incentive programs" were used by U.S. producers during most of the 1968 model year, as shown in Table 14.

TABLE 14   NUMBER OF INDUSTRY-WIDE MARKETING AND SALES INCENTIVE PROGRAMS IN EFFECT DURING EACH MONTH OF THE 1968 MODEL YEAR

	CASH INCENTIVES	MERCHANDISE AND TRIPS	PRODUCT PROMOTION ALLOWANCES	TOTAL INCENTIVE PROGRAMS
1967 *October*	—	—	—	—
November	—	—	1	1
December	—	5	2	7
1968 *January*	—	11	13	24
February	4	12	16	32
March	5	13	18	36
April	6	12	16	34
May	8	16	14	37
June	8	14	11	33
July	10	8	10	28
August	8	3	10	21
September	7	3	10	20

SOURCE   Statement by General Motors, "The Automobile Industry: A Case Study of Competition," October 1968, p. 50.

TABLE 15   CONSUMER PRICE INDEX (CPI), U.S. city average for
urban wage earners and clerical workers: NEW CARS (1957–1959 = 100)
(seasonally unadjusted)[a]; *and* WHOLESALE PRICE INDEXES (WPI) for
commodity groups, subgroups, product classes, and individual items:
PASSENGER CARS (1957–1959 = 100) (seasonally unadjusted)[b]

	1965		1966		1967		1968	
	CPI	WPI	CPI	WPI	CPI	WPI	CPI	WPI
January	101.5	98.5	97.4	97.7	97.6	97.8	100.1	100.3
February	101.0	98.5	97.2	97.5	97.3	97.7	100.8	100.0
March	100.8	98.3	97.1	97.4	97.2	97.5	100.6	100.0
April	100.7	98.3	97.4	97.2	97.0	97.6	100.3	99.4
May	100.2	98.2	97.0	97.0	96.9	97.6	100.3	99.3
June	97.4	98.1	96.8	96.7	96.8	97.1	100.1	99.5
July	97.2	98.1	96.7	96.8	97.0	97.1	99.8	99.3
August	97.1	98.1	95.8	96.3	96.9	97.2	99.1	99.2
September	96.5	97.9	94.4	95.7	96.1	97.3	98.4	98.9
October	97.7	97.8	98.4	98.0	101.1	99.9	102.8	99.5
November	98.7	97.8	99.3	98.0	101.4	99.9	103.8	(NA)
December	98.7	97.7	98.6	98.0	101.3	99.9	(NA)	(NA)

SOURCES   a   *The Consumer Price Index: U.S. City Average and Selected Areas,*
United States Department of Labor, Bureau of Labor Statistics (Washington, D.C.:
Monthly, 1965–1968).   b   *Wholesale Prices and Price Indexes,* United States
Department of Labor, Bureau of Labor Statistics (Washington, D.C.: Monthly,
1965–1968).

Some of these efforts may indeed constitute cost reductions to dealers
on product lines or particular models, but others merely shift the focus of
competition into less desirable forms. Moreover, precisely how much this
competition affects transaction prices at retail is uncertain. Interestingly,
during the period covered by the sales incentive programs of Chevrolet,
Ford, and Plymouth listed above, wholesale and retail prices of new cars
(as measured by the BLS index) remained relatively constant until September
1968, when they declined by approximately 1 per cent (see Table 15).

IV. MARKET PERFORMANCE
NONPRICE COMPETITION

With the disappearance of significant price differentials on comparable
models, "nonprice" competition thus has become increasingly intense.
Particular emphasis has been placed on design changes and advertising. At
one time, model changes emerged from significant developments in technology, but today they are largely merchandising devices designed to enhance sales. The industry custom is annual model changes—i.e., a complete
retooling of the line every 2 years, with a "facelifting" in alternate years.
John Keats puts it very succinctly:

The basic shell is bent a little bit this way, this year, and is bent slightly that way next year. The headlights are higher one year, lower the next, or grow in double. . . . The door knobs are hidden, or recessed, or turned into buttons or bars. . . . Tail fins grow higher, or may be, grow in sidewise. A chiropodist has remarked that the [late] Edsel's fins resemble ingrown toenails.

Meanwhile, no significant changes take place, except in price, and the change there is certainly significant. . . .[42]

The apparent objective of this kind of product variation is to make this year's models unstylish in the next 3 or 4 years so that owners will trade them for a new model. Standard styling, the hallmark of most foreign models, is rejected on the premise that the public does not want it. It seems also that the Big Three have advertised themselves into a position where each must, or at least believes it must, make a substantial annual model change in order to hold its position.

The magnitude of the cost of design changes perhaps can be appreciated by noting that General Motors alone spent $840 million in 1967 for restyling and retooling costs, or approximately $134 per car. Changes in design are closely interwoven with advertising, so that an annual model change entails at least $75 a car more (at the manufacturing level alone) to make the public aware of the new model and to broaden the public appeal.

AUTO QUALITY An automotive consultant of Consumers Union (which tests 30–40 cars per year and has thoroughly tested over 600 cars since the end of World War II) reported that new car quality, in the sense of workmanship and freedom from mechanical imperfections at the time of delivery "is, on the whole, going downhill."[43] This view of deterioration in quality and quality control by manufacturers was also held by a large percentage of buyers. An economist for one of the major producers reported a survey disclosing that 22 per cent of potential car buyers believed European autos to be "mechanically more reliable" and 31 per cent say they have "better workmanship" than American cars. Moreover, a survey conducted by the National Automobile Dealers Association reveals that among buyers of cars priced in the $2,500 and up brackets, 71 per cent cited "better workmanship" as the reason for their purchase of a foreign car.[44] An occasional U.S. auto executive is willing to admit there is something in these impressions held by buyers and testing organizations.[45]

---

42 *The Insolent Chariots* (New York: Lippincott, 1958), pp. 54 and 55.

43 *Administered Prices* (Hearings), op. cit., pp. 3071 and 3072; 3086.

44 "Does Europe Top U.S. in Car Workmanship? Many Folks Think So," *Wall Street Journal* (August 20, 1959), p. 1.

45 *Time* magazine reports that "Detroit wags recalled the time when Big Bill Knudsen, G.M.'s late president, boasted to adman Bruce Barton that a

INNOVATIONS   Innovations—their source and the speed with which they are adopted—are another aspect of nonprice competition significant for public policy. These are not matters that lend themselves to precise measurement, especially the relative values of different innovations; furthermore, several companies often claim credit for what is substantially the same development.[46] Not all of these claims are true "firsts," however. Most of the recent improvements have come from outside the large firms. Many, like the new suspension systems, were pioneered by small European concerns, and others, like the automatic transmissions and power steering, were largely the result of work by independent inventors.[47] Moreover, the small producers have done more than a proportionate share of pioneering.[48] They perform an important function in the market in this regard, displaying a competitive vigor born of necessity. In fact, the high mortality rate among small firms has been partly due to a large amount of unsuccessful innovation.

With all this effort devoted to improving product performance, only little attention seems to be given to producing a somewhat safer product. This raises an important public policy question which will be discussed in a later section. In 1955, Professor Maclaurin summarized the general innovative record of the industry as follows:

The automobile industry has certainly been one of the most vigorous new industries in America. Yet by the late 1920's the innovative characteristics of the industry began to change. There can be no simple

---

certain new-model Chevy was 'almost the perfect low-priced car—and it will really become perfect next year when we make one small change.' Barton bit hard. 'What change?' Deadpanned Bill Knudsen: 'We're just going to hang a small hammock under the chassis. Catch all the goddam parts that fall out.'" October 5, 1959, p. 92.

46 Hearings before the Subcommittee on Antitrust and Monopoly, Senate Judiciary Committee, 84th Congress, 1st Session, "General Motors," *A Study of the Antitrust Laws*, Pt. 7 (Washington, D.C.: U.S. Government Printing Office, 1957), pp. 3507–3509; *Administered Prices: Automobiles*, op. cit., p. 23.

47 For example, the original outstanding inventions in the development of the automatic transmission were made by an electrical engineer employed by a shipbuilding company. The principal contribution of General Motors was the development of a combination of converter-coupling and epicycling gearing.

Cf. J. Jewkes, D. Sawyers, and R. Stillerman, *The Sources of Inventions* (London: Macmillan & Co., 1958), and D. Hamberg, "Size of Firm, Monopoly, and Economic Growth," *Employment Growth, and Price Levels* (Washington, D.C.: U.S. Government Printing Office, 1959); Hearings Before the Joint Economic Committee, 86th Congress, 1st Session, Pt. 7 "The Effects of Monopolistic and Quasi-Monopolistic Practices," pp. 2342, 2354.

48 The Automobile Manufacturers Association publication *A Chronicle of the Automotive Industry* (Detroit: Automobile Manufacturers Association, 1949), seems to confirm this merely by recording the origins of successful innovations. Among the innovations originating with or introduced by the smaller auto companies are all-steel body, noiseless rear axles, adjustable front seats, 4-wheel brakes, rubber engine mounts, overdrive, hydraulic valve lifters, turn signal indicators, and single-unit construction. Cf. *Administered Prices: Automobiles*, op. cit., p. 24.

explanation of this fact. But a partial answer lies in the quality of entrepreneurial leadership, the absence of a research conception, the explosive rate of previous growth, and the success of the established oligopoly.

... If the automobile pioneers had believed in and understood research, they could have provided a more interesting innovative record since 1930.[49]

TABLE 16 RATES OF RETURN (AFTER TAXES) ON STOCKHOLDERS' INVESTMENT FOR AUTOMOBILE COMPANIES, 1940 AND 1947–1967

YEAR	GENERAL MOTORS	FORD	CHRYSLER	AMERICAN MOTORS [a]		STUDEBAKER-PACKARD [b]
				NASH	HUDSON	
1940	19.2	n.a.[c]	22.1	3.7	−6.6	8.9
1947	20.2	8.5	23.6	30.4	13.0	20.6
1948	27.1	12.1	26.2	28.1	25.1	34.3
1949	33.4	19.5	32.0	29.6	16.3	37.0
1950	37.5	24.3	26.7	28.4	17.3	24.3
1951	21.7	10.5	15.2	13.8	−1.6	12.3
1952	20.0	9.1	16.7	10.4	11.4	13.4
1953	19.7	11.9	15.8	11.2	—	2.4
1954	24.5	15.0	5.8	−6.1		−16.0
1955	30.5	24.3	16.0	−4.5		−22.2
1956	18.9	12.3	3.1	−23.4		−64.4
1957	17.1	13.7	17.4	−8.9		−110.9
1958	12.6	3.9	−4.2	22.3		−41.3
1959	16.6	18.3	−0.8	36.8		38.1
1960	16.9	15.6	4.6			
1961	14.9	13.4	1.6			
1962	21.3	14.6	8.8	14.4		0.4
1963	23.0	13.6	18.2	14.5		−21.9
1964	23.5	12.9	20.4	9.1		19.5
1965	26.8	16.4	16.8	1.9		—
1966	21.2	13.3	11.4	−5.9		—
1967	18.1	1.9	10.4	−34.6		—

a American Motors formed in 1954 as a merger of Nash and Hudson.
b Studebaker and Packard merged in 1954. Data before 1954 for Studebaker only.
c Not available.
SOURCE "Report of the Federal Trade Commission on Rates of Return for Identical Companies in Selected Manufacturing Industries, 1940, 1947–1958"; and "Report of the Federal Trade Commission on Rates of Return for Identical Companies in Selected Manufacturing Industries, 1958–1967."

---

49 Rupert Maclaurin, "Innovation and Capital Formation in Some American Industries," *Capital Formation and Economic Growth*, (Princeton, N.J.: Princeton University Press, 1955), pp. 554 and 557.

PROFITS

The rates of return on stockholders investment (after taxes) for the Big Three automobile companies have been exceptionally good both before and after World War II. As Table 16 shows, since the end of World War II General Motors has averaged around 20 to 25 per cent (after taxes), and rarely has its return dropped below 20 per cent. Ford's return has generally been higher than Chrysler's, although both have been unsteady relative to General Motors. The independents have experienced the most variable returns, a fairly good performance in the late 1940's, but steadily deteriorating since 1950. Both American Motors and Studebaker-Packard have gone through a string of years with sustained losses. The Government-approved mergers leading to the formation of American Motors and Studebaker-Packard were made in the hope that the new companies might have a better chance of surviving the costly competition of the times. The discontinuation of auto production by Studebaker in 1963 ended this hope.

V. PUBLIC POLICY

The high degree of concentration in automobile production and the market practices which emerge pose a number of public policy issues. At one time, the industry was characterized by rather vigorous competition. As of 1939, the Federal Trade Commission reported

> Consumer benefits in the automobile manufacturing industry have probably been more substantial than in any other large industry studied by the Commission.[50]

A decade later, Professor Edward S. Mason, in commenting on the possibility of making informed judgments regarding a set of performance criteria for industry, concluded ". . . it is possible from the record of the last two or three decades to determine that the performance of the automobile industry is relatively good."[51] Another decade later, in 1958, Simon N. Whitney reached a similar conclusion.[52] But a 1958 report by the Subcommittee on Antitrust and Monopoly of the Senate Judiciary Committee offered contrary conclusions:

50 Federal Trade Commission, op. cit., p. 1074.
51 "The Current Status of the Monopoly Problem in the United States," *Harvard Law Review*, **62**:1281–1282 (June 1949). See also Mason, *Economic*
Concentration and the Monopoly Problem (Cambridge, Mass.: Harvard University Press, 1957), pp. 367 and 368.
52 Whitney, *Antitrust Policies*, op. cit., p. 522.

The evidence adduced in the hearings at least affords indications that monopoly power is extant in the industry. . . . . The subcommittee believes that the record of its recent hearings and those held in 1955 leaves little doubt that the hard core of the monopoly problem in the automobile industry is in the concentration of production and power held by G.M. This concentration appears neither compatible with nor conducive to a free market in which the public must buy automobiles. . . .[53]

How can these conflicting findings be reconciled? In part, it is a question of whether one focuses attention on the "structure of the market," or "performance" of the industry. For competition to be workable or acceptable in any economically significant sense, the market and market processes should not only *permit* but, more important, must *induce* the desired market results.[54]

PROBLEM OF CONCENTRATION

It will be recalled that Durant originally planned to extend his control over every producer of importance in the industry. Had events and personalities, differed slightly, Durant might have succeeded and Ford, Chrysler, Reo, and Dodge could conceivably have become parts of a General Motors monopoly. The fact that only four domestic producers remain raises the question whether the economics of the industry are such as to make the trend toward fewer and larger firms unavoidable. Given the mass production and consumption characteristics of the industry, Durant's logic would appear to be unassailable. There are definite and important scale economies associated with body and engine production and assembly operations. The conditions bearing on operational efficiency already discussed in Section II suggest that the present level of consumer demand would justify an industry consisting of *at least* ten firms of optimum size.[55] This estimate is a minimum, since a large number would be feasible if firms could secure bodies and engines from other firms specializing in the production of these components. As long as

53   *Administered Prices: Automobiles* pp. 182 and 183.

54   See statements of Ben W. Lewis and Walter Adams, Hearings before the Subcommittee on Antitrust and Monopoly, Senate Judiciary Committee, 86th Congress, 1st Session, "Administered Price Inflation: Alternative Public Policies," *Administered Prices*, Pt. 9 (Washington, D.C.: U.S. Government Printing Office, 1959), pp. 4715–4719; 4782–4783.

55   General Motors' automotive divisions alone could be divided into three or four efficient companies, Chrysler into two, and Ford into two. General Motors reportedly had a plan of its own for dividing its automobile divisions if required by antitrust action, under which separate companies would be formed of both Chevrolet and Buick, whereas Oldsmobile, Pontiac, and Cadillac divisions would remain as General Motors. *Business Week*, **1536**:23 (February 7, 1959).

such specialty firms do not exist, an automobile manufacturer must perforce produce its own engines and bodies.[56]

Two basic questions for public policy are (1) whether the fact that the three major producers account for approximately 97 per cent of domestic production, and the leading firm for more than 50 per cent, is attributable to economies of scale and natural forces of competition; and (2) whether this level of concentration violates the Sherman or Clayton Act. The issue has not been subjected to a legal test. Indeed, with the exception of the suit charging Checker Cab with monopolizing the market for taxicabs in a half-dozen cities and the suit challenging Chrysler's proposed merger with Mack Truck,[57] no *structural* suit has been brought against the automobile industry. Most of the cases brought by the Antitrust Division of the Department of Justice and the Federal Trade Commission have concerned alleged "abuses" of market power or trade restraints; e.g., franchise withdrawals, exclusive dealing arrangements, tying clauses, price-fixing, price discrimination, coercion, and allocation of territories.[58]

Two earlier decisions might appear to offer some grounds for initiating a complaint against General Motors, but no grand jury has returned an indictment: (1) Judge Hand's 1945 Alcoa decision ("Size was not only evidence of violation, or of potential violation . . . it was the essence of the offense") and (2) the court's ruling in the 1946 *Tobacco* case ("Neither proof of the power to exclude nor proof of actual exclusion of existing or potential competitors is essential to sustain a charge of monopolization under the Sherman Act").[59] The auto industry has never been charged with parallelism on price and product policies similar to those practiced by the Big Three of tobacco. The crucial factors that would have to be weighed under present judicial interpretations would seem to be the following.

1. Whether the Big Three *have* the power (i.e., the *existence*, not the *exertion*) as a group substantially to influence the price of automobiles, and whether that power has been maintained for the purpose of enjoying and preserving the advantage of market position.
2. Whether a "combination" can be inferred from a course of dealing or parallel action in response to stimuli of the market, or concerted action on such things as price, product, and distribution policies.[60]

---

56   There are, however, some technological developments on the horizon that could reduce the minimum scale of plant for efficient operations and justify an even larger number of independent producers—e.g., the substitution of plastics for steel in body components and the use of an electric motor in place of the present internal combustion engine.

57   *U.S.* v. *Yellow Cab Company* 332 U.S. 218 (1947), and *U.S.* v. *Yellow Cab Company, et al.*, 338 U.S. 338 (1949).

58   Cf. Whitney, *Antitrust Policies*, op. cit., p. 435–452.

59   *American Tobacco Company* v. *United States*, 328 U.S. 781 at 810 (1946).

60   Cf. Eugene Rostow, "Monopoly Under the Sherman Act," *Illinois Law Review*, 43:762 (1949).

Some students of antitrust law believe that even under the current interpretations recognizing the nature of oligopoly structures some abuse of power must be found in the form of predatory, exclusionary, or discriminatory practices. This history of concentrated industries suggests that market power is inevitably abused, intentionally or "unintentionally," that is, if market power *can* be abused, it probably is.

The only other case that has involved an important structural issue was the General Motors-du Pont decision of 1957, decided under the original Section 7 of the Clayton Act, but concerned a vertical acquisition.[61] The Supreme Court ruled that the 23 per cent stock acquisition made by du Pont back in 1917–1918, gave du Pont what in effect was a monopoly of the automotive paints and fabrics business of General Motors—a reciprocity arrangement that was beneficial to both General Motors and du Pont. The control exercised by du Pont was found to cut off competition and exclude competitors from General Motors business; hence the court ruled that it had not merely a potential but an actual anticompetitive effect.[62]

AUTO DEALERS AND THE
FRANCHISE SYSTEM

Auto dealers raised frequent complaints against the practices of the auto manufacturers.[63] The principal charges have been "forcing" and arbitrary cancellation of franchises. "Forcing" has taken several forms, e.g., the assignment of new-car "quotas" to the dealer with or without his consent, manufacturer's insistence that only "genuine" (i.e., the manufacturer's) parts and accessories be stocked, forcing the dealers to accept a minimum "quota" of parts and accessories, and requiring dealers to contribute an annual sum for advertising.

The franchise creating the dealership and the conditions for cancellation of franchises have been bones of contention. The franchise requires that the dealer meet certain specified capital, character, and experience qualifications, and that he follow certain manufacturer-prescribed business and accounting practices. Also, the franchise establishes "exclusive" dealerships, i.e., generally it ties the dealer to a single manufacturer. Dealers have charged that franchises have been cancelled at the will of the manufacturer, without hearing or for causes not clearly agreed upon by both parties. In some cases cancellations were based upon serious dealer malpractices, but in other cases cancellation was merely a reprisal against dealers refusing to

---

61 *U.S.* v. *E. I. duPont deNemours & Co.*, 353 U.S. 586 (1957).

62 For a penetrating analysis of the decision, see Joel B. Dirlam and Irwin M. Stelzer, "The duPont-General Motors Decision: In the Antitrust Grain," *Columbia Law Review*, **58**: 24 (January 1958).

63 Federal Trade Commission, op. cit., Chs. 3–11.

accept some type of forcing.[64] Many of the difficulties between manufacturers have been resolved as a result of the passage of the Automobile Dealers Franchise Act (the "good faith act") of 1956, which provided a remedy at law if the manufacturer failed to act in good faith in the termination of a franchise. The burden of proof still rests with the dealer, however.

Listening to an automobile dealer whine about his cruel fate at the hands of a manufacturer would, as John Keats says, "ordinarily send a reasonable man into gales of laughter." Sympathy for the dealer doing business with "giants" has been tempered by painful consumer experiences with "sharp" dealer practices, especially the 1946–1949 period when dealers had too few cars to sell and sold them mercilessly, and the price-deception "pack" of 1955 when the dealers had too many cars on hand. The difficulty here is that the dealer finds himself in the uncomfortable position between the powerful manufacturer on the one hand, and a demanding and not too understanding public on the other. The public appears to gain from such practices as automobile forcing through lower prices more closely related to dealer's actual cost, but may lose as much from parts and accessory forcing and from high repair charges dealers use to offset low margins on new-car sales. Both situations arise out of the degree of market power possessed by the car manufacturers, who have passed some of that power on to their dealers through exclusive franchise arrangements.

AUTO SAFETY

Considering the emphasis on product differentiation and product performance, manufacturers gave little attention and precious few dollars for research on safer automobiles, until prodded by committee hearings and the appearance of Ralph Nader's book in 1965. [65] The basic issue raised by the hearings is the responsibility of the automobile manufacturer for putting safety features into an automobile. Manufacturers' policy characteristically had been to offer safety items as an option, but under testimony auto executive after auto executive stated that unfortunately safety options simply

---

64 Cf. Hearings before the Subcommittee on Antitrust and Monopoly Senate Judiciary Committee, 85th Congress, 1st Session, Pt. 7, 1955, pp. 3156–3189, and Pt. 8, pp. 4060–4143. The weight of publicity on General Motors' practices led to a suspension of its dealer advertising fund plan (regarding forced advertising contributions) and the extension of 1 year contracts for 5 years. Ibid., Pt. 7, p. 3556, and Department of Justice announcement, December 3, 1956. See also Pashigian, op. cit., especially pp. 33 ff.

65 For example, General Motors indicated that in 1964 it spent $1¼ millions strictly for safety reasearch, in relation to profits of $1.7 billion. See Hearings before the Subcommittee on Executive Reorganization of the Committee on Government Operations, 89th Congress, 1st Session, *Federal Role in Traffic Safety* (Washington, D.C.: U.S. Government Printing Office, 1965) (hereinafter "Ribicoff Hearings"), and Ralph I. Nader, *Unsafe at Any Speed* (New York: Grossman, 1965).

"do not sell." Hence, from the company's marketing policy standpoint, it made little sense to engineer safety features into cars as standard equipment.[66] This attitude, plus aroused Congressional concern over some 50,000 deaths annually in auto accidents, contributed to the passage of the National Traffic Motor Vehicle Act of 1966, establishing the National Highway Safety Bureau (in the Department of Transportation) with authority to write "safety standards" for automobiles. Senator Ribicoff set forth the rationale for government regulation in this area as follows:

> *Senator Ribicoff:* The question is not does he [the public] want them [safety features]. . . . What is an automobile manufacturer's responsibility to produce a safe car? If he wants to? Do we ask an airplane manufacturer if he wants to produce a safe airplane? Do we ask the person who produces a locomotive or a train whether he wants a safe train? Do we ask the person who drives a truck or a bus does he want a safe truck, does he want a safe bus? Do we ask the man who builds a ship to carry passengers whether he wants a safe ship? You are talking about an item which injured 3.5 million Americans. You are talking about an item that involved $8 billion in property damage. So it is not a question of does a person want to. What is the responsibility of the automobile manufacturer for putting safety features in an automobile? Is it a question of selling him safety or do you have a responsibility of producing a safe car with safety items?[67]

The Ribicoff Hearings established that although traffic accidents are caused by a combination of considerations—principally driver habits (carelessness, intoxication, signal violations, and so on), plus highway design, lack of standardization of state laws, and vehicle design—our current technical knowledge on building safer vehicles exceeds our ability to make motorists drive more carefully and responsibly.[68] Thus, emphasis in the National Vehicle Safety Act was placed upon establishing national standards for "crashworthy" automobiles as the safety measure that was most feasible and most likely to produce the quickest and greatest results in saving lives and minimizing injuries. Twenty initial standards were written in 1967, covering (a) features that affect the likelihood of crashes (e.g., position of controls, tires and tire rims, braking systems, windshield wipers, and so on); (b) features that may reduce the frequency and severity of injuries during the

---

66   Ribicoff Hearings, ibid., pp. 656–657, 678, 825–830, and 876 ff.

67   Ibid., pp. 829–830.

68   For example, research on 57 accidents over a 23 month period in Washtenaw County, Michigan, involving 79 deaths disclosed that 63 per cent of the victims ejected would have been saved with lap-type seat belts. (Also, 50 per cent of the fatally injured drivers were intoxicated, and a substantial number of these drivers had a record of belligerency while intoxicated.) Yet, a 1965 Gallup poll indicated that after years of publicizing the benefits of seat belts, only one in seven drivers was using belts regularly. *Ribicoff Hearings*, op. cit., pp. 822 and 958.

crash (so-called "second collision"), e.g., collapsing steering column, protection against interior projections, seat belts, head restraints, door latches and hinges; (c) safety features for after the crash (fire hazard reduction from fuel system rupture); and (d) other features including exhaust emission control system, standard gear quadrant on automatic transmissions, back-up lights, and so on.

After a careful analysis of standards implemented through the 1968 model cars, *Consumer Reports* suggested that auto safety still had a long way to go. In particular, it suggested some new standards: (a) a series of tests to establish minimum levels of handling and steering performance; (b) improvement in the structural design of hardtop and convertible models by a standard requiring greater protection to occupants in rollovers; and (c) a standard covering self-pollution through excessive penetration of carbon monoxide into the passenger compartment, especially on station wagons.[69]

AUTO WARRANTIES A 1969 Federal Trade Commission (FTC) study of automobile warranties addressed itself to two basic questions: (1) Have the manufacturers and dealers made sufficient effort, using modern technology and mechanical skill, to put cars in top-notch operating condition? (2) Has the new car owner received the kind of service which the terms of the warranty led him to expect? Based upon its findings, the Commission study answered the first question, "no," and the second, "yes" and "no."[70]

Two surveys of buyer satisfaction with condition of new cars at delivery were used by the FTC. A Consumers Union study disclosed that 35.7 per cent of 50,000 members who had purchased 1963–1966 models when new stated their cars were not delivered "in satisfactory condition," and that the percentage expressing dissatisfaction rose from 30.7 per cent for the 1963 models to 37.2 per cent for the 1966 models.[71] However, a *Newsweek* study found that 2.9 per cent of those buying *imported* cars found them mechanically unreliable, as against 9.3 per cent who bought American-made cars.[72]

Perhaps the best available indicator of quality control by manufacturers is the fact that one out of every six of the 7.8 million cars were involved in "recalls" during the 1967 model year. Such statistics speak well of the diligence of auto firms in carrying out safety standards in voluntary compliance with Federal legislation, but reflect poorly on the manufacturing quality control. As of February 1969, *Consumer Reports* indicated it was "finding more assembly deficiencies per car, on the average," than in January, which it said "stem directly from the car manufacturer's carelessness during assembly and from his dealers' failure to prepare a car meticulously for sale."[73]

---

69 *Consumers Reports*, **33**:183 (April 1968).
70 Federal Trade Commission, *Staff Report on Automobile Warranties* (Washington, D.C.: Federal Trade Commission, 1969).

71 Ibid., p. 165.
72 Ibid., p. 166.
73 *Consumer Reports*, **34**:79 (February 1969).

On the second question, the FTC study found that performance of repairs under manufacturers' warranties "too often falls short of the level of adequacy that may properly be expected of manufacturers and their dealers." Available evidence indicates dealers often refuse warranty work or fail to make "warranty-covered" repairs, or make it inconvenient for owners to bring cars in for warranty work. In part, this is due to manufacturers' attempts to hold down warranty costs by following policies that encourage their regional representatives to compete in minimizing warranty claims. The desire to keep warranty costs down and to refuse extravagant or unrealistic claims by buyers is reasonable and understandable, but the result of such pressures all too often makes the customer the loser.

The FTC study also found that for the period studied with the possible exception of American Motors, auto companies do not strictly enforce service standards given to dealers. The 1956 Automobile Dealers Franchise Act makes it more difficult for manufacturers since their efforts may subject them to complaints of coercion or arbitrary behavior. This should not be the case, but it evidently is. Part of the problem is that dealers complain that manufacturers pay less for warranty work than a car owner would pay for the same repair work done outside the warranty.[74] In addition, the FTC found that dealers generally need more space and equipment as well as trained mechanics. The institution of the longer-term warranties in the 1960's aggravated this situation. To illustrate, the total number of dealers has declined as new-car sales increased, with the result that there has been a sharp rise in the new car sales per dealer from 125 cars in 1958, to 285 in 1966.[75] Also, dealers were found to be assigning their best mechanics to nonwarranty work because dealers estimate it costs more to make predelivery service inspection than manufacturers allow.[76]

As a practical matter, the Automobile Dealers Franchise Act and state laws covering the licensing of vehicle manufacturers and dealers, tend to weaken the manufacturer's ability to enforce standards for dealer service by limiting the use of franchise termination. In effect, this situation represents another instance of a public policy designed to protect one economic group from another with the result that the car buyer ends up the net loser—by paying higher real costs for service (through delays, repeat visits for service, and higher charges) than when warranty work is done as "regular" repair service at high rates. Put differently, manufacturers have shifted a greater

---

74 Federal Trade Commission, *Staff Report*, op. cit., p. 85 ff.

75 Federal Trade Commission, *Staff Report*, op. cit., p. 90.

76 For example, where the regular wage rate on service is $7.00 per hour and the factory allowance is based on $6.00, for a 1-hour job the mechanic (who usually receives about one-half of the rate charged) would get $3.50, and the dealer would net $2.50. Dealers efforts to maintain their margin by shifting the highest-paid mechanics to nonwarranty work may be shortsighted if higher-paid mechanics are more efficient than other mechanics—which, of course, does not necessarily follow.

proportion of service costs to dealers who, in turn, have shifted a greater proportion on to the buyers.

Another area of public policy concern is installment financing. There are several hundred relatively small finance companies, and a Big Three consisting of General Motors Acceptance Corporation (GMAC) (a General Motors subsidiary), Commercial Credit Corporation (owned by Chrysler until 1938), and Commercial Investment Trust (to which Ford sold its subsidiary Universal Credit in 1933). One aspect of the installment financing problem has to do with the advertising of finance costs. Most finance companies buy the customer's installment purchase contract from the dealers. In addition to carrying charges, dealers often add a "dealer's loss reserve" charge, and, in some cases, sell automobile insurance as a tie-in requirement. The last two items are excellent sources of dealer "packs."

In the 1930's, the three large finance companies, on the insistence of the auto manufacturers, reduced or eliminated the "pack," and reduced carrying charges to 6 per cent of the full amount financed; the so-called "6 per cent plan." As originally advertised, this plan was misleading—actual simple interest amounted to nearly 12 per cent on the unpaid balance—later enjoined by the FTC. A related problem that prompted government action arose out of the auto manufacturers' forcing or encouraging the use of the Big Three finance companies through pressure on the dealers. In November 1939, General Motors, GMAC, and two other General Motors subsidiaries were found guilty of forcing GMAC financing on dealers and customers. Ford and Chrysler earlier voluntarily severed their relationships with installment finance affiliates under a consent decree arrangement. Recently, however, Ford has announced its intention to form a finance company, and Chrysler is expected to follow suit.

The basic problem here is not simply one of practices as such. It is part of the problem of concentration and the possibilities that credit terms and charges will be dictated not by the economics of financing, but by the exigencies of selling cars.[77] The situation points up something of a public policy dilemma in that the competitive market for financing permitted excessive charges, whereas the "restrained" market reduced them. Interestingly, Ford and Chrysler entered into consent decrees with the Department of Justice prohibiting their being affiliated with finance companies, whereas General Motors successfully contested divestiture of GMAC.

---

77 See the hearings on two bills to prohibit auto manufacturers from engaging in financing and insuring automobiles, Hearings before Subcommittee on Antitrust and Monopoly, Senate Judiciary Committee, 86th Congress, 1st Session, *Auto Financing Legislation* (Washington, D.C.: U.S. Government Printing Office, 1959), especially the testimonies of Thurman Arnold, former head of the Antitrust Division of the Department of Justice, and Donald F. Turner, pp. 256–286, 363–371.

PARTS SUPPLIERS

The position of parts manufacturers has already been mentioned. By virtue of their vertical integration, the major auto companies buy parts from (1) independent suppliers, (2) their own parts producing subsidiaries, or (3) "outside" firms that are closely tied to the auto companies through ownership or contractual arrangements. That this multiple relationship in the supply channels can result in an abuse of market power against the independent parts producers is indicated by a long list of cases tried by the Federal Trade Commission. For example, in July 1953, the FTC charged General Motors, Electric Auto-Lite, and Champion Spark Plug (who together produce around 90 per cent of the nation's spark plugs) with price discrimination in the sale of spark plugs to competing purchasers. The Commission also alleged that Champion and General Motors had induced distributors to agree to handle their lines exclusively. The latter was apparently a repetition of the 1939 violation under which General Motors and its A.C. Spark Plug Division were cited for forcing and maintenance of resale prices, requiring minimum inventories and purchases, and exclusive handling of their spark plugs and oil filters. The upshot of the spark plug cases was to enjoin all arrangements for exclusive dealing and Champion was ordered to justify, or cease and desist from maintaining, the extreme price differential between plugs for new cars (6 cents) and those for replacement use (21 cents and 31 cents).[78]

The prominence of price discrimination in many of these complaints calls attention to the possible effects of the intrafirm pricing system employed by integrated producers. Since the demand for a given automobile model tends to be more elastic than the demand for replacement parts, this may lead to marginal-cost pricing for component parts, with high-profit margins on replacement parts sales, which in turn may reinforce the dealer practice of trading down on new cars and holding up repair costs. Since all auto firms are not able to avail themselves of this technique, the commanding position of the larger manufacturers may be even greater than their size indicates, and the position of the small parts producers and dealers worse than in a more competitive situation.[79] In addition, when both integrated and inde-

---

78   Federal Trade Commission Dockets 3977, 5620, and 5624.

79   General Motors, being the largest supplier of automotive parts and components to nonintegrated and partially integrated firms, is in a much stronger position in this respect than any of its rivals. The corporation's policy is to price its parts so as to yield 20 to 30 per cent on capital invested in parts production, and results in larger overall profits on General Motors' integrated operations than those realized by less integrated competitors. This, of course, is nothing more than "normal, prudent" pursuit of the advantages inherent in General Motors' integration, but it is just this sort of pricing policy that is one of the factors that tends to keep the independents of the auto industry weak and poor. Cf. Joe S. Bain, *Industrial Organization*, op. cit., pp. 328 and 329.

pendent parts producers agree on the same discriminatory pricing system, the consumer can hardly escape high charges for repairs and service.

CONCLUSION

The automobile industry represents one of the nation's most difficult current antitrust dilemmas—industry concentration ratios on their face are disturbingly high, industry pricing policies are the source of annual crises for the Council of Economic Advisors and the President, problems of auto safety and auto warranties have become matters of continuing Congressional concern, consumers complain about quality and service of dealers, grand juries have been empanelled for consideration of possible Sherman and Clayton Act violations, without results, and even Justice Department "draft" complaints for restructuring General Motors are rumored. Yet, the fact remains that no suit aimed at the structure of the auto industry is imminent or likely. If Galbraith is correct, the industry is probably immune from antitrust action that seeks to restructure "achieved market power" as against attempts to increase market power through mergers and acquisitions.[80] In brief, current antitrust policy, insofar as the automobile industry is concerned, seems to be saying that the 1946 Tobacco case rule (*supra*) is not applicable—that is, both proof of *power to exclude* and proof of *actual exclusion* of existing and potential competitors *are* necessary to sustain a charge of monopolization under the Sherman Act. The Department of Justice has not, to date, assembled such proof, and it appears unlikely that it will be able to do so. Whether the available economic evidence on market structure, competitive behavior, and industry performance indicates the Department *should* make an attempt, is something else again.

SUGGESTED READINGS

BOOKS AND PAMPHLETS

Automobile Manufacturers Association. *Automobile Facts and Figures*. Detroit: Automobile Manufacturers Association (annual issues).
————. *A Chronicle of the Automotive Industry*. Detroit: Automobile Manufacturers Association, 1949.
Automotive News. Detroit (annual Almanac issue).
Bain, Joe S. *Barriers to Competition*. Cambridge, Mass.: Harvard University Press, 1956.
Cleveland, R. G., and S. T. Williamson. *The Road is Yours*. New York: Hawthorn Books Inc., 1951.

---

80   John K. Galbraith, *The New Industrial State* (Boston: Houghton   Mifflin, 1967), pp. 186–188.

Drucker, P. F. *Concept of the Corporation*. New York: The John Day Co., 1946.

Epstein, R. C. *The Automobile Industry*. New York: Shaw, 1928.

Factors Affecting Determination of Market Shares in the American Automobile Industry. Ed. by Frederic Stuart. New York: Hofstra University Yearbook, 1967. Vol. 3, Series 2.

Ford, H. *My Life and Work*. New York: Doubleday & Company, Inc., 1923.

———. *My Philosophy of Industry*. New York: Coward-McCann, Inc., 1929.

Galbraith, John K. *The New Industrial State*. Boston: Houghton-Mifflin Company, 1967.

General Motors. *Dynamics of Automobile Demand*. New York: General Motors, 1939.

———. "The Automobile Industry: A Case Study of Competition." October 1968.

Greenleaf, William. *Monopoly on Wheels*. Detroit: Wayne State University Press, 1961.

Keats, John. *The Insolent Chariots*. New York: J. B. Lippincott Company, 1958.

Kettering, C. F., and A. Orth. *The New Necessity*. Baltimore: the Williams & Wilkins Company, 1932.

Lewis, E. W. *Motor Memories*. Detroit: Alved Publishers, 1947.

Musselman, M. M. *Get A Horse*. New York: J. B. Lippincott Company, 1950.

Nader, Ralph. *Unsafe At Any Speed*. New York: Grossman Publishers, Inc., 1965.

Nevins, A., and F. E. Hill. *Ford, Expansion and Challenge, 1915–33*. New York: Charles Schribner's Sons, 1957.

Whitney, Simon N. *Antitrust Policies: American Experience in Twenty Industries*. Vol. 1. New York. Twentieth Century Fund, 1958. Ch. 8.

GOVERNMENT PUBLICATIONS

Federal Trade Commission. *Report on the Motor Vehicle Industry*. Washington, D.C.: U.S. Government Printing Office, 1939.

———. "Staff Report on Automobile Warranties." Washington, D.C.: (mimeo), 1969.

Hearings before the Subcommittee on Antitrust and Monopoly, Senate Judiciary Committee, Eighty-fourth Congress, 1st Session, Pt. 7, *A Study of the Antitrust Laws*. "General Motors," Washington, D.C.: U.S. Government Printing Office, 1957.

Hearings before the Subcommittee on Antitrust and Monopoly, Senate Judiciary Committee, 2nd Session, Pt. 6 *Administered Prices*. "Automobiles," Washington, D.C.: U.S. Government Printing Office, 1958.

Hearings before the Subcommittee on Antitrust and Monopoly, Senate Judiciary Committee, Eighty-sixth Congress, 1st Session, *Auto Financing Legislation*, Washington, D.C.: U.S. Government Printing Office, 1959.

Hearings before the Temporary National Economic Committee, Seventy-fifth Congress, 2nd Session, Pt. 2, *Investigation of Concentration of Economic Power*, Washington, D.C.: U.S. Government Printing Office, 1938.

Hearings before the Subcommittee on Executive Reorganization of the Senate Committee on Government Operations, Eighty-ninth Congress, 1st Session, *Federal Role in Traffic Safety*, Washington, D.C.: U.S. Government Printing Office, 1955–1958.

Staff Report, Subcommittee on Antitrust and Monopoly, Senate Judiciary Committee, Eighty-fourth Congress, 1st Session, *Bigness and Concentration of Economic Power—A Case Study of General Motors Corporation*. Washington, D.C.: U.S. Government Printing Office, 1956.

Staff Report, Subcommittee on Antitrust and Monopoly, Senate Judiciary Committee, Eighty-fifth Congress, 2nd Session, *Administered Prices: Automobiles*, Washington, D.C.: U.S. Government Printing Office, 1958.

United States v. *E. I. du Pont de Nemours & Co*. 353 U.S. 586 (1957).

JOURNAL AND MAGAZINE ARTICLES

"A New Kind of Car Market," *Fortune*, **48** (September 1953), 98.

"The Chrysler Operation," *Fortune*, **38** (October 1948), 103.

"Profits Margins at General Motors: A Background Study in Management Action," *The Corporate Director*, **6**, 3:1 (July 1956).

"Ford's Fight for First," *Fortune*, **50** (September 1954), 123.

"General Motors III," *Fortune*, **19** (February 1939), 71.

"Kaiser-Frazer," *Fortune*, **44** (July 1951), 74.

"Lincoln-Mercury Moves Up," *Fortune*, **45** (March 1952), 97.

Mason, E. S. "Current Status of the Monopoly Problem," *Harvard Law Review*, **62**:1265 (June 1949).

"SAE," *Fortune*, **38** (August 1948), 79.

"Success Story," *Fortune*, **12** (December 1935), 115.

"Super-Luxury Cars," *Fortune*, **55** (June 1957), 160.

Vanderblue, H. B. "Pricing Policies in the Automobile Industry," *Harvard Business Review*, **17**:385 (Summer 1939).

Vatter, H. G. "The Closure of Entry in the American Automobile Industry." *Oxford Economic Papers*, **4**:213 (October 1952).

Williams, Walter. "A Theory of the Declining Buick," *Current Economic Comment*, **21**:43 (November 1959).

"Will Success Spoil American Motors," *Fortune*, **59** (January 1959), 97.

9. Charles H. Hession
METAL CONTAINER INDUSTRY

I. INTRODUCTION
THE PACKAGING REVOLUTION

Although it is not generally recognized, packaging is one of the most important sectors of the American economy. In fact, it is the fourth largest manufacturing industry in the United States, surpassed in value of product only by steel, automobiles, and petroleum. The industry's sales for 1968 are expected to total $18.5 billion. The growing importance of packaging in our way of life is demonstrated by the fact that in the last 30 years the sales volume of packaging has tripled, whereas the Nation's population has risen about 54 per cent.

Americans increasingly understand that packaging in all its forms is an integral part of modern mass production and distribution. Packages are necessary to move the myriad products of our widely dispersed factories and farms to the points of consumption with dispatch and efficiency. In a mass consumption society, such as that of the United States, with considerable self-service merchandising, "the adequate package must be one that will both protect and 'sell' the product . . . ."[1]

The metal container industry is by far the biggest supplier of rigid containers in the nation. In 1968 metal containers and components comprised 20 per cent of estimated packaging sales. This industry has been the pacemaker in the packaging revolution that started at about the turn of this century. Technologically, the first half of the century was devoted to improvements in food preservation. Today, in this highly competitive field, the package maker must also "seek methods that will aid in merchandising the product held by the container; the emphasis is on shelf display and easy opening."[2]

---

[1] *The Role of Packaging in the United States Economy* (Cambridge, Mass.: Arthur D. Little, Inc., 1965), p. 38, privately published. This interesting study shows convincingly that the size and growth of the packaging industry in a nation is definitely related to the structural complexity of the economy. Its correlation analysis demonstrates that "there is a high degree of correlation between tin plate consumption and the degree of industrialization in an economy." (Ibid., page 35.)

[2] G. A. Vaughan, "Metal Cans," *Modern Packaging Encyclopedia* (New York: McGraw-Hill, 1968). Vol. 41, No. 7A, p. 295.

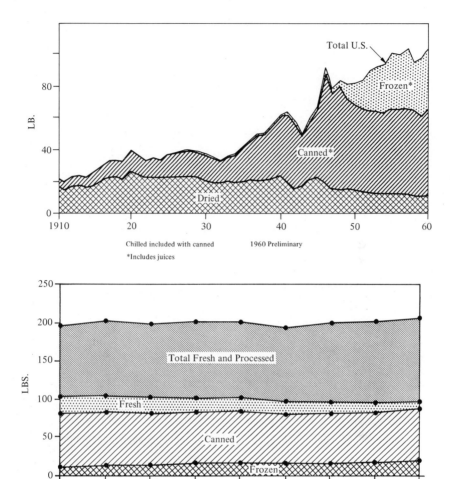

Figure 1

PROCESSED FRUIT CONSUMPTION
Use of processed fruit per person continues to increase.

SOURCE From M. S. Peterson and D. K. Tressler, *Food Technology the World Over*, Westport, Conn.: The Avi Publishing Co., 1963, p. 376.

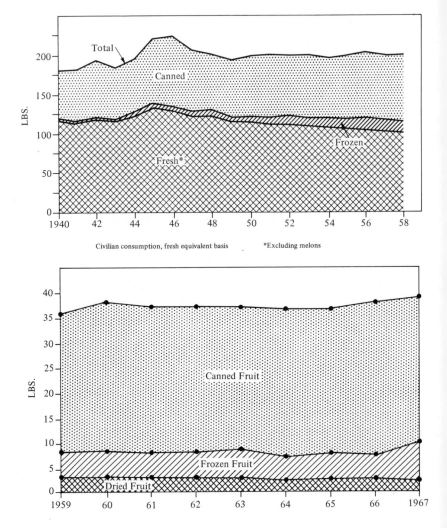

Figure 2

TOTAL VEGETABLE CONSUMPTION PER PERSON
Use of vegetables per person fairly stable since 1950.

SOURCE   From M. S. Peterson and D. K. Tressler, *Food Technology the World Over*, Westport, Conn.: The Avi Publishing Co., 1963, p. 376.

The metal can of today is rapidly changing both in its composition and method of manufacture. Challenged by other materials such as glass, plastics, and aluminum, the historic "tin can" is being transformed; the latest innovation, one of the industry's greatest technological "breakthroughs," is a tin-free steel can.[3]

The magnitude of the industry's production is stupendous; in 1967, it produced over 47 billion cans, using some million tons of steel for this purpose. This prodigious output meant that on a per capita basis the average American used about 252 cans a year. As a group, each family in the nation annually emptied the contents of nearly 850 metal containers—600 of them for food alone.[4]

TABLE 1 END-USE DISTRIBUTION OF METAL CANS, 1956 AND 1964 (PERCENTAGE OF TOTAL SHIPMENTS)

	1956	1964
Fruit and vegetables (including juice)	34.1%	29.7%
Evaporated and condensed milk	5.1	3.6
Other dairy products	1.1	0.5
Meat, including poultry	3.2	3.4
Fish and seafood	2.4	2.4
Coffee	4.1	3.9
Lard and shortening	2.3	1.8
Soft drinks	0.6	4.8
Beer	16.0	18.8
Baby food, including formulas, and all		
all other foods, including soup	10.1	11.1
Pet foods	3.5	4.2
Oil—open top, 1-, 4–5 quart	6.1	2.8
Paint, antifreeze, pressure cooking		
(valve type), and all other nonfood	11.4	12.3
	100.0	100.0

SOURCE   U.S. Department of Commerce, *Annual Review of Containers and Packaging*, **18**:13 (June 1965).

3   Actually, through much of its history, the tin can has been mostly a steel container, disguised and protected by a thin coating of tin. In 1960 the steel industry developed double-reduced tin plate, which made possible "thin" tin cans. In 1965, in a further effort to stave off the inroads of aluminum from its markets, tin-free steel cans were introduced; the latter are said to be cheaper than aluminum by about $2 per 1,000 cans. In 1967, aluminum was used in only about 4 per cent of metal cans produced, but it is estimated that 30 per cent of can production may be of aluminum by 1972. For the early history of the canning industry, see E. C. May, *The Canning Clan* (New York: Macmillan, 1937). For more recent analysis of the metal container industry, see J. W. McKie, *Tin Cans and Tin Plate* (Cambridge, Mass.: Harvard University Press, 1959), and the author's older study, *Competition in the Metal Food Container Industry, 1916–1946*, privately published, 1949.

4   Modern Packaging Encyclopedia, *op. cit.*, 1967, p. 352.

The industry's growth in the post-World War II years has been profoundly conditioned by significant changes in American consumption patterns. The rising popularity of frozen food, the increased use of plastic containers, the development of nonreturnable bottles and of composite containers have drastically affected the market for metal cans. Over the years 1947–1967, annual shipments of metal cans rose 81 per cent or at a rate of less than 4 per cent per year. The changing end-use distribution of metal cans is shown for the years 1956 and 1964 in percentage terms in Table 1. The most rapidly growing markets for metal cans in recent years have been for beer, soft drinks, and aerosol containers. As Table 1 shows, in percentage terms, the industry's most important outlet for its product, fruit and vegetable canning, has been declining in its relative standing. The industry has been able to raise its production and sales only by finding new markets with greater growth potentials than that of food canning. Although the tin can is becoming obsolete in some of its older uses, the modern metal container demonstrates its versatility and efficiency in many new forms almost daily. Currently, metal cans are used to package more than 2,500 products manufactured by over 135 industries.

HISTORY: THE INDUSTRY'S
CHANGING STRUCTURE

What is the nature of competition in this industry? Has the industry, which is a classic case of oligopoly, operated in the public interest or not? To answer these questions, we shall first examine the industry's market structure as it evolved up to 1950, the year of a court decision that had major effects on subsequent economic developments in this field.

The modern history of the metal container industry began in 1901 with the formation of the American Can Company. This combination was comprised of 95 of the leading can manufacturers and controlled at least 90 per cent of the nation's can-producing capacity. Indeed, in its early years American Can was popularly referred to as "the 100 per cent trust." The corporate financiers who dominated the new giant tried to capitalize on their monopolistic position by raising prices—and not by modest amounts. They succeeded merely in attracting a new and ultimately powerful competitor into the industry—the Continental Can Company, organized in 1904.

American Can had apparently attempted at the time of its formation to buttress its monopoly position by acquiring 13 of the principal manufacturers of can-making machinery and by making exclusive contracts with three others. It had also obtained control of major patents on such machinery. In addition, after 1901 it continued acquiring new competitors, and, most important, it received substantial rebates on its purchases of tin plate from the tin plate trust, the American Sheet and Tin Plate Company. Testimony in a later antitrust suit revealed that these rebates amounted to $9 million over the years 1902–1913 or, on an annual basis, an amount that was never below 20 per cent of the net profit of the company. Nevertheless, all these efforts to block new entry in the industry proved to be in vain. Patent control was futile because most of the basic patents on can-making had expired by 1901. The pace of technological development in the industry was so rapid that rivals were able to devise means to circumvent American Can's barriers. New entrants were also able to obtain their principal raw material, tin plate, on such terms as to make entry possible and even profitable. So it was that when the Federal Government finally brought suit in 1913 to dissolve American Can, the erstwhile monopoly had only about 63 per cent of the industry's sales. Continental Can sold 11.8 per cent of the packers' and general-line cans in that year.[5] Nine other firms accounted for the remaining 24.8 per cent of the sales; however, only four of them manufactured a full line of products.

After a long trial filling 8,700 pages of testimony, a lower court judge opined that he was "frankly reluctant to destroy so finely adjusted an industrial machine as the record shows the defendant to be."[6] The court found evidence of an attempt to establish a monopoly, but decided that it had failed. Impressed by American Can's technical services to the canning industry and by its research activities, it concluded: "In this case it appears probable that *all potential restraints upon free competition now imposed by the size and power of the defendant will pass away as speedily without as with dissolution,* and dissolution will cause far more loss and business disturbance than will attend the *gradual reestablishment of competitive conditions* by the free play of economic forces."[7] This decision, upholding the legality of the defendant because of its "good" behavior (after a misspent youth) and stressing the inexpediency of dissolution from a business point of view, foreshadowed the line of argument in the more well-known case against the United States Steel Corporation.[8] But what of the court's prognostication of a "gradual reestablishment of competitive conditions" in the industry? Did time bear out its prediction? Or, was this simply another example of a naive faith in the beneficent working of *laissez faire*?

Analysis of the changes in the competitive standing of the major tin can companies between 1916 and 1939 indicates, in fact, that a decided drift toward duopoly took place in the industry. By the later year, American Can still accounted for more than one half of tin container production (55.4 per cent of total sales of all types of cans). Continental Can, on the other hand, had increased its share of the business from 11.8 per cent in 1913 to more

---

5 Metal cans have customarily been classified into two main types: (1) food, or packer's cans; (2) general-line cans, such as those used to pack nonfood products which do not require heat treatment in the packaging process.

6 *United States* v. *American Can Co.,* 234 Fed. 1019 (1916).

7 *United States* v. *American Can Co., Supplemental Opinion and Decree,* July 7, 1916, p. 6 (Italics in original).

8 *United States* v. *United States Steel Corporation,* 251 U.S. 417 (1920).

than one fourth of the total sales in 1939.[9] Together, the two leading companies were doing more than 80 per cent of the business in that year. The remainder of the trade was shared by much smaller companies, none of which accounted for more than 5 per cent of sales.

American Can's expansion in the years 1916–1949 was practically all "from within," as the president of the company expressed it in his 1944 report to the stockholders. No outside interests or corporations were acquired in this country, perhaps out of fear that such acquisitions would be frowned on by the government. The company's huge physical growth in these years was financed almost entirely from profits.

In contrast, Continental Can grew to its 1949 scale by an ambitious process of merger and purchase of other concerns. These consolidations started in 1927 during the aggressive presidency of Carl C. Conway. Within 3 years Continental had absorbed 19 smaller companies, providing it with production facilities in the rapidly growing Pacific coast canning region and in other parts of the nation, and further diversifying its output of general-line cans. Between 1942 and 1950, Continental expanded heavily (again through merger) in the fields of paper and fiber cans, metal crowns (i.e., bottle caps and closures), cork products, and molded plastics.

II. MARKET STRUCTURE

The present structure of the metal container industry is the result of a process of continuous historical change. We have seen thus far how the practically complete monopoly of American Can at the beginning of this century evolved into a limited duopoly by 1949. To comprehend how this came about, we shall first analyze the conditions of entry in the industry because they have vitally affected its structure. Then, we shall consider to what extent economic concentration in the industry has changed since the so-called San Francisco judgments of 1950.

CONDITIONS OF ENTRY
IN THE YEARS 1916–1949

In 1916, the American Can Company stood accused of efforts to block entry into this industry by acquiring monopolistic control of patents and can-making machinery. The court concluded, however, that the company had failed in its objective. How free was entry into this industry in the years between 1916 and 1949? We need to know the answer to this question to understand the court decree of 1950.

---

9 U.S. Department of Justice, *Western Steel Plants and the Tin Plate Industry*, 79th Congress, 1st Session, Document No. 95 (Washington, D.C.: U.S. Government Printing Office, 1945), p. L1.

Theoretically, restriction of entry into an industry is really significant only when excess profits can be earned, since new firms are not likely to attempt to enter unless the rate of profits exceeds the normal rate of return on capital in enterprises of similar risk. In this connection, it is noteworthy that both American and Continental earned slightly higher profit rates during the 1920's than the average manufacturing corporation. American averaged 10.1 per cent and Continental 11.5 per cent on their respective capital investments for the years 1922–1928 inclusive; the average for 2,046 manufacturing corporations during the same years was 9.7 per cent.[10] Furthermore, the profit rate of American and Continental showed greater stability in the depression of the 1930's than that of the average manufacturing corporation; neither company earned less than 6 per cent on its capital investment during the worst years of that period.

Apart from the inducement of profits, another entry condition is the existence of persons or firms with the necessary, minimum "know-how." The manufacturers of general-line cans who were relatively numerous (there were 85 of them in 1939) had the technological knowledge required for packers' can production; the manufacturing methods used in making the two types of container are essentially similar. Yet, despite the apparent advantages in combining production of the two types of container, hardly any of the smaller general-line producers undertook manufacture of packers' cans in the period 1916–1949. As a matter of fact, there were just three new ventures in the latter field during those years—those of Crown Can, Owens-Illinois Can, and the Pacific Can Companies. Crown Can has survived to the present since its entry into the business in 1927. Owens-Illinois (a subsidiary of the important glass container company of the same name), on the other hand, was sold to Continental in 1944, after 8 years of unsuccessful effort to establish itself in the field. Pacific Can enjoyed a steady expansion in its sales and profits from 1934 until 1954 when it was acquired by the National Can Company.

The experience of the new entrants sheds a revealing light on the conditions of entry in this business in the period under consideration. For example, Crown Cork and Seal, the parent concern of Crown Can, was forced to sustain heavy losses during the 3 years of its existence (1936–1939). These losses were attributed in the trade to the company's efforts to "buy its way" into the industry by quoting prices some 6 per cent below those of the leading companies. Owens-Illinois laid its failure partly to its "incompatible position of attempting to promote sales of both types of containers," though the opinion in the canning business at the time was that there were other more substantial reasons.

---

10   R. Epstein, *Industrial Profits in the United States* (New York: National Bureau of Economic Research, 1935), p. 56.

In 1950, the Federal Government obtained identical court judgments against the two big can manufacturers that fundamentally affected the conditions of entry in this industry. We shall examine the provisions and consequences of these decrees, but it is important that we understand first the factors that apparently impeded entry in the years 1916–1949.

1. Control of patents or can-making machinery by the leading companies did not constitute an insuperable obstacle to entry. The three can makers that entered the packers' can industry between 1916 and 1949 were obviously able to obtain the necessary can-making and can-closing machinery. Nevertheless, in view of the "Big Two's" dominant patent position, newcomers did not have access to the most up-to-date machinery and hence could not hope to produce at the same speed and efficiency as they. (American Can boasted in its news magazine in 1937 that it had ten types of vacuum machines, whereas no competitor had more than two.) Unless a new enterprise could match the large companies' research and development efforts, its continued existence in the industry must have been precarious indeed.

2. A more serious impediment to entry in the years before 1950 was the industry's practice of leasing its can-closing machinery on a "tying clause" basis. Many of the can companies leased their machinery only on the condition that the lessee purchase all the containers he needed from the lessor. Although such leasing policies did not completely block new firms from entering the industry, they undoubtedly were major hurdles. These arrangements had the effect of emphasizing the type of nonprice competition in which American and Continental excelled. Closing machines require a considerable amount of servicing. In rendering that service—the leading companies had elaborate service organizations—they could entrench themselves in their customers' favor and thus ensure the continued sale of their containers. The practice of leasing the closing machines enabled the dominant companies to sell more cans by stressing the value of these services rather than the relative prices of the containers themselves. Entry into the industry was made more difficult because a new entrant, to be successful, had to offer his cans at competitive prices and attempt to duplicate the expensive services of the established companies as well. The size of the initial capital investment required was also increased because a considerable outlay had to be made for the machines that were leased to customers.

3. The long-term requirements contract in use in this industry before 1950 strongly militated against new entry. This barrier to new competition became even more effective in 1946 when American Can extended the length of its general supply contract for both metal and fiber cans from 3 to 5 years. Again, when the brewers turned, in part, from glass bottles to cans, American Can is reported to have insisted on 10-year contracts

before it would invest in the new manufacturing facilities to make such cans. Deductive reasoning suggests that the longer the term of such contracts, the smaller the number likely to expire in any one year. The conclusion seems inescapable: the extension of the term of the sales contract reduces the frequency with which a buyer reconsiders his source of supply and therefore narrows the opportunities for new firms.[11]

4. Another factor affecting entry in this industry is the amount of capital required for successful operation. In any industry the size of the initial investment required depends upon whether very large plants are needed to secure the economies of large-scale production and, secondly, whether there are economies of scale in the operation of multiple plants by one firm. In can manufacturing, reasonably efficient production is possible in small plant units. For example, it was reported in 1957 that a typical can-making line capable of producing 500 cans a minute cost about $1 million, including auxiliary equipment.[12] Further evidence of the fact that technology does not require huge plants for efficient can production is found in the policy of the can manufacturers dispersing their production in numerous plants throughout the nation. If efficiency were only possible in the very largest units, this decentralization of operations would be inadvisable.

All this means that the technical requirements of production do not explain the present size of the leading firms in can manufacturing. Other factors are certainly involved. What advantages (other than proximity to markets) are obtainable by the ownership of multiple plants that would be impossible for a new entrant to achieve, unless he organized on a similar basis? Economic analysis suggests that there are several types of economy that a multiple-plant firm might obtain. Among these are (1) larger quantity discounts in the purchase of raw materials; (2) savings in the cost of such "overhead" functions as research, financing, legal work, and advertising; (3) reduction of costs through ability to keep plants operating closer to capacity by meeting excess demand in some localities by shipping from plants that have idle capacity.

Subsequent analysis will reveal that the two leading can companies have marked advantages over their smaller rivals and over potential new entrants in some of these very respects. The volume production of these multiple-plant firms enabled them in the past to demand maximum quantity discounts on their tin plate purchases; however, the Robinson-Patman Act of 1936 drastically curbed the granting of unwarranted price concessions. New entrants were also probably discouraged by the amount of capital that was

---

11 For a general discussion of the economic consequences of requirements contracts, see G. Shillinglaw, "The Effects of Requirements Contracts on Competition," *Journal of Industrial Economics*, 2:147 (April 1954).

12 "Tin Cans Hustle to Hold Their Own," *Business Week*, 1445:179 (May 11, 1957).

needed to finance distribution and research facilities comparable to those of American or Continental. The economic barriers to entry in this industry were very formidable prior to the 1950 decrees that reformed many of the industry's market practices. On the favorable side, however, was the fact that the marked secular increase in the demand for packers' cans offered more opportunities for new concerns to grow than might otherwise have been the case. In general, the imperfections in the market for packers' cans before 1950, particularly as regards freedom of entry, definitely seem to warrant the conclusion that there were elements of monopoly profit in the earnings of the two major can companies in that period.

THE SAN FRANCISCO JUDGMENTS—THEIR IMPACT ON MARKET STRUCTURE
The so-called San Francisco judgments, resulting from the civil suits instituted against American and Continental by the Department of Justice in 1946, have had a fundamental bearing on the market structure, and especially on the conditions of entry in this industry. According to the government complaint, a triple-threat combination of policies had destroyed competition in can manufacture and in the can-closing field.[13] It was the defendant's policy, the government charged, to "lease machines only to customers, lease so far below cost that the customer must (in the economic sense) lease them, and contract with them on the basis of their total requirements for a long period of time. The intent and result: a monopolized market from which actual and potential competition are excluded."[14] By way of relief the government asked for cancellation of the offending machine leases and of the total requirements contracts and, most important, for divestiture of the can-closing part of the defendant's business.

In its decision the district court upheld most of the government's charges. It concluded that the 5-year requirements contract had unreasonably restricted trade in violation of the Sherman Act. It decided, however, contrary to the government's view, that a reasonable period for such contracts was 1 year. Further, such sales contracts in the future had to be negotiated and executed on the basis of the individual plants of each customer. Thus, it was hoped that the smaller can manufacturers would be able to bid at least for the business of a single plant of a multiplant firm.

The government regarded the machine leases of the can companies with their tying clauses as "the strategic bottleneck of the industry" and it asked for divestiture of this phase of the business from the sale of containers. But the court refused to divest the Big Two of their closing machines; instead, it

---

13 87 F. Suppl. 18 (1949) A consent decree containing provisions identical with those in the American Can judgment was entered against Continental Can on June 26, 1950. It will be understood that the discussion above pertains to both companies. For an excellent and more complete analysis of the practices against which the decrees were aimed as well as of their provisions, see J. W. McKie, *Tin Cans and Tin Plate*, op. cit., Ch. VIII.

14 *Brief for the United States of America*, Civil Action No. 2364H, p. 264.

ordered them for a period of 10 years to sell them to anyone and for 5 years to lease them to anyone other than a container manufacturer. Further, in order to facilitate entry of new independent firms into the manufacture of closing machines, the defendants were required to issue royalty-free non-restrictive licenses on them to any applicant and also provide the necessary "know-how" at cost. If machines were leased, the rentals could not be less than reasonable under all circumstances and after January 1, 1954, they had to be compensatory to the lessor. Thus, below-cost rentals could no longer be used by the dominant can companies as an inducement to lease. The most important provision of the decrees regulating the selling practices of the two companies was that which prohibited the granting of any annual cumulative-volume discounts for 5 years.

What were the effects of these judgments on entry and on the structure of the industry generally? What happened to the machine leases and the plan to have the can companies sell their closing equipment to the canners? Contrary to the district court's expectations, most canners were willing to purchase the closing machines on the terms offered. This was not altogether surprising, since the price formula set by the court was well below the replacement value of the machines. With rentals scheduled to rise to a compensatory level, it was logical for even the small canners to buy, which they did. By the middle of 1954, over 75 per cent of the closing machines of both American and Continental had been sold, and nearly all of them had been disposed of by the close of the following year. However, most of the buyers did not set up their own servicing departments, preferring to rely on those of the two big can manufacturers.

Although fundamental changes have taken place with respect to the machine leases and other practices, no major outsiders have entered the commercial manufacture of packers' cans since the 1950 decree.[15] According to one student of the industry,[16] the large packers now allocate their orders for cans to several suppliers rather than dealing exclusively with one seller; there was an enormous growth in open-order purchasing instead of by contract; and the smaller manufacturers were able to detach "fragments" of business from the two principal suppliers of cans with the result that their

---

15 The United States Hoffman Machinery Company entered the industry in 1955 by purchasing control of four small container manufacturers. This company is not really a competitor of the major food container makers because of its production of packers' cans is inconsequential. Starting in 1952, when it acquired a new management, National Can has become a more successful and aggressive competitor. In 1955 it acquired the Pacific Can Company. [See "Growth at National Can," *Financial World*, 128:5 (September 27, 1967).] Many of the self-manufacturers cited above produce only part of their requirements (tapered integration) and some, such as Sherwin-Williams, sell substantial quantities to outside buyers. On integrated manufacture of packers' and general-line cans, see McKie, *Tin Cans and Tin Plate*, op. cit., pp. 102–105.

16 J. W. McKie, "The Decline of Monopoly in the Metal Container Industry," *American Economic Review*, 45:506 (May 1955).

market position has been strengthened. The concentration of the industry's sales in the post-World War II years will be analyzed in a later section of the chapter.

THE ECONOMICS OF "SELF-MANUFACTURE" Perhaps the most important effect of the decrees was the impetus that they gave to the manufacture of cans by concerns for their own use. In the early years of this century, a large proportion of cans were made in captive plants; for example, in 1913 an estimated 29.4 per cent were so made. Manufacture for self-use declined in the intervening years until in 1954 it amounted to only 11.7 per cent of the total. This decline in self-manufacture was often cited in that period as an indication of the can industry's efficiency and overall performance. However, the enforcement of the Robinson-Patman Act with its ban on discriminatory prices led some users to change their methods of doing business. For instance, Campbell Soup, for a long time Continental's largest customer, began in 1937 to purchase tin plate and allow the can company to manufacture it into cans under contract. After the 1950 decree, Campbell bought machinery and by producing for its own use, became the nation's third largest can manufacturer. Self-manufacture has steadily grown in importance; by 1967, 23 per cent of can production was in this category. Besides Campbell Soup, the companies having captive can plants include H. J. Heinz, Pet Milk, the Carnation Company, California Packaging, Borden, Sherwin-Williams, Anheuser-Busch, and Texaco.

The big brewers have been the latest to manufacture their own cans; they have been urged by the aluminum companies to make their own containers from that light metal, and by using such threats they have wrung large concessions from the can makers. "Customers in the less well-organized food packing industry resent 'the favors that beer is getting' and talk of setting up their own canning operations."[17] Integration of can manufacture with food processing has been stimulated by several factors other than the 1950 decree. Interviews with food processors reveal that the main incentive pushing them into making their own cans was the need to cut costs. They cite the fact that can prices have more than doubled since World War II. Some of them anonymously claimed savings of as much as 10–20 per cent from self-manufacture, after depreciation. "A machinery supplier [not an impartial adviser, to be sure] claims the equipment pays for itself in as little as four years." On the other hand, the president of American Can ridiculed expectations of such large economies.[18]

Two fundamental factors affecting the decision "to make or buy" containers are (1) the prospective annual volume of production and (2) the regularity of container requirements over the year. Without adequate volume,

---

17 "Canners Profit from Price War," *Business Week*, **1537**: 54 (February 14, 1959).

18 "Captive Cans," *Wall Street Journal* (April 8, 1959).

the initial investment in can-making equipment would not be justified, and unless production is reasonably stable over the year idle plant and overhead costs would destroy the profitability of the operation. Despite these problems, many packers believed that they could achieve the necessary volume (40 million cans of one size per year), and that they could stabilize their operations by packing a variety of crops from different picking seasons, by storing cans for later use, or by selling their surplus can production on the open market. Integration, they claim, is profitable because it yields the following economies: (1) transportation costs are less because tin plate packages are compact and cost less to ship by railroad than bulky, easily damaged cans. (2) Handling costs are reduced. An executive of Stokely-Van Camp, a leading food packer, remarks: "We go direct from manufacturing right into production lines." (3) Canners also claim they avoid some of the overhead costs that the commercial can-makers must add to their selling prices.

If the economies of integration are as large as claimed, the movement is likely to spread. Given the small margins of profit in food processing, "savings from can-making enjoyed by one firm tend to draw others into similar ventures." The big can manufacturers, of course, have been aware of this possibility and they have taken a number of steps to counteract it. They have located new plants closer to their customers in order to save freight costs and they have also offered extra services, such as free warehousing space, to hold their accounts. Their research and engineering work has been intensified to improve can-manufacturing methods. In 1959 the major companies took drastic action in the field of price policy to discourage the establishment of captive plants.

The hazards in self-manufacture have been recently illustrated by the introduction of the tin-free can. This development, hailed by one top executive as "the biggest breakthrough in fifty years," was patented by American Can in 1965; Continental developed an alternative method of manufacture, the welded seam, in 1966. American was reported to be licensing other commercial can-makers to use its process, but not canners who make their own cans.[19] The tin-less can is said to cost 8–10 per cent less than the conventional container. One commentator stated: "Self-manufacturing canners may eventually be obliged to increase their business with can-makers if they cannot find a way of counteracting American Can's policy through the courts."[20]

In summarizing this brief analysis of the consequences of the 1950 judgments, we may merely note how they disturbed the economic equilibrium of the can industry. They did this not so much by enticing new entrants to undertake commercial production of cans, but by encouraging integration by the large buyers.

---

19 F. Lachelier, "As Container Industry Benefits from Mammoth Sales in Foods and Beverages," *Magazine of Wall Street*, **118**:316 (June 11, 1966).
20 Ibid., p. 318.

ECONOMIC CONCENTRATION
SINCE 1950

Although the industry's leaders have been shaken by the development of self-manufacture since 1950, their superior market position has not been seriously damaged; in addition, they have grown tremendously through diversification into other lines of manufacture. The changes in the industry's concentration ratios are presented in Table 2. We note that the concentration ratio for the four largest concerns did not show any major change until 1963 when there was an unaccountable drop to 74 per cent. As of 1967, the four leading metal-can manufacturers were reported to have the following shares of the industry's sales: American Can (38 per cent), Continental Can (31 per cent), National Can (about 7 per cent), and Crown Cork and Seal (4 per cent).[21] The two leading companies, on the basis of these statistics, had 69 per cent of total sales as compared with the 80 per cent they had in 1939. National Can's share of total sales of metal cans increased from 2.5 per cent in 1946 to 7 per cent as of 1967. Crown Cork and Seal suffered a slight decline in its share of the business over the same years.

TABLE 2 CONCENTRATION IN THE VALUE OF SHIPMENTS, TIN CANS AND OTHER TINWARE, 1935–1963 (SELECTED YEARS) (VALUE OF SHIPMENTS IN THOUSANDS OF DOLLARS)

YEAR	NUMBER OF COMPANIES	VALUE OF SHIPMENTS	VALUE OF SHIPMENTS (%)	
			FOUR LARGEST	EIGHT LARGEST
1935	NA[a]	NA[a]	80	85
1947	102	678,924	78	86
1954	109	1,366,766	80	88
1958	84	1,803,672	80	89
1963	99	2,075,000	74	85

a NA—means "not available." The above figures include the shipments of many small manufacturers of general line cans, most of which do not produce packers' cans.

SOURCE Subcommittee on Antitrust and Monopoly, *Concentration Ratios in Manufacturing Industry* (Washington, D.C.: U.S. Government Printing Office, 1962), pp. 11, 31; 1963 statistics from *Statistical Abstract for 1968* (Washington, D.C.: U.S. Government Printing Office), pp. 729, 730.

21 Standard and Poor's Industry Surveys, *Containers—Basic Analysis* (New York: Standard and Poor's, 1968), Sec. 4, p. C72.

THE BUYER'S SIDE OF THE MARKET   To understand the process of price formation in this industry, we need to consider the structure of the industries that purchase metal containers. The largest single user of metal cans is the fruit and vegetable canning industry. Concentration of production and sales is much less pronounced in this industry than in can manufacture. As of 1963, the Census Bureau reported that there were 1,135 packers of fruits and vegetables. These food packers vary greatly in financial strength, ranging from concerns with net tangible assets of as little as $15,000 to those with many millions of dollars. In 1963, the four largest packers controlled 24 per cent of the value of shipments; the eight largest, 34 per cent.[22] In considering the significance of these figures, it must be noted that the leading canners have turned to self-manufacture for most of their container needs. The can companies, on the whole, are dealing in the market with the smaller concerns.

The canning industry in the past has been described as "the most harshly competitive industry in America." Actually, each packer has a "monopoly" of his own brand, but brands are numerous and substitution relatively easy. In addition, canned food must compete with frozen, dehydrated, and fresh products. Therefore, despite the relatively high degree of concentration that exists in the sale of some products, it seems reasonable to conclude that food canning is predominantly competitive. In general, the canning industry contrasts sharply with that of can manufacture with respect to the number of producers and the concentration of sales. The bargaining power of most canners is weakened by their relatively small size, the peculiar risks of the industry, the comparatively inelastic demand for their products, and the intense price competition that often characterizes their sale. On the other hand, the bargaining position of the largest canners is enhanced by their ability to manufacture their own cans.

The brewing industry is also less concentrated than can manufacturing, but in its bargaining with the can companies it has shown an enviable degree of unity. According to *Business Week*, "The canmakers' beer business is spread among a relatively small number of big-volume customers—and they have proved to be tough customers . . . 'When it comes to cans, the boys [i.e., the brewers] don't compete,' says an industry expert. 'When one brewer wrangles a price concession, it's just about five minutes before the others are around asking for theirs, too.'"[23] The can companies' problems in dealing with the brewers are complicated by the fact that the aluminum companies, notably Reynolds, have been pressing for their business; some of them have also turned to self-manufacture. Soft drinks, another growing market for cans, includes some big companies equally capable of hard bargaining.

22   *Statistical Abstract of the United States* (Washington, D.C.: U.S. Government Printing Office, 1968), p. 730.

23   "Canners Profit from Price War, *Business Week*, **1537**:54 (February 14, 1959).

III. MARKET CONDUCT

Market conduct refers to business behavior in changing prices, output, product characteristics, selling and research expenditures. Such conduct is often thought to be circumscribed by market structure, but in many instances there is room for a large element of policy or discretion. Generally, the theory of market conduct is regarded as linking the industry's structure to the quality of its performance.[24] Thus, one economist writes: "In some industries the conduct of sellers seems almost a conditioned reaction, so clearly does the configuration of structural elements force a certain pattern of behavior on the firms." But he quickly adds: "In the metal can industry the matter is not so clear-cut as that. Although market structure has influenced the behavior of the large firms, it has not thrust upon them the policies that they have actually followed."[25]

The structural elements involved in the market practices of the can industry have been very complex and in recent years they have been subject to extensive change. As a matter of fact, the structures of at least three industries have been basic to the market practices we are concerned with—can manufacturing, canning, and the tin plate production. Essentially, can manufacturers in the past have simply been converters—they have turned tin plate into containers for a wide diversity of customers in a variety of industries. Perhaps we may best begin to unravel some of these complexities by considering the historic relationship of can manufacture to the tin plate industry.

In the past, the price of tin plate has been of controlling importance in the economics of the can industry because that raw material was, by far, the principal item of cost in the manufacture of metal containers. The cost of tin plate has traditionally averaged between 60 and 65 per cent of the selling prices of cans made from that material.

The market for tin plate is especially interesting to economists because it is a striking illustration of bilateral oligopoly. As J. W. McKie has pointed out: "This whole industry from top to bottom is characterized by substantial buying power at each stage; the makers of tin plate are the chief buyers of tin, and purchase it from a cartelized industry; they sell in turn in an oligopolistic market, while the buyers of tin plate themselves face some influential purchasers among canners, and the canners are subject to pressure from chain stores. . . ."[26]

---

24 R. Caves, *American Industry: Structure, Conduct, Performance* (Englewood Cliffs, N.J.: Prentice-Hall, 1964), p. 36.

25 J. W. McKie, *Tin Cans and Tin Plate*, op. cit., p. 145.

26 J. W. McKie, *Bilateral Oligopoly in Industrial Product Markets*, unpublished doctoral dissertation, Harvard University, 1951, p. 284.

The "rung" of this ladder of buying power which is of immediate interest to us is that involving the sale of tin plate. This product, characterized by a high degree of concentration in its sale, is produced in the United States by the large integrated steel companies almost exclusively. In recent years, the four largest producers have shipped more than three quarters of all the electrolytic tin plate made in this country. The sellers' side of the market, therefore, is definitely oligopolistic, whereas the concentration in the metal container industry makes for oligopsony (few buyers). In short, tin plate is bought and sold under conditions of bilateral oligopoly.

In the pre-World War II period tin plate was sold on the basis of long-term contracts, which usually ran for 5 or 10 years. These contracts did not specify a definite price, but provided that it should be the seller's ruling current price at the time the order for the product was placed, less certain discounts. The price of tin plate was usually published about December 1 and it was effective for the following 9 months; actually, it was good for 12 months. During that period, the price could not go any higher, but it might be lowered; in effect, it was a ceiling price.

The contracts under which the leading can companies secured their tin plate further stated that the price for the year should be "the officially announced domestic base price of the Carnegie Illinois Steel Corporation [a U.S. Steel subsidiary]. . . ." This was one of the few instances in American industry in which a system of price leadership was embodied explicitly in the sales contracts, with the price leader specified as such. By this device the other tin plate producers partially abdicated their price-making function to the largest manufacturer of the product. (We say "partially" because there is evidence that in time of slack demand the smaller producers often shaded the leader's price.) The can companies, in turn, apparently delegated American Can to negotiate for them with Carnegie Illinois. In other words, the leadership principle was followed on both sides of the market.

In the years since 1946, inflationary pressures, strikes, and material shortages have generally made for a seller's market. Buyers and sellers have negotiated with each other separately over the price of tin plate. The steel industry continued to announce tin plate prices annually until 1956, when it went on a 6-month contractual basis, with prices published on May 1 and November 1. Later, U.S. Steel announced that it was discontinuing the practice and that, after January 1, 1958, all revisions of tin mill products would be made not less than 35 days prior to the effective date of the changes. Buyers would pay the price in effect at the time of shipment. This departure from the traditional long-term pricing of tin plate reflected the need of producers for more flexibility to meet their changing costs. Can makers opposed the change, but their objections were to no avail.

In pricing tin cans, American Can early in this century began to use an escalator clause under which the quoted price of cans was tied to the quoted price of tin plate. When the posted price of tin plate changed, the whole price structure for cans would change at once. In the years before World War II, tin plate prices were announced annually and the container prices based on them were generally stable over the course of the canning season. This seasonal stabilization of can prices eliminated one element of cost uncertainty for the canners. In the post-World War II inflationary years, these pricing practices were modified and finally abandoned altogether. In 1946, American Can added a labor-escalator clause to its long-term contract. The Labor Cost Index of the Department of Labor was used in adjusting can prices; for each change of $.025 in the index the price of cans changed by a differential appropriate to the type of can. By this means American Can could raise its can prices to reflect the general wage inflation without giving the buyer the right to cancel the contract.[27] In 1950, as we have seen, the 5-year contract gave way to the 1-year contract as ordered by the court in the antitrust case of that year. Since then both tin plate and tin can prices have been changing more frequently than in the past, even within the canning season. The seasonal stabilization of can prices which lasted for half a century is no more.

The other market practices which prevailed in the can industry before 1950 were (1) the long-term requirements contract; (2) the granting of price discounts and, prior to 1937, of special concessions to large buyers; (3) the tied purchase of cans to the lease on closing machinery. The first of these practices was modified by the 1950 decree; the second was drastically affected by the Robinson-Patman Act; and the third has been abolished altogether. These changes in the industry's conduct have had revolutionary effects on the objectives and performance of its leading firms.

Prior to 1950, American Can tended to minimize the importance of can prices. Its can contracts placed the focus on the provision of services. Under the standard packers' contract, prices to every buyer fluctuated with tin plate and labor costs, on a standard formula basis. American Can emphasized its technical services, technological improvements and the seasonal price stability it provided the canners. It did not appear to think in terms of a given target rate of return on its investment, but was concerned more with maintaining its share of the market.[28] In the more dynamic and competitive conditions which have prevailed in the industry since 1950, American Can seems to have placed more stress on a policy of meeting competition rather than one of pricing to finance services and technological progress.

Apart from the development of self-manufacture, the most important trend in this industry since the 1950 decree has been the move toward further diversification by the leading companies. American and Continental had ventured in this direction before World War II, but the tendency has become

---

27 Continental did not add a labor-escalator clause at this time. It retained the right to change prices during the term of the contract instead. The customer could cancel, however, if Continental changed prices for any reason other than a change in tin plate prices. National and Crown changed prices more frequently and did not employ the escalator clause.

28 A. D. H. Kaplan et. al., *Pricing in Big Business* (Washington, D.C.: The Brookings Institution, 1958), pp. 208–209.

more pronounced in recent years. The factors underlying this policy are several. The growth of user-manufacture, the competition of such dynamic industries as frozen foods, plastics, and so on, the relative slow growth rate of the canning industry, the advent of more sales-oriented management and the development of organizational maturity have all played a part. In the midst of this highly competitive packaging revolution, the big companies had of necessity to redefine their objectives, if they were to continue to grow. Continental began to diversify in 1942, acquiring about a dozen firms in fiber containers, glass, plastics, paper bags, and other products. The acquisition of Hazel-Atlas Glass Company and the Robert Gair Company in 1956 were part of this aggressive search for growth. By 1967 Continental derived only about 57 per cent of its sales from metal cans.

American Can had entered fiber production as early as 1913 and later became one of the leading producers of fiber milk containers. It set out on its modern course of diversification in 1951. It moved into paper cups, plastic tubes, and so on, and in 1960 it also ventured into glass container manufacture. By 1968 metal cans accounted for 55 per cent of the American Can sales, as compared with 85 per cent a decade earlier. In that year American Can moved further toward a conglomerate operation when it acquired the Printing Corporation of America (printer of numerous trade and business periodicals) and the Butterick Company, Inc., world-famous pattern maker. According to American Can's annual report, these acquisitions "demonstrates its commitment in the growing fields of education and leisure-time activities."[29]

Since the 1950 decree, if not before, the leading can companies have increasingly conceived themselves as packaging manufacturers rather than being confined to the sale of one basic product. Like many other large American corporations, they have become multiproduct and multinational in the scope of their operations. They too have sought the economies of growth[30] and in so doing they have become market oriented rather than product oriented. Their concern with growth and performance have led them, in effect, to redefine their industrial environment. If we are to understand how the structure of the markets in which they operate affects them, we must comprehend how they *perceive* that environment. For in social psychology, if not in pure economics, behavior is a response not to the objective, but to the perceived or subjective environment. The new field of organizational analysis attempts to understand business behavior in these terms.[31]

---

29 American Can Company, *Annual Report*, 1967, p. 6.

30 On this, see E. Penrose, *The Theory of the Growth of the Firm* (New York: Wiley, 1959), pp. 99–103.

31 For an analysis of pricing in the can industry along these lines, see R. M. Cyert and J. C. March, *A Behavioral Theory of the Firm* (Englewood Cliffs, N.J.: Prentice-Hall, 1963), p. 93 ff.

IV. MARKET PERFORMANCE
PRICE POLICIES

$\mathbf{T}$hree phases of the price policies of the metal container industry will be treated in this section, namely, (1) price leadership, (2) price discrimination, and (3) the stability of can prices.

1. Price leadership   Price leadership has been one of the common practices resorted to by oligopolists to avoid the uncertainty and possible cut-throat competition which often prevail in a highly competitive type of market structure. This pattern of concurrent pricing, as it has been called, existed for many years in the metal container industry. For example, in the 1916 antitrust suit against the industry's leading firm the court said: "The American Can Company practically establishes the market price for packers' cans. . . . The competitors of the American Can Company manufacturing packers' cans, as a rule, adopt the published prices."[32] The court qualified this finding by noting that Continental and Wheeling Can Companies had strictly adhered to American's prices, whereas the smaller companies frequently gave concession of from 2 to 6 per cent off the leader's prices. American Can's published prices established the base line of competition, so to speak, for the minor concerns as well as for Continental, but because of the successful differentiation of product by the two leaders (especially in terms of service) the smaller companies had to resort to price reductions to obtain business.

In 1946, the Federal Government charged that the identity between American and Continental Can in California was due to direct collusion rather than to the practice of price leadership.[33] The indictment alleged that the observed price uniformity was the result of "a continuing agreement and concert of action among the defendants" from approximately 1935 to 1946. American and Continental pleaded *nolo contendere*, and paid the maximum but insignificant fines that were imposed by the court: $25,000 for American Can and $20,000 for Continental Can.

Although the prices charged by the two major can companies tended to be uniform in the years 1916 to 1946, indirect price concessions, such as liberal credit terms, generous treatment of customers' spoilage claims, low rentals for closing machines and the like, were common in time of slack business; but usually competition was diverted into nonprice forms, and the close harmony on prices between the two giants of the industry was preserved.

In the post-World War II years and especially after the 1950 decrees, the rivalry between American and Continental became more intense—climaxed by the revolutionary price developments of 1958–1959. For the first time in more than 50 years, American Can's price leadership was defied and rejected by its arch rival. It all started conventionally enough when U.S. Steel an-

---

32   *U.S.* v. *American Can*, 234 Fed. 168.

33   *U.S.* v. *American Can et al.*, Cr. 30323-A (N.D. Calif., 1946), par. 20.

nounced another increase in tin plate prices, 35 cents more per base box, effective November 1, 1958. In anticipation of this action, American Can had announced in September a 6 per cent increase on all can lines. At the same time, American Can stated that starting November 1, it would break with traditional industry pricing practice by establishing a policy under which changes would be made in can prices in direct relationship to the costs involved in each type of can. Formerly, the company explained, a flat percentage increase had been applied. According to *Business Week*, "Instead of mirroring this price change, Continental announced it would impose only a 3 per cent increase. Then the price war began." [34]

American Can retaliated against its recalcitrant follower with a series of direct price cuts averaging 2–5 per cent, depending upon the size and type of can; these changes were estimated as saving buyers more than $9 million. Starting January 1, 1959, the new prices were to be based on separate f.o.b. quotations at each of its 68 plants for each type and size of can. (Previously, the industry had two general pricing areas—east and west of the Rocky Mountains.) Under the revised policy, American Can's prices were to be based on the actual transportation costs of steel and tin plate delivered to the company's plants, as well as the cost of delivery to the company's customers. Continental promptly matched these price changes, including the breweries in its concessions, and moved the effective date ahead 2 weeks. American Can, then, with equal promptness, matched its rival's earlier date.

According to some trade sources, the price cutting went on after this, though there was little mention of it in business journals. The president of the National Can Company, largest of the independents, was quoted as saying: "American and Continental are cutting their own throats—and ours along with them. Every price line has been cut at least twice; there have been six cuts in beer cans. And I'll be surprised if they don't cut down even further." [35]

These fears were soon realized. On April 2, 1959, general reductions of from 4 to 10 per cent in prices were made by American Can on packers' cans; Continental and National Can immediately announced similar reductions. American Can in large newspaper ads presented this action to the public as being its contribution to the fight against inflation as well as reflecting its efficiency and desire to have cans made by expert can makers. A Continental Can spokesman frankly said its cuts were designed to keep packers from manufacturing their own cans.

A week later the president of American Can told reporters that the industry was not engaged in a price war, but conceded that the primary reason for the price reductions was to halt the growth of can manufacture by individual food processors. Terming self-manufacture "a very serious threat to the future of our can business," he disclosed that the company's January

---

34 "Canners Profit from Price War," *Business Week*, **1537**: 54 (February 14, 1959).

35 Ibid., p. 55.

price reductions had staved off plans of six large customers to make their own cans.

In retrospect, it would seem that the price upheaval was due fundamentally to the abolition of aggregate price discounts under the terms of the 1950 decrees, the threats to integrate by the big users as container costs went up because of inflation, and American Can's adoption of the coil processing method. The latter step probably made its cost of plate sufficiently lower at specific plants relative to those of competitors that it was induced to establish its new method of price quotation. The disruption of price uniformity seems to have stemmed basically from disagreement between the Big Two as to the proper level of "limit pricing" they should follow to deter self-manufacture by their customers. This disagreement may readily be understood in terms of differences in the size of their respective customers and their related abilities to produce cans for themselves.

Since 1959 the price front in the can industry has not been as disturbed as it was in that extraordinary year. As Table 3 shows, tin plate prices were advanced twice between November 1958 and January 1967 for an increase of about 5.5 per cent. During the same period the selling price of No. 2 cans increased seven times, part of the advances being necessary to offset higher labor costs incurred by the March 1965 contract settlements with the United

TABLE 3　TIN PLATE COSTS AND CAN PRICES IN THE UNITED STATES, 1958–1967 (DATES SHOWN ARE WHEN PRICE CHANGES BECAME EFFECTIVE)

TIN PLATE (NO. 25 POUND ELECTROLYTIC PER BASE BOX OF 100 SHEETS)		NO. 2 CANS (ON A NO. 25 POUND ELECTROLYTIC PLAIN BASIS PER 1,000 CANS)	
	($)		($)
Nov. 1, 1958	9.10	*March 10, 1958*	35.62
Nov. 17, 1965	9.35	*Nov. 15, 1958*	35.62
Oct. 16, 1967	9.60	*Jan. 1, 1959*	34.22
		April 1, 1959	32.82
		Jan. 15, 1960	33.31
		Jan. 1, 1961	34.03
		Jan. 1, 1962	35.10
		Feb. 1, 1964	35.95
		May 1, 1965	37.19
		Dec. 1, 1967	37.84
		Jan. 1, 1967	38.99

SOURCE　Standard and Poor's Industry Surveys, *Containers—Basic Analysis* (New York: Standard and Poor's Corp., November 14, 1968), Section 4, p. C75.

Steel Workers. The total price increase over this time works out to a gain of 9.4 per cent for that size can. As one financial analysis of the industry reported: "Aided by strong demand generated by the high level of economic activity, [profit] margins widened notably in the 1964–1966 period. However, the threat of self-manufacture, especially by large vegetable and fruit producers, had a restrictive influence on margins over the past decade. This seems likely to ease in the years ahead as more packers will probably want to maintain their container flexibility, and many realize that rapidly changing technology could obsolete their captive lines. . . ."[36]

2. Price discrimination   In the past the most important form of price discrimination in this industry has been the granting of excessive quantity discounts to large buyers. The adjective "excessive" is basic here, because discriminatory quantity discounts can only be said to exist when the varying amounts that a seller offers cannot be justified in terms of the identifiable production and marketing costs incurred in the handling of different-sized orders. The economic conditions that are conducive to this form of price discrimination are pronounced in the canning industry; we refer to the great differences in size, bargaining power, and the consequent varying elasticity of demand of individual packers. The very large concerns, as we have seen, have real possibilities of choice in deciding whether to buy cans or to manufacture for their own use. This fact in itself makes their demand for cans potentially more elastic (at least in the long run) than that of the small canner, and makes the granting of price concessions to the former more probable.

Before the passage of the Robinson-Patman Anti-Price Discrimination Act of 1936, American Can was the defendant in two such suits. In both of them, the courts held that a large packer had received discounts on its can purchases of 18 and 20 per cent, respectively, which were prejudicial to its smaller competitors.[37] After the new law was passed, it is said that American Can was happy to be able to tell its large customers who were demanding "free closing machinery, credit without interest, freight rebates, and indiscriminate discounts" that such "wild cards" were now prohibited. At that time, the company discontinued its practice of giving discounts by private negotiation and published a schedule under which 1 per cent was allowed to firms buying $500,000 worth of containers in a year, 2 per cent to those buying $1 million, 3 per cent to those buying $3 million, and 4 per cent to those buying $5 million or more. The biggest buyers thus lost discounts that were later shown to have ranged up to 14 per cent. Concurrently, American Can cut its base prices to all customers by 8 per cent; this move was probably designed to prevent its large customers from manufacturing their own cans.

---

36   Standard and Poor's Industry Surveys, *Containers—Basic Analysis* (New York: Standard and Poor's Corp., November 14, 1968), Sec. 4, p. C76.

37   *George Van Camp and Sons* v. *American Can Co.*, 278 US 245 (1929) and *American Can Co.* v. *Ladoga Canning Co.* 44 F. 2nd 763 (7th Circuit, 1930).

In 1946, American Can issued a new schedule of quantity discounts that applied, for the first time, to the smaller buyers. The revised list started with purchases of $50,000 on which 0.2 per cent was granted and rose gradually to 3 per cent on purchases of $4 million and over.

After World War II, American had to defend itself against two treble damage suits filed by small customers. In *Bruce's Juices*, the plaintiff eventually lost its appeal to the Supreme Court because of its refusal to pay for cans for which American was charging it more than it charged other competing firms.[38] In its treble damage action in Florida, however, Bruce's Juices was more successful; the district court there found that American Can was evading the prohibitions of the Robinson-Patman Act and the court of appeal sustained the decision.[39] In the second case,[40] American Can's discount system was ultimately held to be satisfactory by the courts, but the company was vulnerable on another issue, and hence made a private settlement of the suit.

In the long run, so far as price discrimination was concerned, these Robinson-Patman cases were much less important that the 1950 decrees that banned cumulative quantity discounts. Those prohibitions, as we have already noted, brought about revolutionary changes in the industry's price structure and contributed greatly to the recent trend toward self-manufacture.

3. Stability of can prices   One of the most obvious characteristics of the published prices of packers' cans prior to World War II was their relative stability over a period of time. The prices of cans were much more stable between 1924 and 1939 than the selling prices canners obtained for their canned fruit and vegetables. This stability was evident over the course of the canning season, i.e., for as long as a year, and for periods as long as three consecutive years prior to wartime price stabilization. The major reason for this pre-World War II stability of can prices was the escalator clause of the packers' can contract, which tied the price of such containers to the price of tin plate, with the result that the former displayed the same degree of price stability as the price of the raw material.

The economic consequences of price stabilization depend very largely on the duration of time over which stability is maintained. Canners have expressed strong support for price stabilization of cans over the canning season.[41] Day-to-day variations in can prices (as under spot pricing) would create intolerable uncertainty for the average canner. Many canners contract

---

38   *Bruce's Juices, Inc.* v. *American Can Co.*, 330 U.S. 743 (1947).

39   87 F. Suppl. 985 (S.D. Fla. 1949) and 187 D. 2nd 923.

40   *Russellville Canning Co.*, v. *American Can Co.*, 87 F. Suppl. 484. (W.D. Ark. 1949); *American Can Co.* v. *Russellville Canning Co.* 191 F. 2nd. 38 (8th Cir. 1951).

41   See Temporary National Economic Committee, *Hearings*, Part 20 (Washington, D.C.: U.S. Government Printing Office, 1940), pp. 10761 and 10762; also *United States* v. *American Can Co.*, 87 F. Supp. 18 (N.D. Cal. 1949), pp. 5391–5392, 5453–5455, 5873–5876, 7011–7014.

in advance for raw produce at definite prices, but with the quantities unspecified. To do this they must be able to predict their can costs within a narrow range. Furthermore, stable can prices enable them to hypothecate their pack or to sell futures in order to obtain short-term financing. The canners prefer to have stable prices during periods of peak demand, even though it means they must forgo lower prices during a time of deficient demand.

Under the new price policies in effect since 1958 tin plate and tin can prices are subject to change within a month's notice. Nevertheless, can prices are still fairly stable during the canning season. The steel producers do not change tin plate prices every month; nor do the can manufacturers raise prices during the season because of increased demand for containers. The degree of price variation that exists is probably much more satisfactory to the canners than what would be likely under spot pricing.

Stabilization of can prices over periods longer than the canning season, i.e., over the period of a business cycle or longer has been more controversial. In the years 1929–1933, for example, it was argued that the relative inflexibility of can prices threw the burden of adjustment on the flexibly priced commodities; the canner was caught in a "squeeze" between relatively rigid prices for his containers and falling prices for his pack. Secular price stabilization (i.e., over periods of time longer than the average business cycle) has not been possible in the post-World War II years of inflation.

NONPRICE COMPETITION

By nonprice competition economists mean the rivalry in service, advertising, and product development and improvement. This kind of competition is very common in oligopolistic industries, and the metal container industry is no exception. In fact, one study of the pricing practices of big business found that "the clearest among those companies surveyed, in its emphasis on nonprice competition as a basis of price policy, was probably American Can. The policy of this company of automatically transmitting to its customers increases or decreases in basic costs—tin plates and wages—removed its prices from the executives' roster of items with which they must have constant concern. Possibly even more important was the emphasis of this company on routine and special services to its customers. American Can, having relegated price to the background, and having enjoyed a position as price leader, was able safely to concentrate on the provision of service and the devising of innovations. . . ."[42] (This summary may have some accuracy in it, as it pertained to conditions before 1958; in the years after 1958, the executives of American Can and other can companies have not been able to be so complacent about prices.)

---

42 A. D. H. Kaplan et al., *Pricing in Big Business* (Washington, D.C.: The Brookings Institution, 1958), pp. 260 and 261.

The can industry's research and development activities have come to be very highly regarded in recent years. For example, in 1957 an authoritative journal of the packaging trade stated that the industry's research facilities are "among the finest and most extensive in the entire packaging field."[43] Indeed, it seems incontrovertible that the rivalry of the Big Two in these areas has been largely responsible for the sensational fifteenfold increase in the demand for metal cans during the first half of this century. Consistently, over the years, their engineers and scientists have made breakthroughs in chemical, metallurgical, and mechanical research to produce numerous "firsts," such as beer cans, motor oil cans, baby food cans, and so on.

The process of innovation has been accelerated in recent years not only by the competition among the can-makers themselves, but by inter-industry competition. The producers of aluminum reduced prices to win markets traditionally supplied by tin plate. The glass container manufacturers developed the nonreturnable bottle, seeking to capture the lucrative market for beer containers. In self-defense, the can-makers in 1961 introduced cans made out of thinner tin plate, and the next year, the lift-tab end for beer containers. In 1965 they scored their greatest triumph with tin-free steel cans.[44] The unremitting competition in packaging among these substitute materials led one chief executive of a can company to express a desire to get into fields other than packaging "where there is a constant battle on the margins."[45]

As to service competition, it is widely recognized that the big can companies are more thoroughly organized and equipped for customer service than most supplier industries. Their former practice of rental of can-closing machinery contributed to their becoming the "technical assistant of the canning industry."

THE INDUSTRY'S PERFORMANCE

IN PROFIT TERMS

In the post-World War II period the industry's profit rate has not been as high as it was in the pre-World War II years. American Can, for example, had a mean rate of operating profit on sales of 12.1 per cent in the 1920's, 13.7 per cent in the 1930's, 10.5 per cent in the 1940's, and 10.0 per cent in the years 1950–1955. In the late 1950's and early 1960's, the earnings of the industry failed to keep pace with sales growth. However, in the 1964–1967 period, widening profit margins and a lower tax rate contributed to higher profit ratios. Profit margins in the 1950's were much lower than those of the late 1920's and early 1930's, whereas rates of return fell much less.[46]

---

43 *Modern Packaging*, 30:104 (January 1957).

44 See, for example, G. J. McManus, "Tinplate Shaken by New Technology," *Iron Age*, 197:57 (January 20, 1966); "Growth Comes in Many Packages," *Business Week*, 1810:68 (May 9, 1964);

"Look at the Action in Metals," *Modern Packaging*, 41:101 (October 1968).

45 "Challenge and Response," *Forbes*, 99:56 (February 15, 1967).

46 J. W. McKie, *Tin Cans and Tin Plate*, op. cit., p. 238.

In the last 10 years the two leading container companies (American and Continental) have had moderate profits on the average. For the years 1958–1967 inclusive, American Can's net income averaged 8.9 per cent on its net worth and Continental Can's was slightly higher (9.6 per cent).[47] As indicated above, the return on these companies' capital investment improved in the last three years (1965–1967) and this served to pull up their respective averages for the longer period.

A comparison of the profitability of American and Continental with that of other major packaging concerns for the years 1959–1966 shows the former to have the lowest ranking for these years. Continental earned 1.7 per cent on sales and 5.1 per cent on stockholders equity, compared with an industry median of 5.0 per cent for profit margin and 5.5 per cent for the earnings rate.[48] These figures suggest that in the 1960's, though their earnings have improved, the two big can companies have earned moderate profits compared to their peers. In the light of these facts, it is not surprising that the can companies have been seeking to improve their profit performance by broadening their product lines, accelerating their marketing efforts, and, in the case of American Can, reorganizing itself internally.[49]

A general evaluation of the performance of this industry since World War II embracing price behavior, nonprice competition, and the profit record of the two leading companies would suggest that it approximates a state of "workable competition" much more so than it did before the 1950 decrees. Though these decrees did not radically reform the oligopolistic structure of the industry, they did greatly encourage self-manufacture, and this has exerted a downward pressure on the industry's selling prices. In addition, Schumpeter's "perennial gale of creative destruction" has been spurred by interindustry rivalry, resulting in a host of product innovations—many of them minor in nature, but some of basic importance.

V. PUBLIC POLICY

Major issues of public policy toward this industry have been presented by the 1950 court decrees reforming its market practices and by the antitrust suit brought by the Department of Justice in 1956 to block the acquisition of the Hazel-Atlas Glass Company by Continental Can. The latter case

47 Computed by the author from data in Moody's *Industrials*, p. 2242 (June 1967).

48 *Forbes'* Nineteenth Annual Report on American Industry, 1966 Profitability Rankings. Container Corp., Diamond International, Owens Illinois Glass Co., Union Camp were the companies included in this comparison.

49 On the recent reorganization of American Can, see "Canco Tightens Up," *Business Week*, **1836**:174 (November 7, 1964); and "The New Package at American Can," *Business Week*, **1933**:94 (September 17, 1966); for an appraisal of the results, see Standard and Poor's, *The Outlook*, **40**:864 (March 25, 1968).

finally resulted in an important decision by the Supreme Court interpreting the Celler-Kefauver Act.[50] In this Section we shall briefly appraise the economic consequences of the 1950 decrees, analyze the Court's decision in the Continental Can case, and conclude with some consideration of possible alternatives in public policy regarding this industry.

THE IMPACT OF THE 1950 DECREES

In retrospect, the 1950 antitrust decrees against American and Continental have assumed the character of legal landmarks in the evolution of public policy toward this industry. Indeed, events since 1950 bear out the assessment made by the president of the American Can Company 10 years ago to the effect that these judgments "have brought about radical changes in the economic patterns and operations of the industry. . . ."[51]

Among the effects of these decrees that must be noted are, first, the purchase of can-closing machinery by the canners gave the latter a new degree of independence in contracting with the can-makers for containers; the big can companies could not longer use the leverage which they formerly derived from their control of this machinery to restrict the can buyer's freedom to purchase. Second, the decrees encouraged "an extensive breakdown of exclusive supplier-customer relations" with the result that price dickering and competition in nonprice terms were stimulated. Third, the self-manufacture of containers, or the threat of it, by large users has meant, in effect, that entry could not be blocked under the decrees, and this has resulted in a pronounced downward pressure on the industry's selling prices. Last, though the oligopolistic structure of the industry remains pretty much intact, the price leadership of American Can on a national basis was practically destroyed after 1958 and 1959.

Early discussion of the effects of the 1950 decrees found students of the industry in disagreement. McKie believed that the decrees "finally knocked out all the remaining artificial props of market control." He stressed that "in an atmosphere of change and growth the two leaders were likely to continue their attempts to overreach each other in capturing new markets and developing new products." He concluded that "a forecast of workable competition for the can market appears to be justified."[52]

Others, including the author, were more skeptical about the prospects for a restoration of workable competition.[53] They stressed the persistence of a

---

50 *United States* v. *Continental Can Co.* 378 U.S. 441 (1964).

51 Quoted in S. N. Whitney, *Antitrust Policies* (New York: Twentieth Century Fund, 1958), Vol. 2, p. 490.

52 McKie, *Tin Cans and Tin Plate*, op. cit., pp. 307–309.

53 G. W. Stocking and M. W. Watkins, *Monopoly and Free Enterprise* (New York: Twentieth Century Fund, 1951), p. 181; C. H. Hession, "The Tin Can Industry," *The Structure of American*

concentrated market structure, impediments to entry, and other factors preventing an acceptable environment for competition. On the whole, the developments since 1950—increased self-manufacture and intensified inter-industry competition—have sustained the soundness of McKie's more optimistic view.

THE CONTINENTAL–HAZEL-ATLAS CASE   The civil suit filed by the government against the Continental Can Company in 1956, contesting its acquisition of the Hazel-Atlas Glass Company, involved policy issues of the utmost importance.[54] The government charged that this merger was a violation of the Anti-Merger Act of 1950. It alleged that the effect of the merger by the second largest manufacturer of metal cans with the third largest manufacturer of glass bottles in the United States would be that actual and potential competition between Continental and Hazel-Atlas in the sale of metal cans and glass bottles, plastic and glass bottles, and metal closures would be eliminated or substantially lessened. The merger of these two companies, it further contended, would give the resulting combination: "a decisive advantage over its less diversified competitors" and would increase industry-wide concentration in the container field.

The district court found that metal and glass containers constituted separate lines of commerce because the containers had different characteristics disqualifying them from particular uses. Judge Bryan held that the case involved a "conglomerate merger" between a manufacturer of metal cans and a producer of glass containers. In a scholarly decision the district court rejected the government's relevant lines of commerce, basing itself closely upon criteria enunciated in the Brown Shoe case, and held that the government had failed to establish reasonable probability of substantial anti-competitive effects.

In the presentation of the case before the Supreme Court, the government in a revised brief stressed the interindustry aspects of the matter. The majority of the court, although noting that metal containers and glass containers were separate markets, held that interindustry competition between manufacturers of metal and glass containers brought both under one combined product market. Its opinion was, in effect, that Continental Can had not moved into a separate market by its merger with Hazel-Atlas, but had strengthened its position in the combined metal and glass container market. In the court's words: "By the acquisition of Hazel-Atlas stock Continental not only increased its own share more than 14 per cent from 21.9 per cent to 25 per cent, but also reduced from five to four the most significant competitors who

Industry, ed. by Walter Adams (New York: MacMillan, 1954), rev. Ed., pp. 438–439; J. H. Stauss, Comment on "The Decline of Monopoly in the metal Container Industry," *American Economic Review*, **45**:528 (May 1955).
54   378 U.S. 441 (1964).

might threaten its dominant position. The resulting percentage of the combined firms approaches that held presumptively bad in *United States* versus *Philadelphia National Bank. . . .*"[55]

A dissenting opinion, written by Justice Harlan and joined in by Justice Stewart, spoke of the majority decision as "a travesty of economics" because it provided "its own definition of a market, unrelated to any market reality whatsoever." With the relevant market being so unclear, Justice Harlan argued that the presumptively illegal market share approach employed in the Philadelphia Bank case was inappropriate.

As a result of its defeat in this case, Continental sold eight glass container plants of Hazel-Atlas to the Brockway Glass Company for 1 million shares of Class B common stock in that company; this gave Continental a 42 per cent equity in Brockway. The remaining plant of this unprofitable business was sold to Alexander H. Kerr and Company. Continental retained the more profitable Hazel-Atlas plant that manufactures glass tableware with the court's permission.[56]

A divestiture such as that ordered in the Continental Can case is a milder remedy than dissolution. Although the latter is one possible alternative for public policy in oligopolized industries such as metal containers, it is not likely to be urged unless the objectives of maintaining workable competition can be attained in no other way. Actually, the dissolution of either American or Continental at the present time would not seem to be a very promising course of action, even if the restoration of workable competition required it. Given the complex interdependency of the tin can and tin plate industries, such a piecemeal approach would create serious imbalances and inequities in the relationships of these industries to each other. An optimum approach

---

55 378 U.S. 461 and 374 U.S. 321 (1963) The percentage of metal and glass container shipments accounted for by Continental and Hazel-Atlas in 1955 were presented by the government as follows:

	CONTINENTAL CAN	HAZEL-ATLAS	CONTINENTAL CAN AND HAZEL-ATLAS COMBINED
Glass containers	None	9.6	9.6
Metal containers	33.0	None	33.0
Glass and metal containers	21.9	3.1	25.0

56 In 1967 American Can disposed of its American Wheaton Glass Corporation (acquired in 1960) to the Midland Glass Company after suffering losses for 7 years in that business. The Chairman of American's Board explained that the sale stemmed not only from the losses, but because of its inability to buy additional facilities to extend its geographical reach, the shortage of technical personnel throughout the glass industry, and more profitable opportunities in other fields of growth. American Can Company, *American Report* (Spring 1968), p. 7.

would necessitate the structural reorganization of the steel industry as well because of its integral relationship to tin plate manufacture.[57]

In any case, with the metal container companies, at least the two largest ones, having turned to radical policies of diversification (American Can speaks of "its commitment to expansion in the growing fields of education and leisure-time activities" in its 1967 Annual Report), the emergent issue of public policy is no longer one of market power in a single industry, but of massive conglomeration spreading over the activities of the whole economy, and into foreign ones as well. With this growing thrust and impact of the packaging giants on our lives, there is a dawning realization, too, of the "neighborhood effects" produced by the profusion of packages in our affluent society. The social costs growing out of the irresponsible use and disposal of containers is growing upon the consciousness of progressive management in this industry.[58] Such leadership is aware that metal containers and other packages must be properly disposed of as well as profitably sold, if our national environment is not to be abominably littered, befouled, and contaminated. Thus, we see that the issues of public policy in an advanced industrialized society are seldom completely and permanently solved; they simply take ever new and more complex forms.

SUGGESTED READINGS
BOOKS AND PAMPHLETS

American Can Company. *Fifty Years of American Can Company, 1901–1951.* New York: American Can Co., 1951.

Collins, J. H. *The Story of Canned Foods.* New York: E. P. Dutton & Co., Inc., 1924.

Containers—Basic Analysis. Standard and Poor's Corporation, Industry Surveys, November 14, 1968.

Hession, C. H. *Competition in the Metal Food Container Industry, 1916–1946.* Brooklyn, N.Y.: privately published, 1948.

McKie, J. W. *Tin Cans and Tin Plate.* Cambridge, Mass.: Harvard University Press, 1959.

Modern Packaging Encyclopedia, July 1968. Vol. 41. New York: McGraw-Hill Book Company, Inc., 1968.

Peterson, M. S., and D. K. Tressler. *Food Technology the World Over.* Westport, Conn.: The Avi Publishing Company, 1963.

---

57 See McKie, *Tin Cans and Tin Plate*, op. cit., pp. 302–305, for a consideration of the problems presented by a hypothetical dissolution of the can industry.

58 See the address by American Can's chairman and president, William F. May, to the 30th annual national packaging forum of the Packaging Institute, October 9, 1968, reproduced in part in American Can Company, *American Report* (Fall, 1968), p. 4 ff.

Singer, E. M. *Antitrust Economies, Selected Legal Cases and Economic Models.* Englewood Cliffs, N.J.: Prentice-Hall, Inc., 1968, pp. 247–249, 251, 258.
Whitney, S. N. *Antitrust Policies.* New York: Twentieth Century Fund, 1958. Vol. 2, Ch. 16.

GOVERNMENT PUBLICATIONS

U.S. v. *American Can Company et al.*, 230 Fed. 859 (d. Md, 1916).
U.S. v. *American Can Company et al.*, 87 Fed. Sup. 18 (1949).
U.S. v. *American Can Company et al.*, Final Judgment, June 22, 1950.
U.S. v. *Continental Can Company*, 217 F. Supp. 761 (D.C. S.D. N.Y.).
U.S. v. *Continental Can Company*, 378 U.S. 441 (1964).
U.S. v. *American Can Company*, 126 F. Supp. 811 (N.D. Cal., 1954).
U.S. v. *Continental Can Company*, 128 F. Supp. 932 (N.D. Cal., 1955).
U.S. v. *Continental Can Company*, 143 F. Supp. 787 (N.D. Cal., 1956).
U.S. Attorney General. *Western Steel Plants and the Tin Plate Industry.* Washington, D.C.: U.S. Government Printing Office, 1945.

COMPANY REPORTS

American Can Company, *Annual Reports*, 1960–1967.
Continental Can Company, *Annual Reports*, 1960–1967.

JOURNAL AND MAGAZINE ARTICLES

"Beer Can Battle," *Wall Street Journal* (September 16, 1965).
Bennett, K. W. "Is TFS Breakthrough Near?" *Iron Age*, 200:45 (September 21, 1967).
"Canco Tightens Up," *Business Week*, 1836:194 (November 7, 1964).
"Challenge and Response," *Forbes*, 99:56 (February 15, 1967).
"The Changing Tin Can Picture," *Financial World*, 136:10 (May 25, 1966).
"Growth Comes in Many Packages," *Business Week*, 1810:68 (May 9, 1964).
"How Much Will the Law Allow?" *Business Week*, 1412:88 (September 22, 1956).
Keay, W. R. "The Revolution in the Container Industry," *Magazine of Wall Street*, 116:339 (June 13, 1964).
Lachelier, F. "As Container Industry Benefits from Mammoth Sales in Foods and Beverages," *Magazine of Wall Street*, 118:316 (June 11, 1966).
"Metals Fight to Hold Their Beer," *Business Week*, 1959:92 (March 18, 1967).
"New Mettle in Cans," *Barrons*, 38:3 (December 8, 1958).
"Tin Cans Hustle to Hold Their Own," *Business Week*, 1445:178 (May 11, 1957).
"Tin Plate Shaken by New Technology," *Iron Age*, 197:57 (January 20, 1966); *Iron Age*, 199:46 (March 2, 1967).

10. Frederic M. Scherer

THE AEROSPACE INDUSTRY

O ne of the largest and most fascinating branches of American industry
is the aerospace industry, or as we shall construe it more broadly, the advanced weapons and space vehicles industry. It has a number of distinctive
characteristics. It includes producers from a variety of more conventionally
defined fields—i.e., aircraft, electronic computers, communications systems,
and ordnance. It is a voracious consumer of the nation's highly skilled scientific and technical resources, employing roughly 45 per cent of all the scientists and engineers engaged in industrial research and development. It sustains
an extraordinarily rapid pace of technological advance, attended by unusually great technological uncertainties concerning product characteristics
and costs. Because of these uncertainties and the large size of individual
defense and space programs, special institutions have been created to shift
from producers to the government what might otherwise be intolerable
financial risks. When it assumes the risks of research and production, the
government tends also to usurp many of the decision-making functions traditionally exercised by sellers. The end result is a set of buyer-seller relationships quite unlike those normally found in the market economy. Indeed,
what goes on in the industry cannot be called private enterprise in any
conventional sense; it lies instead in the grey area between private and
public enterprise. Much of what follows in this chapter will be concerned
with elucidating the nature of this unique "nonmarket" buyer-seller relationship.

THE SIZE AND SCOPE OF THE INDUSTRY

The Federal Government's demands for products of the aerospace and related
industries are implemented through four principal agencies: the Department
of Defense (DOD), the National Aeronautics and Space Administration
(NASA), the Atomic Energy Commission (AEC), and the Federal Aviation
Administration (FAA). In the government fiscal year ending June 30, 1965—
before the full effect of the Vietnamese war escalation was felt—these four

agencies spent approximately $26 billion, or about 4.0 per cent of gross national product (GNP), on aircraft, missiles, other advanced weapons and supplies, and the exploration of space. By 1968, their outlays for comparable items had risen to approximately $36 billion, or 4.2 per cent of the GNP.

By far the largest proportion of these demands was supplied by privately owned industrial corporations. The existence of an identifiable, specialized, weapons industry populated by ostensibly private firms is a relatively new phenomenon in the United States. Throughout the nineteenth century and during the first quarter of the twentieth century, the Army and Navy relied in peacetime primarily on government-owned arsenals and shipyards for specialized military equipment. They turned to private industry only for standard items (such as food, clothing, and rifles) sold also in civilian markets, and in wartime in order to supplement their production capacity when the arsenals and shipyards became overloaded. With the advent of aviation, this traditional pattern was challenged. Civilian inventors and entrepreneurs pioneered the development of the airplane, which initially could be used almost interchangeably for military purposes, sport, and mail or passenger transportation. The arsenals and shipyards, dominated by military officers unreceptive to the new technology, shunned aircraft design and production. As a result, the government by necessity turned to private industry to meet its aircraft demands, which were modest before 1915 and in the interwar period, but soared to great heights during the two World Wars.[1]

Following World War II, and especially after the Cold War stabilized armaments demands at relatively high levels, private industry began to play an increasingly important role. There were two main reasons. First, private firms had greater flexibility than government entities in offering salaries to attract the large numbers of engineers and skilled technicians needed. Also, contracting-out offered subtle political advantages. Through its industrial suppliers, dispersed throughout several populous states, the newly organized Air Force found a potent and enthusiastic source of political support for its programs, with more freedom to lobby and mount promotional campaigns than arsenals and shipyards. These advantages did not escape notice of the other services, which gradually tempered their advocacy of the arsenal approach and began to depend more and more upon private contractors. Similar considerations led the NASA to contract out the lion's share of its program, even though the Redstone Arsenal team headed by Wernher von Braun and the former National Advisory Committee for Aeronautics laboratories, which it inherited, had traditionally favored a dominant role for intramural government operations.

The result can be seen in recent statistics on the relative distribution of

---

1 For a survey of the aircraft industry's early history, see Gene R. Simonson, "The Demand for Aircraft and the Aircraft Industry, 1907–1958," *Journal of Economic History* (September 1960), pp. 361–382.

"in house" versus "contracted-out" activity. In 1965, approximately 10 per cent of the DOD total research, development, and weapons production effort was conducted intramurally; the balance was contracted out.[2] Breakdowns for specific product lines reflect the divergent traditions. In-house units accounted for only 1 per cent of the DOD spending on aircraft and only 4 per cent for communications equipment. But some 26 per cent of total expenditures for ship development, construction, and repair went to naval shipyards, while the share of ordnance items (such as ammunition, fire control devices, and tanks) supplied by Army arsenals and related intramural establishments approximated 37 per cent. NASA programs in 1965 consisted largely of research and development activity, of which 18 per cent was conducted intramurally.[3] The AEC relied even more heavily upon contractors, fulfilling none of its production responsibilities and only 3 per cent of its research and development intramurally.

Any definition of the industry encompassing the private firms that supply the government with weapons and space equipment is arbitrary. The most common definition, reflected in the title of this chapter, would include only the suppliers of aircraft, missiles, space vehicles, and such supporting paraphernalia as guidance systems and special maintenance equipment. However, the methods by which aerospace items are procured and the problems encountered differ little from those prevailing in the acquisition of nuclear submarines, aircraft carriers, hydrogen bombs, radio communication networks, armored personnel carriers, and so on. The analysis in this chapter applies equally well to the development and production of the whole spectrum of technically advanced, complex, specialized weapons, weapon systems, and space systems; and we shall normally construe the "industry" in this broader sense.

Table 1 reveals in greater detail the product orientation of government contract awards to private industry in fiscal year 1965. It includes a full breakdown of DOD and NASA domestic procurement obligations plus selected items from the AEC and Federal Aviation Administration (FAA) budgets. The bottom fourth of Table 1 consists largely of standard commodities sold in civilian markets. These fall outside the advanced weapons and space vehicles industry by any reasonable definition. Items in the top half of Table 1 clearly belong within the industry's bounds. The remaining items can be categorized only ambiguously.

The commodities covered by Table 1 are supplied by enterprises classified in numerous conventionally defined manufacturing industries. Table 2

---

2   Estimated from U.S. Department of Commerce, Bureau of the Census, "Shipments of Defense-Oriented Industries: 1965," *Current Industrial Reports*, MA-175(65)-2 (July 1967), pp. 6–8 and 68 and 69.

3   U.S. National Science Foundation, *Federal Funds for Research, Development, and Other Scientific Activities: Fiscal Years 1964, 1965, and 1966* (Washington, D.C.: U.S. Government Printing Office, 1965), pp. 88 and 89.

TABLE 1 MILITARY, AVIATION, AND SPACE
PROCUREMENT OBLIGATIONS TO DOMESTIC INDUSTRIAL
CONTRACTORS: FISCAL YEAR 1965

CATEGORY	$ MILLIONS	CUMULATIVE PERCENTAGE
1. *Military aircraft development and production*	5,781	20.1
2. *Military missile and space systems*	4,233	34.9
3. *Military electronics and communications* *equipment*	2,788	44.6
4. *Military research and development in non-* *profit institutions, other than educational* *institutions*	263	45.5
5. *NASA space systems development*	4,166	59.9
6. *AEC weapons development and fabrication*	753	62.5
7. *AEC military and space reactor development*	332	63.7
8. *AEC production of fissionable materials,* *less sales and leases to civilian reactor* *users*	371	65.0
9. *FAA research, development, and production* *of electronic control systems and navigation* *equipment*	101	65.4
10. *Military combat vehicles*	262	66.3
11. *Military ships*	1,691	72.2
12. *Conventional weapons (i.e., rifles, torpedoes)*	299	73.2
13. *Military ammunition*	759	75.8
14. *DOD miscellaneous hard goods*	307	76.9
15. *DOD: miscellaneous services (including some* *engineering services)*	1,740	83.0
16. *Military construction, including missile bases*	767	85.7
17. *DOD noncombat vehicles*	588	87.7
18. *AEC acquisition of raw materials (natural* *uranium, etc.)*	267	88.6
19. *Military textiles, clothing, and equipage*	361	89.9
20. *DOD orders of less than $10,000 each*	3,395	94.8
21. *DOD: fuels and lubricants*	818	97.7
22. *Military subsistence*	647	100.0
Total	28,689	

SOURCES   Department of Defense and NASA procurement reports and
federal budget documents.

shows the distribution of government prime contract and subcontract shipments in the 12 four-digit census industries having the highest government
sales, as estimated through a 1965 survey of plants in 76 defense-oriented
industries. The leading four industries—aircraft, communications equipment (i.e., radar units and guidance systems), aircraft engines, and guided

TABLE 2   GOVERNMENT CONTRACT SHIPMENTS OF THE 12
MOST ACTIVE DEFENSE AND SPACE-ORIENTED INDUSTRIES,
CALENDAR YEAR 1965

STANDARD INDUSTRIAL CLASSIFICATION		COMBINED PRIME AND SUBCONTRACT SHIPMENTS ($ MILLIONS)	CUMULATIVE PERCENTAGE OF SURVEY TOTAL
CODE	NAME		
3721	*Aircraft*	5,299	18.4
3662	*Communications equipment*	3,514	30.6
3722	*Aircraft engines and parts*	3,150	41.6
1925	*Complete guided missiles*	3,044	52.1
3723	*Aircraft propellers and parts*	2,286	60.1
3731	*Shipbuilding and repairing*	1,285	64.5
2819	*Miscellaneous organic chemicals*	639	66.8
2911	*Petroleum refining*	636	69.0
3679	*Miscellaneous electronic components*	529	70.8
1999	*Miscellaneous ordnance and accessories*	399	72.2
3571	*Computing and related machines*	397	73.6
1929	*Ammunition, other than small arms*	362	74.8
	All 76 industries surveyed	28,785	100.0

SOURCE   U.S. Department of Commerce, Bureau of the Census, "Shipments of Defense-Oriented Industries: 1965," *Current Industrial Reports*,
MA-175(65)-2 (July 1967).

missiles—accounted for 41.6 per cent of all surveyed government shipments.

In addition to their domestic sales, U.S. weapons makers have in recent
years experienced considerable success in export markets. Between 1961 and
1967 sales by American munitions producers to foreign countries amounted
to more than $12.6 billion, or roughly $2 billion per year.[4] Surprisingly,
defense contractors are said to have displayed little enthusiasm at first about
plunging into the export trade. They were encouraged to do so by the DOD
through its Deputy Assistant Secretary for International Logistics Negotiation Henry Kuss, who in 1965 received the Meritorious Civilian Service
medal for his "unparalleled ability as a negotiator."[5]

One further component of the weapons and space vehicles industry
deserves mention. Many American universities are heavily involved in

4 See U.S. Senate, Committee on
Foreign Relations, Staff Study, "Arms
Sales and Foreign Policy" (Washington,
D.C.: U.S. Government Printing Office,
1967); "Pentagon Escalates War on
Payments Gap," *Business Week*, p. 22

(January 13, 1968); and the series of
articles commencing in the *New York
Times* (July 19, 1967), p. 2.
5 "U.S. Arms Salesman," *New York
Times* (July 19, 1967), p. 2.

providing research, development, and engineering services to military and space agencies. Examples include the University of California's Livermore and Los Alamos Laboratories, working on nuclear weapons; California Institute of Technology's Jet Propulsion Laboratory, which conducts and manages space programs for NASA; and MIT's Instrumentation Laboratory, which designed guidance systems for the Polaris missile system and the Apollo space vehicle program. Other university contributions range from the execution of specific operations research studies through the conduct of basic research only loosely related to sponsor objectives. Counting only development and applied research activities, university work under contract to the DOD, NASA, and the AEC involved fiscal year 1967 obligations of $600 million.[6] In the same year those three agencies committed $534 million for the support of basic research in universities.

II. MARKET STRUCTURE

For most advanced weapons and space systems the Federal Government is the sole domestic buyer, and it also regulates the sale of weapons by U.S. firms to foreign governments. The industry's structure on the buying side might appear therefore to be monopsonistic. This view slightly oversimplifies the situation, however, since the Air Force, Army, Navy, NASA, AEC, and FAA have often displayed considerable independence as purchasers, competing with one another both for program authorizations and contractor resources. Still it is clearly accurate to say that power is highly concentrated on the buying side of the market.

Several distinctions must be drawn before the structure of the sellers' side can be examined. The most fundamental is the distinction between prime contractors and subcontractors. Prime contractors sell directly to government purchasing agencies, but after receiving their contracts, they in turn purchase subassemblies, components, and materials from other specialist firms who act as subcontractors. A survey disclosed that 61 major prime contractors subcontracted somewhat more than half of all the defense prime contract dollars that they received between 1956 and 1959.[7] Most major defense and space vendors serve both as prime contractors on some items and as subcontractors to other firms on other items.

---

6 Estimated from U.S. National Science Foundation, *Federal Funds for Research, Development, and Other Scientific Activities: Fiscal Years 1967, 1968, and 1969* (Washington, D.C.: U.S. Government Printing Office, 1968), pp. 168–169 and 193–194; and *Federal Support to Universities and Colleges: Fiscal Years 1963–66* (Washington, D.C.: U.S. Government Printing Office, 1967), pp. 7 and 41.

7 M. J. Peck and F. M. Scherer, *The Weapons Acquisition Process: An Economic Analysis* (Boston: Harvard Business School Division of Research, 1962), pp. 150–151 and 624–625.

Contractors also accept a diversity of assignments. In some cases, the prime contractor assumes responsibility for integrating and assembling an entire system (i.e., a guided missile system, or a radar detection system). Others undertake the development and production of a subsystem, such as the computer for a missile tracking radar system or the nuclear reactor controls for an aircraft carrier. Still others supply component parts such as gyroscopes, landing gear struts, and high-powered electron tubes; or materials such as titanium sheets and insulated silver wire. Since weapons and space systems are complex aggregations of component parts, system and subsystem prime contractors normally do more subcontracting than component and materials suppliers. Components and materials are more frequently bought under subcontract arrangements, whereas systems and (to a lesser degree) subsystems are developed and produced under prime contracts. Finally, certain organizations—notably such not-for-profit entities as the Aerospace Corporation and Cal Tech's Jet Propulsion Laboratory, but also on occasion (as in the Apollo program) profit-making firms like Boeing—have received "systems integration" or "systems management" contracts to oversee, coordinate, and second-guess the operations of other systems development prime contractors.

THE CONCENTRATION OF
PRIME CONTRACT AWARDS

Complete statistics on the distribution of defense and space orders among industrial firms are available only at the prime contract level, although adjustments to take into account interfirm subcontract transactions do not appear to alter the picture significantly.[8] Table 3 presents data on the concentration of defense prime contract awards in the hands of the leading 25 and 100 recipients for several time periods. The share of the leading 25 firms has varied between 43 and 55 per cent over time, while the share of the top 100 firms ranged between 64 and 74 per cent. The concentration of orders is relatively high during peacetime, when a nucleus of faithful specialists serves most of the government's needs. It falls during shooting wars, when the government must call upon firms normally preoccupied in civilian pursuits to meet its peak demands for uniforms, rations, personnel carriers, fuel, and ammunition. The NASA, with a small number of programs, a few of which are extremely large, has concentrated its industrial contracts more tightly than the more diversified DOD. During the mid-1960's, the top ten NASA prime contractors received between 66 and 70 per cent of the Space Administration's industrial prime contracts by dollar volume, while the share of the leading 100 NASA contractors ranged between 91 and 94 per cent. Given the special characteristics of both DOD and NASA procurement

---

8 Ibid., pp. 152–158.

TABLE 3   THE SHARE OF THE LARGEST
PRIME CONTRACTORS IN ALL MILITARY
PRIME CONTRACT AWARDS, BY DOLLAR
VOLUME: WORLD WAR II TO 1968

TIME PERIOD (FISCAL YEAR)	PERCENTAGE SHARE OF TOP 25 FIRMS	PERCENTAGE SHARE OF TOP 100 FIRMS
World War II[a]	46.5	67.2
Korean War (1951–1953)	45.5	64.0
1958–1960	55.3	73.7
1961	54.8	74.2
1962	50.8	72.3
1963	51.9	73.9
1964	52.9	73.4
1965	48.2	68.9
1966	43.0	63.8
1967	44.5	65.5
1968	45.6	67.4

a   The data for World War II include only prime
contracts of $50,000 or more and exclude the procurement
of subsistence. The more recent data cover all contracts of
$10,000 or more, including subsistence. If the data were
fully comparable, the World War II concentration ratios
would be relatively lower.

SOURCES   M. J. Peck and F. M. Scherer, *The Weapons
Acquisition Process: An Economic Analysis* (Boston:
Harvard Business School, 1962), p. 117; and annual
reports of the Department of Defense.

programs, it is difficult to determine objectively whether the observed levels
of prime contract concentration are necessary and desirable.

Firms leading the list of defense and space prime contractors tend naturally enough to be large corporations, although there is not a close correlation
between rankings of industrial firms by total civilian and government sales
and rankings of the leading government contractors. Table 4 indicates the
total volume of DOD and NASA prime contract awards received by the
15 top defense and space producers during fiscal years 1965 through 1967,
along with the approximate share of those firms' sales attributable directly
and through subcontracts to Federal Government orders. Eight of the 15
producers were aircraft and missile specialists, typically (with the exception
of Boeing and United Aircraft, holding strong positions in the civilian jet
airliner market) dependent upon the government for an overwhelming fraction of their sales. Three others were electrical and electronic equipment
makers operating extensively in both civilian and government fields. General
Motors and Ford appear on the list partly because of their electronics sub-

TABLE 4 THE LEADING 15 DEFENSE AND SPACE PRIME
CONTRACTORS: FISCAL YEARS 1965–1967

RANK	COMPANY	TOTAL VALUE OF DOD AND NASA PRIME CONTRACTS: 1965–1967 ($ MILLIONS)	PERCENT OF TOTAL SALES ATTRIBUTABLE TO GOVERNMENT PRIME AND SUBCON- TRACTS, CIRCA 1966
1	*Lockheed Aircraft*	5,176	95
2	*North American Aviation*	5,167	95
3	*McDonnell-Douglas*[a]	5,127	77
4	*General Dynamics*	4,410	83
5	*General Electric*	3,897	20
6	*Boeing*	3,303	50[b]
7	*United Aircraft*	2,992	65[c]
8	*Grumman Aircraft*	2,293	95
9	*AT & T—Western Electric*	1,981	16[d]
10	*General Motors*	1,648	3
11	*Sperry-Rand*	1,337	30
12	*Textron*	1,248	45
13	*Ford-Philco*	1,243	5[e]
14	*General Tire-Aerojet General*	1,221	45
15	*Ling-Temco-Vought*	1,201	73[f]
	Total 1965–1967 awards to top fifteen	——— 42,244	

a Consolidated figures, due to merger in 1967.
b Nearer 90 per cent in 1957, before Boeing's rise in the airliner field.
c Nearer 80 per cent in 1960, before increase in demand for jet airliner engines.
d Western Electric sales only.
e Approximately 35 per cent of Philco Division sales.
f Excludes Wilson and Company, acquired in 1967. With Wilson sales weighted
on the basis of LTV's ownership share, government sales approximated 30 per cent of
total consolidated sales.
SOURCES Annual procurement reports of the Department of Defense and NASA
and company annual reports.

sidiaries, and partly because of heavy Vietnamese war demands for automotive and related equipment. Textron's position is largely a result of
wartime orders for its Bell division's helicopters, and General Tire owes its
prime contract awards largely to its rocket-making subsidiary, Aerojet-
General.

At the other extreme of the prime contract spectrum are the so-called small
business concerns, defined by law as firms with fewer than 500 or 1,000
employees, depending upon the industry. The small business share of all
defense prime contracts has ranged between 16 and 25 per cent, rising when
the DOD is buying large quantities of material for a conventional shooting

TABLE 5   THE PROPORTION OF DEFENSE PRIME CONTRACT
AWARDS BY DOLLAR VOLUME RECEIVED BY "SMALL
BUSINESS," FISCAL YEAR 1965

CATEGORY	PERCENTAGE SHARE	CATEGORY	PERCENTAGE SHARE
Construction	67.6	Tanks and automotive	
Textiles, clothing, and		vehicles	12.3
equipage	66.7	Electronics and	
Subsistence	51.2	communication	
DOD procurements of		equipment	13.0
less than $10,000	51.0	Ships	8.3
Ordnance weapons	30.4	Aircraft	3.6
Fuels and lubricants	25.3	Missiles and military	
Services	20.6	space systems	1.5
Ammunition	15.8		

SOURCE   U.S. Department of Defense, *Military Prime Contract Awards and
Subcontract Payments*, July 1964–June 1965 (Washington, D.C.: U.S. Department
of Defense, 1965).

war and falling when it is not. In NASA programs, small businesses have
secured from 6 to 12 per cent of total prime contract dollars. The success
of small businesses in winning orders varies with the type of item purchased.
As Table 5 shows, small firms do relatively well obtaining contracts for construction and the supply of clothing and food products—operations characterized by modest scale economies, where small enterprises also thrive in
the civilian economy. But they receive only a tiny fraction of the government's orders for missiles, space vehicles, aircraft, and complex electronic
systems, where the scale of the typical project is apparently too large to be
accommodated by a company with only a handful of employees. Even then,
smaller producers participate in major weapons and space vehicle programs
through subcontracting. Firms classified as small businesses received from
37 to 43 per cent of the subcontract awards made by large DOD and NASA
prime contractors during the 1960's.

THE GEOGRAPHIC CONCENTRATION OF DEFENSE AND SPACE WORK   Defense
and space procurement is concentrated regionally as well as by corporate
beneficiaries. In 1965, four large industrial states—California, New York,
Connecticut, and Ohio—accounted for 46 per cent of all defense, space,
and military atomic energy contract employment, as estimated in a Census
Bureau survey.[9] California alone, traditional seat of the aircraft industry,

---

9   U.S. Department of Commerce,
"Shipments of Defense-Oriented Industries: 1965," op. cit., pp. 18–25.

**TABLE 6 TEN STATES ESPECIALLY DEPENDENT
UPON DEFENSE AND SPACE CONTRACTS:
CALENDAR YEAR 1965**

STATE	DEFENSE AND SPACE EMPLOYMENT AS A PERCENTAGE OF TOTAL MANUFACTURING EMPLOYMENT IN STATE[a]	STATE'S SHARE OF TOTAL U.S. DEFENSE AND SPACE EMPLOYMENT (%)
New Mexico	112.4[b]	1.3
California	27.3	27.1
Utah	21.8	0.7
Idaho	21.5[c]	0.5[c]
Washington	19.6[c]	3.0[c]
Arizona	19.1	0.8
Connecticut	17.3	5.4
Colorado	14.9	1.0
Florida	14.6	2.4
Kansas	13.8	1.2
All other states	5.2	66.5

a Since the defense-oriented survey did not cover all industries and excluded establishments with fewer than 100 employees, the percentages in the first column are biased downward. The data cover employment in government-owned, contractor-operated facilities, but exclude government-operated industrial facilities.

b Includes the Los Alamos Laboratories, operated by the University of California, whose employment is not counted in the manufacturing sector in the *Survey of Manufactures*.

c Approximate estimate.

SOURCES U.S. Department of Commerce, Bureau of the Census, "Shipments of Defense-Oriented Industries: 1965," *Current Industrial Reports* (Washington, D.C.: Bureau of the Census, 1967); and idem. *Annual Survey of Manufactures: 1964–65* (Washington, D.C.: U.S. Government Printing Office, 1968).

enjoyed 27 per cent of the U.S. total. During the early and mid-1960's, it regularly received between 20 and 24 per cent of all DOD prime contract dollars, an even larger share of the first-tier subcontracting volume,[10] and roughly 44 per cent of all NASA prime contract awards. These figures reflect California's specialization in defense and space tasks, and not just its large size. As Table 6 reveals, 27.3 per cent of the total California manufacturing

---

10 See "The Pentagon Shot That Misfired," *Business Week*, **1962**:38 (April 8, 1967). It is probable that a larger share of second- and third-tier subcontract work flows out of California, but no satisfactory data are available.

TABLE 7   THE LEADING 15 DEFENSE AND SPACE PRIME
CONTRACTORS IN FOUR PERIODS, 1940–1967

RANK	WORLD WAR II (1940–1944)	KOREAN CONFLICT (1951–1953)	FISCAL YEARS 1958–1960	FISCAL YEARS 1965–1967
1	General Motors	General Motors	Boeing	Lockheed
2	Curtiss-Wright	Boeing	General Dynamics[a]	North American
3	Ford Motor Co.	General Electric	Lockheed	McDonnell-Douglas
4	Consolidated-Vultee	Douglas	General Electric	General Dynamics
5	Douglas	United Aircraft	North American	General Electric
6	United Aircraft	Chrysler	United Aircraft	Boeing
7	Bethlehem Steel	Lockheed	AT&T	United Aircraft
8	Chrysler	Consolidated-Vultee	Douglas	Grumman
9	General Electric	North American	Martin	AT&T
10	Lockheed	Republic Aviation	Hughes Aircraft	General Motors
11	North American	Curtiss-Wright	Sperry-Rand	Sperry-Rand
12	Boeing	Ford Motor Co.	Raytheon	Textron
13	AT&T (mostly Western Electric)	AT&T	McDonnell	Ford-Philco
14	Martin	Westinghouse	RCA	General Tire
15	du Pont	Grumman	IBM	Ling-Temco-Vought

a   Formed through merger, of which Consolidated-Vultee was a main component.
SOURCES   M. J. Peck and F. M. Scherer, *The Weapons Acquisition Process: An
Economic Analysis* (Boston: Harvard Business School Division of Research, 1962),
pp. 613–621; and annual procurement reports of the Defense Department and NASA
for 1965 through 1967.

sector work force was engaged directly in defense and space contract activities during 1965. For the United States as a whole, the comparable average
was 7.8 per cent. Dependence upon military and space work is even stronger
in a number of metropolitan areas in California, Washington, and Connecticut. Nearly half of San Diego manufacturing establishment employees and
31 per cent of those in Los Angeles and Long Beach owed their jobs to defense and space contracts in 1965.

The heavy dependence of certain localities and regions upon specialized
defense work could be troublesome if major steps toward disarmament were
taken. Cities like San Diego, Los Angeles, Seattle, Oak Ridge, and New
London would experience severe unemployment shocks. Persons who have
spent most of their adult lives designing warhead fusing devices or hyper-
sonic reentry vehicles would find few civilian jobs fully utilizing their skills.

The economic impact of disarmament would depend upon how readily such individuals adjust to new, less-skilled, lower-paying jobs; and how promptly firms in defense-dependent regions adapt to produce peacetime commodities. What evidence we have on this problem, which differs from the World War II readjustment experience because of the higher skill content of missile and aircraft jobs during the 1960's, is not particularly encouraging.[11]

TURNOVER AND DIVERSIFICATION   Not all who rise to the top of the defense and space prime contractor lists manage to stay there. A considerable amount of turnover is evident.[12] Table 7 provides one view of the situation, listing the leading 15 DOD and (for 1965–1967 only) NASA prime contractors in four periods roughly 7 years apart. Seven of the firms or their corporate descendants remained on all four lists. Three companies dropped out for reasons other than merger between World War II and the Korean conflict; seven dropped from the list between the Korean conflict and 1958–1960; and five disappeared between 1958–1960 and 1965–1967. Most of the shifts in position were gradual; for instance, Grumman rose from 22nd during World War II to 15th during the Korean action, dropping back to 17th in 1958–1960 and then ascending to eighth in 1965–1967. But a few were more dramatic—i.e., Curtiss-Wright's steady fall from second place during World War II to 66th on the defense list for 1967, largely because of its failure to make the transition from reciprocating engine technology to jets and rockets. Recurring revolutions in military technology have been one major cause of turnover among the leading contractors; another has been the oscillation of the United States between hot and cold war footings, carrying with it changes in the mix of equipment procured. There is reason to believe that aerospace specialists are becoming more adaptable to such changes, so that turnover may be less rapid in future years.

With few exceptions, the companies which lost position in defense and space contracting did not do so because they wanted to.[13] Most contractors have tried hard, though not always successfully, to maintain their defense sales. However, many have attempted to reduce their *relative* dependence upon volatile military orders by diversifying into related or unrelated civilian and government markets.

---

11   See Leslie Fishman et al., *Reemployment Experiences of Defense Workers*, U.S. Arms Control and Disarmament Agency report E-113 (Washington, D.C.: U.S. Government Printing Office, 1968); and the *Report of the Committee on the Economic Impact of Defense and Disarmament* (Washington, D.C.: U.S. Government Printing Office, July 1965).

12   For diverse views, see Peck and Scherer, op. cit., pp. 123–128; and

W. L. Baldwin, *The Structure of the Defense Market: 1955–1964* (Durham, N.C.; Duke University Press 1967), pp. 16–24 and 41–51.

13   The only clear exceptions among firms listed in Table 7 are du Pont, which made a deliberate policy decision to emphasize commercial products following World War II; and Bethlehem Steel, which gradually declined in rank and finally sold its shipbuilding division to General Dynamics.

The last column of Table 2 offers a static view of the leading defense producers' diversification positions as of 1966. The degree of government dependence varies widely, ranging from the low government sales ratio of General Motors to the almost total dependence of Grumman and (before its merger with Rockwell-Standard) North American. A similar pattern exists among smaller defense contractors.[14]

Firms with very high government sales ratios have been particularly eager to strike a more even balance. For the aircraft companies, civilian airliner production had been a traditional hedge. The jet age brought a new scramble for market position, with strikingly mixed results. General Dynamics sustained losses of $425 million on its ill-starred 880 and 990 models—the largest single loss ever recorded in U.S. industrial history.[15] Douglas and Lockheed, who had previously shared leadership of the airliner market, fared only slightly better during the late 1950's and most of the 1960's. Only Boeing, rich in experience from producing B-47 and B-52 jet bombers and KC-135 tankers, achieved significant success in civilian sales during the first 10 years of the jet airliner era.

The old-line aircraft makers were somewhat more successful, diversifying into new government markets related to their original specialities. Most survived the transition into guided missiles, and many were able to lessen their military dependence by becoming NASA suppliers. Some integrated vertically into the production of electronic subsystems and components and rocket propulsion units. A few aerospace firms—notably, General Dynamics, Lockheed, and Litton Industries—also acquired shipbuilding concerns.

In all these instances, there were technical and managerial links between the new fields entered and traditional specialties. Aircraft makers have also attempted to develop products for completely unrelated civilian markets, but here they made little headway. There have been two main stumbling blocks.[16] First, sophisticated product design and high reliability have been the overriding indexes of success in the advanced weapons field, whereas cost control was of much less importance. The aerospace firms found it difficult to depart from this orientation with their civilian products, which tended to embody more sophistication than buyers desired at a price they were unwilling to pay. Second, the organizational structures of aerospace

---

14 See Baldwin, op. cit., p. 76; and Peck and Scherer, op. cit., pp. 628–630.

15 See Richard Austin Smith, *Corporations in Crisis* (New York: Doubleday, 1963), Chaps. III and IV. On more recent problems, see Dan Cordtz, "The Withering Aircraft Industry," *Fortune*, **82**:114 (Sept. 1970).

16 See report prepared for the U.S. Arms Control and Disarmament Agency,

John S. Gilmore and Dean C. Codding- ton, *Defense Industry Diversification: An Analysis with 12 Case Studies*, (Washington, D.C.: U.S. Arms Control and Disarmament Agency, 1966); and Thomas G. Miller, Jr., *Strategies for Survival in the Aerospace Industry* (Cambridge, Mass.: Arthur D. Little, 1964), pp. 27– 29.

firms were geared to serving a monolithic buyer group able to state with some precision what it wished to buy. Absent were the marketing channels and skills needed to discover and tap the demands of widely dispersed buyers accustomed to letting suppliers take the initiative. Because of these weaknesses, aerospace specialists have for the most part been able to diversify into orthodox civilian markets only by merging with established civilian goods suppliers—e.g., in the mergers of General Dynamics with the Material Service Corporation, North American with Rockwell-Standard, Martin with American Marietta, and Ling-Temco-Vought with Jones & Laughlin Steel and the Okonite Co. These civilian acquisitions have then been operated independently of the government divisions, with their own sales forces, management teams, and accounting systems. By the same token, large diversified civilian firms, such as General Electric and Ford, conduct most of their defense business in divisions segregated physically and philosophically from commercial operations.

ENTRY, EXIT, AND PROFITS These developments had important repercussions on the structure and performance of the weapons industry. Few firms exited voluntarily. But there was an enormous amount of new entry, especially during the 1950's, as old-line aircraft makers diversified into missile and space work, component vendors expanded into the design and production of complete systems, civilian goods producers established new military products subsidiaries, and thousands of small new defense-oriented enterprises were founded. Indeed, the rate of new entry outpaced the growth of military and space demand, so that by the early 1960's there was evidence of considerable excess capacity in the manned aircraft, guided missile, guidance system, and related electronic subsystem fields.

Several interacting factors contributed to this result. First, the new technologies required new skills and facilities. Scientific analysis, advanced engineering, high precision metal-working, and delicate electronic assembly operations became more important, while the need for mass-production capabilities declined. Second, defense work under Cold War conditions was profitable. Between 1950 and 1957 aerospace producers realized after-tax returns on invested capital averaging approximately 19 per cent—well above the 12 per cent mean for all manufacturing corporations. Enhancing the profitability of defense work was the Federal Government's willingness to assume most of the burden of financing plants, equipment, research, and work in progress.[17] Finally, many firms saw entry into technically advanced

---

17 Cf. Herman O. Stekler, *The Structure and Performance of the Aerospace Industry* (Berkeley, Calif.: University of California Press, 1965), pp. 9–11; and Stanford Research Institute, *The Industry-Government Aerospace Relationship* (Menlo Park, Calif.: Stanford Research Institute, 1963), Vol. 1, p. 44.

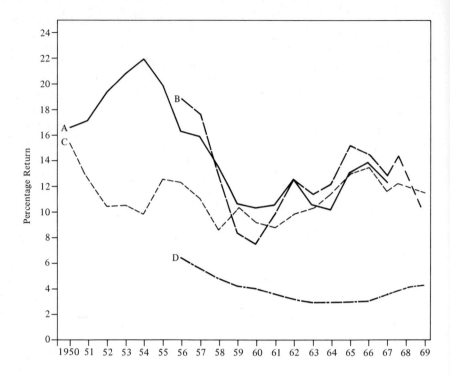

Figure 1

PROFIT RETURNS OF SELECTED AEROSPACE AND
DEFENSE INDUSTRY GROUPS: 1950–1969

A   Return after taxes on stockholders equity, selected aerospace
industry leaders, adjusted for commercial airliner losses.*
B   Return after taxes on stockholder equity, all aircraft and parts
firms.†
C   Return after taxes on stockholder equity, all manufacturing
corporations.†
D   Pre-tax return on sales of firms subject to renegotiation.‡

* Compiled from annual financial reports of from 14 to 23 companies
primarily engaged in defense and space contracting. Surviving firms have
been included after mergers which did not dilute the predominant
government orientation and deleted when commercial operations out-
weighed government sales. To exclude the impact of commercial losses,
the following deletions were made: Martin in 1951, Douglas in 1959,
1960, and 1966; General Dynamics in 1960 and 1961; Ling-Temco-
Vought in 1961, McDonnell-Douglas in 1967, and Fairchild in 1958.
Adjustment were made for commercial losses or income tax credits on
past losses for Avco in 1956, Fairchild in 1960, Lockheed in 1960, and
General Dynamics in 1962.

† SOURCE   U.S. Federal Trade Commission and Securities and
Exchange Commission, *Quarterly Financial Report for Manufacturing
Corporations*, various years. Data were published for the aircraft and
parts industry only beginning in 1956.

‡ SOURCE   Annual reports of the Renegotiation Board. There is a lag of
about a year between accrual of profits and reporting to the Renegotiation
Board.

defense activities as a means of gaining subsidized know-how which could then be applied in civilian markets.

Like all booms, the defense-space boom of the 1950's sowed the seeds of its own undoing. As excess capacity mounted, profits began to fall. It is impossible to trace the decline precisely because of the huge airliner losses suffered by aircraft makers during the late 1950's and because the defense contract profits of diversified corporations are not segregated from commercial returns in financial reports. Figure 1 attempts to circumvent these obstacles by presenting three alternative data series on defense industry profits. All three series show a steady decline throughout the late 1950's, followed by a moderate recovery in the mid-1960's.

The decline in profits was partly the result of intensified competition. In addition, several more subtle forces were at work. With the advent of the guided missile, a rising share of the total contracting effort involved research, development, and complex job-shop production, for which relatively low-profit rates were traditionally negotiated. There was a relative fall in the volume of mass production contracts, for which high profit rates were customary. The government began exploiting contractors' weakened bargaining position by demanding that they finance the bulk of their new plant investment, so that the industry's investment base rose while profits were stagnating. It also refused increasingly to reimburse contractor expenditures for such activities as bid preparation, advertising, and independent research. "Disallowances" of this sort rose from 0.4 per cent of government sales for 15 leading contractors in 1953 to 1.0 per cent in 1960.[18]

By 1961, aerospace industry leaders were alarmed over the erosion of their profits. Incoming Secretary of Defense Robert S. McNamara was also concerned. In the hope of raising efficiency and profits simultaneously, he instituted several contracting policy reforms, including increased use of contracts bearing higher profit margins (as well as enhanced risk) and the adoption of a "weighted guidelines" procedure for negotiating profit rates. The public statements and reports supporting these changes reflect scant awareness that low profits were the consequence of excess capacity and that an increase in profits would merely inhibit the withdrawal of resources, delaying correction of the underlying malady. Nor was there a well-reasoned economic rationale for paying "normal" and even supranormal profits to firms with no attractive alternative opportunities for employing their redundant resources. Still, even in defense contracting the forces of competition have a way of overriding well-meaning but misguided policy decisions. When commercial profits and losses are excluded, as in the Renegotiation Board series of Figure 1, the McNamara profit policy appears to have done no more than arrest the declining trend. Only when defense procurement

---

18 Stanford Research Institute, op. cit., p. 46.

outlays shot upward as a result of the Vietnamese war escalation did a clear-cut upturn materialize.[19]

We have no solid evidence on the response of entry and exit rates during the 1960's to these profit developments. Impressionistic observation suggests that the rate of new entry tapered off, while exit proceeded at a snail's pace. Most defense specialists simply had nowhere else to go, and they continued to earn higher returns in defense than the average of all manufacturing corporations combined. However, in a few special situations the government did experience difficulty attracting desired resources. The most striking example occurred in the nuclear reactor and steam turbine field, where submarine propulsion system suppliers found it more lucrative to use their skilled engineers on civilian power reactor work than to accept defense contracts at standard profit rates. Their services were secured for the Navy reactor program only when profit rates as high as 15 to 25 per cent were allowed, or when intense political pressures were brought to bear.[20]

THE DEMAND FOR ADVANCED WEAPONS

The government's demand for products from the advanced weapons and space vehicles industry has fluctuated widely over time. No comprehensive statistics on military procurement outlays for a long span of years are available. However, a general impression can be gleaned by examining data on total national defense expenditures, given for eleven relevant periods in Table 8. Procurement outlays ranged from about 48 per cent of these totals between 1954 and 1966 to roughly two thirds of the total during World War II.

The most striking feature of Table 8, apart from the enormous share of GNP allocated to the World War II military effort, is the sharp difference between peacetime preparedness expenditure levels before the Cold War and after it began. Prior to 1939, peacetime outlays varied from three quarters of a per cent to 1 per cent of GNP. After 1949, they jumped to an order of magnitude higher.

This change reflects three phenomena: the U.S. decision to abandon isolationism and pursue an active role in the world power struggle; changes

---

19 For other evidence on profits, see U.S. Congress, Joint Economic Committee, Subcommittee on Economy in Government, Hearings, *Economics of Military Procurement*, Part 1 (Washington, D.C.: U.S. Government Printing Office, 1969), pp. 60–62 and 105–119. See also "Easing the Cash-Flow Problems," *Business Week*, **2006**:25 (February 10, 1968); "Defense Profits Lag," *Business Week*,

2053:22 (January 4, 1969); and "Aerospace: The Dark Side of the Moon," *New York Times*, **118**:84 (January 6, 1969).

20 Cf. "Rickover Tells GE to Weigh Anchor," *Business Week*, **1973**:105 (June 24, 1967); "Pentagon Scored on Atomic Fleet," *New York Times* (February 26, 1968); and "Rickover, Alleging Waste, Asks Overhaul of Pentagon's Policies," *New York Times* (January 17, 1969).

TABLE 8 RELATIVE LEVELS OF NATIONAL
DEFENSE SPENDING IN SELECTED PERIODS,
1910 TO 1969

PERIOD	$ BILLIONS EXPENDED PER YEAR[a]	PERCENTAGE OF GNP
July 1909–June 1916	0.3	0.75
July 1917–June 1920	8.2	10.26
July 1921–June 1929	0.7	0.74
July 1929–June 1939	0.8	1.04
July 1939–June 1941	3.8	3.64
July 1941–June 1945	61.3	32.50
July 1946–June 1950	13.0	5.18
July 1950–June 1953	38.9	11.59
July 1953–June 1959	43.7	10.34
July 1959–June 1966	51.7	8.61
July 1966–June 1969	77.2[b]	9.13[b]

    a Includes atomic weapons outlays and military
assistance abroad, but excludes NASA, veterans benefits,
and interest on the war debt.
    b Preliminary estimates.
    SOURCES U.S. Bureau of the Census, *Historical
Statistics of the United States, Colonial Times to 1957*
(Washington, D.C.: U.S. Government Printing Office,
1960), pp. 719–720; idem, *Long Term Economic Growth:
1860–1965* (Washington, D.C.: U.S. Government
Printing Office, 1966), pp. 166–167; *Economic Report of
the President* (Washington, D.C.: U.S. Government
Printing Office, January 1969); and various editions of
the Federal budget.

in military technology; and accompanying changes in military strategy. The
last two points warrant elaboration. Before World War II, the United States
was sheltered from potential enemies by vast expanses of ocean. To mobilize
a debilitating attack on the U.S. mainland would have been a most expensive
and time-consuming undertaking. It was believed therefore that the United
States could rest secure with a mere skeleton military force, which could be
expanded in time to ward off any potential attack or to intervene in wars
underway abroad if desired. This strategy was successful in World Wars
I and II. But it became obsolete with the development of hydrogen bombs
and the long-range bombers and missiles to carry them, making it possible
to carry out a devastating attack in a few swift blows. U.S. military policy
reacted to these events by shifting from the emphasis on possessing an
expansible "mobilization base" to having on hand a "forces-in-being,"

ready to respond immediately to any conceivable attack and to retaliate with great force against an aggressor's homeland.

At first it was hoped that maintaining powerful nuclear deterrent forces-in-being would be less expensive than supporting conventional armed forces of sufficient size, expansibility, and mobility to cope with aggression in a less violent way. This belief soon proved to be illusory. As rival nations acquired their own stockpiles of nuclear weapons and the means to deliver them, the threat to use nuclear weapons to punish an attack by ground forces or guerillas became excessively risky. Reciprocal fear of nuclear counterattack and escalation led to a nuclear stalemate, so that conventional armed forces were still needed to deal with nonnuclear aggression.[21] Moreover, the technology of nuclear weapons offense and defense continued to advance by leaps and bounds, spurring major powers to invest in repeated rounds of an intense qualitative and quantitative arms race. The outcome was more spending on arms, not less. And for arms suppliers, business was good.

THE LOGIC OF THE ARMS RACE   It is extraordinarily difficult to avoid arms races of this character in the absence of iron-clad disarmament agreements. When the decision to develop or produce a new weapon is confronted, it is generally accepted that the United States should pursue a conservative strategy—one which makes the best of potentially adverse rival actions.[22] Weapons are normally developed in an environment of secrecy both in the United States and in such closed societies as Red China and the Soviet Union. Weapons development is also marked by long "lead times." It takes from 4 to 10 years to bring an ambitious program from inception to the stage where significant quantities of the new weapon are ready for use. If a rival nation secretly gets the jump in a new field, the United States may be unable to escape several years of distressing technological inferiority. When new possibilities appear on the horizon, therefore, the prudent decision-maker is likely to assume that rivals may quickly exploit them.

However, in the Soviet Union and other nations similar reasoning prevails. Soviet rulers are not anxious to be caught in an inferior position, so they, too, are prone to exploit new development possibilities quickly. Indeed, when they see the United States proceeding in the fear that they might secretly be coming up with a new threat, they are compelled by prudence to commence a countervailing program. And so both nations end up develop-

---

21   The pioneering intellectual contribution was Henry A. Kissinger, *Nuclear Weapons and Foreign Policy* (New York: Harper, 1957).
22   See the explicit statement of this principle in the address of Robert S. McNamara, quoted in full in the *New York Times* (September 19, 1967), p. 18; and in a speech by his successor, "Excerpts from Talk by Clifford," *New York Times* (September 6, 1968), p. 2. See also *Analysis for Military Decisions*, ed. by E. S. Quade (Chicago: Rand McNally, 1964), and my review in the *American Economic Review*, **55**:1191 (December 1965).

ing and deploying the new weapon, expending vast sums on maintaining something approximating parity of forces. Each nation would be better off if all would refrain from taking new steps, preserving the status quo and avoiding the heavy burden of weapons development and production outlays. Yet fear that others will not exercise restraint impels repeated departures from the current equilibrium. Such is the nature of arms races.[23]

The United States has frequently aggravated the problem by attempting to attain a position of qualitative and quantitative superiority relative to the Soviet Union. It did so, for example, by keeping its World War II atomic bomb effort secret from the Russians,[24] by building up a large bomb stockpile immediately after the war, by stationing thousands of strategic bombers at bases encircling the U.S.S.R., and by deploying 1,050 ICBM's and 650 Polaris submarine-launched missiles during the late 1950's and early 1960's. It can be argued that these actions were taken in a kind of innocent good faith, in the firm belief that the United States would never commit aggression, but was merely seeking to defend itself and its allies. Yet from the standpoint of Soviet leaders, paranoid (like Stalin) or fully rational, it was hardly reasonable to perceive the situation in this benign manner. Rather, they viewed the American arms buildup as formidable threats to which they had to respond—most recently, by expanding ICBM inventories from approximately 150 missiles in 1962 and 340 in 1966 to roughly 1,000 in 1969.[25] It was this action-reaction process, and not anything inherent in the political conflicts between the United States and Russia, that fueled the demand for advanced weapons in both nations.

When he became Secretary of Defense in 1961, Robert S. McNamara was insensitive to the dynamics of the arms race. But he was willing to learn. In 1967, two gigantic new steps in the race—the development of multiple independent reentry vehicle missiles (MIRV) and an antiballistic missile (ABM) system—were at the decision point. Each had the potential of propelling U.S., Soviet, and Chinese arms stockpiles to unprecedented levels. In a major policy address, McNamara acknowledged that his early ICBM force level decisions had evoked a strong Soviet reaction:

---

23 On the history and theory of arms races, see Samuel P. Huntington, "Arms Races: Prerequisites and Results," *Public Policy*, Vol. 8 (Harvard University Graduate School of Public Administration, 1958), pp. 41–86; Philip Noel-Baker, *The Arms Race* (New York: Oceana, 1958); Lewis F. Richardson, *Arms and Insecurity* (Chicago: Boxwood Press, 1960); Malcolm Hoag, "On Stability in Deterrent Races," *World Politics*, 13:505 (July 1961); Martin C. McGuire, *Secrecy and the Arms Race* (Cambridge, Mass.: Harvard University Press, 1965), and F. M. Scherer, "Was the Nuclear Arms Race Inevitable?" *Co-existence*, 3:59 (January 1966).

24 On the Soviet perceptions and reactions, see Arnold Kramish, *Atomic Energy in the Soviet Union* (Stanford, Calif.: Stanford University Press, 1959); and the translation of articles by A. P. Alexandrov and Igor Golovin, *Bulletin of the Atomic Scientists*, 23:8 (December 1967).

25 Cf. "Clifford Disturbed by Rise in Russian Missile Force," *New York Times*, p. 1 (January 19, 1969).

Clearly, the Soviet buildup is in part a reaction to our own buildup since the beginning of this decade. Soviet strategic planners undoubtedly reasoned that if our buildup were to continue at its accelerated pace, we might conceivably reach, in time, a credible first strike capability against the Soviet Union. This was not in fact our intention . . . . But they could not read our intentions with any greater accuracy than we could read theirs. And thus the result has been that we have both built up our forces to a point that far exceeds a credible second-strike capability against the forces we each started with.[26]

He went on to argue that a similar arms race process was the underlying rationale for expenditures on ballistic missile defense, which could easily escalate to $40 billion:

Were we to deploy a heavy A.B.M. system throughout the United States, the Soviets would clearly be strongly motivated to so increase their offensive capability as to cancel out our defensive advantage. It is futile for each of us to spend $4 billion, $40 billion, or $400 billion— and at the end of all the spending . . . to be relatively at the same point of balance on the security scale that we are now. In point of fact, we have already initiated offensive weapons programs costing several billions in order to offset the small present Soviet A.B.M. deployment, and the possibly more extensive future Soviet A.B.M. deployments. That is money well spent; and it is necessary. But we should bear in mind that it is money spent because of the action-reaction phenomenon. If we in turn hope for heavy A.B.M. deployment—at whatever price— we can be certain that the Soviets will react to offset the advantage we would hope to gain.

Mr. McNamara concluded that the United States should limit its ABM effort stringently and that urgent steps should be taken through negotiation to curb the "mad momentum" of the nuclear weapons race.

Never before had a high official of the U.S. government characterized with such perception the nature of the demand for advanced weapons. It is difficult to escape the fear that what McNamara learned will be ignored by his followers. The attitudes Defense Secretary Melvin Laird brought into his new job in 1969 were strikingly different. Criticizing McNamara's "strategy of response," he urged earlier as a Congressman that:

The best way to insure that [general war] will never come is to return the United States to a full commitment behind the maintenance of a

---

26   *New York Times* (September 19, 1967), p. 18.

decisively superior defense posture. . . . To build our future defenses on the imagined good will of the potential adversary or on the belief that he shares a common interest with the free world in avoiding a nuclear exchange at all costs is, it seems to me, a grave mistake that gambles with the future security of the United States.[27]

Should this view of defense strategy persist, and should steps toward negotiated arms limitations falter as they have in the past, one can be sure that the demand for advanced weapons will continue to be strong.

THE MILITARY-INDUSTRIAL COMPLEX

In his farewell address, George Washington warned against the danger to liberty of "overgrown military establishments." Dwight D. Eisenhower resumed the theme in his final presidential address on January 17, 1961:

This conjunction of an immense military establishment and a large arms industry is new in the American experience. The total influence —economic, political, even spiritual—is felt in every city, every state-house, every office of the federal government. We recognize the imperative need for this development. Yet we must not fail to comprehend its grave implications. . . . In the councils of government we must guard against the acquisition of unwarranted influence, whether sought or unsought, by the military-industrial complex. The potential for the disastrous rise of misplaced power exists and will persist.

Do these warnings have some bearing in explaining why the level of arms spending is so high? The term "military-industrial complex" chosen by President Eisenhower calls to mind tales of payola, political logrolling, and sinister coalitions to deplete the Federal treasury through defense contracting largesse. There are indeed some grounds for concern, but blatant influence peddling and logrolling have only a peripheral impact on the demand for weapons. The main stimulant is a widely shared consensus that military superiority is the key to national security. This consensus is reinforced by chauvinistic oratory before American Legion conventions and by grossly exaggerated claims, leaked to a receptive press, of a bomber gap, a missile gap, and a ballistic missile defense gap. These, combined with the inexorable dynamics of the arms race and the perverse beneficence of modern science, are sufficient to keep the weapons industry operating at a healthy clip.

---

27 *Congressional Record,* 112:14539, 14534 (June 28, 1966). See also "Laird Predicts Delay on Arms Talks as Hearings on Cabinet Open," *New York Times* (January 15, 1969), p. 24.

Nevertheless, there are certain features of the decision-making process in which coalitions of vested interests play a particularly disturbing role. It is not easy to get a major new weapons development program going. Costs are high, risks and uncertainties substantial. Recognizing this, industrialists and military officers are inclined to view a program's future prospects through rose-tinted glasses, and there is a common belief at intermediate levels of the military decision-making hierarchy that one should not rock the boat too vigorously through criticism at the start of a program. Troubles can be pinpointed and corrected later, when the program has its own momentum. As we shall see, the nature of competition among weapons producers aggravates this propensity toward excessive optimism. The result may be seriously defective decisions.

The history of the Skybolt guided missile program provides an especially vivid illustration.[28] Prime contractor for Skybolt was the Douglas Aircraft Company. How it came to that role is an important part of the story. In the spring of 1959, when 14 firms were competing for the Skybolt job, Douglas was in trouble. It had been one of the first aircraft manufacturers to enter the guided missile field, and it had done extraordinarily well. Its responsibilities in the Nike Ajax, Nike Hercules, and Thor missile programs were discharged with admirable dispatch and efficiency, but the flow of production orders from those programs was ebbing. To fill the gap, Douglas competed strenuously for the Minuteman ICBM prime contractor's job in 1958, but the award went instead to Boeing, which had experience in only one prior missile program—the Bomarc anti-aircraft effort, generally acknowledged to have been a dismal failure. After this defeat, Douglas found its backlog situation desperate.

Skybolt, a proposed medium-range missile to be launched from B-52 bombers, seemed its best new opportunity, and it went all-out in the design competition. It abandoned its traditionally conservative engineering philosophy, accepting extreme technical risks in order to promise maximum technical performance to the Air Force contractor selection board. It underestimated the difficulty of the Skybolt development tasks, submitting optimistic cost and delivery date estimates in the expectation that it would be "bailed out" a year or so later when final contract provisions were negotiated. That Douglas' estimates were unduly optimistic was well known in aerospace industry circles at the time. Whether this knowledge permeated the Air Force general staff is not clear. That it did seems probable, however, for Air Force Chief of Staff Thomas White nearly let the cat out of the bag in 1960 by announcing that the Skybolt development program would last

---

28 This account is pieced together from published reports and from interviews the author had with military and industrial officials during the early months of the Skybolt program. A more comprehensive case study was prepared by Professor Richard Neustadt, at the request of President Kennedy, in 1963. Unfortunately, it was still classified top secret when this chapter was written.

8 years. This "accidental mistake" was quickly corrected by a Pentagon spokesman, who set the "correct" estimate at 4 or 5 years.[29]

Full understanding of Douglas' optimism evidently did not reach the very top of the government decision-making structure, for in April and May of 1960 the United States negotiated with Great Britain an agreement to supply Skybolt missiles to extend the operational life of England's deterrent force mainstay, the Vulcan bomber. Doubts soon arose, however. George Brown of the opposition Labour Party asserted in September 1960 that the Skybolt development had already slipped behind schedule by 10 months, but the Air Force vehemently denied delay of any "significant event" in the program.[30] Thus the program and the agreement with Great Britain continued through 1961 and into 1962.

The rest is history. By late 1962, the truth had become too compelling to deny. The cost of the program, originally estimated at $890 million, had risen to $3 billion and was still climbing. The delivery schedule was slipping steadily. Rumors of cancellation arose in early December, drawing heated protests from the British, who would have to spend large sums to maintain an independent strategic deterrent if Skybolt missiles were not available for their Vulcan bombers. Nevertheless, on December 13 Pentagon officials announced that the program would be continued only if the British agreed to pay the remaining development costs, estimated to be at least $500 million, plus the steadily rising costs of producing the operational missiles they needed. To resolve the dispute, President Kennedy and Prime Minister Macmillan agreed at their pre-Christmas Nassau meeting cooperatively to build up in place of Skybolt a "multilateral force" of submarines armed with Polaris missiles. France was invited to join the MLF effort. But President de Gaulle was infuriated that England and the United States had made this crucial decision of NATO policy without the simultaneous participation and consent of his country. He saw the MLF idea as a return to "special relations" between Britain and the U.S., and it is probable that the Skybolt-MLF affair cemented his determination to block British entry into the European Common Market. On January 1, 1963, de Gaulle flatly rejected the invitation to join the proposed MLF, and in the years thereafter the MLF issue contributed significantly to a deterioration of relations among NATO allies.

The moral of this story can be stated tersely. The military-industrial complex—a coalition of industrial executives and military officers—held back from the nation's leaders accurate information about a weapons program

---

29 "U.S.—British Deal on Missiles Is Set," *New York Times* (June 2, 1960), p. 3.
   30 "Delay on Skybolt Seen," *New York Times* (September 2, 1960), p. 2. See also the account of Arthur M. Schlesinger, Jr., *A Thousand Days* (Boston: Houghton-Mifflin, 1965), pp. 858–862. According to Schlesinger, Secretary McNamara twice chose not to press for more accurate information to avoid a fight with Air Force generals, whom he had angered in his ICBM and B-70 bomber decisions.

they were promoting, causing the United States to enter into an international agreement which subsequently collapsed, engendering much ill will. The repercussions of this incident are with us still.

III. MARKET CONDUCT
COMPETITION IN WEAPONS AND
SPACE VEHICLE PROCUREMENT

We turn now to a more detailed examination of how advanced weapons and space vehicles are acquired. Let us begin by examining the role competition plays.

Weapons contractors are exposed to powerful forces of competition. It is not, however, the kind of competition prescribed as the norm in Federal procurement laws, nor does it resemble the price competition observed when industrial product markets are working effectively. During the 1960's, the share of defense prime contract dollars awarded under advertised competitive bidding procedures ranged between 12 and 18 per cent.[31] Roughly 50-60 per cent of the awards were made without any formal competition at all—typically because a single firm had unique capabilities for meeting the government's demands. The remaining contract obligations were let under a variety of procedures blending competition, negotiation, and limits on entry. These ranged from design competitions, in which price was only one of many variables considered, to the purchase of perishable foodstuffs at the prices prevailing in local wholesale markets. Price competition is used most frequently in the procurement of standard commercial commodities and military items of an especially simple character. For the purchase of technically sophisticated weapons and space systems, straightforward price competition is more the exception than the rule.

However unhappy Congressmen may proclaim themselves to be over this state of affairs, it is virtually unavoidable. There are three main reasons for the inappropriateness of simple price competition in advanced weapons contracting. First, the purchases entail inherently multidimensional choices. The offerings of different contractors are almost never homogeneous; they vary with respect to countless technical performance features, reliability, and speed of delivery as well as price. The government must choose the best mix of these attributes; it cannot consider price alone. Second, know-how

---

31   See the testimony of Comptroller General Elmer B. Staats and Deputy Assistant Defense Secretary John M. Malloy in U.S. Senate, Committee on the Judiciary, Subcommittee on Antitrust and Monopoly, Hearings, *Competition in Defense Procurement* (Washington, D.C.: U.S. Government Printing Office, 1969), pp. 98–100, 107, and 139–145. NASA, buying fewer standardized commodities than the Defense Department, used advertised competitive bidding even less frequently—i.e., in from 3 to 6 per cent of its awards by dollar volume during the 1960's.

is extremely important. Once a particular firm has gained considerable experience with a design or product, it may have a decisive cost advantage over less experienced suppliers. Third, and perhaps most important, at the early stages of an ambitious development program technological uncertainty is high. Even if the government were to choose the contractor who seemingly met all qualitative specifications at the lowest price, it could not be sure that it would actually obtain what was promised. This last point deserves elaboration.

TECHNOLOGICAL UNCERTAINTY   The paramount distinguishing characteristic of the weapons and space vehicles industry is the vigor with which, backed by government funds and spurred by the dynamics of the qualitative arms race and the race to explore space, it probes the limits of technology. This is manifested in an extraordinary emphasis on research and development. In fiscal year 1966, $5.1 billion, or 14.7 per cent of the DOD total domestic procurement obligations, were earmarked for research and development activities. Fully 84 per cent of NASA's spending involved work of a sufficiently novel and experimental character to be called research and development (R&D). Furthermore, even after the R&D stage has been completed in aircraft, missile, radar, and similar programs, the production tasks tend to be intricate, and replete with routine-disrupting design changes—a far cry from cranking out sausages, aluminum ingots, or television sets.

Technological uncertainties abound in this research-oriented environment. Usually they are of a quantitative rather than a qualitative nature. That is, the issue is not whether a particular weapon system can be built at all, but how well it will perform, how reliable it will be, how long it will take to achieve desired levels of performance, and how much the effort will cost. Since as a rule there is greater stress on meeting performance goals than on cost control, the consequences of technological uncertainty show up with special force in the form of unpredicted cost increases. A study of 12 major weapon systems development programs conducted during the late 1940's and the 1950's revealed that on the average, actual R&D costs turned out to be 3.2 times higher than originally estimated.[32] Similar errors occurred in predicting costs of producing operational equipment. For the same sample of programs, development schedules averaged 36 per cent longer than initially predicted.

---

32 Peck and Scherer, op. cit., p. 22. See also A. W. Marshall and W. H. Meckling, "Predictability of the Costs, Time, and Success of Development," in the National Bureau of Economic Research Conference volume, *The Rate and Direction of Inventive Activity* (Princeton, N.J.: Princeton University Press, 1962), pp. 461–475; and Robert Summers, "Cost Estimates as Predictors of Actual Weapon Costs," Rand Corporation document RM-3061-PR (Santa Monica, Calif.: Rand Corporation, 1965).

Strenuous efforts by Secretary of Defense McNamara to improve matters during the 1960's were not particularly successful.[33] Two widely acclaimed test cases of McNamara's cost control techniques were the F-111 fighter and C-5A transport programs. The cost of developing the F-111 was originally estimated at $700 million by General Dynamics and $900 million by military analysts.[34] But by 1968, actual development costs had soared to $2 billion. The Phoenix air-to-air missile for the Navy version of the F-111 was to be developed for $175 million; actual costs were nearing $420 million when the program was terminated. In the C-5A transport program, tight cost control was sought by avoiding risky technical approaches and by negotiating a contract which placed unusually heavy responsibility for absorbing cost increases upon the prime contractor. Yet the actual cost of producing the first 58 units exceeded the contractor's original $1.3 billion estimate by at least $900 million.[35]

Experiences like these are a reality which cannot be ignored in shaping the institutions within which competition among weapons and space vehicle contractors operates. At the same time, government procurement agencies are under heavy pressure from Congress to employ fair, impartial competitive methods to the fullest possible extent. The result is often an uneasy compromise satisfactory to no one.

SOURCE SELECTION COMPETITIONS   Competition between rival contractors can arise at any point in the life of a program, but the most dramatic moment of confrontation usually occurs at the very outset, when major developmental responsibilities are assigned. This is the so-called "source selection competition" stage. Along with many variants and mixtures, three main types of source selection competition, depending upon the choice criteria emphasized, can be identified: selection on the basis of the quality of design proposals submitted; selection on the basis of available technical and managerial resources; and selection on the basis of demonstrated past performance.

The first approach is exemplified in the "design competition." Qualified firms are invited to prepare more or less detailed design proposals, complete

---

33 For evidence that the operating reliability of 1960's vintage weapons actually deteriorated relative to the 1950's see Richard A. Stubbing, "Improving the Acquisition Process for High-Risk Military Electronic Systems," reprinted in the *Congressional Record* (February 7, 1969), pp. S1449–1455.

34 For an extensive analysis of the F-111 program's inception and consequences, see U.S. Senate, Committee on Government Operations, Permanent Subcommittee on Investigations, hearings, *TFX Contract Investigation* (Washing-

ton, D.C.: U.S. Government Printing Office, 1963 and later years). See also Robert J. Art, *The TFX decision: McNamara and the Military* (Boston: Little, Brown, 1968); and Richard A. Smith, *Corporations in Crisis*, op. cit., Chaps. IX and X.

35 Contrast John Mecklin, "The Ordeal of the Plane Makers," *Fortune*, **72**:158 (December 1965); and the Joint Economic Committee Hearings, *Economics of Military Procurement*, op. cit., pp. 200–209, 253–259, and 293–319.

with development and production cost estimates, for review by a government evaluation board. Design competitions have two prime advantages. The government obtains a diversity of proposed technical approaches, from which it may choose the most promising. And at least ideally, its choice can be made on the basis of objective engineering analyses, without delving into political ramifications or subjective personality judgments. But with these benefits come three significant drawbacks.

For one, technical uncertainties often preclude choosing a true "winner" at the early design stage, while prolonging the competition until uncertainty has been reduced through design refinement and prototype testing may be excessively costly.[36] Normally many design changes are made after a winner is selected, and it is not unusual for the winning entrant to scrap its original approach altogether.[37] The only thing that can be deduced confidently from preliminary design proposals in ambitious programs is whether the bidder really understands the technical problems at hand. But this is usually known anyway by well-informed government engineers. In a study of 48 government design competitions in which the government scientist reponsible for issuing requests for bidding ranked the potential bidders in advance, it was found that in 39 cases, the first or second most favored bidder ultimately won the technical evaluation.[38] This suggests that when the technical alternatives and their exponents are well known, as they usually are, the government might do as well be selecting a contractor informally and then working closely with him to evolve a suitable final design.

Another problem is the propensity of design competition entrants to submit excessively optimistic proposals, since they recognize that cost estimates biased on the low side are less likely to stir up the opposition of budget-minded officials. Indeed, design competitions are often called "bidding and lying" competitions in the trade. When decisions are taken on the basis of these distorted projections, resource misallocation and waste result.

A third disadvantage of design competitions is the enormous drain on technical talent they impose. Winning source selection competitions is the *sine qua non* of existence for a defense and space specialist. As long as its order backlog is slender, a firm is compelled to assign its most creative scientists and engineers to design proposal work, entering one competition

---

36   But see Burton Klein, "A Radical Proposal for Military R&D," *Fortune*, 57:112 (May 1958), who urges a return to the "prototype competition" approach used before World War II and in the immediate postwar period in aircraft procurement.

37   See, for example, Charles J. V. Murphy, "Boeing's Ordeal with the SST," *Fortune*, 78:129 (October 1968).

38   Cf. Edward B. Roberts, "Questioning the Cost/Effectiveness of the R&D Procurement Process," ed. by M. C. Yovits et al., *Research Program Effectiveness* (New York: Gordon and Breach, 1966), pp. 93–113; and "Facts and Folklore in Research and Development Management," *Industrial Management Review*, 8:5 (Spring 1967).

after another until a sufficient number of contracts is in hand. When a company has considerable excess capacity, as was true in many advanced weapons fields during the late 1950's and early 1960's, proposal preparation may become a permanent assignment for these people. They are backed up by large numbers of less talented engineers, since the design brochures presented for government evaluation are often extremely detailed, running to thousands of pages. In the first stage of the F-111 source selection competition, before the field was narrowed to General Dynamics and Boeing, the six entrants spent from $4 million to $7 million each on their proposals. Furthermore, Air Force and Navy technical personnel consumed some 100-man years evaluating the submissions. For there to be six or so entrants is commonplace in major manned aircraft and guided missile system source selection competitions. On less demanding missile projects and subsystem contracts, the number of competitors may run as high as 30 or 40. Since in most cases equally good designs could be obtained through a much more limited and informal screening, the upshot is a tremendous waste of scarce scientific and engineering talent.[39]

Aware of this, government procurement agencies have tried to discourage overly elaborate design preparation, putting increasing stress on other criteria such as the availability of suitable technical, managerial, and plant resources. The attempt to restrain contractors' proposal work has borne little fruit, since an eager bidder invariably hopes he can win by outclassing his rivals in design refinement. Moreover, the resource availability approach creates its own set of problems. If the firm with engineers and craftsmen in reserve is favored when new contracts are given out, there emerges a strong incentive to hoard talent. When technology is changing rapidly, top management finds it worthwhile to divert its attention from conducting on-going programs efficiently to building capabilities that lure contracts in new fields. The preoccupation of aerospace producers with diversification during the late 1950's contributed markedly to the emergence of excess capacity in many lines, aggravating the inherent insecurity of defense contractors and causing them to scurry all the more frantically for additional orders.

A third possible criterion approach is to reward firms which have performed well in the past with attractive new contracts while penalizing poor performers by withholding orders. It has one compelling advantage: it generates the strongest possible incentives for efficient, innovative performance of on-going programs. But it too has limitations. Good performance in one program does not necessarily guarantee good performance on the next round. A successful contractor may become complacent or committed to obsolescent technical approaches, whereas the unsuccessful may learn from their mistakes. More important, evaluating the performance of con-

---

39 On the relationship between the number of rivals and the vigor of their efforts in weapon systems designing, see F. M. Scherer, *The Weapons Acquisition Process: Economic Incentives* (Boston: Harvard Business School, 1964), pp. 44–49.

tractors in pioneering research and development assignments is not easy. It is impossible to avoid some element of subjective judgment. If the evaluation job were done poorly, it could damage morale and nullify the system's incentive value.[40]

To sum up, implementing an effective system of competition in contractor selection poses myriad difficulties. The best hope for the future would appear to lie in deemphasizing formalized, ritualistic selection processes and placing more stress on past performance. During the 1950's there was no consistent policy of rewarding good performance. Somewhat more attention was paid to past performance in selection decisions of the 1960's, and a few weapons specialists with particularly weak records were allowed to wither and die. A great deal can still be done, however, to make the forces of competition channel contractor energies in more constructive directions.

COMPETITION WHEN PROGRAMS ARE UNDERWAY   Being chosen to develop a new weapon or space system does not confer total immunity from further competition. Other more or less close substitute systems in varying stages of development may raise a planned or unplanned competitive challenge. However, as new weapons have become increasingly complex and costly, the government has found itself able to support fewer and fewer competing alternatives at any moment in time. Even then, unlike programs compete with one another for support from a finite defense budget. The contractor that allows its program's costs to approach benefits too closely risks total loss of budgetary support.

If its program succeeds in weathering the storms of close substitute competition and in maintaining budgetary support, a contractor usually faces little or no direct competitive challenge to its role in producing what it has developed, at least during the early stages of a production program. This is true for several reasons. When the production of a new device or system is just getting underway, information on operational "bugs" gained from tests inspires a steady stream of design changes. To introduce these improvements efficiently requires close coordination of the engineering and production functions, and this is most easily accomplished when the two functions are integrated organizationally. The original development contractor has the advantage of possessing special jigs, fixtures, and test equipment which could be duplicated by a competing producer only at considerable cost. The original contractor also accumulates manufacturing know-how, permitting production of subsequent units at reduced cost, whereas a new producer would have to start from scratch, at the top of its "learning curve." Because the original development contractor has these advantages over outsiders, "follow-on" production contracts are often awarded by the government without any attempt to seek competition from alternative sources.

---

40   But the task probably can be and will if a sincere effort is made. See the proposal in Scherer, op. cit., pp. 327–362.

Most advanced weapons and space vehicles, serving specialized demands and exposed to rapid technological obsolescence, have short production runs and never emerge from this "sole source" stage. Still there are exceptions. When a long production run is expected after designs are stabilized, the gains from putting competitive pressure on costs and prices can more than repay the government's cost in setting up a new production operation. In no major weapon systems program known to the author has the original prime development contractor had its production responsibilities completely usurped by a competitive challenger. However, in numerous programs the government has established a "second source" to produce part of its requirements in competition with the original source. The share of the total order allocated to each source is then determined on the basis of cost and price comparisons. This method has generated strong incentives for cost reduction, and more widespread use has been urged.[41]

Price competition has been sought more aggressively on weapon systems component production. The simplest parts are often "broken out" for competitive bidding early in a production program, and gradually the effort is extended to include fairly complicated components and subassemblies. Nearly half of all replenishment spare parts for weapons and a smaller but not inconsequential fraction of all original equipment items have been procured in this way.[42] Price reductions resulting from the introduction of competitive bidding have averaged more than 25 per cent, according to DOD surveys.[43] Weapons producers at first tried to protect themselves by insisting that their designs and the know-how underlying them were "proprietary," but this claim was rejected by the DOD and contractors are now required to supply "data packages" sufficiently detailed to permit other firms to manufacture the product when the government so desires.

PRICE FORMATION
AND CONTRACTUAL INCENTIVES

Another respect in which the weapons and space vehicles industry differs from most of American manufacturing industry is in the methods by which prices and profits are determined. Except on that small share of the procurement volume awarded through orthodox competitive bidding, contract prices are usually set through bilateral negotiation. Moreover, because of the technological uncertainties pervading development and production programs,

---

41 See ibid., pp. 117–126; and the testimony of R. E. Johnson, G. R. Hall, and Ralph C. Nash, Jr., before the Senate Antitrust Subcommittee in *Competition in Defense Procurement*, op. cit., pp. 34–81 and 193–198.
42 See the testimony of John M.

Malloy in the same hearings, ibid., pp. 145–146.
43 See the testimony of Assistant Secretary of Defense Paul R. Ignatius in the Joint Economic Committee hearings, *Economic Impact of Federal Procurement* (Washington, D.C.: U.S. Government Printing Office, 1966), pp. 73–74.

special contractual instruments have been devised to shift risk from the contractor to the government. These include the infamous cost-plus-fixed-fee (CPFF) contract and various hybrid forms known as "incentive" contracts.[44]

THE PRINCIPAL CONTRACT TYPES   The differences between the principal contract types can best be characterized in terms of a simple equation. The contractor's total realized profit from a contract is given by the following relationship:

$$Realized\ profit = Target\ profit + \alpha\,(Target\ cost - Actual\ cost)$$

Ideally before any work on the contract has begun, but sometimes much later, the government and its contractor negotiate the target cost, the target profit, and α, which is known as the sharing proportion. The sharing proportion α can vary from 0 to 1.0. When $\alpha = 1.0$, a "firm fixed price" contractual relationship obtains. If actual cost upon contract completion then proves to be higher than the original target (an "overrun" situation), the contractor absorbs the excess dollar-for-dollar as a deduction from its realized profit. Obversely, if actual cost turns out to be less than the original target (an "underrun" situation), the contractor retains the full savings as added profit. For CPFF contracts, $\alpha = 0$. Then the contractor's profit realization is fixed at the target profit amount, whether actual costs equal target cost, exceed it, or fall below it. With CPFF coverage the government bears the full burden of cost overruns and enjoys the full benefit of any cost underruns. "Incentive" contracts represent a compromise between these two extremes, with α values lying between 0 and 1.0—most commonly, in the neighborhood of 0.20–0.35. Under a cost incentive contract, the contractor absorbs as a deduction from profits the fraction α of any cost overrun, the government paying the balance; whereas the contractor retains 100α per cent of an underrun, the government receiving the rest of the saving. A further distinction is drawn over the handling of very large cost overruns. If costs rise above some negotiated ceiling, the contractor absorbs 100 per cent of the increment under "fixed-price incentive" contracts. Under "cost-plus-incentive-fee" contracts, the government is responsible for reimbursing fully any costs exceeding the negotiated ceiling.

If all other elements of the contractual relationship are held constant, the contractor's incentive to control and reduce costs is strongest under a firm fixed price contract, with $\alpha = 1.0$. It is weakest under a CPFF contract. Should costs get out of control under a firm fixed price arrangement, the contractor may incur severe losses—a prospect avoided with CPFF contractual

---

44 For a more intensive analysis of the implications of various contract types, see Scherer, op. cit., Chaps. 6–8; and Frederick T. Moore, *Military Procure-* *ment and Contracting: An Economic Analysis*, Rand Corporation publication RM-2948-PR (Santa Monica, Calif.: Rand Corporation, 1962).

coverage. Because they tend to be risk averters, defense and space contractors have generally preferred to operate under CPFF contracts or incentive contracts with very low α values when they face substantial cost uncertainties. In some respects risk also increases with the value of α from the buyer's viewpoint, for if actual costs turn out to be much less than the target under a firm fixed price or similar contract, the contractor can end up earning very high profits. This may embarrass the government contracting officer before his superiors and Congress, so that government negotiators often display a preference toward low values of α when uncertainty is high. This preference may be countervened, however, by pressures from higher headquarters to employ contracts with the strongest possible incentive effect.

To induce contractor acceptance of contracts with relatively high α values, the government pays a risk premium in the target profit. A study of defense contracts negotiated during the 1950's revealed the following relationships between the contract type and the average target profit, expressed as a percentage of the negotiated target cost[45]:

Cost-plus-fixed-fee	6.4 per cent
Cost-plus-incentive-fee	7.0 per cent
Fixed price incentive	8.6 per cent
Firm fixed price	11.5 per cent

The premium for shifting from one polar extreme, CPFF, to the firm fixed price pole appears to have been on the order of five percentage points. In determining what kind of contract to seek, government negotiators must weigh the increased cost associated with paying the risk premium on high-α contracts against the cost savings expected from exposing the contractor to more potent incentives.

The type of contract negotiated in any given situation depends upon the expectations of the contracting parties concerning costs and their variability, the attitudes of the parties toward risk bearing, the relative bargaining power of the parties, and overall government policy. During World War II, CPFF contracts accounted for approximately 30 per cent of the value of all defense contracts.[46] This fairly heavy reliance upon the riskless CPFF form reflected the inexperience of most contractors in producing war goods, which in turn implied a high degree of uncertainty in predicting costs. Since then there have been marked variations over time in the extent to which the various contract types have been utilized, as Table 9 reveals. In fiscal year 1952, at the peak of the Korean war procurement effort, 18 per cent of total obligations were committed under CPFF instruments. The production of CPFF work rose steadily through the 1950's as increasing stress was placed on research, development, and the production of complex sophisticated weapon systems and subsystems. It then fell sharply during the 1960's after Secretary

45   Scherer, op. cit., p. 273.
46   See John Perry Miller, *Pricing*   *of Military Procurements* (New Haven: Yale University Press, 1949), p. 127.

TABLE 9 PROPORTION OF MILITARY PROCUREMENT
DOLLARS OBLIGATED UNDER THE PRINCIPAL
CONTRACT TYPES, FISCAL YEARS (FY) 1952–1968

CONTRACT TYPE	FY 1952 (%)	FY 1956 (%)	FY 1960 (%)	FY 1964 (%)	FY 1968 (%)
Firm fixed price	29.8	36.4	31.4	46.3	52.7
Fixed price incentive	12.0	19.2	13.6	18.5	18.7
Cost-plus-incentive-fee	0.0	1.9	3.2	14.1	9.0
Cost-plus-fixed-fee[a]	17.8	28.0	39.0	14.3	12.8
All other types[b]	40.4	14.5	12.8	6.8	6.8

   a Includes cost-plus-no-fee.
   b Includes time and materials, escalation, and redeterminable contracts.
The last form, which permits the price to be readjusted when the contract is par-
tially or sometimes fully executed, poses special incentive problems. See F. M.
Scherer, *The Weapons Acquisition Process: Economic Incentives* (Boston:
Harvard Business School, 1964), pp. 137–140.
   SOURCE U.S. Department of Defense, *Military Prime Contract Awards and Sub-
contract Payments* (Washington, D.C.: U.S. Department of Defense, annually).

McNamara began a drive to negotiate contracts with stronger cost-reduction
incentives. NASA, with an even sharper research and development orientation than DOD, spent only 10 to 12 per cent of its procurement funds under
firm fixed price contracts between 1963 and 1967. However, it too caught the
incentive contracting bug, reducing its use of CPFF contracts from 79 per
cent of total procurement volume in 1964 to 21 per cent in 1967, compensating
with increased application of cost-plus-incentive-fee and fixed-price incentive
instruments.

IV. MARKET PERFORMANCE

The Department of Defense has claimed multibillion dollar cost savings
as a consequence of its shift from CPFF to incentive-type contracts. Its
official statements estimate the saving at 10 per cent of actual contract outlays when incentive provisions (i.e., α on the order of 0.30) are employed in
place of CPFF terms.[47] This conjecture stemmed from observation that
CPFF contracts have historically tended to end in an overrun condition,
whereas actual cost turned out on the average to be less than target cost under
fixed price incentive and firm fixed price contracts. That firms try harder to
reduce costs when they share in the savings appears indisputable. However,

---

47 See the testimony of Secretary
McNamara in the Joint Economic Com-
mittee hearings, *Economic Impact of*
Federal Procurement (Washington, D.C.:
U.S. Government Printing Office, 1966),
pp. 21–23 and 37.

most economists studying the operation of contractual incentives believe that the 10 per cent saving claim is exaggerated.[48] Their skepticism is based upon two main propositions.

First, case studies of defense contractor operations under diverse contractual arrangements have yielded little evidence of significant behavioral changes when the organization moved from a CPFF situation to the kind of fixed price incentive contract customarily negotiated. This is so partly because project managers are reluctant to cut corners on quality, endangering company reputation; and partly because "organizational slack" is an advantage toward winning source selection competitions. Also, corporate management has difficulty instilling in line supervisors a sense of urgency with respect to cost-reducing, profit-increasing measures, whereas the man on the line knows much better than top managers where costs can be cut without sacrificing product quality or delivery schedules. As a result, contractors appeared willing and able to lay off surplus personnel only when the danger of outright financial loss was great.

Skepticism is called for in addition because the cost outcomes of differently structured incentive contracts depend critically upon the balance of bargaining power in cost target negotiations. It is easier to gain high profits by bamboozling the government negotiator into accepting a generously padded cost target than through an all-out effort to reduce actual costs once the target is set. Even when the contractor has no such rapacious intent, large cost underruns may be due more to good luck on the outcome of events, which could be predicted in advance only within a substantial range of uncertainty, than to conscious, deliberate, cost-reducing actions by the contractor.[49]

This dependence of incentive and firm fixed price contract profits on chance and success in negotiations is the chief pitfall in the incentive contract approach. Naturally, contractors try to make the best of contract bargaining. Theory, case study evidence, and experimental gaming results all indicate that the contractors are more willing to accept contracts with high sharing proportions when they are fairly confident that actual costs will be less than the established target.[50] Obversely, they fight hard for a

---

48 See Scherer, op. cit., pp. 191–270; John G. Cross, "A Reappraisal of Cost Incentives in Defense Contracts," *Western Economic Journal*, 6:205 (June 1968). Edward B. Roberts, "Fact and Folklore in Research and Development Management," *Industrial Management Review*, 8:15 (Spring 1967); Sloan School of Management, Massachusetts Institute of Technology, E. B. Roberts and J. Barry Sloat, "Effects of Incentive Contracts in Research and Development: A Preliminary Research Report," Working Paper 186-66 (Cambridge, Mass.: Massachusetts Institute of Technology, April 1966); and I. N. Fisher, "An Evaluation of Incentive Contracting Experience," *Naval Research Logistics Quarterly*, 16:63 (March 1969).

49 See Scherer, op. cit., for evidence from several groups of contracts.

50 The gaming findings are reported in G. J. Feeney, W. H. McGlothlin, and R. J. Wolfson, *Risk Aversion in Incentive Contracting: An Experiment*, Rand Corporation publication RM-4231-PR (Santa Monica, Calif.: Rand Corporation, August 1964).

low α value when a substantial overrun is anticipated. When the government insists upon a high sharing ratio, they seek cost targets with ample elbow room, resisting reductions in the target with all the bargaining resources they can mobilize. To the extent that they are successful, one would expect the contracts which *ex post facto* show the largest underruns to be those on which high sharing proportions were accepted—precisely what the historical evidence reveals.

In contrast, government negotiators seeking to minimize total contract outlays will press for low α values when an underrun is likely, while a high α value is optimal when a sizable overrun is expected.[51] Except when both parties are so strongly risk averse that they mutually crave the security of low sharing ratios, there is a conflict between the contractor's set of cost target and α preferences and that of the government. How this conflict is resolved depends upon the relative bargaining power and skill the two parties bring into negotiations.

At the start of a program, the government holds most of the trump cards. Competition from other firms seeking a role in the program may still be at work, or if the final source-selection decisions have been made, memory of promises made in the heat of rivalry constrains the contractor's cost estimates. High-level support for the program is not yet solidified, and for this reason, too, the contractor must be careful not to seek too generous a cost target. Thus, in the early stages of weapons and space vehicle programs there is a strong tendency for cost target estimates to be optimistic, rendering an ultimate contract cost overrun probable. The contractor escapes paying a heavy financial penalty for its optimism only because government negotiators are also risk averters, preferring low α values in the face of significant technological uncertainty, and perhaps also because government project officers fear that the contractor might default or cut corners on quality if heavy losses were imminent.

As a program progresses into the production stage, the advantage in negotiations usually shifts to the contractor. With a change to other producers inhibited by the contractor's technological advantage, the contractor is locked together with his buyer in a bilateral monopoly relationship. If close substitutes pose no immediate competitive threat and if the program has a sufficiently high priority to be assured of budgetary support, the bargaining outcome is indeterminate over a wide range of possible cost targets. Where the actual bargain falls within this range can depend crucially upon knowledge of costs. The contractor nearly always has much better information than the government negotiator on what future costs will be, and so the contractor enjoys a distinct advantage in securing contract terms

---

51 See F. M. Scherer, "The Theory of Contractual Incentives for Cost Reduction," *Quarterly Journal of Economics*, **78**:271 (May 1964); and O. Hagen, "Risk Aversion and Incentive Contracting," *Economic Record*, **12**:416 (September 1966).

that promise a generous profit return or at least minimize the risk of loss. It is largely because of this knowledge disparity that the incentive contracts negotiated in advanced weapons production programs have ended in under-runs more often than overruns, and why outright financial losses under such contracts have been rare.

There may, nevertheless, be an important exception to the rule. When a contractor has considerable excess capacity, it will be hard-pressed for orders to keep its staff busy. If the government negotiator is astute, he can take advantage of this weakness. He may stall, delay the initiation of progress payments, and when the delivery schedule is not urgent, even refuse to authorize further work, so that the contractor is forced either to stop pro-ducing and lay off workers or continue without the assurance of any payment at all. Confronted with such pressures, the contractor may accede to a tight cost target and at the same time a high α value.

Cases of this sort seem to have proliferated during the 1960's. The use of incentive and firm fixed price contracts for weapons production rose sharply, but for the first time in recent history, overruns became more com-mon than underruns as pressure on cost targets mounted. Negotiated profit rates on all DOD CPFF and incentive contracts rose from an average of 8.0 per cent in fiscal years 1959–1963 to 8.8 per cent in fiscal years 1964–1968, largely because of the shift away from CPFF toward incentive contracts bearing relatively high profit targets. But *realized* profit rates remained constant at 7.7 per cent due to the increasing incidence of cost overruns.[52] This was why Secretary McNamara's drive to raise defense industry profits was largely unsuccessful. Competitive pressures, operating indirectly on negotiated cost targets rather than directly on profit margins, simply would not support the desired increase. Still the policy of substituting incentive contracts for CPFF instruments undoubtedly stimulated some incremental reduction, satisfying one of McNamara's two original objectives.

This survey of broad central tendencies belies the wide variation among individual contract outcomes. A few incentive contracts end in outright financial losses; a larger fraction yield profits well in excess of the originally negotiated target. Although some of the highly profitable outcomes may be the result of diligent cost reduction efforts, it seems more likely that loose cost target negotiation and good luck on unpredictable contingencies are the primary causes. This has not escaped the notice of Congress, which has consistently refused to accept a "law of averages" approach to defense contract profits. Especially profitable contracts have been singled out for investigation and criticism. Elaborate prenegotiation and post-execution audits have been enforced to guard against abuse. When these failed to solve the problem, Congress in 1962 passed a "truth in negotiations" bill requiring prime contractors and major subcontractors to certify that the cost data

---

52   Cf. "Defense Profits Lag," *Business Week*, **2053**:22 (January 4, 1969).

they submit for negotiations are "current, accurate, and complete." As a further check, Congress has demanded the maintenance of a renegotiation procedure under which the reasonableness of sizable government contractors' profits is reviewed annually. Excessive profit refunds ordered by the Renegotiation Board since World War II have ranged from a high of $167 million in 1955 to a low of $8 million in 1962. There is reason to believe that the profit review and recapture practices of the Renegotiation Board may in some instances weaken incentives for efficiency, and the whole question has been debated hotly.[53] But as long as it is possible to gain high defense contract profits through cost padding and chance, Congress is likely to continue supporting some kind of renegotiation system.

MULTIDIMENSIONAL INCENTIVE CONTRACTS   One further aspect of contracting policy merits briefer treatment. The Department of Defense and NASA have begun to use "multidimensional" incentive contracts with increasing frequency in their research and development programs. Such contracts tie the contractor's realized profit to its success in meeting technical performance and reliability targets and in maintaining delivery schedules, as well as to the contractor's control of costs. This approach has the obvious virtue of providing balanced rewards and penalties on all dimensions of contract performance important to the government. However, it also has some disadvantages.

For one, many of the incentives it creates are redundant. Most defense and space contractors are strongly motivated to deliver a high-performance product, for their reputations and the ability to secure future contracts might suffer if they fail to do so. Case studies of defense and space vehicle development programs identified no significant constructive behavioral changes when quality incentives were introduced into contracts.[54] In view of this, and given that contractors have historically been more successful in meeting performance goals than cost targets under research and development contracts, the main effect of multidimensional incentive contracts seems to have been to raise profits slightly by paying contractors bonuses for what they would have done in any event.

Second, the incentive provisions can be subverted. In the B-58 bomber development program, for example, General Dynamics received an incentive payment for delivering all its bomb pods on time, even though deliveries of the aircraft itself fell badly behind schedule, so that there were no bombers to carry the pods. In the F-111 program, the same firm received an $875,000 bonus for demonstrating that a prototype airplane's wings could be pivoted

---

53 For a survey of the issues, see Scherer, *The Weapons Acquisition Process: Economic Incentives*, op. cit., pp. 252–268.

54 Ibid., pp. 166–171; A. L. Baker, "A Study of the Managerial Decision Process under Multi-Incentive Contracts," unpublished master's thesis, Sloan School of Management, Massachusetts Institute of Technology (Cambridge, 1965).

backwards and forwards in flight.[55] It was only later that tests disclosed flaws in the pivot mechanism. Since the whole point of the program was to develop a fighter embodying the variable wing sweep technique, the bonus arrangement was not unlike paying a refrigerator manufacturer a bonus because his product keeps one's milk cold.

Absurdities such as these can be avoided by thoughtful contract negotiation, but this poses a third problem. The negotiation of multidimensional incentive provisions is an enormously complicated affair, draining untold quantities of technical and managerial talent away from more productive work. Once the contract is negotiated, it serves as a kind of straightjacket, forcing project managers to forgo unplanned design improvements that conflict with the incentive formula, to go ahead with the changes and suffer reduced profits, or to renegotiate the contract. Since the third alternative is most apt to be chosen in important matters, the end result is an increase in bureaucratic paper shuffling which at best raises costs and at worst diverts management's energies from getting the substantive job at hand done.

V. PUBLIC POLICY

On this dreary note we end our detailed examination of contracting practices and step back to survey the larger picture. How good or bad has the performance of the weapons and space vehicles industry been? What can be done to improve matters?

Reaching a balanced appraisal of industry performance is peculiarly difficult, since the standard theories and measures of industrial organization analysis are largely inapplicable. Profit levels, for instance, say little about the caliber of performance, because they depend in part upon government contracting policies, and government agencies have made no concerted effort to relate returns to the efficiency of specific contractors or to the aggregate balance between demand and resource supply. Nor do data on costs and prices tell us much, since the products of different suppliers are typically unique, preventing interfirm and intertemporal comparison. Whatever summary judgment we reach must be crude, qualitative, and even impressionistic.

When one is preoccupied with the industry's manifest problems, as we have been at times, it is hard to avoid a sense of wonder that anything gets done at all. Technological uncertainties abound. Competition impels contract-seekers to distort the data on which program decisions are based and to divert talent from creative research and development into salesmanship.

---

55   See "New Fuss Over F-111," *Business Week*, **2003**:32 (January 20, 1968), and "New Flaw Found in F-111 Planes," *New York Times*, p. 1 (Dec. 20, 1969).

Workers and engineers are hoarded in unproductive uses. Contractual instruments grow to unbelievable complexity, but have only peripheral effects on behavior. The bureaucracy increases, multiplies, and fills the earth.

Yet things do get done. The industry is responsible for many of the most spectacular technological achievements of all time. That men have been able to land on the moon and return home safely is astonishing even to the most callous science watcher. The arsenal of missiles, nuclear submarines, hydrogen bombs, supersonic fighters, infrared detection devices, and so on, amassed cannot help but impress. The chauvinist's acid test is passed with flying colors, for the United States has managed to maintain leadership among world powers in most areas of military technology. All this has been accomplished at a very high expenditure of resources; cost control is undoubtedly the dimension along which performance has been least satisfactory. There is an extraordinary amount of waste, but the process does generate results.

No easy solutions to the problems of the industry exist. However, three broad lines of possible attack can be identified. First, the system of incentives guiding and stimulating contractor behavior might be improved. Second, controls might be imposed to ensure that contractor actions and decisions do not stray too far from acceptable norms. Third, the whole structure of the industry might be radically altered—i.e., by encouraging large-scale mergers or by nationalizing substantial segments.

Incentive system reforms are clearly desirable. To improve competitive incentives, greater flexibility should be introduced into the process of selecting contractors for new programs. More stress should be placed on rewarding good past performance in selection decisions and less should be put on costly but inherently unreliable design proposals. In the realm of contracting policy, and especially for research and development contracts, there should be less reliance on "Rube Goldberg" contracts with a carrot for every conceivable accomplishment. Instead, a continuing effort should be exerted systematically to assess the quality of contractors' performance and to award high profits to firms with especially good records and to penalize those who fall below the norm.

Direct controls over contractor operations have already been extended to a considerable degree, partly in response to the acknowledged failure of incentive mechanisms. Government program management offices monitor contractor activities in detail, initiating or reviewing all significant decisions on product design, specifications, design changes, the choice of subcontractors, quality control procedures, and even methods of financing new equipment. Contractors are hired by the government to oversee the work of other contractors. Hoards of auditors roam contractor plants, and so on. Many of these measures are essential. Yet too much control can stifle creativity and initiative, and it certainly adds to the mounting bureaucratic costs of defense and space work. Whether the controls actually imposed have been excessive is difficult to determine. Nevertheless, to the extent that the two are substitutes rather than complements, it seems clearly desirable to expend more energy on improving incentives so that the more oppressive controls can be eliminated.

Finally, more drastic structural remedies might be effected. The United States might imitate British policy of the late 1950's by encouraging mergers which lead ultimately to an industry dominated by a few very large, fully integrated weapons supply firms directly susceptible to government shaping and control. Already during the 1960's such important weapons producers as Chance-Vought, Republic, and Douglas surrendered their independence through merger with other aerospace companies. More consolidations can be expected in the future, unless the Justice Department or the Defense Department prevent them.[56] Within wide limits, such mergers have less of an adverse effect on competition than they might in industries producing homogeneous products, since the multidimensional character of weapons procurement decisions makes it possible to achieve vigorous rivalry even when only two firms are vying for an order. Still it is not clear that concentration-increasing mergers in the weapons industry would yield much in the way of social benefits, for the government already has the power to mold industry structure in desired directions through its source selection actions, and it can eliminate tendencies toward wasteful competition by altering its selection criteria. Therefore, it is no doubt better to retain a general presumption against aerospace mergers that substantially increase concentration, relaxing it only when the benefits of a proposed merger are patent and compelling.

Nationalization is a final possibility. As we have observed, the United States has moved in the opposite direction over the past half century. Existing shipyards, arsenals, and laboratories have been allowed to languish and die, in part through explicit closure decisions made on essentially ideological grounds,[57] and partly through a process of erosion in which the most challenging engineering assignments were allocated to private industry, leaving only the dregs for in-house groups.[58] Whether substantial segments

---

56 Only the merger of Chance-Vought with Ling-Temco Electronics was challenged, and the ensuing litigation produced one of the Justice Department's rare defeats in enforcing the Celler-Kefauver Act. *U.S.* v. *Ling-Temco Electronics, Inc., et al.,* CCH 1961 Trade Cases, Para. 70,160. The Douglas and Republic mergers were apparently not challenged because those firms were in serious financial trouble at the time they were acquired.

57 An especially striking case was the closing of the Army's Springfield Arsenal in 1968, leaving the Army with no in-house small arms design and de-

velopment group. See Edward C. Ezell, "The Death of the Arsenal System? The Decision To Close Springfield Armory," paper presented at the annual meeting of the Organization of American Historians in 1968, summarized in *Technology and Culture,* 9:576 (October 1968).

58 This practice was criticized in the so-called Bell Report. See U.S. Senate, Committee on Government Operations, document prepared by the Bureau of the Budget, *Report to the President on Government Contracting for Research and Development* (Washington, D.C.: U.S. Government Printing Office, May 1962), p. 21.

of the defense and space vehicle industry would function more efficiently if nationalized is uncertain, since the evidence available is meager. Along with the distortions and inefficiency associated with the present contracting system come such advantages as aggressiveness and flexibility. Neither virtue is always maintained easily in a nationalized framework. To determine how the advantages and disadvantages of nationalization balance out would require a study much more ambitious than this one. Certainly, however, the government should doff its ideological blinders and experiment with a wider variety of organizational approaches.

SUGGESTED READINGS
BOOKS AND MONOGRAPHS

How Sick Is the Defense Industry? Cambridge, Mass.: Arthur D. Little, Inc., 1963.

Baldwin, William L. *The Structure of the Defense Market: 1945–1964.* Durham, N.C.: Duke University Press, 1967.

Hitch, Charles J. and Roland N. McKean. *The Economics of Defense in the Nuclear Age.* Cambridge, Mass.: Harvard University Press, 1960.

Miller, John Perry. *Pricing of Military Procurements.* New Haven: Yale University Press, 1949.

Miller, Thomas G., Jr. *Strategies for Survival in the Aerospace Industry.* Cambridge, Mass.: Arthur D. Little, Inc., 1964.

Moore, Frederick T. *Military Procurement and Contracting: An Economic Analysis.* Rand Corporation Memorandum RM-2948-PR. Santa Monica, Calif.: The Rand Corporation, June 1962.

Peck, M. J. and F. M. Scherer. *The Weapons Acquisition Process: An Economic Analysis.* Boston, Mass.: Harvard Business School Division of Research, 1962.

Scherer, F. M. *The Weapons Acquisition Process: Economic Incentives.* Boston, Mass.: Harvard Business School Division of Research, 1964.

Schlaifer, Robert. *Development of Aircraft Engines.* Boston Mass.: Harvard Business School Division of Research, 1950.

Smith, Richard A. *Corporations in Crisis.* New York: Doubleday & Company, Inc., 1963.

Stanford Research Institute. *The Industry-Government Aerospace Relationship.* Vols. I and II. Menlo Park, Calif.: Stanford Research Institute, May 1963.

Stekler, Herman O. *The Structure and Performance of the Aerospace Industry.* Berkeley, Calif.: University of California Press, 1965.

Tybout, Richard A. *Government Contracting in Atomic Energy.* Ann Arbor, Mich.: University of Michigan Press, 1965.

GOVERNMENT PUBLICATIONS

Battelle Memorial Institute. *The Implications of Reduced Defense Demand for the Electronics Industry.* Washington, D.C.: U.S. Arms Control and Disarmament Agency, September 1965.

Donnelly, Charles H. *The United States Guided Missile Program*, study prepared for the Preparedness Investigating Subcommittee of the Senate Armed Services Committee (Washington, D.C.: U.S. Government Printing Office, January 1959).

Fishman, Leslie. *Reemployment Experiences of Defense Workers: A Statistical Analysis of the Boeing, Martin, and Republic Layoffs.* Washington, D.C.: U.S. Arms Control and Disarmament Agency, December 1968.

Gilmore, John S., and Dean C. Coddington. *Defense Industry Diversification: An Analysis with 12 Case Studies.* Washington, D.C.: U.S. Arms Control and Disarmament Agency, January 1966.

Logistics Management Institute. *Study of Profit or Fee Policy.* Washington, D.C.: mimeograph, 1963.

U.S. Congress, Joint Economic Committee, Subcommittee on Federal Procurement and Regulation. Hearings, *Economic Impact of Federal Procurement.* Washington, D.C.: U.S. Government Printing Office, 1966.

U.S. Congress, Joint Economic Committee, Subcommittee on Economy in Government. Hearings, *Economics of Military Procurement*, Parts 1 and 2. Washington, D.C.: U.S. Government Printing Office, 1969.

U.S. House of Representatives, Committee on Government Operations. Report, *Organization and Management of Missile Programs.* Washington, D.C.: U.S. Government Printing Office, 1959.

U.S. House of Representatives, Committee on Government Operations. Report, *Air Force Ballistic Missile Management.* Washington, D.C.: U.S. Government Printing Office, 1961.

U.S. Senate, Committee on Government Operations, document prepared by the Bureau of the Budget. *Report to the President on Government Contracting for Research and Development.* Washington, D.C.: U.S. Government Printing Office, 1962.

U.S. Senate, Committee on Government Operations, Permanent Subcommittee on Investigations. Hearings, *TFX Contract Investigation.* Parts 1–10. Washington, D.C.: U.S. Government Printing Office, 1963.

U.S. Senate, Committee on the Judiciary, Subcommittee on Antitrust and Monopoly. Hearings, *Competition in Defense Procurement.* Washington, D.C.: U.S. Government Printing Office, 1969.

U.S. Department of Commerce, Bureau of the Census. Current Industrial Reports, *Shipments of Defense-Oriented Industries.* 1965, 1966, and 1967. Washington, D.C.: Bureau of the Census, 1967, 1968, and 1969.

U.S. Department of Defense. *Military Prime Contract Awards and Subcontract Payments.* Washington, D.C.: U.S. Department of Defense, annually.

U.S. Department of Defense. *100 Companies and Their Subsidiary Corporations Listed According to Net Value of Military Prime Contract Awards.* Washington, D.C.: U.S. Department of Defense, annually.

U.S. National Aeronautics and Space Administration. *Annual Procurement Report.* Washington, D.C.: National Aeronautics and Space Administration, annually.

11. Manley R. Irwin
THE COMMUNICATIONS INDUSTRY

I. INTRODUCTION

The communication common carrier industry is a regulated industry. Unlike firms in the unregulated sector of the economy, the carriers are public utilities endowed with franchises of public convenience and necessity. Whether imposed by state commissions or by the Federal Communications Commission (FCC), regulation of telephone and telegraph service distinguishes and separates the communication carriers from firms in the steel, automobile, or textile industries. Indeed, regulation shapes and conditions this industry's structure and conduct, and thus bears ultimate responsibility for the industry's performance.

II. MARKET STRUCTURE
THE COMMON CARRIERS
AND THEIR SERVICES

Market structure on the supply side identifies the number of firms, their service offerings, their vertical relationship, and conditions of market entry. Market structure on the demand side classifies service offerings by customer groups and attempts to assess consumer responsiveness to price changes.

The Bell Telephone System, independent or non-Bell telephone companies, and the Western Union Telegraph Company account for the nation's telephone and telegraph service. With the exception of Western Union, the industry's structure is dominated by the telephone holding company. The holding company does not exist to render communication service per se, but rather controls stock in utilities who render telephone service and in manufacturers who supply communications equipment.

The American Telephone and Telegraph Company (AT & T) exemplifies the holding company relationship. AT & T controls some 24 telephone operating companies throughout the United States; owns 100 per cent of Western Electric, a manufacturing and supply unit; and together with Western Electric, shares ownership of the Bell Telephone Laboratory. Within AT & T, the General Department provides advice and assistance in plant, traffic, accounting, and capital and legal services to Bell's local telephone companies who provide intrastate toll and local exchange services. The Long Lines Department supplies toll telephone service both within the U.S. and overseas. This combination of serivce, research, and manufacturing make up what is commonly known as the Bell System.

As a giant among giants, the Bell System serves 100 million customers from a plant investment of $43 billion. Bell's total operating expenses exceed $15 billion; net operating revenue exceeds $6 billion. Bell accounts for some 90 per cent of toll or long distance telephone calls and 85 per cent of local exchange service in the U.S.; the system's manufacturing affiliate, Western Electric, accounts for 84 per cent of the domestic production of communications equipment.[1]

The Bell System was built on patents. The original Bell patents were filed in 1876 and 1877 and were offered to Western Union for $100,000. The telegraph company turned down the offer, but later acquired the rival telephone patents of Elisha Gray, Thomas A. Edison, and Amos Dolbear. A Supreme Court decision (4 to 3) awarded the basic patent right of the telephone instrument to the Bell interests in 1876. In subsequent negotiations Western Union acknowledged the validity of the Bell patent, withdrew from the telephone field, licensed Bell its own Gray patents, agreed not to enter the telephone industry, and promised to pay 20 per cent of the costs of Bell's new patents developed or acquired by the Bell interests. In turn, Bell agreed not to enter the telegraph field and to reimburse Western Union of all royalties on Bell patents.[2]

Once the patent grant was secured, Bell filed over 600 patent suits against competing companies and individuals, some 200 alone against the American Cushman Telephone Company.[3] Most firms went out of business. Only five suits reached the Supreme Court. Moreover, Bell's patent portfolio was carefully cultivated. By the 1930's, AT & T had acquired or developed some 9,000 patents, had filed 1,200 patents, and was licensed to some 6,000 others.[4] These patents gave Bell virtual monopoly in the technology of long distance transmission.

In 1894, the original telephone patent expired and independent companies began entering the industry. Although these firms accounted for nearly half

1 The State of California is an exception. See California Utility Commission, Investigation on the Commission's own motion on the rates, tolls, rules, charges, operations, practices, and telegraph company, Decision No. 67369, Case No. 7409 (July 26, 1962), p. 33. (Hereafter cited as California Rate Case.) See also *Moody's Public Utility Manual* (New York: Moody's Investors Service, 1968), p. 1344.

2 Federal Communications Commission, "Report on the Investigation of the Telephone Industry in the United States," H. R. Doc. No. 340, 76th Congress, 1st Session, 196–97 Table 40 (1939).

3 *United States* v. *Western Electric Co.*, Civil No. 17–49 (D.N.J., filed February 14, 1949).

4 Federal Communications Commission, "Report on the Investigation of the Telephone Industry in the United States," op. cit., p. 234.

the telephone market by 1910, the position of the independents nevertheless remained precarious. Bell occupied large metropolitan areas, refused to connect its long distance facilities, and banned equipment sales to independent telephone firms.[5] These policies combined with a policy of uninterrupted acquisitions accorded Bell's predominance in both domestic voice and record service.

The independent telephone market is also experiencing a trend toward consolidation and merger. Since 1940, the number of independents have declined from 6400 to just over 1800. As of 1967, five telephone holding companies accounted for 70 per cent of the non-Bell stations in the U.S.[6] General Telephone and Electronics, Inc.; United Utilities, Inc.; the Continental Telephone Co.; and the Mid-Continent Telephone Co. typify the holding company trend. The largest of the independents, General Telephone, owns some 30 operating companies, serves some 6.943 million telephones in 32 states, and holds roughly half of the non-Bell market (some 8% of the total market). United Utility operates some 970,410 telephones in 17 states; Continental operates 662,505 telephones in 36 states; and Mid-Continent operates 192,252 telephone stations in six states.

Finally, Western Union has adopted the holding company structure. The subsidiary telegraph company renders public message service (PMS), a teletypewriter switched service (TELEX), and private line communications service to the public. Recently, the FCC has sanctioned Western Union's purchase of Bell's Teletypewriter Exchange Service (TWX).

Western Union's share of the total record market, including message exchange service, TELEX system (a teletypewriter exchange service), and private-line telegraph services, has declined from 80 to 57 per cent between 1940 and 1963.[7] Much of that decline can be traced to a persistent fall in the PMS service or telegrams. Since diversification into private wire service has not compensated for decline in PMS, Western Union's growth has predictably suffered, averaging some 1.6 per cent growth in recent years (1957 and 1967). Nevertheless, Western Union has attempted to stake its future on a market that is growing 20 per cent annually, namely, leasing lines to commercial and government users; but in doing so, the telegraph company finds itself relying on the Bell System for local and toll telephone lines and dependent upon

---

5   Ibid., p. 134.

6   U.S. Department of Commerce, *Statistical Abstract of the United States, 1968* (Washington, D.C.: U.S. Government Printing Office). See United States Independent Telephone Association, *Holding Company Report* (Washington, D.C.: U.S. Independent Telephone Association, April 15, 1968). At the end of 1963, 25 companies controlled 70.0 per cent of the stations in the Independent telephone industry; this percentage increased to 71.3 per cent at the end of 1964, 72.8 per cent by the end of 1965, 75.1 per cent by the end of 1966, and 78.23 per cent by the end of 1967.

7   Federal Communications Commission, Report of the Telephone and Telegraph Committee of the Federal Communications Commission on the Domestic Telegraph Investigation, Docket No. 14650, p. 81. (Hereafter cited as Federal Communications Commission Telegraph Investigation.)

Western Electric for its supply teleprinter equipment.[8] Beset with delays in responding to markets blessed with opportunities, Western Union continues as the sick carrier of the industry.

THE FUTURE   It is relatively easy to summarize the existing market structure of the industry, quite another task to assess its future. Certainly the growth of the domestic common carriers is tied to the computer revolution. By 1975, most computers are expected to have time-sharing capability, some three-fourths of the nation's computers are expected to be tied into the nation's telephone lines, data modem sets are expected to grow 50 per cent annually, and remote teleprocessing services are expanding at an annual pace of 75 per cent.[9] These trends portend a gradual shift from voice traffic to nonvoice traffic. Although video, facsimile, and so on, are likely to make important contributions, the expansion and growth of computers linked to telephone lines is expected to be fundamental to the industry's future growth, including the Bell System, Western Union, and the independents.[10]

The Bell System is installing electronic switching systems or special purpose computers which perform abbreviated calling, conference calling, and automatic call routing. Bell is now introducing digital transmission systems: the so-called T-1, T-2, T-3, and T-4 series capable of handling 24, 96, 672, and 1344 voice circuits, respectively. Together with pulse code modulation techniques (time division multiplexing) AT & T expects to increase its traffic handling capability.[11] Bell also manufactures and leases data subsets or modems, devices that enable business machines to access the analog or voice network. Today, approximately 50,000 sets are in use and by 1972 Bell expects its production to approach 750,000 units.[12]

As computer information systems gain momentum, Bell's Touchstone card dialers can serve as data inquiry devices, accessing data files, querying computers, and facilitating financial transactions among and between users; and AT & T's picture-phone poses as a potential data display device, particularly when information is fed by remote computers.

Despite its investment in computers, switching and input/output devices and transmission, AT & T has announced that it does not intend to offer data processing services to the public. Whether such diversification is conditioned by inadequate capital, competition from the computer industry, or antitrust considerations, it is clear that AT & T possesses the constituent parts that make up nationwide computer information network.

---

8   J. Wolpert, "Western Union," *Barrons*, **49**:9 (January 27, 1969).

9   See Data Processing Management, Proceedings of the 1963 International Data Processing Conference and Business Exposition, *Data Processing* (Washington, D.C.: Data Processing Management Association, 1969), Vol. 13, p. 344 and 345.

10   See J. R. Pierce, "The Transmission of Computer Data," *Scientific American*, **215**:144 (1966).

11   John W. Geils, "A Current View of Research and Development," *Symposium on Economics of Public Utilities*, Georgetown University (Washington, D.C., 1967), p. 18.

12   *Wall Street Journal* (August 30, 1968), p. 5.

Western Union, under no antitrust constraint, has attempted to diversify from its declining public message market into remote data processing services. As a first step, Western Union inaugurated a plan to provide turn-key management information systems to its subscribers, systems that would include computer hardware, software, terminals, and communication lines as a package. Second, the telegraph company regards itself as the information utility of the future, employing time-sharing computer centers to render a series of services, legal retrieval, job matching, as well as conventional data processing services to the public at large.[13] Third, tariff filings mark a further step in this direction. SICOM and INFOCOM tariffs are shared line and computer switching services to private lease customers.[14] (SICOM is directed to the needs of the securities or stock market; INFOCOM is a generalized version of SICOM to all users.) Fourth, the telegraph company, in acquiring AT & T's TWX service, will hopefully combine that service with TELEX to give the telegraph company additional customers for remote teleprocessing services.[15] Fifth, the telegraph company has formed Western Union Computer Utilities—a joint venture with the Advance Computer Utilities Corporation —as a vehicle to offer remote teleprocessing services. And finally, the telegraph company recently began diversifying into the manufacturing of communication equipment.

The independent telephone industry has also seized upon remote computer-based services as a source for market diversification. General Telephone has acquired Ultronics Electric—a firm selling a computerized stock quotation— and has formed a data-processing affiliate for commercial services—an affiliate separate and apart from GT & E, the parent corporation.[16] United Utilities has also established a time-sharing data-processing subsidiary. A pattern of carrier diversification is thus emerging: carriers are employing a horizontal, vertical, or joint venture approach in exploiting their entry into computer-based services. Whether such entry carries with it a potential extension of regulation is, of course, one of many policy issues now under study. In a tentative decision, the Commission has sanctioned wholly-owned data processing affiliates by non-Bell carriers. On the other hand, the FCC has held that in the case of hybrid communication/computer services, the carriers must file tariffs if the data-processing segment is rendered as an incidental service.[17]

---

13   *Western Union Annual Report* (New York: Western Union Co., Inc., 1965).

14   Federal Communications Commission, In Re Western Union Telegraph Company Tariff FCC No. 251, Applicable to SICOM Service, *Memorandum, Opinion and Order* (1967).

15   *Telecommunications Reports*, 35:1 (January 20, 1969).

16   *Wall Street Journal* (May 16, 1968), p. 14. Besides servicing some 30 telephone operating companies of the GT & E System, GT & E Data Services Corporation will use the computers to offer outside customers such services as bank loan and deposit accounting, credit verification, billing, and inventory control.

17   Federal Communications Com-

COMMUNICATIONS EQUIPMENT   The holding company as noted embraces both communications equipment as well as communication service. Generally speaking, communications equipment falls under four categories. Switching equipment consists of manual or automatic switching devices used in central office exchanges or supplied on a private lease basis to subscribers. Terminal equipment, or station apparatus, consists of telephone instruments, teletypewriter sets, and related terminal devices. Transmission and distribution apparatus includes wire, cable, and microwave radio equipment employed in conveying communications signals between and among users.

Western Electric, the manufacturing unit of the Bell System, accounts for 84 per cent of the domestic market, enjoys gross revenues of $3 billion, and ranks eleventh among U.S. corporations in sales.[18] Western's sales are confined largely to AT & T and Bell operating companies (excluding defense contracts), and the Bell carriers buy the bulk of their equipment and related supply needs from or through their supply affiliate.

Western Electric's history parallels the Bell System. Purchased by Bell in 1881, the company received exclusive patent licenses to manufacture related telephone hardware. Western refused to sell equipment to independents—a policy which stimulated the formation and growth of independent manufacturers. In 1908 Bell reversed its selling practice and Western Electric attempted to acquire ownership in leading independent suppliers, a move apparently frustrated by state antitrust laws.[19] In the late 1920's the nation's only suppliers of teleprinter equipment—the Morkrum Company and Kleinschmidt Company—merged to become the Teletype Corporation. In 1930, Teletype was purchased by Western Electric and continues today as its operating subsidiary.

For the most part, manufacturing affiliates of independent telephone companies supply the remaining 15 per cent of the equipment market, specifically, General Telephone, United Utilities, and Continental Telephone.[20] In recent years General has acquired Leich Electric Company, the Alphaduct Wire and Cable Company, Sylvania Electric, Lenkurt Electric Company, and the Automatic Electric Company. General's subsidiaries alone account for about half of the non-Western equipment market. United Utilities has also integrated backwards by its controlling interest in North Electric, a supplier of related

mission, "In the Matter of the Regulatory and Policy Problems Presented by the Interdependence of Computer and Communication Services and Facilities," Docket No. 16979, *Notice of Inquiry* (1966). (Hereafter cited as Federal Communications Commission Computer Inquiry.)

18   Florida Public Utility Commission, *General Investigation of Southern Bell Bell Telephone & Telegraph Co.*, Order No. 3715, Nov. 30, 1964, at 4. (Testimony of of General Services Administration.)

19   "Integration and Exclusion in the Telephone Equipment Industry," 70 *Quarterly Journal of Economics*, **70**:252 (May, 1965).

20   R. E. McKee and M. R. Irwin, "Vertical Integration and the Relevant Market: A Critique," *Antitrust Bulletin*, **11**:1015 (September–December 1966). See also *Complaint, United States* v. *General Telephone and Electronics Corporation*; Civ. No. 64-1912 (S.D. N.Y., June 19, 1964).

switching equipment; and Continental Telephone has acquired the stock of Superior Cable and the Communication Apparatus Corporation. Thus, to the extent that over 90 per cent of the equipment market is integrated with operating carriers and to the extent that the carriers buy their equipment in-house, the independent equipment market has become merely an extension of the telephone holding company.

III. MARKET ENTRY: CAPITAL REQUIREMENTS, DECREASING COSTS, AND FREQUENCY ALLOCATION

CAPITAL REQUIREMENTS

Entry into the communication common carrier market is conditioned by several factors. They include capital requirements, economies of scale, availability of frequency spectrum, and the regulatory process. Like many utilities, the industry is capital intensive. Bell's capital turnover ratio is 0.40, which is equal to natural gas pipelines, greater than electric utilities, but less than 2.00 for all manufacturing.[21] Distribution of plant investment cost is shown by Table 1.

Switching makes up the largest component in terms of total plant investment. For all telephone calls, switching accounts for 22 per cent, but for long distance calls, switching costs approach 60 per cent. Central exchange plant is characterized by heavy capital outlays and has experienced several generations of development—from manual to automatic mechanical relays, to cross-bar switching, to the present generation of computer-aided switching or the ESS. Despite heavy capital costs associated with switching plant, decreasing cost tendencies are not altogether clear. On one hand, a 16,000

TABLE 1   TELEPHONE INVESTMENT MIX

	INVESTMENT COST (%)	INVESTMENT PER CALL	
		ALL CALLS (%)	LONG DISTANCE (%)
Transmission	23	2	19
Switching	28	22	58
Station sets	21	46	14
Local distribution	26	30	9

SOURCE   Staff paper, President's Task Force on Communication Policy, *Technology, Demand and New Services* (Washington, D.C.: unpublished, 1968).

---

21   Paul J. Garfield and Wallace F. Lovejoy, *Public Utility Economics* (Englewood Cliffs, N.J.: Prentice-Hall, 1964), p. 23.

trunk circuit costs only half again as much as a 3,000 trunk center, leading one to believe that increasing returns are present. On the other hand, recent studies indicate average cost per subscriber line (local exchange service) rises beyond 50,000 trunk lines—a rise attributed to additional central office and telephone loops.[22] Moreover, new switching technology, although permitting a host of new services, does not appear to effect major cost reductions.

Transmission accounts for 23 per cent of plant investment, but only 2 per cent of the per unit cost of calls, and 19 per cent of long distance calls. On long-haul heavy traffic routes, transmission facilities can require large capital expenditures. A single Bell relay station requires an investment in land, buildings, power plant, and so on, of some $330,000 per repeater station. Equipment for 600 voice grade circuits adds another $40,000 or some $600 per voice circuit. On the other hand, capital requirements do not pose as formidable entry barriers—particularly in microwave transmission. That individual corporations have constructed radio links to supplement their communications requirements suggests that any natural monopoly status of transmission has eroded. Moreover, transmission is amenable to technological cost reduction. The L1 series of Bell, new generations of microwave, and the potential of satellites, suggest that transmission costs per circuit may fall to 35 cents per circuit mile.[23]

Local distribution costs include the carrying of signals between local exchanges and the user's terminal device, and accounts for some 26 per cent of investment plant. Much of this cost is multiplexing equipment—devices which enable wire or radio facilities to carry several voice conversations simultaneously. Terminal costs of some 21 per cent are made up of telephone handsets, teletypewriters, as well as data terminals or modems, which enable data signals to get on and off the voice or analog network.

Another element conditioning market entry is the limited supply of microwave frequencies used in point-to-point radio relay systems. If regulatory policy regards the radio spectrum as a scarce resource, then a policy of frequency rationing automatically limits the number of firms who can exploit radio relay technology. On the other hand, if the spectrum is judged to be relatively unlimited then a major resource input, the microwave spectrum, is removed as a condition of entry. Since 1959, the FCC has relaxed its microwave licensing and this resource has been reduced as a barrier to market entry.[24]

---

22 D. A. Bowers and W. F. Lovejoy, "Disequilibrium and Increasing Costs: A Study of Local Telephone Service," *Land Economics*, **41**:36 (Feb. 1965). See also testimony of W. H. Melody, FCC Docket No. 16258, Federal Communications Commission, Exhibit No. 52 (Nov. 25, 1968), p. 22.

23 President's Task Force on Com-munication Policy, Staff Paper on *Technology, Demand and Services* (Washington, D.C., 1968), p. 16.

24 Federal Communications Commission, "In the Matter of Allocating of of Frequencies in the Bands Above 890 Megacycles," Docket No. 11866, *Memorandum, Opinion and Order* (Washington, D.C., September, 1960).

Finally, entry is conditioned by regulatory policy. Existing communication carriers operate in exclusive franchised areas. As monopolies endowed with licenses of public convenience and necessity competition is held undesirable on grounds that duplication of services and facilities is wasteful and inefficient. Any new entrant faces formidable burdens: the opposition of existing carriers, the burden of proving unmet need, demonstration of technological competence and financial capability, and the like. Moreover, the problem of overcoming the cost of the adjudicatory process is obviously an important entry deterrent since the carriers' legal expenses constitute an allowable and hence recoverable expense. In a very real sense, telephone subscribers subsidize carrier efforts to discourage existing or potential market entry.[25]

In sum, the holding company and the utility/supplier integration stand as the structural hallmark of the domestic common carrier industry. That relationship is exemplified by the Bell Telephone System, replicated to a lesser extent by the General, United Utilities, and Continental Systems. This structure coupled with uninterrupted mergers and acquisitions has given both communication service and communications hardware a bias toward concentration unique in American corporate history.

DEMAND

Demand for communication services can be classified as exchange and private line service, toll and local service, and business and residential service. Table 2 segregates demand on the basis of exchange and private line. The Bell System provides the bulk of the nation's interstate and intrastate message telephone service; Western Union, the nation's telegraph service.

As noted, users have in the past had a choice between AT & T's TWX service and Western Union's TELEX service. Private lines for telephone, telegraph, TELPAK, program and other uses are leased for users on a dedicated basis. TELPAK is a private line service offering bulk or volume users communication channels in excess of 64 voice grade circuits. Finally, program service includes radio and video transmission service for broadcast purposes.

By contrast, Western Union's public message service has declined from 191,000 messages in 1940 to 92,000 in 1966; and TELEX has experienced continued growth since its inauguration in 1958.

ELASTICITY

The common carriers have made available few studies that deal with consumer responsiveness to price changes. Perhaps part of the problem is the difficulty

---

25   See Hearings on Activities of Regulatory and Enforcement Agencies Relating to Small Business Before Subcommittee No. 6 of the House Select Committee on Small Business, 89th Congress, 2nd Session (1966) (Testimony of John Goeken, President, Microwave Communications, Inc.).

TABLE 2 REVENUES AND MESSAGES BY TYPE OF SERVICE, 1962–1966

	1962	1963	1964	1965	1966
FCC TELEPHONE CARRIERS					
Revenues:					
Local telephone	5,275	5,583	5,919	6,264	6,696
Toll telephone	3,185	3,419	3,769	4,134	4,704
WATS	64	113	162	209	259
TWX	70	72	74	75	79
Private line	476	501	530	561	644
Messages:					
Local telephone	108,924	112,034	117,916	125,790	134,494
Toll telephone	4,532	4,852	5,310	5,921	6,655
BELL SYSTEM					
Revenues:					
Local telephone	5,088	5,375	5,692	6,022	6,430
Toll telephone	3,072	3,290	3,626	3,971	4,510
WATS	64	112	161	207	257
TWX	70	71	72	73	78
Private line	464	489	515	544	621
Messages:					
Local telephone	102,736	106,332	111,698	119,351	127,448
Toll telephone	4,338	4,638	5,072	5,655	6,350

SOURCE   Federal Communications Commission, *Statistics of Communications Common Carriers* (Washington, D.C.: U.S. Government Printing Office, 1967); also FCC Staff Paper, President's Task Force on Communications Policy (Washington, D.C.: unpublished, 1968).

of agreeing upon the proper unit of communication service because of variables of time, distance, and length of conversation (station to station, person to person). Perhaps the absence of studies results from the tacit assumption that demand is price inelastic. A study of West Virginia customers' reaction to changes in local rate increases does confirm that users' response to rate increases is "practically nonexistent."[26] Certainly the telephone carriers tend to treat local exchange service as price inelastic—since 1940 local exchange rates have risen by over 40 per cent.[27]

---

26 "Price Elasticity of Local Telephone Service Demand," *Public Utility Fortnightly*, **75**:31 (Feb. 4, 1965).
27 Richard Gabel, *Development of Separations Principles in the Telephone Industry*, Institute of Public Utilities, Michigan State University, Division of Research, Graduate School of Business Administration (East Lansing, Mich.: Michigan State University Press, 1967), p. 137. [Since 1940.]

On the other hand, there is some indication that local telephone service is sensitive to personal income. In 1966, 81 per cent of all U.S. households had telephone service; yet, more than one fourth of households with family income under $5,000 were without telephone service, suggesting that price effectively excluded lower income families from telephone service.[28]

The carriers insist that interstate toll long distance service is slightly inelastic. On the other hand, a study by Gabel on station-to-station calls indicate elasticities greater than unity, i.e., increased communications outweigh price cuts, certainly the phenomenal rise in flat-rate station calls for after 9 P.M. service reveals an elasticity that belies an insensitivity to price changes.

As one moves from public service to private lease service, the users become exposed to a greater array of choice, For example, demand is less elastic for low volume subscribers who have the option of leasing carrier services or going without the service altogether. Volume users, on the other hand, may turn to Bell and Western Union facilities or even consider the possibility of building their own private microwave system. As we shall see, this latter market has experienced price competition.

Turning to public message telegraph service it is interesting that most of the published work on demand elasticity has originated with the FCC. The FCC's historical coefficient of elasticity studies of Western Union's public message service (PMS) attempted to explain the 60 per cent decline in telegram service from 1944 to 1964. Western Union had apparently assumed that PMS service was price inelastic during that period, but FCC studies discovered that the telegraph company's assumption of its demand was both correct and incorrect. From 1945 to 1957 the FCC study tended to confirm Western's view of its demand slope. But after 1957 the FCC found that competitive substitutes from jet air mail and toll telephone service had pushed the PMS historical coefficient of elasticity to 1.6.[29] A medium distance full-rate telegram, less costly than either a comparable TWX or a toll telephone call in 1945, was by 1963 one third more expensive. In short, the telegraph company had priced PMS service out of the market (160 per cent increase since 1945). Not surprisingly, the FCC has recommended that Western Union consider promotional pricing as part of its marketing strategy.[30]

In sum, price elasticity of demand for telephone and telegraph service confirm what are generally regarded as the determinants of consumer sensitivity to price changes; namely, the nature of service (a necessity or luxury), the proportion of cost to total expenditures, and in particular, the availability of competitive substitutes.

---

28 Ibid., p. 137.

29 Federal Communications Commission, *Telegraphy Investigation*, op. cit., p. 89.

30 Harry Trebing, "Plight of the Telegraph Service," *MSU Business Topics*, **15**:44 (Summer 1967).

IV. MARKET CONDUCT
PRICE COMPETITION

As an outgrowth of the industry's market structure, the conduct of the domestic common carriers embrace several facets. Two, however, are outstanding—price competition and nonprice competition. On its face, price competition appears contradictory. By definition, communication services are limited to carriers holding franchised monopolies and assigned exclusive geographic territories. The carriers, nevertheless, inhabit submarkets, particularly in the private lease market, where they compete with each other as well as with private microwave communication systems. It is in this latter market—the carrier-microwave segment—or bulk communications that price competition has erupted.

Microwave radio transmits information-bearing signals by a chain of repeater towers spaced some 30 miles apart. Standing apart from conventional wire facilities, microwave possesses several advantages; namely, the absence of pole line rights-of-way, an abundance of channel capacity, a flexibility in circuit use among data, voice, and video, and a minimal expansion cost. These traits combined to make microwave point-to-point communications systems an attractive alternative to conventional wire line facilities. Some of the carriers began introducing radio transmission equipment into their plant after World War II.

Despite carrier microwave, private users also sought to exploit economies of radio relay. They were prevented from doing so under FCC rationing policy which limited frequency bands to the common carriers. An FCC petition by the American Trucking Association to operate a microwave system on hitherto excluded frequency bands in effect challenged that rationing policy, and the request, joined by manufacturers, retailers, and suppliers of radio relay equipment, precipitated a dispute that focused on the size of the radio spectrum and the feasibility of liberalizing spectrum allocation.[31]

The carriers opposed any relaxation of FCC frequency policy. They argued that bands in the microwave spectrum constituted a fixed and limited resource whose consumption should be confined to common carrier needs alone. The carriers noted further that their facilities satisfied the nation's communication requirements, and that private microwave would threaten the carriers with revenue losses, ultimately leading to a rise in telephone rates to the public. Proponents of private microwave countered by insisting that frequency spectrum size was sufficiently large to remove any rationing by the FCC, that consumers ought to be accorded a choice between leasing circuits and owning circuits, and that private microwave would stimulate competition

---

31 Federal Communications Commission, "In the Matter of Allocating of Frequencies in the Bands Above 890 Megacycles," Docket No. 11866, *Report and Order* (1959).

TABLE 3 MONTHLY RATE COMPARISON BETWEEN THE BASE
CAPACITY OF TELPAK CLASSIFICATIONS AND A LIKE NUMBER OF
INDIVUAL PRIVATE LINES (EQUIPPED FOR VOICE ONLY FOR 100
MILES)

	INDIVIDUAL PRIVATE LINE	TELPAK	DIFFERENCE	PER CENT DIFFERENCE
(A) 12 Voice grade channels	3,780	1,860	1,920	51
(B) 24 Voice grade channels	7,560	2,720	4,840	64
(C) 60 Voice grade channels	18,900	4,300	14,600	77
(D) 240 Voice grade channels	75,600	11,700	63,900	85

SOURCE The FCC TELPAK Docket 14251, *Tentative Decision* (Washington, D.C.:
Federal Communications Commission, 1964).

in the communications equipment market, thereby benefiting the supplier, the
user, and ultimately the state of the communications art.

In 1959 and again in 1960, the FCC ruled to liberalize its frequencies so
as to permit users to construct and own private microwave systems. This
decision represented a defeat for the carriers; and having lost the battle on
the frequency front, the carriers shifted to a reassessment of their lease line
charges. Specifically, AT & T introduced TELPAK—a bulk lease service
consisting of four packages of 12, 24, 60, and 240 voice grade circuits and
designated TELPAKS A, B, C, and D, respectively. The TELPAK tariff
reduced private lease charges in some cases by over 80 per cent of previous
line rates (Table 3). In filing its new service the Bell System explained that the
TELPAK discount resulted from its innovation of its own low-cost, or broadband facilities, as well as an intent to accept the competitive challenge of
microwave.

The TELPAK tariff found former coalitions posed as adversaries. Predictably, large private line users were elated with TELPAK price cuts.
Motorola, a microwave equipment supplier, and Western Union Telegraph
Company, on the other hand, challenged the tariff's cost and the competitive
necessity in a dispute that erupted before the FCC.

In retrospect, the FCC embarked on two major crossroads by permitting
first the discount to take effect while Bell solicited customers, and second, by
declaring 4 years later that TELPAKS A and B were unlawful. The FCC
reasoned that the Bell physical plant facilities employed in supplying TELPAK
and non-TELPAK circuits were identical, therefore no cost differences could
be identified, the profit on TELPAK services was sufficiently low to question
compensatoriness. Also, since one private microwave system had been built
from the time of the tariff's introduction, considerable doubt attended their
competitive necessity—at least on TELPAKS A and B.[32] In short, the FCC

32 Federal Communications Com-
mission, "In the Matter of American
Telephone and Telegraph Company,"
Tariff FCC No. 250. TELPAK Service
and Channels, Docket No. 14251,
Tentative Decision, p. 379 (1965).

concluded that TELPAKS A and B, justified neither by their alleged economies nor by rivalry from customer-owned private microwave, were judged to
be discriminatory.[33] The FCC ruling accorded AT & T two choices: raise
TELPAK prices to former private line rates or cut private line rates to TEL-
PAK levels. Bell elected the former.

Perhaps Bell's pricing policy would have incurred less controversy were it
not for the economic plight of the Western Union Telegraph Company.
Caught between TELPAK on one side and private microwave on the other,
the telegraph company attempted to diversify into private lease services beset
by severe price cuts. Western Union complaints prompted an FCC inquiry
known as the Telegraph Inquiry—an inquiry in which the FCC requested
Bell to undertake a cross-section study of its seven interstate services on a
fully distributed cost basis.[34] The study, the Seven-Way Cost Study, identified
Bell's net earnings for each of these services. It revealed that profits from
Bell's competitive services—TWX, private line telegraph, the TELPAK—
average 2.9, 1.4, and 0.3 per cent, respectively. On the other hand, in Bell's
noncompetitive services—WATS, for example—profits exceeded 10 per cent
(Table 4). (Two additional studies substantially confirm these results.) The
study was obviously laden with controversy; but the evidence was highly
persuasive that Bell had employed its monopoly markets to underwrite losses
in its competitive markets. Indeed, the FCC felt compelled to investigate
AT & T's rate of return, rate structure, rate base, and so on—a move unprecedented in FCC history.

Controversy surrounding the Seven-Way Cost Study has not abated.
AT & T contends that the FCC is overly restrictive in assigning fully distributed costs to Bell's interstate services. Moreover, Bell submits that if the FCC
seeks to encourage microwave competition as a policy decision, the carriers
ought to be free to respond and confront that competition. Although Bell
asserts that a fully additional cost concept is not unlike the economist's
concept of long-run marginal cost, critics assert that whereas incremental
pricing is to be encouraged for stimulated off-peak public telephone usage, it
is illegitimate as a means to foreclose entry in competitive submarkets; and
if marginal cost pricing is to be employed as a pricing guide, such pricing

---

33 Ibid., p. 379.
34 Federal Communications Commission, Telegraph Investigation, op. cit.,
p. 202. That AT & T was not unaware of
the impact of its rate cut on Western
Union can be seen by the following Bell
observation:
"They can be expected to oppose such
an offering with attack on our costs, unfair
competition, etc., unless we can find a way
to diminish the impact. We are faced with a
dilemma here in that while the broadband's
objective is to compete with private microwave, it has the unintended result of
potential harm to Western Union. The
interests of Western Union and the Bell
System are to a great extent harmonious in
that both common carriers should be
meeting the microwave competition
together, and we should not miss that
primary objective by inadvertently damaging Western Union's viability."
AT & T Broadband Rate Planning Group
(September 1960); made public in Federal
Communications Commission Docket No.
16509–16519 (Washington, D.C., 1967).

TABLE 4 BELL SYSTEM INTERSTATE SERVICES FOR 12 MONTH PERIOD SEPTEMBER 1, 1963 TO AUGUST 31, 1964 EARNINGS STATEMENT SUMMARY (THOUSANDS OF DOLLARS)

TOTAL DAY	MESSAGE TOLL TELEPHONE	TELETYPE-WRITER EXCHANGE SERVICE	WIDE AREA TELEPHONE SERVICE	TELEPHONE GRADE PRIVATE LINE	TELEGRAPH GRADE PRIVATE LINE	TELPAK	ALL OTHER	TOTAL
Revenues and other income								
Operating revenues	2,116,211	62,820	113,796	103,485	90,630	89,281	91,093	2,667,316
Other income	21,311	915	1,515	1,929	1,262	2,901	2,725	32,558
Total	2,137,522	63,735	115,311	105,414	91,892	92,182	93,818	2,699,874
Expenses, income charges and operating taxes								
Expenses, income charges and operating taxes except Federal income taxes	1,343,598	53,589	58,224	76,805	87,795	98,159	91,679	1,809,849
Federal income taxes	367,201	3,351	26,403	11,472	(317)	(7,639)	(3,035)	397,436
Total	1,710,799	56,940	84,627	88,277	87,478	90,520	88,644	2,207,285
Net operating earnings	426,723	6,795	30,684	17,137	4,414	1,662	5,174	492,589
Net investment	4,286,702	237,584	303,004	362,758	313,324	564,742	490,292	6,588,406
Ratio of net operating earnings to net investment (%)	10.0	2.9	10.1	4.7	1.4	1.3	1.1	7.5

SOURCE Report of the Telephone and Telegraph Committee of the Federal Communications Commission in the Domestic Telegraph Investigation, Docket 14650, 1965.

should be extended to all telephone services rather than reserved to merely competitive ones.[35] Whatever the rationale, it is instructive that TELPAK as a price has effectively rescinded the FCC's policy to encourage competition from user-owned circuits and independent manufacturers.

TELPAK SHARING   TELPAK sharing—a second variation of price competition—dates back to the FCC private microwave decision. In that ruling, the FCC held that government entities, right-of-way companies, and other regulated companies could share or collectively own microwave communications facilities. Bell's TELPAK offering matched that sharing provision thus laying the groundwork for a dispute over circuit sharing.

The dispute was triggered in 1965 when several petroleum companies petitioned the FCC to broaden microwave sharing in order to collectively operate microwave for drilling operations. A year later, the FCC ruled that cross-sharing be extended for public safety and regulated entities, and that sharing be made available to the manufacturing of petroleum, forest products, construction, mining, and farming as well as sharing certain megacycles to banks, department stores, and retailers, and so on.[36] This ruling combined with the FCC declaration that TELPAKS A and B were illegal precipitated an inquiry into the sharing of TELPAKS C and D. Users experienced excess line capacity for TELPAKS C and D, and sharing would enable them to reduce their communication line charges.

AT & T, in refusing to expand sharing eligibility, contended that no discrimination existed for those not eligible to share TELPAK, that TELPAK sharing could not be justified by the competitive necessity of private microwave, and that expanded sharing would introduce unregulated "third parties" into the communications business who would buy and resell circuits to the subscribing public.[37] In addition, the carrier held that sharing provisions would cause users of telephone and telegraph lines to shift to bulk circuits, thus eliminating some $50–100 million in telephone revenues.[38] The result of these revenue losses would prompt an increase in TELPAK rates, thus effectively eliminating TELPAK as a service altogether.

35   See AT & T's Statement in Federal Communications Commission Telegraph Investigation, Docket No. 14650; See also, H. Trebing and W. Melody, "Pricing Policies in the Common Carrier Industry," *Report to the President's Task Force on Communications Policy* (Springfield, Va.: U.S. Department of Commerce, Clearing House, 1968).

36   Federal Communications Commission, "In the Matter of Amendment of Parts 87, 89, 91 and 93 of the Commission's Rules to Prevent Expanded Co-operative Sharing of Operational Fixed Stations," Docket No. 16218, 1966.

37   Federal Communications Commission, "In the Matter of TELPAK Sharing Provisions of American Telephone and Telegraph Company and the Western Union Telegraph Company," Docket No. 17457, 1967. (Hereafter cited as FCC TELPAK Sharing.)

38   Federal Communications Commission, ibid., p. 19, 1967. Testimony of AT & T Assistant Vice-president W. B. Kelly.

Proponents of TELPAK sharing argued, nonetheless, that Bell's sharing provisions favor large communication users at the expense of small users, that sharing provisions constituted an artificial market separation leading to price discrimination, and that the prohibition of sharing prohibited arbitrage as a check to discriminatory rate practices.[39]

The issue of TELPAK sharing is still pending before the FCC, but to the extent that the ban on sharing prevents users from reselling circuits, the ban prevents intramodal price competition.

Price strategy and the entry of specialized carriers are equally controversial. In August 1969, the FCC granted a license to Microwave Communications, Inc. to render a customized point to point service between Chicago and St. Louis. Subsequent to that decision, some 1700 station applications have been filed for approval. The Commission's Common Carrier Bureau has recommended a policy of competitive entry to all. Notwithstanding carrier opposition to such a policy and notwithstanding their assertion that a market need has not been demonstrated, AT & T has nevertheless promulgated deep price reductions to its point to point customers (Tariff Series 11,000), and announced its intention to construct a digital transmission system on a private lease basis; and Western Union's recent DATACOM tariff contemplates a rate reduction of up to 80 per cent for private lease subscribers. Such price counter-punching inevitably adds fuel to the controversy of cross-subsidization between carrier monopoly and competitive markets.

NONPRICE COMPETITION

The carriers have long promulgated policies that insulate them from direct price competition. These practices include interconnection policies, foreign attachments, the ban on reselling of circuits, intrafirm transactions, as well as market negotiations.

INTERCONNECTION Interconnection consists in the physical interfacing, attachment, or tying together of two communication facilities. Traditionally, the carriers have exercised almost unlimited discretion as to who may and who may not interconnect lines with the public telephone network. Generally, Bell has defended any refusal to interconnect on several grounds, namely, that such systems do not meet the quality essential for a public telephone network, that such systems lead to wasteful duplication and higher cost, and that the interconnection would prompt users to build on high-profit routes but turn to the carriers for low-profit routes, ultimately translating into higher prices

---

39 Federal Communications Commission, TELPAK Sharing, op. cit., p. 13, 1968. Testimony of Dr. W. H. Melody, FCC Common Carrier Bureau.

to the consuming public. Those critical of carrier refusal to interconnect hold that the carriers do not alone possess manufacturing expertise, that publication of performance standards or specifications would enable carrier network to interface with noncarrier network without degradation in quality, and that refusal to interconnect precludes market entry and hence market competition. The merits of these positions aside, interconnection has been crucial as a variable of market conduct, particularly as it relates to independent telephone companies, Western Union, and private microwave systems.

1. Independents Until 1914, AT & T generally denied interconnection to independent telephone companies. Given Bell's monopoly in long distance transmission, the policy isolated independence into geographical pockets, and required subscribers to rent two phones, one for local service and one for long distance. Not surprisingly, public pressure grew for the elimination of redundant phones, and for a communication service from one entity. In this case as in others, interconnection was not unimportant in structuring the carrier industry.[40]

2. TV transmission Interconnection has been critical in the development of transmission facilities for TV signals. In the 1940's the country experienced an explosion in television. Whereas AT & T constructed underground coaxial cable facilities, Western Union and private TV networks attempted to introduce microwave radio relay facilities. The latter group—Philco and Dumont, among others—were, in the absence of common carrier facilities, permitted to build microwave relays to relay TV signals to outlying geographical areas. Although the FCC permitted the broadcasters to interconnect with the common carrier facilities, the FCC warned the broadcasters to "amortize their investment at the earliest possible date."[41] Once the carriers elected to construct parallel facilities, the FCC held that broadcasters would be under obligation to lease those facilities, thus abandoning their own investment in communications plant and equipment.[42]

The struggle then shifted to the common carriers. Again, the interconnection role was decisive. Western Union's construction of a microwave relay triangle was based on the assumption that it could gain interconnection with Bell System coaxial cable facilities. When Bell's refusal to interconnect was upheld by the FCC, Western Union's microwave system became for all

---

40 J. C. Goulden, *Monopoly* (New York: Putnam, 1968), p. 71.

41 The Federal Communications Commission, "In the Matter of American Telephone and Telegraph Company and Western Union Telegraph Company, Charges and Regulations for Television Transmission Services and Facilities," Docket No. 8963; Quoted from Docket No. 6651. (5 Pike and Fisher, 1950.) "The Commission desires to emphasize this special provision for intercity tv relaying is a purely temporary measure designed to assist the tv industry until such time as a permanent common carrier facility is generally available, and those broadcasters who venture into the business of relaying television programs in these frequency bands should plan to amortize their investments at the earliest possible date."

42 Ibid., p. 663.

practical purposes isolated and redundant.[43] Today, Bell accounts for almost 100 per cent of the programmed transmission facilities throughout the United States.

3. Private microwave Finally, interconnection bears on the growth and innovation of private microwave systems. As noted, the FCC liberalized frequencies to permit private user ownership. With few exceptions (rails and pipelines) the carriers have refused to permit users to tie their facilities into the nation's toll and local telephone network. The denial of interconnection confronts the users with two choices—build a microwave system without interconnection, thus making such a communications network essentially an intercom system, or lease communications facilities from the carriers and thus gain full interconnection. Not unexpectedly, the interconnection privilege artificially shifts the comparative advantage toward leasing all communications facilities from the common carriers and their supply affiliates.[44]

FOREIGN ATTACHMENTS As a corollary to interconnection, the carriers refused to permit customers to attach telephone instruments or related devices to the public network. Noncarrier equipment is termed "foreign," hence the name foreign attachment tariff. Users who persist in tying their own instruments into the telephone network risk service disconnection and loss. Thus, the carrier's policy of leasing equipment only, together with the practice of destroying old equipment, gives them control over competitive substitutes.[45]

Although the carriers have softened foreign attachment restrictions on lines leased to some private lease customers, the policy of nonattachment has been vigorously defended on the public network. The carriers hold that

43 Federal Communications Commission, "In the Matter of the Western Union Telegraph Company and the American Telephone Company, *et. al.* Establishment of Physical Connections and Through Routes and Charges Applicable Thereto Pursuant to Section 201 (a) and the Communications Act of 1934 as amended with respect to Intercity Video Transmission Service," Docket 9539, 1951. See also Donald C. Beelar, "Cables in the Sky and the Struggle for their Control," *Federal Communications Bar Journal*, 21:32 (Jan. 1967). See also Federal Communications Commission, "In the Matter of American Telephone and Telegraph Company and Western Union Telegraph Company Charges and Regulations for Television Transmission Services and Facilities," Docket No. 8963, 1949. Commissioner Hyde observed:

"The decision of the majority while it states in its conclusion that it is not intended to support the claim which the Bell System has made to monopoly in the field of intercity transmission effectively does grant a monopoly to Bell. Moreover, this de facto monopoly is granted without specific recognition by the Commission of such effect and without a finding that such a result would be in the public interest . . . . The Commission is establishing a precedent which cannot but have the effect of discouraging for all time competition in this vital television relay field."

44 See Federal Communications Commission, "In the Matter of American Telephone and Telegraph Regulations Relating to the Connection of Telephone Company Facilities with Certain Facilities of Customers," Docket No. 12940, *Memorandum, Order and Opinion* (Washington, D.C.: Federal Communications Commission, 1967).

45 Western Electric's affiliate, NASSAU Smelting and Refining Co., scraps old equipment.

customer-owned equipment may be technically inferior, that the user is under no obligation to repair or update his equipment, and that total system quality is synonymous with total responsibility and control.

Those opposing the foreign attachment tariff insist that the ban effects a tie-in between communication lines and communication equipment, that AT & T, by interfacing its equipment with independent telephone companies, connects facilities with non-Western Electric equipment, that the issue of quality could be resolved by publication of technical standards, and that the maintenance and repair of telephone equipment might well be submitted to the test of market competition.

RESELLING OF CIRCUITS   A third practice falling under nonprice competition is again the question of reselling carrier lines by private parties. Although both AT & T and Western Union generally prohibit users from reselling communication lines, a firm may resell to select customers. If a third party receives "authorized user" status, then a middleman may buy and resell circuits to that third party at no price markup. This condition had been granted by the carriers to firms in the stock market quotation business. Specifically, the Bunker-Ramo Corporation sold a computerized information service to subscribers of the securities market industry.[46] Customers queried Bunker-Ramo's computers via leased telephone lines linked to remote terminal devices.

The carriers refused to lease circuits, however, when Bunker-Ramo added computer routing of administrative data to its data information service. AT & T and Western Union implied that Bunker-Ramo was engaged in communications switching, and hence impinged on regulated communications activity.[47] Despite Bunker-Ramo's insistence that its computer-routed message service was incidental to its quotation service, the firm has not been permitted to offer this service to the public.

INTRAFIRM TRANSACTIONS   Finally, transactions within subsidiaries of the telephone holding company mark a fourth area of nonprice competition. These transactions—conducted, absent, arm's-length bargaining—include fees for patent licenses and research and management services paid to operating telephone carriers to their parent holding company and prices on equipment and supplies sold by affiliated manufacturers to operating telephone

---

46   M. R. Irwin, "The Computer Utility: Competition or Regulation," *Yale Law Journal,* **76**:1307 (July 1967).
47   Letter from the Western Union Company to the Federal Communications Commission, Dec. 1965; also AT & T Letter to Federal Communications Commission, September 29, 1965. "It would appear that the transmission of com- munications is the heart of its [Bunker-Ramo] proposals for 'message switching' services, which services might prove in fact to be a most significant element of Telequote IV." See also M. R. Irwin, "Time-shared Information Systems: Market Entry in Search of Policy," *Proceedings of the Fall Joint Computer Conference* (Thompson Publications, November 1967).

companies. In the first instance, carrier payments represent flat rates of some 1 per cent of their operating revenues. Few regulatory agencies examine the value rendered by holding company services, and fewer still challenge the reasonableness of such payments with the possible exception of the California Public Utility Commission.

A second variation of intracarrier transactions (communications hardware and supplies) between manufacturing affiliates and regulated carriers. The operating subsidiaries of Bell and General buy 90 per cent of their equipment from their captive suppliers.[48] In fact, once a new supplier is merged into the holding company arrangement, the new firm finds it irresistible not to funnel its equipment orders in-house. In-house procurement is defended on grounds that the utility supplier manifests overwhelming economies of scale. But if the carriers were confident of these economies, one would expect they would welcome competitive bidding as proof. To date they have opposed such a test vigorously.

On the other hand, in-house transactions do not pose an absolute ban to outside manufacturers; for integrated suppliers serve as purchasing agents for their utility affiliates. Indeed, a study by the FCC in the 1930's revealed that nearly 40 per cent of the sales of six major independent equipment suppliers came from Western Electric subcontracts (1926 to 1934).[49] To the extent that such subcontracts continue today, independent equipment firms are unlikely to act aggressively in competing with holding company subsidiaries who pose as important customers as well as obvious competitors.

MARKET BARGAINING AND DEEP POCKET MONEY   Finally, buying or selling of corporate assets can serve to identify spheres of market interests—either in communication services or communications equipment. Deep pocket money, for example, effectively forestalled earlier attempts by the Telephone, Telegraph and Cable Company in 1899 to establish a long distance telephone network. The purpose of the company was to interconnect independent telephone firms. However, the company was purchased by the New Amsterdam Trust Company, and was later disbanded. An FCC report observed that Bell System funds had financed the trust company's action as a means of eliminating a competitive transmission network.[50]

Second, the ability ot trade on patents is equally critical in market bargaining. This capability was illustrated by AT & T negotiations with private corporations as well as the government. Following World War I, the Navy Department urged formation of a holding company for radio patents. The participants, General Electric, Westinghouse, and American Telephone and

---

48 *General Telephone Company of Upstate New York, Inc.* v. *James Lundy, et al., Constituting New York Public Service Commission,* 22 AD2d, 256 NYS 2d 87, February 2, 1965.

49 Federal Communications Commission, Report on the Investigation of the Telephone Industry in the United States, op. cit., p. 145.

50 Ibid., p. 132.

Telegraph Company, then allocated the market: manufacturing of sets was assigned on a 60 to 40 basis to GE and Westinghouse; RCA was given sole distribution of radio sets, and the Bell System was assigned patents on radio and telephone transmission equipment and broadcasting equipment. With the rush to establish radio networks the cartel broke down. General Electric, Westinghouse, and RCA attempted to link their radio stations by telephone lines, but upon AT & T refusal they turned to Western Union's telegraph lines. Bell countered by establishing its own radio broadcast networks.

An accommodation was reached by the middle 1920's. Bell agreed to withdraw from the broadcast field and to sell its chain to RCA (who in turn formed a subsidiary known as NBC). RCA then entered an exclusive agreement with AT & T to lease Bell telephone lines to interconnect its radio network.[51]

Third, cartelization of the communications equipment market has not been immune from asset or patent negotiations. On the domestic side, Western Electric sold its generator and power plant division to General Electric and Westinghouse after the turn of the century; and in the 1920's, both firms found it convenient to stay out of the communication transmission equipment market.[52] On the overseas side, Western Electric sold its international manufacturer to International Telephone and Telegraph in 1925, assigning ITT an exclusive 15-patent right. Perhaps this sale was an unnecessary embellishment, since a 40 per cent *ad valorem* duty on imported equipment had already been prescribed by the Tariff Act of 1922.[53]

Fourth and finally, the patent is a commanding asset in negotiating with government agencies. An attempt by the Department of Justice to spin Western Electric off from AT & T was finally resolved by a 1956 consent decree. AT & T bargained to retain Western Electric in exchange for opening its patent portfolio on a royalty-free basis together with forfeiting of some 0.02 per cent of its sales. (Teletypesetter Corporation, a subsidiary of Teletype Corporation; Westrex Corporation.)[54]

In sum, the carriers have employed price and nonprice competition which serve to augment and protect their plant investment and their market structure. Denial of interconnection with other carriers or private communications facilities insulates that investment life from competitive threat (23 per cent of the carrier's plant and equipment is embedded in transmission plant). Refusal to permit circuit reselling enables the carriers to inhibit computer-based switching as well as preclude price competition in circuits (28 per cent of carrier plant is switching equipment). The foreign attachment tariff bans equipment competition or competitors. Combined with carrier leasing

51 Ibid., p. 226–228.
52 Ibid., p. 244; See also Goulden, *Monopoly*, op. cit., p. 84.
53 *U.S. Statutes at Large*, 67th Congress, 1922, Tariff Act of 1922.
54 "Consent Decree Program of the Department of Justice," Hearings Before the Antitrust Subcommittee (Subcommittee No. 5) of the Committee on the Judiciary, House of Representatives, 85th Congress, 2nd Session (Washington, D.C.: U.S. Government Printing Office, 1958).

of equipment, their procurement practices together with the destruction of old equipment enables the carriers to hold virtual discretion over competitive substitutes (21 per cent of the carrier's investment is devoted to terminal equipment). The above stratagems, combined with the ability to manipulate procurement awards, accords the holding company power to either discipline nonintegrated suppliers from market entry or discourage incipient market entry outright.[55] Such practices are defended on grounds that communication service, research, repair, procurement, and manufacturing must reside within holding company control alone.

V. MARKET PERFORMANCE
PRICES—SERVICE

Any assessment of the industry's performance whether measured in terms of prices, profits, research, productivity, or innovation, necessarily embraces both communication equipment and communication service. It is also important to note that performance is monitored and hence shared by regulatory agencies who stand between the monopoly firm on one side and the consumer on the other.

Consider first the trend in carrier-pricing policy. Rates for interstate toll telephone calls have on the average experienced a secular decline. Using a 3-minute station-to-station call from New York as a unit of measure, from 1940 to 1967 toll rates to Chicago declined from $1.90 to $1.40; to Denver from $3.25 to $1.60; and to San Francisco from $4.00 to $1.75.[56] Moreover, Bell has introduced new services such as Wide Area Telephone Service, Centrex, Direct Distance Dialing, as well as flat station-to-station rates after 9 P.M.

Rates for public message telegraph service, on the other hand, have experienced a persistent rise. Again, if a minimum charge of 15 textwords from New York is used as a measure, then between the years 1919 and 1948 prices have increased from 30 cents to $1.25 to Philadelphia, from 60 cents to $1.75 to Chicago, from 90 cents to $2.23 to Denver, and from $1.20 to $2.23 to San Francisco.[57] In toll calls versus the telegram, at least the telephone companies have been able to share some of their productivity with the consumer.

---

55 The following statement of a Motorola witness in the Federal Communications Commission Docket No. 11866 is instructive:

MR. BAKER: Isn't it true that manufacturers—such as Motorola other than Western Electric—provide microwave equipment for common carriers?

MOTOROLA WITNESS: Yes, yes. That may be a temporary situation, however, because Western Electric is moving towards a condition where they will supply their own equipment.

56 U.S. Department of Commerce, *Statistical Abstract of the United States* (Washington, D.C.: U.S. Government Printing Office, 1968).

57 Ibid., p. 497.

The price trends in telephone calls, however, mask two problems, namely, the averaging of telephone costs, and the disparity between toll and local charges. As to the first, telephone rates are derived as an average of old and new plant investment as well as an admixture of route densities. Facilities and geographical averaging means that specific costs cannot be assigned to specific rates. Over and above the issue of accuracy there is some question whether the carriers possess undue discretion in customer cross-subsidization, because of the causal relationship between price and cost.

The disparity between local and toll telephone rates poses a second problem. A 1963 conference of state regulatory commissions estimates that comparable intrastate toll calls exceeded interstate by $270 million, or 17.1 per cent of intrastate revenue.[58] Studies as recent as 1966 indicate that a 6-minute, 100-mile, person-to-person call intrastate cost twice that of a comparable interstate call. Part of the discrepancy may be assigned to rising labor and material costs, but much of the gap has been said to arise from improper separation of joint costs between plant used for both purposes—a discrepancy that shifts the pricing burden to the local telephone user. Indeed, the price of local exchange service has increased 40 per cent since 1940.

Another facet of communication service is quality. Here any index of measurement is not only elusive but dependent upon the class of user concerned. If complaints to regulatory agencies are any criteria, millions of residential telephone subscribers have in the past regarded their quality as satisfactory. On the contrary, some assert that excess quality and reliability is built into carrier plant since the utility incurs no penalty, indeed vests an interest in an expanded investment rate base.[59]

Still, one user's adequacy may pose as another's inadequacy. Cross-talk, fading, noise, and outages quite tolerable in a voice conversation mode take on a different order of magnitude when data processing machines "talk" over toll telephone facilities. Subscribers of computer-based services tend to be much more critical of the quality of toll and exchange facilities than the general public.[60] It is true that the carriers will provide "conditioned" or distortion-free lines at an extra charge, but forcing high volume data over voice lines is regarded as a compromise at best. What is needed, they submit, is a separate transmission network for data traffic requirements.[61] A more serious question is the imposition of digital traffic on a transmission and switching plant built essentially around analog or voice requirements. The

---

58 *Report of Staff Subcommittee on Separations and Toll Disparity* (Washington, D.C., NARUC, 1963). Reported in the 75th National Association of Railroad Utilities Commission Proceedings, p. 461, cited in Gabel's Separation Study.

59 H. Averich and L. Johnson, "Behavior of the Firm Under Regulatory Restraint," *American Economic Review*, **52**:1052 (December 1962).

60 See S. L. Mathison and P. M. Walker, *Computers and Communications: Issues in Public Policy* (Englewood Cliffs, N.J.: Prentice-Hall, 1969), Chap. 9.

61 Paul Baran, "On Distributed Networks," *Rand Corporation Paper*, p. 2626.

carriers assure their skeptics that a telephone line cares not whether the subscriber is a computer terminal or a teenager. But service degradation bordering on "telephone blackouts" have in some cities approached crisis proportions.[62] Whatever the cause, the carriers insist that higher rates of return will yield improved service. The quality of the nation's public message service has deteriorated markedly over the years. The FCC has found it necessary on several occasions to issue letters of warning to Western Union; and recently the FCC has decided to look into the quality and delivery time of Western Union's telegrams on a more formal basis.[63]

PRICES—EQUIPMENT

Price trends in communication equipment vary from product to product. Immediately after World War II, Western Electric price increases ranged from 26 per cent on switchboards to 63 per cent on line wire. Since then, Western prices have generally experienced a decline.[64] If cost comparisons between Western Electric and the independents are regarded as valid, then Western Electric prices are below comparable prices of outside suppliers. But these studies originate with the Bell System; with the possible exception of the FCC in the 1930's, few regulatory bodies have attempted a thorough assessment of Western's cost. In that investigation, Western's record was mixed. Telephone handsets and lead-covered cable were lower than suppliers outside AT & T. But independent prices were lower for telephone equipment components and the production of specialized equipment.[65]

The real question is, of course, the assumption of comparability. The California Public Utility Commission has rejected Bell cost comparisons on grounds of Western Electric's size and its captive market.[66] Other critics have

---

62   M. Flood, "Commercial Information Processing Networks—Prospects and Problems in Perspective," *U.S. National Commission on Technology Automation and Economic Progress*, Technology and the American Economy (1966). See also The Network of University Computing Co., *Forbes*, **102**:45 (Dec. 1, 1968); on the other hand an AT & T Assistant Vice-president stated: "There isn't any technological sense in asserting a need for two networks—one for telephone calls, and a parallel structure for data."

63   See *Telecommunication Reports*, **34**:14 (Oct. 14, 1968).

64   National Association of Railroad Utilities Commission, Data for 1964 Prepared by Western Electric Company, Inc. at request of joint NARUC-FCC Subcommittee, April 1965; see also Report on Preliminary Survey and Investigation of Western Electric Co., Inc., National

Association of Railroad Utilities Commission, July 15, 1948.

65   Federal Communications Commission, "Report on the Investigation of the Telephone Industry in the United States," op. cit., pp. 321–322. For a typical defense of Western Electric price studies, see Phillips, "Some Observations on the FCC's Telephone Investigation," *Public Utility Fortnightly*, **77**:23, 32 (Feb. 17, 1966):

"With respect to the reasonableness of Western Electric's prices and profits, what additional proof can a vertically integrated company offer to justify 'internal' prices that are not subject to a direct market test (i.e., that are not subject to arm's-length bargaining) beyond the price comparisons and reasonableness of profit standards laid down by the Supreme Court in Smith v. Illinois Bell Tel. Co., Id. at 33."

66   California Rate Case, op. cit., p. 35.

observed that the test used to measure Western Electric is question begging, inasmuch as the independents have no market and experience low volume and high cost, given the integration and procurement policies of Bell and General.[67] Perhaps Western is dispassionate in showing that its prices are reasonable, but when the FCC attempted to look at Western's cost data in the 1930's, it observed:

> As a result of improperly treating some cost as part of manufacturing expense applicable to current production and because of the loose method following and allocating variations between standard and actual cost, Western's computed cost for individual products does not provide an authentic basis for testing the reasonableness of prices of these products.[68]

Nevertheless, the acid test is cost disallowance. To the extent that the FCC has never seen fit to disallow such prices, Western Electric has passed that test easily.

PROFITS AND RATE OF RETURN

Profits in the telephone industry vary from state to state and from commission to commission. Generally, profits have ranged from 6.5 per cent to 8 per cent, depending on the particular state involved. The FCC has ruled that the proper range should fall between 7 per cent and 7.5 per cent on interstate voice traffic.[69] It must be remembered that profits are added to the carrier's investment rate base. Without any test or probing of the optimality of carrier's investment decisions or depreciation policies, not to mention operating expenses, profit ceilings may not necessarily be the test of carrier performance.

Profits in the equipment market are another matter. Western Electric's profits have averaged between 9 and 11 per cent on net investment over a 20-year period.[70] Profits earned by General Telephone's manufacturing affiliate appear even higher. In 1963, Automatic Electric earned an 18 per cent return on its average net investment and some 23.5 per cent on average common equity.[71] GT & E disputes this method of calculation, however. The company holds that the profit on Automatic Electric should be based on

---

67 M. R. Irwin and R. McKee, "Vertical Integration in the Communication Equipment Market: A Public Policy Critique," *Cornell Law Review*, **53**: 449 (Feb. 1968).

68 Federal Communications Commission, Report on the Investigation of the Telephone Industry in the United States, op. cit., p. 322.

69 Federal Communications Commission, "In the Matter of American Telephone and Telegraph Company and Associated Bell System Companies, Charges for Interstate and Foreign Communication Service," Docket No. 16258, *Memorandum, Order and Opinion* (1967).

70 National Association of Railroad Utilities Commission Study, op. cit., p. 24.

71 National Association of Railroad and Utilities Commissioners *Report of the Committee on Communications Problems* (1964), pp. 9–10.

GT & E's cost of buying Automatic Electric at its date of acquisition. According to this measure, GT & E submits its rate of return on its automatic electronics investment as 10.4 per cent in 1963.

What is of interest is that profits in the equipment market are inserted on top of costs rather than posing as a residual, as is the case under competitive conditions. Western Electric begins with standard or predetermined costs which include labor and materials. Cost variations are added to research, development, engineering expenses, and taxes. Finally, a profit margin is added. According to Professor Sheahan, "market forces play no significant role—the rate of return is a matter of management choice." One is thus left with the impression that Western's prices function to meet a target profit on investment.[72]

Other than as management prerogative, it is difficult to identify any force that prevents cost inefficiencies on the hardware-market side from being passed forward into the carrier's rate base This issue is not without its implications to the subscribing public. Some 65 per cent of AT & T's net investment and 55 per cent of the Bell operating carriers' investment result from hardware purchases from Western Electric, an investment upon which the carriers assert they are entitled to earn a reasonable return.[73] Thus, in the absence of regulatory and market checks, there is no guarantee that the consumer does not bear the unique burden of a dual rate base.

RESEARCH AND DEVELOPMENT
—PRODUCTIVITY

In 1965, the Bell System spent approximately $253 million in research and development, a figure that represents 3 per cent of gross product (value added) of the Bell System, roughly the same proportion as total research and development is to Gross National Product.[74] Most of this research was conducted by Bell Laboratories, a laboratory that has made significant contributions in practically every facet of the communications art and whose reputation for excellence is worldwide.

On the other hand, government-sponsored contracts are not unimportant in the electronics and communications fields. About 50 per cent of Bell Lab's contracts are government-funded; and next to the aerospace industry, some 65 per cent of the research and development in the electronics and communications industry is financed under Federal contract.[75]

72 Sheahan, op. cit., p. 255.
73 *Moody's Public Utility Manual* (Washington, D.C.: Moody's Investors Service, 1968), p. 1348.
74 John Kendrick, "Productivity and Changes in Economic Structure Since 1948," Paper given at Symposium of Public Utilities (Georgetown University), 1967.

(Cited as Kendrick Symposium Paper.)
75 *Moody's Public Utility Manual*, op. cit., 1958, p. 204. See also "Research and Development in the Electrical Equipment and Communication Industry, 1956–62," *Reviews of Data on Science Resources* (1965), Vol. 2.

Measuring productivity is elusive. Studies by Kendrick from 1899 to 1953 (1929 = 100) rank productivity as measured by output per labor in the following order: the electrical utilities, gas utilities, railroads, local transit, manufacturing, telephone communications, and farming.[76] In terms of output per unit of capital, Kendrick observes that the telephone industry experienced its greatest period of productivity between 1899 and 1909. The coincidence between the patent expiration and the industry's period of greatest competition is more than coincidental.

Kendrick also notes that the Bell System experienced a 14 per cent increase in productivity from 1948 to 1966, and the physical volume of real output in the communications industry was 6.7 per cent a year compared with 4.9 per cent for the private domestic sector from 1948 to 1965.[77] For Bell System alone, the rate of increase in real productivity has been at least twice that of the private economy.

The difficulty that besets any recitation of these studies is that they largely exist in a vacuum. One may be able to assign a number to research and development. What is missing is a standard to judge the optimality of that performance. Moreover, the relevant test is not research and development expenditures alone, but the introduction of new facilities and services into the marketplace—the innovation process—a process that yields cost efficiencies due to new technology rather than mere size (scale).

Although the carriers assert their innovation record is above reproach, the Justice Department has contended otherwise, alleging that unattended switching was introduced in non-Bell markets by Automatic Electric in 1904, whereas Bell introduced it in 1919; that unattended dial central office equipment for smaller offices was made available to the independents in 1914, whereas Bell introduced it in 1927; that telephone handsets were introduced in Europe in 1905, whereas Bell introduced them in 1927.[78] Whatever the record, several factors seriously compromise market incentives identified with innovation process. These include rate-base economics, depreciation policy, vertical integration, procurement policy, and tariff practices.

The absolute size of the carrier's rate base mitigates optimum resource allocation. Firms are placed in the dilemma of choosing between the innovation of low-cost plant versus high-cost plant and its attendant revenue requirements.[79] Thus, to the extent the carriers are successful in rejecting challenges to their investment either by incorporating competitive substitutes or discouraging market entry, their control over innovation remains secure. Moreover, rate-base economies are further exacerbated by a refusal to take advantage of rapid depreciation write-offs or investment tax credits.

---

76 John W. Kendrick, *Productivity Trends in the United States*, National Bureau of Economic Research (Princeton, N.J.: Princeton University Press, 1961), p. 167.

77 Kendrick's Symposium Paper, op. cit., p. 4.
78 *United States* v. *Western Electric Civil* No. 17–49, op. cit., pp. 4–8.
79 Averich and Johnson, *American Economic Review*, op. cit., p. 18.

A second disincentive to innovation is the utility-supplier relationship. Once the vertical relationship is consummated and insulated from competitive bidding, access by nonaffiliated research firms as well as independent suppliers of equipment tends to be foreclosed.[80] The independent supplier has, of necessity, subsisted on a diet of shrinking markets and/or subcontracts from their integrated competitor. However valid in the past, vertical integration as a deterrent to the innovative process is now assuming a new order of magnitude. The potential entrant consists not of a few random firms, but of an entire industry—suppliers of computer and peripheral equipment. No one, not even the carriers, has had the temerity to imply that the computer industry is ill prepared to make contributions to the state of the telecommunications art.

Tariff restrictions mark a third disincentive. Restrictions on circuit use, denial of noncarrier-provided services, refusal to attach user-owned hardware, and so on, again act to throttle the innovation process. It is true that the introduction of carrier microwave was spurred by potential competition in the 1940's and 1950's, that carrier-sponsored satellites plan was rejected when measured against systems developed by the aerospace industry, that the computer industry has placed data modems in competition with carrier modems, but these cases indicate that the process of innovation is not built into the industry's structure.[81] Pressure from the market or from regulation tends to be infrequent and ad hoc. All of this suggests that the disparity between the actual and the possible constitutes the cost of opportunities foregone. In sum, the array of disincentives to the innovation process persists as a central deterrent to industry performance.

VI. PUBLIC POLICY
THE PAST

In a narrow sense, state and Federal regulatory agencies condition the economic behavior of communications common carriers. In a broad sense the industry's structure, conduct, and performance have been shaped by policies promulgated by Congress, the Executive Office of the Presidency, and

---

80 International Telephone & Telegraph Letter to Federal Communications Commission, Nov. 22, 1967; subject FCC File Nos. 1757–1745–Cl–TC–68, "A domestic nonintegrated supplier of ITT alleged the following . . . GT & E has not developed a line of common control crossbar switching equipment produced by Western Electric, ITT, and other leading telephone equipment manufacturers throughout the world, but has instead clung stubbornly to the manufacture and use within the general system of the old-fashioned step-by-step switching equipment manufactured by GT & E's subsidiary, Automatic Electric."

81 F. M. Scherer, "The Development of the TD-X and TD-2 Microwave Radio Relay Systems in Bell Telephone Laboratories," Remarks at Communication Conference, *Brookings Institute* (Spring 1968).

the Department of Justice. As a prelude to examining public policy alternatives in this industry, it is necessary to identify policies which have led to the formation of the holding company.

THE COMMUNICATIONS HOLDING COMPANY   Although the holding company preceded regulation, regulation has neither challenged nor inhibited holding company growth. Indeed, regulation has enabled the holding company to extend, tighten, and consolidate its control over major facets of the communications industry. The Mann-Elkins Act (1910), for example, first extended Federal jurisdiction over interstate communications carriers at a time when the market shares of the Bell System and the independent telephone industry stood at 50 per cent each. The record indicates that the Interstate Commerce Commission (ICC) imposed little restraint on carrier merger policies. Perhaps as one observer noted: "The ICC was so engaged in railroad regulatory problems that it had little time to investigate communication affairs."[82] Whatever the reason, merger and concentration continued under ICC jurisdiction.

It is true that Bell's unrelenting acquisition of independents prompted threat of antitrust action in 1914. The Justice Department and AT & T entered the so-called Kingsbury Agreement, an agreement in which Bell agreed to forgo acquisition of independent telephone companies, to connect its toll lines to noncompeting independent companies, and to sell controlling interests of its Western Union stock.[83] But Congress rescinded this policy with passage of the Willis-Graham Act of 1921—an act that approved carrier mergers when sanctioned by the ICC or state commissions.[84] Later, the Justice Department notified AT & T its merger policy would be free from antitrust action. The result was that Bell experienced a net increase of over 400 independent telephone companies from 1920 to 1930.[85] The 50 per cent market penetration by independents thus represented their high-water mark.

If horizontal integration has prospered under regulation, public policy has challenged the utility-supplier tie-in at least once. A 1949 antitrust suit, in charging Western Electric with monopolization of the telephone equipment market, sought to divest Western Electric from AT & T, attempted to dissolve Western into three competing companies, and sought to require Bell operating companies to buy equipment on an arm's-length basis.[86] Seven years later, a consent decree crystallized Bell's vertical relationship. The Justice Department did require Bell to make its patent portfolio available to all comers on

---

82   Harold T. Koontz, *Government Control of Business* (Boston: Houghton-Mifflin, 1941), p. 380.

83   Federal Communications Commission, Report on the Investigation of the Telephone Industry in the United States, op. cit., 1939, p. 144.

84   Ibid., p. 158.

85   Ibid., p. 158.

86   *Complaint, United States* v. *Western Electric*, Civ. No. 17–49 (D.N.J. February 14, 1949).

a royalty-free basis; but critics contend the company's buying practices effectively destroy any market incentive to exploit those patents.[87]

The decree, of course, did more. By approval of the utility-supplier tie-in, it promoted a parallel integration among the independents—specifically the mergers of General, Continental, and United Telephone Systems. To be sure, the Department of Justice challenged General Tel's purchase of Hawaiian Telephone on grounds of vertical foreclosure in 1964, but 2 years later, the Department commented "that it would be inappropriate to prosecute its suit against a single company at this time."[88] Public policy thus tends to be circular on the market structure issue; Bell's vertical integration is approved, non-Bell mergers are challenged, but the latter dismissed on grounds of the former. The result is that franchised utilities have extended their monopoly into the manufacturing of communications hardware.

PROCUREMENT   Attempts to impose arm's length bargaining within holding company transactions have met with repeated failure. As early as 1914, the Clayton Act (Section 10) held that the carriers holding interlocking directorates be required to purchase supplies and equipment on an arm's-length basis. Presumably, the 1914 Clayton Act applied to communications as well as to rail carriers. However, when the ICC initiated hearings, Bell maintained that its affiliates did not qualify as common carriers.[89] Although the ICC competi-

---

87 *Consent Decree in United States* v. *Western Electric*, Civ. No. 17–49 (D.N.J. Jan. 23, 1956). See Celler Committee Report, op. cit., p. 108.

"At the outset it must be observed that nothing in the Decree assures manufacturers of any opportunity whatever to supply directly the needs of the Bell Operating Companies or requires a Bell Operating Company to buy any equipment competitively from any source other than Western Electric."

88 *United States* v. *General Telephone & Electronics Corp.*, Civil No. 64–1912 (S.D.N.Y., filed June 19, 1964). See also *Wall Street Journal* (November 15, 1966). After dismissal by the Justice Department, GT & E merged with Hawaiian Telephone Company and Northern Ohio Telephone Company. Thereupon ITT brought suit. Complaint at 9–10, *International Tel. & Tel. Corp.* v. *General Tel. & Electronics Corp.*, Civil No. 2754 (D. Hawaii, filed October 18, 1967):

"Plaintiff (ITT) has been and now is foreclosed from selling telephone equipment to the operating companies of the Bell System, the General System, and the UUI

System except to the limited extent that particular products are not manufactured by the affiliated system companies. The foreclosure of the market available to plaintiff (ITT) has been severe and now threatens to become so substantial that plaintiff may be forced to withdraw from the business of manufacturing and selling telephone equipment in the United States. General Telephone operating companies, including Hawaiian, represent a substantial portion of plaintiff's actual and potential sales of telephone equipment which will be foreclosed by General Telephone unless appropriate injunctive relief is granted by this Court."

89 Regulation Relative to Bids of Carriers Subject to the Clayton Antitrust Act for Securities, Supplies, or Other Articles of Commerce, Interstate Commerce Commission, ex parte No. 54 (October 4, 1916), Letter from AT & T to Interstate Commerce Commission, June 5, 1916.

"Neither the American Telephone Company nor the Western Electric Company, Inc., nor any of our associated companies is a common carrier. Consequently, none of our companies comes within the inhibition of the statute. (86)."

tive rules failed to distinguish between rail or communications carriers alike, in practice the distinction proved quite real.[90] Communications carriers generally escaped imposition of competitive buying practices.

Competitive buying erupted again during hearings prior to the Communications Act of 1934. In fact, an original bill proposed that all carriers entertain competitive buying whether they owned integrated affiliates or not. In testifying against this section (Section 215), President Gifford of AT & T observed:

> We regard this section as a dangerous extension of regulated authority without precedent in the country and a radical departure from all past practice and an unwarranted invasion on the rights of management.[91]

Congress acceded to this theory of management rights and Section 215 of the Communications Act directed the Commission to study and make its recommendations. A first report, the Walker Report, requested legislative authority to regulate the cost and prices of telephone equipment, implying that Western Electric had somehow attained quasi-utility status.[92] A year later, however, a final report dropped the request with a statement that "the instituting of an active program of telephone regulation need not await the enactment of further laws by Congress."[93] The most recent episode, the Consent Decree of 1956, of course, cancelled the Justice Department's plea that arm's-length bargaining be injected into Bell and Western Electric dealings.

On the other side, the FCC did seek authority to require competitive bidding on communication satellite equipment and research and development contracts. Congress gave that authority without hesitation. Indeed, FCC procurement rules apply not merely to prime contracts but to lower subcontracting tiers.[94] All of this suggests that equipment policy is ad hoc if not somewhat contradictory. On conventional facilities the carriers may buy in-house; on satellite facilities the carriers must entertain competitive bids. In the meantime

---

90 *Ex parte* No. 54, ibid. (October 4, 1920).

91 Hearings on a Commission on Communications, Senate Committee on Commerce, 71st Congress, 1st Session, 1934, p. 86.

92 Federal Communications Commission, Telephone Investigation, *Proposed Report* (Washington, D.C., 1938), p. 700. The Commission requested additional legislation to "review, approve or disapprove all Bell System policies and practices promulgated by the central management group of the American Company; to regulate the costs and prices of telephone apparatus and equipment; and to review, approve or disapprove all intercompany contracts."

93 Federal Communications Commission, *Investigation of the Telephone Industry in the United States*, 1939; see also Telephone Investigation Docket No. 1, *Brief of Bell System Companies on Commissioner Walker's Proposed Report on the Telephone Investigation*, p. 112.

94 Federal Communications Commission, "In the Matter of Amendment of Part 25 of the Commission's Rules and Regulations with Respect to the Procurement of Apparatus, Equipment and Services Required for the Establishment and Operation of the Communication Satellite System and the Satellite Terminal Stations," Docket No. 151231, *Report and Order* (1964).

the carriers hold that both facilities serving a common end should be commonly owned.

TARIFFS AND CARRIER PRACTICES   The practices of the carriers in refusing interconnection to competing carriers, private microwave, customer-provided equipment, and the reselling of circuits have grown, evolved, and been sanctioned under state and Federal regulation. These practices give the carrier virtual control over competitive substitutes, and accord the utility discretion over technological obsolescence. Only recently has the FCC (opposed by the National Association of Railroad and Utilities Commissions) challenged the premise, much less assessed the implications, of these practices. The first, the FCC Computer Inquiry, sought information on the relevance of carrier tariffs to the data processing community.[95] The response to these long-standing tariffs was perhaps as surprising to the FCC as it was unsettling to the communications industry. Indeed, the computer industry sought freedom to switch circuits, to share lines, to purchase as well as lease equipment, and to interconnect communication systems.[96] Still more recently, the FCC Carterphone case—directed specifically to the lawfulness of the foreign attach ment tariffs—marks a significant policy reversal.[97] The FCC ruled that such tariffs had always been illegal—that Bell's filing before the FCC was in no way equivalent to FCC approval. Although these decisions are historic, they are of recent vintage. The real question is whether these policies are a trend or a random factor.

TECHNOLOGY AND MARKET ENTRY   Finally, the policy record in terms of market entry and new technology is obviously mixed. Certainly, in the past the FCC has been biased in favor of the monopoly solution. The FCC, restricting facilities to the common carriers alone, thwarted the development of microwave links by the television industry. Then by upholding Bell's refusal to interconnect Western Union microwave facilities the FCC prevented Western Union from building a national microwave communication system. To the extent the FCC has promoted microwave and microwave sharing, the FCC has attempted to preserve some choice for the private line subscriber. On the other hand, by acceding to carrier noninterconnection policy and by permitting TELPAK to take effect, although its legality lay undetermined, it effectively delayed the development of private microwave.

The FCC's stance during the Communication Satellite Controversy led many observers to charge that the Commission was overly solicitous, if not

---

95   Federal Communications Commission, Computer Inquiry, op. cit., p. 6.

96   Ibid., Response of BEMA.

97   Federal Communications Commission, "In the Matter of Use of the Carterphone Device in Message Toll Telephone Service," Docket No. 16942; and

"In the Matter of *Thomas F. Carter and Carter Electronics, Complainants* v. *American Telephone and Telegraph Co. et al., Defendants*," Docket No. 17073, *Brief for the United States as amicus curiae Department of Justice* (1967). (Hereafter cited as Carterphone case.)

outright protective, of carrier undersea cable facilities.[98] Indeed, the Commission adopted the carrier's position that satellites were complementary rather than competitive transmission links.[99] And despite Congressional approval of a separate entity—the Communication Satellite Corporation—the FCC has prevented Com Sat from direct competition with the international voice and record carriers.[100] That the satellite issue will not disappear can be seen in the current statement over domestic introduction and use. Indeed, it took the Commission less than six months to elect the overseas carriers as sole participants of satellite systems. By contrast, the domestic introduction of satellite relay is now entering its seventh year of delay.

THE PRESENT—EFFECTIVE REGULATION

It is perhaps inevitable that these policies pose two questions with respect to the holding company and regulation. First, is the holding company being regulated? The answer is yes and no. With respect to General Telephone and Electronics, the FCC views its jurisdiction as limited to actual telephone operating companies.

Apparently GT & E has the best of two worlds with regard to horizontal mergers. If it is apprehensive of FCC reaction, the parent holding company will acquire the operating company, and only the antitrust enforcement by the Justice Department will remain an obstacle. If antitrust is the primary concern, then one of the subsidiary interstate operating companies will acquire the new firm, and the Commission could insulate the merger from antitrust possibilities under Section 221.[101]

A second question follows. If holding companies fall within state or Federal jurisdiction, can regulation be imposed with any degree of effectiveness? In response to this query, Commissioner Johnson has observed that Bell's operating revenues are "several times larger than the budgets of all the

98 Hearings on Space Satellite Communications Before the Senate Subcommittee on Monopoly of the Select Commission on Small Business, 87th Congress, 1st Session, 370 (1961). See testimony of Commissioner Craven: "The main thing I want to emphasize is that if we try to establish a separate system by satellites in competition with existing things, I am quite certain, ultimately, the existing means of communications which are going to be necessary are not going to survive economically." p. 473. See also Walter Adams, "The Role of Competition in the Regulated Industries," *American Economic Review*, **48**:530 (1958).

99 Federal Communications Commission, "In the Matter of an Inquiry into the Administrative and Regulatory Problems Relating to the Authorization of Commercially Operable Space Communications Systems," Docket No. 14024, *Second Report* (1961). See also Report of the Ad Hoc Carrier Committee, October 12, 1961.

100 Federal Communications Commission, "In the Matter of Authorized Entities and Users Under the Communications Satellite Act of 1962," Docket No. 16058, July 1966.

101 M. R. Irwin, R. E. McKee, *Cornell Law Review*, **53**:467, op. cit.

Federal regulatory agencies, the Federal court system, and the U.S. Congress combined, larger than the budgets of each of the 50 states, 6,000 times larger than the total budget of the FCC Common Carrier Bureau."[102] Not surprisingly, regulation in the past has tended to be casual and informal rather than rigorous and adjudicatory. "Continual surveillance" has been held the modern tool of regulation, a tool in which rate reductions or increases are negotiated between regulator and regulatee in private—the results subsequently announced to the public.[103] A less charitable view has described this process as "shaking the apple tree."

Recently the FCC has attempted to break from this tradition. But the FCC suffers from inadequate budgets, regulates less than 30 per cent of AT & T's revenues, exercised no regulation over General Telephone & Electronics, and devotes less than 11 per cent of its staff to the common carrier field.[104] There is, moreover, the pervasive threat of political retaliation. Gains attributed to effective regulation may actually yield budget cuts and personnel transfers. (A $150 million telephone rate reduction by the Transportation and Public Utility Service unit of the General Service Administration resulted in that unit's dismemberment.)[105] Thus, operating against the burden of divided regulatory jurisdiction, carrier advertising, and political expertise, it is questionable whether examining the utility's investment rate base and operating expenditures can be much more than an exercise in frustration

It is also clear that the identities of integrated manufacturing units have become equally blurred. For example, is Western Electric a utility, a quasi-utility, or a nonutility? Obviously, the carriers prefer to let sleeping dogs lie, and only occasionally has serious policy discussion turned on the performance and conduct of utility-owned suppliers. Certainly the integrated supplier enjoys a unique position, insulated from the test of the competitive market, yet residing outside the reach of direct regulation. Informal glances at annual reports pose an inadequate substitute for the market place. The FCC failure to disallow Western Electric prices to AT & T may be because it is thoroughly convinced that Western's prices are demonstrably reasonable. But a Bureau of the Budget study observed:

Apart from the occasional review of periodic reports, no examination of Western Electric nor the leading telephone equipment manufacturers has

---

102 Federal Communications Commission, "In the Matter of American Telephone and Telegraph Company and Associated Bell System Companies, Charges for Interstate and Foreign Communication Service," Docket No. 16258, *Concurring Opinion of Commissioner*, Nicholas Johnson, July 5, 1967, p. 34. (Hereafter cited as FCC Telephone Rate Case).

103 For a Defense of Continual Surveillance, see Francis X. Welch, "Constant Surveillance: a Modern Regulatory Tool," *Villanova Law Review*, 8:430 (1963).

104 N. L. Parks, "Who Will Bell the Colossus," *Nation*, 205:391 (October 23, 1967).

105 *Congressional Record*, August 13, 1962; Remarks of Senator Bartlett, Docket No. 142, p. 15307; also J. Goulden, *Monopoly*, op. cit., pp. 209–218.

been undertaken to determine the reasonableness of charges to the Bell System.[106]

Nor does state regulation act to supplement the burden of regulation. Although 20 states have authority to regulate the competitive bidding or impose competitive bidding, only two states do so; and only one state requires competitive bidding in the purchase of materials and supplies.[107]

In sum, the rationale of public regulation as both a substitute for the market and as an institution to serve the ends of the consumer appears misplaced. More often than not, corporate power is permitted to assume the role of arbiter in determining the direction and content of the public interest.

POLICY ALTERNATIVES

What alternatives are available for public policy? Certainly maintaining the status quo is one choice. Perhaps it is sufficient to leave well enough alone. The problem is that the industry is beset by one policy crisis after another. Whether that crisis turns on the introduction of common carrier microwave, the innovation of private microwave, the use of communication satellites, the innovation of domestic satellites, the feasibility of private satellites, the growth in computer switching, the proliferation of data terminals, the application of specialized common carriers, the call for a separate digital transmission network, the maturity of community antenna systems—innovation by new firms finds the carriers united in opposition. Eventually conflict in the innovation process surfaces before the FCC, runs the gamut of adjudicatory proceedings, becomes subject to judicial review, is taken over by Congress, or requires the formation of a Presidential Task Force. The carriers find themselves in the awkward position of pleading that new entrants will be cream-skimming revenues, will threaten the carrier's financial health, will offer redundant services, will be technically incompetent and financially weak, and will compromise the quality of the nation's communications system. Indeed, the carriers often assume the stance that competitive technology is not new technology; and that what is new will be introduced when the carrier sees fit. The public, in short, is counselled patience.

All of this suggests that the holding company acts as an impediment to the industry's ability to adjust to the imperatives of technological change. Indeed, the recurring crises in the communications field pose still another question, is the holding company the norm for regulated industries in general?

A cursory glance suggests that it is not. The Air Mail Act of 1934, for

---

106 Booz, Allen, and Hamilton, *Organization and Management Survey of the Federal Communications Commission*, for the Bureau of the Budget (1962), p. 283.

107 Federal Power Commission, *Federal and State Commission Jurisdiction and Regulation*, Electric, Gas and Telephone Utilities (1967), p. 25.

example, bans vertical tie-ins between air carriers and air suppliers.[108] The Public Utility Holding Act parallels the air transport policy by prohibiting electrical utility holding companies from acquiring or maintaining interest in equipment suppliers.[109] And although the ICC requires arm's-length bargaining between carriers and supply affiliates who hold common interlocks, in practice the ICC has gone beyond this interpretation of Section 10 of the Clayton Act. According to Professor Fulda:

> The Interstate Commerce Commission has gone beyond what Section 10 ordains by requiring competitive bidding in practically all instances including the flotation of bonds and equipment trust certificates without any inquiry into whether there are any interlocking directorates.[110]

In the final analysis, policy is left with the ultimate dilemma. Can an industry possessed with formidable corporate power be held accountable for the exercise of that power? To the extent that Federal and state jurisdiction is divided, to the extent that resources devoted to regulation are inadequate, to the extent that public policy is biased toward the monopoly solution, to the extent that labor and management power continue to coalesce, to the extent that the industry holds discretionary power over its investment and expenses, and to the extent the innovative process is narrowed and constricted, the answer is not reassuring.[111] Perhaps it is enough to trust to the benevolence of the monopoly firm. But it must be recognized that this prescription is both unique and hazardous. It is not only alien to the traditions of a market economy but alien to the firm itself; for disproportionate economic power inevitably preludes still another policy alternative—public ownership.

---

108 An Act to Revise Air Mail Laws and to Establish a Commission to Make a Report to the Congress Recommending an Aviation Policy, U.S. Statutes at Large, Vol. 38, Part 1, 73rd Congress. See also J. Howard Hamstra, "Two Decades—Federal Aero-Regulation in Perspective," *The Journal of Air Law and Commerce*, **12**:113 (April 1941); also Richard Caves, *Air Transport and Its Regulators* (Cambridge, Mass.: Harvard University Press, 1962), pp. 99–101. Hamstra comments: ". . . Holding company control was broken, interlocking relationships disestablished and manufacturing and sales decisions divorced from air transport."

109 Report, Committee on Interstate Commerce, U.S. Senate, 74th Congress, 1st Session, Report No. 621, *Public Utility Act of 1935* (1936). Also *Control of Power Companies, Electric Power Industry*, Federal Trade Commission in Response to Senate Resolution No. 329, 68th Congress (1927), p. 12.

110 Remarks of Carl Fulda, "Proceedings of the Conference in the Law of Space and of Satellite Communications, a part of the Third National Conference on the Peaceful Use of Space," *National Aeronautics and Space Administration* (Washington, D.C.: U.S. Government Printing Office), p. 92. See also Carl Fulda, *Competition in the Regulated Industries—Transportation* (Boston: Little, Brown and Company, 1961), p. 56.

111 Both the Carriers and the Communications Workers of America (CWA, AFL-CIO) are united in their opposition to competitive satellite systems (Ford Foundation), a broad ownership participation of Satellite Systems, and any "Fragmentation" of the Bell System. See *Telephone Engineer and Management*, **72**:32 (July 15, 1968).

SUGGESTED READINGS

BOOKS

Goulden, J. C. *Monopoly.* New York: G. P. Putnam's Sons, 1968.
Irwin, M. R. *Telecommunications Policy: Integration vs. Competition.* New York: Frederick Praeger, Inc., 1970.
Mathison, S., and P. Walker. *Computers and Communications: Issues in Public Policy.* Englewood Cliffs, N.J.: Prentice Hall, Inc., 1970.
Phillips, Charles E. *The Economics of Regulation,* Rev. Ed. Homewood, Ill.: Richard D. Irwin, Inc., 1969.
Trebing, H. M. (Ed.). *Essays on Public Utility Pricing and Regulation.* Graduate School of Business Administration, Michigan State University, East Lansing, Michigan, Institute of Public Utilities, 1970.
Trebing, H. M. (Ed.). *Performance Under Regulation.* Graduate School of Business Administration, Michigan State University, East Lansing, Michigan, Institute of Public Utilities, 1968.
Wilcox, Claire. *Public Policies Toward Business.* Homewood, Ill.: Richard D. Irwin, Inc., 1966.

GOVERNMENT PUBLICATIONS

Federal Communications Commission. Telephone Investigation of the Telephone Industry in the United States (Pursuant to Public Resolution No. 8, 74th Congress). Washington, D.C.: U.S. Government Printing Office, 1938.
Final Report, President's Task Force on Communications Policy, December 7, 1968.
Hearings on Consent Decree Program of the Department of Justice, before Subcommittee (Subcommittee No. 5) of the Committee on the Judiciary, House of Representatives, 85th Congress, 2nd Session, 1956.
Hearings on Space Satellite Communications Before the Senate, Subcommittee of the Select Committee on Small Business, 87th Congress, 1st Session, 1961.
Report of the Telephone and Telegraph Committee of the Federal Communications Commission in the Domestic Telegraph Investigation, Docket 14650 (1965) GPO.
Stanford Research Institute. *Policy Issues Presented by the Interdependence of Computer and Communication Services,* Docket No. 19979, Contract RC-10056, SRI Project 7379B, Clearinghouse for Federal Scientific and Technical Information, Department of Commerce, February 1969.
Staff Paper V, President's Task Force on Communication Policy Part 2, U.S. Department of Commerce, Clearinghouse for Scientific and Technical Information, GPO, Washington, June 1969; Harry Trebing and William H. Melody, "An Evaluation of Domestic Pricing Practices."

JOURNAL AND MAGAZINE ARTICLES

Averich, H., and L. Johnson. "Behavior of the Firm Under Regulatory Restraint," *American Economic Review*, **52**:1052 (December 1962).

Booz, Allen, and Hamilton. *Organization and Management Survey of the Federal Communications Commission*, for the Bureau of the Budget (1962).

Demaree, Allen T. "The Age of Anxiety," *Fortune*, **81**:156 (May 1970).

Gable, Richard. "The Early Competitive Era in Telephone Communications 1893–1920," *Law and Contemporary Problems* **34**:340 (Spring 1969).

Irwin, M. R. "The Computer Utility: Competition or Regulation," *Yale Law Journal*, **76**:1299 (June 1967).

————. "The Computer Utility: Market Entry in Search of Public Policy," *Journal of Industrial Economics*, **27**:239 (July 1969).

————. "Vertical Integration and the Communications Industry: Separation of Western Electric and AT & T?" *Antitrust Law and Economics Review*, **3**:31 (Fall 1969).

Lessing, L. "Cinderella in the Sky," *Fortune*, **76**:131 (October 1967).

Licklider, J. C. R., et al. "The Computer as a Communication Device," *Science and Technology*, **76**:21 (April 1968).

McWhirter, William A. "What Hath God Rung," *Life*, **68**:86A (December 5, 1969).

Melody, William H. *Market Structure and Public Policy In Communication*, paper presented to the American Economic Association (December 1969).

Pierce, J. R. "The Transmission of Computer Data," *Scientific American*, **215**:144 (September 1966).

Sheahan, John. "Integration and Exclusion in the Telephone Equipment Industry," *Quarterly Journal of Economics*, **70**:249 (1956).

Trebing, Harry. "Common Carrier Regulation: The Silent Crisis," *Law and Contemporary Problems*, **34**:299 (Spring 1969).

Westfield, Fred. "Regulation and Conspiracy," *American Economic Review*, **55**:424 (1965).

"Why You Hear a Busy Signal at AT & T," *Business Week* (December 27, 1969).

12. Elton Rayack

THE PHYSICIANS' SERVICE INDUSTRY

"F rom a 'blessed benevolence' or a 'private luxury' medical care has gradually assumed the status of a necessity and a 'civic right.'"[1] The changed attitude toward medical care, the increase in population, and rapidly rising personal incomes have generated a pronounced growth in the demand for medical services. In 1929, private and public expenditures for medical care amounted to $3.6 billion, or 3.6 per cent of the gross national product (GNP); by 1967 they exceeded $47 billion and their share of the GNP had risen to 6.2 per cent.

Although private expenditures on medical care have increased tenfold since 1929, a growing share of the costs of medical care is being borne by the public sector. Public care as a per cent of total medical care expenditures doubled—from 13 to 26 per cent—between 1929 and 1966. The role of the public sector increased at an even more rapid rate with the start of the Federal Medicare program in July 1966, so that in 1967 government expenditures accounted for more than 34 per cent of the nation's medical costs. Two thirds of a $5.1 billion rise in public expenditures in 1966–1967 was due to the Medicare program. The major share of public funds for medical care comes from the Federal Government—61 per cent in 1967. Since 1960, Federal expenditures have increased 147 per cent compared with a 55 per cent increase in state and local funds. Given Medicare and its probable extension the Federal Government is destined to play an even larger role in the medical market in future years.

Medical care services and products are provided by four major interrelated yet quite distinct industries—physicians' service, hospital service, drug, and dental service—and a number of subsidiary industries. This chapter will concern itself primarily with the physicians' service industry which, in 1966, attracted 29 per cent of the private consumers' medical dollar, about the same amount spent on hospitals, the number one recipient (see Table 1).

I. INTRODUCTION

---

1 Herman M. Somers and Anne R. Somers, *Doctors, Patients, and Health* *Insurance* (Washington, D.C.: The Brookings Institute, 1961), p. 133.

TABLE 1   PRIVATE CONSUMER
EXPENDITURES FOR HEALTH SERVICES
AND SUPPLIES, BY TYPE OF EXPENDITURE,
1950 AND 1966

	1950 ($)	1966 ($)
Total	8,501	30,082
Hospital care	1,965	8,772
Physicians' services	2,597	8,608
Dentists' services	961	2,959
Other professional services	370	905
Drugs	1,716	5,049
Eyeglasses and appliances	482	1,560
Nursing-home care	110	807
Expense for prepayment	300	1,422

SOURCE   U.S. Department of Health, Education, and
Welfare, *Social Security Bulletin*, **31**:18 (April 1968).

The $8.6 billion spent by consumers on the services of physicians, as large as
it is, understates the economic significance of the doctor's role. For not only
is the physician a supplier of services, but he also determines, in great part,
the extent to which hospitals are utilized as well as the type and quantity of
drugs consumed.

The idea of medical care as a basic necessity is of relatively recent origin.
Only 75 years ago, poor patients were sent to hospitals to die. Nor could the
patient at the turn of the century find much solace in the fact that he would
receive the services of a physician, for, as a distinguished medical authority
has stated: "I think it was about the year 1910 or 1912 when it became possible to say of the United States that a random patient with a random disease
consulting a doctor chosen at random stood better than a fifty-fifty chance of
benefiting from the encounter."[2] Under those conditions, the absence of any
great public outcry for medical care is readily understandable.

During the past 50 years, the science and technology of modern medicine
have created an incredible array of new tools and methods for controlling
the forces of nature related to health—new and complex laboratory tests for
accurate diagnoses, electronic and radar devices for pinpointing organic processes, heart-lung machines, the artificial kidney, organ transplantation, the
electron microscope, and perhaps the most revolutionary event in the history
of medicine, the discovery of antibiotics. All these developments and hundreds more, along with the general rise in the standard of living, produced
dramatic decreases in death rates and increases in life expectancy. Crude death

---

2   L. J. Henderson, as quoted in Alan
Gregg, MD, *Challenges to Contemporary*
Medicine (New York: Columbia University
Press, 1956), p. 13.

rates fell from 17.2 per 1,000 population in 1900 to 9.4 in 1964. In 1900 an infant had a life expectancy of 47 years; by 1964 he could look forward to 70 years of life, an increase of almost 50 per cent.

Yet despite these advances, the available data suggest that *morbidity rates have actually risen*! The paradox of longer life and more illness may in great part be explained by the increased significance of the aged in our population. The increased life span has led to a higher incidence of the chronic degenerative diseases, associated primarily with the aged, and to a decline in the acute infectious diseases, which attack primarily the young. Influenza and pneumonia, tuberculosis and enteritis—all acute infectious diseases which attack primarily the young—were the "killers" at the beginning of the century. Recently, the leading causes of death have been diseases of the heart, cancer, and vascular lesions of the central nervous system—chronic diseases associated primarily with older age groups. Since the chronic diseases are frequently of long duration, they add significantly to the demand for medical care.

Despite the enormous benefits reaped from the medical revolution, and paradoxically in part because of it, for more than two decades there has been considerable controversy concerning the adequacy of the operation of the market for medical services. The debate has focused on several major interrelated problems:

1. The sharp growth in demand for physicians' services has not been matched by a sufficient increase in supply. The resulting shortage is reflected in enormous increases in the incomes of doctors and heavy reliance on the use of foreign-trained physicians. Since the latter are often less adequately trained than graduates of American medical schools, there is serious concern about a possible deterioration in the quality of medical care.

2. The medical care component of the Bureau of Labor Statistics (BLS) Consumer Price Index (CPI) has, since the end of World War II, risen more rapidly than any other item priced. The increases in hospital daily service charges has been particularly sharp, but physicians' fees, the item of primary concern in this chapter, have also bolted upward. Since the CPI 1957–1959 base period, physicians' fees have increased at a rate more than twice that of "all items."

3. There is a real need to develop new techniques in the methods of producing and financing medical care. Discussion of alternatives has focused on several key questions: Does group practice offer opportunities for reducing costs and improving the quality and the quantity of medical services? Has the profession gone too far in the direction of specialization? Would it be desirable to develop health practitioners less highly trained than the medical doctor to take over some of the tasks of the expensively produced physician? Are there insurance techniques or methods of reimbursing the physician, that might place a check on rising medical costs?

4. Serious doubts have been raised concerning the quality of American medical care. Major studies have been conducted indicating physicians

engage in substantial amounts of unnecessary surgery and that the quality of the care provided by many general practitioners leaves much to be desired. Data on infant mortality, life expectancy, and death rates suggest that there are serious deficiencies in American medical care. In 1965 the United States had higher infant mortality rates than 15 other countries. Life expectancy for American males ranges from about 1.2–5 years behind that of males in Norway, Sweden, Denmark, the Netherlands, France, England, and Canada. Of particular economic significance, the United States had significantly higher death rates for males between the ages of 40 and 55—the most productive years—than did 11 other well-developed nations.[3]

II. MARKET STRUCTURE

In 1965 there were 288,671 physicians in active practice in the United States. Of these 190,748 (66 per cent) were in private practice, 44,276 (16 per cent) in training as interns or residents in hospitals, and 53,647 (18 per cent) in other types of practice such as Federal service, full-time staff in hospitals, full-time medical school faculty, administrative medicine, laboratory medicine, preventative medicine, or research.

Despite enormous technological changes in the industry, the most common type of firm remains that of the solo practitioner, the man with a solely owned private practice. Sixty per cent of the private practitioners are in solo practice, about 19 per cent are in two-man partnerships or in some type of informal relationship with one or more physicians, another 19 per cent are working under some formal relationship with three or more physicians, and the remaining 2 per cent are physicians employed by other physicians or by organizations other than hospitals.[4]

Although solo practice continues as the dominant form of business organization, the scientific and technological revolutions in medicine have forced sweeping changes in other characteristics of medical practice. Perhaps no other development so dramatically reflects the twentieth-century revolution in medical practice as the growth of specialization. No longer is it possible for the general practitioner to effectively meet the medical needs of the public with his accumulated knowledge and the few tools carried in his proverbial "little black bag." So vast is the amount of medical knowledge amassed during this century that it is virtually impossible for any single physician to master all but a small portion of the science and art of modern medicine. As

---

3   The United Nations, *Demographic Yearbook, 1966* (New York: The United Nations, 1967).

4   Christ N. Theodore and Gerald E. Sutter, "A Report on the First Periodic Survey of Physicians," *Journal of the American Medical Association*, **202**:520 (Nov. 6, 1967).

recently as 1931 about 80 per cent of all physicians were in general practice or part-time specialties; by 1965 only 29 per cent were in general practice and 71 per cent were full-time specialists.

An inevitable concomitant of specialization is mutual dependence. Interdependence is not limited to physicians organized in groups. Even the solo practitioner must depend upon other physicians in various specialties to whom he can refer patients with ailments beyond his knowledge or ability to treat successfully. Nor is the specialist independent, for almost his entire practice flows from the referral of general practitioners and physicians in other specialties.

Another major development increasing the dependence of physicians on others has been the phenomenal growth in number of other health personnel. In 1900 for every physician in practice, there was one other health practitioner. Today the ratio of professional and technical workers in the health field to physicians is almost four and one-half to one.

Dependence of the physician on others has also increased because it is no longer financially possible for him to acquire more than an infinitesimal fraction of the costly tools so essential for modern medical care; laboratory, diagnostic, medical, and surgical equipment are so expensive that they impose heavy burdens even on the resources of entire communities. As a result, the hospital, to a substantial extent has become the workshop of the doctor. Doctors now earn nearly half their income from hospital connected work.[5]

The large number of firms in the physicians' service industry and the small size of each might suggest that we are dealing with an industry closely approximating perfectly competitive conditions. However, there are other elements in the market structure—the nature of the product, consumer ignorance, and the various powers vested in the industry's key professional organization, the American Medical Association—which combine to make the industry one of the most highly monopolistic in the country. Let us turn to an examination of these factors.

CONSUMER IGNORANCE AND PROFESSIONAL POWER

A prerequisite for the effective operation of any market is that the consumer have considerable knowledge concerning the nature of the product so that he can make a rational choice in attempting to maximize his satisfaction. A fundamental characteristic of the medical services' market, however, is the the relative lack of knowledge on the part of the consumer. Medical knowledge is extraordinarily complex, so complex that the knowledge possessed by the physician concerning the necessity for or consequences of treatment is tremendously greater than that possessed by the consumer.

---

5 George Bugbee, "Administration and the Professional in the Hospital," Address for the Upper Midwest Hospital Conference, May 1960, Health Information Foundation (mimeo), p. 2, cited by Somers and Somers, op. cit., pp. 68–69.

It is the physician who decides whether or not drugs are required, whether or not hospitalization is desirable, whether or not surgery is necessary, and by his recommendation he can create a demand for his own product. The consumer has no way of knowing which alternative is best for him—he must rely upon his faith in the integrity and competence of the physician. Moreover, the consequences of a wrong choice on the part of the consumer can be disastrous.

In recognition of the inevitable baneful consequences of permitting *caveat emptor* to prevail in the medical market place, society has granted considerable power to organized medicine to maintain quality standards and to police the profession.[6] And it is precisely this delegation of authority that is the seminal source of the American Medical Association's (AMA) power.

MEMBERSHIP AND FORMAL STRUCTURE OF THE AMA   Approximately 75 per cent of America's 288,671 physicians are in the ranks of organized medicine. Aside from southern Negro physicians barred because of color, nonmembers are primarily physicians outside private practice—in the armed services, medical school professors, physicians engaged in research, doctors-in-training, and public health officers. A 1960 study indicated that only 35 per cent of the physicians not in private practice were AMA members. Of physicians engaged in private practice, however, probably about 90 per cent are members of the AMA.

The formal structure of the AMA is roughly patterned after the American federal system, with governing bodies at the federal, state, and county levels. At the base of organized medicine's political pyramid are almost 2,000 county medical societies. The county societies are "component" bodies of the 54 autonomous state and territorial associations, and the latter are, in turn, "constituent" associations of the summit federation, the AMA. Except in rare instances, it is not possible for a physician to join the AMA directly; he must first be admitted to the county or state medical society. The county societies select delegates to the governing body of their state societies and the latter—not the membership—choose representatives to the AMA policy-making House of Delegates.

Although the AMA constitution designates the 238-member House of Delegates as its legislative and policy-making body, much if not most of the effective power at the national level rests with the House-elected Board of Trustees. Since the House meets for a few days semiannually, many of the basic policy and administrative decisions are of necessity left to the board. Although technically responsible to the House of Delegates, the board functions with practically no supervision when the House is not in session, and

---

6 For a brilliant analysis of the significance and implications of consumer ignorance and uncertainty in the purchase of medical care, see Kenneth J. Arrow, "Uncertainty and the Welfare Economics of Medical Care," *American Economic Review*, **53**:941 (December 1963).

the AMA constitution gives the board a blank check on organized medicine's substantial treasury. The members of the board, in effect, "perform the typical role of corporate directors."[7]

MEDICAL LICENSURE, MEDICAL SCHOOLS, AND HOSPITALS

The laudable social goal of medical licensure is to ensure practitioner competence through tests, minimum education requirements, or some other demonstration of ability. In order to practice in a particular state or territory a physician must meet the requirements of that political unit's medical examining board. The policies of the various state boards of medical examiners are virtually identical with those of the AMA; this is an inevitable product of the fact that in about half the states the medical society recommends appointees to the state board, in others the society nominates candidates for the office, and in one the State Medical Society Board of Censors itself constitutes the State Board of Medical Examiners.

In granting sole authority to the boards to issue licenses, society has in effect given considerable power to organized medicine to restrict the supply of physicians and to influence the patterns of medical care for the benefit of the profession. As Professor Milton Friedman has argued, licensure is the "key to the control" that the AMA exercises over the number of physicians trained. Its essential control is at the stage of admission to medical school. Medical schools are approved by the AMA Council on Medical Education, and to stay on the approved list a school must meet the standards set up by the council. The council's approval is crucial for the existence of a medical school, since in almost every state in the United States, a person must be licensed to practice medicine, and to get the license he must be a graduate of an approved school. Generally, the list of approved schools is identical with the list of schools approved by the council. Loss of approval would make it extremely difficult for a school's graduates to obtain licenses. That is why the licensure procedure is the key to the effective control of admission.[8] By directly exerting pressure on schools to restrict admissions, or by requiring very high quality standards, the AMA can restrict the supply of physicians.

State licensure laws together with the activities of the AMA Council on Medical Education and Hospitals also make it possible for organized medicine to exercise control over admission to practice in hospitals. The council approves hospitals as well as medical schools. Of crucial significance is the fact

---

7 David R. Hyde, Payson Wolff, Anne Gross, and Elliott Lee Hoffman, "The American Medical Association: Power, Purpose and Politics in Organized Medicine," *Yale Law Journal*, **43**:943 (May 1954). This article is a classic in the field and a basic source of primary data on organized medicine.

8 Milton Friedman, *Capitalism and Freedom* (Chicago: University of Chicago Press, 1962), pp. 150–155.

that the council has "final responsibility for approval of internship programs."[9] State licensure generally requires a candidate to complete an internship in an "approved" hospital before being admitted to practice, and the licensing boards' lists of approved schools are generally identical with that of the AMA council list. Loss of council approval would be a deadly blow to a hospital since it would then be virtually impossible for it to obtain the staff of interns so vital for the operation of a hospital today. The threat of council disapproval has been an effective weapon to exert pressure on hospitals to follow the AMA line in organized medicine's many battles against the development of group practice.

In addition to being regulated by the medical practices acts of the various states, the physician is governed by the AMA *Principles of Medical Ethics*. Frequently, "unethical" practices have been interpreted by AMA leadership to include such acts as participation in local insurance schemes not approved by organized medicine, association with health practitioners the AMA refers to derogatorily as "cultists" (e.g. osteopaths, chiropractors, and optometrists), and acceptance of salaried arrangements that are not in accord with the AMA sacrosanct fee-for-service principle.

Organized medicine's power over the physician to make him conform to its standards exists for the most part at the county society level. Not only does the county society have the sole authority to admit a physician to membership, "there is no right to a hearing and no appeal from the society's verdict" to deny membership.[10] In addition, most discipline cases have been handled at the county level with not even so much as a report being made to the state society.

AMA ethical standards can often be enforced against an offending physician at the county society level without any formal action. As Garceau pointed out 25 years ago in discussing the sanctions available to organized medicine:

> First, of course, and never out of use, is social pressure in a small group. The social life of the county society is important to some doctors. Few can wholly disregard it, simply because a doctor can ill afford more than a few enemies, certainly not the hostility of an organized group in positions of local prominence. His reputation is a fragile thing, and his income and practice depend upon being called in consultation, though perhaps more vitally on being able to call his colleagues in emergencies. Ostracism becomes a terrible weapon in such a business.[11]

---

9 American Medical Association, *Directory of Approved Internships and Residencies* (Chicago: American Medical Association, 1964), p. 1.

10 Hyde and Wolff, op. cit., p. 950.

11 Oliver Garceau, *The Political Life of the American Medical Association* (Cambridge, Mass.: Harvard University Press, 1941), p. 103.

What Garceau wrote in 1940 has even greater validity today due to the fantastic growth in medical specialization since then. Under present conditions denial of patient referrals and consultation can drastically reduce a specialist's income.

Should informal pressures prove inadequate to compel a recalcitrant physician to mend his ways, formal sanctions may be invoked by the county society's board of censors. Formal action could result in denial of membership application or expulsion from the county medical society, actions which can have dire consequences for the offending physician. Nonmembership may prevent an applicant from taking advantage of reciprocal licensing provisions to practice in other states. In Delaware a physician moving from Chester, Pennsylvania, was recently denied licensure "because he was not affiliated with any of the hospitals in Chester and he did not belong to the Medical Society in the county in which he practiced." [12]

A nonmember may also find it very costly or impossible to purchase malpractice insurance. Insurance rates are sometimes 20–100 per cent higher for nonmembers and some insurance companies refuse to issue them policies. [13] According to 1958 AMA data, one in seven living physicians had been the target of a malpractice suit or claim, with the annual cost of damages, settlements, and legal fees estimated at $50 million! Since such claims are so frequent and costly, adequate insurance is a necessity for the physician.

Nonmembership has it greatest impact in the severe limits it places on the opportunity to practice. A nonmember may be blocked from specialty certification and hence barred from the more lucrative specialty practice. Most damaging of all, he will be denied the use of most hospital facilities. Since perhaps about half the average doctor's income is derived from hospital connected work, being barred from the use of hospitals can be a devastating blow.

THE MEDICAL LOBBY

In addition to the economic power the AMA derives from its position as a professional association, it has substantial financial resources, which enable it to engage in costly propaganda campaigns, extensive political activity, and vigorous lobbying. Over the past 20 years, the AMA has spent millions—more than any other single pressure group—for maintaining a highly effective Washington lobby. In 1949 and 1950, AMA lobbying expenditures were almost double those of the second-ranked lobbyist and greater than those of such big spenders as the National Association of Manufacturers, the AFL-CIO, and the various veterans' organizations. In 1951 and 1952, the AMA finished a strong third and second, respectively, [14] as it successfully fought

---

12 *Federation Bulletin*, p. 205 (June 1965).

13 Hyde and Wolff, op. cit., p. 951.

14 *Legislators and the Lobbyists* (Washington, D.C.: Congressional Quarterly Service, 1965), pp. 33, 34, and 37.

President Truman's national health insurance proposals and legislation, which would have provided much-needed Federal aid for medical schools.

The AMA's 1965 campaign against medicare broke all recent records for expenditures by lobbyists. In the *first quarter* of 1965 the AMA spent more than $950,000. During the past 20 years there have been only two occasions when spending by any organization for any full year reached or exceeded $900,000—and on both those occasions, as in 1965, the AMA was the group involved. None of this, it should be noted, includes the spending of state and county medical societies affiliated with the AMA.

Moreover, the AMA budget does not include all the expenditures by organized medicine in fighting legislation it considers inimical to its interests. In September 1961, the AMA created the American Medical Political Action Committee (AMPAC) as an independent operation for the purpose of organizing doctors into an effective political action group. AMPAC was formed by the AMA because the latter, as a corporation, is forbidden to make direct campaign contributions for political candidates. The Board of Directors of AMPAC was appointed by the AMA Board of Trustees,[15] and in 1962 the AMA supported AMPAC with a $50,000 contribution. By mid-1963 AMPAC had helped establish political action committees in all states but Mississippi and Ohio, and in the 1962 elections it distributed to congressional candidates about $250,000, a figure that does not include the expenditures of committees at the state and local level.[16] The funds in 1962 were devoted to 4 key Senate races and 75–80 House races, with most of the money going to support members of the House Ways and Means Committee who were opposed to the King-Anderson bill.[17] In the 1964 political campaign, AMPAC spent $402,000 and was seventeenth in a list of 164 organizations filing reports with the U.S. House of Representatives.[18]

III. MARKET CONDUCT

Analysis of the behavior of physicians and their professional organizations reveals a long history of price discrimination, severe restrictions on entry into the field, widespread opposition to marketing innovations particularly with respect to the development of voluntary health insurance, restrictive practice by specialists vis-à-vis general practitioners and among specialists, and restrictions imposed on the activities of health practitioners who are not medical doctors.

---

15 *New York Times* (March 18, 1962), p. 70.
16 *Wall Street Journal* (July 2, 1963), p. 12.
17 *Medical Economics*, p. 267 (November 6, 1962).
18 *Congressional Quarterly Weekly Report*, Part I, p. 72 (January 21, 1966).

PRICE DISCRIMINATION   Price discrimination by physicians, i.e., varying fees with the income of patients, has become the classic textbook illustration of the discriminating monopolist. By charging higher prices for the rich and lower prices for the poor, the physician is increasing his income by taking advantage of the smaller elasticity of demand for medical services on the part of the wealthy.

Price discrimination by physicians is not, as doctors argue, merely a charitable activity to aid the poor. A Health Information Foundation—National Opinion Research Center survey of family doctors in 1955 revealed that 63 per cent take "ability to pay" into account when setting fees. The survey also found that such price discrimination is more common among members of specialized societies, big-city practitioners and those in the far West than among general practitioners in small communities where doctors are likely to be in the best position to evaluate the patient's income and wealth. In commenting on this survey, the Somers concluded that "apparently [sliding fees] are now used primarily as a device for raising fees above the standard, as increasingly established by health insurance practices, rather than for lowering them for the poor, their major historical justification."[19] Furthermore, as Kessel points out: "Existing evidence indicates that if income and wealth differences are held constant, people who have medical insurance pay more for the same service than people who do not have such insurance. Union leaders have found that the fees charged have risen as a result of the acquisition of medical insurance by their members. . . . Members of the insurance industry have found that 'the greater the benefit provided the higher the surgical bill.' This suggests that the principle used for the determination of fees is . . . what the traffic will bear."[20]

RESTRICTIONS ON ENTRY   In 1925 the Association of American Medical Colleges (AAMC) organized the Commission on Medical Education to make a study of the education principles involved in medical education and licensure. The work of the commission was in great part financed by the AMA. The commission's *Final Report*, released in 1932, stated: "It is clear that in the immediate past there has been a larger production [of physicians] than necessary and that at the present time we have an oversupply . . . of at least 25,000 physicians in this country. . . . An over-supply is likely to introduce excessive economic competition, the performance of unnecessary services, an elevated total cost of medical care, and conditions in the profession which will not encourage students of superior ability and character to enter the profession."[21] The concern of the commission over "excessive economic

---

19   Somers and Somers, op. cit., pp. 53–54.

20   Reuben A. Kessel, "Price Discrimination in Medicine," reprinted from the *Journal of Law and Economics* in *Readings in Microeconomics*, ed. by William Breit and Harold M. Hochman (New York: Holt, 1968), pp. 320–321.

21   *Final Report of the Commission on Medical Education* (New York, 1932), pp. 89, 93, 100.

competition" was undoubtedly a product of sharply falling medical income. Between 1929 and 1932 the incomes of physicians fell almost 40 per cent.

In a not too veiled recommendation for a restrictionist policy, the report concluded: "Those responsible for medical education and for the licensure of physicians, particularly for graduates from foreign medical schools, should have the situation clearly before them."[22] The commission's *Final Report* laid the ground work for organized medicine's drive to restrict the production of physicians during the 1930's.

In an editorial in August 1932 the *Journal of the American Medical Association* (*JAMA*) stated that "the United States already has more doctors in proportion to its population than any other country in the world," and that "if this ratio is still further increased it is evident that an oversupply of doctors threatens with an inevitable lowering of the standards of the profession." The editorial concluded prophetically that "perhaps there is need for professional birth control."[23]

In his presidential address before the AMA convention in mid-1933, Dr. Dean D. Lewis asserted: "There apparently is an over-production of doctors. How such an over-production can be controlled is a problem for the Council on Medical Education and Hospitals."[24] A year later there was no question in the mind of the new president of the AMA, Dr. Walter L. Bierring, concerning both the over-production of doctors and what to do about it:

> one is forced to the conviction that more doctors are being turned out than society needs and can comfortably reward. . . . The time has arrived for the American Medical Association to take the initiative and point the way. During the coming year the Association, through the Council on Medical Education and Hospitals, will institute a resurvey of the medical schools of the country . . . it will require real courage and tenacity to bend the educational processes to the urgent social and economic needs of the changing order. A fine piece of educational work could well be done if we were to use only half of the seventy-odd medical schools in the United States.[25]

The mechanism for exerting pressure on the medical colleges with respect to admission policy was the survey of medical schools conducted by the AMA Council on Medical Education in cooperation with the Federation of State Medical Boards and the AAMC. During the years 1934 to 1936 the council visited and evaluated 89 schools in the United States and Canada. In reporting on its survey to the Annual Congress on Medical Education, Medi-

---

22 Ibid., p. 100.
23 *Journal of the American Medical Association*, **99**:765 (August 27, 1932).
24 *Journal of the American Medical Association*, **100**:1908 (June 17, 1933).

25 Walter L. Bierring, "The Family Doctor and the Changing Order," *Journal of the American Medical Association*, **102**:1997 (June 16, 1934).

cal Licensure, and Hospitals in 1936, the council was able to state: "Most of the schools . . . which . . . allowed themselves to yield to the demands of this increasing number of applicants and to take in larger numbers of students than they have been able to care for properly . . . have expressed their readiness to cooperate with us by reducing the size of their student body." In 1937 the chairman of the council reported: "A reduction in the quota of students received for admission is now being made by a number of our medical schools."[26]

The AMA pressure on medical schools had a substantial impact. Despite the fact that there was virtually no change in the number of applicants between the academic years 1933–1934 and 1938–1939, the number of acceptances fell 1,355, a decline of 17.9 per cent, and the percentage of applicants accepted fell by 17.8 per cent. Fully 74 per cent of the decline in the number of applicants accepted occurred within 2 years of the AMA's Council on Medical Education's 1935 warning to medical schools against the admission of larger classes.[27] The success of organized medicine's restrictionist activities during the 1930's contributed to the shortage of physicians which has persisted since the end of World War II.

In the post-World War II years the demand for medical services continued to grow, and there was a pronounced rise in the number of applicants to medical schools. Pressure for medical education grew tremendously, but the inadequacy of existing facilities set an upper limit to the number of students who could be enrolled. Although the annual number of applicants for the years 1947 through 1950 was about double the pre-World War II annual rate, the increase in the number accepted was relatively small; whereas in the pre-World War II years more than 50 per cent of the applicants were accepted annually, in the post-World War II years acceptances dropped to about the 30 per cent level.

In the face of rising demand for medical education and the resultant stresses and strains imposed on existing medical school facilities, the AMA again turned toward restrictionism. However, instead of exerting direct pressure on medical schools to curtail enrollment as it did in the 1930's—this was not necessary since a ceiling on admission was already effectively established by the limited facilities—the AMA in the post-World War II years turned toward slowing down the growth in the number of doctors by vigorously opposing the provision of much-needed Federal aid to medical education:

1. Between 1946 and 1950 the AMA vigorously and vehemently opposed all forms of federal aid to medical education that would tend to increase the

26 *Journal of the American Medical Association,* **106**:1393 (April 18, 1936); **108**:771 (March 6, 1937).

27 *Journal of Medical Education,* **35**: 224 (March 1960). It is of more than pass-

ing interest that the AMA's own detailed 1,200-page official history, published in 1947, contains not a single word of reference to its restrictionist objectives of the 1930's!

supply of physicians, arguing not only that there was no danger of a shortage of physicians but that there was even the possibility of a surplus by 1960.

2. As the pressures for federal aid grew, organized medicine retreated somewhat and in the years from 1951 to 1958 reluctantly accepted the principle of such aid for one-time construction grants when there was a "demonstrated emergency." However, it continued to deny there was any danger of a physician shortage and maintained its strong opposition to federal aid for the operational expenses of medical schools. To still demands for federal aid, the AMA pressed its program of seeking funds for medical schools from private sources.

3. In the years since 1958 the AMA finally conceded there was a real danger of a serious physician shortage, that medical schools were in dire financial need, and, therefore, federal assistance for construction purposes was necessary. It was, nevertheless, still opposed to federal aid for scholarships and for operational expenses. However, so successful in preventing an adequate growth of medical schools was organized medicine's twenty-year campaign against federal aid that even the AMA finally admitted that it would take prompt and massive aid to prevent a serious shortage of physicians.[28]

RESTRICTIVE PRACTICES AND
VOLUNTARY INSURANCE

Despite the recent denials of organized medicine, there is abundant evidence to demonstrate that the AMA was a vigorous opponent of private health insurance in the early 1930's. The AMA then argued that "all such schemes are contrary to sound public policy and that the shortest road to the commercialization of the practice of medicine is through the supposed rosy path of insurance." By 1949, private health insurance—"the voluntary way"— had become to the AMA "the American way." The metamorphosis from the passionate enemy to reluctant lover had been completed with the threat of compulsory insurance functioning as the catalytic agent. The purpose of this section is to examine the practices of organized medicine as it responded to the development of voluntary health insurance.

FARMERS UNION HOSPITAL ASSOCIATION   In 1929 Dr. Michael Shadid contributed $20,000 to the Farmers Union Hospital Association, enabling it to establish the Community Hospital Clinic of Elk City, Oklahoma, perhaps the first consumer cooperative in the field of medical care. The members of the cooperative own the hospital, pay the staff doctors fixed salaries, and receive

---

28   A detailed discussion of the AMA opposition to Federal aid to medical schools is presented in the author's   *Professional Power and American Medicine* (New York: World Publishing, 1967), pp. 81–101.

medical care on a prepaid basis. From its inception and for more than two decades, the cooperative was harassed by the local county medical society, Dr. Shadid, the hospital's first medical director, was the medical society's prime target. Despite the fact that he had been a respected member of the medical society for 20 years, organized medicine tried to destroy him and his hospital. Since the society's members had no legitimate reason for expelling Dr. Shadid, they resorted to the incredibly ludicrous procedure of dissolving six months and then reorganizing without him! The county society also tried to get legislation passed that would have had the effect of outlawing the Community Hospital Clinic. For more than 20 years other members of the hospital's staff were barred from the local medical society. Finally, in 1950, the Farmers Union Hospital Association brought suit against the county society and its members. Charging its opponents with being involved in a conspiracy in restraint of trade, the union sued for $300,000 in damages and threatened to carry the case to the U.S. Supreme Court. Although the county society employed delaying tactics, it finally agreed to settle out of court. The damage suit was dropped as the medical society agreed to admit the cooperative's doctors to membership.[29]

THE GROUP HEALTH ASSOCIATION In 1937, employees of the Federal Home Owners' Loan Corporation in Washington, D.C. formed a nonprofit cooperative—the Group Health Association (GHA). Aided by a $40,000 grant from the loan corporation, they equipped a clinic, engaged doctors, and assessed themselves monthly prepayments to finance medical care and hospitalization for themselves and their families, and sought members in other Federal agencies. Almost immediately GHA was attacked on legal grounds by the District of Columbia Medical Society as being improperly engaged in the insurance business and in the "corporate practice of medicine."[30]

Two basic characteristics of the GHA plan aroused (and still arouses) the ire of organized medicine: (1) "Closed panel" practice—that is, subscribers to the insurance plan, if they are to receive its benefits, must use doctors associated with the plan—and (2) the use of "prepayment" rather than the fee-for-service system. Under "prepayment" the subscriber, for a fixed premium paid in advance, is guaranteed certain specific services. Organized medicine much prefers the fee-for-service system since it gives the physician

---

29 James Howard Means, *Doctors, People and Government* (Boston: Little, Brown, 1953), pp. 175–176; U.S. Congress, Senate Subcommittee on Health of the Committee on Labor and Public Welfare, *Hearings on S.1805, Cooperative Health Act,* 81st Congress, 2nd Session (Washington, D.C.: U.S. Government Printing Office, 1950), pp. 213–217; U.S. Congress, House Committee on Interstate and Foreign Commerce, *Hearings, Health Inquiry,* Part 6, 83rd Congress, 2nd Session (Washington, D.C.: U.S. Government Printing Office, 1954), p. 1787.

30 Committee on Research in Medical Economics, *Restrictions on Free Enterprise in Medicine* (New York: 1949), p. 12.

considerably more control over the price—he can charge what the market will bear.

When the attempt to destroy the GHA by legal action in the courts failed, the medical society resorted to direct action. The District society ruled that GHA doctors were "unethical" for participating in closed-panel practice and refused them admission to the medical society, or, if they were already in it, expelled them. Doctors who consulted with GHA physicians were threatened with expulsion from the medical society. Pressure was brought to bear on local hospitals to close their doors to GHA physicians, and as a result the doctors were unable to treat the GHA patients in those hospitals. The press reported stories of sick people denied treatment, consultation, or operations. Some of the doctors resigned under the pressure, but most stood by the GHA. The AMA national office condemned the GHA plan as "unethical," sent staff members to advise the District of Columbia Medical Society, and instructed the *JAMA* editor to bring the situation to the attention of the entire medical profession.[31]

The actions of organized medicine made it very difficult for the GHA to recruit physicians and to assure its subscribers the quality care for which they had paid. On July 31, 1938, Assistant Attorney General Thurman Arnold announced that the Department of Justice proposed to prosecute the District society and the AMA under the Federal antitrust laws if a grand jury investigation resulted in an indictment. In less than 3 months a special grand jury returned indictments. In a subsequent hearing before Justice James M. Proctor in the U.S. District Court for the District of Columbia, the indictment was quashed on the grounds that medical practice was not a "trade" and hence not subject to the antitrust laws. In March 1940, the U.S. Court of Appeals reversed the decision by Justice Proctor, a trial was held, and in April 1941 the jury found the medical associations guilty as charged. Organized medicine then carried the case to the U.S. Court of Appeals which, by a unanimous vote, upheld the jury's decision. In a ringing indictment Associate Justice Justin Miller, who delivered the opinion, blasted organized medicine in words that went to the heart of the problem:

> Professions exist because the people believe they will be better served by licensing especially prepared experts to minister their needs. The licensed monopolies which professions enjoy constitute in themselves severe restraints upon competition. But they are restraints which depend upon capacity and training, not special privilege.
>
> Neither do they justify concentrated criminal action to prevent the people from developing new methods of serving their needs. There is sufficient historical evidence of professional inadequacy to justify occasional popular protest.

---

31   Morris Fishbein, *A History of the American Medical Association* (Philadelphia: Saunders, 1947), p. 545.

The better educated laity of today questions the adequacy of present-day medicine. Their challenge finds support from substantial portions of the medical profession itself. The people give the privilege of professional monopoly and the people may take it away.[32]

The decision, upheld by a unanimous United States Supreme Court opinion on January 18, 1943, pointed out that the medical societies had combined and conspired to prevent the successful operation of the GHA by taking the following steps: "(1) to impose restraints on physicians affiliated with Group Health by threat of expulsion or actual expulsion from the societies; (2) to deny them the essential professional contacts with other physicians, and (3) to use coercive power of the societies to deprive them of hospital facilities for their patients."[33] The loss of the case was a serious blow to the prestige and power of organized medicine and a crucial victory for the "independent" insurance plans.

HEALTH INSURANCE PLAN OF GREATER NEW YORK (HIP)   HIP was the product of several years of planning aimed at providing prepaid comprehensive medical service of high quality for persons of moderate means in the New York metropolitan area. The initial impetus for the plan came from New York's Mayor LaGuardia, when in 1944, he announced that the city would pay half the premiums of group health insurance for municipal employees if the coverage could be truly comprehensive. With the help of $855,000 in loans (subsequently repaid in full) supplied by several philanthropic foundations, HIP began to operate in March 1947. The services are currently provided by 31 medical groups scattered throughout New York City and Nassau County. HIP does not cover hospital expenses, only doctor's bills, but the plan requires its members to join Blue Cross or some other hospitalization plan.

From its inception, HIP ran into difficulties with organized medicine, which again raised the cry that "free choice of physician" was being denied. The local medical societies subjected HIP to the same kind of pressure exerted against prepaid group practice plans in other parts of the country. The situation came to a head in 1960 and exploded in the press when a hospital-accredited obstetrician in Staten Island died of an ulcer worsened by what his colleagues said was cruel overwork. A staff position for a badly needed assistant for the doctor had been refused. About 30 months prior to his death, Staten Island's three large hospitals "suddenly closed their doors" and until the controversy flared up in the press, did not permit a single additional HIP physician to have staff privileges. This despite the fact that 24,000 of HIP subscribers lived on Staten Island.

---

32   Committee on Research in Medical Economics, op. cit., pp. 13 and 14, and *New York Times* (June 16, 1942), p. 1.
33   *A.M.A.* v. *United States*, 317 U.S. 519 (1943), as quoted in Franz Goldmann, *Voluntary Medical Care Plans in the United States* (New York: Columbia University Press, 1948), pp. 55–61.

Aroused by these developments, the New York State Legislative Committee on Health Insurance Plans held public hearings. As the *New York Times* stated in reviewing the hearings:

> There is no doubt that, for the past thirty months, no HIP physician has been given the privilege of admitting patients to any of the three non-profit Staten Island hospitals. This has been a formidable handicap for HIP in giving its subscribers the best and promptest hospital care. It is clear also, from the testimony of the hospital representatives themselves, that this has come about primarily because of their dislike of, and opposition to, the group practice, prepayment types of medical service—"a repugnant ideology" as one of them called it. As usual ideological differences bred personal antagonism that led to ostracism. No evidence was given that the denial of hospital privileges in any case is based on a lack of professional skill.[34]

Under public pressure, the hospitals on the island agreed to appoint to their staffs five physicians associated with HIP.[35]

The fight over hospital appointments for HIP physicians however, was not over. Two years later, the presiding supervisor of the town of Hempstead asserted that it is an "irrefutable fact that there is serious discrimination and it must be ended." In response, Nassau County, with 60,000 HIP subscribers, on October 29, 1962, became the first county in the nation to prohibit discrimination against physicians associated with group medical plans.[36] About a year later the New York state legislature took similar action.[37]

THE RUSSELLTON MEDICAL GROUP   The Russellton Medical Group is a comprehensive prepaid direct-service organization which operates clinics in several towns in Western Pennsylvania. After "long and persistent" efforts to obtain courtesy staff privileges for its physicians at a New Kensington hospital, the group filed suit on March 29, 1967 in the U.S. District Court of Pittsburgh. The suit asked for $2.4 million in damages, charging that the hospital violated the 5th and 14th amendments to the Constitution as well as other Federal statutes in denying staff privileges to its physicians. The complaint asked that the hospitals be permanently enjoined from denying the plaintiffs admission to its medical staff, and charged that the executive committee of the hospital medical staff adopted a secret resolution stating: "No member of the medical staff shall endorse any application, vote for or

---

34   *New York Times* (June 17, 1960), as quoted in *Public Health Economics and Medical Care Abstracts*, University of Michigan School of Public Health, p. 396 (August 1960).

35   *Public Health Economics*, p. 6. (September 1960).

36   *Public Health Economics*, p. 6 (July 1963).

37   *New York Times* (November 11, 1964), p. 45.

otherwise directly or indirectly assist any physician associated with the Russellton Medical Group in obtaining any medical staff privileges at the hospital."

Aided in its legal battle by the Group Health Association of America, the Russellton group late in 1967 won an agreement admitting seven additional Russellton physicians to the staff of the hospital. The settlement also stated: "No such physician shall be discriminated against or denied appointment to or membership on the medical staff, because of his association with or participation in any medical group practice or health insurance plan, program or fund." The group expressed satisfaction that the case was settled without litigation and the District Court dismissed the suit.[38]

Numerous other cases could be discussed that demonstrate the aggressive tactics of the AMA in opposing various kinds of insurance—the Kaiser Permanente Health Plan in California, the Civic Medical Center in Chicago, Blue Cross in Wisconsin, the Complete Service Bureau in San Diego, the United Mine Workers Welfare and Retirement Fund in several states, the Union Medical Fund of the hotel industry in New York City, and many more. However, presentation of these cases would add nothing new to our discussion,[39] since the fundamental reason for organized medicine's opposition (protection of its vested economic interest through control of the medical market) and the tactics employed (threats of coercion, expulsion from the membership in the medical society, denial of consultation and hospital privileges) follow a pattern similar to those in the cases already discussed.

There is, however, another tactic of considerable effectiveness which organized medicine has used in its war on prepaid medical service plans. After initial reluctance, the AMA encouraged growth of the doctor-dominated Blue Shield plans to maintain organized medicine's control over the medical market. In 26 states the medical societies induced state legislatures to pass restrictive legislation that made it extremely difficult for plans other than Blue Shield to operate. In 15 of these states the restrictive legislation actually granted professional-controlled plans a virtual monopoly in the prepayment medical care field.[40] Organized medicine's control is ensured through various means by these states. In some the directors of the plan must be doctors or approved by the medical society. In others the incorporators must be doctors, thus blocking lay formation of medical service plans.

There are important indications that the legislative barriers erected against lay-sponsored plans are beginning to crumble. In 1959, the Ohio legislature

---

38 *Group Health and Welfare News* (April 2, 1967); and (November 1, 1967).

39 U.S. Congress, Hearings, *National Health Program*, Part 5 (Washington, D.C.: U.S. Government Printing Office, 1946), pp. 2630–2646; U.S. Congressional Record, 81st Congress, 2nd Session, November 27, 1950 to January 2, 1951, Vol. 94, Part 12, pp. 16862–16863; Carter, op. cit., pp. 170–183; *Medical World News* (June 7, 1963).

40 U.S. Congress, Hearings, *Health Inquiry*, Part 6 (Washington, D.C.: U.S. Government Printing Office), p. 1779.

passed a new enabling act authorizing lay-sponsored plans to provide subscribers with medical, hospital, and dental services.[41] The previous enabling act, in existence since 1941, was among the most restrictive in the country as far as the non-Blue Shield plans were concerned.

Organized medicine received an even more severe blow in New Jersey where the state law had given the state medical society complete control over medical service plans. The Group Health Insurance Plan of New Jersey had sought a license in 1961 and was turned down because it did not have the approval of the state medical society. Group Health initiated a test case and, in 1961, the state supreme court ruled that the section of the law that gave the state medical society the authority to approve medical-surgical plans was unconstitutional. The law also required that an approved medical-surgical plan must have 51 per cent of the doctors in a county as member physicians. The court, in 1961, did not rule on the 51 per cent requirement.

In what may well be a major decision setting a precedent for other states, the court, on July 16, 1964, found the 51 per cent rule also unconstitutional. On the basis of this opinion, the court ordered the state to reconsider the Group Health Insurance Plan's application. A quote from the New Jersey supreme court opinion succinctly brings into focus the fundamental theme of this section:

> We think that such a power to restrict, or indeed, to prohibit competition in a field so vitally connected with the public welfare may not constitutionally be placed in the hands of a private organization such as the medical society, which has an interest in promoting the welfare of the only existing medical service corporation (Blue Shield) in the state.[42]

But the AMA is not giving up on its attempt to control health insurance. Late in 1967, the National Association of Blue Shield Plans (NABSP) took an action permitting the operation of a plan without approval by the medical society. The AMA House of Delegates requested the NABSP to rescind the action and asked quite bluntly that all plans "continue to serve as economic arm of the medical profession in offering sound alternatives to the public in the voluntary financing of health care."[43]

JURISDICTION DISPUTES AMONG
THE HEALTH PROFESSIONS

Despite its demonstrated unity against outside pressures, the AMA is far from a monolithic organization. Internally it is a house divided; general

---

41 Somers and Somers, op. cit., p. 357.
42 University of Michigan, School of Public Health, *Public Health and Economics and Medical Care Abstracts*, pp. 378–379

(August 1963); p. 477 (September 1963).
43 *The A.M.A. News*, p. 5 (December 11, 1967).

practitioners battle specialists and various types of specialists battle one another, as each group is engaged in a struggle to protect or expand its domain over segments of the human anatomy. The conflict is an ancient one, almost as old as the practice of medicine itself.

Scientific, technical, and demographic changes during the past several decades have fragmented the profession into a number of competing specialties. The general practitioner (GP), who formerly claimed as his jurisdiction the treatment of all health problems of the individual—medical, surgical, psychiatric, diagnostic, and therapeutic—has seen his job territory steadily whittled down by the emergent specialties. Yet, according to the AMA the general practitioner engages in "treatment of the whole body, largely through non-surgical means."

Therein lies the heart of the conflict. Since the whole body is the sum of its parts, the GP frequently finds himself in conflict with the various "parts" specialists over the right to practice. Furthermore, since the parts are highly interrelated—and in rather close proximity to each other—specialists frequently transgress each others' anatomical or therapeutic jurisdictions. The boundary lines between one specialty and another are often indistinct. The difficulty of defining jurisdiction is reflected in a survey of 1,084 specialists conducted by *Medical Economics*. Ninety-one per cent conceded they were "uncertain" about fringe areas of their field where the question at issue is this: "Which of two specialists is better able to handle a given procedure?" At what age level should the pediatrician's "right" to treat the patient end and the internist's begin? When does the general surgeon invade the rightful territory of the thoracic, orthopedic, or gynecological surgeon? Since definitive answers to these questions cannot be given, the present organization of medicine, largely on a fee-for-service, basis makes conflict among practitioners inevitable.

Internally, as the GP's battle the specialists and the specialists battle each other, organized medicine is faced with a dilemma similar to that which bedevils society in its relationship with organized medicine as a whole: When does the power to set quality standards—a power considered socially desirable to delegate to professionals—become a device for restricting practice with socially undesirable results.

CONFLICTS WITHIN THE PROFESSION In June 1964, the physicians at Mary's Help Hospital adopted the following hospital bylaw:

From the date of the opening of the new Mary's Help Hospital in Dale City, California, an applicant may be considered for surgical and obstetrical privileges only if he meets one of the following qualifications:

a. Is a fellow of his respective American college, or
b. Is a diplomate of his respective American board, or

c. Has the requisite training necessary to become a diplomate of his respective American board and can present a letter from such speciality board stating that he is qualified for examination in that board.

The qualifications in (a), (b), and (c) above shall not be required in order that an applicant may be considered for privileges as a surgical assistant.

"To put it another way," commented *Medical Economics*, "No G.P.'s need apply!"[44]

The GP's in the dispute proposed a bylaws amendment which provided for acceptance of an applicant who "has been individually evaluated and upon the basis of his training and experience and demonstrated ability is deemed competent to be granted the privileges sought." Despite a year of GP lobbying, the amendment was rejected.

Such restrictions on the right to practice are common throughout much of our hospital system. Many hospitals function under a "closed staff" arrangement whereby a list of physicians is maintained and only those on the list are authorized to admit patients; all other physicians are automatically barred. Generally, university, teaching, and government operated hospitals invite physicians to join the staff; physicians themselves do not initiate applications. Community and church related hospitals are more open in that any physician may apply for admitting privileges. However, the license to practice does not carry with it automatic admitting privileges.

The widespread existence of restrictions on hospital staff privileges is reflected in a survey of the staffing patterns of hospitals in eight communities located in various sections of the United States, with populations ranging from 62,000 to over 2.5 million. The survey revealed that most of the hospitals imposed various kinds of restrictions on privileges. Personal interviews with physicians in the communities brought to the surface deeply held feelings of "bitterness, resentment, and jealousy" on the part of those against whom barriers had been erected.[45] The prevalence of restrictive staff arrangements is also borne out by the hundreds of articles on the problem which have appeared in medical journals since the end of World War II and the numerous professional society committees which have been periodically established to find a "solution." The GP, it must be emphasized, is not the only physician against whom barriers are erected; similar restrictions are imposed against specialists who have not been "certified" by one of the 19 American specialty boards.

The bitterness among GP and non-certified specialists is readily understandable. Barred completely from some of the better teaching hospitals or

---

44 *Medical Economics*, p. 88 (February 15, 1960).

45 Patricia L. Kendall, "The Relationship Between Medical Educators and Medical Practitioners," *Journal of Medical Education*, Part 2, **40**:187 (January 1965).

restricted to minor care, they are also locked out from many voluntary hospitals and severely limited in their staff privileges in others. Without staff privileges or with privileges severely limited, the practitioner must relinquish a patient requiring hospitalization to a specialist having access to a hospital. At best, the noncertified doctor, in a case involving his hospitalized patient, may be given the opportunity to act as an assistant to a certified specialist who then takes on the major responsibility in the care of the patient. Since nearly half of medical incomes are earned in hospitals, the threat posed by staff restrictions to the earnings and status of a physician could be substantial.

THE QUESTION OF QUALITY   Are restrictions on staff privileges an attempt to raise standards in hospitals, as the specialists with privileges hold? Or, as many hospital-barred physicians argue, are they monopolistic devices for limiting competition?

There is some strong evidence that the quality of much general practice is in fact inadequate. In a careful in-depth interview survey of general practice in North Carolina, a medical team from the University of North Carolina, found numerous serious deficiencies. This report and others[46] indicate that the conditions found in North Carolina are also common far beyond that state's border.

Reports of inferior practice, however, are not limited to general practitioners. Specialists also have come in for considerable criticism. Three major studies in recent years demonstrated the existence of a substantial amount of unnecessary surgery and inferior surgical treatment, particularly with respect to appendectomies and hysterectomies.[47]

It is clear from such studies of both general practitioners *and* specialists that some kind of quality control is necessary to protect the patient. The studies are equally clear in indicating that specialty board certification for hospital privileges is no guarantee of adequate quality.

SPECIALTY BOARD CERTIFICATION AS A RESTRICTIVE DEVICE   That board certified specialists have used high quality standards as a device to maintain or increase their incomes through restriction of competition is indicated by two kinds of evidence: (1) Particular specialty board rules for certification

---

46   Oscar L. Peterson, MD, *et al.*, "An Analytical Study of North Carolina General Practice 1953–1954," *Journal of Medical Education*, Part 2, **31**:22 (December 1956); Kendall, op. cit., pp. 181–186; Oscar L. Peterson, "Medical Care Research," *Hospitals, Doctors, and the Public Interest*, ed. by John H. Knowles (Cambridge, Mass.: Harvard University Press, 1965). Peterson cites Canadian and Australian studies that came up with similar findings.

47   Ray E. Trussell, MD, MPH, *The Quantity, Quality and Costs of Medical and Hospital Care Secured by a Sample of Teamster Families in the New York Area* (New York: Columbia University School of Public Health and Administrative Medicine, 1962), p. 3; *Journal of the American Medical Association*, **151**:360 (January 1953); J. Frederick Sparling, MD, "Measuring Medical Care Quality," *Hospitals*, **36**:62 (March 16, 1962).

that are clearly aimed at restriction of competition and have no bearing on quality; (2) specific cases in which certification requirements have been used to suppress competition.[48]

Several specialty boards require *applicants* for certification to be American citizens, a requirement that bars foreign doctors from even applying for certification for at least 5 years (the residency requirement for United States citizenship). The burden on the foreign doctor is especially great since, even after the application for certification is filed, the other requirements are such that it may take several more years before he is actually certified. With the recent influx of foreign physicians into the United States, the citizenship requirement barrier takes on added significance. That a number of specialty boards do not have citizenship requirements suggests that those which do are not simply concerned with quality. Whatever else citizenship may confer on an individual, it does not improve his ability as a physician.

The provisions of certification of foreign doctors by the American Board of Dermatology are particularly revealing: "Graduates of Foreign Medical Schools, not citizens of the United States or Canada, who will return to their homeland after completion of approved residency training in dermatology are eligible for non-resident certification." However, to get such certification the foreign doctor must present "A notarized statement that the applicant is (a) returning to his homeland to remain and to practice there; (b) that he will surrender his special certification should he ever return to practice in the United States or Canada." The speciality boards for internal medicine and orthopedic surgery have similar provisions for foreign physicians. The neurological surgery board grants to foreign doctors special "Foreign Certificates," which are issued only *after* the doctor has returned to his home country.

A number of boards want the applicant for certification to submit letters of reference and some require that the letters be from board-certified specialists in the applicant's community. This makes it possible for a certified specialist to block a potential competitor. In *Medical Economics'* survey of 1,084 board-certified specialists, one of the most frequently cited "arbitrary" requirements was the letter of reference from a certified man in the community.[49]

There are other arbitrary rules of the various boards that indicate more of a concern for competition than for quality. Both the boards of anesthesiology and of ophthalmology reserve "the right to limit the number of candidates to be admitted to any examination." The former also "reserves the right to reject any applicant for any reason deemed advisable and without stating the same." The Otolaryngology Board has a similar provision; since this board also requires that an applicant present letters of reference from certified

---

48 The speciality board requirements discussed in this section are in *Directory of Medical Specialists*, Vol. 12 (Chicago: Marquis-Who's Who, Inc., 1965–1966).
49 *Medical Economics*, p. 278 (May 23, 1960).

specialists in his community, the arbitrary power to deny certification is particularly suspect. The Board of Dermatology states that its "records are confidential throughout," that "examination marks will not be divulged to the applicant," and that "the findings of the board are subject to its discretion and are final." Clearly, none of these provisions can be defended on grounds that they maintain quality.

Most of the specialty boards, in their descriptions of certification requirements, include a passage similar to the following found in the American Board of Surgery statement:

> The American Board of Surgery has never been concerned with measures that might gain special privileges or recognition for its diplomates in the practice of surgery. *It is neither the intent nor has it been the purpose of the board to define requirements for membership on the staffs of hospitals.* The prime object of the board is to pass judgment on the education and training of broadly competent and responsible surgeons, not who shall or shall not perform surgical operations. The board specifically disclaims interest in or recognition of differential emoluments that may be based on certification. [Italics in original.][50]

Since specialty board certification is so widely used throughout the United States as a criterion for hospital staff privileges, how can we explain the emphatic disclaimers noted above? In part the disclaimers may be an attempt to forestall an attack on the specialty boards from breaking out among GP and uncertified specialists within the ranks of organized medicine. Perhaps even more important is a desire to avoid becoming embroiled in the large number of court battles between hospitals and barred physicians. Furthermore, the explicit restriction disclaimer may be a useful device for preventing the boards from being subjected to prosecution under the antitrust laws as conspiracies in restraint of trade.

The most significant characteristic of the disclaimer, however, is that *it does not say that the boards will oppose the use of specialty board certification as a requirement for staff privileges.* A hospital medical staff, using "the maintenance of standards" as a justification, can with impunity bar non-certified physicians from hospital privileges, and the specialty board can then hide behind the ploy that these are "local" matters over which it has no rightful control.

A recent court case illustrates the nature of the problem. A physician's application for staff privileges was rejected by the governing board of a nonprofit hospital upon recommendation of the medical staff. The doctor was able to convince the local judge to order the hospital to admit him. On appeal, the Kansas Supreme Court reversed the trial judge and restated the basic rule of law applicable to the situation:

---

50 *Journal of American Medical Association* **150**:414 (September 29, 1952).

It seems to be practically the unanimous opinion that private hospitals have the right to exclude licensed physicians from the use of the hospital, and that such exclusion rests within the sound discretion of the managing authorities.[51]

In a recent issue of *Hospitals,* attorney James E. Ludlam reported: "Either by circumstances or default, the ultimate control of medical standards has become the function of the medical staff. It is in this setting that the quality of the individual physician's practice can be subject to continuous audit. More important, the continuation of his medical staff privileges usually has important economic meaning to the individual doctor." How widespread are the conflicts over staff privileges is also indicated by Mr. Ludlam: "A reported legal case involving medical staff privileges was a rarity 20 or 30 years ago, but now the number of cases in the books is increasing at a geometric rate. . . . Even more serious, these reported cases are only the exposed part of the iceberg . . ."[52]

The desire to restrict competition is reflected in a revealing round-table discussion conducted by the journal *Medical Economics.* One of its editors asked the panelists whether they had ever run into situations "when a horde of staff doctors, such as G.P.'s have suddenly had their privileges withdrawn." Dr. Charles E. Letourneau, president of the American College of Legal Medicine, replied, "Yes, typically this happens when a horde of surgical specialists moves into an area only to discover there's not enough surgery around. I've seen it affect four or five hospitals in the same community. Board-certified men tried to freeze out the competition completely, although local G.P.'s have been there for thirty years doing good work."

Nor are the conflicts limited to specialists versus GP. When Dr. Letourneau, who has been called into resolve "literally hundreds of staff conflicts," was asked how they arise, he commented as follows:

Many of them have to do with privileges—the question of who should be allowed to do what. Wherever specialties overlap there's likely to be contention. General surgeons clash with gynecologists. Plastic surgeons clash with nose and throat men.

Take two board certified men, one in surgery and one in OBG (obstetrics and gynecology). The general surgeon says he can do a procedure as well as the next fellow. Not in his special field, says the gynecologist . . .

I remember one case where we decided to give all the fractures to the orthopods (orthopedic surgeons). No go. The general surgeons decided they just weren't going to hand over all those cases. Eventually there may

51 *Foote* v. *Community Hospital of Beloit, Kansas* (September 9, 1965), as reported in *Hospitals,* **39**:96 (November 1, 1965).

52 James E. Ludlam, "Legal Snares for the Hospital," *Hospitals,* **38**:38 (August 1, 1964).

be enough orthopods to change the ground rules and make them stick. Meanwhile both factions have access to the disputed area of fractures.[53]

Clearly, the physician's income was at issue and not the quality of medical care.

Even certification, however, is no guarantee of hospital staff privileges, particularly if a physician takes a position opposed to the wishes of organized medicine. A 13-year physician-hospital dispute which received some national notoriety was finally settled out of court in Bellaire, Ohio, in 1965. The fight began in 1952 with the establishment of the Bellaire Clinic and the Bellaire Medical Group, a prepaid group insurance plan of the United Mine Worker's Welfare and Retirement Fund. The clinic's doctors are members of the medical group. Because of organized medicine's long standing opposition to prepaid group-practice plans, clinic doctors had difficulty becoming admitted to staff privileges in the Bellaire Hospital and were barred from medical society membership. One of the clinic doctors was Dr. James E. Sams. His application for membership in the local medical society was rejected, even though he was certified by the American Board of Obstetrics and Gynecology and the county had no other specialists in obstetrics and gynecology. As a direct consequence of the rejection of his membership application by the medical society, he was denied hospital privileges. In March 1963, the clinic and its physicians accused the society and the hospital of "a 10-year history of harassment, discrimination, and obstruction" and filed two suits —one for $2.5 million in damages for conspiracy and restraint of trade, and another seeking to end the discrimination. After a 2-year struggle, the case was settled out of court: Dr. Sams won courtesy staff privileges in the hospital and the local medical society agreed to amend its bylaws to allow any physician whose membership is rejected to request binding arbitration to determine whether the rejection was justified.[54]

ORGANIZED MEDICINE AND
OTHER HEALTH PROFESSIONS

This brief section merely summarizes the main points fully developed in Chapter 6 of my book *Professional Power and American Medicine*.

1. Osteopaths In its harassment of America's 12,000 osteopathic physicians, organized medicine has employed all of its traditional weapons. The AMA has branded osteopaths as "cultists," fought against their receiving recognition through licensure, barred them from membership in local medical societies, denied them the right to practice in AMA dominated

---

53 *Medical Economics* (April 5, 1965), pp. 90 and 103.

54 *Hospitals*, **39**:116 (June 16, 1965); Group Health Association of America, *Group Health and Welfare News*, **6**:7 (March 1965); **6**:1 (May 1965).

hospitals, and prevented physicians from associating with them professionally, from lecturing in their medical schools, and from participating in their
professional meetings.

2. Chiropractors For about 5 decades the AMA and its state and county
societies have pressed a relentless war against chiropractors. It has attacked
them publicly as "frauds" and "quacks" and fought vigorously against
giving them recognition through state licensure. When unsuccessful in preventing licensure, organized medicine has pursued a program of containment
through securing statutory limits on the ailments chiropractors could treat
and on the techniques they could employ. The AMA has lobbied against
Federal payment of tuition for veterans seeking chiropractic training under
the GI Bill, against approval of chiropractic schools by the U.S. Department
of Labor, against Veterans Administration recognition of—and reimburse-
ment for—chiropractic care, against deferment of chiropractic students
under the Selective Service System, and against the appointment of doctors
of chiropractic in the department of medicine and surgery of the Veterans
Administration. Although the AMA has made considerable concessions to the
osteopathic profession in recent years, there does not seem to be any prospect
for a similar modification in its attitude toward chiropractic as a "dangerous
cult."

3. Optometrists Optometrists and physicians, particularly ophthalmol-
ogists, have been engaged in bitter jurisdictional disputes for decades.
Despite the fact that optometrists have long been generally recognized as
legitimate health practitioners—the optomery act of the District of Columbia
in 1924 completed optometric licensing coverage for the entire nation—their
right to practice has for decades been challenged by the AMA and they have
been subjected to the same kind of harassing tactics employed by organized
medicine against osteopaths and chiropractors.

IV. MARKET PERFORMANCE

As we have shown, organized medicine—the AMA and the various
specialty boards—plays a fundamental role in the production and distribution
of medical care. By its restrictions on entry into medicine it has inflicted heavy
social costs both on individuals who were prevented from practicing medicine
and on the general public, which was unable to buy all the medical services
it wanted. The success of those restrictionist policies has, during the past
couple of decades, contributed to a serious shortage of physicians' services
and to an extraordinarily sharp rise in the incomes of doctors. Furthermore,
AMA opposition to certain technological and organizational changes in the
production and distribution of medical care has had an adverse effect on the
quality of medical care and made it more difficult to reduce its cost. Let us
turn to an examination of these points.

THE SHORTAGE OF PHYSICIANS' SERVICES, PHYSICIANS' INCOMES, AND THE SEARCH FOR SUBSTITUTES   For analysis of physicians' services, a useful definition of shortage, i.e., one that makes it possible to test for its presence, is that a shortage exists when the quantity of physicians' services supplied increases less rapidly than the quantity demanded at incomes received by physicians in the recent past. Under such conditions, the income of physicians relative to the incomes of others will tend to rise. As the relative income of physicians rises, there will be attempts to substitute less costly services for the services of physicians. The following discussion indicates that there has been a persistent and marked rise in the relative income of physicians and that the pressure of unsatisfied demand has been channeled into a search for less costly substitutes, i.e., the analysis shows that a shortage does currently exist.

Table 2 indicates clearly the pronounced rise in the relative income of physicians since 1939. Between 1939 and 1951 the mean income of physicians (column 1) increased 218 per cent. This increase exceeded the percentage increase for other occupational classes by the following percentages: non-salaried dentists, 42 per cent; nonsalaried lawyers, 113 per cent; professional, technical and kindred workers, 74 per cent; managers, officials and proprietors, 132 per cent; full-time employees, all industries, 40 per cent (percentage calculated from data in Table 2, columns 1, 3, 4, 5, 6, and 7).

The analysis can be further extended to 1966 using median rather than mean income data: Between 1947—the first year for which median income data are available—and 1966, physicians' incomes rose 268 per cent. During those years the percentage rise in doctors' incomes was 66 per cent greater than the percentage rise for "managers, officials and proprietors" and 106 per cent greater than the percentage rise in the average annual earnings for full-time employees in all industries.

The earnings data of Table 2 take no account of the increased specialization and training of physicians. Since specialists earn higher incomes than general practitioners, the rise in the relative incomes of physicians as a whole could be, it might be argued, a product of the trend toward specialization rather than of shortages. In addition, part of the rise in medical incomes may be explained by the necessity for paying physicians additional compensation for the income loss during the greater training period, characteristic of recent years.

The effects of specialization on the income data cannot be separated out from the effect of the longer training period, since the latter is primarily a result of increased specialization. The average length of training for doctors after completion of medical school has increased from about 2 years in 1940 to about $3\frac{1}{2}$ years in 1959. Specialty board certification of specialists requires from 2 to 6 years, depending on the specialty, of residency training beyond the internship. Since the number of specialists as a percentage of private practitioners has risen from 24 to 71 per cent since 1940, the increase in the

TABLE 2 INCOME OF PHYSICIANS AND SELECTED OCCUPATIONAL CLASSES, FOR SELECTED YEARS, 1939–1966

	(1) MEAN NET INCOME OF NON-SALARIED PHYSICIANS ($)	(2) MEDIAN NET INCOME OF NON-SALARIED PHYSICIANS ($)	(3) MEAN NET INCOME OF NON-SALARIED DENTISTS ($)	(4) MEAN NET INCOME OF NON-SALARIED LAWYERS ($)	(5) MEDIAN WAGE OR SALARY INCOME OF: PROFESSIONAL, TECHNICAL, AND KINDRED WORKERS ($)	(6) MANAGERS, OFFICIALS, AND PROPRIETORS (NONFARM) ($)	(7) AVERAGE ANNUAL EARNINGS PER FULL-TIME EMPLOYEES, ALL INDUSTRIES ($)
YEAR							
1939	4,229		3,096	4,391	1,809	2,136	1,264
1943	8,370	8,744	5,715	5,945			1,951
1947	10,726	13,150	6,610	7,437		3,345	2,589
1951	13,432	16,107	7,820	8,855	4,071	4,134	3,231
1955		22,100			5,055	5,290	3,847
1959		25,050			6,287	6,670	4,557
1963		28,380			7,182	7,411	5,190
1964		28,960			7,460	7,560	5,503
1965		32,170			7,572	8,175	5,710
1966					8,204	8,730	5,959

SOURCE For columns 1, 3, and 4: U.S. Department of Commerce, *Survey of Current Business*, **29**:18 (August 1949), Tables 1 and 2; **30**:9 (January 1950), Table 2; **31**:11 (July 1951), Table 1; **32**:6 (July 1952), Table 3; for column 2: *Medical Economics*, pp. 112, 128, 129 (October 1946) and *Physicians' Earnings and Expenses* (reprint of articles based on *Medical Economics* continuing survey), 1960, p. 8; for columns 5 and 6: U.S. Bureau of the Census, *Current Population Reports Series* P-60, various issues; for column 7, U.S. Department of Commerce, *Survey of Current Business*, **39**:37 (July 1959); **44**:30 (July 1964). The 1963 median net incomes in column 2 are from *Medical Economics*, p. 64 (November 2, 1964) and the 1965 and 1966 figures are from *Medical Economics*, p. 69 (December 11, 1967).

TABLE 3 MEAN NET INCOME OF FULL SPECIALISTS AND GENERAL PRACTITIONERS, 1939–1959

PHYSICIANS	INCOME ($)						PER CENT INCREASE
	1939	1943	1947	1951	1955	1959	1939–59
Full Specialists	6,184	11,808	14,442	17,112	20,010	26,800	333
General Practitioners[a]	3,940	7,511	10,254	14,467	16,317	21,500	446

a For 1939 through 1951, the incomes of the GP and partial specialists have been combined by weighting each in accordance with their respective numbers in the 1939 *Medical Economics* survey. For 1955 and 1959, *Medical Economics* presented median net incomes for partial specialists and the GP combined and for full specialists. Those median net income figures have been adjusted upward by $2,000 for specialists and $1,500 for the GP by the author to arrive at the estimated mean net incomes for 1955 and 1959. The upward adjustment was based on the average difference between median and mean net incomes of $1,892 in 1955 and 1959 for doctors as a whole (see Table 5, columns 2 and 4). The resulting mean net incomes of full specialists and the GP, when averaged for 1955 and 1959 to arrive at the mean net income for doctors as a whole, differ by 0.2 and 1 per cent respectively, from the mean net incomes for doctors as a whole, indicating an insignificant error in the estimate.

SOURCE *Medical Economics* "Quadrennial Surveys."

average period of training for physicians as a whole is essentially a product of the trend toward specialization. Hence, if an examination of the relevant data can eliminate greater specialization as the explanation of the rise in the relative incomes of physicians as a whole, such as examination would at the same time rule out the longer training period as a basic cause of the rise.

The relative incomes of both specialists and the GP have increased markedly (see Tables 3 and 4). However, between 1939 and 1959 the percentage increase in the mean income of the GP was 37 per cent greater than the percentage increase for specialists. Since 1959 the median incomes of specialists and the GP increased at about the same rate. These facts suggest a shortage of *both* the specialists and the GP and, furthermore, that the rise in the relative incomes of physicians as a whole did not result from the trend toward specialization and increased training.

TABLE 4 MEDIAN NET INCOME OF SPECIALISTS AND GENERAL PRACTITIONERS, 1959–1966

	INCOME ($)		PER CENT INCREASE
	1959	1966	
General Practitioners	20,000	27,720	39
Specialists	24,800	34,325	38

SOURCE *Medical Economics*, "Quadrennial Surveys" (October 21, 1960); pp. 69 ff. (December 11, 1967).

The shortage in the supply of physicians' services, reflected in their rapidly rising relative incomes, had led to a pronounced movement in the direction of substituting for the services of doctors the cheaper services of personnel with less training and experience. The attempt at substitution has been particularly marked in the use of foreign trained personnel. With the passage of the U.S. Information and Education Exchange Act of 1947 (effective July 1949), there began a steadily rising influx of foreign trained physicians. Between 1950 and 1966 the number of interns and residents rose from about 21,500 to 41,600. Over the same period the per cent of intern and resident positions filled by foreign personnel rose almost threefold, from 9.6 to 27.7 per cent.

The high failure rate of 50 to 70 per cent on tests given to foreign trainees by the Educational Council for Foreign Medical Graduates (ECFMG) compares dismally with a failure rate on licensure exams of about 3 per cent for graduates of approved schools in the United States. That the high failure rate of foreign-trained personnel is largely a reflection of their relatively inadequate training and skill is borne out by the evidence and testimony of many who have studied the problem. When hospitals, staffed by foreign medical graduates who had not passed the ECFMG examination were threatened with loss of approval of their internship and residency programs, it was reported: "Many hospitals, believing that the situation is hopeless without uncertified foreign graduates, will defy the ban and risk losing accreditation."[55] As the U.S. Department Director of the Office of Cultural Exchange has observed: "Some [hospitals] see the foreign physicians as a source of cheap labor" and "turn to the Exchange Visitor Program . . . to meet staffing problems . . ."[56]

The impact of immigration is also shown in medical licensure data. Between 1959 and 1966 more than 17 per cent of the physicians licensed were foreign graduates. Since 1950 more than 20,000 graduates of foreign medical schools have been licensed for practice in the United States. In 1967 almost one out of four newly licensed physicians were foreign graduates.

Approximately 75 per cent of the foreign medical graduates now serving in internship and residency programs and most of the newly licensed foreign physicians are from developing countries.[57] Thus, ironically, the world's richest country finds itself heavily dependent upon the poorest nations of the world for providing a substantial amount of its medical care.

The shortage of physicians' service has led to a search for substitutes in unusual directions. Hospitals in increasing numbers are relying on third and fourth year medical school students to take histories and do physicals under

---

55 *House Physician Reporter*, p. 2 (January 1962).

56 *Journal of the American Medical Association*, **179**:44 (February 24, 1962).

57 Harold Margulies, Lucille S. Block, and Francis K. Cholko, "Random Survey of U.S. Hospitals with Approved Internships and Residencies," *Journal of Medical Education*, **43**:713 (June 1968).

supervision. Lacking adequate house staff, hospitals are letting registered nurses perform many services once performed only by doctors, despite the fact that this is a practice barred by a number of state laws. A number of hospitals are welcoming graduates of osteopathic schools to house-staff positions formerly barred to them by long standing and rigid AMA policy. Despite the vigorous opposition of organized medicine, the number of chiropractors increased 127 per cent between 1940 and 1960, more than three times the percentage increase in the number of doctors.

THE RISING COST OF MEDICAL CARE   Perhaps no other development has contributed more to the controversy over the provision of medical services during the past couple of decades than the spiraling prices of medical care.

During the depression decade of 1929–1940, the "all items" index fell by 18 per cent whereas medical care prices showed practically no change (see Table 5). That medical prices did not fall may be because the industry is characterized by "customary prices" which are relatively slow in responding to economic pressures. When the general price level turned sharply upward during the World War II years, medical prices again lagged. In the post-World War II period, down through 1968, however, the prices of medical care caught up. As a result, over the entire 1929–1968 period, the percentage increases for "all medical care items," physicians' fees, and hospital daily service charges were considerably greater than the percentage increase for "all items"—by 84, 57, and 696 per cent, respectively. Furthermore, a breakdown of the post-World War II period shows clearly that the relatively large increases in medical care prices have continued to the present.

RESISTANCE TO INNOVATION   For about half a century, organized medicine has resisted the development of "group practice," particularly when the practice has been tied to a prepayment insurance scheme. Group practice has been defined by the Public Health Service as "a formal association of three or more physicians providing services in more than one field or specialty,

TABLE 5   PERCENTAGE INCREASES IN PRICES OF SELECTED ITEMS IN THE CONSUMER PRICE INDEX, SELECTED PERIODS, 1929–1965

EXPENDITURES	1929–1940	1940–1945	1945–1968	1929–1968	1957–59 TO 1968
All items	−18	28	93	103	21
All medical care items	1	14	151	189	44
Physicians' fees	2	16	129	162	45
Hospital daily service charges	1	28	591	820	125

SOURCE   U.S. Bureau of Labor Statistics, *Consumer Price Index* (Washington, D.C.: U.S. Government Printing Office, various years).

with income from medical practice pooled and redistributed to the members according to some prearranged plan." There are a number of possible advantages to group practice: (1) the pooling of skills of a number of specialists to serve the needs of the patient; (2) salutary effects of the doctor being subject to observation by his peers; (3) easy access to the services of specialists at little or no additional costs; (4) lower costs through economies of scale resulting from the pooling of capital investment; and (5) further use of ancillary personnel and equipment.

Despite the possible advantages of group practice, it has shown no significant growth. In 1965, only 6.6 per cent of American physicians were practicing in multi-specialty groups, 3.5 per cent in single specialty groups, and 0.9 per cent in general practice groups. Furthermore, only about 2 per cent of all the groups used the prepayment mechanism.[58] A major reason for this slow growth, as already discussed in this chapter, has been the opposition of the AMA.

Thus, in addition to restricting the supply of physicians' services, organized medicine has attempted to control the medical market structure in order to maintain the fee-for-service system, a system under which the price-discriminating solo-practitioner can exercise monopolistic power. In pursuit of this goal, the AMA opposed the development of voluntary insurance and came reluctantly to its support only when confronted with the threat of compulsory health insurance. The AMA was particularly adamant in its opposition to voluntary insurance that took the form of prepaid group practice, a method of medical cost financing that lessens the control the individual physician has over fees. In discussing the AMA opposition to experimentation in the organization and financing of medical care, Professor Milton Friedman has commented sharply: "These methods of practice may have good features and bad features, but they are technological innovations that people ought to be free to try out if they wish. There is no basis for saying conclusively that the optimal technical method is practice by an independent physician. Maybe it is group practice, may be it is by corporations. One ought to have a system under which all varieties can be tried."[59]

Specialty restrictionism has been a factor contributing to a decline in the number of GP's. Authorities who have studied the causes of the decline invariably point to restrictions on hospital privileges as one of the key factors discouraging students from pursuing a career in general practice. Recent studies also indicate that specialists are increasingly taking over the functions of general practitioners since families are turning toward specialists for *basic* medical care as well as specialized services.

But is not this development socially desirable? Is it not *always* better for the patient to use a specialist rather than a general practitioner? The answer is

---

58 *Survey of Medical Groups in U.S.*, 1965 (Chicago: American Medical Association, 1968), p. 11.

59 Friedman, op. cit., p. 154.

no! To the extent that specialty restrictionism has led to the use of the higher priced services of the specialist as a substitute for the general practitioners' services, *on the assumption that the GP could have provided services of equal quality*, there is definitely a malallocation of resources. The loss is not simply in terms of the higher prices paid by the consumers for medical services; even more significant is the waste of resources involved in training specialists when the smaller amount of resources devoted to the training of the GP would have been adequate. If a patient has a brain tumor, it is obvious that it would be more desirable for him to be operated on by a neurosurgeon than by a GP. However, most common ailments, normal deliveries of babies, minor surgery, and even much uncomplicated major surgery can surely be handled by the GP; in these cases, to compel the use of the costly services of specialists is to waste resources. Furthermore, if there is to be efficient use of our medical resources, *specialists should specialize*, because as Dr. Ratner notes, "if a special doesn't see special cases, he's not going to remain a specialist since he will lack experience. We see this in pediatrics, where, as we all know, the pediatrician who was trained extensively to take care of these very serious illnesses ends up spending most of his time parading a series of well babies through an assembly line setup."[60]

Another effect of the vacuum created by the decline of the GP is that the patient often "becomes his own diagnostician and decides which kind of specialist he should approach."[61] The kind of treatment he gets may be less a function of what his medical condition requires than of the particular specialist he chooses. Suppose, for example, a patient has an ulcer. A surgeon may properly recommend surgery, a psychiatrist analysis, and an internist treatment by medicine. What is appropriate from the viewpoint of the patient depends upon the nature of his medical condition. But whether he receives surgery, analysis, or medication—given the consumer's lack of knowledge in medical matters—may depend upon whether he goes to the surgeon, the psychiatrist, or the internist. The specialist, because of consumer ignorance, has considerable power to create a demand for his services. The GP, acting as a family physician in such situations, can, because he has vastly greater medical knowledge than the consumer, help him make a rational choice among competing specialists. There is enough evidence of unnecessary surgery to indicate that this is in fact a serious problem.

Another undesirable effect of hospital medical staff restrictionism is that the noncertified specialist and GP tend to be barred from the better teaching hospitals. As a result they are channeled into proprietary hospitals, and increasingly, in recent years, have turned toward building hospitals of their own where they are able to treat their patients. Cut off from the better teaching hospitals, the noncertified physician or GP loses out on the intellectual

---

60 Herbert Ratner, MD, "Deficiencies in Present Day Medical Education," *General Practitioner,* **32**:187 (July 1965).

61 "The Graduate Education of Physicians," op. cit., p. 34.

stimulation and educational opportunities such an institution can provide. Such isolation can only produce a deterioration in the quality of medical care.

V. PUBLIC POLICY

Society has delegated considerable power to the AMA and its constituent societies and, as we have seen, they have all too frequently used that power in a socially undesirable manner. Organized medicine has restricted entry into the medical profession, thereby imposing heavy costs both on individuals barred from practicing medicine, and on society, which is getting less medical care than it needs. It has often, and with considerable success, opposed technological changes in the organization and distribution of medical services, innovations that could have raised the quality and reduced the costs of medical care.

Many proposals for improving the quality and reducing the cost of American medical care are currently being discussed—group practice; techniques for reducing unnecessary utilization of hospitals; expanding the opportunities for increasing the efficiency of medical education; the use of "new types of personnel to relieve the physician of those tasks not requiring the long (and extremely costly) period of education and training that characterizes medicine in the United States;[62] comprehensive systems of financing medical care with universal compulsory coverage—employer-employee plans financed with Federal subsidies to cover low-income groups, or some variant of a national health insurance scheme paid by general taxation. But no matter what proposals are made for technological innovation or the financing of medical care, no matter how desirable these changes might be, whether they are tried or how successful they will be if tried will to a significant extent depend upon the response of organized medicine. Unfortunately, the way the AMA has used its market power in the past leaves little reason for society to be sanguine about the cooperativeness of organized medicine in the future.

What, then, can be done to curb the power of organized medicine? A basic requirement is the elimination of its control over licensing. As Professor Milton Friedman has argued, and as we have discussed, licensure is the key to AMA power. After surveying the effects of organized medicine's activities, Professor Friedman concluded:

> When these effects are taken into account, I am myself persuaded that licensure has reduced both the quantity and quality of medical practice; that it has reduced the opportunities available to people who would like

---

62   Rashi Fein, *The Doctor Shortage* (Washington, D.C.:
The Brookings Institution, 1967), p. 11.

to be physicians, forcing them to pursue occupations they regard as less attractive; that it has forced the public to pay more for less satisfactory medical service, and that it has retarded technological development both in medicine itself and in the organization of medical practice. I conclude that licensure should be eliminated as a requirement for the practice of medicine.[63]

Few would be prepared to go as far as Professor Friedman's vigorous laissez-faire position. The social acceptance of licensing in medicine indicates general belief in the desirability of providing protection for the consumer through the maintenance of standards. Fortunately, however, it is not necessary to go as far as Professor Friedman suggests. A more moderate approach is possible whereby AMA power can be curbed and at the same time socially acceptable medical standards maintained.

"In occupational licensing," as Professor Gellhorn has stated, "the choice is not between some regulation and none. The choice is between licensing for the sake of the occupations and on the other hand, licensing for the sake of the public at large." The argument generally made in support of having licensing boards controlled by professionals drawn from the regulated occupation is that only those professionals can have the technical competence required for evaluation of license applicants. Professor Gellhorn points the way out of this dilemma: "The solution of this difficulty . . . lies in creating a responsible administrative body that, if need be, may employ vocationally experienced staff members and *that should in all instances recruit suitable advisory groups from within the affected occupations*" [italics provided].[64] The italicized words hold the key to curbing the power of organized medicine. The physician's role on a medical licensing board should be in an *advisory* capacity; his control over licensing *policy* should be eliminated.

The principle of using physicians only in an advisory capacity has general applicability. The principle is applicable to the machinery for accrediting medical schools, to the determination of staff privileges in hospitals, to the limitations imposed on nonmedical health practitioners, to the operation of utilization review procedures, and to the determination of "reasonable charges" under the Medicare programs. Only if this principle is vigorously and generally applied can the social problems created by the contradictions in the concept of professionalism be resolved in society's interest. *Wherever there is a need to set standards in the medical market and the possibility of a conflict of interest exists, physicians should not be in policy-making positions.*

---

63 Friedman, op. cit., p. 158.
64 Walter Gellhorn, *Individual Freedom and Governmental Restraints* (Baton Rouge, La.: State University Press, 1956), pp. 143 and 151.

SUGGESTED READINGS

BOOKS AND PAMPHLETS

Fein, R. *The Doctor Shortage*. Washington, D.C.: The Brookings Institution, 1967.

Friedman, M. *Capitalism and Freedom*. Chicago: University of Chicago Press, 1962.

Garceau, O. *The Political Life of the American Medical Association*. Cambridge, Mass.: Harvard University Press, 1941.

Klarman, H. *The Economics of Health*. New York: Columbia University Press, 1965.

Rayack, E. *Professional Power and American Medicine*. Cleveland, Ohio: World Publishing Co., 1967.

Somers, H., and A. Somers. *Doctors, Patients, and Health Insurance*. Washington, D.C.: The Brookings Institution, 1961.

GOVERNMENT PUBLICATIONS

U.S. Department of Health, Education and Welfare. *Physicians for a Growing America*. Report of the Surgeon General's Consultant Group on Medical Education, Washington, D.C.: 1959.

U.S. Department of Health, Education and Welfare. *Report of the National Conference on Medical Costs*. Washington, D.C., 1967.

U.S. Department of Health, Education and Welfare. *Health Manpower Perspective: 1967*. Public Health Service Publication No. 1667. Washington, D.C., 1967.

JOURNAL AND MAGAZINE ARTICLES

Arrow, K. J. "Uncertainty and the Welfare Economics of Medical Care," *American Economic Review*, **53**:941 (December 1963).

Hyde, D. R., P. Wolff, A. Gross, and E. L. Hoffman. "The American Medical Association: Power, Purpose and Politics in Organized Medicine," *Yale Law Journal*, **43**:938 (May 1954).

Kessel, R. "Price Discrimination in Medicine," *Journal of Law and Economics*, 1:20 (October 1958).

Muller, C. "Economic Analysis of Medical Care in the United States," *American Journal* of Public Health, 51:31 (January 1961).

13. Walter Adams

PUBLIC POLICY IN A
FREE ENTERPRISE ECONOMY

W hen Congress passed the Sherman Act of 1890 it created what was then—and what has remained to this day—a uniquely American institution. Heralded as a magna carta of economic freedom, the Sherman Act sought to preserve competitive free enterprise by imposing legal prohibitions on monopoly and restraint of trade. The objective of the Act, according to Judge Learned Hand, was not to condone *good* trusts or condemn *bad* trusts, but to forbid *all* trusts. Its basic philosophy and principal purpose was "to perpetuate and preserve, for its own sake and in spite of possible cost, an organization of industry in small units which can effectively compete with each other."[1]

THE ANTIMONOPOLY LAWS

Specifically, the Sherman Act outlawed two major types of interference with free enterprise, viz., collusion and monopolization. Section 1 of the Act,

---

1 *U.S.* v. *Aluminum Company of America*, 148 F.2d 416 (C.C.A. 2d, 1945). In elaborating on the goals of the Sherman Act, Judge Hand stated:

"Many people believe that possession of unchallenged economic power deadens initiative, discourages thrift and depresses energy; that immunity from competition is a narcotic, and rivalry is a stimulant, to industrial progress; that the spur of constant stress is necessary to counteract an inevitable disposition to let well enough alone. Such people believe that competitors, versed in the craft as no consumer can be, will be quick to detect opportunities for saving and new shifts in production, and be eager to profit by them. . . . True, it might have been thought adequate to condemn only those monopolies which could not show that they had exercised the highest

possible ingenuity, had adopted every possible economy, had anticipated every conceivable improvement, stimulated every possible demand. . . . Be that as it may, that was not the way that Congress chose; it did not condone 'good' trusts and condemn 'bad' ones; it forbade all. Moreover, in so doing it was not necessarily actuated by economic motives alone. It is possible, because of its indirect social or moral effect, to prefer a system of small producers, each dependent for his success upon his own skill and character, to one in which the great mass of those engaged must accept the direction of a few. These considerations, which we have suggested only as possible purposes of the Act, we think the decisions prove to have been in fact its purposes." (Ibid.)

457

dealing with collusion, stated: "Every contract, combination . . . or conspiracy, in restraint of trade or commerce among the several States, or with foreign nations, is hereby declared illegal." As interpreted by the courts, this made it unlawful for businessmen to engage in such collusive action as agreements to fix prices; agreements to restrict output or productive capacity; agreements to divide markets or allocate customers; agreements to exclude competitors by systematic resort to oppressive tactics and discriminatory policies—in short, any joint action by competitors to influence the market. Thus Section 1 was, in a sense, a response to Adam Smith's warning that "people of the same trade seldom meet together even for merriment and diversion, but the conversation ends in a conspiracy against the public, or in some contrivance to raise prices."[2]

Section 2 of the Sherman Act, dealing with monopolization, provided: "Every person who shall monopolize or attempt to monopolize, or combine or conspire with any other person or persons to monopolize any part of the trade or commerce among the several States, or with foreign nations, shall be deemed guilty of a misdemeanor, and . . . punished." This meant that businessmen were deprived of an important freedom, the freedom to monopolize. Section 2 made it unlawful for anyone to obtain a stranglehold on the market either by forcing rivals out of business or by absorbing them. It forbade a single firm (or a group of firms acting jointly) to gain a substantially exclusive domination of an industry or a market area. Positively stated, Section 2 attempted to encourage an industry structure in which there are enough independent competitors to assure bona fide and effective market rivalry.

As is obvious from even a cursory examination of the Sherman Act, its provisions were general, perhaps even vague, and essentially negative. Directed primarily against *existing* monopolies and *existing* trade restraints, the Sherman Act could not cope with specific practices which were, and could be, used to effectuate the unlawful results. Armed with the power to dissolve

---

2 *The Wealth of Nations*, Book 1, Chapter 10. Here it should be pointed out that businessmen engage in trade restraints and organize monopolies not because of any vicious and anti-social motives, but rather because of a desire to increase personal profits. As George Comer, former chief economist of the Antitrust Division, once observed, monopolies are formed "not because businessmen are criminals, but because the reports from the bookkeeping department indicate, in the short run at least, that monopoly and restraints of trade will pay if you can get away with it. It will pay a large corporation to agree with its competitors on price fixing. It pays to operate a basing-point or zone-price system. If patent pools can be organized, especially with hundreds or thousands of patents covering a whole industry, the profits will be enormous. If an international cartel can be formed which really works, the very peak of stabilization and rationalism is reached. If the management of all the large units in an industry can get together with the labor unions in the industry, a number of birds can be killed with one stone. And finally, if the government can be persuaded to legalize the restrictive practices, the theory of 'enlightened competition' is complete." ("The Outlook for Effective Competition," *American Economic Review, Papers and Proceedings*, 36:154 (May 1946).)

existing monopolies, the enforcement authorities could not, under the Sherman Act, attack the *growth* of monopoly. They could not nip it in the bud. For this reason Congress passed, in 1914, supplementary legislation "to arrest the creation of trusts, conspiracies and monopolies *in their incipiency and before consummation.*"[3] In the Federal Trade Commission Act of 1914, Congress set up an independent regulatory commission to police the industrial field against "all unfair methods of competition." In the Clayton Act of the same year Congress singled out four specific practices which past experience had shown to be favorite weapons of the would-be monopolist: (1) price discrimination, i.e., local price cutting and cut-throat competition; (2) tying contracts and exclusive dealer arrangements; (3) the acquisition of stock in competing companies; and (4) the formation of interlocking directorates between competing corporations. These practices were to be unlawful whenever their effect was to substantially lessen competition or to create tendencies toward monopoly. Thus price discrimination, for example, was not made illegal per se; it was to be illegal only if used as a systematic device for destroying competition—in a manner typical of the old Standard Oil and American Tobacco trusts.[4] The emphasis throughout was to be on prevention rather than cure. The hope was that—given the provisions of the 1914 laws to supplement the provisions of the Sherman Act—the antitrust authorities could effectively eliminate the economic evils against which the antitrust laws were directed. The thrust of the Celler-Kefauver Anti-Merger Act of 1950 was aimed at the same objectives.

THE CHARGES AGAINST MONOPOLY

What those evils were has never been clearly stated, and perhaps never been clearly conceived, by the sponsors of antitrust legislation. In general, however,

---

3 Senate Report No. 695, 63rd Congress, 2nd Session, 1914, p. 1 (italics supplied).

4 A Congressional Committee explained the background of the price discrimination provision of the Clayton Act as follows:

"In the past it has been a most common practice of great and powerful combinations engaged in commerce—notably the Standard Oil Company and the American Tobacco Company, and others of less notoriety, but of great influence—to lower prices of their commodities, oftentimes below the cost of production in certain communities and sections where they had competition, with the intent to destroy and make unprofitable the business of their competitors, and with the ultimate purpose in view of thereby acquiring a monopoly in the particular locality or section in which the discriminating price is made.

"Every concern that engages in this evil practice must of necessity recoup its losses in the particular communities or sections where their commodities are sold below cost or without a fair profit by raising the price of this same class of commodities above their fair market value in other sections or communities.

"Such a system or practice is so manifestly unfair and unjust, not only to competitors who are directly injured thereby but to the general public, that your committee is strongly of the opinion that the present antitrust laws ought to be supplemented by making this particular form of discrimination a specific offense under the law when practiced by those engaged in commerce."

(House Report No. 627, 63rd Congress, 2nd Session, 1914, pp. 8–9.)

the objections to monopoly and trade restraints—found in literally tons of antitrust literature—can be summarized as follows:[5]

1. Monopoly affords the consumer little protection against exorbitant prices. As Adam Smith put it, "the price of monopoly is, upon every occasion, the highest which can be got. The natural price, or the price of free competition, on the contrary is the lowest which can be taken, not upon every occasion indeed, but for any considerable time taken together. The one is upon every occasion the highest which can be squeezed out of the buyers, of which, it is supposed, they will consent to give; the other is the lowest which the sellers can commonly afford to take, and at the same time continue their business."[6] The consumer is, under these conditions, open prey to extortion and exploitation—protected only by such tenuous self-restraint as the monopolist may choose to exercise because of benevolence, irrationality, concern over government reprisals, or fear of potential competition.

The monopolist can generally charge all the traffic will bear, simply because the consumer has no alternative sources of supply. The consumer is forced to pay the monopolist's price, turn to a less desirable substitute, or go without. His freedom is impaired, because his range of choice is artificially limited.

An example, while admittedly extreme, serves to illustrate this point. It involves tungsten carbide, a hard-metal composition of considerable importance in such industrial uses as cutting tools, dies, and so on. In 1927, tungsten carbide sold in the United States at $50 per pound; but after a world monopoly was established by the General Electric Company and Friedrich Krupp A.G. of Germany, under which GE was granted the right to set prices in the American market, the price promptly rose to a maximum of $453 per pound. During most of the 1930's the price fluctuated between $225 and $453 per pound, and not until 1942—when an indictment was issued under the antitrust laws—did the price come down. Thereafter, it fluctuated between $27 and $45 per pound.[7]

2. Monopoly causes a restriction of economic opportunity and a misallocation of productive resources. Under free competition, it is the consumer who —through his dollar votes in the market place—decides how society's land, labor, and capital are to be used. Consumer tastes generally determine whether more cotton and less wool, more cigarettes and less pipe tobacco, more aluminum and less steel shall be produced. Under free competition the

---

5 For a good summary of the charges against monopoly as well as the claims made in support of monopoly, see C. Wilcox, *Competition and Monopoly in the American Economy*, Temporary National Economic Committee Monograph No. 21 (Washington, D.C.: U.S. Government Printing Office, 1941), pp. 15–18. (Hereafter referred to as TNEC Monograph.)

6 Smith, op. cit., Book I, Chapter VII.

7 See C. D. Edwards, *Economic and Political Aspects of International Cartels*, Monograph No. 1, Senate Committee on Military Affairs, 78th Congress, 2nd Session (Washington, D.C.: U.S. Government Printing Office, 1946), pp. 12–13.

Economics of a Free Market

Producers   Consumer

Economics of Security

Producers   Consumer

Figure 1

FREE COMPETITION VERSUS PRICE FIXING

SOURCE   Thurman W. Arnold. *Cartels or Free Enterprise?* Public Affairs
Pamphlet No. 103, 1945; reproduced by courtesy of Public Affairs
Commission, Inc.

consumer is in this strategic position because businessmen must, if they want to make profits, do as the consumer demands. Since a businessman, under competition, is free to enter any field and to produce any type and quantity of goods he desires, the tendency will be for him to do those things which the consuming public (in its wisdom or ignorance) deems most valuable. In short, under a truly competitive system, the businessman can improve himself only by serving others. He can earn profits only by obeying the wishes of the community as expressed in the market.

Under monopoly, by contrast, the individual businessman finds his freedom of enterprise limited. He cannot do as he pleases, because the monopolist has the power of excluding newcomers or stipulating the terms under which newcomers are permitted to survive in an industry. The monopolist can interfere with a consumer-oriented allocation of resources. He, instead of the market, can determine the type and quantity of goods that shall be produced. He, and not the forces of supply and demand, can decree who shall produce what, for whom, and at what price. In the absence of competition, it is the monopolist who decides what *other* businessmen shall be allowed to do and what benefits the consuming public shall be allowed to receive.

A good illustration of this is the Hartford-Empire Company which once was an undisputed monopolist in the glass bottle industry. Through its patent control over glass bottling machinery, Hartford-Empire held life-and-death power both over the producers already in the industry and those attempting to enter it. As one observer described the situation,[8] Hartford had become benevolent despot to the glass container. Only by its leave could a firm come into the industry; the ticket of admission was to be had only upon its terms; and from its studied decision there was no appeal. The candidate had to subscribe to Hartford's articles of faith; he could not be a price-cutter or a trouble-maker. He could not venture beyond his assigned bailiwick or undermine the market of his partners in the conspiracy. Each concern had to accept the restrictions and limitations imposed by Hartford. Thus the Buck Glass Company was authorized to manufacture wine bottles for sacramental purposes only. The Sayre Glass Works were restricted to producing "such bottles, jugs, and demijohns as are used for vinegar, ciders, sirups, bleaching fluids, hair tonics, barber supplies and fluid extracts." Knox Glass Bottle Company was allowed to make only amber colored ginger ale bottles. Mary Card Glass Company could not make products weighing more than 82 ounces. Baurens Glass Works Inc. was licensed to provide bottles for castor oil and turpentine, but none to exceed 4 ounces in capacity. Here indeed was a shackling of free enterprise and a usurpation of the market—a private government more powerful than that of many states. Here indeed was a tight little island, where the law of the monopolist was supreme and unchallenged.

---

8 See W. H. Hamilton, *Patents and Free Enterprise*, TNEC Monograph No. 31 (Washington, D.C.: U.S. Government Printing Office, 1941), pp. 109–115.

Only through antitrust prosecution were the channels of trade reopened, and the Hartford dictatorship dissipated.[9]

3. Monopoly often restrains technological advances and thus impedes economic progress. As Clair Wilcox points out, "the monopolist may engage in research and invent new materials, methods, and machines, but he will be reluctant to make use of these inventions if they would compel him to scrap existing equipment or if he believes that their ultimate profitability is in doubt. He may introduce innovations and cut costs, but instead of moving goods by price reduction he is prone to spend large sums on alternative methods of promoting sales; his refusal to cut prices deprives the community of any gain. The monopolist may voluntarily improve the quality of his product and reduce its price, but no threat of competition compels him to do so."[10]

Our experience with the hydrogenation and synthetic rubber processes is a case in point. This, one of the less illustrious chapters in our industrial history, dates back to 1926 when I. G. Farben of Germany developed the hydrogenation process for making oil out of coal—a development which obviously threatened the entrenched position of the major international oil companies. Soon after this process was patented, Standard Oil Company of New Jersey concluded an agreement with I. G. Farben, under which Farben promised to stay out of the world's oil business (except inside Germany) and Standard agreed to stay out of the world's chemical business. "By this agreement, control of the hydrogenation process for making oil outside Germany was transferred to the Standard Oil Company in order that Standard's petroleum investment might be fully protected. In the United States, Standard licensed only the large oil companies which had no interest in exploiting hydrogenation. Outside the United States, Standard . . . proceeded to limit use of the process so far as the threat of competing processes and governmental interest [of foreign countries] permitted."[11] As a result, this revolutionary process was almost completely suppressed except in Germany where it became an effective tool for promoting the military ambitions of the Nazi government.

The development of synthetic rubber production in the United States was similarly retarded by the I. G.-Standard marriage of 1928. Since Buna rubber, under the agreement of 1928, was considered a chemical process, it came under the exclusive control of I. G. Farben—both in- and outside Germany. Farben, however, was not interested in promoting the manufacture of synthetic rubber anywhere except in Germany, and proceeded therefore—both for commercial (i.e., monopolistic) and nationalistic reasons—to forestall its development in the United States. In this purpose, Farben had at least

---

9 See *U.S.* v. *Hartford-Empire Co. et al.*, 323 U.S. 386 (1945).

10 Wilcox, op. cit., pp. 16–17.

11 Edwards, op. cit., p. 36. For a popular discussion of the I. G.-Standard

marriage, see also G. W. Stocking and M. W. Watkins, *Cartels in Action* (New York: Twentieth Century Fund, 1946), Chap. 11, especially pp. 491–505.

the tacit support of its American partner. As a result, the outbreak of World War II found the United States without production experience or know-how in the vital synthetic rubber field. In fact, when the Goodrich and Goodyear tire companies attempted to embark on synthetic rubber production, the former was sued for patent infringement and the latter formally threatened with such a suit by Standard Oil Company (acting under the authority of the Farben patents). This happened in November 1941, one month before Pearl Harbor. Not until after our formal entry into World War II was the Farben-Standard alliance broken under the impact of antitrust prosecution, and the production of vital synthetic rubber started in the United States. Here, as in the case of hydrogenation, monopolistic control over technology had serious implications not only for the nation's economic progress but also its military security.[12]

4. *Monopoly tends to impede the effectiveness of general stabilization measures and to distort their structural impact on the economy.* Monopolistic and oligopolistic firms, as Galbraith suggests, may insulate themselves against credit restrictions designed to curb investment and check inflation. They may do so by raising prices to offset higher interest costs, by raising prices to finance investment out of increased profits, or by resorting to the capital market rather than to banks for their supply of loanable funds. Competitive firms, by contrast, cannot raise prices to compensate for higher interest charges. They cannot raise prices to finance investment out of higher profits. They cannot readily turn to the capital market for funds. Their lack of market control makes them the weakest borrowers and poorest credit risks, and they must therefore bear the brunt of any "tight money" policy. In short, monopolistic and oligopolistic firms not only can undermine the effectiveness of monetary control in their sector of the economy, but also shift the burden of credit restrictions to the competitive sector and thus stifle its growth. The implications for concentration need not be belabored.[13]

5. *Monopoly threatens not only the existence of a free economy, but also the survival chances of free political institutions.* Enterprise which is not competitive cannot for long remain free, and a community which refuses to

---

12 See W. Berge, *Cartels: Challenge to a Free World* (Washington, D.C.: Public Affairs Press, 1944), pp. 210–214; G. W. Stocking and M. W. Watkins, *Cartels or Competition* (New York: Twentieth Century Fund, 1948), pp. 114–117; J. Borkin and C. A. Welsh, *Germany's Master Plan* (New York: Duell, Sloan & Pearce, 1943). For a contrary view, see F. A. Howard, *Buna Rubber* (New York: D. Van Nostrand Co., 1947).

13 "Market Structure and Stabilization Policy," *The Review of Economics and Statistics*, 39:131, 133 (May 1957). For further discussion of "sellers' inflation," "administered price inflation," and "inflation in the midst of recession"—in short, the relation between market structure and general price stability—see also *Hearings before the Subcommittee on Antitrust and Monopoly, Senate Judiciary Committee, Administered Prices*, Part I (1957), and Parts 9 and 10 (1959); and *The Relationship of Prices to Economic Stability and Growth*, compendium of papers submitted by panelists appearing before the Joint Economic Committee, 85th Congress, 2nd Session, 1958.

accept the discipline of competition inevitably exposes itself to the discipline of absolute authority. As Mutual Security Administrator Harold Stassen once observed, "world economic history has shown that nationalization and socialization have come when there has been complete consolidation and combination of industry, not when enterprise is manifold and small in its units. . . . We must not permit major political power to be added to the other great powers that are accumulated by big business units. Excessive concentration of power is a threat to the individual freedoms and liberties of men, whether that excessive power is in the hands of government or of capital or of labor."[14] The enemy of democracy is monopoly in all its forms, and political liberty can survive only within an effective competitive system. If concentrated power is tolerated, giant pressure groups will ultimately gain control of the government or the government will institute direct regulation of organized pressure groups. In either event, free enterprise will then have to make way for collectivism, and democracy will be superseded by some form of authoritarianism.

This objection to monopoly, this fear of concentrated economic power, is deeply rooted in American traditions—the tradition of federalism, the separation of church and state, the tripartite organization of our governmental machinery. It is the expression of a socio-political philosophy which believes in the decentralization of power, a broad base for the class structure of society, and the economic freedom and opportunity for new men, new ideas, and new organizations to spearhead the forces of progress. It stands in stark contrast to the European varieties of free enterprise, which involve merely curbs on governmental powers without similar checks on excessive private power.[15]

---

14 Address reprinted on *Congressional Record*, February 12, 1947, p. A545. See also H. C. Simons, *Economic Policy for a Free Society* (Chicago: University of Chicago Press, 1948); F. A. Hayek, *The Road to Serfdom* (Chicago: University of Chicago Press, 1945); R. A. Brady, *Business as a System of Power* (New York: Columbia University Press, 1943); G. W. Stocking, "Saving Free Enterprise from Its Friends," *Southern Economic Journal,* **19**:431 (April 1953). Also relevant in this connection are the repeated warnings by the Federal Trade Commission to the effect that "the capitalist system of free initiative is not immortal, but is capable of dying and dragging down with it the system of democratic government. Monopoly constitutes the death of capitalism and the genesis of authoritarian government." (*The Basing Point Problem,* TNEC Monograph No. 42, 1941, p. 9.)

15 This point was well made by Senator Cummins in 1914, when he pressed for adoption of the Federal Trade Commission Act and the Clayton Act:

"We have adopted in this country the policy of competition. We are trying to preserve competition as a living, real force in our industrial life; that is to say, we are endeavoring to maintain among our business people that honorable rivalry which will prevent one from exacting undue profits from those who may deal with him. . . . We are practically alone, however, in this policy. . . . England long ago became indifferent to it; and while that great country has not specifically adjusted her laws so as to permit monopoly they are so administered as to practically eliminate competition when the trade affected so desires. France has pursued a like course.

"Austria, Italy, Spain, Norway, Sweden, as well as Belgium, have all pursued the course of permitting combinations and

By way of illustrating this charge against monopoly some students contend that the rise of Hitler in Germany was facilitated by the pervasive cartelization of the German economy—by the absence of competitive freedom in German business and the lack of democratic freedom in German government. Similarly, they point out that unregulated private monopoly was the breeding ground for Italian fascism and Japanese totalitarianism. Whether or not these correlations are scientifically valid is difficult to determine. Certainly, the seriousness of a danger is not easy to evaluate. "Who can say whether any particular warning is due to overcautiousness, timidity or even superstition or, on the other hand, to prudence and foresight? . . . It is, of course, possible that 'monopoly' is merely a bugbear frightening the believers in free enterprise and free society; but it is equally possible that we have underestimated the danger and have allowed the situation to deteriorate to such a degree that only a very radical effort can still save our social and political system."[16]

---

relations which practically annihilate competition, and Germany, our most formidable rival, so far as commerce is concerned, not only authorizes by her law the formation of monopolies, the creation of combinations which restrain trade and which destroy competition, but oftentimes compels her people to enter into combinations which are in effect monopolies. We are, therefore, pursuing a course which rather distinguishes us from the remainder of the commercial world.

"I pause here to say, and I say it emphatically and earnestly, that I believe in our course; I believe in the preservation of competition, I believe in the maintenance of the rule that opens the channels of trade fairly and fully to all comers. I believe it because it seems to me obvious that any other course must inevitably lead us into complete State socialism. The only monopoly which civilized mankind will ever permanently endure is the monopoly of all the people represented in the Government itself." (*Congressional Record*, June 30, 1914, p. 11379.)

Since World War II, the contrast between the American and European approaches to the monopoly problem has been considerably reduced. Several nations in Western Europe have enacted restrictive practices legislation which, though not as far-reaching as the American prototype, nevertheless reflects a growing awareness of the problem. See European Productivity Agency, *Guide to Legislation on Restrictive Business Practices*, 2 vols. (Paris: Organiza-tion for Economic Cooperation and Development, 1960).

16 F. Machlup, *The Political Economy of Monopoly* (Baltimore: Johns Hopkins Press, 1952), pp. 77–78. Many students of the concentration movement, including the distinguished historian Charles A. Beard, feel that monopoly is to a considerable extent the creature of government action and inaction. Professor Beard explained his position to a Congressional Committee as follows:

"I should like to emphasize the fact that our state and national governments have a responsibility for the corporate abuses and economic distress in which we now flounder. It is a matter of common knowledge that corporations are not natural persons. They are artificial persons. They are the creatures of government. Only with the sanction of government can they perform any acts, good or bad. The corporate abuses which have occurred, the concentration of wealth which has come about under their operations, all can be laid directly and immediately at the door of government. The states of the American Union and the Congress of the United States, by their actions and their inaction, have made possible the situation and the calamities in which we now find ourselves." (*Hearings before a Subcommittee on the Judiciary*, Seventy-fifth Congress, 1st Session, 1937, Part I, p. 72.)

See also W. Adams and H. M. Gray, *Monopoly in America: The Government as Promoter* (New York: The Macmillan Company, 1955).

THE EXTENT OF CONCENTRATION

In discussing the concentration of economic power, it is important to distinguish between *market* concentration[17] and *aggregate* concentration.

Market concentration indicates the share of business held by the leading firms in an industry—usually the top 4 or 8 firms. Although concentration ratios cannot fully describe the number and size distribution of companies in an industry, they do serve as a convenient index or proxy of the degree of market power held by the largest firms. Like any other single statistic, of course, they are not the last word on the subject.

Concentration ratios are usually computed with reference to the SIC classification system which ranges from 2-digit major industry groups to 7-digit product categories. The following example illustrates the point:

SIC CODE	DESIGNATION	NAME
20	Major industry group	Food and kindred products
208	Industry group	Beverages
2085	Industry	Distilled liquors
20853	Product class	Bottled liquors
20853–51	Product	Whiskey
–55	Product	Gin
–57	Product	Vodka

The most readily available and widely used concentration ratios are those computed for 4-digit industries. These ratios show a pattern of the richest variation, ranging from "extremely high" to "relatively low" concentration. Among the "extremely concentrated" industries in 1966, where the four largest producers account for 75 per cent or more of total industry shipments, are: locomotives (98 per cent), aircraft propellers and parts (96 per cent), flat glass (96 per cent), telephone apparatus (94 per cent), electric lamps (93 per cent), chewing gum (88 per cent), steam engines and turbines (87 per cent), cereal preparations (87 per cent), organic fibers (85 per cent), cigarettes (81 per cent), typewriters (79 per cent).

"Highly concentrated" industries, where the four largest producers account for 50–74 per cent of total industry shipments, include: industrial gases (72 per cent), soap and detergents (72 per cent), explosives (72 per cent), metal cans (71 per cent), tires and inner tubes (71 per cent), beet sugar (68 per cent), photo equipment (67 per cent), transformers (66 per cent), automatic vending machines (61 per cent), storage batteries (60 per cent), biscuits and

---

17 For conflicting views on the extent of concentration in the American economy, see M. A. Adelman, "The Measurement of Industrial Concentration," *Review of Economics and Statistics*, 33:269 (November 1951); and J. M. Blair, "The Measurement of Industrial Concentration: A Reply," *Review of Economics and Statistics*, 34:343 (November 1952).

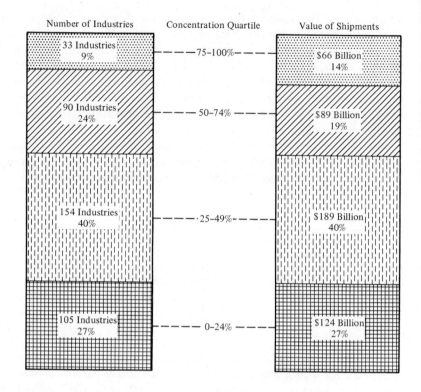

Number of Industries	Concentration Quartile	Value of Shipments
33 Industries 9%	75–100%	$66 Billion 14%
90 Industries 24%	50–74%	$89 Billion 19%
154 Industries 40%	25–49%	$189 Billion 40%
105 Industries 27%	0–24%	$124 Billion 27%

Chart 1

DISTRIBUTION OF MANUFACTURING INDUSTRIES BY 4-FIRM CONCENTRATION-RATIO QUARTILES, 1966

NOTE   The manufacturing sector is composed of 417 industry categories. Excluded from the above tabulation are: 15 industry categories composed of products "not elsewhere classified" within major industry groups; 18 local or small regional industries; and the newspaper and periodical industries. The Census did not publish 1966 concentration ratios for 29 industries. For these 29 industries, 1963 concentration ratios were used.

SOURCE   Annual Survey of Manufacturers: 1966, Value-of-Shipment Concentration Ratios by Industry, U.S. Bureau of the Census.

crackers (59 per cent), synthetic rubber (56 per cent), distilled liquor (55 per cent), semiconductors (51 per cent).

"Moderately concentrated" industries, where the four largest producers account for 25–49 per cent of total industry shipments, include: construction machinery (45 per cent), fertilizers (34 per cent), petroleum refining (32 per cent), envelopes (32 per cent), dehydrated food products (31 per cent), periodicals (28 per cent), costume jewelry (25 per cent).

Industries with "relatively low" concentration, where the four largest firms account for less than 25 per cent of total industry shipments, are represented by the following: fluid milk (23 per cent), games and toys (22 per cent), lighting fixtures (18 per cent), knit fabric mills (16 per cent), newspapers (14 per cent), dresses (8 per cent), special dies and tools (5 per cent), ready mixed concrete (5 per cent), fur goods (4 per cent).

The frequency distribution of manufacturing industries according to the foregoing concentration categories is summarized in Chart 1. It is clear that a significant number of industries are highly concentrated, but market concentration is nevertheless moderate or relatively low in the greater part of manufacturing.

Certain caveats are recommended to guard against unwarranted conclusions based on the above figures. First, it is difficult to define an "industry," and high concentration in one industry may not be very significant if its product competes actively with that of another industry (i.e., where the cross elasticity of demand is high). For example, concentration in the field of textile fibers, taken as a whole, may, for public policy purposes, be more relevant than concentration in silk, wool, cotton, rayon, nylon, orlon, acrilan, dynel, dacron, and so on taken separately. Second, some giant firms are listed as members of one industry, although their capital assets are spread over a number of other industries. General Motors, for example, is listed as an automobile producer, although some of its capital investment lies in such fields as diesel engines, electric appliances, refrigerators, and so on—a fact which results in partial overstatement of the degree of concentration in the automobile industry. Third, imports are not reflected in the concentration ratios, although their significance may be substantial in some industries like chemicals, cameras, typewriters, clocks and watches, toilet preparations, and so on. Fourth, the ratios apply to concentration in national markets, but fail to reflect concentration in regional or local markets. Thus, the top four producers in the bread industry account for only 25 per cent of the national market, although their sales in some 23 states exceed 50 per cent, and run still higher in individual cities. Finally, concentration must not be confused with monopoly. The mere fact that an industry is highly concentrated is not positive proof that the industry is monopolized or that its firms are in active collusion. Under extreme circumstances, it is even conceivable that as few as two companies are enough to provide effective competition in an industry. As Dexter Keezer, vice-president of the McGraw-Hill Company, points out:

"If the heads of the two surviving firms were the hard-driving, fiercely independent type of businessman who has played such a large part in the industrial development of the U.S.A., two of them would be enough to create a ruggedly competitive situation. But," Dr. Keezer adds, "if the two were of the genteel, clubby and take-it-easy type which is also known in the high reaches of American business, two companies might get together and tend to sleep together indefinitely. When the number of firms involved is small, the chances of having the industry animated by vigorously competitive leadership also seem to me to be small."[18]

As for trends since World War II, it is clear that average market concentration in manufacturing industries has shown no marked tendency to increase or decrease. This was the finding of the Cabinet Committee on Price Stability which prepared an analysis of 213 essentially comparable industries between 1947 and 1966, and it is corroborated by other studies. As Table 1 shows, the 4-firm concentration ratios increased by more than 3 percentage points in 88 industries, whereas it declined by the same amount in 78 industries—remaining essentially unchanged in 47 industries. The 8-firm concentration ratios show a slightly different pattern, with a significantly larger number of industries experiencing an increase rather than a decrease.

Nevertheless, Table 1 does indicate an interesting divergence in the trend of market concentration in producer goods and consumer goods industries. In the former, declines in concentration were substantially more frequent than increases, while in the latter precisely the opposite was true. Moreover, when the changes in market concentration in the consumer goods sector are broken down according to the degree of product differentiation, we find that increasing concentration was clearly associated with high product differentiation. Again, according to the Cabinet Committee, "between 1947 and 1963 average 4-firm concentration of highly differentiated consumer product industries rose 16.8 percentage points. . . . The average 8-firm concentration ratio of these industries increased 17.5 percentage points. In other words, . . . high differentiation was associated with an increase in concentration of nearly one percentage point per year over the postwar period."[19] On the basis of these statistics, one might well argue that product differentiation (in consumer goods industries) proved a more formidable "entry" barrier than the alleged economies-of-scale imperatives in the producer goods sector.

Aggregate concentration, as distinct from market concentration, measures the centralized control which a group of firms exercises over more than one industry, product, or market. It measures the relative control that giant firms have over an entire sector of economic activity, like manufacturing and mining, or trade and commerce, or transportation and public utilities, and so on. It is an index of the conglomerate concentration of power, and a first

---

18 "Antitrust Symposium," *American Economic Review*, **39**:718 (June 1949).

19 Cabinet Committee on Price Stability, *Studies by the Staff* (Washington, D.C.: U.S. Government Printing Office, 1969), p. 62.

TABLE 1 CHANGE IN CONCENTRATION BETWEEN 1947 AND 1966 IN 213 MANUFACTURING INDUSTRIES[a]

A. NUMBER OF INDUSTRIES

TYPE OF INDUSTRY	NUMBER OF INDUSTRIES	NUMBER OF INDUSTRIES IN WHICH 4-FIRM CONCENTRATION			NUMBER OF INDUSTRIES IN WHICH 8-FIRM CONCENTRATION		
		INCREASED 3 PERCENTAGE POINTS OR MORE	CHANGED LESS THAN 3 PERCENTAGE POINTS	DECREASED 3 PERCENTAGE POINTS OR MORE	INCREASED 3 PERCENTAGE POINTS OR MORE	CHANGED LESS THAN 3 PERCENTAGE POINTS	DECREASED 3 PERCENTAGE POINTS OR MORE
Total	213	88	47	78	97	52	63
Producer goods	132	41	31	60	47	36	48
Consumer goods	81	47	16	18	50	16	15
Undifferentiated	28	12	7	9	14	7	7
Moderately differentiated	36	21	9	6	22	8	6
Highly differentiated	17	14	0	3	14	1	2

B. VALUE OF SHIPMENTS

TYPE OF INDUSTRY	INDUSTRY SHIPMENTS ($ MILLIONS)	PER CENT DISTRIBUTION OF SHIPMENTS			PER CENT DISTRIBUTION OF SHIPMENTS		
		INCREASED 3 PERCENTAGE POINTS OR MORE	CHANGED LESS THAN 3 PERCENTAGE POINTS	DECREASED 3 PERCENTAGE POINTS OR MORE	INCREASED 3 PERCENTAGE POINTS OR MORE	CHANGED LESS THAN 3 PERCENTAGE POINTS	DECREASED 3 PERCENTAGE POINTS OR MORE
Total	222,353	37	20	43	41	29	30
Producer goods	134,659	20	25	55	25	38	37
Consumer goods	87,694	63	11	26	65	16	19
Undifferentiated	14,197	29	15	56	30	16	59
Moderately differentiated	33,449	59	24	17	66	26	8
Highly differentiated	40,048	78	0	22	79	7	14

a Table reflects 1947 to 1963 concentration changes in 24 industries for which the Census did not report 1966 concentration data.
SOURCE Annual Survey of Manufactures: 1966, Value-of-Shipment Concentration Ratios by Industry, U.S. Bureau of the Census; and Industry Classification and Concentration, Federal Trade Commission, March, 1967.

TABLE 2   AGGREGATE
CONCENTRATION, ALTERNATIVE
LEVELS, 1941, 1964, AND 1968
(PER CENT OF CORPORATE
MANUFACTURING ASSETS)

LARGEST	1941	1964	1968
100	38.4	46.8	49.4
200	46.2	57.2	61.1
300	50.2	62.9	67.3
400	53.0	66.6	71.1
500	55.3	69.3	73.8
600	57.0	71.4	75.9
700	58.4	73.1	77.5
800	59.6	74.5	78.8
900	60.7	75.6	79.9
1,000	61.6	76.6	80.8

SOURCE   Bureau of Economics, Federal
Trade Commission.

approximation of the discretionary power that may accompany such forms of structural organization.

The level of aggregate concentration is high and—unlike the case of market concentration—the trend is persistently and substantially upward. Table 2, for example, shows the steadily increasing proportion of total manufacturing assets controlled by the largest companies in that sector. Note that, between 1941 and 1968, the 100 largest manufacturers had increased their share of assets by 11 percentage points, and the 1,000 largest by almost 20 points. Viewed differently, the 100 largest controlled a larger share of assets in 1968 than the 200 largest did in 1941. The significant increases in concentration during the 4-year period between 1964 and 1968 are also significant.

This trend is directly, and almost entirely, attributable to the magnitude, velocity, and character of the post-World War II merger movement, especially in the 1960's. Table 3 shows the growing volume of "large" mergers since 1948—i.e., mergers where the acquired assets exceeded $10 million—and the proportion of such mergers consummated by the largest companies. In nearly every year since 1948, the 200 largest were responsible for about two thirds of the assets of "large" manufacturing and mining companies acquired. Over the entire period covered in Table 3, the top 100 accounted for 44 per cent, whereas the top 200 acquired 64 per cent of the assets involved in these mergers. If acquisitions are ranked by the size of the acquiring company, it is again clear that the very largest companies negotiated the lion's share of these mergers—both by number and by assets acquired (see Chart 2).

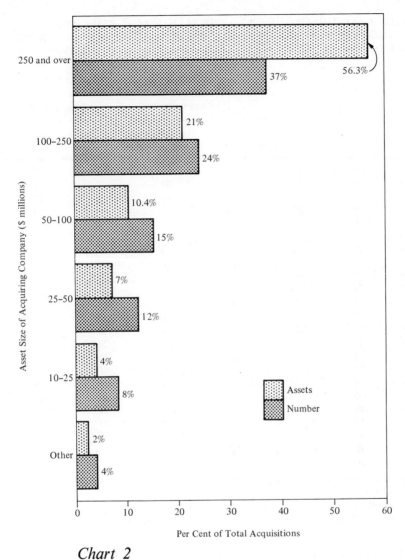

Chart 2

ACQUISITIONS BY SIZE OF ACQUIRING COMPANY, 1948–1968

NOTE   Includes all manufacturing and mining acquisitions of $10 million or more.

SOURCE   Bureau of Economics, Federal Trade Commission.

TABLE 3   ACQUISITIONS OF LARGE MANUFACTURING AND
MINING FIRMS[a] BY COMPANIES RANKED AMONG THE 100 LARGEST
AND THE 200 LARGEST MANUFACTURERS OF 1968, 1948–1968

	TOTAL		ACQUIRED BY 100 LARGEST MANUFACTURERS		ACQUIRED BY 200 LARGEST MANUFACTURERS	
	NO.	ASSETS ($ MILLIONS)	NO.	ASSETS ($ MILLIONS)	NO.	ASSETS ($ MILLIONS)
1948	6	101	4	65	4	65
1949	5	67	4	45	4	45
1950	4	173	1	20	1	20
1951	9	201	1	12	5	125
1952	14	338	4	142	6	176
1953	23	679	6	120	15	438
1954	35	1,426	7	490	16	916
1955	67	2,117	21	900	36	1,298
1956	55	1,991	22	1,096	34	1,486
1957	51	1,442	13	548	26	951
1958	37	1,077	15	563	21	755
1959	64	1,959	19	872	33	1,350
1960	62	1,708	19	591	32	1,043
1961	55	2,056	17	880	24	1,295
1962	72	2,174	20	889	34	1,312
1963	71	2,956	27	1,563	40	2,081
1964	89	2,707	30	1,147	41	1,378
1965	90	3,827	17	1,541	27	2,009
1966	99	4,167	19	1,911	36	2,470
1967	167	9,062	36	4,025	71	6,431
1968	201	12,800	45	6,168	88	8,257
Total	1,276	53,025[b]	347	23,587[b]	594	33,900[b]

   a   Large acquired companies are those that had $10 million in total assets at the time
they were acquired.
   b   Detail does not add to total due to rounding.
   SOURCE   Bureau of Economics, Federal Trade Commission.

Some of the companies acquired were large indeed. Between 1948 and
1968, some 1,206 manufacturing and mining corporations disappeared. Of
these, 372 ranked among the 1,000 largest manufacturers in 1950, but by 1968
they had disappeared and bequeathed some commanding market positions
to their acquirers. As a group, these 327 companies held one of the four top
positions in 619 separate product classes.

The extent to which mergers have contributed to aggregate concentration can
also be seen in Chart 3, which isolates the merger component in the growth
of the 200 largest manufacturing corporations. Over the 1947–1968 period,
these corporations increased their share of assets held by 11.7 percentage

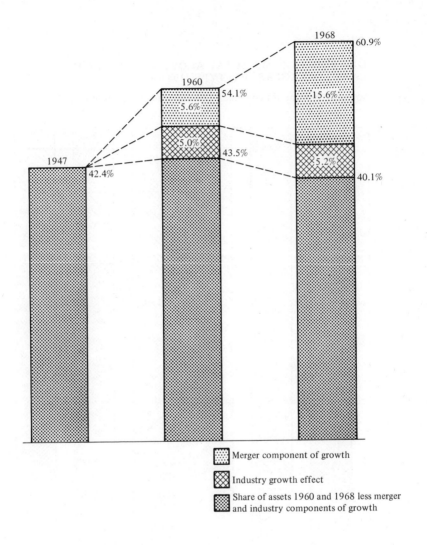

Chart 3

SHARE OF ASSETS OF 200 LARGEST MANUFACTURING
CORPORATIONS OF 1968 AND ACCUMULATIVE
COMPONENTS OF GROWTH; 1947, 1960 AND 1968

SOURCE   Bureau of Economics, Federal Trade Commission.

Chart 4

DISTRIBUTION OF TOTAL ACQUIRED ASSETS IN
LARGE MERGERS, BY TYPE, 1948–1968

SOURCE Bureau of Economics, Federal Trade Commission.

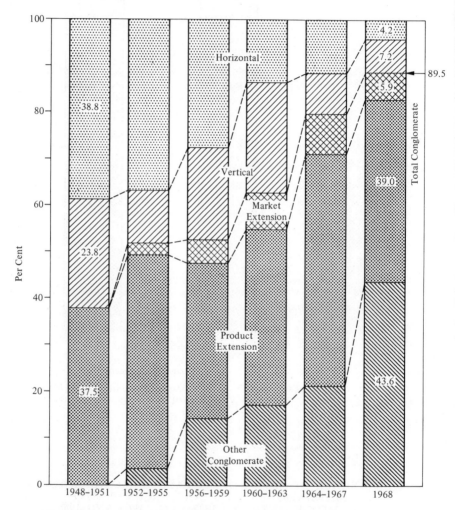

*Firms with assets of $10 million or more

points, of which 5.6 points were attributable to mergers. The change between 1960 and 1968 is even more dramatic.

The character of the merger movement between 1948 and 1968 also explains an apparent paradox, viz., that, despite the movement's magnitude, average market concentration remained relatively stable, although aggregate concentration rose appreciably. Chart 4, which shows a breakdown by types of merger during this period, illustrates this point. It highlights the relative decline of horizontal mergers—the only ones which register an effect on market concentration ratios—in the face of a startling rise in the relative importance of all types of conglomerate mergers.[20]

Spearheading this most recent phase of the merger movement have been the so-called "new conglomerates." Five of these acquired more than $1 billion each by merger between 1961 and 1968, and in many cases bought out companies with leading positions in their industries. International Telephone & Telegraph Corporation, for example, acquired 47 companies with combined assets of $1,487 million, including Continental Baking Company, the nation's largest baking firm; Sheraton Corporation of America, the largest owner-operator of guest rooms in the U.S.; Levitt & Sons, the largest home builder in the U.S.; and Avis, the second largest car rental firm. Ling-Temco-Vought acquired 23 companies with combined assets of $1,901 million, including Wilson & Company, a major meat packer as well as a leader in sporting goods, drugs, and pharmaceuticals; Jones & Laughlin, a major steel company; and Braniff, a leading airline (which, of course, is not listed as a manufacturing corporation). Gulf & Western acquired 67 companies with combined assets of $2,882 million, including leading companies in the zinc, motion picture, sugar, cigar, rolling mill machinery, and other industries. Tenneco acquired 31 companies with assets of $1,196 million, and Teledyne Inc. acquired 125 companies with $1,026 million. Such mergers tend not only to increase aggregate concentration, but to give the 100 or 200 largest a leading market position in diverse industries.

One final observation. The foregoing data understate the degree of aggregate concentration, because many of the largest manufacturing corporations are not fully independent business units. Thus, the following ties were known to exist among the roughly 900 largest manufacturing companies:

---

20 Conglomerate mergers of the *geographic market-extension* type involve companies manufacturing the same product, but selling it in different geographic markets; for example, a bakery in New York and Chicago. (Such mergers are sometimes called "chain" horizontals because of their close resemblance to horizontal mergers.) Conglomerate mergers of the *product-extension* variety involve companies which are functionally related in production and/or distribution but do not sell products in direct competition with each other; for example, the union of soap and bleach manufacturers. Other conglomerate mergers involve companies having neither a buyer-seller relationship nor a functional connection in manufacturing or distribution, such as a ship builder and an ice cream manufacturer.

(1) Twenty-eight companies with combined assets of $2,699 million are joint ventures owned by other industrial corporations. Twenty-two of these corporations, with combined assets of $2,436 million, were progeny of one or more of the 200 largest corporations. Eight of the joint ventures had assets exceeding $100 million.

(2) Thirty-two corporations with combined assets of $6,746 million were totally owned by or had a substantial share of their common stock held by other large manufacturing corporations. Seventeen of these companies, with combined assets of $5,439 million, were controlled by other corporations among the 200 largest.

(3) Forty-three corporations with combined assets of $6,150 million were controlled or were subsidiaries of non-manufacturing corporations. Sixteen of these had assets exceeding $100 million.[21]

Finally, of course, these companies are often interlocked through common directors or managers with their suppliers, customers, potential competitors, and the financial institutions from which they borrow funds. The top 50, for example, had 520 interlocks with companies ranking among the 1,000 largest manufacturing corporations; of these, 134 were interlocks with companies producing in the same 5-digit product class.

In summary, then, joint ventures and interlocking ties further escalate the degree of aggregate concentration.

The significance of all this is still the subject of violent controversy, and all we can say—as Machlup suggests—is that economists regard the current degree of concentration either as (a) desirable and avoidable; (b) desirable and unavoidable; (c) undesirable and avoidable; or (d) undesirable and unavoidable.

PUBLIC POLICY ALTERNATIVES

Depending on which of these views is accepted, economists will then recommend one of the following policy alternatives with respect to concentrated industries: (1) maintenance of the status quo which, by and large, is regarded as satisfactory; (2) imposition of public regulation or public ownership; or (3) rejection of both private and public monopoly, and the promotion of vigorous competition under the antitrust laws. It is these policy alternatives which shall now be examined in greater detail.

THE STATUS QUO

The defenders of the status quo generally advocate a policy of noninterference with respect to our concentrated industries. They seem satisfied with

---

21 Federal Trade Commission, *Economic Report on Corporate Mergers* (Washington, D.C.: U.S. Government Printing Office, 1969).

the prevailing industrial structure, either because they believe that bigness and concentration are now controlled by the "right" people or because they refuse to regard concentration as indicative of pervasive monopolization.

Three distinct, though related, facets of this position are discernible. One is the belief that the business leader of today is a far cry from the robber baron of yesterday; the belief that industrial statesmanship, social responsibility, enlightened self-restraint, and progressive labor, customer, and supplier relations have replaced the exploitative behavior, the sharpshooting competitive practice, and the "public-be-damned" attitude of a bygone age; in short, the belief that the present managers of giant corporate enterprise have demonstrated their capacity for exercising industrial stewardship.[22]

The second facet of the status quo position is the "workable competition" thesis.[23] Its supporters hold that bigness and concentration are no cause for alarm, because competition is present and *working* in an economy such as ours where constant technological progress is reflected in ever-increasing output, lower prices, and new and improved products. They urge that the effectiveness of competition be judged not in terms of market structure (i.e., the degree of concentration in particular industries) but rather by market results (i.e., performance in the public interest). They suggest that an industry is "workably competitive"—regardless of the fewness of sellers in it—if it shows, among other things, "a progressive technology, the passing on to consumers of the results of this progressiveness in the form of lower prices, larger output, improved products, etc."[24] The emphasis here is on performance and results rather than on structural organization which *compels* such performance and results.

---

22 David E. Lilienthal, in his *Big Business: A New Era* (New York: Harper & Brothers, 1953), argues that the antitrust philosophy is no longer applicable and that the antitrust laws are, in fact, crippling America. He feels that the newer type of American big businessman is in little need of the restraints imposed by the antitrust laws. In contrast to Mr. Lilienthal's position, it is interesting to note that a distinguished Wall Street attorney, General William J. Donovan, disagrees. Mr. Donovan's warning, sounded in 1936, is still relevant today:

"Those who would remove the inhibitions of existing law must recognize that the alternative is not between the Sherman Act on the one hand and the regulation of industry by industry on the other. The alternative is between the continuance of the competitive system as a proper safeguard to the public, and the closest supervision and control of industry by the government. The self-interest of business in such matters would often be antagonistic to the interest of the public as a whole. The recent experience under the NRA shows the abuses that may arise by vesting in business the power of self-regulation without at the same time providing for adequate and capable supervision and control by a government agency." Address before the American Bar Association, 1936, quoted in V. A. Mund, *Government and Business* (New York: Harper, 1950), pp. 628–629.

23 See primarily J. M. Clark, "Toward a Concept of Workable Competition," *American Economic Review*, **30**:241 (June 1940).

24 E. S. Mason, "Antitrust Symposium," op. cit., p. 713. See also C. E. Griffin, *An Economic Approach to Antitrust Problems* (New York: American Enterprise Association, 1951).

The believers in workable competition usually buttress their position with the suggestion that "old-fashioned" competition—i.e., competition among sellers and among buyers *within* an industry—be replaced with a more dynamic concept of interindustry or technological competition. Their argument is this: classical, intraindustry competition tends to promote maximum output, minimum prices, and optimum utilization of capacity; in short, it stimulates efficiency. But this efficiency is static and unprogressive in character. It makes no allowance for the research, development, and innovation required for economic growth. While it prevents concentration, it stifles progress. To have progress we need more, not less, concentration. Only bigness can provide the sizable funds necessary for technological experimentation and innovation in the industrial milieu of the twentieth century. Only monopoly earnings can provide the bait that lures capital to untried trails. Although progress may thus require high power concentrations in many industries, this need not be a source of concern to society at large. Technological development will serve as an offset against any short-run position of entrenchment which may be established. The monopoly of glass bottles will be subverted by the introduction of the tin can; and the dominance of the latter will, in turn, be undermined by the introduction of the paper container. The consumer need not rely, therefore, on the static competition between large numbers of small firms as protection against exploitation. In the long run, he can find greater safety—and better things for better living to boot—in the technological competition of a small number of large firms which, through research and innovation, eventually destroy any position of market control which may be established.[25]

The third facet of the status quo position is the rather ingenious "countervailing power" thesis which concedes the pervasiveness of concentration and monopoly, but maintains that the dangers of exploitation are minimized by certain built-in safeguards in our economy.[26] According to this thesis, the actual or real restraints on a firm's market power are vested not in its competitors, but in its customers and suppliers. These restraints are imposed not from the same side of the market (as under classical competition), but from the opposite side. Thus "private economic power is held in check by the countervailing power of those subject to it. The first begets the second."[27] A monopoly on one side of the market offers an inducement to both suppliers and customers to develop the power with which they can defend themselves against exploitation. For example, concentration in the steel industry will stimulate concentration among the industry's customers (automobile manufacturers) as well as among its suppliers (steel workers). The result will be, so the argument runs, a balance of power within the economy—the creation of

---

25 See J. A. Schumpeter, *Capitalism, Socialism, and Democracy* (New York: Harper, 1943), p. 79 ff.

26 See J. K. Galbraith, *American Capitalism: The Concept of Countervailing Power* (Boston: Houghton Mifflin, 1952).
27 Ibid., p. 118.

almost automatic checks and balances requiring a minimum of interference or "tampering."

The foregoing arguments in defense of the status quo are subject to a number of criticisms. As to the beneficence of industrial stewardship and workable competition, we should note that "results alone throw no light on the really significant question: have these results been *compelled* by the system—by competition—or do they represent simply the dispensations of managements which, with a wide latitude of policy choices at their disposal, happened for the moment to be benevolent or smart?"[28] In other words, what assurance do we have that the workable competition of today will not be transformed into the abusive monopoly or oppressive conspiracy of tomorrow? How, in the absence of competition or constant and detailed supervision, can we ever determine whether the performance of industrial giants does, in fact, serve the public interest and will continue to do so in the future? By what concrete yardsticks do we measure the workability of competition?

Secondly, with regard to the countervailing power thesis, it can be argued (1) that countervailing power is often undermined by vertical integration and top level financial control which blend the opposing sides of the market into one; (2) that the bilateral monopolies created through the countervailance process often conclude bargains prejudicial to the consumer interest (witness, for example, wage increases for the CIO steelworkers followed by price increases for the steel industry); (3) that the countervailing influence of technological or interindustry competition is often subverted by a combination of the potential competitors (witness, for example, the merger between motion picture houses and television networks); (4) that any countervailance through government action is often undermined by unduly intimate affiliation between regulator and regulatee (witness, for example, the ICC which seems to have degenerated into a lobby on behalf of railroad interests); and finally (5) that the whole thesis rests on the dubious assumption that industrial giantism is inevitable under modern technological conditions—an assumption which still awaits scientific validation.[29]

PUBLIC REGULATION OR
PUBLIC OWNERSHIP

The advocates of public regulation or public ownership hope simultaneously to ensure industrial efficiency and to avoid the abuses of private monopoly—not by the dissolution of monopoly but by its social control. Their argument runs along these lines: Competition in many basic industries is a thing of the

---

28 Ben W. Lewis, "Antitrust Symposium," op. cit., p. 707.
29 For a more comprehensive critique of the countervailing power thesis, see

W. Adams, "Competition, Monopoly and Countervailing Power," *Quarterly Journal of Economics*, 67:469 (November 1953).

past and has been replaced by trade agreements and price fixing, cartels, and monopolies. While legislation to eliminate specific abuses of monopoly power can do some good, it cannot compel a return to competition in industries where it would be wasteful and undesirable. The facts of life are that efficient organization in mass production and mass distribution fields requires unification, coordination, and rationalization. Only monopoly can bring this about. But private monopoly is no guarantee of efficiency. By fixing prices, allocating production, imposing levies on the efficient to keep the inefficient in production, the general level of prices is kept high, and incentives to modernization may be lacking. Hence, if monopoly is inevitable, it is preferable that such monopoly be publicly supervised or publicly owned.[30]

Basic to this argument is the assumption that monopoly, or at least cooperation on a comprehensive scale, is necessary in many industries—the assumption that monopoly is inevitable under modern industrial conditions. It is this belief in the inevitability of monopoly which had led men of such distinguished position, unimpeachable integrity, and obvious sincerity as Judge Gary (former president of the U.S. Steel Corporation) to advocate a public-utility-type regulation for concentrated industries. Thus Judge Gary, as long ago as 1911, offered the following testimony to a Congressional committee investigating the steel industry:

> I realize as fully, I think, as this committee that it is very important to consider how the people shall be protected against imposition or oppression as the possible result of great aggregations of capital, whether in the possession of corporations or individuals. I believe that is a very important question, and personally I believe that the Sherman Act does not meet and will never fully prevent that. I believe we must come to enforced publicity and governmental control, even as to prices, and, so far as I am concerned, speaking for our company, so far as I have the right, I would be very glad if we had some place where we could go, to a responsible governmental authority, and say to them, "Here are our facts and figures, here is our property, here our cost of production; now you tell us what we have the right to do and what prices we have the right to charge." I know this is a very extreme view, and I know that the railroads objected to it for a long time; but whether the standpoint of making the most money is concerned or not, whether it is the wise thing, I believe it is the necessary thing, and it seems to me corporations have no right to disregard these public questions and these public interests.

"Your idea then," said Congressman Littleton of the committee,

---

30 For this formulation of the argument, see the work of the British socialist, E. Davies, *National Enterprise* (London: Gollancz, 1946), p. 16.

"is that cooperation is bound to take the place of competition and that cooperation requires strict governmental supervision?"

"That is a very good statement," replied the Judge.[31]

Unfortunately, Judge Gary's faith in independent regulatory commissions has, in the light of American experience, not proved justified. These commissions—the Interstate Commerce Commission,[32] the Civil Aeronautics Board,[33] the Federal Power Commission,[34] the Federal Communications Commission[35]—have at times failed to regulate their respective industries in the public interest. Often these commissions adopted regulatory techniques which did little to promote operational efficiency and innovative progress; which were ineffective, costly, and debilitating; and which suffered from administrative incompetence, unimaginativeness, and dishonesty. Moreover, no satisfactory solution seems yet to have been found for the vexing problem of watching the watchers. (*Quis ipsos custodes custodiet?*) As ex-Senator Wheeler once sadly observed, "It seems to invariably happen, that when Congress attempts to regulate some group, the intended regulatees wind up doing the regulating."[36]

Dissatisfied with the past record of regulatory commissions, some groups have gone further and advocated the nationalization, i.e., outright government ownership, of concentrated industries. Typical of these groups is the British Labour Party which, in 1948, demanded nationalization of the steel industry on the grounds that the public supervision of private monopoly is unworkable. Said the Labour Party:[37]

A board controlling a private monopoly must in the long run be ineffective. Its activities must be negative. It can, for example, refuse to recommend a price increase, but it cannot force the industry to take steps to cheapen production. It has no power to make the monopoly spend money on new plant or scrap old plant. A supervised private

---

31 Special Committee to Investigate the United States Steel Corporation, House Report No. 1127, 62nd Congress, 2nd Session, 1911, quoted in W. Adams and L. E. Traywick, *Readings in Economics* (New York: Macmillan, 1948), p. 223.

32 See, for example, S. P. Huntington, "The Marasmus of the I.C.C.," *Yale Law Journal*, **61**:467 (April 1952); and Senate Small Business Committee, *Competition, Regulation, and the Public Interest in the Motor Carrier Industry*, Report No. 1693, 84th Congress, 2nd Session, 1956.

33 See, for example, Senate Small Business Committee, *Report on Role of Irregular Airlines in United States Air Transportation Industry*, Report No. 540,

82nd Congress, 1st Session, 1951.

34 See, for example, Federal Power Commission, *In the Matter of the Phillips Petroleum Company*, Opinion No. 217, Docket No. G-1148, August 16, 1951.

35 See, for example, Federal Communications Commission, *In the Matter of American Broadcasting Company Inc. and United Paramount Theatres, Inc.*, Docket No. 10046, 1953; also B. Schwartz, *The Professor and the Commissions* (New York: Knopf, 1959).

36 Quoted in B. Bolles, *How to Get Rich in Washington* (New York: Dell, 1952), p. 23.

37 *British Steel at Britain's Service*, quoted in Mund, op. cit., p. 548.

> monopoly can be prevented from doing the wrong things, but it cannot
> be forced to do the right things. In the future, the control of steel must
> be dynamic and purposeful, not negative and preventive. . . . There is
> no hope, then, in a supervised monopoly. The only answer is that steel
> must be made a public enterprise.

According to the socialist, then, nationalization is preferable both to public
regulation and to private monopoly. It is better than public regulation, because the latter has proved generally ineffective. It is better than private
monopoly, because the power to control basic industries, and hence the
economy, must be "democratized."[38] Such power must, according to the
socialist, be held by the many and not as hitherto concentrated—without
corresponding responsibility—in the hands of a few. There must be assurance
that monopoly—a system which can be used for good or evil—will be used
in the public interest. According to the socialist, a nationalized industry
affords such assurance, simply because its management will be motivated by
considerations of public service and not private profit.

The disadvantages of public ownership are fairly obvious: administrators
in nationalized industries may easily succumb to the disease of security,
conservatism, procrastination, and bureaucracy. Their enterprises, as a result
of supercentralization and lack of competitive incentives, may come to suffer
from inflexibility and inelasticity. Moreover, the public enterprise may develop
a tendency of using its monopoly power as a cloak for inefficient operation
by resorting to the ready device of raising prices to meet increased costs, and
thus avoid showing a deficit. Finally, there is the distinct possibility that the
very people in whose interest a particular industry may originally have been
nationalized will eventually lose control of it. This result is probable for two
reasons: (1) general elections are no substitute for the market as an agency of
social control (because people cannot indicate their dissatisfaction with a
particular public enterprise by means of the ballot); and (2) the public enterprise, if it is to operate efficiently, must be "taken out of politics" and put in
the hands of an autonomous body—again with the result of removing such
enterprise from the direct control of the electorate.[39]

---

38 See Ben W. Lewis, *British
Planning and Nationalization* (New York:
Twentieth Century Fund, 1952), pp. 43–45.
   39 See F. A. Hayek, *The Road to
Serfdom* (Chicago: University of Chicago
Press, 1945); L. Von Mises, *Planned Chaos*
(New York: Foundation for Economic
Education, 1947); C. E. Griffin, *Britain:
A Case Study for Americans* (Ann Arbor,
Mich.: University of Michigan Press,
1950). These criticisms of public ownership
are confirmed by the distinguished British
scholar, W. Arthur Lewis. In his "Recent
British Experience of Nationalization as
an Alternative to Monopoly Control"

(a paper presented to the International
Economic Association in 1951), Professor
Lewis makes the following comments on
Britain's experiment in socialism:
   "The appointment of public directors to
manage an undertaking is not sufficient
public control. . . . Parliament is handicapped in controlling corporations by its
lack of time. . . . Neither have Members of
Parliament the competence to supervise
these great industries. . . . Parliament is
further handicapped . . . by paucity of
information . . . for example, less information is now published about the railways
than was available before they were

In summary, public regulation and public ownership suffer from the same basic drawback as private monopoly, viz., the concentration of power in the hands of a few. Such power may be used benignly or dangerously, depending on the men who possess and control it. They may be good men, benevolent men, and socially minded men; but society still confronts the danger of which Lord Acton so eloquently warned: power corrupts, and absolute power corrupts absolutely.

THE PROMOTION OF
EFFECTIVE COMPETITION

The advocates for greater competition through vigorous antitrust enforcement reject both the Scylla of private monopoly and the Charybdis of public ownership. Believing that the preservation of competitive free enterprise is both desirable and possible, they point out that this does not mean a return to the horse-and-buggy age, nor a strict adherence to the textbook theories of "perfect" or "pure" competition. What they advocate is a structural arrangement in private industry characterized by decentralized decision-making and "effective" competition.

Among the ingredients necessary for effective competition, the following are considered of primary importance:[40] (1) an appreciable number of sellers and buyers for substantially the same product, so that both sellers and buyers have meaningful alternatives of choice; (2) the economic, as well as legal, freedom to enter the market and gain access to essential raw materials; (3) the absence of tacit or open collusion between rivals in the market; (4) the absence of explicit or implicit coercion of rivals by a dominant firm or a groups of dominant firms; (5) the absence of "substantial preferential status within the market for any important trader or group of traders on the basis of law, politics, or commercial alliances";[41] (6) the absence of diversification, subsidization, and political motivation to an extent where giant firms may escape the commercial discipline of a *particular* market or a *particular* operation.

---

nationalized. . . . Except in the case of transport, the British government has resisted proposals that public corporations should be treated in the same way [as private monopolies], with the result that the consumer is formally less well protected vis-à-vis public corporations than he was vis-à-vis private firms operating public utilities. . . . The [public] corporation's Board, though publicly appointed, has many loyalties in addition to its loyalty to the public. It has also a loyalty to itself, and to its own staff, which may well conflict with the interests of the consumer. . . . Public corporations have not found it easy to dismiss redundant workers, or even to close down inefficient units or to expand more efficient units in some other place (e.g. railways, mines). It may well turn out that public corporations are less able to promote this kind of efficiency than are private corporations, in the British atmosphere of tenderness towards established sources of income." (Quoted in Machlup, op. cit., p. 50.)

40 See C. D. Edwards, *Maintaining Competition* (New York: McGraw-Hill, 1949), pp. 9–10.

41 Ibid., p. 10.

Some economists feel that the maintenance of this type of competition may, under modern conditions, be difficult if not impossible. They contend that antitrusters are faced with the dilemma of choosing between "(1) firms of the most efficient size but operating under conditions where there is inadequate pressure to compel firms to continue to be efficient and pass on to the consumer the benefits of efficiency, and (2) a system in which the firms are numerous enough to be competitive but too small to be efficient." [42] According to this view our choice is between monopoly and efficiency, on the one hand, and competition and relative inefficiency, on the other.

The supporters of vigorous antitrust enforcement deny that such a choice is necessary, at least in many of our highly concentrated industries. The following reasons are usually given for rejecting the ostensible conflict between competition and efficiency. First, large firms, although technologically imperative in many industries, need not assume the Brobdingnagian proportions of some present-day giants. The unit of technological efficiency is the plant and not the firm. This means that, although there are undisputed advantages in the large-scale integrated steel operations at Gary or Pittsburgh or Birmingham, there seems little technological justification for combining these functionally separate plant units into a single administrative giant. [43]

Second, it seems significant that many of our colossal firms were not formed to gain the technical advantages of scale, but organized instead to achieve monopolistic control over the market and to reap profits from the sale of inflated securities. Giantism in industry today is not unrelated to the investment banker's inclination of yesteryear to merge and combine competing companies for the sake of promoter's profits.

Third, there is mounting evidence that industrial concentration is not necessarily the result of spontaneous generation or natural selection, but often the end-product of unwise, man-made, discriminatory, and privilege-creating governmental action. In an era of "big government," when the structural impact of federal activity is no longer neutral, the government's spending, taxing, proprietary, legislative, and regulatory powers have often been used—unintentionally, in some instances—to throttle competition and restrict opportunity. Especially in the regulated industries, government has

---

42 A. R. Burns, "Antitrust Symposium," op. cit., p. 603.

43 In his definitive study of 20 representative industries, Joe S. Bain found that, in 11 out of 20 cases, the lowest-cost (most efficient) plant would account for less than $2\frac{1}{2}$ per cent of the industry's national sales; in 15 out of 20 cases, for less than $7\frac{1}{2}$ per cent; and in only one case, for more than 15 per cent. Moreover, in estimating multiplant economies, Bain concluded that in 6 out of 20 industries, the cost advantages of multiplant firms were "either negligible or totally absent"; in another 6 industries, the advantages were "perceptible" but "fairly small"; and in the remaining 8 industries, no estimates could be obtained. (*Barriers to New Competition* (Cambridge: Harvard University Press, 1956), pp. 73, 85–88 ff.) These findings hardly support the contention that existing concentration in American industry can be explained in terms of technological imperatives.

become an instrument for promoting concentration far beyond the impera-tives of technology and economics.[44]

Finally, to the extent that profit figures are valid as measures of com-parative efficiency, it seems that in a number of cases medium-sized and small firms outperform their giant rivals. Moreover, a breaking down of huge firms does not necessarily have fatal effects on efficiency *or* profitability. In the public utility field, for example, the comprehensive dissolution program carried out under the Public Utility Holding Company Act of 1935 has resulted in increased efficiency and profitability among the successor com-panies. This was demonstrated in the above average appreciation in the security values of the successor companies which occurred despite declining utility rates, higher costs, and the inevitably higher taxes.[45] On the basis of experience, therefore, it may not be unreasonable to suggest, as *Fortune* does, that there are areas in American industry where an unmerging process among the giants can contribute both to increased efficiency and more vigorous competition.[46]

If such an unmerging process were to be accomplished through antitrust action, three types of market structure would have to be identified and dealt with, viz., horizontal, vertical, and conglomerate integration. (1) The hori-zontal size of *some* firms would have to be reduced, if competition is to be promoted, because an oligopolistic industry structure often results in con-scious or unconscious parallelism among the giant firms. Price leadership, live-and-let-live policies, nonprice competition, and so on—in short, the type of gentlemanly behavior which imposes higher and more inflexible prices on the consumer—are common among firms of oligopolistic size, because each fears retaliation by its large rivals as punishment for independence and non-conformity. (2) Vertically integrated size would, in some cases, have to be reduced because the large integrated concern can apply the squeeze—both on prices and supplies—to its smaller rivals who are both its customers and competitors.[47] A case in point here would be a fully integrated aluminum firm which simultaneously supplies independent fabricators with aluminum ingot and then competes with them in the market for fabricated products.[48] (3) Conglomerate integration would pose a problem, because the widely diversified giant can exercise undue power as a buyer of materials, energy, transportation, credit, and labor; and also because such a concern often en-joys special advantages in litigation, politics, public relations, and finance.[49]

---

44 See Adams and Gray, op. cit., especially Ch. 3.

45 See W. Adams, "The Dilemma of Antitrust Aims: A Reply," *American Economic Review*, **42**:895 (December 1952).

46 See editorials in *Fortune* (March and April 1938).

47 Senate Small Business Committee, *Monopolistic Practices and Small Business*, 82nd Congress, 2nd Session, 1952,

pp. 21–55; also, *The Distribution of Steel Consumption, 1949–50*, 82nd Congress, 2nd Session, 1952.

48 See *U.S.* v. *Aluminum Company of America*, 148 F.2d 416 (C.C.A. 2d, 1945).

49 See Edwards, *Maintaining Competition*, op. cit., pp. 99–108. It has been said, for example, that General Motors has so much conglomerate power that it could successfully enter the ice cream

In launching a comprehensive program against these forms of integration a case-by-case approach seems preferable to any absolute prohibition on size per se. Moreover, to avoid any major conflicts with vested interests, enforcement might at first be confined to new industries where the problem of concentration is not yet extreme and where structural arrangements have not yet been solidified. This may have significant results, since ours is a dynamic economy in which new industries—if they remain competitive—can substantially curb the power of older and more entrenched interests. Finally, to forestall any possible interference with industrial efficiency, antitrust prosecution might be confined to cases where the goals of competition and efficiency are not in conflict. Toward that end, the antitrust laws can be amended to provide that "any corporation whose size and power are such as to substantially lessen competition and tend to create a monopoly in any line of commerce shall be dissolved into its component parts, *unless* such corporation can demonstrate that its present size is necessary for the maintenance of efficiency."[50] Given a provision of this sort, the dilemma of antitrust may be resolved and our twin goals of competition and efficiency actively promoted.

Antitrust enforcement along the above lines, however, is not enough if competitive free enterprise is to be maintained. Competition must become the core of an integrated national economic policy.[51] It must be positively promoted, rather than negatively preserved.[52] It must have an environment which provides opportunity for new men, and is receptive to new ideas. To

---

industry and capture a predetermined share of the business. "It would matter little whether General Motors is an efficient ice cream manufacturer or whether its ice cream is indeed tastier than more established brands. By discrete price concessions, by saturation advertising, by attractive promotional deals, it could commit its gargantuan financial power to the battle until only so much competition as General Motors is prepared to tolerate would be left in the industry. . . . Put differently, in a poker game with unlimited stakes, the player who commands disproportionately large funds is likely to emerge victorious." (Testimony of Walter Adams in *Hearings before the Subcommittee on Antitrust and Monopoly, Senate Judiciary Committee,* 86th Congress, 1st Session, 1959, p. 4780.)

50   Cf. Monopoly Subcommittee of the House Judiciary Committee, *Hearings,* Part 2-B, 81st Congress, 1st Session, 1949, pp. 1311–1339, 1600–1625. For an endorsement of this general position, see C. Kaysen and D. F. Turner, *Antitrust Policy* (Cambridge, Mass.: Harvard University Press, 1959).

51   See House Small Business Committee, *United States* v. *Economic Concentration and Monopoly,* 79th Congress, 2nd Session, 1947.

52   As Vernon Mund observes, "a policy of individual enterprise and price competition is a highly elaborate and complex plan for organizing the conduct of economic activity. It is a plan, however, which is not self-enforcing. When the policy of competition is accepted, it must be implemented by positive measures to provide for its creation, maintenance, and preservation. Competition is a form of human behavior; and like other behavior it should be conducted according to good manners and morals. The big mistake which government has made with respect to economic regulation is in thinking that in the absence of direct price control (as in the case of public utilities) government intervention is not necessary. The lessons of history clearly show that we cannot have fair competition unless positive measures are taken to create and maintain it." (Mund, op. cit., p. 642.)

create such an environment, a number of recommendations merit consideration:

1. Defense contracts, accelerated amortization privileges, and other wartime bonanzas coming down the government pike should not be restricted to a favored few, but distributed to many firms so as to assure the nation of a broad industrial base for future defense efforts.[53]
2. In the disposal of government property—whether war surplus, synthetic rubber plants, or atomic energy installations—to private industry, sales should be made in a manner calculated to encourage competitive newcomers rather than to rigidify existing patterns of industrial control.
3. The corporate tax structure should be overhauled so as to remove present penalties on the growth and expansion of small business.[54]
4. Government financing of small business should be more than polite encouragement for prospective hot-dog stands and gasoline stations.
5. The patent laws should be revised so as to prevent monopolistic abuse of the patent grant without destroying the incentives for invention. This may entail compulsory licensing of patents on a royalty-free basis in cases involving violations of the antitrust laws; compulsory licensing of patents on a reasonable-royalty basis in cases of patent suppression and nonuse; and outright prohibition of restrictive and exclusive licensing provisions in private patent agreements. In any event, an invention made as a result of government financing or subsidy should become part of the public domain and not allowed to accrue as private property to the corporation doing the contract research.[55]

---

53 See, for example, Senate Small Business Committee, *Concentration of Defense Contracts*, Report No. 551, 82nd Congress, 1st Session, 1951; House Committee on Expenditures in the Executive Departments, *Inquiry into the Procurement of Automotive Spare Parts by the United States Government*, 82nd Congress, 2nd Session, House Report No. 1811, 1952; Attorney General, *Report Prepared Pursuant to Section 708(e) of the Defense Production Act of 1950*, 1950; Joint Committee on Defense Production, *Hearings on Tax Amortization*, 82nd Congress, 1st Session, 1951.

54 See Senate Small Business Committee, *Tax Problems of Small Business*, Report No. 442, 83rd Congress, 1st Session, 1953; J. K. Butters and J. Lintner, *Effect of Federal Taxes on Growing Enterprises* (Boston: Harvard Business School, 1945); J. K. Butters, J. Lintner, and W. Carey, *Effects of Taxation: Corporate Mergers* (Boston: Harvard Business School, 1951).

55 In this connection the Attorney General has recommended that "where patentable inventions are made in the course of performing a Government-financed contract for research and development, the public interest requires that all rights to such inventions be assigned to the Government and not left to the private ownership of the contractor. Public control will assure free and equal availability of the inventions to American industry and science; will eliminate any competitive advantage to the contractor chosen to perform the research work; will avoid undue concentration of economic power in the hands of a few large corporations; will tend to increase and diversify available research facilities within the United States to the advantage of the Government and of the national economy; and will thus strengthen our American system of free, competitive enterprise." [*Investigation of Government Patent Practices and Policies* (Washington, D.C.: U.S. Government Printing Office,

6. Any further exemptions from the antitrust laws should be discouraged, and some existing exemptions re-examined.[56] We must stop what Leverett S. Lyon has called the "growing tendency in the United States for special groups to identify their limited good with the national good and to ask government for subsidy, support, or special protection rather than for laws which increase competitive opportunity."[57] Such laws as the Webb-Pomerene Act, for example, which exempts foreign trade associations from the Sherman Act, should be drastically revised or altogether repealed.[58]

7. Protective tariffs, quotas, and similar restrictions that serve to shield highly concentrated industries from the potential inroads of foreign competition should be reduced or repealed.

8. Incorporation and licensing laws should not be made a front for monopolistic privilege and restrictive practices.

9. The advisability of a progressive tax on advertising—with a generous exemption—should be examined, in an effort to prevent excessive advertising expenditures from acting as an obstacle to free entry in some concentrated industries.[59]

1947), Vol. I, p. 4. [Obviously, it makes little sense to permit—as in the past—"publicly-financed technology to be supressed, used restrictively, or made the basis of an exaction from the public to serve private interests." (Ibid., p. 2.)

56 The problem of exceptions from the antitrust laws is well illustrated in the following story about a Polish ghetto, told by Congressman Celler:

"The rabbi of the synagogue said: 'There is a very poor family on the other end of the ghetto. They have not raiment, they have not food, and they have not shelter. You are too poor yourselves'—he said to his congregation—'to help them, but I have an idea. . . . On the Sabbath eve when you praise the Lord for the fruitage of the earth' and you praise him by drinking a glass of wine, do not drink the full glass of wine. Drink a half a glass of wine, and the next morning when you come to the temple, I will have a barrel, and as you all come in, you will pour the half glass of wine that you left from the night before in the barrel. The Lord will not mind being blessed by the drinking of half a glass of wine, and at a given time the barrel will be filled. I will sell the barrel of wine and give the proceeds to this poor family. You will

not be hurt; nobody will be harmed, and even the good Lord will bless you for it.' At a given time the barrel was opened and lo and behold, it was all water, and the rabbi reprimanded every member in the congregation, and they all had this answer: 'We figured what difference would a half glass of water make in a full barrel of wine.' . . . That is what is happening here. If we keep whittling away, and whittling away, and everybody asks to be exempted, everybody asks to put the half a glass of water in the full barrel of wine, we will have a barrel of water, and we will have no antitrust laws left." (Subcommittee on the Study of Monopoly Power, *Hearings*, 81st Congress, 1st Session, Serial No. 14, Part I, 1949, pp. 267–268.)

57 "Government and American Economic Life," *Journal of Business*, **22**:89 (April 1949).

58 Committee on the Webb-Pomerene Act, American Economic Association, "The Webb-Pomerene Law: A Consensus Report," *American Economic Review*, **37**:848 (December 1947).

59 See W. H. Nicholls, *Pricing Policies in the Cigarette Industry* (Nashville, Tenn.: Vanderbilt University Press, 1951), pp. 412–415.

Security Through
Government Control

Free
Enterprise

Security Through
Monopoly

?

We

Figure 2

PUBLIC POLICY ALTERNATIVES: "THE ROAD AHEAD"

SOURCE Thurman W. Arnold. *Cartels or Free Enterprise?* Public Affairs Pamphlet No. 103, 1945; reproduced by courtesy of the Public Affairs Committee, Inc.

491

Such steps as these—and the list is by no means complete—may serve to stimulate an environment favorable to genuine free enterprise. The task is not easy, for we must strike a delicate balance between the businessman's search for profit and economic security, and society's insistence on freedom and opportunity for the newcomer. Although the task is difficult, it is not insuperable. Given a comprehensive and imaginative economic policy, it is likely that competition can be maintained (or revived), for the record shows that free enterprise in our generation has not failed; it has never been tried.

A hard look at the choice before us is indicated because, in the absence of positive action, we can expect little but aimless drifting and a gradual erosion of our traditional values. As Stocking and Watkins point out, "either the people must call a halt to the concentration—whether in governmental or private hands—of economic power, or they must be prepared to give up a competitive economy, bit by bit, year by year, until it is beyond recall. They will then be obliged to accept some collectivistic alternative that may give more short-run basic security but in the long run will almost certainly provide less freedom, less opportunity for experiment, less variety, less economic progress, and less total abundance."[60]

SUGGESTED READINGS
BOOKS AND PAMPHLETS

Adams, W., and H. M. Gray. *Monopoly in America: The Government as Promoter.* New York: The Macmillan Company, 1955.

American Economic Association. *Readings in the Social Control of Industry.* New York: McGraw-Hill Book Company, Inc., 1942.

Bain, J. S. *Barriers to New Competition.* Cambridge, Mass.: Harvard University Press, 1956.

Caves, R. *American Industry: Structure, Conduct, Performance.* 2nd ed. Englewood Cliffs, N.J.: Prentice-Hall, Inc., 1967.

Dirlam, J. B., and A. E. Kahn. *The Law and Economics of Fair Competition: An Appraisal of Antitrust Policy.* Ithaca, N.Y.: Cornell University Press, 1954.

---

60   G. W. Stocking and M. W. Watkins, *Monopoly and Free Enterprise* (New York: Twentieth Century Fund, 1952), p. 526. We might profit from British experience, which the conservative London *Economist* has summarized as follows: "The fact is that British industrialists, under the deliberate leadership of the Tory Party in its Baldwin-Chamberlain era, have become distinguishable from British Socialists only by the fact that they still believe in private profits. Both believe in 'organizing' industry; both believe in protecting it, when organized, against any competition, either from foreigners or from native newcomers; both believe in standard prices for what they sell; both unite in condemning competition, the one as 'wasteful,' the other as 'destructive.' If free, competitive, private-enterprise capitalism is to continue to exist, not throughout the national economy, but in any part of it, then it needs rescuing from the capitalists fully as much as from the Socialists." [*The Economist*, London, **139**:22 (June 29, 1946). Copyright *The Economist*. Reprinted by permission of the publishers.]

Edwards, C. D. *Maintaining Competition.* New York: McGraw-Hill Book Company, Inc., 1949.

Fellner, W. *Competition Among the Few.* New York: Alfred A. Knopf, Inc., 1949.

Galbraith, J. K. *American Capitalism: The Concept of Countervailing Power.* Boston: Houghton Mifflin Company, 1952.

Galbraith, J. K. *The New Industrial State.* Boston: Houghton Mifflin Company, 1967.

Hamberg, D. *R & D: Essays on the Economics of Research and Development.* New York: Random House, Inc., 1966.

Heflebower, R. B., and G. W. Stocking. *Readings in Industrial Organization and Public Policy.* Homewood, Ill.: Richard D. Irwin, Inc., 1958.

Kaysen, C., and D. F. Turner. *Antitrust Policy.* Cambridge, Mass.: Harvard University Press, 1959.

Lilienthal, D. E. *Big Business: A New Era.* New York: Harper and Row Publishers, Inc., 1952.

Machlup, F. *The Political Economy of Monopoly.* Baltimore: Johns Hopkins Press, 1952.

Mason, E. S. *Economic Concentration and the Monopoly Problem.* Cambridge: Harvard University Press, 1957.

Nelson, R. C. *Merger Movements in American Industry, 1896–1956.* Princeton: Princeton University Press, 1959.

Scherer, F. M. *Industrial Market Structure and Economic Performance.* Chicago: Rand McNally & Company, 1970.

Schumpeter, J. A. *Capitalism, Socialism and Democracy.* New York: Harper and Row Publishers, Inc., 1942.

Shepherd, W. G. *Market Power and Economic Welfare.* New York: Random House, Inc., 1970.

Simons, H. C. *Economic Policy for a Free Society.* Chicago: University of Chicago Press, 1948.

Singer, E. M. *Antitrust Economics: Selected Legal Cases and Economic Models.* Englewood Cliffs, N.J.: Prentice-Hall, Inc., 1968.

Stigler, G. J. *The Organization of Industry.* Homewood, Ill.: Richard D. Irwin, Inc., 1968.

Stocking, G. W., and M. W. Watkins. *Cartels in Action.* New York: Twentieth Century Fund, 1946.

———. *Cartels or Competition?* New York: Twentieth Century Fund, 1948.

———. *Monopoly and Free Enterprise.* New York: Twentieth Century Fund, 1951.

Whitney, S. N. *Antitrust Policies.* New York: Twentieth Century Fund, 1958.

GOVERNMENT PUBLICATIONS

Federal Trade Commission. *Economic Report on Corporate Mergers.* Washington, D.C.: U.S. Government Printing Office, 1969.

Hamilton, W. H. *Antitrust in Action*, Temporary National Economic Committee, Monograph No. 16. Washington, D.C.: U.S. Government Printing Office, 1940.

Hearings before the Subcommittee on the Study of Monopoly Power, House Judiciary Committee. *Study of Monopoly Power*. Serial 14, Parts 1, 2-A, 2-B, Eighty-first Congress, 1st Session, 1949.

Hearings before the Subcommittee on Antitrust and Monopoly, Senate Judiciary Committee. Parts 1–10, Eighty-fifth and Eighty-sixth Congress, 1957–1960.

Hearings before the Subcommittee on Antitrust and Monopoly, Senate Judiciary Committee, *Economic Concentration*, Parts 1–8A, Eighty-eighth through Ninety-first Congresses, 1964–1970.

Nelson, S., and W. Keim. *Price Behavior and Business Policy*. Temporary National Economic Committee. Monograph No. 1. Washington, D.C.: U.S. Government Printing Office, 1940.

Wilcox, C. *Competition and Monopoly in American Industry*. Temporary National Economic Committee. Monograph No. 21. Washington, D.C.: U.S. Government Printing Office, 1940.

JOURNAL AND MAGAZINE ARTICLES

Adams, W. "Dissolution, Divorcement, Divestiture: The Pyrrhic Victories of Antitrust." *Indiana Law Journal*. **27** (Fall 1951).

Adams, W. "The Military-Industrial Complex and The New Industrial State," **58**, *American Economic Review* (May 1968).

Adams, W. J. "Firm Size and Research Activity: France and the United States," **84**, *Quarterly Journal of Economics* (August 1970).

Adelman, M. A. "Integration and Antitrust Policy." *Harvard Law Review*. **63** (November 1949).

Comanor, W. S., and T. A. Wilson. "Advertising and the Advantages of Size," **59**, *American Economic Review* (May 1969).

Heflebower, R. "Economics of Size." *Journal of Business of the University of Chicago*. **24** (April 1951).

Keezer, D. (ed.). "The Antitrust Laws: A Symposium." *American Economic Review*. **39** (June 1949).

Mason, E. S. "Current Status of the Monopoly Problem." *Harvard Law Review*. **62** (June 1949).

Scherer, F. M. "Firm Size, Market Structure, Opportunity, and the Output of Patented Inventions," **55**, *American Economic Review* (December 1965).

Stigler, G. J. "The Case Against Big Business." *Fortune*. **45** (May 1952).

Stocking, G. W. "Saving Free Enterprise from Its Friends." *Southern Economic Journal*. **29** (April 1953).

Wilcox, C. "On the Alleged Ubiquity of Monopoly." *American Economic Review*. **40** (May 1950).

SUBJECT INDEX